More praise for
Robber Barons and Radicals

"Stiles's dramatic and complex tapestry of characters and incidents illuminates with poignancy, eloquence, and clarity a period of vast economic, social, and racial change in American life between Lincoln's assassination and Teddy Roosevelt's inauguration."

—Bertram Wyatt-Brown,
   Richard J. Milbauer Professor of History,
   University of Florida

Critical acclaim for
In Their Own Words

"Contemporary concerns in the study of history have made primary-source material from eyewitnesses increasingly interesting to a vast audience. . . . What makes Stiles's work so important is the quality of his editing."

—*Library Journal*

About the Series:

In Their Own Words offers a multivolume account of American history, told through the words of those who lived it. In each volume, historian T. J. Stiles weaves primary-source materials together with his own writing, creating a gripping historical narrative. The first book in the series, *Civil War Commanders,* follows the war through the recollections of senior officers from both sides. *Warriors and Pioneers,* the second volume, provides a history of the conquest of the West in the words of settlers, soldiers, and Native Americans.

Civil War Commanders: "A valuable addition to the literature of the American *Iliad.*"

—James M. McPherson, bestselling author of
Battle Cry of Freedom

Warriors and Pioneers: "An absorbing but rigorously realistic account of conflict and conquest in the Old West."

—Richard Maxwell Brown, Beekman Professor
Emeritus of Northwest and Pacific History,
University of Oregon

About the Author:

T. J. Stiles is the author of *Warriors and Pioneers; Civil War Commanders; The Citizen's Handbook: Essential Documents and Speeches from American History*; and *Jesse James.* His work has appeared in such publications as *The Los Angeles Times, The Denver Post, The New York Daily News,* and *The People's Almanac Presents the Twentieth Century.* A native of Benton County, Minnesota, he studied history at Carleton College and Columbia University, and now lives in Brooklyn.

About the Introducer:

Edward Countryman is professor in the Clements Department of History at Southern Methodist University. He has also taught at the University of Canterbury (New Zealand), the universities of Cambridge and Warwick (England), and Yale University. His most recent book is *Americans: A Collision of Histories.* He won the Bancroft Prize for *A People in Revolution.*

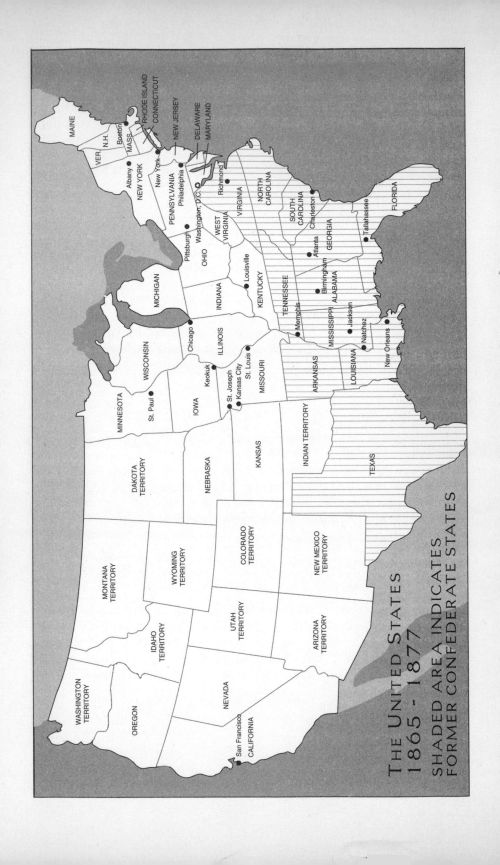

THE UNITED STATES
1865 - 1877

SHADED AREA INDICATES
FORMER CONFEDERATE STATES

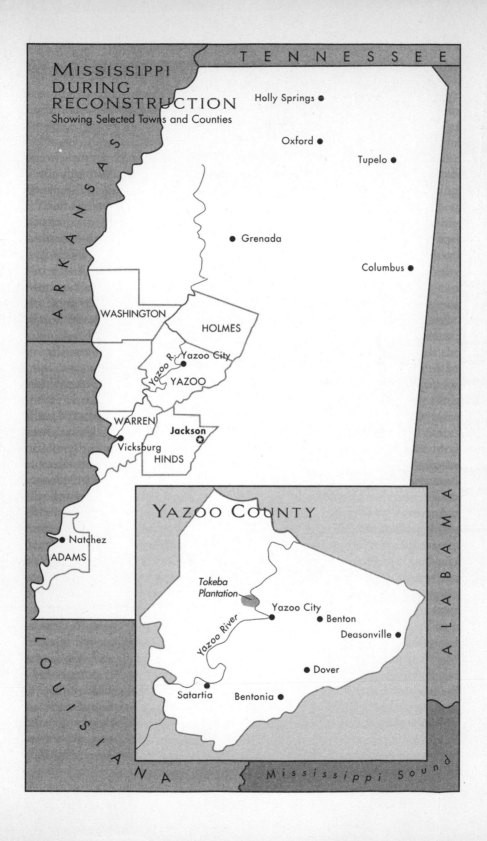

MISSISSIPPI
DURING
RECONSTRUCTION
Showing Selected Towns and Counties

TENNESSEE

ARKANSAS

Holly Springs ●

Oxford ●

Tupelo ●

Grenada ●

Columbus ●

WASHINGTON

HOLMES

Yazoo R. Yazoo City ●
YAZOO

WARREN

Jackson ★

Vicksburg ●
HINDS

Natchez ●
ADAMS

LOUISIANA

ALABAMA

Mississippi Sound

YAZOO COUNTY

Tokeba
Plantation

Yazoo City ●

Benton ●

Deasonville ●

Yazoo River

Dover ●

Satartia ●

Bentonia ●

IN THEIR OWN WORDS

ROBBER BARONS AND RADICALS

Collected and Edited by

T. J. Stiles

With an Introduction by Edward Countryman

A PERIGEE BOOK

Excerpts from *The Personal Memoirs of
Julia Dent Grant* copyright © 1975 by
U.S. Grant Association, reprinted by permission
of the publisher, Southern Illinois University Press.

A Perigee Book
Published by The Berkley Publishing Group
200 Madison Avenue
New York, NY 10016

First edition: April 1997

Published simultaneously in Canada.

The Putnam Berkley World Wide Web site address is
http://www.berkley.com/berkley

Library of Congress Cataloging-in-Publication Data

Robber barons and radicals / collected and edited by T. J. Stiles ;
    with an introduction by Edward Countryman. — 1st ed.
        p.   cm. — (In their own words)
    "A Perigee book."
    Includes bibliographical references.
    ISBN 0-399-52279-4
    1.   United States—History—1865–1898—Sources.   2. Reconstruction—
Sources.   I. Stiles, T. J.   II. Series: In their own words
(Berkley Publishing Group)
E666.R78   1997
973.8—DC20   96-41567
                                                                CIP

Printed in the United States of America

10   9   8   7   6   5   4   3   2   1

CONTENTS

II. Money
THE CUTTHROAT ECONOMY

III. Crisis
THE YEAR 1868

IV. Hope
A REPUBLICAN IN THE WHITE HOUSE, 1869

VIII. Darkness
THE REPUBLICAN FAILURE, 1875–1877

IX. Epilogues

PREFACE

This book is not an anthology—at least not in the traditional sense. It is a continuous, chronological history of the twelve years following the Civil War, woven out of both my own narrative and numerous first-person accounts. With a few exceptions, the individual eyewitness selections do not stand up well on their own. If you dip into Part IV to read about Yazoo County, Mississippi, for example, you will probably end up confused; if you reach that chapter after reading from the beginning, however, you might be very interested, perhaps even moved.

Yes, moved. The tale that emerges from these pages may well be the classical tragedy of our national history. If the Civil War is America's *Iliad,* then the era of Reconstruction and the Gilded Age[1] is our *Oedipus Rex:* a story of struggle, apparent triumph, fatal flaws, and catastrophic loss. *Robber Barons and Radicals* covers this period with careful attention to the most recent scholarship—but it has been written for much more than an academic audience. I seek to draw out the dramatic impact as well as the historical importance of this age by following the lives of a few individuals as they experienced these climactic dozen years in Washington, New York, Pittsburgh, and Yazoo City, Mississippi.

If you are well versed in recent studies of this period (Eric Foner's *Reconstruction* is an outstanding example), then you will still find much to arouse your interest here, for many of these individuals' accounts are as gripping as anything historians have written. If you have not read much about it recently, however, you will almost certainly be surprised, perhaps even shocked. This is the lost era of American history, a time drowned out between the cannons of the Civil War and the tub-thumping roar of Teddy Roosevelt, a time largely ignored by the history-reading public. Such a shame: this period rivals any other in drama and importance, with its debates over the meaning of freedom, its confrontations between African Americans and the Ku Klux Klan, its corporate skulduggery, its political plots. Indeed, the Gilded Age could well be renamed the Age of Conspiracy.

There is another, more disturbing reason why this era has been forgotten: the memory of Reconstruction was hijacked long ago by the very

[1]The Gilded Age is often thought of as falling just before the turn of the century, taking its name from the opulent wealth of the new industrial magnates. But the term comes from Mark Twain's novel of the same name (published in 1873), which parodied government corruption, not wealth, and addresses the years immediately following the Civil War.

forces that had snuffed it out. Fortunately, historians have recovered a very accurate understanding of this era over the last thirty years or so, reviving its dignity and importance. But the academic world has scarcely touched the popular image, an image fostered by generations of racially biased scholars, by Southern apologists such as D.W. Griffith and Margaret Mitchell, and by the same demagogues who overthrew racial equality. Conventional wisdom still holds that Reconstruction was a time when vengeful Northern Republicans persecuted peaceful Southern whites with military rule, when thieving carpetbaggers and collaborating scalawags duped ignorant blacks to gain power and the public purse.

In *Robber Barons and Radicals,* I join the relatively recent effort to more accurately depict the age. The picture that emerges is of a complex era, one filled with bitter ironies and terrible mistakes, but still a breathtaking moment when the recently freed slaves had a brief chance at real freedom and opportunity. It was a chance they made the most of, but the flaws in those charged with protecting that freedom led to its downfall, as Reconstruction was crushed by sheer racist brutality.

There are many who tell that story in these pages—General Oliver O. Howard, commissioner of the Freedmen's Bureau; John R. Lynch, who rose from slavery to Congress; and Radical Massachusetts Congressman George S. Boutwell, among others—but at the heart of it all is the unforgettable account of Albert T. Morgan. Morgan was a white Wisconsin man who served in the Union army through all four years of war despite near-crippling wounds and malaria, then moved with his brother to Yazoo City, Mississippi. The two men invested their life savings in a cotton and lumber operation; driven out of business by vengeful whites, who controlled the local courts and government machinery, they took to politics. Through circumstances and force of personality, Albert Morgan emerged as the leading Republican in Yazoo, and one of the great statesmen of Mississippi. His memoirs brilliantly capture the experience of Reconstruction in this one small town.

My choice of a white man as the main character in the story of the struggle for black freedom might strike some as odd. Many might well prefer that the tale be told primarily by an African American; indeed, I myself wish to stress that blacks played a leading role in fighting for their rights, and Congressman John R. Lynch's memoirs are a critical ingredient in this book. But I have three very important reasons for giving so much space to Morgan's account. First, he is searingly honest, and his accuracy is unusual for most personal memoirs (he wrote the book only eight years after Reconstruction came to an end in Mississippi). Second, his portrait of ten years in Yazoo County brings to life the many grassroots black leaders—now forgotten by the public—who made this revolution happen.

Third, and most important, his life epitomized the spirit of Reconstruction at its best—a spirit that transcended racial divisions. It is true that many other whites in the South, including Republicans, thought in terms of white vs. black—but Morgan did not. Nor did the recently freed African Americans who were his allies. Together, they sought to build a movement that would erase racial lines. Morgan broke with fellow white Republicans to run for office on the same ticket with black candidates; he both appointed and willingly served under black officials; and (to give away a surprise) he married a black woman, after securing a change in state law to be able to do so. In selecting Albert Morgan as my protagonist, I am seeking to evoke a movement for freedom and justice: its foes made it a racial fight, to our misfortune.

However, this was not the only movement of the day. This was also the age of incorporation, as Alan Trachtenberg has named it.[2] A nation of self-employed farmers, artisans, and shopkeepers began to fade away with the rise of massive railroad corporations and vertically integrated, industrial empires. A handful of men amassed immense concentrations of wealth—and they used it unscrupulously, both in Wall Street and the lobbies of legislatures. The change was reflected in the evolution of President Ulysses S. Grant from an apolitical general, a man of humble origins, to an avid political partisan, indulging in intrigues against his Congressional foes as well as in even darker conspiracies, while hobnobbing with the rich and powerful. The fatal flaws in his once-promising administration brought Reconstruction crashing down, as elite Southern whites came to terms with the wealthy establishment that now dominated the North.

I must, of course, thank the many people who made my work on this book possible. Foremost among them is Professor Edward Countryman, who has written an outstanding introductory essay for this volume. Following the path set out in his excellent work *Americans,* he offers an insightful look at American identity. My research was directly aided by Mr. John Parras, as he labored on his dissertation at Columbia University and looked forward to the birth of his baby girl. Mr. Peter Miller also proved a critical help: he always seemed to know just the right person to help me find a crucial book or article. Mr. Miller was also one of those who read all or part of the manuscript and offered almost no comments, along with Mr. Geoffrey Feinberg and Mr. Dana Lowell, who has been my first reader for all the *In Their Own Words* books. I must thank Professor Richard Maxwell Brown, who wrote the introduction to *In Their Own Words: Warriors and Pioneers,* for directing me to the work of Professor Trachtenberg. I owe a great deal to my editor, Mr. John Schline, for his expansive interest and encouragement, and his enthusiasm for the *In*

[2] For an account of the incorporation of the Western frontier at this time, see *In Their Own Words: Warriors and Pioneers,* the previous book in this series.

Their Own Words series. And most of all, I thank my wife, Nadine Spence, for her love, for her distaste for nonsense, and for her own commitment to a world much as Albert Morgan, John Lynch, and Elizabeth Cady Stanton would have wanted it.

T. J. Stiles

SOURCES

Adams, Charles Francis, Jr.: "A Chapter of Erie," *North American Review* (No. 142, July 1869)

Boutwell, George S.: *Reminiscences of Sixty Years in Public Affairs* (New York: McClure, Phillips, & Co., 1902)

Carnegie, Andrew: *Autobiography of Andrew Carnegie* (Boston: Houghton Mifflin Co., 1920)

Chamberlain, Daniel H.: "Reconstruction and the Negro," *North American Review* (No. 267, February 1879)

Childs, George W.: *Recollections* (Philadelphia: J.B. Lippincott, 1890)

Cox, Jacob D.: "How Judge Hoar Ceased to be Attorney–General," *The Atlantic Monthly* (August 1895)

Cullom, Shelby M.: *Fifty Years of Public Service: Personal Recollections of Shelby M. Cullom* (Chicago: A.C. McClurg & Co., 1911)

Grant, Julia Dent: *Memoirs of Julia Dent Grant* (Edited by John Y. Simon, © 1975 by the Ulysses S. Grant Association; excerpted by permission of the publisher, Southern Illinois University Press, Carbondale, IL, and the Ulysses S. Grant Association)

Howard, Oliver Otis: *Autobiography of Oliver Otis Howard,* Volume II (New York: Baker & Taylor Company, 1907)

Lamar, Lucius Q. C.: "Ought the Negro to be Disfranchised? Ought he to have been Enfranchised?", *North American Review* (No. 268, March, 1879)

Lynch, John R.: *The Facts of Reconstruction* (New York: Neale Publishing, 1913)

McDonald, John: *Secrets of the Great Whiskey Ring and Eighteen Months in the Penitentiary* (St. Louis: W.S. Bryan, 1880)

Miller, Thomas N.: Letter to the Editor, *Pittsburgh Leader,* September 25, 1903.

Morgan, Albert T.: *Yazoo: or, On the Picket Line of Freedom in the South: A Personal Narrative* (Washington, D.C.: Published by the Author, 1884)

Sherman, John: *Recollections of Forty Years in the House, Senate, and Cabinet;* Volume I (Chicago: Werner Company, 1895)

Stanton, Elizabeth Cady: *Eighty Years and More (1815–1897): Reminiscences of Elizabeth Cady Stanton* (New York: European Publishing Co., 1898)

Taylor, Richard: *Destruction and Reconstruction: Personal Experiences of the Late War* (New York: D. Appleton and Company, 1900)

Washington, Booker T.: *Up From Slavery* (New York: Doubleday, Page, & Co., 1901)

THE WRITERS AND THEIR POSITIONS
AT THE TIME

Writers, Observers, and Activists

Booker T. Washington, child freed from slavery; later founder of Tuskegee Institute.

Elizabeth Cady Stanton, leading campaigner for women's right to vote.

Charles Francis Adams, Jr., essayist and journalist.

Julia Dent Grant, wife of General Ulysses S. Grant and later First Lady.

George W. Childs, publisher and confidant of President Grant.

Industrialists

Andrew Carnegie, railroad executive, investor, and later steel industrialist.

Thomas Miller, investor in iron manufacturing.

Congressmen, Cabinet Members, and Federal Officials

Shelby M. Cullom, U.S. representative from Illinois.

George S. Boutwell, U.S. representative from Massachusetts, later treasury secretary under President Grant.

John Sherman, U.S. senator from Ohio, later treasury secretary under President Rutherford B. Hayes.

Jacob D. Cox, U.S. interior secretary under President Grant.

Oliver O. Howard, U.S. Army general and head of the Freedmen's Bureau.

John McDonald, Supervisor of Internal Revenue, St. Louis, under President Grant, and leader of the Whiskey Ring.

Southern Republican Leaders

Albert T. Morgan, immigrant to Mississippi from Wisconsin; plantation operator in Yazoo County; later State senator, head of the Yazoo County Board of Supervisors, and Yazoo County sheriff.

John R. Lynch, freed from slavery to become a photographer and Republican activist; later justice of the peace in Natchez, Mississippi, Speaker of the Mississippi House of Representatives, and U.S. Representative.

Daniel H. Chamberlain, former governor of South Carolina.

Southern Democratic Leaders

Richard Taylor, former Confederate general.

L. Q. C. Lamar, Mississippi Democratic party leader, U.S. representative, and U.S. senator.

INTRODUCTION
The Enemy, Ourselves

Are Americans one people? Late in the twentieth century, few would doubt that proposition. Traveling overseas or serving in our far-flung outposts of military or corporate power, we recognize one another readily, even with pleasure, whatever our differences of region, gender, political party, social class, or, to invoke that most bitter of categories, race. We understand (at least implicitly) that over the nearly four centuries since Europeans and Africans first began arriving in what is now the United States, what began as an utterly diverse mosaic of strangers has turned into a single entity. Unless we are totally alienated, we feel an identity with the American polity. At some level, we recognize that whatever our differences, we cannot escape one another, and that our only viable option is to share the space we inhabit. If we move beyond felt identity, we might reflect on the consequences that failing to do so could bring, especially given what has happened in the former Yugoslavia and much of the former Soviet Union.

The nation's public rhetoric reinforces our feeling of identity. Whether we look at formal pronouncements like the Declaration of Independence, the Constitution, or Abraham Lincoln's Gettysburg address, at patriotic songs such as "America" (sung to the tune of the *British* national anthem), at rituals such as the pledge of allegiance, or at historical notions such as the "frontier" or the "melting pot," we are told again and again that the American Republic has an infinite capacity to include. The greatest poetic expression of our nationhood, Walt Whitman's "Song of Myself," celebrates a unity that is founded on diversity, not on sameness. In page after page of dense verse, Whitman elaborates on the nation's own motto, *e pluribus unum* (out of many, one). His whole project is to make us not-strangers to ourselves, however little we may look, talk, eat, dress, or remember like one another.

Yet when Whitman was writing "Song of Myself" there was good reason to think that the American Republic would not survive. Between 1850 and 1861 the ties of emotion, politics, and finally government that bound white Americans (as they thought) into one people stretched taut and snapped. Between 1861 and 1865, red, white, and black Americans tore at one another's bodies and communities in a cataclysmic war of destruction. The Civil War was not the first such general conflict in our history. The War of American Independence likewise pitted everyone within the thirteen British colonies/young United States against virtually everyone else. Nor were these epochs of formal warfare the only times when violence has determined the conditions of our existence. The long, drawn-out dispossession of the First Americans from what had been entirely theirs, the institutionalized violence of slavery, massive strife between capital and labor, ethnic rioting, gang warfare: all of these have turned on the question of who should belong, in America, and to what.

Our words, too, have served as weapons that exclude and divide, as much as they have served to unite us. Even before there was an American Republic, the British colonizers who would give it shape were arguing with themselves about the terms and meaning of their own existence. One effect of the American Revolution was to open that argument up to people rendered more or less silent by race and sex until then. Since the Revolution the argument has gone on in pamphlets, newspapers, poetry, music, paintings, fiction, films, and the jurisprudence of the United States Supreme Court, so much so that the argument itself seems to form one of the reasons why we exist. In my own lifetime the political repression of the 1950s, the times that were a-changin' of the 1960s, and the conservative resurgence of the 1980s have formed chapters within it. Our present disputes about the history that we should remember and the terms we should use to address one another do not spring from shallow "multiculturalism" or facile "political correctness." They emerge from a long history of America finding itself in the act of arguing with itself about itself.

Robber Barons and Radicals brings one of the most striking chapters in our long history of arguing with ourselves about ourselves into glowing, three-dimensional, full-color life. When silence fell at Appomattox on April 9, 1865, it ended only the military phase of an all-engulfing crisis. Just one point was established as General Robert E. Lee surrendered what was left of Confederate power to General Ulysses S. Grant and as Jefferson Davis fled the capital of his failed slave republic. In military terms, at least, the white South would fight no more, forever. Nothing else was resolved at all. That slavery was in its final moments seemed clear, but the institution still did legally exist in states that had permitted it but that had not joined the Confederacy. It even survived in states that had seceded. Not until "Juneteenth" (June 19, 1865) was its abolition proclaimed in Texas.

Where slavery was in fact gone, the condition of the former slaves remained uncertain. In 1857 Chief Justice Roger B. Taney had decreed from the bench that free or slave, black people were not part of the American People. They had no citizenship under the Constitution, no recourse to Federal courts, no rights that white Americans were bound to respect. Taney's point applied as much to highly visible African Americans who were working for slavery's destruction—Frederick Douglass, the Reverend Henry Highland Garnet, Sojourner Truth—as it did to the hundreds of thousands of slaves who built and sustained the Cotton Kingdom. The slaveholding chief justice was dead by 1865. The war he had unwittingly helped bring on had seen slaves begin to free themselves as early as 1861 by crossing Union lines and becoming "contrabands." It had seen 170,000 black men wear the Union's uniform. But it was still not clear in 1865 that these people did belong to the United States on terms of full equality that the notion of citizenship implies.

Just as uncertain was the condition of former Confederates, both in their separate capacities as individuals and in their collective capacities of the citizenrics of Virginia, Georgia, Alabama, Mississippi, or Arkansas. Both as individuals and as members of their polities they had renounced the United States and waged war against it. That their military defeat required their reintegration on some terms was obvious, but what those terms would be could not have been less certain.

The greatest, most hopeful, and most tragic story of the era took place in the former Confederacy. By the story's end a dozen years after Lee's surrender, the white South had regained an astonishingly large portion of what had seemed totally lost in April 1865. "Redemption," the final removal of Reconstruction governments, Union military power, and Northern will to carry on in the South, left former slaves effectively at the mercy of their former masters. Slavery itself may have been dead, but white supremacy would endure until the Civil Rights movement led to a "second reconstruction" a full century later. White Southerners had lost their grip on power in Washington (though, as this book shows, the architect of Mississippi secession *and* Mississippi "redemption" found his way into the House of Representatives, the Senate, the Cabinet, and finally the Supreme Court). But former slaveholders regained control of their counties, their states, and their region.

Much of *Robber Barons and Radicals* is devoted to that story, and some astonishing characters appear within it. We meet predictable figures (from traditional accounts) such as Lucius Quintus Cincinnatus Lamar, the Mississippian who moved from ardent secessionism to the Supreme Court. We also meet the former slave John R. Lynch, who won a Mississippi congressional election as late as 1882, and the white "carpetbagger" Albert T. Morgan, who traveled downriver from Wisconsin to the Mississippi/Yazoo Delta in 1865, tried planting with free labor (and failed at it because of white opposition), entered state politics and succeeded at it, and married an African-American woman before "redemption" finally drove him out.

Generally "meeting" such people in historical texts means getting a brief reading of their words and perhaps a snapshot view of their faces. T. J. Stiles takes us into their worlds, in the fullest possible detail. Secessionist/Congressman/Senator/Justice Lamar had ample opportunity before his death in 1893 to tell his story in a way that would justify the ways of himself and his kind to the world, and the world heard. Lynch and Morgan fell from the high positions they enjoyed for a time and endured the complete ruin of the high hopes they had entertained. Each died forgotten, and in despair. But they did not go quietly or gently, and after their defeat they set out to show what had happened, as they had seen it. Each wrote at length, and what they wrote provides a compellingly different picture of the Reconstruction era in what one historian has described as "the most Southern place on earth."

The final freeing of black America after two and a half centuries of enslavement and the terrible realization that "nothing but freedom" would be the final result is the main story. But the years between the white South's great military disaster and its astonishing political triumph saw many other stories underway as well. Conventional accounts of Reconstruction harp ceaselessly on the theme of corruption in very high places. We see it here in the cases of two successive failed Presidents, Andrew Johnson and Ulysses S. Grant. Each found himself in the White House because he had won great success in other ways, Johnson as the Unionist governor of his native Tennessee and Grant as the architect of the Union victory. Each man found himself out of place. In Johnson's case the fault sprang from a combination of his own personality and his complete inability to accept the principles for which the Republican party stood at the time of his succession. Grant was personally unsuited to the White House as well, but he had touched greatness (in the words of his biographer), and his tragedy was greater too. Stiles shows us both presidential failures, again at length, again through the eyes of witnesses who stood very close to them and who are themselves as fascinating as the Presidents whose stories they recount.

A third great story of the era is the emergence of truly big business as the dominant economic force in American life. The Union won the Civil War not just because of Grant's military genius but also because its vibrant capitalism, well-developed industry, and free-labor system allowed it to amass the enormous resources that Grant's strategy required. The economic energies released during the war grew even stronger when the guns stopped firing. One direction was through the emergence of finance capitalism, as Wall Street became the nation's economic heart. Another direction was through the use of the fruits of high finance for genuinely creative purposes. Great opportunity, however, readily slides into great temptation. We see the finance side here in the schemes of Jay Gould, Jay Cooke, and Jim Fisk, all of whom pyramided speculations into fortunes before tumbling from fortune to failure. We see the creative side in the redoubtable Andrew Carnegie and the makers of steel whom he gathered around him. In his own memoirs, which Stiles excerpts at length, Carnegie would have the reader believe that speculative finance and creative industry were two different things. But for a time he was just as much a denizen of the world of insider deals as any speculator. As in the hopes and failures of Southern Reconstruction, the "great barbecue" presents a complex story of human history, achievement, and tragedy, rather than a melodrama that pitted good against bad.

Nor is this all. The era before the war's outbreak saw the emergence of gender as a major category in American discussion. It saw the place and the role of women within the Republic become major items on the American agenda. As with former slaves, former masters, carpetbaggers, Washington politicians, and capitalists, the actual story is full of contradiction. Harriet Beecher Stowe forcefully articulated the relationship between the issue of gender and slavery in her great novel *Uncle Tom's Cabin* (1852). Yet she backed off from asserting that women might claim a place in the public sphere for themselves. Elizabeth Cady Stanton did make that assertion, and she campaigned just as forcefully as Stowe did against slavery. Her disappointed bitterness when the end of slavery and the achievement of black citizenship by Constitutional amendment also brought the introduction of gender discrimination into the Constitution is understandable. Her willingness thereafter to traffic in racism for the sake of the "woman movement" looks less well.

Stanton, too, appears in these pages. So do (in passing) Indians in the far Southwest and northern Great Plains who were entirely surrounded by whites, grotesquely outnumbered, bereft of all possible allies, and on the verge of the final end of their way of life. Their story too is part of the era (and is covered in detail in *Warriors and Pioneers*, the previous book in this series). The same United States army that offered only fitful protection to former slaves such as John Lynch and to radical reconstructors such as Albert Morgan, and that eventually abandoned them entirely, moved to defeat Apaches, Comanches, Cheyennes, Sioux, Nez Percés, and Arapahos. The establishment of absolute white supremacy took place in the Dakotas and Arizona as well as in Alabama and Louisiana.

Not even a really long volume—and this one is not short—could possibly tell all these stories. But *Robber Barons and Radicals* makes very compelling reading. Despite its formidable length, I devoured it in only a few days. It tells a very complex, very American story through the voices of people who took direct part, who realized they were making history, and who wanted what they had done to be recalled. We still live with the consequences of their victories and of their defeats.

—Edward Countryman
Clements Department of History
Southern Methodist University

A NOTE TO THE READER

In addition to providing introductions to the first-person accounts in this book, the editor has included original narrative to connect the selections and offer critical commentary. A heavy line appears at the beginning and end of these sections, marking off the editor's words from those of the historical writers. Within the first-person accounts, of course, the editor's insertions appear in brackets.

I

OUT OF THE ASHES

THE BATTLE FOR
RECONSTRUCTION
1865–1867

1

FOOT SOLDIERS OF FREEDOM:
THE OTHER SOUTHERNERS

On April 2, Richmond burned. As darkness fell, the streets filled with horses, with mules, with coaches, with wagons, lashed ahead by government officials and panicked civilians, all lit by flames that roared through the city. Through four years of war, the stately capital of that entity called the Confederate States of America had stood untouched, as town after town fell to Union forces. Now, in 1865, the end had finally come; federal troops were only hours away. The ragged army of General Robert E. Lee had already fled west; the rebel leadership followed in its wake, torching what it could not carry away; now mobs crowded the cobblestones, and the city burned.

The next day it was over. In many places, fire still clawed at the walls of offices and warehouses; in others, nothing was left but ashes, blackened chimneys, and empty shells of brick. The fighting shifted away from the city; in a few days, General Ulysses S. Grant would trap Lee and force him to surrender at Appomattox Courthouse. In the fallen capital, the citizens watched as their conquerors marched through the streets in tightly disciplined order, erect and proud in the blue uniforms of the United States Army. But the people of Richmond noticed less the color of the uniforms than that of the men, for they were soldiers of the all-black 25th Corps.

Following those first Union troops came another unlikely visitor, in the person of Abraham Lincoln. He had been visiting Grant's forces when Lee's line collapsed; now, with a simple escort of ten sailors, the Great Emancipator strolled through the prize his soldiers had suffered and died for through four long years. With every step, he attracted a growing crowd of people—people who up to that very moment had been held in slavery—and they shouted thanks to God and praises for their liberator. When one man fell to his knees, Lincoln bent his tall body and said, "Don't kneel to me. That is not right. You must kneel to God only, and thank Him for the liberty you will enjoy hereafter."[1]

[1] This and all other quotes from Lincoln (and Frederick Douglass) in this chapter are from James M. McPherson's *Battle Cry of Freedom: The Civil War Era* (New York: Oxford University Press, 1988). Most of the statistics and detailed information on Reconstruction and the status of the South at war's end can be found in Eric Foner's excellent *Reconstruction: America's Unfinished Revolution, 1863–1877* (New York: Harper & Row, 1988). Another important, readable account of the period is William S. McFeely's *Grant: A Biography* (New York: W.W. Norton, 1982).

If only the story could end at that moment of euphoria and triumph, on that note of thanksgiving and humility. But the Union victory carried within it problems that dwarfed the wartime quandary of capturing Richmond. Indeed, it was virtually a Trojan horse delivered by the hand of history to Lincoln and his government—a gift of peace harboring the agents of catastrophe.

As the African-American soldiers of the 25th Corps put out the remaining fires of Richmond, Lincoln faced a peace made tenuous by the methods that had made victory certain. During the war the President had encouraged his generals to win by any means necessary; though a man of unsurpassed compassion, he had summed up his orders in a terse phrase: "Destroy the rebel army." In an age of modern industry and equipment, facing a hostile public as well as an army, his commanders had won by taking the war to the heart of the South, destroying both its will to resist and its ability to sustain men in the field. Far from Grant's battles with Lee, such generals as William T. Sherman and Philip H. Sheridan had marched through the countryside, burning, destroying, burning.

The Shenandoah Valley, the jewel of Virginia and the breadbasket of Lee's forces, had been methodically leveled by Sheridan's men in 1864. Crops, buildings, fences, and livestock were gone. North Carolina, Georgia, and especially South Carolina had yet to recover from damage wrought by Sherman's army. The commercial and manufacturing centers of Atlanta and Columbia had been thoroughly torched. Railways and farmland in Alabama, Mississippi, and Louisiana were torn up and ravaged by Yankee troops. Even five years after the end of the war, the former Confederate states would not yet reach prewar levels of land value, livestock, acres of cultivated farmland, and economic output.

Much of the devastation was almost certainly necessary to the Union victory; but Lincoln's generals were not alone at fault. Confederate raids behind Union lines (though still in Southern states) had added to the direct destruction. And the Southerners had thrown away much of their wealth in the drive to establish a slave republic below Mason-Dixon. Their financial capital had gone into Confederate bonds—now worthless. They had expended vast sums for the purchase of arms, uniforms, and supplies for the troops, not to mention fortifications, ships, and other materiel of war. Meanwhile they had neglected roads, levees, and irrigation works, eroding the South's already underdeveloped infrastructure.

Perhaps worst of all was the bitterness left by the war. The rebels' savage losses had driven the Confederacy to defeat, but they only increased Southern anger and resentment. Approximately 260,000 men—more than 20 percent of the adult white male population of the South—died while under arms for the rebel government. Many more were badly wounded; Mississippi, for example, spent one-fifth of its budget in 1865 on artificial limbs for veterans. Perhaps no one felt the bitterness of war more deeply than the people of Missouri—a state that had not even joined the Confederacy. Far from the front lines for most of the war, the state had endured what is usually called guerrilla warfare, though a more precise description would be terror and counterterror. Butchering gangs of scalp-taking Confederate bushwhackers and almost equally brutal Union cavalrymen had ravaged the once-rich countryside, shooting prisoners, looting farms, and burning crops, buildings, and fences. They depopulated and devastated vast areas. By 1865, one out of three Missourians had died in battle, been murdered, or fled the state. As the war ended, near anarchy reigned in many of the state's rural counties.

Anarchy was almost undoubtedly a shadow that haunted Lincoln's mind as he returned to Washington in the second week of April. Throughout the South, state governments existed in a legal limbo: the President had argued that states could never secede from the Union, yet it would scarcely be possible for him to recognize governors and legislators who had made war on the Constitution. Lincoln made this point directly on April 11 in a speech delivered from a White House balcony to an enthusiastic crowd. "There is no authorized organ for us to treat with," he declared. "We must simply begin with, and mould from, disorganized and discordant elements."

The President's choice of words suggests how deeply he had begun to think about the great quandary before him—a depth of thought sometimes missed by succeeding generations. In the almost century and a half since his death, a great deal has been written about how Lincoln's forgiving nature and desire for reconciliation put him at odds with vengeful Republicans in Congress. The implication has been that Lincoln would have been so kind to the fallen South that no crisis would have ensued. Yet the man from Illinois did not indulge in such simplistic, wishful thinking. His speech clearly indicated that he was unwilling to simply restore the old regime in the South (after all, he had recently pushed Congress to launch the Thirteenth Amendment to the Constitution, abolishing slavery). Nor was he under any illusion that he would have an easy task in moulding the South's "disorganized and discordant elements."

But he never had the chance to try. On April 14, 1865, as Lincoln sat in a box in Ford's Theater watching *Our American Cousin,* actor John Wilkes Booth fired a bullet into his brain. The assassin then leaped to the stage (breaking his leg), and shouted, "*Sic semper tyrannis!* The South is avenged!"[2] It was a telling start to the postwar era—for the grisly murder was part of an insidious conspiracy, a conspiracy to launch an age of conspiracy. That same night, Secretary of State William H. Seward was severely wounded by one of Booth's friends, Lewis Thornton Powell.

---

[2] *Sic semper tyrranis* ("Thus always to tyrants") was (and still is) the state motto of Virginia.

The plotters also planned an assault on Vice-President Andrew Johnson, but the assigned killer lost his nerve. In the months to come, many Americans might well have wished that the nervous assassin had traded targets with the straight-shooting Booth.

The North's worst fears about the bitterness of the defeated South were now realized—a stark omen of confrontations yet to come. For two weeks the public mourned their loss and chattered about the conspiracy as the search for Booth went on. Finally, on April 26, the actor was found in a barn near Bowling Green, Virginia. His pursuers set the building on fire, then shot him down as he tried to escape.

In a crisis compounded by crisis, one of the strangest men ever to occupy the White House took the oath of office. The question of who Andrew Johnson was, and what he would do, gripped the leaders of the day—from Republican congressmen such as Thaddeus Stevens and Charles Sumner to General Ulysses S. Grant and his wife Julia Dent Grant, who now heard the first whispered suggestions that the army commander might run for the presidency himself. Still others watched expectantly, wondering where the events would take the nation: Elizabeth Cady Stanton, who longed to renew her campaign for women's rights now that the war had ended; the rising, ruthless financier Jay Gould; a little-known railroad manager and investor named Andrew Carnegie; and a recently freed slave, now in the employ of the army, named John R. Lynch. In the days and months and years to come, these individuals would help shape the country's future as it moved in directions no one could have predicted when Lincoln's body was laid to rest.

But the most important problem left by the war was not physical destruction, the legitimacy of state governments, or even the political leanings of the new President: it was a question of four million. That vast number of African Americans had been released from bondage—a number greater than the total population of the American colonies a century earlier. To Lincoln, the abolition of slavery had been a happy result of the conflict, but not its first purpose. Deeply moral in his character, repulsed by slavery, Lincoln had nevertheless been a resolutely practical politician: his overriding goal had been victory, which meant placating border-state slaveowners who remained loyal to the Union. Yet the war waged by the South to preserve slavery led inexorably to its destruction. As the fighting stretched on, Lincoln had come to conclusions in the political realm much like those reached by General Sherman in military matters: the Southern war effort had to be undermined in every way possible, and that meant eliminating slavery. The Emancipation Proclamation (which freed the slaves in Confederate territory) and the Thirteenth Amendment (which outlawed slavery everywhere), ratified in 1865, were the legal fruits of thinking driven by the war itself.

And yet, freedom was hardly a gift handed down to black people from the white government in Washington. In many ways, the legal abolishment of slavery was simply a recognition that freedom had already been earned, and *taken,* by African Americans themselves. Wherever the federal armies had advanced during the war—from the Missouri River basin east of Kansas City to the sea islands of South Carolina—slaves had fled to the light of Union campfires. Yankee troops called them "contrabands," in an ironic twist on the term for seized enemy property—for here the property was unseizing itself. These freed people set about helping the Union effort, providing information on the Confederate armies, building fortifications, repairing railroads, and finally serving as soldiers themselves.

The enrollment of black troops in 1862 had shocked the South. In American democracy, service as a soldier was a fundamental expression of citizenship. Frederick Douglass exulted in what white Southerners feared, saying, "Once let the black man get upon his person the brass letters, U.S.; let him get an eagle on his button, and a musket on his shoulder and bullets in his pocket, and there is no power on earth which can deny that he has earned the right to citizenship." The Confederates showed how seriously they took this threat by selling captured black soldiers into slavery and summarily shooting their officers. In the North, the opposite reaction took place—the bravery of the tens of thousands of African-American soldiers helped erode Yankee racism, and added to the sentiment that blacks deserved a place at the political table.

But at war's end, sentiment had yet to be turned into action. Lincoln, who might have provided practical yet principled leadership on the issue, was dead. Johnson, a man with untested qualities, was in the White House with no known policy. The Republican-dominated Congress had recessed for the summer. In the South, the future was unreadable—a social and economic system built up over two centuries had been overturned virtually overnight. And yet, for four million African Americans, the *meaning* of freedom, as historian Eric Foner has put it, was yet to be established. No greater change in our society has ever taken place in so short a time, and how it would affect people's lives and where it would take the South was unclear to everyone.

Booker T. Washington was one man who lived through the tumultuous transition from slavery to freedom as a young child in Virginia. In later years, he wrote a direct, unaffected memoir that recalled his early life in bondage. As a small boy, he missed some of the worst horrors visited upon slaves in the South, yet the hardships he describes speak for themselves. He also begins to sketch the life that blacks made for themselves under the pressure of slavery, in a world where education was forbidden and travel prohibited, and he illuminates their yearning for Union victory as the Civil War neared its conclusion. He also memorably recalls the splendid moment of emancipation. Perhaps most important, Washington provides insight into the meaning of freedom for African Americans, as they tested the basic elements of liberty—beginning with the right to a name of one's own.

Up From Slavery
by Booker T. Washington

I was born a slave on a plantation in Franklin County, Virginia. I am not quite sure of the exact place or exact date of my birth, but at any rate I suspect I must have been born somewhere and at some time. As nearly as I have been able to learn, I was born near a cross-roads post-office called Hale's Ford, and the year was 1858 or 1859. I do not know the month or the day.

The earliest impressions I can now recall are of the plantation and the slave quarters—the latter being the part of the plantation where the slaves had their cabins. My life had its beginning in the midst of the most miserable, desolate, and discouraging surroundings. This was so, however, not because my owners were especially cruel, for they were not as compared with many others. I was born in a typical log cabin, about fourteen by sixteen feet square. In this cabin I lived with my mother and a brother and sister till after the Civil War, when we were all declared free.

Of my ancestry I know almost nothing. In the slave quarters, and even later, I heard whispered conversations among the colored people of the torture which the slaves, including, no doubt, my ancestors on my mother's side, suffered in the middle passage of the slave ship while being conveyed from Africa to America. I have been unsuccessful in securing any information that would throw an accurate light upon the history of my family beyond my mother. She, I remember, had a half-brother and a half-sister. In the days of slavery not very much attention was given to family history and family records—that is, black family records.

My mother, I suppose, attracted the attention of a purchaser who was afterward my owner and hers. Her addition to the slave family attracted about as much attention as the purchase of a new horse or cow. Of my father I know even less than of my mother. I do not even know his name. I have heard reports to the effect that he was a white man who lived on one of the nearby plantations. Whoever he was, I never heard of his taking the least interest in me or providing in any way for my rearing. But I do not find especial fault with him. He was simply another unfortunate victim of the institution which the nation unhappily had engrafted upon it at that time.

The cabin was not only our living-place, but was also used as the kitchen for the plantation. My mother was the plantation cook. The cabin was without glass windows; it had only openings in the side which let in the light, and also the cold, chilly air of winter. There was a door to the cabin—that is, something that was called a door—but the uncertain hinges by which it was hung, and the large cracks in it, to say nothing of the fact that it was too small, made the room a very uncomfortable one. . . . There was no wooden floor in our cabin, the naked earth being used as a floor. In the center of the earthen floor there was a large, deep opening covered with boards, which was used as a place in which to store sweet potatoes during the winter. . . . There was no cooking-stove on our plantation, and all the cooking for the whites and slaves my mother had to do over an open fireplace, mostly in pots and skillets. While the poorly built cabin caused us to suffer with cold in the winter, the heat from the open fireplace in summer was equally trying.

The early years of my life, which were spent in this little cabin, were not very different from those of thousands of other slaves. My mother, of course, had little time in which to give attention to the training of her children during the day. She snatched a few moments for our care in the early morning before her work began, and at night after the day's work was done. One of my earliest recollections is that of my mother cooking a chicken late at night, and awakening her children for the purpose of feeding them. How or where she got it I do not know. I presume, however, it was procured from our owner's farm. Some people may call this theft. If such a thing were to happen now, I should condemn it as theft myself. But taking place at the time it did, and for the reason that it did, no one could ever make me believe that my mother was guilty of thieving. She was simply a victim of the system of slavery.

I cannot remember having slept in a bed until after our family was declared free by the Emancipation Proclamation. Three children—John, my older brother, Amanda, my sister, and myself—had a pallet on the dirt floor, or, to be more correct, we slept in and on a bundle of filthy rags laid upon the dirt floor. . . .

I had no schooling whatever while I was a slave, though I remember on several occasions I went as far as the schoolhouse door with one of my young mistresses to carry her books. The picture of several dozen boys and girls in a schoolroom engaged in study made a deep impression upon me, and I had the feeling that to get into a schoolhouse and study in this way would be about the same as getting into paradise.

As far as I can now recall, the first knowledge that I got of the fact that we were slaves, and that the freedom of the slaves was being discussed, was early one morning before day, when I was awakened by my mother kneeling over her children and fervently praying that Lincoln and his armies might be successful, and that one day she and her children might be free. In this connection I have never been able to understand how the slaves throughout the South, completely ignorant as were the masses so far as books or newspapers were concerned, were able to keep themselves so accurately and completely informed about the great national questions that were agitating the country. From the time that Garrison, Lovejoy, and others began to agitate for freedom, the slaves throughout the South kept in close touch with the progress of the movement. Though I was a mere child during the preparation for the Civil War and during the war itself, I now recall the many late-at-night whispered discussions that I heard my mother and the other slaves on the plantation indulge in. These discussions showed that they understood the situation, and that they kept themselves informed of events by what was termed the "grape-vine telegraph."

During the campaign when Lincoln was first a candidate for the presidency, the slaves on our far-off plantation, miles from any railroad or large city or daily newspaper, knew what the issues involved were. When war was begun between the North and the South, every slave on our plantation felt and knew that, though other issues were discussed, the primal one was that of slavery. Even the most ignorant members of my race on the remote plantations felt in their hearts, with a certainty that admitted no doubt, that the freedom of the slaves would be the one great result of the war, if the Northern armies conquered.

Every success of the Federal armies and every defeat of the Confederate forces was watched with the keenest and most intense interest. Often the slaves got knowledge of the results of great battles before the white people received it. This news was usually gotten from the colored man who was sent to the post-office for the mail. In our case the post-office was about three miles from the plantation, and the mail came once or twice a week. The man who was sent to the office would linger about the place long enough to get the drift of the conversation from the group of white people who naturally congregated there, after receiving their mail, to receive the latest news. The mail-carrier on his way back to our master's house would as naturally retail the news that he had secured among the slaves, and in this sway they often heard of important events before the white people at the "big house," as the master's house was called. . . .

Finally the war closed, and the day of freedom came. It was a momentous and eventful day to all upon our plantation. We had been expecting it. Freedom was in the air, and had been for months. Deserting soldiers returning to their homes were to be seen every day. Others who had been discharged, or whose regiments had been paroled,[3] were constantly passing near our place. The "grape-vine telegraph" was kept busy night and day. The news and mutterings of great events were swiftly carried from one plantation to another. . . .

The slaves would give the Yankee soldiers food, drink, clothing—anything but that which had been specifically trusted to their care and honor. As the great day drew nearer, there was more singing in the slave quar-

---

[3] During the Civil War, the two armies would often parole their prisoners, allowing them to return home on the condition that they would not fight again.

ters than usual. It was bolder, had more ring, and lasted later into the night. Most of the verses of the plantation songs had some reference to freedom. True, they had sung those same verses before, but they had been careful to explain that the "freedom" in these songs referred to the next world, and had no connection with life in this world. Now they gradually threw off the mask, and were not afraid to let it be known that the freedom in their songs meant freedom of the body in this world.

The night before the eventful day, word was sent to the slave quarters to the effect that something unusual was going to take place at the "big house" the next morning. There was little, if any, sleep that night. All was excitement and expectancy. Early the next morning word was sent to all the slaves, old and young, to gather at the house. In company with my mother, brother, and sister, and a large number of other slaves, I went to the master's house. All of our master's family were either standing or seated on the veranda of the house, where they could see what was to take place and hear what was said. There was a feeling of deep interest, or perhaps sadness, in their faces, but not bitterness. As I now recall the impression they made upon me, they did not at the moment seem to be sad because of the loss of property, but rather because of parting with those whom they had reared and who were in many ways very close to them. The most distinct thing that I now recall in connection with the scene was that some man who seemed to be a stranger (a United States officer, I presume) made a little speech and then read a rather long paper—the Emancipation Proclamation, I think. After the reading we were told that we were all free, and could go when and where we pleased. My mother, who was standing by my side, leaned over and kissed her children, while tears of joy ran down her cheeks. She explained to us what it all meant, that this was the day for which she had been so long praying, but fearing that she would never live to see.

For some minutes there was great rejoicing, and thanksgiving, and wild scenes of ecstacy. But there was no feeling of bitterness. In fact, there was pity among the slaves for our former owners. The wild rejoicing on the part of the emancipated colored people lasted but for a brief period, for I noticed that by the time they returned to their cabins there was a change in their feelings. The great responsibility of being free, of having charge of themselves, of having to think and plan for themselves and their children, seemed to have taken possession of them. It was very much like suddenly turning a youth of ten or twelve years old out into the world to provide for himself. In a few hours the great questions with which the Anglo-Saxon race had been grappling for centuries had been thrown upon these people to be solved. These were the questions of a home, a living, the rearing of children, education, citizenship, and the establishment and support of churches. Was it any wonder that within a few hours the wild rejoicing ceased and a feeling of deep gloom seemed to pervade the slave quarters? . . .

After the coming of freedom there were two points upon which practically all the people on our place agreed, and I find this was generally true throughout the South: that they must change their names, and that they must leave the old plantation for at least a few days or weeks in order that they might really feel sure that they were free.

In some way a feeling got among the colored people that it was far from proper for them to bear the surname of their former owners, and a great many of them took other surnames. This was one of the first signs of freedom. When they were slaves, a colored person was simply called "John" or "Susan." There was seldom occasion for more than the use of the one name. If "John" or "Susan" belonged to a white man by the name of "Hatcher," sometimes he was called "John Hatcher," or as often "Hatcher's John." But there was a feeling that "John Hatcher" or "Hatcher's John" was not the proper title by which to denote a freeman; and so in many cases "John Hatcher" was changed to "John S. Lincoln" or "John S. Sherman," the initial "S" standing for no name, it being simply a part of what the colored man proudly called his "entitles."

As I have stated, most of the colored people left the old plantation for a short while at least, so as to be sure, it seemed, that they could leave and try their freedom on to see how it felt. After they had remained away for a time, many of the older slaves, especially, returned to their old homes and made some kind of contract with their former owners by which they remained on the estate.

EVEN AS YOUNG Booker—now Booker *T. Washington*—departed the plantation with his mother, millions of African Americans remained behind in a dense fog of uncertainty. Everything—from the most basic rules of social conduct to the ownership of the land the slaves had worked for so long—was thrown into question. Rumors burned through the same grapevine telegraph that had once transmitted news of Union victories: in particular, rumors of a great redistribution of farmland to the freed people at Christmas. Meanwhile, African Americans proudly chose their own names, often selecting those most closely linked to liberty: Washington, Jefferson, and Lincoln. Many refused to submit to the social subservience still expected of them from Southern whites. Returning black veterans in particular stood up to the old conventions; they had learned their power and proven their dignity, just as Frederick Douglass had predicted.

Meanwhile the confusion that hung over the South was exacerbated by the silence of Andrew Johnson, the new President, whose policy toward the defeated Confederates seemed in doubt as spring pushed toward summer in 1865. The initial lack of direction from Washington agitated Southern whites, who were as uncertain about the future as their former slaves. Virtually overnight, the worst fears of the old slaveholders had been realized: a race of millions that had been held down by force was now free among them. Beyond any possible threat of revenge from the freed people (a threat many whites loudly and frequently trumpeted), their greatest concern was, as they put it, the "control of labor." Accustomed to coercing, not contracting with, their laborers, plantation owners refused to believe that African Americans would work for wages. And many blacks refused to sign labor contracts—though the real reason was often the rumored division of land at the end of the year. Expecting their own farms, some preferred to wait and see.

But a feeling deeper than fear of a labor shortage agitated whites: it was their sense that it was not *right* for blacks to move about without restrictions, working wherever the best wages could be found. Feelings of ownership and mastery persisted among former slaveholders. African Americans had hardly finished shouting in jubilation at their liberation when local governments (especially in South Carolina, Mississippi, and Louisiana, where blacks were a majority of the population) began passing laws to control and restrict them. A new battle loomed across the region after the Civil War—a battle to define the meaning of freedom in everyday life.

But to describe race relations and working conditions in the South in such broad terms drains history of its life—the bitterness, hope, and anger, the tensions between individuals, the plans and calculations of both blacks and whites. For that, we need to follow the path of another traveler, one who journeyed south even as Booker T. Washington went north.

In the fall of 1865, this young man stepped off a steamboat onto a landing in Vicksburg, Mississippi—setting foot in a state that was to change his life for good. Little as he knew it at the time, he was to undergo the full experience of Reconstruction condensed into one small town, where circumstances would thrust him to the forefront of the battle for the soul of the South. Fortunately, this man later wrote a moving, highly accurate account of his time in Mississippi, leaving us with a burning portrait of how the sweeping events of this era affected the lives of real people in one particular community.

His name was Albert T. Morgan, and though the public has long forgotten him, he was destined to become one of the most famous (and important) Northern immigrants in the state of Mississippi. When he set foot in Vicksburg, he was accompanied by his older brother Charles; the two had neither politics nor race relations on their minds, but rather the possibility of making a fortune growing cotton. America was a nation on the move, and after the Civil War the westward tide of migration briefly shifted south, where many saw rich new lives to be made in rebuilding the shattered region. Such men as Albert and his brother have come to be known as "carpetbaggers"—a hateful insult wielded by their conservative white opponents, a term that has unfortunately been perpetuated by historians. The implication was that these southbound migrants were somehow different from those who went west; that they were penniless, unscrupulous opportunists who had packed all their meager belongings in old bags made of carpet. But in the case of the Morgans, nothing could be farther from the truth—for like so many Yankees who went south in 1865, they came ready to invest thousands of dollars to reinvigorate the lands of their former enemies.

To the eye, Albert made a poor protagonist for the great political battles he so little expected in the months ahead. At only twenty-three, he had all the markings of a man in poor health: he stood five feet ten inches, but weighed a mere 145 pounds, with a virtually lame leg that he often had to drag along. Yet his eyes betrayed a fierce will that had driven him into danger many times before, and would many times again in the months and years ahead.[4]

Only four years before, Morgan had been a strapping eighteen-year-old weighing 175 pounds. The son of a successful Wisconsin agricultural warehouse owner, he was a devout Baptist who had enrolled at Oberlin College in Ohio. When the Civil War broke out that year, he promptly dropped out of school and enlisted in Company A of the Second Wisconsin Regiment. In those early days, volunteer regiments elected their officers; Albert so impressed his fellows that he quickly rose in rank. And his record in the years that followed bears testimony to his idealism and determination. After being captured at the Second Battle of Bull Run, he went free in a prisoner exchange, then quickly returned to the front. At the Battle of Gettysburg, he fought bravely for long hours on the first day, only to fall when a Confederate rifleman shot him through the left thigh, shattering the bone. He took months to heal, and he was left with a limp for the rest of his life. Even so, he joined the battle once more, fighting through the horrendous Wilderness campaign where tens of thousands died, rising through a field promotion to lieutenant colonel. Finally he succumbed to illness in the trenches around Petersburg. Yet upon his recovery he once again went back to the war, serving with Grant's forces until well after Lee surrendered in April 1865.

His health badly damaged, the boy colonel put aside the idealism that had nearly killed him and joined his brother Charles on a trip south to make money. If Albert was the hothead of the family, Charles was the operator—the cool-thinking businessman who saw opportunities and made the most of them. It had been Charles who pushed for the move to the South: cotton prices soared during the Civil War, and they remained high

---

[4] Perhaps the finest and most thorough possible biographical portrait of Albert Morgan appears in *Those Terrible Carpetbaggers: A Reinterpretation* by Richard Nelson Current (New York: Oxford University Press, 1988). Almost all information about Morgan and Yazoo County that appears in these pages can be found in Current's book, if not in Morgan's own memoirs.

afterward, thanks to greatly reduced production. Charles was sure that if they could find a good plantation to rent, he could line up capital among investors in the North to back their venture.

And so Albert and Charles Morgan boarded their steamboat, bound for Vicksburg. As revealed in the account that follows, the brothers found their plantation in Yazoo County, on the rim of the rich Mississippi Delta.[5] But as Albert organized their venture into cotton farming, he soon learned the depth of bitterness—perhaps hatred is a better word—in the county that was to be his home for the next tumultuous decade.

A Yankee in Yazoo County
by Albert T. Morgan

In these pages the reader will find faithfully set out a simple and truthful narrative of the principal incidents and events in the public and private life of the author during his residence in Yazoo County, Mississippi, together with occasional pictures illustrative of the social conditions of the people of that State. The *characters* are real persons, whose true names are given only in cases where it was found impossible to disguise their identity. The conversations quoted, of course, are not verbatim. They are, nevertheless, strictly within the line of truth.

Both in gathering the material and preparing it for the public, the author has encountered certain obstacles which many never will be able adequately to appreciate, because it will be impossible for them to stand in his place. Nothing is asked or expected, however, more than an honest judgment upon his motive and his work.

SOUTHWARD, HO!

Charles and I were strangers in Mississippi. Although born in New York, we were raised in Wisconsin on a farm of what, in that State, is called "openings" and prairie land. Therefore we knew something about farming. I had some experience in my father's store and wheat warehouse. Perfectly

---

[5] The Delta is not, as might be thought, the mouth of the Mississippi River down in Louisiana, but rather a semicircular region in the state of Mississippi, bounded by Memphis in the north and Vicksburg in the south, with the Yazoo River as its eastern boundary. This region had rich soil, perfect for cotton farming; as a result, it was filled with large plantations—along with a large population of poor blacks, and a small population of rich whites.

familiar with the crops and the soils of Wisconsin, we knew nothing about those of the Mississippi lowlands, and until we went South with the Union armies neither of us had seen a cotton boll. During the last two years of the war many Union soldiers, tempted by the large returns on the capital invested in cultivating cotton, remained behind when their commands returned home to be mustered out, and engaged in that business.

Charles's service had been in the army which occupied the cotton territory, and it was what he had seen, as well as the information that he had gained from these Yankee planters during his three years with the armies of Thomas and Sherman, that tempted him, when the last armed rebel had surrendered, to seek a permanent home in the far South.

To me, brother Charles always seemed possessed of a wonderful power of self-control. He never lost his head. My affection for him was only less than my love for father, and I know that his love for me was very great. I had an abiding faith in him; in his clear head, sound judgment, and good heart. Therefore, he did not have to persuade me to accompany him. I was only too glad of his offer to take me along as an equal partner with himself. . . .

It was early autumn when we landed at Vicksburg, 1865. Nearly every steamer from above brought large quantities of freight and many prospectors like ourselves. The town was astir with young life, and new vigor everywhere manifested itself. New stores and residences were building, the levees were being repaired, and, though the works of the two armies had been dismantled, they had not yet been leveled down. The caves in which the citizens had taken refuge during the siege and the point where Pemberton met Grant and arranged the terms of surrender were objects of great interest to all strangers.[6] The hotels were full; they overflowed, and we had been obliged to seek accommodation with a private family, known to our agent to be highly respectable, but so reduced in circumstances by the war that they were willing to accept such means of gaining a livelihood.

Several days were spent in "doing" the town and surrounding country. Thus we became acquainted with several old and new settlers, and with the general business and commercial interests of the place. Land agents were numerous. Each one had lengthy lists of "plantations for sale," and "plantations for rent." These varied in size from a hundred to ten thousand acres. Nearly all were amply described, their varied attractions set forth with great apparent exactness, and owners or agents were always only too glad to show their premises to whomsoever might come along.

We had spent about a month examining such as we could hope, from the description of them in the hands of the agent, might meet our re-

[6] For an account of the campaign and siege that led to Vicksburg's capture, see *In Their Own Words: Civil War Commanders,* the first book in this series. Vicksburg's downfall was a great turning point in the Civil War.

quirements, without success, when one day Mrs. —— , the only other guest of our hostess, received a letter from a "dear old friend" of hers, living "up the Yazoo," at Yazoo City, announcing that she had been "utterly ruined by the war"—all her slaves had run off with the first Yankee troops that came into that section.

This was true of most of her neighbors. She had not been able to educate her daughters as she had hoped. Indeed, they did not know how they were to live, unless it could be made of "Tokeba" [the plantation].[7] Her husband was not suited to the task of organizing a new force for the plantation under the "free system," and if he were, where was the money coming from? It could not be borrowed on the plantation for security. It was not to be had of anyone in that region; for they all were as good as bankrupt. She had racked her brain for weeks, aye, months, for some way out of the dilemma. . . .

She had come to the conclusions there was no use "trying to hold out any longer." The negroes were free, and the sooner the fact was recognized by them [the whites] the better. They might talk if they pleased, but she was going to look out for herself and her children. If she could find some "suitable Northern gentlemen of means" to take it, she would lease Tokeba. . . .

The upshot of it all was that the next day, armed with a letter from Mrs. —— to her old friend, "Mrs. Charlotte Black, Yazoo City, Miss.,"[8] Charles took the Yazoo River packet, bound for that town. . . . Two days afterward Charles returned. He took occasion to see Mrs. —— at once, and inform her that he had rented Tokeba for three years, subject to my approval.

She was "perfectly delighted."

That evening Charles and I sat up until after midnight talking over the matter. He gave me a detailed account of his trip, beginning with incidents of the journey to Yazoo City, in the course of which he had met several Northern men en route to different points on the Yazoo River, and with a purpose similar to his own. He had also met and conversed with several citizens of Yazoo City returning from Vicksburg with supplies for their plantations and stores. All seemed to vie with each other in expressions of welcome to him, on learning the object of his visit. As to Tokeba, it offered greater advantages for the development of our plans

7 Morgan wrote that the name was an Indian word, but that some said it came from the phrase "took a bar" (bear), which suggests the pronunciation.

8 Mrs. Black's real name was White (along with her husband, Colonel J.J.B. White, a Confederate veteran). Colonel and Mrs. White play a central role in Albert Morgan's story, and he couldn't resist the obvious play on their names. For clarity, they will be referred to consistently by the name Morgan gives them (Black).

than he had seen anywhere else, and he gave me a minute description of it. . . .

We had already been able to form pretty accurate notions of the fertility of the region, but my mind had not taken it all in before. . . . Prior to coming South, to give me the benefit of comparison, we had, upon my brother's motion, taken a trip through Missouri into Kansas, as far as we could go by rail. Not far beyond Sedalia we spent three days, prospecting upon the prairie lands of that region. . . . Charles was strongly tempted to stop there. But anxious to know more of the "wonderful" soils of the Mississippi bottoms, after going on into Kansas, we concluded to postpone purchase until after we had made a close personal inspection of the cotton territory.

For some months the influential newspapers of the North had contained glowing descriptions of parts of the South, and editorials encouraging immigration into that region. The former cry, "Go West, young man," had undergone just enough variation by the substitution of "South" for "West," to effect a change, already quite apparent, in the purposes of those of the North who were seeking new homes, and as Charles touched this point he grew eloquent indeed.

In his view he saw such a tide of thrifty emigrants and others with capital setting southward, as within twenty-five years would make the two million people of the Mississippi lowlands twenty millions, and in a century a hundred millions. "Thanks to the overthrow of slavery," my brother exclaimed, "these great natural advantages can no longer be hidden from the home-seekers of the world." In his opinion we were fortunate beyond measure in having presented to us an opportunity to precede, if we could not lead, this vast host, in the work of laying the foundations of this new empire by building canals, railroads, and other facilities for its development. . . .

At last, and as a clincher, my brother related how the price at first demanded was ten dollars an acre for the open or plowed lands, being the same as that asked by other owners. But as our plans embraced permanent residence in the community where we should determine to locate as renters, and as the lease was to be for three years instead of one, Mrs. Black had been the first to consent to a reduction to seven dollars per acre: Charles's offer. She had even thrown in a cypress brake of several thousand trees, with permission to cut from it all the timber for our purposes we might wish, including the manufacture of all kinds of lumber for the market. This, to Charles, was the best feature of the bargain. For, as he declared, should the crop from any cause fail, the profits from this branch of the business [lumber] could be relied upon to save us from very great losses. . . .

His representations . . . helped to banish my doubts as to the place he had selected for our new home. The next day we separated, he to the North for supplies, and the evening following I took the "good steamer"

Martin Walt for Tokeba, via Yazoo City, where I was to remain at least over the Sunday following.

I was then twenty-three. Charles was ten years older. . . . My faith in him was limitless. He was the successful boy of our family. He never made mistakes. I cannot now recall any undertaking of his life, up to that time, in which he had not succeeded according to his plans, and his confidence in the future of Yazoo City amounted to enthusiasm. I had been but illy able to disguise my own as he advanced from point to point in the unfolding of his plans for Tokeba, Yazoo, and the great Delta. . . .

FIRST LESSONS

Tokeba plantation, in 1865, contained nine hundred acres of open land, "more or less," for so it was described in the contract, which the lawyers of Mrs. Charlotte Black, wife of Colonel J.J.B. Black, wrote out, and which, having been signed by the Colonel as "agent in fact" for Mrs. Black, "of the first part," and by Charles, one of the "parties of the second part," lay in their hands awaiting my signature. In that instrument we promised to pay to Mrs. Black, for Tokeba, seven dollars per acre per annum for a term of three years, one-half of the annual rental to be paid in advance. It was upon the west bank of the Yazoo River, and lay in a compact body, bounded on the north by a bayou, from which it derived its name, and upon the south by the cypress brake. It was two and a half miles above Yazoo City, which nestled at the foot of the bluffs that crowded to the water's edge at that point, on the east bank of the river. . . .

I had been heartily welcomed by the Black family. They would not allow me to remain at the hotel, where I had taken lodgings upon leaving the *Martin Walt* that glorious Sabbath morning, but insisted I should make their home mine "for the present." My first impression of them was favorable. The next morning, bright and early, the Colonel, mounted on a little, old bay horse, and myself, mounted on a smart, mouse-colored mule, were off for the plantation. Our route lay over the alluvion fringing the east bank of the river for many miles, along the point of land formed by the bend which the river makes for the accommodation of Tokeba. . . .

We had scarcely gone a mile when the Colonel began to halloa: "Ho-ou-ou-ou-pee!" long drawn out. It sounded in the cool, clear air through the forest, shrill and loud as a blast from a hunter's horn. Long practice had made him expert. His horse understood its meaning, pricked up his ears, and struck into a smart canter. It was the Colonel's call to the ferryman on Tokeba, and was repeated every minute or two, so that when we reached the ferry-landing the "flat," guided and propelled by an old black man, bent in body and with legs all awry, promptly scrambled out and made the flat fast to a peg in the ground, pending which the following conversation took place:

"Good morning, Bristol," said Colonel Black cheerily.

"Good mornin', marstah," was the man's response.

"This gentleman is Captain Morgan's brother, Bristol. We're going over to take a look at Tokeba this morning. How's aunt—"

But at this point he abruptly ceased speaking, and turning upon the freedman a most wrathful countenance, exclaimed: "Hi, you black rascal! Don't go putting on the airs of gentleman about me. D'ye-y'hear? Mind that!"

At the first word Bristol seized his long pole, scrambled on to the flat, upon which we had led our horses, and humbly ejaculating: "Ye-a-as, Mars Jeems," began pushing us out into the stream.

Meanwhile the Colonel continued: "These Yankees have come down, y'hear, to make money, God damn[9] you. D'you ever see a Yankee who didn't love money? You'll have to quit yo' damned free nigger notions around them, d'ye-y'hear? and me too, or by God I'll see ye in hell befoah I'll give ye a recommend to them."

What had the poor fellow done? For the life of me, I had not observed anything to criticize in his deportment. . . .

Colonel Black consumed the time of our trip over in imparting to me the information that he knew "the whole damned nigro[10] tribe. Give them an inch and they'll take an ell. They can be governed only by fear. You'll not be able to do anything with them unless you start right. They are by nature a lazy, thieving, treacherous people. I wouldn't trust one of them. This fellow, Bristol, is tainted, like all the rest, with those damned notions about freedom, which you damned Yankees—" Here he checked himself, apologized, and resumed: "It is true that Bristol did not run off with the rest to the first Yankee soldiers that came along. The grand rascal had good reasons for not doing so. He was my carpenter—sort of jack-of-all-trades, and has kept this ferry so long, I reckon he preferred

9 [Original author's footnote] It will be impossible for me to present to the reader a perfect likeness of Colonel Black. He has been dead some years. He was a slaveholder, a rebel, my host, my landlord, and my most implacable foe. He has been dead some years. I long ago forgave him. Under ordinary circumstances I would cover all his faults with that mantle of charity which belongs of right to ordinary mortals after death. But Colonel Black was so conspicuous a personage at a time when the foundations of a newer and better civilization were being laid there, that I should be false to essential truths were I, from feelings of delicacy, or of regard for sensitive readers, to fail to paint him in native colors.

10 [Original author's footnote] Englishmen say "negro." Many Yankees and "poor white trash" have accustomed themselves to say "nigger" or "darkey." The real Southern lady or gentleman pronounces the word with a snap, denoting mastery, thus, "nigro."

to remain on the place where he is sho' of a living. But he is not one whit better than the rest."

Landing at the mouth of the bayou, we rode out to the gin-house, only a few rods distant, thence over the spot he said Charles had selected for a mill-site, thence to the "quarter," two hundred yards further on, and from the quarter thence to the knoll where stood the family residence, embowered in China and magnolia trees. . . .

The plantation was all Charles had claimed for it. Such trees as there were in the brake I had never seen before. Many of them were six to eight feet in diameter above the bulging roots, and ran up skyward straight as an arrow, eighty feet or more to the first limb. That which impressed me most, however, was the deserted "quarter." There were cabins of one and two rooms for a force of 125 or more hands. Only two of them were now occupied. In one was an old man, no longer "serviceable," but who was taking care of and supporting his mother who, they said, was several years more than a century old. In the other were Sallie and her nursing babe. She was not more than thirty-two, and had lost a leg. . . .

During our ride Colonel Black endeavored to entertain me with incidents in the life of a slave-owner. These were illustrative of the "humanity" and "chivalry" of the master, and of the barbarity of the slave. The story of the trip, however, the one of which he seemed to have stored the fondest recollections, was an account of his canvass before the war as the nominee of the "Old-Line Whigs," for a seat in the State Senate.

It was made by him on horseback with two mules following behind, upon which he had packed "that gal, Sal, by God, sir," together with an ample supply of whisky and tobacco. That was before Sallie lost her leg, and when she was a "likely gal." Thus equipped he was able to offer to the suffragans [voters] of Yazoo weightier arguments than his opponent on the Democratic ticket, for he could bid them "choose to their taste" from the greater variety of the "creature comforts" which he "toted about" with him. "By God, sir, that did the business for me, and I was the first Whig Senator ever sent to the legislature from this county."[11] . . .

These "stories" caused me to wonder greatly whether this man had exhibited the same side to my brother, that he was now without reserve uncovering to me. I could not bring myself to think he had. . . .

The following morning I accompanied him to the office of Mrs.

11 [Original author's footnote] On the threshold of this narrative I beg the reader to remember that I have set out to tell the whole truth about the state of society in Yazoo. At this late date therefore, it is but right that the facts be stated in language so plain that the average American woman or man may readily comprehend how I was impressed by personal contact with the people of Yazoo.

Black's lawyers, where I examined the contract, found my brother's well-known signature, and under it placed my own.[12]

While I was engaged with the lawyers, the Colonel went out upon the streets, and by the time our legal business was concluded a number of his friends had dropped in. On all sides there was apparently a desire to give me a hearty welcome to Yazoo, and I spent some time in pleasant conversation with them. . . . I found both of Mrs. Black's lawyers to be courteous and apparently skillful attorneys. Their office was in a one-story structure, opening out on Main Street. It was a sort of rendezvous for the "leading citizens" of the county, as well as of the town.

I also observed that the opinions of these lawyers upon almost all subjects in which the planters and merchants were interested at that time, were received as law by those who sought them, and I could not fail to see that the legal profession, in which they were evidently the local aristocrats, was highly esteemed in Yazoo. They did not seem to care to discuss the war. Others did, and as many as said anything upon the subject agreed that the "wah is over," the "nigros are free," "we wor whipped!" "we don't want any mo' of it in ourn." The silence of these astute lawyers and an occasional shrug or wise look, struck me as indicating a mental reservation, at least, on their part in their sort of involuntary acquiescence in the opinion prevailing on this point. . . .

A FIRST DAY WITH THE FREEDMEN OF YAZOO

It had been arranged by Charles and myself before we separated at Vicksburg, that during his absence I should endeavor to gather together the labor required for Tokeba. Should he be able to arrange for a saw-mill it was our purpose to bring trained men from the North to operate it. . . .

There were daily many freedmen in town in search of work. But Colonel Black assured me that these were mostly restless, "no-account nigros," who were taking advantage of their freedom to leave their masters, or were those who had "run off with the Yankees," and were waiting for their "forty acres and a mule." I did not lack for advisers, and was struck by the unanimity of sentiment and opinion upon this subject. But the holidays were rapidly approaching, and as many Northerners were prospecting for favorable locations on the Yazoo River, I deemed it wise to set about my task without further delay.

In the crowd of freed people I had observed standing about the street corners, or in front of store doors, there were few seeking homes for them-

---

12 [Original author's footnote] It was Mrs. Black, and not the Colonel, we were dealing with, and I thought we should be able to get on with her.

selves alone. Most of them appeared well behaved, orderly, able bodied, and as though they had not long been idle. On closer inquiry I found that many of them had homes and had but recently quit work. In such cases the family remained with the old master, and their abandonment of him was wholly dependent upon the success of their representative in his efforts to find an employer for himself and them. In no case was he willing to hire himself for more than a brief period without his family. . . .

I had expected to be able to go into the labor market, and buy and pay for the labor required for Tokeba in the ordinary way—the one in which I had been reared. It had not occurred to either Charles or myself, while discussing the subject of labor for Tokeba, that in order to secure a force of one hundred or so hands for the place, it would be necessary to make provision for food and clothes for any greater number than was actually required for its cultivation. . . .

When next I went among them, to the first man who asked me to employ his wife and children to work in the fields I put this question: "Why will you freedmen all insist that your wives shall work in the field?"

He seemed not to understand me, so I repeated it. The poor fellow looked about him as if to see whether we were likely to be overheard, and replied: "Bees you a Yankee?[13] I know you is, do, kase I done seed it. Laws! Kunnel; I specs yo' is a Kunnel. We col'ud folks is too po'. Mars ain't done tole us we is free yit, an' we got no money, an' no close, nor nuffin, 'cept'n what we eat and what we wahr. We done heerd 'bout de Yankees comin' 'bout de Azoo, an' brerer Jon'than he 'lowd mout ez well come down y'hea and see fur ouah own self."

"Well," said I, "should you go with us we will pay you wages, you know, and that will enable you to support your wife."

"How much ye 'low ter pay me?" inquired the freedman.

"Fifteen dollars per month."

"He! Dat's heap mo' money den I done seed dis blessed yeah. But ye see, Kunnel, none on us niggers got no lan', nor no mooles, no nuffin, 'cep'n wot we eat an' wot we wahr, an' Uncle Jon'than, he 'low'd ef 'twar so dat de Yankees comin' in y'hea, and we is all free, dat de o'omin folks an all on um jes go 'way from dah. He 'low'd, he did, dat we all better wuk, little an' big, t'wel we got hole some ob dis y'hea lan' what we is stan'in' on, and I 'low'd ter do jes dat we way fust, Kunnel. Ole Uncle Si, he 'low'd niggers nebber will own no lan'. Kase dey ain't none fur um, an' de white folks won' nebber gi'e us none daern, nur sell us none nuther;

---

[13] The speech of nineteenth-century African Americans (especially freed slaves) has often been rendered mockingly by white writers, to imply that they lacked intelligence and dignity. It is clear from Morgan's account that this was not his intent, that he was trying to put down as exactly as possible the speech of both whites and blacks in the South. He freely admired the thoughts of many of the blacks he quotes, as here. These passages can be difficult to read, but are worth the effort.

kase dey 'feared de bottom rail mout come on de top. But de Yankee sojas wor dar lookin' arter 'fedrit cotting an' gobment mooles, jes fo' de s'render, an' dey 'low'd dat we mout own lan' jes 'e same ez de white folks, wen we done buy it, an' pay fur it out'en ouah own money. . . ."

The foregoing was drawn out of Pomp [the freedman] by the questions I from time to time put to him, until I had obtained the whole story of his escape, and that of his fellow servants, from that slavery which all agreed was annihilated at Appomattox. . . .[14]

There he stood, a man full six feet tall, with brawny muscles and a frank, honest, open countenance. His hat was a mere remnant of one. His coat, made of some sort of homespun cotton, had been patched with so many different colors and kinds of cloth, it was difficult to make out the texture of the original garment. His pants, of some sort of bagging stuff, had received less care, for the original patches were worn until they hung in strings, and his shoes, brogans, of the color of raw hide, glazed with wear, made but a feeble pretence of covering his feet.

This man, all his life, had been the slave of a minister of the gospel of the Son of God, and had faithfully served him. When the war came, his young master, Henry, this minister's son, had enrolled himself in a regiment of infantry, and served in the rebel army of northern Virginia to its close. He had been twice severely wounded, and had been at home on that account several weeks when Lee's army surrendered. Nearly all the young white men in his county and many of the old ones had rendered similar service. During their absence, this man before me had remained, faithfully serving his master. . . . All he received for this service was his food and what I saw upon his person. Yet this man looked forward to a future which, to him, was full of promise; a future in which he saw himself the possible owner of land, if only he could find honest employment for himself, wife, and children in the cotton or corn fields. Neither in his speech nor in his manner was there any sign of bitterness toward his old master, nor any desire to take by force any part of his past earnings, nor any wish to have any part of the land of another that he could not pay for, nor any disposition to ask any lands or mules or food from the Government, or from private citizens, as a forfeit or a gift. This man might beg for work; he would never beg for bread; neither would he steal it. He now appears to me as I saw him then, a nobleman in the highest sense of the word.

[14] This man's former master, a planter in Holmes County, had tried to keep the news of the Confederate surrender and the subsequent emancipation secret from his workers.

JEALOUS "JOHNNY REBS"

I did not mention the interview to Colonel Black or to the ladies, nor my reflections upon it either, while at dinner that day or ever afterward; from regard for their feelings—and—well, the war was over. I thought it a very serious matter, however, and it raised a flood of apprehension in my mind. . . .

Whenever I asked [freedmen] the question, "Why do you wish to leave your old master?" the response generally was a sullen, far away look, or simply: "Ole marstah an' me doan 'gree no mo'."[15]

Occasionally one would reply in plain English: "I'm free now and I want to work for my own self." As a rule this latter class were quite comfortably dressed, and bore the appearance of having had good treatment. They held up their heads and did not have that timid, shy look, which so many wore whose old homes were farther back toward the interior. The true explanation of this did not occur to me for some time afterward. I am now certain that it was entirely due to the fact that they had seen, talked with, and probably spent some time in the employ of Yankee planters on the Mississippi, or had been with the Yankee soldiers. However, there were not many of that class in Yazoo then.

Some of the ladies whom I met at the Colonel's, also his daughters, thought I ought not to be doing this work myself. "It must be very disagreeable," said one. "Don't you 'low to have an overseer?" said another. "I reckon you'll have to have one."

On two occasions, while thus seeking labor for Tokeba, the Colonel accompanied me. I observed that whenever he addressed a freedman he would say: "Here, you, boy!" or "Hi! boy." Sometimes in his blandest manner he would salute one thus: "Well, Mr. Washington," or "Mr. Julius Augustus," or "Caesar," as the case might be, "how do you do today? How's your good lady?"

This I accepted as a hint to me not to be nice in my manner of addressing the freed people—that I should fall in with the ways of the country. . . .[16] The Colonel, however, soon became satisfied that I was either not an apt pupil, or that he was not very well fitted to be my instructor in such matters, and abandoned all further efforts in that direction, venting his spleen in an extra number of oaths. It speedily became known to the planters who came to town, as well as to the townspeople, that I was

---

[15] [Original author's footnote] I was not long in finding out the importance of the form in which I put my questions to the freed people. "Why do you wish to leave your old master?" was apprehended by them as implying that they were under some sort of obligation to that personage.

[16] [Original author's footnote] The fact is, it was intended as a criticism upon my manner.

"the Yankee who had rented the Black plantation"—and that I was "Colonel Black's Yankee guest."

Now this latter fact was of the utmost importance: First, because the Black family, being of the bluest old South Carolina stock, were at the very top of the best society of Yazoo. There were those who did not like the Colonel, but there was no doubt of his standing. . . . The sheriff, the judges, and all in the trades or professions recognized this fact. . . . Second, as Colonel Black's guest I was absolutely protected against insult, and could go where I pleased. These facts made me quite a conspicuous figure, and quite an important personage in the little town.

I had not long been engaged in the work of hiring the labor for Tokeba before it became evident to me that my manner toward the freed people was being unfavorably commented upon by the "best citizens."[17]

Occasionally, some planter in town on similar business as my own, observing me in conversation with a group of freed people, would stop, and after listening a short while, speak to some one he might know and ask who I was. Upon being informed he would mutter: "I thought so," then walk on a few steps, halt, turn about, scowl gloomily upon us, and always turn finally to go away, with a nervous jerk of his head or shoulder, or some deprecatory wave of the hand.

I well recollect once when thus engaged, a man whom I shall call Wicks, because it as completely disguises his real name as any I can think of would. Ben Wicks, owner of several thousand acres of cotton land, and formerly a thousand or so slaves, offensively and violently elbowed his way right in among a group with whom I was arranging for their hire, and exclaimed: "What er you all doing y'here? You nigros better go back whar ye b'long, and quit running after these y'here damn Yankees."

"Hi, yo black rascal!" he continued, in a still more venomous tone, if possible, and addressing a freedman in the group who had on a blue military cap and coat: "Yo'r kind'll be damn skase about y'here befo' a gret while." Then, without having apparently looked at me, he walked angrily away. . . .

But few of the residents of the town then carried weapons exposed. Those who kept them on their persons wore them concealed. But a great majority of the country white people wore theirs strapped outside their pants, and many outside their coats. They generally came to town on horseback, in groups of from two or three to six or eight, sometimes even a greater number, and dressed in old Confederate gray, or what appeared

---

[17] [Author's original footnote] The freed people at that time were just beginning to adopt surnames, and out of regard to the custom of the country, I had purposely avoided addressing them by any other title than that given to them by their late owners, as Pomp, Tom, Dick, etc. It was not possible, however, for me to so soon acquire the style of address, and the manner of the Southron.

to be homespun goods. . . . Sometimes, as they rode out or passed by where I might be standing, some one of them would shout to another, some epithet applied to Yankees, in a sufficiently loud tone for me distinctly to hear. . . .

Another cause of ill-feeling toward me I discovered to be in the fact that, whereas I was succeeding beyond my expectations in restocking Tokeba, many old planters, or their overseers, were not having any success at all, and it was being acknowledged on all sides, what indeed had long been feared by the native planters, that the freedmen preferred to hire to the newcomers, even at less wages than native planters were offering. This fact was made a pretext for unfriendly criticism of the means employed by the newcomers to "entice the nigros from their masters," as it was called. The fact was, I did not have to use persuasion at all. My chief difficulty was to select from the great number willing to go with me the very best. . . .

All this information about my conduct reached me through Colonel and Mrs. Black, who appeared to watch over me with anxious solicitude. One morning at breakfast this solicitude manifested itself in open but friendly criticism.

The Colonel began by assuring me of his desire that I should endeavor to make myself popular with "our people." . . . Then he told me that several of his acquaintances had spoken to him of the "unfavorable impression" I had made by my "treatment of the nigros on the street," and my "manner of speech while among them." Some of these rumors were exceedingly disagreeable to himself. . . . But he regretted exceedingly to say that the nigros themselves were quoting me as their friend, as against their old masters, and if what some of them reported of my remarks to them was true, I was not only doing myself a great injury, but should be regarded by the community as willfully engaged in stirring up bad blood between the races. . . .

Very soon after this conversation occurred, the Holmes County "runaway" [Pomp] reported himself, wife, and children, Uncle Jonathan, his wife, their children, and two other grown persons and several children. They had gone straight to Tokeba, and each family had already selected a cabin. . . . They had "slipped off" in the night. This appeared to be the prudent course, because several young men in their neighborhood had organized a sort of patrol[18] for the purpose of preventing any "rising" that the blacks might contemplate . . . and had whipped one young man of the company in the most cruel manner, because he was "found away from home" without a pass, and were said to have threatened to kill Jonathan and Pomp, should they ever show themselves in those parts again. . . .

[18] [Original author's footnote] This was the beginning of that organization in Mississippi which afterward became known by the name of Ku Klux Klan—click, cluck, clack, or the three sharp sounds caused by the cocking of a gun.

A NEW DEPARTURE

I could get along with the family well enough. The accommodations were excellent. In the parlor their neighbors, male and female, were courteous enough, and socially very companionable indeed. I would not "talk politics." The war was over with me, in deed and in truth. I was there to make money, it is true, but the getting of money was not my only object. . . .

While at Vicksburg, I had heard that large camps formerly occupied by Federal soldiers were now full of freed people who were dependent for support upon government aid, and I resolved to try my luck in that quarter. At one of those camps on the Mississippi River, just above Vicksburg, I found many of Colonel Black's former slaves. From their number I was quickly able to select all the labor we were likely to need.

The camp was on an island, where I was compelled to remain all night, and it was then and there, and from the lips of these "runaways" from Tokeba, that I first learned the truth about both the Colonel and Mrs. Black. There was no hesitation on the part of the runaways, either in their recognition of me or their talk about the old home place, for my dress, complexion, and speech could not well be disguised. They took to me at once, and manifested their joy at the prospect of going back to Tokeba to work for the "Yankees," in various ways. Indeed, they had already heard "the wud put out" that "ole Mars Jeems [Colonel Black] h'd done gone rent Tokeba to de Yankees." But they could hardly believe "de tale, kase why! Mars Jeems wor' so mighty down on de Yankees, he done swor' of'n, dat no damn Yank should eb'r put dey feet ont'er Tokeba. He'd shed de las' drap ob he blood fus', an' meet dem all in hell's fire an' b'imstun. Fo' God he said it! Kunnel, of'n an' of'n, b'efo Gen'l Herron com'd dat ar' way. Den we all le'f um, an' been long wid' de Yankees dat day ter dis. Did ye see dat are ole jail dar on Tok'ba?"

"No." I had seen no *jail* on Tokeba.

"Well, den, it's dah all same, 'low he nebber tote it arway. 'Twas dar when we all le'f um, sartin. Mars Jeems nebber tole ye widout ye ax him, an' den he mout a tole ye hit wor only a chik'n coop, 'cept'n' he know'd you mount a know'd better'n dat. . . . Dars ole Brister! Did yo' see Brister? Well, he good fur nuth'n cept'n choin' bout, kase his legs, ye know. Wall, Brister he mout' tole ye all bout'n dat ar' jail, ef'n ye ax *him*."

This all sounded to me so like the stories I had read before the war, and to which I had sometimes listened from the contrabands who came into our camps while the war was being fought, that I became deeply interested, and nearly the whole night was spent around a huge log-fire listening to the history of Tokeba from the lips of the slaves who had wrought it out of the dense wilderness years before the war. . . .

What shocked me most, however, was the unanimous opinion of these people that Mrs. Black was more cruel and tyrannical than the Colonel, and their accounts of cruel floggings, brandings, and starvings inflicted upon them by order of Mrs. Black were simply incredible. My estimate of that lady, based upon what I had seen in her own home, forbade belief in such stories, and I secretly attributed them to a habit of recounting their wrongs to Federal soldiers until they had learned to exaggerate them in order to deepen a soldier's sympathy for themselves.

Of the numerous tales was one which painted the Colonel as having ordered several—I forget the number now—of his slaves to be locked up in the jail with cornmeal and water only, and then himself going on a trip to New Orleans, where he remained for several days with the key to the jail in his pocket. No one, not even the overseer, dared release them or give them food could it have been got to them, and so when the Colonel returned one or two had already died, some died soon after, and others were crippled for life. . . .

Returning to Yazoo, I at once informed Colonel Black of my success, and that I had brought back his old servants. His face became a study worthy of a master artist. However, his philosophical temperament triumphed over his wrath and indignation before these found audible expression. . . . Finally, he broke out in a most comical laugh, and with a round of ridiculous oaths, declared that I had now "capped the climax," for of all the "worthless, good-for-nothing, thieving gang," there was "not one, by God sir, from old Aggaby to that scape-grace boy of Sal's, worth a tinker's baubee."

WITH THESE WORDS, Colonel J.J.B. Black set the stage for a conflict that loomed only months away in Yazoo County: a battle between white Southerners on one side and blacks and immigrant Northerners on the other. Such former slaveowners as Colonel Black and Ben Wicks had long made subjugation the defining theme of race relations; far from being reconciled to the sudden collapse of their system, they climbed to new heights of anger. Colonel Black himself was under bond to the local Freedmen's Bureau agent for threatening to kill an African-American veteran of the Union army. Albert Morgan, as a tenant of Colonel and Mrs. Black, was in a position to closely observe these hostilities as they built up in the white community—tensions that would soon burst upon himself and his brother, along with the freed people who returned to Tokeba as his paid employees.

Mention of the Freedmen's Bureau, however, points to the other field of battle in the reshaping of the South: Washington, D.C. There, in the victorious capital, a larger conflict was taking shape, one that would frame the daily struggle in places such as Yazoo County. On the banks of the Potomac River, the Republican Congress was learning that their new President was not what they had hoped, but what they most feared.

2

THE STRUGGLE IN WASHINGTON, PART I: THE FORCES GATHER

In the spring of 1865, a few months before Albert Morgan journeyed to Yazoo County, the leaders of Congress made their way, in ones and twos, to meet the new President. It was an extraordinary moment, and no one knew quite how to act or what to do. Never before had an American President been assassinated—and Lincoln had been shot while Congress was in recess, where it would stay for the rest of the year. So the Republican legislators went to the White House informally to see if the new man could work with the Republican majority.

That majority was a mixed lot, as any set of congressmen must be. The Republican party itself was still fairly new in 1865: barely a decade old, it had been soldered together from elements of the old Whig party, organizations of abolitionists, the Free Soil party, and other bits and pieces of the American political body. The question of what the Republicans stood for was somewhat cloudy: certainly many believed, as the Whigs had, in a strong central government that would expand and improve what we would now call the nation's infrastructure. They were all guided (as historian Eric Foner has shown) by a deep belief in free labor.[19] But until the South tried to secede, most Republicans were prepared to move cautiously regarding slavery; like Lincoln, they sought first to limit its expansion, and then to proceed with a slow process of gradual emancipation.

But war changes everything in politics. The spectacle of a nation struggling for its very life throws together political groups that would be at odds during peace. And as a war drags on, the need to achieve victory radicalizes the most lukewarm moderates; the ever more stringent measures required to win the conflict lead to legal steps that would have been unthinkable only months before. Never has this been more true than during the Civil War. The demands of war led to the rise of a federal bureaucracy overnight. As historian James M. McPherson has noted, the post office had been the only U.S. agency that actually touched most people's lives; now there was a direct income tax, an internal revenue bureau, a national paper currency (the greenback was a wartime innova-

---

[19] The ideology of free labor went far beyond abolitionism. It was based on the idea that every individual could (and should be free to) lift himself up economically through his own efforts.

tion), a national banking system, a military draft, and army control (and construction) of much of the railway system. The first twelve amendments to the Constitution had *limited* the power of the federal government; but the Thirteenth Amendment (abolishing slavery) suggested a different trend. Together, these developments formed quite a legacy for postwar congressmen—but whether it would be permanent or temporary remained to be seen.

Within the Republican party, a new faction arose during the conflict: the Radicals. Like the income tax, like legal tender, like the Thirteenth Amendment itself, the Radicals were a product of the war, a product almost unimaginable before the first shots were fired at Fort Sumter in 1861. Led by such men as the fire-eating Thaddeus Stevens in the House and the erudite and polished Charles Sumner in the Senate, they formed the leading element in the battle about to break, and so deserve careful consideration.

To this day, the popular imagination sees the Radicals as an unreasonable, almost vicious group of demagogues—an image fostered by contemporary Southern whites, along with such figures as D.W. Griffith and generations of historians. In fact, the Radicals were a diverse group with a wide range of convictions, united in one thing: a demand for justice for the African American. Some, such as Senator Sumner, had strong ties to the abolitionist movement before the war; others were driven to an expansive view of civil rights by the tide of battle, by seeing black troops fight for their freedom; others were simply determined to destroy the old power of the slaveowners who had caused this terrible war.

Were they extremists? Certainly not by the standards of today—or even of 1865. At war's end, most Radicals still believed that only limited numbers of African Americans should get the vote—those who had fought for the Union, for example. Nor was their hostility to the power of rich Southern planters hard to understand: after all, those same Southerners had just launched the bloodiest war in the nation's history, in the name of defending slavery. Furthermore, the South had long dominated the national government, despite the greater population and economic power of the North. McPherson has also pointed out that Southerners held the presidency for two-thirds of the nation's history before the start of the Civil War; they provided twenty-three of the thirty-six speakers of the House, as well as twenty-four of the presidents pro tem of the Senate; and they had always formed a majority of the Supreme Court. Before judging the Radicals harshly, it should be remembered that, just before the war, the Southern-dominated Congress had voted to allow the extension of slavery into Western territories, and had passed an unusual *expansion* of federal power at the expense of the states—the Fugitive Slave Act, which required the return of those who had escaped north. The Southern-led Supreme Court had even declared in the Dred Scott decision of 1857 that blacks could *never* be American citizens.

After considering all this, after considering the 360,000 Union soldiers who died during the war, after considering the assassination of Lincoln and the fear and suspicion it engendered, after considering the eloquence of such spokesmen for freedom as Frederick Douglass, the wonder is that most Radicals did not press even harder in the spring of 1865.

The new President, however, was the man of the hour, and as he settled into his unexpected office, the Republicans respectfully sought out his views on what to do with the defeated South. At first, they swelled with hope; though a Southerner himself, Andrew Johnson had been outspoken in his denunciation of secession as treason. "Treason is a crime," Johnson had told Radical Senator Benjamin F. Wade, "and crime must be punished." At the end of May, however, Johnson issued a series of proclamations that laid out his policy toward the South—showing that he had a very different view of Reconstruction than the Republicans had. Before the summer was over, he would fire the first shots in a battle with Congress that would end in his own impeachment and trial.

Two of the Republican congressmen who took part in that battle were Shelby M. Cullom and George S. Boutwell—the first a moderate, the second a leading Radical. Both were members of the House of Representatives; Cullom was only in his first term as a representative from Illinois, while Boutwell was an established force in Congress who had previously been governor of Massachusetts (the center of the abolitionist movement). In the selections that follow, the two congressmen recall the start of the great conflict over how to reconstruct the South—a conflict so distinctly shaped by the rigid personality of President Johnson. Cullom's account is the most personal; though suspicious of the Radical leaders himself, he deftly sums up the quirks in Johnson's personality that helped spark the conflagration. He also includes a shrewd contrast between Lincoln and his successor. Events in the South would soon drive even such moderates as Cullom into the Radical camp, as the President sided with conservative Southern whites. Boutwell's account is more formal, yet more informative; a loyal Republican, he sums up the mistake in nominating Johnson in the first place, then describes the opposing theories of how to rebuild the South—and the disturbing implications of Johnson's surprise policy.

Congress and Mr. Johnson
by Shelby M. Cullom

As I look back now over the vista of the years that have come and gone, it seems to me that I entered the lower House of Congress just at the beginning of the most important period in all our history. The great President had been assassinated; the war was over; Andrew Johnson, a Union Democrat, was President of the United States. Reconstruction was the problem which confronted us, how to heal up the nation's wounds and re-make a Union which would endure for all time to come. These were the difficult conditions that had to be dealt with by the Thirty-Ninth Congress.

Andrew Johnson was the queerest character that ever occupied the White House, and, with the exception of Lincoln only, he entered it under the most trying and difficult circumstances in all our history; but Lincoln had what Johnson lacked, the support and confidence of the great Republican party. Johnson was never a Republican, and never pre-tended to be one. He was a lifelong Democrat, and a slave-holder as well; but he was loyal to the Union, no man living more so. As a Senator from Tennessee, alone of all the Southern Senators he faced his colleagues from the South in denouncing secession as treason. His subsequent phe-nomenal course in armed opposition to the rebellion brought about his nomination for the Vice-Presidency as a shrewd stroke to secure the sup-port of the War Democrats of the North and the Union men of his state and section.

He came to the Presidency under the cloud of President Lincoln's as-sassination, when the majority of the North believed that a Southern conspiracy had laid the great President low. The seceding states hated him as a traitor to his own section; the North distrusted him as a Dem-ocrat. At first I believe the very radical element of the Republican party in Congress, led by old Ben Wade of Ohio, than whom there was no more unsafe man in either house of Congress, were disposed, if not openly to rejoice, which they dared not do, to see with some secret sat-isfaction the entrance of Johnson into the White House. It is well known that Wade did say in his first interview with President Johnson, when, as a member of the committee on the conduct of the war, he waited on him, "Johnson, we have faith in you. By the gods, there will be no more trou-ble in running the Government." . . .

There were two striking points in Johnson's character, and I knew him well: first, his loyalty to the Union; and second, his utter fearlessness of character. He could not be cowed; old Ben Wade, Sumner, Stevens, all the great leaders of that day could not, through fear, influence him one particle. . . . He sought rather than avoided a fight. Headstrong, domi-neering, having fought his way in a state filled with aristocratic South-erners from the class of so-called "low whites" to the highest position in the United States, he did not readily yield to the dictates of the domi-nating forces in Congress. . . .

Congress was not in session when Johnson came to the Presidency in April, 1865. To do him no more than simple justice, I firmly believe that he wanted to follow out, in reconstruction, what he thought was the pol-icy of Mr. Lincoln, and in this he was guided largely by the advice of Mr.

[Secretary of State William H.] Seward. But there was this difference. Johnson was, probably in good faith, pursuing the Lincoln policy of reconstruction; but when the legislatures and executives of the Southern states began openly passing laws and executing them so that the negro was substantially placed back into slavery, practically nullifying the results of the awful struggle, the untold loss of life and treasure, Mr. Lincoln certainly would have receded and would have dealt with the South with an iron hand, as Congress had determined to do, and as General Grant was compelled to do when he assumed the Presidency.

From April to the reassembling of Congress in December, Johnson had a free hand in dealing with the seceding states, and he was not slow to take advantage of it. He seemed disposed to recognize the old state governments; to restrict the suffrage to the whites; to exercise freely the pardoning power in the way of extending executive clemency not only to almost all classes, but to every individual who would apply for it.

The result was, it seemed to be certain that if the Johnson policy were carried out to the fullest extent, the supremacy of the Republican party in the councils of the nation would be at stake. To express it in a word, the motive of the opposition to the Johnson plan of reconstruction was the firm conviction that its success would wreck the Republican party, and by restoring the Democrats to power bring back Southern supremacy and Northern vassalage.

The Proclamations
by George S. Boutwell

Mr. Johnson never identified himself with the Republican Party; and neither in June 1864, nor at any other period of his life, had the Republican Party a right to treat him as an associate member. He was, in fact, what he often proclaimed himself to be—a Jacksonian Democrat. He was a Southern Union Democrat. He was an opponent, and a bitter opponent, of the project for the dissolution of the Union, and a vindictive enemy of those who threatened its destruction. . . . It is manifest that he was not an advocate of the doctrine of political equality as it came to be taught by the leaders of the Republican Party. When he became President, he was an opponent of negro suffrage. . . .

Without representing in his history or in his person the slave-holding interest of the South, Mr. Johnson was yet a Southern man with Union sentiments. The impression was received therefrom that his influence would be considerable in restraining, if not in conciliating, the slaveholders in what were called the "border states." These facts tended to his nomination for the Vice-Presidency. . . .

The incidents of the inauguration of Mr. Johnson in the Senate Chamber, and especially his speech on the occasion, which was directed, apparently, to the diplomatic corps, excited apprehensions in those who were present, and the confidence of the country was diminished materially concerning his qualifications for the office to which he had been elected. Without delay these apprehensions circulated widely, and they were deepened in the public mind by the assassination of Mr. Lincoln and the elevation of Mr. Johnson to the Presidency.

The public confidence received a further serious shock by his proclamation of May 29, 1865, for the reorganization of the state government in North Carolina. That proclamation contained provisions in harmony with what has been set forth in this paper concerning the political principles of Mr. Johnson. First of all, he limited the franchise to persons "qualified as prescribed by the constitution and laws of the State of North Carolina in force immediately before the 20th day of May, 1861, the date of the so-called Ordinance of Secession." This provision was a limitation of the suffrage, as it excluded necessarily the negro population of the state. It was also a recognition of the right of the state to reappear as a state in the Union. It was, indeed, an early assertion of the phrase which afterwards became controlling with many persons—"Once a state, always a state." He further recognized the right of the state to reappear as a state in the organization and powers of the convention [for a new state constitution] which was to be called under the proclamation. . . . There were further instructions given in the proclamation as to the duties of the various officers of the United States to aid Governor Holden, who by the same proclamation was appointed "Provisional Governor of the State of North Carolina."

Upon the publication of this proclamation, I was so much disturbed that I proceeded at once to Washington, but without any definite idea as to what could be done to arrest the step which seemed to me a dangerous step towards the reorganization of the government upon an unsound basis. At that time I had had no conversation with Mr. Johnson, either before or after he came to the Presidency, upon any subject whatever. The interview which I secured upon that visit was the sole personal interview that ever occurred between us. I called upon Senator Morrill of Vermont, and together we made a visit to the President.

I spoke of the features of the proclamation that seemed to me objectionable. He said that "the measure was tentative" only, and that until the experiment had been tried no other proclamation would be issued. Upon that I said in substance that the Republican Party might accept the proclamation as an experiment, but that it was contrary to the ideas of the party, and that a continuance of the policy would work a disruption of the party. He assured us that nothing further would be done until the experiment had been tested. With that assurance we left the Executive Mansion.

On the 13th day of June, 1865, a similar proclamation was issued in reference to the State of Mississippi, and on the 17th day of June, the 21st and 30th of June, and the 13th day of July, corresponding proclamations were issued in reference to the States of Georgia, Texas, Alabama, South Carolina, and Florida. In each State a person was named as provisional governor. This action led to a division of the party and to its subsequent reorganization against the President's policy. . . .

The controversy with Mr. Johnson had its origin in the difference of opinion as to the nature of the Government. That difference led him to the conclusion that the rebellion had not worked any change in the legal relations of the seceding states to the National Government. His motto was this: "Once a state, always a state," whatever might be its conduct either of peace or of war. There were, however, differences of opinion among those who adhered to the Republican Party. Mr. Stevens, who was a recognized, if not the recognized, leader of the Republican Party, advocated the doctrine that the eleven states were to be treated as enemy's territory, and to be governed upon whatever system might be acceptable to the states that had remained true to the Union. Mr. Sumner maintained the doctrine that the eleven states were territories, and that they were to be subject to the General Government until Congress should admit the several territories as state organizations.

The fourth day of May, 1864, I presented a series of resolutions in the House of Representatives, in which I asserted this doctrine: The communities that have been in rebellion can be organized into states only by the will of the loyal people expressed freely and in the absence of all coercion; that states so organized can become states of the American Union only when they shall have applied for admission and their admission shall have been authorized by the existing National Government.

A small number of persons who were identified with the Republican Party sustained the policy of Mr. Johnson. Others were of the opinion that the eleven states were out of their proper relation to the Union, as was declared by Mr. Lincoln in his last speech, and that they could become members of the American Union only by the organized action of each, and the concurrent action of the National Government. . . .

The difference of opinion was a vital one with Mr. Johnson. Whatever view might be taken of his moral qualities, it is to be said that he was not deficient in his intellectual ability, that his courage passed far beyond the line of obstinacy, and that from first to last he was prepared to resist the claims of the large majority of the Republican Party. The issue began with his proclamation of May, 1865, and the contest continued to the end of his term. The nature of the issue explains the character and violence of his speeches, especially that of the twenty-second day of February, 1866, when he spoke of Congress as a "body hanging on the verge of the Government."

JOHNSON'S PROCLAMATIONS LAID the basis for what is known as Presidential Reconstruction—that is, his attempt to rebuild the Union without Congress, which was in recess most of the year. They also marked the start of his epic battle with the Radical Republicans. At first, as Cullom noted, the Radicals thought they had a President who was determined to punish the leaders of the rebellion and truly remake the South; instead, they discovered a deeply conservative man who wished to restore the old Union (minus slavery) and roll back federal power.

There was another twist to Johnson's personality as well—for in 1865, being deeply conservative meant being deeply racist. As Boutwell pointed out, the President's proclamations implicitly restricted the ballot to white citizens. Johnson soon became quite forthright on the matter, telling one senator, "White men alone must manage the South." As a former tailor's apprentice and an old enemy of the Southern elite, he did make some attempt to limit the power of the planter class. For example, he granted a presidential pardon to virtually all rebels except those whose taxable property exceeded $20,000 in value. This feature of his proclamations gave some Radicals hope. As the summer progressed, however, he began to grant pardons to these individuals in large numbers, and before autumn had ended Johnson had restored the legal standing of almost every wealthy Confederate.

Johnson also tried to reach beyond the rich planters when he appointed provisional governors in the South—but he only furthered his alienation of the Radicals and African Americans. The President selected men who had opposed secession in their home states in 1860–61; some, such as South Carolina's Benjamin F. Perry, North Carolina's William W. Holden, and Alabama's Lewis E. Parsons, had close ties to small farmers and businessmen who opposed the power of the old plantation owners. But, like Johnson himself, these governors soon decided that they needed to expand their power base—there were not enough white men who had opposed the war, and the planters still had the most money.

Their main tool in this attempt to broaden their support was the power of political appointment: as Eric Foner writes, "In nineteenth-century America, patronage oiled the machinery of politics, and Johnson's governors possessed unprecedented patronage powers. Every state and local office stood vacant." The provisional governors turned to men who had been leaders in the secession movement, who had held high office in the Confederacy. Thousands upon thousands of offices, from county sheriff to tax assessor to state supreme court justice, went to individuals who had fought against the federal government in the defense of slavery.

Before the leaves had begun to change in late 1865, Northerners discovered that President Johnson had handed control of the South back to many of those who had started the Civil War in the first place. Johnson's policies allowed the ex-Confederate states to function as they had before the war, with the single exception of slavery. Union army generals were still military administrators throughout the region; but Johnson removed any who disagreed with the actions of the provisional governors. Where there were black troops stationed in the South, Johnson removed them, too. The devastating defeat suffered by Southern whites in the war had left them at first somewhat willing to accept Washington's dictates (one ex-member of the Confederate cabinet even advocated limited black suffrage); but the President's actions filled them with new hope for firmly reestablishing "white man's government."

As the state constitutional conventions (mandated by Johnson's proclamations) began to meet in the summer and fall of 1865, white militancy rose up once again throughout the South. As one Mississippi delegate remarked, " 'tis nature's law that the superior race must rule and rule they will." While there *was* some shift of power in the new state constitutions away from the wealthy planters, there was no attempt whatever to offer the vote to blacks. Far from it: starting in late 1865, the new state legislatures in Mississippi and South Carolina passed the first of what became known as the "Black Codes"—laws that strictly controlled all areas of life for African-Americans. Blacks were required to show proof of employment for the coming year (which usually meant a contract to work for their former masters); if they left their jobs early, they would forfeit all their wages, and could be arrested by any white citizen. A sharp fine prevented anyone from offering work to someone already under contract. To limit their chances to earn extra money or take up skilled trades, the laws prevented blacks from renting urban land or selling goods after dark; South Carolina imposed a heavy tax on any African American who was not a farmer or a servant. Vagrancy laws strictly limited the freedom of movement. Apprenticeship laws bound orphans (or those deemed orphans) to unpaid labor, usually at the hands of their former owners.

Not surprisingly, African Americans and many Northern whites viewed the Black Codes as an attempt to reinstate slavery in all but name. While these laws were unevenly enforced, they still had a powerful effect on the freed people. Blacks in the South were already suffering on a tremendous scale when the war ended in April: tens of thousands were impoverished refugees, having fled to the light of Union army campfires during the war. Now they found work where they could, or lived off army rations in dismal camps. Those who returned home often found themselves forced to work for their old masters.

Fortunately, Congress tried to do something for the freed people before it recessed in the spring of 1865. After long haggling, it launched an experiment unprecedented in the history of the national government—a social welfare agency known as the Freedmen's Bureau. Starting literally from scratch (in this case, scratch paper), commissioner General Oliver O. Howard built up the first federal effort to directly help individuals in need.

He faced a multitude of problems: the lack of resources, the hostility of Southern whites, the often byzantine opposition of President Johnson. Howard himself was somewhat conservative: he often took a patronizing approach to African Americans, and he believed that the bureau should complete its work and be shut down as soon as possible. In keeping with the times and the Republican ideology of free labor, the general took a dim view of offering government help to able-bodied adults. Despite these limitations, Howard's agency offered a solitary federal lifeline to blacks suffering in a sea of oppression.

The Founding of the Freedmen's Bureau
by General Oliver O. Howard

The evening of May 10, 1865, found me in Washington. I went the next day to the Secretary's office in the War Department and reported to him as I had been instructed. This was not my first interview with Edwin M. Stanton. He had been at times very kind to me. . . . He now appeared hearty, in good humor, and glad to see me; but, after a few brief words of greeting, as was usual with him, went straight to the business in hand. We had hardly taken seats when he took from his desk and handed me a copy of the Freedmen's Bureau Act, and said substantially: "We have been delaying the execution of this law because it has been difficult to find a commissioner. You notice that he can be detailed from the army. Mr. Lincoln before his death expressed a decided wish that you should have the office; but he was not willing to detail you till you could be spared from the army in the field. Now, as the war is ended, the way is clear. The place will be given to you if you are willing to accept it."

After a few more words of conversation, and understanding that I wished time for reflection and consultation with my friends, he said: "Take the document and look it over and let me know as soon as you can whether or not you are willing to undertake the business."

Naturally, as the great war drew to a close, I had been pondering the subject of my future work. Should I remain in the army or not? What as a young man of thirty-four had I better to do? The opportunity afforded by this offer appeared to me at once to answer my anxious inquiries. Indeed, it seemed providential; so in my consciousness my mind was virtually made up even before I left the War Office; my custom in war had never suffered me to hold decisions long in abeyance.

The morning of May 12th, I returned to Mr. Stanton and said: "I have concluded to accept the duty you offer me." He briefly expressed his satisfaction and sent for the papers, chiefly letters from correspondents, widely separated, and reports, official and unofficial, touching upon matters which pertained to refugees and freedmen. The clerk in charge brought in a large, oblong, bushel basket heaped with letters and documents. Mr. Stanton, with both hands holding the handles at each end, took the basket and extended it to me and with a smile said: "Here, General, *here's your Bureau!*" He told me that I could use the officers of my Tennessee army for Bureau assistants as far as I wished, or submit recommendations for any helpers. He further said that the house of a prominent Senator who had joined the Confederacy, situated at the northeast corner of Nineteenth and I Streets in Washington, was ready for my immediate use as an office. The next day Mr. Stanton caused the following War Department order to be formally issued, entitled "Order organizing the Bureau of Refugees, Freedmen, and Abandoned Lands." . . .

By Monday morning, May 15th, the new Bureau was sufficiently equipped for me to issue a circular letter. As this letter affords a glimpse of the situation thus early in my administration, I here insert the substance of it:

> "In accordance with orders, I enter immediately upon the duties of the Commissioner of Refugees, Freedmen, and Abandoned Lands. . . .
>
> "I earnestly solicit cooperation from all officers and agents whose position or duty renders it possible for them to aid me. The negro should understand that he is really free but on no account, if able to work, should he harbor the thought that the Government will support him in idleness."

As yet I had no organization, properly so named, outside of the Washington office, and so by correspondence and officers sent out I began to collect the information already much needed. This first letter was published over the country extensively, and on account of the views in the last paragraph brought upon me many attacks from radical newspapers which were friendly to the negro, indicating that they had sentimental views in regard to the relation of the United States to the freedmen; the logical result of those views was that under my circular letter the negro had merely changed masters from the Southern slave owners to the United States; they implied that the Government should support the emancipated even if idle. But the enemies of free labor approved all my compulsory language.

The Bureau, standing between these two extremes as to the negro, entered upon its work naturally under the fire of hostile newspapers and some congressional criticism from both sides. Long before this period of experience I had learned that I could not suit everybody.

My own reason for introducing into the circular letter the paragraph relating to labor was that many thought the Bureau would "feed niggers in idleness," as they expressed it, and I wished to start right. There was found in Mr. Stanton's basket evidence that the military authorities were then feeding immense groups of refugees and freedmen in Washington and vicinity as well as in different parts of the South and West. The daily issue then amounted to upward of 144,000 rations. For the ensuing June, July, and August, the indigent groups, though constantly shifting ground, were in the aggregate somewhat increased. The number of persons relieved by our Bureau commissariat daily during August was 148,120. Without doubt many freedmen and poor whites, from the seeming helplessness of their condition, like pensioners, were through this source expecting permanent support.

By September 1865, when the Bureau had been sufficiently organized and at work so as to take entire charge of all gratuitous relief, by a rigid examination of every applicant, by the rejection of all who could support themselves by labor, and by the process of finding work for the willing, the number assisted was reduced to 74,951; and from that time on, there was a constant reduction. . . .

On May 19th from my office was made the next substantial public announcement. By this, assistant commissioners were located. To them were entrusted the supervision of abandoned lands, and the control of subjects relating to refugees and freedmen within their districts. . . . The educational and moral condition of these people was never forgotten. The officers of the Bureau should afford the utmost facility to benevolent and religious organizations, and to State authorities, where they exist, in the maintenance of good schools. Do everything possible, was my constant cry, to keep schools on foot till free schools shall be established by reorganized local governments. "In all this work," I announced, "it is not my purpose to supersede the benevolent agencies already engaged, but to systematize and facilitate them."

By May 22nd the freedmen were largely at work, cultivating plantations and abandoned lands; but owners who were called "disloyal" to the Government were already seeking recovery of their farms and forcibly to displace the freedmen. So with Mr. Stanton's sanction I ordered that all such land under cultivation by the freedmen be retained in their possession until the growing crops should be secured for their benefit, unless full and just compensation were made for their labor and its products, and for expenditures. . . . My proposed instructions were submitted to the President. He favored them. Beneath my signature it is written: "Approved June 2, 1865. *Andrew Johnson*, President of the United States." . . .

Upon their appointment[20] the assistant commissioners of freedmen were enjoined to use every proper means to quicken the industries of the States under their charge. They held indeed a broad commission. Negroes were declared in my letters sent them to be free to choose employers and receive pay for their labor. The old system of overseers was abolished. Cruelty and oppression were to be suppressed. It was easy to write and publish, but hard to carry such orders into execution.

From all directions anxious employers poured in letters upon me urging me to fix prices and enable the employer to exercise power, in one way or another, over the laborer. The majority did not believe the negro would work unless under compulsion. One prominent gentleman came all the way from Louisiana to Washington. He had been delegated by a score or more planters to visit me and show a schedule of prices which they had drawn up as liberal as they could make them *and live*. He asked for a formal approval.

Much to the astonishment and chagrin of the suggestors and their agent, the statement made and reiterated by me that *wages* must be free was adhered to, and that they were to be regulated by the assent of both parties to a contract verbal or written, or adjusted from the common market value. I repeatedly cautioned my officers against any substitute whatever for slavery. . . .

Naturally enough, exaggerated stories were always rife, a rumor was circulated among the freedmen quite generally that they would finally get somehow all the lands of disloyal owners. The wording of the Bureau law unfortunately fostered the idea. Were not forty acres to be set apart to every male citizen, colored and white, whether refugee or freedman? Soldiers, colored and white, magnified the report till the belief became prevalent that the Government intended, at the Christmas of 1865, to effect this division. Speculators who desired to cheapen the lands added to their tales their own exaggerations. The result was that toward the autumn great numbers of freedmen became averse to making any contracts whatever with property holders, verbal or written, for the coming year. Our officers and agents at once set themselves to disabuse the minds of the working people of impressions so detrimental to their interests, entreating them to hasten and get places of support, and then aiding them to obtain fair wages. But even the correction of false reports did not always produce willingness to contract. . . .

The work of my officers in obtaining recognition of the negro as a man instead of a chattel before the civil and criminal courts took the lead; we took the initiative in influencing the South in its transition into the new order of things. In land and labor matters the Bureau found existing conditions the settlement of which would brook no delay if we were to pre-

---

[20] This and the following several paragraphs have been moved for continuity.

vent race wars or starvation; but under the title of justice was the first active endeavor to put the colored man or woman on a permanent basis on a higher plane.

Here is the way the process began: Quite early in my administration as commissioner I paid a visit to Virginia, and not far from Charlottesville met a small assembly of planters. Some of them said they could not work negroes when free. Others asked what was to hinder men from running off and leaving a crop half gathered? The most of them appeared quite in despair over how to make or execute contracts with ex-slaves.

After having drawn out quite generally an expression of opinion and feeling on their part, I addressed them: "Gentlemen, no one of us alone is responsible for emancipation. The negro is *free*. This is a fact. Now cannot we blue-eyed Anglo-Saxons devise some method by which we can live with him as a free man?" I then made a suggestion. "Suppose for all minor cases, say within one or two hundred dollars of value, we organize a court. My agent being one member may represent the Government; the planters of a district can elect another; and the freedmen a third. In nine cases out of ten the freedmen will choose an intelligent white man who has always seemed to be their friend. Thus in our court so constituted, every interest will be fairly represented." The hearers were pleased. They were astonished to find me a friend and not an enemy, and they said with feeling: "General, why didn't you come down here before?"

After this talk the court was started here, and similar courts extended in orders to all my jurisdiction. For the whole field for some months minor justice was administered by these Bureau courts constituted wholly or partially from officers or agents of the Bureau; but everywhere when practicable we associated civilians with our officials. By orders, the power as to punishment was limited to not exceed $100 fine, or thirty days' imprisonment. All cases of capital crimes, felonies, or questions relating to titles to real estate were referred to some State court, if such existed where the case occurred, or to a court of the United States, or to military commissions. . . .

The Bureau had hardly begun its work when it encountered unexpected opposition. At first President Johnson was apparently very friendly to me, yet, while Mr. Stanton favored our strong educational proclivities, the President declared that the true relief was only in work. One member of the Cabinet, Secretary William Dennison, said about the time I took charge: "General, it is feared that the Freedmen's Bureau will do more harm than good." These gentlemen and their followers thought relief was in work alone. It was hard for them to realize that the training of the mind and hand, particularly with negroes, could go on together.

Before many days, when the rehabilitation of the old State governments and the appointment of governors was under consideration in the President's Cabinet, the military possession of all the late insurrectionary

States was made complete by having a military commander for each State, stationed either at the capital or in one of its largest cities. Each commander had under him a considerable force, so that he divided his State into districts and had an officer in charge of each. Fortunately for the Bureau work, Mr. Stanton and General Grant, in sympathy with each other in the main, managed this force, and both sustained me. This, however, did not prevent some friction in the field. In places the military commander of a district absorbed the functions of the Bureau agent and in others would not cooperate with him and give him needed military support in his work. Some officers, hostile to negroes, took the part of unfriendly employers and sought at times with success to bring the Bureau agent's work into contempt.

It was not many months before the President himself in his contest with Congress began to show a steady, though underhanded, opposition to the execution of the Bureau law. Open resistance to the law by the Chief Executive could be impeached, but indirect obstacles might be thrown in the way of its execution. To keep publishing charges against the commissioner, the assistant commissioners, and all other Bureau officers appeared to be at one time a settled policy.

———

THE BUREAU AGENTS did what they could across the South to protect African Americans, to advance their opportunities—but the combined hostility of the President and the white population formed a tide that could not be held back. As 1865 passed away, the battle had been joined. Two visions of a republic without slavery were emerging, emerging from a combination of idealism, hatred, and bitter partisan politics. It was a struggle that would arouse the best—and the very worst—in the American people.

———

3

THE SOUTHERN BATTLEGROUND

Far from the troubled halls of Washington, Albert Morgan welcomed his returning brother Charles on the rich soil of Tokeba plantation in Yazoo County, Mississippi. Albert was worried by what he had learned of Colonel Black and his wife—more than worried, in fact, for the young Union army veteran had a ferocious temper and a stringent sense of justice, instilled in him by his devout Baptist parents. But Charles was as much a diplomat as Albert was a hothead, and he quickly quieted his younger brother down. Besides, he brought with him an investor from the North, as well as a crew of skilled lumbermen for their new sawmill. The future looked bright for Morgan, Ross, & Company, as the plantation operators called themselves.

Had the Morgan brothers been paying attention to national politics, they might have seen the shadows ahead. As 1865 gave way to 1866, running a business in the heart of the deep South would prove more than a matter of planting, harvesting, and settling accounts. President Johnson's policies sparked a new spirit of resistance, even arrogance, among those who had fought for the Confederacy only a year ago. Through his proclamations and speeches, he opened the gate for Southern whites: with slavery repealed, they could run their own states—and control the freed blacks in their own way.

Federal garrisons still dotted the South; Freedmen's Bureau agents still worked where they could. But the defeated rebels saw the opening Johnson had made for them: in locations such as Yazoo County they decided that they no longer had to tolerate Yankees like the Morgans or African Americans like those the brothers employed. For blacks, it was the beginning of a titanic struggle that would bring unprecedented victories as well as stunning defeats. For Albert Morgan, it was the start of another turn in his dramatic life, one that would fill him with a renewed sense of purpose on the front line of freedom.

Persecution
by Albert T. Morgan

The incidents recounted in the former chapter occurred only a few days prior to my brother's return. Of course, I told him of them and dwelt significantly upon the temper of the people. He had often allowed me to see that he had great faith in my ability to win friends. At school I had always been a match for the best of my fellows in a wrestle, "side holt," "square holt," or "rough and tumble." I had as often as any other carried off the prize in my class and in our debating and other societies. I had enlisted in the ranks in spite of the suggestion of my father and of influential friends that if I would wait for a later regiment I could go as a commissioned officer. And I had got my first promotion from "high private" to sergeant, upon the request of my company, by a vote of fully four-fifths of the privates, over all the corporals, of whom a majority voted for me for the vacancy. Therefore, he was somewhat surprised at what I told him, and I could plainly see also annoyed. In seeking for an explanation of it he prodded me with all manner of questions, putting much stress upon the way in which I had conducted the financial part of the business at my end of the line. . . . I was able to give entirely satisfactory answers to all of these interrogatories, even to so exacting and rigid an examiner as my brother. . . .

But we were in for it, and would make the best of it. Besides, whatever their [the Black family's] feelings might be, they were only natural after all. If for no other reason, their poverty would, for a time at least, compel compliance with the new order of things. During this time, the tide of immigration which, Charles observed, was setting strongly southward, especially the more thrifty and intelligent portion from the East, of itself would in a very few years work a complete change in the elements of society. Charles had no fear. . . .

My brother's negotiations at the North succeeded beyond his anticipations. He arranged with an old lumberman to come down at once and bring with him his sawmill, fixtures, and entire force of skilled hands, and very soon things were so lively on Tokeba that occupation banished . . . the apprehensions which my experience during his absence had awakened. . . . As the business was wholly new to us and our employees, all strangers, it may be readily seen that we really had no time for anything else.

In less than ninety days things were "just smoking" on Tokeba, as Charles, in one of his happy veins, declared. There stood the sawmill, just where Charles had planned for it, and it proved to be the very best kind of site. . . . The old mill was just "singing away lively." It could be heard on a calm day at Yazoo City, more than two miles away. On the plantation our hands were doing equally well, and the best of feeling existed between the laborers and ourselves. . . . "Old Uncle Bristol" still kept the ferry and worked in the carpenter shop, repairing plow frames or making new ones, while the kling-klang of the anvil at the blacksmith's shop kept him to his task; for the work of the blacksmith was crowding him.

Altogether it *was* "just smoking" on Tokeba. The mill could not supply the local demand for lumber, which we readily sold in town, delivered on the levee or to steamers that took it from the mill for customers at way landings on the Yazoo River, at prices ranging from thirty-five to eighty dollars per thousand feet, according to kind and quality. Neighbors from far and near passing Tokeba would rein in their horses, halt, take a look at things, and ride on evidently in a brown study. Having no leisure for entertaining them, "nor anything good to drink," we seldom invited them to alight[21]—we were busy.

The merchants in Yazoo City, anxious for our custom, held out such inducements as led us to make our purchases of general supplies for the place and for our hands in that town, instead of sending abroad for them, and their orders on us for lumber for their other customers often exceeded our weekly bills with them for supplies for Tokeba. Ours was the only sawmill in operation in that region, and for a time proved a real blessing to Yazoo City and the country round about. We were not asking credit ourselves, being able to pay our way as we went, either with greenbacks, which were quite popular in Yazoo at the time of which I write,[22] or with good cypress lumber, which was almost as popular as greenbacks. . . .

During the winter and spring of 1866, nothing occurred to mar the *entente cordiale* which circumstances, aided by our sawmill, had established between "those Yankees on Tokeba" and "our people."[23]

THE WOLF SHOWS HIS TEETH

We were not getting on with Colonel Black quite as smoothly as we could have wished. The following will serve to illustrate some of the annoyances to which he subjected us: It was not long after the incidents related in the foregoing chapter that, happening in town one day, on one of those errands connected with the supplying of the place, Colonel Black met me, and calling me aside into a small court, where we were out of hearing of the passers-by on the street, but in plain view of a group of men lounging at a store front, with an air of deep mystery and importance, informed me that it was rumored in the town that one day while his guest I had told Mistress Black that a "nigro wench" was as "good as a white lady."

I had never said any such thing, but resolved to keep silent until I had learned more of his purpose on this occasion. Accordingly, after a brief

21 [Original author's footnote] This was a violation of one of the ways of the country, but it was business.

22 Paper currency as legal tender (the "greenback") was first issued as a war measure under Lincoln. In some areas, prejudices in favor of "hard money" (gold coins or banknotes redeemable in gold) caused greenbacks to be less popular.

23 [Original author's footnote] From the day of our arrival in Yazoo to this date, summer of 1866, I had not heard the phrase "our people" used by the native whites in any other sense than one which embraced themselves alone. Neither freed people nor Yankees were meant to be included in it.

pause, he reminded me of the pains Mrs. Black and himself had been to, in order that our introduction to Yazoo should lack nothing of the elements requisite to insure us a good start in our new home. . . .

"But," he continued, "ouah people are very sensitive upon one question, and cannot tolerate in ouah midst any division of sentiment upon it, or opinion either, without tearing down the only props remaining to ouah social fabric, by God, sir, and consenting to the destruction of all present prospects for any tol'able solution of the great labor question thrust upon us by Lincoln's proclamation. . . . I knew from the outset that secession was but a piece of damn foolishness, and meant emancipation, and I opposed it, by God, sir. But now that he's free, we have nothing to hope from any policy that does not leave the control of the nigro to the wisdom of his fo'mer masters, by God, sir." And a number of rapid thumps with his cane upon the ground evinced his sincerity no less than his earnestness. "And we are bound to look upon any man as a public enemy, by God, sir, I care not who he is or whence he comes, who does not consent to this. Yo' have had no experience with the nigro, and, by God, sir, yo' can't be expected to know the nature of the beast."

Then he resumed his assumed air of gentle dignity. "In your treatment of him, therefore, yo' must allow me to say yo' ought to govern yo'r conduct by the opinions and wishes of we all who do know him. The nigro is an animal, by God, and by God, sir, he must be kept in his place; and who knows better how to manage a horse or a steer than one who is familiar with his raising? . . .

"Why," said he, "my deah sir, I recognize the fact that ouah ways, at first blush, may appeah distasteful to yo' who wor raised on the high God-and-morality notions of Wendell Phillips and Henry Ward Beecher, but, by God, sir, it will be easier for yo' to adapt yo'r ways to ouahs than for we all to change. You must be governed by the example of the apostle of old and while in Rome do as the Romans do, by God, sir-r-r. Why, sir! must we surrender our cherished theories and dearest interests to please a handful of Yankee immigrants, by God, sir-r? By—I beg yo' pardon, sir, those who come amongst us? No sir-r-r, by God, sir-r-r-r-r."

Still no response.

Then he despairingly resumed, but in a whining tone: "We were prosperous and happy, and at peace with ouah nigros and all the world, before a lot of damned fanatics took it into their heads—got an *idee,* by God, sir— that slavery was wrong. Wrong hell! The nigros wor' never so well off in Timbuctoo or any of the wilds of their native jungles as with us, by God, sir-r-r-r. Wrong be damned! . . . I tell yo' sir, now as then, the prosperity of the country and the peace of this Union depends on we all being left to manage ouah nigros in ouah own way, by God, sir-r-r-r-r-r."

But as the Colonel was likely never to let go, and the situation was becoming too monotonous to be longer endured, I gave way and exclaimed, rather impatiently I fear: "Well, who has proposed to hinder you?"

This staggered him. But he quickly rallied, and a smile lit up his sinister countenance as he sneeringly replied: "Well, sir, by God, sir, yo' may not understand the effect of youah own example. It was only a few days ago that I saw you as I passed by Tokeba at work with some nigros repairing a fence. And Mistress Black says that the other day, she drove on to Tokeba to see how things wor' going, and, by God, sir, yo' brother was working at the mill with the nigros, and came to speak to her in his shirt sleeves, by God, sir. I learn that you allow yo'r nigros to call you Colonel Morgan. By God, sir, they shall call me Master! Besides, it's all over town that yo' have been heard to call youah blacksmith's wife Mrs. Smith. Mrs. Hell! By god, sir, this must be stopped or yo' all will be ruined." . . .

"Colonel Black, you say the negroes are all free?"

"Yes, by God, sir," he exclaimed excitedly.

"Well, you'll grant that I am a free man, too, will you not?"

"Well, sir, by God, sir, what d'yo' mean, sir-r-r-r?"

But I kept cool, saying only: "We hold the lease of Tokeba for three years from the legal owner on a contract to pay a certain annual rent. We have paid the rent according to the contract, and we have a right to the management of that place. I grant to you and to all the right to control your own labor in your own way without interference from me. I claim for our firm only such privileges as we cheerfully accord to others. We believe that we can get more and better labor for the same money out of our hands by treating them as though they too had rights"—at this point the clouds began to deepen on his face—"than if we treated them as though they were brutes." And now he leaned with both hands upon his stick—a heavy hickory—in front of him, trembling with wrath. "We have meant no more by it than our similar treatment of white men would mean." Now he began to grin.

"We have not dreamed that it would be considered revolutionary, nor even thought of it in that light. But we may as well understand each other on this subject. I am sure that no member of our firm is sorry for what we have done in this regard. Recollect, it is our money, not yours, now running Tokeba. We recognize the obligation each individual member of society is under, so to conduct himself that he shall not jeopardize the good of others while pursuing his own ends. Therefore, we shall make no display of our views or example; but at the same time we shall not hide our light under a bushel. We shall continue to treat our people as though they were worthy of their hire, so long as they shall continue so, in *our* opinion; and a *large share* of a laborer's hire is respectful consideration from his employer."

At this point the Colonel grunted out "bah!" but I continued. "We shall never forget that Mrs. Smith is a member of our community, nor can I understand why we should be disturbed in our lawful and peaceful pursuits by reason thereof."

The Colonel was completely beside himself. While listening to me he had turned red and white by turns, and as I concluded, he leaned forward on his cane, while his hands trembled as with palsy in his efforts to control himself. The muscles of his face relaxed until a fiend-like grin appeared. Then turning on his heel he left me, with the simple taunt, "Well, by God, sir, as you make yo're bed yo' must lie. I took yo' for a *gentleman;* yo' are only a scalawag." As I passed out upon the street the group of men by the store uttered deep groans. . . .

We had not intended to credit out much lumber, nor did we. But it was quite impossible to decline the orders of men who appeared to be large property-owners and of gilt-edged business reputation, high-toned, honorable gentlemen, and by fall we had out several bills of this character. In all such cases it had been our custom to ask payment whenever, from any cause, we were in need of money. . . .

It was late in the fall, after quite a severe and prolonged "spell of the ague," and while I was barely able to ride on horseback.[24] But Captain Telsub's bill was overdue. We needed cash; and so I called at that gentleman's drug store, and presented our bill to him. He had received the lumber and already put it to the uses for which he intended it. He was in his counting-room at the time, received me pleasantly, and, saying that they were short of funds just then, begged me to send or call again. I informed him that he need not "put himself out" to pay the bill at once, but to indicate when he would be prepared to meet it, and I would cheerfully oblige him. . . .

Passing out upon the street, on my way to the post office, I had not gone more than half the square, when I heard my name spoken, and someone walking quite rapidly behind me. I half turned, stopped, and, leaning on my sunshade, which I was at that time using as a cane, waited until he came up; for I saw it was the Captain. Although he appeared a little flustered, there was no show of violence in his manner. But, as he came nearer, his face grew red, and he began:

"What in the hell do you mean, you Yankee son of a bitch? By God, sir, I'll have you to bear in mind that I pay my debts; I'm a gentleman, by God, sir, and if you don't know it, I'll teach you how to conduct yourself toward one, damn you."

Now, this sudden and unexpected assault quite upset me. I was a noncombatant; had been brought up by parents who believed in the law of love, and in the power of gentleness and truth to protect the innocent anywhere. I had never raised my hand against any human being. But had it been otherwise, in my feeble state I could have been no match for the large, powerfully built man who now confronted me with his great fists almost under my nose. Almost in mortal terror I replied in a half-dazed sort of way: "Well, sir, a gentleman would hardly assault one in my condition in a manner such as this."

---

24 Morgan, whose health may have been permanently damaged by his severe wounds and illness in the Civil War, was probably sick with malaria.

But before the sentence was uttered, he hit me such a blow under my ear that I fell to the pavement. Then he jumped upon me and continued his strokes upon my head and face, while the crowd of "gentlemen," whom I had observed in and about his store as I came out, gathered in a sort of ring around us, shouting: "Fair play, here! Fair play! Kill the damn Yankee! Kill him, damn him."

But at this juncture the ring parted, scattered, and the postmaster, who had been a Federal officer, in company with two other Yankee ex-army officers who were planting near our place, rushed in, picked me up, and carrying me to the post office, washed the blood from my face . . . and, after doing all they could to comfort me, insisted that I must abandon my puritanical notions there, and never be seen in public without weapons of some sort; that *they* carried them, and they had taken pains to let the fact be known; that I would have not been attacked had it been known that I was armed, etc.

THAT "NIGGER SCHOOL"

That night, while we sat by the great fireplace in our sitting room in the old mansion on Tokeba, overlooking the turbid Yazoo, sullenly winding its way through the gloaming, I gave Charles an account of this "affair" with Captain Telsub. Many things had occurred of an unpleasant nature during the few months that had passed since we began housekeeping on Tokeba—Charles and I—which I had not cared to mention, remembering his predilections. But the situation, it appeared to me, was becoming critical, and I could no longer hide my anxiety from him. . . .

[While they were speaking,] one of our carpenters, a white man who had formed quite an extensive acquaintance among the loungers in town, called and, being seated, Charles said to him, "Tom, I wish you would tell the Colonel what you have told me."

"Well, Cap'n, there's no more to it than I've told ye already, unless it's my opinion you want."

"Well, let's have your opinion then."

"I think they'll raid the place."

"Pshaw!" said Charles, "you don't believe that, do you? What has put that into their heads?"

"Well, Cap'n, they all treat me well enough—always have, 'cept'n when that bully tried to make me say that if you was bound to build that nigger school-house, I'd bolt and not strike a lick on it."

I soon found out what the trouble was. Some days prior to this, Charles had told me of a contract he had made with a commissioner of the Freedman's Bureau to furnish the lumber for a school-building in town, for the freed people.

The situation was this: The freed people had long been anxious to have a church of their own, but did not feel able to pay the cost of such a one as they desired. This commissioner had seen and arranged with their leaders to contribute to the cost of one, if they would consent that it might also be used as a school-building.[25] In furtherance of this plan, Charles, after consulting with Mr. Ross [the partner from the North], had subscribed liberally to the fund. . . . As the Bureau commissioner could get none of the mechanics in the place to do that part of the work "for love or money," Charles had contracted to have our carpenters do it, and Tom was bossing the job. In Tom's opinion, they were going to raid the plantation, hoping by that means to remove the cause of "this outrage" as they were pleased to term it.

They had at first threatened to "kill any damned Yankee son of a bitch" who would "dare to strike a lick" on such a job. But there were six of our white mill hands, all told, who had been in the Federal army; they were "heeled"[26] too, and were not going to be bluffed. That very day they had laid the foundation and commenced to build. None of them had been harmed, however, and Tom's opinion as to the purpose of the rebs, as he called them, to "raid Tokeba," was based on remarks he had heard made by a crowd of loungers who had hung about there the greater part of the day.

While this talk was going on between Charles, Tom, and myself, Uncle Stephen called with a long story about what one of his "feller-servants of slave time" had overheard between his young masters, the substance of which was, that the Yankees must all be "driven out" or the country would be "ruined," and something about a plan to "raid the Morgans."[27] Uncle Stephen's fellow-servant lived with his old master in Holmes County, twenty-five or more miles away.

While Stephen was making his report, two of our Yankee neighbors dropped in and soon after another. One of them had been an officer of negro troops and afterwards of the Freedman's Bureau. The feeling against him had become so bitter that he did not often venture to town. . . . In reply to Charles's inquiry as to the probable cause of all this feeling, the ex-

25 [Original author's footnote] Sometime afterward I learned that a movement had been for some months under way among the freed people, looking to their separation from the "white folks'" churches, where their position had always been a servile one, and that the white folks had been making very strenuous exertions indeed to prevent such a result. They were not willing, of course, to receive their former slaves into full Christian fellowship, nor were they willing to tear down the railing in their places of worship which marked the arbitrary line the master class had drawn between white and black worshipers. They wished them all to continue, at least in their worship of God, the same as "in the good old days befo' the wah."

26 [Original author's footnote] Armed with pistols.

27 [Original author's footnote] The kuklux germ in that county had been developing.

bureau officer declared it had all the time existed, and was open now only because of the fight between the President and the known leaders of his party; that the rebels felt sure of Johnson's secret, if not open encouragement, and believed they would have to hold out but a short while before he would be able, by a judicious use of his patronage, to control Congress when it should assemble. . . .

Brother Charles and I had heard that there was a difference of some sort between the President and the national leaders of the Republican party, but had not followed it up, and knew nothing of its scope or probable effect. We had given no thought whatever to politics. . . .

All agreed that the assault upon me was likely to be repeated, and that other Northerners were in equal danger. It was also agreed that the crowd had scattered upon the approach of the postmaster and friends solely because *he* was a Yankee *in office* and supposed to have influence. . . . They had no fear of the Northern settler *out of office*. The ex-bureau agent attributed his security thus far in part to the fact that the postmaster was his partner in planting. . . .

Within a very few days after this event, a number of revolvers found their way to Tokeba, and, as the hands had been given to understand that we had no objections to their having weapons, Uncle Taylor brought out his old army rifle and handled it with such dexterity and skill in the manual of arms, that he became quite a hero at Tokeba.

THE STRAW THAT BROKE OUR CAMEL'S BACK

Not many days after . . . , a squad of Federal troops arrived at Yazoo City. It was understood that they had been sent there by direction of General O.O. Howard to prevent interference with the erection of a schoolhouse for the freed people.

The angry, snarling wolves all at once became lambs in manners and appearance, and the proud "American eagle" [Colonel Black] ruffled his own feathers until they stood erect, in indignant protest against the "outrage" put upon "we all best citizens" by the hostile presence "in ouah midst" of "ahmed soldiery" in a time of "profound peace." The officer in command of the squad was something more than "a gentleman, by God, sir," he was "discreet." From the moment they "sot eyes onto him" and got a glimpse of his face, Yazoo's "best citizens," females and males, began to coddle him, and dined and wined that "discreet Yankee ahmy officer," *ad nauseam* for us. . . . They were powerless to prevent their coming, now they were there. Therefore it would be the part of wisdom to make the visit of these "Yankee soldiers" as harmless as under the circumstances would be possible. Secretly they cursed General Howard and held him, not Mr. Johnson—it was *Mr.* Johnson now—responsible for the "outrage." . . .

Then, too, Colonel Black and his friends managed the whole thing so adroitly there was perfect peace in Yazoo; there were no longer anywhere apparent signs of ill-feeling towards the negroes; no groups of angry, threatening whites at the landing when a raft of lumber arrived for the "nigger school"; nor about "the people" who were at work on the school-house that was to be, and Charles declared that he could walk all the way from the levee to the post office and not hear his name called nor yet a polecat's. So, without consulting with us, or with the ex-bureau agent, or with any of "we all Yankees," so far as I was able to learn, this very "discreet" officer of the United States army reported to his superior that there was no need for him or his soldiers there, and he and they were soon afterward recalled.

But our point had been gained. The building had been completed, and a teacher, furnished by the Bureau, duly installed before the officer could "tear himself away" from such "hospitable, high-toned" people as welcomed *him*—and was he not a Yankee?—to Yazoo City. . . .

Our crop that year was a failure. The proceeds barely paid for gathering and working it. The sawmill, however, had been doing a good business right along, and in this crisis proved to be our stalwart friend. . . . In June following [1867], we had as fine a stand of cotton on six hundred acres of Tokeba as had ever been seen on the plantation. At least so Colonel Black's former slaves declared. In one respect the overflow had proved a blessing to us, for it enabled us to float a large number of as fine cypress trees as were ever brought out of the brakes in that region, and the mill was just "coining money" for us. . . . In compliance with our promise to have a school on the place, the old quarter jail had been torn down and the same logs used in the building of a house for that purpose. Colonel Black's old slaves recognized and greatly enjoyed the poetic justice in the use of that old jail. . . .

HOW TO GET "RID A THE DAMN YANKEES"

During the first days of September, Uncle David thought he saw signs of the army worm in his "crap" [crop]. David was planting "on shares" that year.[28] In less than ten days, nearly all of the six hundred acres looked as though they had been swept by fire; all the green leaves and shoots had been eaten off, and the crop was ruined. Only our "stalwart friend" [the sawmill] remained steadfast. . . .

Although the crop was a failure, in all probability there would be enough corn and cotton made to pay the rent. Besides, there were upon the planta-

---

[28] In later years, sharecropping became an appropriate symbol of the subjugation of the black farmer. In the years immediately after the Civil War, however, many African Americans eagerly sought out sharecropping deals as a way of winning more autonomy, compared to old-fashioned plantation gang labor.

tion, belonging to our firm, several head of work cattle, twenty-nine head of horses and mules, and wagons and plows, harness, etc., etc. The only lien of any kind against this property was that of the landlord for his rent.

Notwithstanding these evidences of our ability to pay the rent when it should become due, Colonel Finley, the sheriff, came to Tokeba and informed my brother that Colonel Black, as agent in fact of his wife, had been before a magistrate and made oath that he had reason to suspect and did verily believe we were about to remove our property beyond the jurisdiction of Yazoo County, "for the purpose of defrauding" him of his rent. Whereupon an attachment writ had been issued, commanding the sheriff to seize the *sawmill and fixtures,* logs, lumber, shingles, etc., and hold them, subject to the further orders of that magistrate's court. He [Sheriff Finley] had called for the purpose of executing the writ.

The purpose of the proceeding was evident. When Colonel Black made that oath, he knew that if we had desired to do so, it would have been impossible for us to remove the property levied on into the adjoining county—the nearest being twenty miles distant—in less time than one week. When the magistrate issued the writ, and when the sheriff executed it, the fact was as evident to them as to Colonel Black or to ourselves. Yet they had done these things. Their only motive was our destruction. . . . Had his only object been to collect the rent, by allowing us to keep the mill running, we readily could have paid it out of the orders for lumber already on hand and from the proceeds of the cargo we were about to send to New Orleans. But this he would not permit; and the sheriff not only forbade us to operate the mill, he also put a guard over it to make sure that we did not. It was evident that Colonel Black, the magistrate, and the sheriff had conspired together to destroy us.

But we had made some few friends during our brief residence in the county, and, notwithstanding the ugly front of the enemy, we resolved to contest with the conspirators their *power* to destroy us, as well as their right to this writ for money not yet due. But at the moment when we thought we were about to defeat them by replevin, the sheriff made another visit to Tokeba, and shortly afterward another, until the writs covered all our property, even including the growing and ungathered crops, and amounted to the whole of the rental for the coming year 1868, in addition to the last installment of the rental for 1867, which itself was not yet due.

The end of it all was that the enemy triumphed, the sheriff sold our property, and the rent remained unpaid still. Unpaid? Yes, unpaid. Why? Because, after the sheriff got his fees, there was not enough money left from the proceeds of the sale to pay it. Then, too, the property was not sold very well. For example, a wagon which cost $125 sold for $28; mules that cost us $130 per head only the year before in St. Louis were knocked off, some of them to Black, at $25–55 per head, and the mill, with fixtures, which had cost us, as it stood when attached, nearly eleven thousand dollars, was sold to Colonel Black for *one hundred dollars*. . . .

Why did we permit all this? We did not; we tried hard to avoid it. How was it done? According to law; and the law of Yazoo on the subject was similar to that of many States of the Union, North as well as South. The difficulty was not in the law, but in the character of our neighbors. . . .

We were now at the end of our pursuit of a legal remedy. It seemed that the feeling against us increased in just proportion to the zeal and skill with which we pursued after our rights, and so it did. Our partner gave out in the race first, I next. Charles was the last to give up. . . .

It came about that when the mill was sold, Colonel Black was the only bidder, which demonstrated to Mr. Ross, Charles, and myself, the futility of laws that are against "the will of the people," and that in Yazoo County the "anti-Yankee" element constituted the people. For as the sheriff triumphantly conducted our animals over Mr. Gosling's ferry, and up through town to the stable where they were to be sold, men, women, and children shouted as they passed by, "Hurrah! Hurrah! for Colonel Black!" and they said to each other, while they shook hands over it, "we'll get rid a the damned Yankees now."

―――――――――

AS THE MORGANS pondered their suddenly impoverished future, others fought back against the resurgent ex-Confederates. African Americans from Virginia to Louisiana organized themselves in bodies ranging from local churches to political clubs and agitated against the reassertion of the old order. In some places, groups of Confederate veterans (the first kernels of the Ku Klux Klan) retaliated against them; in others, the authorities responded to black activism with brute force. President Johnson had set the tone: white men must rule the South. The need to please the conquering North, Southern whites felt, had been lifted.

The legal conspiracies that swallowed the Morgans and other white Northerners were dwarfed by the atrocities against blacks across the South in 1866. Memphis saw the first great battle—or massacre, as it might well be called. The city had absorbed a massive influx of African Americans during and after the war, which agitated local whites. On May 1, 1866, tensions erupted when two horse-drawn cabs ran into each other. One driver was white, the other black. A number of black veterans intervened in the quarrel—and the white police force responded brutally. For three days, police-led mobs ran through the streets of largely black south Memphis. African-American troops were assaulted, along with their families. As Eric Foner writes, "Before the rioting subsided, at least forty-eight persons (all but two of them black) lay dead, five black women had been raped, and hundreds of black dwellings, churches, and schools were pillaged or destroyed by fire."

President Johnson's policies were discredited in the North by the Memphis riot—but they were about to be clouded by an even greater tragedy. This time, the setting was New Orleans. In 1864, a Unionist but whites-only government had been set up in the Union-occupied parts of the state with the blessing of Lincoln's administration (eager to undermine rebel resistance, Lincoln wanted to establish rival, loyal state governments in the South). Johnson's provisional governor for the state, James M. Wells, had sought to broaden his support by appointing former Confederates to a host of public offices. By the summer of 1866, however, even Governor Wells had grown alarmed at the power of the ex-rebels, and he called for a reconvening of the constitutional convention that had set up the state government in 1864. Intransigent local whites, however, had other ideas.

On July 30, a small number of delegates began to march to the convention hall, backed by a parade of more than 200 black supporters. The New Orleans mayor (who had run the city under the Confederacy) had already prepared the police force, a body of mostly Confederate veterans. The police launched a full-scale assault on the convention hall, shooting down even those who tried to flee or surrender. Troops from the federal garrison rushed to the scene, but it was already too late: the local authorities had butchered thirty-four black and three white Radicals, and had caused an additional 100 or so casualties. The military commander for Louisiana, General Philip H. Sheridan, had been out of the city during the riot, but he quickly returned and launched a searching investigation. In the end, he suspended the civil authorities who had caused the bloodshed. Andrew Johnson's response was to send Sheridan to Kansas to fight Indians and replace him with General Winfield Scott Hancock, a much more conservative man.

In later years, the violence of these dying months of President Johnson's plan for Reconstruction would be downplayed by Southern apologists. Often historians and popular writers implied that poor whites—not sophisticated planters and political leaders—were behind the atrocities. Even darker suggestions were made from time to time that blacks somehow deserved what they got. Any confusion on that question can quickly be cleared up by the memoirs of Confederate General Richard Taylor—the son of a U.S. president, a wealthy and educated planter, the true flower of Southern chivalry.

Atrocities—A Defense
By General Richard Taylor

Doubtless there were many acts of violence. When ignorant negroes, instigated by pestilent emissaries [from the North], went beyond endurance, the whites killed them; and this was to be expected. The breed to which these whites belong has for eight centuries been the master of the earth wherever it has planted its foot. A handful conquered and holds in subjection the crowded millions of India. Another and smaller bridles the fierce Caffre tribes of South Africa. Place but a score of them on the middle course of the Congo, and they will rule unless exterminated; and all the armies and all the humanitarians cannot change this, until the appointed time arrives for Ham to dominate Japhet. . . .

While the excitement growing out of the untoward event mentioned [the massacre in New Orleans] was at its height, President Johnson summoned me to Washington, where I explained all the circumstances, as far as I knew them, of the recent murders, and urged him to send General [Winfield Scott] Hancock to command in New Orleans. He was sent, and immediately restored order and confidence.

AS JOHNSON'S GOVERNORS appealed to the ex-Confederates, as local mobs and paramilitary patrols lashed out at Southern blacks, one force stood in the way: the Freedmen's Bureau. In spite of the President's interference, in spite of the conservatism of many army officers, in spite of the conservatism of Commissioner Oliver O. Howard himself, this experimental agency offered the only whisper of hope for African Americans in the angry, shouting South during 1865 and 1866.

Unfortunately, President Johnson soon went beyond merely meddling with the Bureau's work—he moved to block its basic mission. The grounds he selected for this obstruction comprised one of the essential reasons for its creation, a matter that filled freed blacks with the greatest hope: the promise of land. The agency itself was formally known as the Bureau of Freedmen, Refugees, and Abandoned Lands; its congressional fathers had envisioned it as a means of distributing to the freed people land seized from prominent Confederate planters who refused to repent, who had failed to pay their taxes, or who had disappeared in the fog of war.

Certainly the project of redistributing land to the former slaves was the most controversial aspect of Radical policies in the North. Many Republicans who later accepted that black men must have the vote balked at undermining the principle of private property by seizing land from its rightful owners and giving it away. Eric Foner has shown that the ideological principle of free labor that motivated many to oppose slavery also filled them with loathing for government interference in the economy—and seizing and redistributing private property is about the most serious interference possible. So the focus remained on lands lost to the owners through due process—in particular, seizure for failure to pay taxes or simple abandonment.

President Johnson saw things differently. He had already begun to curry favor among whites in the South to build support for his election campaign in 1868. In his eyes, blacks were only fit to work for whites, either as field hands or personal servants. Nor would he allow any such creation of the Republicans as the Freedmen's Bureau to tamper with the social structure of the South. As a result, General Howard was thrown onto the horns of a dilemma: on one hand he faced the opposition of the President, and his own conservatism; on the other hand, this vocally Christian soldier felt a strong sense of responsibility for seeing that justice was done to the freed people. With conflicting feelings, he did what he could against widespread hostility, even as the dream of forty acres for every freedman evaporated across the South.

No Forty Acres
by General Oliver O. Howard

Perhaps nothing excited higher hopes in the minds of those who had for years suffered and labored for emancipation, than the provision of law that was to open up the abandoned estates and certain public lands for prompt settlement by the newly emancipated.

Much in vogue at the end of the war was that plan of allotting abandoned lands to freedmen. This course the Government during the latter part of the war, as we have seen, for those lands along the Atlantic coast and in the Mississippi Valley had constantly followed first in legislative and then in executive action.[29] Only about one five-hundredth, however, of the entire amount of land in the States seceding was available; it was all that had ever been held by the United States as abandoned. . . . There was, however, some public wild land in the South which might have answered; but undoubtedly the land intended by the lawmakers was that of those Confederates who had been in arms against the National Government. Such use, however, of even the small amount which was turned over to the Freedmen's Bureau, was nullified by the President's pardon, granted to those who had abandoned the lands in order to engage in the war; orders of restoration to all such immediately followed the presentation of the executive pardon; this was very soon after I had obtained the control of Bureau matters. . . .

We had in December 1865 already under cultivation 161,331 acres; and for the use of the refugees and freedmen there were 768,590 acres not yet

[29] During the war Confederate plantation owners fled from these areas as the Union army moved in. The federal commanders settled freed slaves on these abandoned lands, leasing them their own farms; the income from the rents eventually went to the Freedmen's Bureau.

surrendered by operation of the President's pardons; but even that early, 88,170 acres and 1,177 pieces of town property had been restored to former owners, thus largely reducing the income of our Bureau from the rents, and making a continued possession of the remainder too uncertain to be of material value. . . . The tenure [of Bureau-run lands] had already become too doubtful to warrant much allotment to individuals or the giving of leases of any considerable length. Thus the provisions of the law were plainly thwarted by unexpected executive action. . . .

In order to establish a definite and uniform policy relative to confiscated and abandoned lands, as commissioner, I issued a circular (July 28th) quoting the law and limiting and regulating the return of the lands to the former owners; I authorized assistant commissioners to restore any real property in their possession not *abandoned;* the cultivators [freedmen living on these lands] were protected in the ownership of growing crops on land to be restored, and careful descriptions were required of such land, and monthly records of amounts which remained in the possession of the Government. I further directed the assistant commissioners to select and set apart in orders, with as little delay as possible, as some had already been doing, such confiscated and abandoned property as they deemed necessary for the immediate use for the life and comfort of refugees and freedmen; and we also provided for rental and sale when that was possible.

Surely the pardon of the President would not be interpreted to extend to the surrender of abandoned or confiscated property which in strict accordance of the law had been "set apart for refugees and freedmen" or was then in use for the employment and general welfare of all such persons within the lines of national military occupation in insurrectionary States. Did not the law apply to all formerly held as slaves, who had become or would become free? This was the legal status and the humane conclusion. Then naturally I took such actions as would protect the *bona fide* occupants, and expected the United States to indemnify by money or otherwise those Confederates who were pardoned; assuredly we would not succor them by displacing the new settlers who lawfully were holding the land.

My circular of instructions did not please President Johnson. . . . He made me draw up another circular worded better to suit his policy and submit it to him before its issue. But he, still dissatisfied, and with a totally different object in view than mine, had the document redrawn at the White House and instructed me September 12, 1865, to send it out as approved by him, and so with reluctance I did. This document in great part rescinded former land circulars. Besides allowing assistant commissioners to return all land not abandoned, it instructed them to return all abandoned lands to owners who were pardoned by the President, and provided no indemnity whatever for the occupants, refugees or freedmen, except a right to the growing crops. In the definition of confiscated estates the words were: "Land will not be regarded as confiscated until it has been condemned and sold by decree of the United States court for the district in which the property may be found, and the title thereto thus vested in the United States."

On the face of it this approved circular appeared fair and right enough; but with masterly adroitness the President's draft had effectually defeated the *intention* of all that legislation which used the abandoned estates and the so-called confiscated property; that intention was to give to loyal refugees and freedmen allotments of and titles to land. In Virginia, a considerable amount had been libeled and was about to be sold, when Mr. Stanton considerately suspended the sales, that these lands might be turned over to the Bureau for the benefit of the freedmen. I insisted that these lands, condemned for sale, though not actually sold, were already the property of the Government; therefore, I made objection to the President against the insertion of the word "sold" into the definition of confiscated property; but after reference to the attorney general, the President decided adversely to me and so the word "sold" was inserted in the definition that was published in the order.

This was what caused the return to former owners of *all property* where sales had been suspended and never consummated. It was further strongly recommended by me to the President that all men of property to whom he was offering pardon should be conditioned to provide a small homestead or something equivalent to each head of family of his former slaves; but President Johnson was amused and gave no heed to this recommendation. My heart ached for our beneficiaries, but I became comparatively helpless to offer them any permanent possession.

When the former owner had not as yet been pardoned the burden was after this time put upon my officers to prove that property had ever been voluntarily abandoned by a disloyal owner. I soon saw that very little, if any, had been confiscated by formal court decision; so that wholesale pardons in a brief time completed the restoration of the remainder of our lands; all done for the advantage of the late Confederates and for the disadvantage and displacement of the freedmen. Very many had in good faith occupied and cultivated the farms guaranteed to them by the provision and promise of the United States.

My heart was sad enough when by constraint I sent out that circular letter; it was chagrined when not a month later I received the following orders issued by President Johnson: "Whereas certain tracts of land, situated on the coast of South Carolina, Georgia, and Florida, at the time for the most part vacant, were set apart by Major General W.T. Sherman's special field order No. 15[30] for the benefit of refugees and freed-

---

[30] During the war General Sherman had issued this order to set aside great stretches of farmland—much of it on the coastal sea islands—for the freed people; tens of thousands took up homesteads as a result. Ironically, Sherman issued the order because he refused to accept black soldiers in his army, and he wished to escape the burden of supporting the people he had freed by his march through the South.

men that had been congregated by the operations of the war, or had been left to take care of themselves by their former owners. . . .

"It is ordered: That Major General Howard, Commissioner of the Bureau of Refugees, Freedmen, and Abandoned Lands, *proceed* to the several above-named States and endeavor to effect an agreement mutually satisfactory to the freedmen and the land owners, and make report. . . ." Why did I not resign? Because I even yet strongly hoped in some way to befriend the freed people.

Obeying my instructions I reached Charleston, S.C., October 17, 1865. General Saxton's headquarters were then in that city. I had a conference with him and with many of the land owners concerned. The truth was soon evident to me that nothing effective could be done without consulting the freedmen themselves who were equally interested. Therefore, accompanied by several officers and by Mr. William Whaley, who represented the planters, I went to Edisto Island, and met the freedmen of that vicinity who came together in a large meeting house.

The auditorium and the galleries were filled. The rumor preceding my coming had reached the people that I was obliged by the President's orders to restore the lands to the old planters, so that strong evidence of dissatisfaction and sorrow were manifested from every part of the assembly. In the noise and confusion no progress was had till a sweet-voiced negro woman began the hymn, "Nobody knows the trouble I feel—Nobody knows but Jesus," which, joined in by all, had a quieting effect on the audience. Then I endeavored as clearly and gently as I could to explain to them the wishes of the President, as they were made known to me in an interview with him just before leaving Washington. Those wishes were also substantially embodied in my instructions.

My address, however kind in manner I rendered it, met with no apparent favor. They did not hiss, but their eyes flashed unpleasantly, and with one voice they cried, *"No, no!"* Speeches full of feeling and rough eloquence came back in response. One very black man, thick set and strong, cried out from the gallery, "Why, General Howard, why do you take away our lands? You take them from us who are true, always true to the Government! You give them to our all-time enemies! That is not right!"

At my request, the assembly chose three of their number, and to them I submitted with explanations the propositions to which the land owners were willing to subscribe. I faithfully reiterated to the whole body the conditions of the existing tenure under our President's action, they having no absolute title but simply occupying the homesteads. I urged them to make the best terms they could with the holders of the titles. . . . But their committee after considering all the matters submitted to them said that on no condition would the freedmen work for their late owners as formerly they did under overseers; but if they could rent lands from them, they would consent to all the other arrangements proposed. Some without overseers would work for wages; but the general desire was to rent lands and work them. At last, to be fair to all parties as possible, I constituted a board of supervisors in which the Government, the planters, and the freedmen were equally represented. This board was to secure and adjust contracts and settle cases of dispute and controversy. . . .

Prior to the President's fuller action in the interest of the land owners, my instructions had been clearly defined, to return estates to those only who could show constant loyalty, past as well as present—a loyalty which could be established by the production of an oath of allegiance, or amnesty, or other evidence. As the Bureau held property by authority of an Act of Congress for certain definite purposes, I had presumed and believed that this tenure would continue until those purposes were accomplished; that such property must be surrendered by us only when it was made evident that our possession and control of it was not proper. But the adverse action of President Johnson and the non-action of Congress caused a complete reversal of the Government's generous provision for the late slaves.

JUST WHO WON the Civil War? Many Northerners and black Southerners asked themselves this question in 1865 and 1866. Within a year after the last shell was fired, it seemed as if every fruit of the federal victory (except the legal abolition of slavery) had been ground into the dirt by the President and the former Confederates who still ran the South. To those who had fought under the Stars and Stripes, it seemed as if the defeated rebels were showing their true colors—and the prevailing hue was blood red. The riots in New Orleans and Memphis, along with those in scores of smaller places, shocked Northern voters. Their newspapers were filled with reports of injustice handed out to Northern men such as the Morgans—men who had served the Union, who had invested their life savings in the South, only to be persecuted because they did not see African Americans as chattel. And President Johnson, through his attacks on the Freedmen's Bureau, had blocked the best chance for helping the black population become a self-sustaining, prosperous community.

Of course, the political situation was complex—more complex than the picture being painted might suggest. Southern whites were split by economics and wartime loyalties; Southern blacks were divided between the elite (who had been free before the war) and the recently freed; Northern Republicans fell into moderate and Radical camps, in addition to divisions over fiscal policy and other matters. But the events of 1866 polarized the nation. Driven by the lash of Southern atrocity and injustice, moderate Republicans joined the Radicals in an unprecedented battle cry: give the black man the vote.

4

THE STRUGGLE IN WASHINGTON, PART II:
CONGRESS ACTS

On April 9, 1868, Colonel William G. Moore, the President's private secretary, noted in his diary that Johnson "has at times exhibited a morbid distress and feeling against the negroes." Col. Moore was being excessively tactful. Only a few months before, Johnson had filled his annual message to Congress with a shocking attack on black people. Africans, he declared, had less "capacity for government than any other race of people. No independent government of any form has ever been successful in their hands. On the contrary, wherever they have been left to their own devices they have shown a constant tendency to barbarism." Give African Americans the vote, and he predicted one thing: "A tyranny such as this continent has never yet witnessed."[31]

In December 1865, those words were more than two years in the future; as Congress assembled for its first session since the Civil War ended, Johnson's views were only gradually becoming clear. The Republicans easily dominated both houses, but the party was split between Radicals and moderates. By the time the representatives and senators assembled in Washington, Radicals such as George Boutwell had already seen enough of Presidential Reconstruction to know they opposed it. As 1865 ended and 1866 began, events such as those described in the last chapter would drive the Radicals into determined hostility—perhaps hatred is not too strong a word—toward the Southern Democrat who held the White House.

The moderates, however, were not so quick to dismiss Johnson's program. Freshman Congressman Shelby Cullom and veteran Senator John Sherman hesitated at the sweeping social realignment sought by Thaddeus Stevens and others. They would be satisfied with an impartial operation of the laws in the South, a fair and rational business climate, and certain restrictions on the rights of the leading Confederate rebels. These men were far more skeptical than the Radicals about black suffrage: most would only consider giving the vote to African Americans who were veterans, literate, or owned some property.

The President saw an opportunity in this attitude, and he delivered a measured, reasonable message to Congress in an effort to split the Republicans.

[31] Quoted in Foner, *Reconstruction*. Eric Foner dryly notes in his excellent commentary that "it is difficult to imagine what regime blacks might impose more tyrannical than chattel slavery."

Unfortunately for Johnson, he soon stumbled on two things. The first was the demon he had helped unleash by restoring whites-only government in the ex-Confederate states. Harassment and outright atrocities horrified Northerners of all stripes, stirring sympathy for blacks. Even the most conservative Republicans began to think that the only hope for justice was to guarantee African-American citizenship. The President's second stumbling block was his own head—his stubborn, mean-spirited, quarreling head. Johnson was no coalition builder. He did one thing and he did it well: attack political opponents without mercy. The vindictive President drove Cullom, Sherman, and the other moderates straight into the Radical camp—and the nation made a giant leap toward universal suffrage.

The Radicals Take Command
by Shelby M. Cullom

When I entered the Thirty-Ninth Congress . . . representatives of the eleven seceding States were there to claim their seats in Congress. The Republican members met in caucus the Saturday evening preceding the meeting of Congress on Monday. I, as a member-elect, was present, and I remember how old Thaddeus Stevens at once assumed the dominating control in opposition to the President's plan. Stevens was a most remarkable character—one of the most remarkable in the legislative history of the United States. He believed firmly in negro equality and negro suffrage. . . .

It was at once determined by the Republican majority in Congress that the representatives of the eleven seceding States should not be admitted. The Constitution expressly gives to the House and Senate the exclusive power to judge of the admission and qualifications of its own members.

We were surprised at the moderation of the President's message, which came in on Tuesday after Congress assembled. In tone and general character the message was wholly unlike Johnson. It was an admirable state document, one of the finest from a literary and probably from every other standpoint that ever came from an Executive to Congress. It was thought at the time that Mr. Seward wrote it, but it has since been asserted that it was the product of that foremost of American historians, J.C. Bancroft, one of Mr. Johnson's close personal friends.

There existed three theories of dealing with the Southern States: one was the President's theory of recognizing State governments, allowing the States to deal with the suffrage question as they might see fit; the Stevens policy of wiping out all State lines and dealing with the regions as conquered military provinces; and the Sumner theory of treating them as organized territories, recognizing the State lines. Johnson dealt in a masterful manner with the subject in his message. He said . . . "The perpetuity of the Constitution brings with it the perpetuity of the States. . . .

The true theory is that all pretended acts of secession were, from the beginning, null and void. The States cannot commit treason. . . ."

But the question was, whether the members from the seceding States should be admitted to the Senate and the House; and he dealt with this most difficult question in a statesmanlike way [by leaving the question to Congress]. . . . On the suffrage question, he said: "On the propriety of making freedmen electors by proclamation of the Executive, I took for my counsel the Constitution itself, the interpretations of that instrument by its authors, and their contemporaries, and the recent legislation of Congress. They all unite in inculcating the doctrine that the regulation of the suffrage is a power exclusively for the States. . . ."

Aside from the worst radicals, the message pleased everyone, the country at large and the majority in Congress; and there was a general disposition to give the President a reasonably free hand in working out his plan of reconstruction. But as I stated, the legislatures of the Southern States and their executives assumed so domineering an attitude, practically wiping out the results of the war, that the Republican majority in Congress assumed it to be its duty to take control from the Executive.

What determined Johnson in his course, I do not know. It was thought that he would be a radical of radicals. Being of the "poor white" class, he may have been flattered by the attentions showered on him by the old Southern aristocrats. Writers of this period have frequently given that as a reason. My own belief has been that he was far too strong a man to be governed in so vital a matter by so trivial a cause. My conviction is that the radical Republican leadership in the House was right: that he believed in the old Democratic party, aside from his loyalty to the union; and was a Democrat determined to turn the government over to the Democratic party, reconstructed on a Union basis.

I cannot undertake to go into all the long details of that memorable struggle. As I look back over the history of it now, it seems to me to bear a close resemblance to the beginning of the French Revolution, to the struggle between the States General of France and Louis XVI. Might we not, if things had turned out differently, have drifted into chaos and revolution? If Johnson had been impeached and refused to submit, adopting the same tactics as Stanton in retaining the War Department; had Ben Wade taken the oath of office and demanded possession, Heaven only knows what might have been the result. . . .

An extension of the Freedmen's Bureau bill was passed, was promptly vetoed by the Executive. . . . I had not the slightest idea that Johnson would dare to veto the Freedmen's Bureau bill, and I made a speech on the subject, declaring a firm conviction to that effect. A veto at that time was almost unheard of. Except during the administration of Tyler, no important bill had ever been vetoed by an Executive. It came as a shock to Congress and the country. Excitement reigned supreme. The question was: "Should the bill pass the veto of the President regardless thereof?"

Not the slightest difficulty existed in the House; Thaddeus Stevens had too complete control of that body to allow any question concerning it there. The bill, therefore, was promptly passed over the veto of the President. But the situation in the Senate was different. At that time the Sumner-Wade radical element did not have the necessary two-thirds majority, and the bill failed to pass over the veto of the President. The war between the executive and legislative departments of the government had fairly commenced, and the first victory had been won by the President.

The Civil Rights bill, drawn and introduced by Judge Trumbull, than whom there was no greater lawyer in the United States Senate, in January 1866, on the reassembling of Congress, was passed.[32] Then began the real struggle on the part of the radicals in the Senate, headed by Sumner and Wade, to muster the necessary two-thirds majority to pass a bill over the veto of the President.

Let me digress to say a word in reference to Charles Sumner. For ten years he was chairman of the Foreign Relations Committee of the United States Senate, and no man, by education, experience, knowledge of world politics, and travel, was ever more fitted to occupy that high position. He was one of the most cultivated men of his day, a radical, and filled one of the most important places in the history of his time. When he entered the Senate, the South dominated this government; the great triumvirate, Webster, Clay, and Calhoun, had just passed. The day he entered, Clay for the last time, feeble, emaciated, appeared on the Senate floor. Compromise was the word, and the Southerners so dominated that it was considered treason to mention the slavery question. Charles Sumner was an abolitionist; he was not afraid, and at the very first opportunity he took the floor and denounced the institution in no unmeasured terms. Chase and Seward were present that day, and quickly followed Sumner's lead. Seward, however, was far more conservative than either Sumner or Chase.

It was the mission of Charles Sumner to awake the public conscience to the horrors of slavery. He performed his duty unfalteringly, and it almost cost him his life. . . . Mr. Sumner's end has always seemed to me most pitiful. Removed from his high position as chairman of the Foreign Relations Committee of the Senate, followed relentlessly by the enmity of President Grant, then at the very acme of his fame; drifting from the Republican party, his own State repudiating him, Charles Sumner died of a broken heart.

But to return to the struggle between the President and Congress. Trumbull, Sumner, Wade, and the leaders were bound in one way or another to get the necessary two-thirds. The vote was taken in the Senate:

[32] The Civil Rights Bill defined all U.S.-born persons (except Indians) as national citizens for the first time in American history, and detailed their rights: regardless of race, citizens could make contracts, bring lawsuits, and receive equal protection of the laws. The federal courts were authorized to try state and local officials who violated anyone's rights. But the bill did not give blacks the vote.

"Shall the Civil Rights bill pass, the veto of the President to the contrary notwithstanding?" It was well understood that the vote would be very close, and the result uncertain.

The excitement was intense. The galleries were crowded; members of the House were on the Senate floor. The result seemed to depend entirely on the vote of Senator Morgan, of New York, and he seemed to be irresolute, uncertain in his own mind which way he would vote. The call of the roll proceeded. When his name was reached there was profound silence. He first voted nay, and then immediately changed to yea.

A wonderful demonstration burst forth, as it was known that the bill would pass over the veto of the President, and that the Republican party in Congress at last had complete control. Senator Trumbull made a remarkable speech on that occasion, and I was never prouder of any living man.

So the struggle went on from day to day and year to year, growing all the time more intense. I have always been disposed to be conservative; I was then; and it was with profound regret that I saw the feeling between the President and Congress becoming more and more strained. I disliked to follow the extreme radical element, and when the row was at its height, Judge Orth, a colleague in the House from Indiana, and I concluded to go and see the President and advise with him, in an attempt to smooth over the differences.

I will never forget the interview. It was at night. He received us politely enough, and without mincing any words he gave us to understand that we were on a fool's errand and that he would not yield. We went away, and naturally joined the extreme radicals, always voting with them afterwards. The row continued in the Fortieth Congress. Bills were passed, promptly vetoed, and the bills were immediately passed over the President's vetoes.

Congress Makes a Plan
by John Sherman

In the beginning of the controversy between Congress and the President, I tried to act as peacemaker. I knew Mr. Johnson personally, his good and his bad qualities. I sat by his side in the Senate chamber during the first two years of the war. I was with him in the canvass of 1864. I sympathized with him in his struggles with the leaders of the Rebellion and admired his courage during the war, when, as Governor of Tennessee, he reorganized the state upon a loyal basis. The defect of his character was his unreasoning pugnacity. He early became involved in wordy warfare with Sumner, Wade, Stevens, and others. In his high position he could have disregarded criticism, but this was not the habit of Johnson. When assailed he fought, and could be as violent and insulting in language or acts as anyone. . . .

I still hoped that the pending Civil Rights Bill would be approved by the President, and that then the controversy would end. On the 17th of March, 1866, I made a speech at Bridgeport, Conn., in which I said . . .

> "On Thursday, the day that I left Washington, we sent to him [President Johnson] a bill which secures to all the colored population of the Southern states equal rights before the law, the Civil Rights Bill. It declares that no state shall exclude any man on account of his color from any of the natural rights which, by the Declaration of Independence, are declared to be inalienable; it provides that every man may sue and be sued, may plead and be impleaded, may acquire and hold property, may purchase, contract, sell, and convey; all those rights are secured to the negro population. That bill is now in the hands of the President. If he signs it, it will be a solemn pledge of the law-making power of the nation that the negroes shall have secured to them all these natural and inalienable rights. I believe the President will sign it."

Unfortunately at the end of ten days the President sent to the Senate the Civil Rights Bill . . . with his message vetoing it. It passed both Houses with the requisite two-thirds majority, and thus became law. This veto was followed by other vetoes, and, practically, the President abandoned his party.[33] From this time forth, I heartily joined with my political associates in the measures adopted to secure a loyal reorganization of the Southern states. I was largely influenced by the harsh treatment of the freedmen in the South under acts adopted by the reconstructed legislatures. The outrages of the Ku Klux Klans seemed to me to be so atrocious and wicked that the men who committed them were not only unworthy to govern, but unfit to live.

The weakness of the position of Congress in the controversy with Mr. Johnson was that it had furnished no plan of reconstruction and he was compelled to act upon the urgency of events. Many efforts were made to provide legislation to take the place of the proclamations and acts of the President, but a wide divergence of opinion in the Republican party manifested itself, and no substantial progress was made until near the close of the 39th Congress. . . . On the 16th of February, [1867,] after consultation with my political colleagues, I moved a substitute for the House [Reconstruction] bill. The fifth section of this substitute embodied a comprehensive plan for the organization of the rebel states with provision for elections in said states, and the conditions required for their admission and restoration to the Union. . . . The substitute was adopted on the same day. . . . It was sent to the President and was not approved by him, but was, on the 2nd of March, passed over his veto by a vote of two-thirds of both Houses.

[33] Johnson existed in a sort of political limbo. He had been elected on Lincoln's ticket, and so he was considered head of the Republican party, if only at first and only technically. However, he was widely seen as an old-style Jacksonian Democrat, and the Democrats were his main source of support.

CONGRESS HAD STRUCK: horrified by the Black Codes and bloodshed in the South, disgusted by Johnson's attitude and policies, it overrode his vetoes and produced its own plan for Reconstruction. As forged by Senator John Sherman and his colleagues, the Reconstruction Act of 1867 did the following: first, it divided ten of the eleven former Confederate states (Tennessee excepted) into five military districts. The army commanders of these districts were charged with maintaining civil order—with their troops, if necessary. Second, in order to be readmitted to the Union, these states were to hold elections open to all adult men—*regardless of color*—for conventions to draw up new state constitutions based on universal manhood suffrage. Then, once the new constitutions were approved by the voters, and the states ratified the Fourteenth Amendment (see the next chapter), Congress would accept them back into full membership in the nation. At the same time, the Republicans passed the Habeas Corpus Act, which made it easier for private citizens to remove their cases from state to federal courts.

A true revolution had begun. In early 1865, most congressmen approached the issue of Reconstruction cautiously; in late 1866 and early 1867, they were driven to unprecedented action. For the first time, the national government intervened in local affairs to guarantee the rights of individuals. But to carry out this dramatic new policy, Congress had to overcome the determined opposition of President Johnson in the capital and white Democrats in the South.

One man fought the battle on both fronts: Freedmen's Bureau Commissioner Oliver O. Howard. In the passage that follows, Howard provides an important perspective on the legislative fight described by Cullom and Sherman. The details of this duel had very real meaning to him and his African-American clients, and he deftly describes the impact of Johnson's opposition on both his agency and the ever-hardening opposition throughout the South. Here, in the last months of the Bureau's brief life, the best qualities of this one-armed, contradictory general came forth, as he and his men fought the rising waters of racism and reaction.

The Bureau vs. the White House
by General Oliver O. Howard

The most annoying things that I, as commissioner, encountered, and they were hitherto unceasing, were the complaints made to President Johnson against officers and agents and referred to me for examination and correction. Any agent who took the part of the freedmen against a Southern planter, especially one who had the hardihood to arrest a white man for misusing a negro, was traduced, and often, I am sorry to say, his discharge was brought about. The President was very anxious to be rid of every prominent officer who was reported to have been long the freedmen's friend. . . .

As I was obliged to execute the law under the direction of his Excellency, little by little his power made itself felt. To give my work the utmost opportunity to succeed I came to the conclusion, first, that all Government agencies within a given State must work in harmony, and so I recommended to the President that the functions of the military commander and that of the assistant commissioner in each State be exercised by the same officer. To this he gladly assented. . . .

Fortunately for me the Secretary of War, Mr. Stanton, and General Grant, the commander of all the geographical departments and garrisons, were friendly to my work; it was, therefore, not difficult to secure in that way unity of organization and action; it was easy enough in and near all towns actually garrisoned, and in places which were reached by rail. Perhaps the needs, the hopes, the fears, the failings, and such progress as was made in the Bureau work for 1866 may be best illustrated by some of the work before the courts that year. . . .

In Mississippi, General T.J. Wood, an able division commander during the war, always of a conservative turn of mind, gave a statement of the conditions of affairs which was not very encouraging. Grievous outrages had been committed. A class of citizens called "regulators" appeared in several States as if by concert of action; the fear of them in some parts of Mississippi was so great that peaceably disposed inhabitants were afraid to give the information necessary for their detection and punishment. The regulators shot freedmen without provocation, drove them, unpaid, from plantations, and committed other crimes. So many outrages of this kind were perpetrated that General Wood at first wondered that the better portion of the community did not take decided measures against the guilty. . . .

The deliberate murder April 30th of that year [1866] of a worthy officer, Lieutenant J.B. Blanding, Twenty-First Regiment Veteran Reserve Corps, while walking on the street at Grenada, Miss., and attempts upon the lives of other men who had been faithful and fearless in the discharge of their delicate and dangerous duties, gave rise to increased anxiety everywhere and seemed to necessitate an increase of military force. . . .

PRESIDENT JOHNSON'S FIRST OPPOSITION

For political reasons, however, the President desired to put before the people a very different view [that is, a negative one] of the Bureau. His plan of reconstruction of the Southern State governments had been discredited by Congress; senators and members of the House applying for seats under it were refused admittance. The plan had been broached of giving negroes a vote, the Bureau to be the means of preparing them for the suffrage and protecting them in it.

It was during this time that the new Bureau bill was being debated in Congress (May, 1866), that he inaugurated a remarkable inspection of the Bureau in the South by two officers in the interest of his policy. One of them, General Steedman, had been a brave officer; but he was a rough character with no sympathy for negroes. The other had been my adjutant general in the field, and afterwards a long time in my Bureau. He was a kind, upright young man, but unaccountably took part in this attack upon the Bureau and upon the administration of some of our best subordinates. The two men set out, reporters with them for the press, generally unfriendly to plans of reconstruction favored by Congress. They passed on from city to city and from place to place, visiting military and Bureau headquarters in each Southern State, and sent their reports, as critical and adverse as possible, broadcast through the newspapers to the entire country.

Before this operation began, General Grant, who had to some extent found out what was to be done, kindly sent for me and said substantially: "Howard, you must not take too much to heart or as against yourself what may be said or reported before long against your Bureau." . . .

THE RECONSTRUCTION ACT, MARCH 2, 1867

The year 1867 for the Freedmen's Bureau was an eventful one. . . . By a law, of date March 2, 1867, the plan of Congress for a reconstruction of the South had been passed over the President's veto. Its preamble read: "Whereas, no legal state governments or adequate protection for life or property now exist in the States of Virginia, North Carolina, South Carolina, Georgia, Mississippi, Alabama, Louisiana, Florida, Texas, and Arkansas; and whereas, it is necessary that peace and good order should be enforced in such States until loyal and republican State governments can be legally established," etc., etc. . . .

Each State was divided into military districts whose commanders were the Bureau agents in matters pertaining to the freedmen, and under them were the sub-districts where the sub-agent, usually without troops present, procured the necessary supplies for the extremely destitute, adjusted labor matters, encouraged negro education, and counteracted the effect of unjust, prejudiced juries and the action of some local courts, which arrested and in many instances practically re-enslaved the negro. I simply conformed to the new law, as I had to President Johnson's previous plans. . . .

Owing to the heated controversy still going on between the President and Congress, it was thought that the President would cause my removal, the air being full of rumors to that effect, so that the work of reconstruction as provided by the several Acts would be retarded by his replacing me by an opponent of Congress. To prevent that, the Act of June 24th was followed by another brief Act, that of July 25, 1868, entitled: "An Act relating to the Freedmen's Bureau, and providing for its discontinuance." The first paragraph provided that I should be continued as commissioner while the Bureau lived; that in case of vacancy by death or resignation, the Secretary of War should nominate and the Senate confirm a new commissioner, or during the recess of Congress that the acting assistant adjutant general of the Bureau should do the work. The second and last paragraph directed me to discontinue the Bureau altogether on January 1, 1869, except the educational department and payment of bounties and other dues to colored soldiers and sailors or their heirs. . . .

Very naturally this bill was vetoed by the President, but was speedily passed by both the Senate and the House over his veto, and so became a law. . . . The necessary orders and instructions were issued very soon after the publication of the Act of Congress which, in fact, was to effect the substantial close of the Freedmen's Bureau. Officers, agents, and clerks were notified that their services would no longer be required after December 31, 1868. The freedmen were generally carefully apprised of the situation, and shown that they must now look to the civil magistrates more directly than heretofore for protection of their rights and redress of wrongs.

GENERAL HOWARD'S BUREAU was through, though its work was not. So unprecedented was the idea of the government directly aiding individuals that not even the Radicals wished to sustain the Freedmen's Bureau past 1868.[34] Some might have done a better job as commissioner than Oliver O. Howard; certainly many would have done worse. He was strongly Christian and deeply conservative; he was compassionate yet patronizing; sympathetic yet rigid. He was not the man to force the issue of redistributing land to the freed people; but neither would he stand by as atrocities wracked the South. For all his flaws, he had done quite a bit of good.

Upon his departure, the general served as president of the all-black Howard University in Washington, D.C., which he had helped found. He also joined in the founding of Lincoln Memorial University in Tennessee. Returning to active duty in the army, he went to the West—where he played yet another contradictory role with the Indians. Howard negotiated with Cochise, forging a just (if temporary) agreement that brought peace with the Chiricahua Apaches. But a few years later, his unyielding stance drove the Nez Percés of Chief Joseph to flee for Canada.

Even before the doors were closed at the Freedmen's Bureau, however, Congress took another bold step toward equality. It passed a proposal for a change in the Constitution, one quickly ratified by the states: the groundbreaking Fourteenth Amendment.

---

[34] It should be noted, however, that Senator Sumner proposed that the Bureau be made a permanent department, and its head be given a cabinet seat.

5

SUFFRAGE

In slightly over a year, a revolution had swept Washington—indeed, the nation itself. Frustrated with Southern white governments and the Johnson administration, moderate and Radical Republicans had leaped ahead to a position unimaginable at war's end: that blacks should have the vote. And to see the program through against Southern opposition, it had enacted the largest peacetime expansion of federal power in American history.

Of course, everything Congress does is a product of politics, and politics tends to erode (if not eradicate) moral principles. So it was with the Reconstruction Act of 1867. For many Northern Republicans, African-American suffrage was merely a means of counterbalancing former Confederates; Congress did not mandate it throughout the Union—only in the South. In 1868, a black man in loyal Ohio would have to emigrate to the formerly rebellious state of Louisiana if he wanted to vote. California's leaders maneuvered to ensure that Chinese immigrants would not inadvertently gain the right to cast ballots—and no one wanted Native Americans at the polls. On the other hand, Senator Charles Sumner was so determined to see that true equal rights be granted to blacks that he obstructed the compromise measures worked out in Congress's endless negotiations.

Republicans of every stripe, however, drew a lesson from their contest with the President and the Southern state legislatures. Their principles and political purposes must be placed beyond the reach of daily politics—they must be enshrined in the Constitution. After much haggling, they came up with a proposal for what became the Fourteenth Amendment. It breaks down into five parts. The first defines citizenship, and guarantees equal protection of the laws to all. The second section punishes states that deny the right to vote to any class of male citizens by reducing that state's congressional representation according to the number of lost voters. The third section forbids anyone who has rebelled against the government from taking federal office. The fourth repudiates Confederate war debts and rules out any payment in compensation for the emancipation of the slaves. The fifth grants Congress the right to enforce the amendment.

A somewhat strange piece of basic law: clearly it was the result of a tangled political struggle over just how far Reconstruction should go. Republican congressmen tiptoed around the issue of forcing the *North* to grant the vote to blacks; it would be another few years before the issue was dealt with directly in the Fifteenth Amendment. The formula for penalizing states for limiting the vote was a lever for creating black suffrage *only* in the South (where almost all African Americans lived at the time). And yet, for all its faults, the Fourteenth Amendment was a revolutionary attempt to define and guarantee the rights of citizens on a national level—to protect individuals against local prejudices.

One of the main forces behind the amendment was Congressman George Boutwell, the Radical from Massachusetts. In the selection below, Boutwell recalls how he maneuvered between the contending forces as he pushed the Fourteenth Amendment forward. On one side were the bulk of the Republicans—most rather doubtful of black suffrage, at least during 1866, but determined to do something to overthrow the Confederate rebels. The war was still deeply felt in the North—many thought that the victory was being thrown away. On the other side was Senator Sumner, a man struggling with his deep principles, who only grudgingly accepted the compromises that made the amendment possible.

The Fourteenth Amendment
by George S. Boutwell

It was impossible in 1866 to go farther than the provisions of the Fourteenth Amendment. That amendment was prepared in form by Senators Conkling and Williams and myself. We were a select committee on Tennessee. The propositions were not ours, but we gave form to the amendment. The part relating to the "privileges and immunities" came from Mr. Bingham of Ohio. Its euphony and indefiniteness of meaning were a charm to him.

When the measure came before the Senate Mr. Sumner opposed its passage and alleged that we proposed to barter the right of the negroes to vote for diminished representation on the part of the old slave States in the House and in the electoral colleges; while in truth the loss of representation was imposed as a penalty upon any State that should deprive any class of its adult male citizens of the right to vote.

Upon this allegation of Mr. Sumner the resolution was defeated in the Senate . . . The defeat of the amendment was followed by bitter criticisms by the Republican press and by Republicans. These criticisms affected Mr. Sumner deeply and he then devoted himself to the preparation of an amendment which he could approve. While he was engaged in that work I called upon him and he read seventeen drafts of a proposition, not one of which was entirely satisfactory to himself, and not one of which would have been accepted by congress or the country.

The difficulty was in the situation. Upon the return of the seceded States their representation would be increased nearly forty votes in the House and in the electoral colleges while the voting force would remain in the white population. The injustice of such a condition was apparent, and there were only two possible remedies. One was to extend the franchise to the blacks. The country—the loyal States—were not then ready for the measure. The alternative was to cut off the representation from States that denied the elective franchise to any class of adult male citizens. Finally Mr. Sumner was compelled to accept the alternative. Some changes of phraseology were made, and Mr. Sumner gave a reluctant vote for the resolution.

Aside from the debates on the constitutional amendments, there were serious differences among Republicans in regard to the exercise of the right of suffrage by the negroes. Previous to the year 1868, there were a majority of Republicans who would have imposed some qualification, some of service in the army or navy, some of property, and some of education. It was with great difficulty that the scheme of limitation was resisted in regard to the District of Columbia. As to the Democrats they could always be counted upon to aid in any measure which tended to keep the negroes in a subordinate condition. This of the majority—there was always a minority, usually a small one, who were ready to aid in the elevation of the negro when his emancipation had been accomplished. I do not recall the name of one man who favored emancipation as a policy and adhered to the Democratic Party. When a man reached the conclusion that the negroes should be free, he could not do otherwise than join the Republican Party.

THE FOURTEENTH AMENDMENT was not the answer to the Radicals' prayers—but it was a sign in the political heavens, a glimpse of the nation's imminent future. George Boutwell would have dearly loved to craft a document that dealt with black suffrage directly (indeed, he actually did so when he helped forge the Fifteenth Amendment a couple of years later), but in 1866 and 1867, the Fourteenth Amendment was the best practical measure that he could hope for. It was clearly a big step toward the Radical ideal of equality.

One political figure, however, was less enthusiastic—in fact, she was enraged. For years, Elizabeth Cady Stanton and her close friend Susan B. Anthony had been campaigning for the woman's right to vote. From careful organizational work to podium-thumping speeches, their efforts had made suffrage for women an unavoidable issue in American politics. When the Civil War broke out, they put aside their work to campaign against the larger evil of slavery. And with the nation, they had celebrated the victory of the Union and the end of that horrible institution.

The mood at the close of the war, as we have seen, led to new thinking about the rights and freedoms due to Americans. Those were heady years for Stanton and Anthony, years when it seemed as if anything were possible, and woman suffrage might only be months, even weeks away. But then came the Fourteenth Amendment, which introduced a new word into the Constitution—a word that crushed the hopes of these dedicated fighters for women's rights.

Suffrage Denied
by Elizabeth Cady Stanton

Liberty, victorious over slavery on the battlefield, had now more powerful enemies to encounter at Washington. The slaves set free, the master conquered, the South desolate; the two races standing face to face, sharing alike the sad results of war, turned with appealing looks to the general government, as if to say, "How stand we now?" "What next?" Questions our statesmen, beset with dangers, with fears for the nation's life, of party divisions, of personal defeat, were wholly unprepared to answer. The reconstruction of the South involved the reconsideration of the fundamental principles of our Government and the natural rights of man. The nation's heart was thrilled with prolonged debates in Congress and State legislatures, in the pulpits and public journals, and at every fireside on these vital questions, which took final shape in the three historic amendments to the Constitution.

The first point, his emancipation, settled, the political status of the negro was next in order; and to this end various propositions were submitted to Congress. But to demand his enfranchisement on the broad principle of natural rights was hedged about by difficulties, as the logical result of such action must be the enfranchisement of all ostracized classes; not only the white women of the entire country, but the slave women of the South. Though our senators and representatives had an honest aversion to any proscriptive legislation against loyal women, in view of their varied and self-sacrificing work during the War, yet the only way they could open the constitutional door just wide enough to let the black man pass in was to introduce the word "male" into the national Constitution [in the Fourteenth Amendment]. After the generous devotion of such women as Anna Carroll and Anna Dickinson in sustaining the policy of the Republicans, both in peace and war, they felt it would come with bad grace from that party to place new barriers in women's path to freedom. But how could the amendment be written without the word "male," was the question.

Robert Dale Owen being in Washington, and behind the scenes at the time, sent copies of the various bills to the officers of the Loyal League in New York, and related to us some of the amusing discussions. One of the committee proposed "persons" instead of "males." "That will never do," said another, "it would enfranchise wenches." "Suffrage for black men will be all the strain the Republican party can stand," said another. Charles Sumner said, years afterward, that he wrote over nineteen pages of foolscap to get rid of the word "male" and yet keep "negro suffrage" as a party measure intact; but it could not be done.

Miss Anthony and I were the first to see the full significance of the word "male" in the Fourteenth Amendment, and we at once sounded the alarm, and sent out petitions for a constitutional amendment to "prohibit the States from disfranchising any of their citizens on the grounds of sex." Miss Anthony, who had spent the year in Kansas, started for New York the moment she saw the proposition before Congress to put the word "male" into the national Constitution, and made haste to rouse the women in the East to the fact that the time had come to begin vigorous work again for woman's enfranchisement. . . . Miss Anthony and I spent all our Christmas holidays in writing letters and addressing appeals and petitions to every part of the country, and before the close of the session of 1865–66, petitions with ten thousand signatures were poured into Congress. . . .

However, women learned one important lesson—namely, that it is impossible for the best of men to understand women's feelings or the humiliation of their position. When they asked us to be silent on our question during the War, and labor for the emancipation of the slave, we did so, and gave five years to his emancipation and enfranchisement. To this proposition my friend, Susan B. Anthony, never consented, but was compelled to yield because no one stood with her. I was convinced, at that time, that it was the true policy. I am now equally sure that it was a blunder, and ever since, I have taken my beloved Susan's judgment against the world. I have always found that, when we see eye to eye, we are sure to be right, and when we pull together we are strong. After we discuss any point together and fully agree, our faith in our united judgment is immovable and no amount of ridicule and opposition has the slightest influence, come from what quarter it may.

Together we withstood the Republicans and abolitionists, when, a second time, they made us the most solemn promises of earnest labor for our enfranchisement, when the slaves were safe beyond peradventure. They never redeemed their promise made during the War, hence, when they urged us to silence, we could not for a moment entertain the proposition. The women generally awoke to their duty themselves. They had been deceived once and could not be again. If the leaders in the Republican and abolition camps could deceive us, whom could we trust?

Again we were urged to be silent on our rights, when the proposition to take the word "white" out of the New York Constitution was submitted to a vote of the people of the State, or, rather, to one-half of the people, as women had no voice in the matter. Again we said, "No, no, gentlemen! If the 'white' comes out of the Constitution, let the 'male' come out also. Women have stood with the negro, thus far, on equal ground as ostracized classes, outside the political paradise; and now, when the door is open, it is but fair that we both should enter and enjoy the fruits of citizenship. Heretofore ranked with idiots, lunatics, and criminals in the Constitution, the negro has been the only respectable compeer we had; so pray do not separate us now for another twenty years, ere the constitutional door will again be opened."

We were persistently urged to give all our efforts to get the word "white" out, and thus secure the enfranchisement of the colored man, as that, they said, would prepare the way for us to follow. Several editors threatened that, unless we did so, their papers should henceforth do their best to defeat every measure we proposed. But we were deaf alike to persuasions and threats, thinking it wiser to labor for women, constituting, as they did, half the people of the State, rather than for a small number of colored men; who, viewing all things from the same standpoint as white men, would be an added power against us.

———

ELIZABETH CADY STANTON'S protests are well taken—but they lured her down a dark path of prejudice. In her anger at the inclusion of the word "male" in the Constitution through the Fourteenth Amendment, she began to lash out at the idea of granting black men the vote before white women. She cast the issue in openly racist terms; she declared that black women should prefer being "the slave of an educated white man, than of a degraded, ignorant black one." Not for the last time in American history, a defeat had led the leaders of one outcast group to attack another.

Meanwhile, the abstract argument over suffrage that dominated the halls and chambers of the Capitol began to change the concrete reality of life in the South. As mandated by the Reconstruction Act, military authorities scheduled elections for constitutional conventions throughout the former Confederacy. In towns, cities, and rural counties, the Congress's airy debates and parliamentary maneuvers were forgotten in excitement at the sight of hundreds of thousands of African Americans going to the polls for the first time in the nation's history.

———

6

A MISSISSIPPI ELECTION

In the darkest hour of his life, Albert Morgan was a man transformed. With his brother Charles, he stood on the rich Mississippi soil without much more than a dollar in his pocket. Their business, so well planned and so conscientiously run, had been destroyed through an extraordinary abuse of the law by a conspiracy of judges, local officials, and their land-lord. Here in Yazoo County, devotion to the Confederacy had been hot-ter than anywhere in the South; now those passions had been fanned into a roaring fire by President Johnson's defiance of the Congressional plan of Reconstruction. Yazoo City was a white supremacist fortress: "The government of this city is particularly faulty and corrupt," judged the local Freedmen's Bureau agent. "The mayor shows no disposition to give justice to the freedmen." Far from it: he charged blacks a dollar a year for a permit to live within the city limits, at a time when few freed people had access to cash in any amount.

And yet, Morgan was a changed man. The foray into planting and lumbering had been his brother's idea; the business may not have suited the hotheaded Albert in the first place. Now that they were driven out of it by the most gross injustice, now that he had seen the cruelty visited upon black people, he rediscovered his sense of mission. He had felt it before as a student at Oberlin College (coincidentally, a leading center of abolitionism). It had burned in him during four years of war, sending him back to the front again and again after near-crippling wounds and bouts with malaria. Now, after having lost so much on what he called "the stubble-ground of slavery," he saw a new path in the light of his de-feat: politics.

In 1867, the Reconstruction Act made itself felt in the heart of in-transigent Mississippi. Military commanders and Freedmen's Bureau agents crossed the countryside, enrolling African American voters for the first time in the history of the South. As dictated by the Act, an election was to be held for a constitutional convention, which would draw up a framework for a new, more egalitarian state government. A fledgling Re-publican party coalesced out of blacks, immigrant Northerners, and na-tive whites who had long hidden their distaste for the Confederacy and the rich planters who ran the state.

Morgan's views were still emerging as he leaped into that first free elec-tion in Mississippi. Always of an egalitarian bent, he now truly discovered both the right and the ability of black people to run public affairs. At the time, however, white men predominated in the party's leadership—and they were not all as honest or perceptive as Albert Morgan. Many condescended to their African-American fellow citizens, judging them incapable of leading the way to a new state.

Yet many black voters willingly cast their ballots for white Republican candidates. Were they ignorant or misled? Quite the contrary: like voters throughout American history, they preferred leaders with experience—and they were painfully aware of their own long-enforced exclusion from politics and education. And they were still largely excluded, for candidates had to post bonds backed by real estate, which virtually no African Americans owned (or *could* own, in areas such as Mississippi). They voted for black candidates where they could—but alongside them they chose white men whom they judged most likely to respect their interests. And Albert Morgan had already shown them where he stood—as a fair employer, as a school builder, as a man who looked them in the eye and called them "Mr." and "Mrs."

And so the young ex-colonel, the limping outcast of Yazoo County, rocketed into the political heavens, propelled by enthusiastic (and shrewd) black support. He faced vicious opposition from most local whites. Steeped in racism, they could hardly believe that the nation would stand for the Radical plan of letting blacks vote. Undaunted, Albert Morgan launched his dramatic political career with the unforgettable election of 1867.

Into Politics
by Albert T. Morgan

While Colonel Black and his allies were engaged in rooting out so many of the Northern settlers in Yazoo as they could get under by hook or by crook, the reconstruction acts of Congress were being put into effect in Mississippi. Registrars had been appointed for Yazoo County. A general registration of all persons entitled under those acts to vote had been concluded, and proclamation had been made of an election to be held for the selection of delegates to a convention to frame a constitution, etc. At this forthcoming election colored men—black, light, and white—were to be allowed to vote along with their former masters.[35]

Had I been called upon two years before to decide for myself whether the freed people ought to be allowed to vote, I presume I should have

[35] Since an individual was considered black even if he had only a trace of African ancestry, some former slaves had extremely light skin.

replied, "Yes, why not?" and doubtless should have dismissed the subject with that. . . . But had the alternative been presented to me, and I required to decide the question for the whole country—"the ballot for the negro or not"—I am quite certain I should have demanded some qualification. . . . My faith in the fidelity of the North to its high purposes, and in the *promises* of the nation to the emancipated slaves, was not one whit less than was my faith in its power. By actual contact with them, I had come into a more perfect knowledge of the true character of "conquered" rebels—especially of slave-holding rebels. And in the same manner I had come to form a juster estimate of the character and capacity of the African in America.

After only two years' contact with him I was able to answer the question—"the ballot for the negro, or not for him"—not only for myself, but also for the country; for, I said, any means that will enable us to live here in peace, and enjoy the fruits of our toil, can but be helpful and good for the whole country. Therefore, with the call for this election, there came to Charles and myself hope of succor through the power of the ballot, backed as it was by the power of the nation. We began to canvass the situation as to the prospect of an application of the means afforded by the "reconstruction plan" for a restoration to ourselves, and to secure to the freed people the right to life, liberty, and the pursuit of happiness.

In proof of the capacity of the negro to enjoy these privileges we had only to look at Tokeba; for during the two years we had been together as "masters and servants," as a whole, our hands had demonstrated their possession of the very best qualities of natural manhood and womanhood. . . . During those two years, of the plantation force of more than one hundred and twenty-five only one had been drunk; only one had been caught stealing . . . ; Uncle Stephen had been taught a new text; Rose, still a "pure" girl, was able to read and write, and her mother had determined to make a true "woman" rather than a "lady" of her; Uncle Bristol, Uncle Jonathan, and Pomp wore new clothes and held their heads up, though Bristol could not yet straighten out his legs; Uncle David had become his own overseer; and Uncle Anderson Henderson, during the whole period, had been Charles's most trusted and faithful mill-hand, while his Judy was universally respected at the quarter and by ourselves as a model wife.

During this time we kept out of debt, except to friends and relatives residing in the North, from whom we had received pecuniary aid, and excepting wages due to our hands. Our friends in the North could not understand things at all, and the sudden winding up of our business—especially the manner of it—was incomprehensible to them. Had we "no *courts* in Mississippi?" some inquired.

"What had we done to bring down upon our business the wrath of the entire community?" some said; others: "No business to have gone down there among those rebels"; while there were those who intimated that "the boys" after all, "had done badly," "no use denying it"; "if there weren't a screw loose somewhere they would have had *some* friends; couldn't talk to me." It would be impossible to bring a whole community against faithful, industrious, and honorable "business men, with the backing we had at the start, unless there was," they said. We could reply to these questionings and insinuations only by silence. We had failed, that was certain. We could feel it in our bones.

SWEET CONSOLATION

The fulfillment of my brother's prophecy seemed to me a long way off; for by the close of 1867 the tide of immigration had ceased to flow southward. Indeed, it was flowing away from Yazoo. But there was one consolation—yes, a real consolation—left to us; for when at last we gave up the struggle with Colonel Black, "agent in fact" for Mrs. Charlotte Black, and that lady's lawyers, we discovered that the negroes on the plantation were all loyal to us. Uncle David, Uncle Anderson, Uncle Stephen, Uncle Aggaby, Uncle Bristol, Mr. Smith and *Mrs.* Smith, and all the other uncles and aunts, voluntarily came forward, each and every one, and forgave us what we owed them! . . .

During the two years we had been on Tokeba the fame of our acts had spread far, carried partly on the tongues of "ole marsa," who ceased in his cursing of the "free nigros," or "that damned radical Congress," or "that damned free nigro bureau," only to curse "them damned nigger-loving, radical Yankee incendiaries" on Tokeba, and partly in the hearts and prayers of such as Jonathan, Pomp, Isam, Mrs. Smith, and others. And now, when the new voters began to look about for candidates to make the new constitution, delegations of them from far and near came and urged us to be their "leaders." Even "yan in de ole Holmes County" sent a delegation.

Our firm had sunk on Tokeba nearly fifty thousand dollars. Mr. Ross, our Illinois partner, thoroughly disgusted, returned North at once. Charles was on the point of doing so, and I think would have left Yazoo and all his bright visions to Colonel Black and his allies at that time, but for the noble conduct of our hands, which had altered the nature of our obligation to them. . . .

One day, after the first shock of Black's treatment had passed, he [Charles] said to me: "Albert, it is evident that Congress is having a pretty hard fight with Andy and these rebels"—he called them rebels now—"and should the plan of reconstruction they have adopted fail to carry the South, there is no telling what the consequences may be to the nation. I am too old"—he was thirty-four—"and too set in my ways ever to hope to succeed in politics, but you are young and have a long future before you.

"Suppose you go to the convention; help to give us a free constitution—you can copy after Massachusetts or Ohio—start a loyal government, and I will remain here and see what I can do toward getting a new start. There are greater natural advantages here, from a business point of view, than anywhere else in the world. All we need is to let these rebels see that their slaves are free in fact, and that they were really whipped. Then things will settle down again to the ways of peace, and this country will prosper."

I had not thought of such a thing as he suggested. I was not old enough; had no knowledge of public men or affairs other than military. Besides, the fight was going to be a long and bitter one. It would require the ablest and best men to be found. The adoption of a new constitution and the setting up of a new government under it would, in my opinion, be but the beginning of the conflict which would continue until the negroes were in a position, by reason of their property, education, and experiences, to protect themselves. I did not look for immigration again to set southward for many years. . . .

While we were debating this question, three Northerners, all ex-Federal officers, announced themselves as candidates on a ticket they called "the Republican ticket." In discussing the question with the Northerners, we had discovered quite a division of opinion among them as to the policy to be pursued in the creation of the new government. Some declared that there were none of the native whites who could be trusted to aid in doing the work, not one; and the freedmen were too ignorant and inexperienced. There were others who believed that it would be organizing for certain defeat, and that it would not be correct in principle to ignore the native [white] population.

When asked to name some Southerner who could be relied on, I suggested Major Snodgrass. The ex-bureau agent suggested another. But strong objections were urged to both these men. Then I suggested that if not one native white man could be found, a negro ought to be put upon the ticket.

At first this suggestion was laughed at. This aroused me to defend my idea, and I said: "Why, gentlemen, the freed people are about the only true friends we have here; remove them out of the country and you will have removed the necessity for a convention. How absurd, then, to laugh at my suggestion! . . ." There were no freedmen present, and not one of our number was able to say whether there were any who desired to have one of their number on the ticket.

"Besides," as was declared, "we don't want either rebels or negroes in that convention." An opportunity is offered us Northern men to take control of the State and run it "loyal and foremost." There was enough talent in the State at large, they said, to do it; and the loyal people of the nation would stand by them, as they believed, to the end. . . . When I related these interviews to Charles he became more urgent than ever in his wishes that I should go to this convention, and I began to feel that it might be my duty to do so.

The ex-bureau agent and myself had several consultations together upon the subject, and he agreed to see Major Snodgrass and the gentleman he had himself mentioned, and endeavor to induce one of them to come out on a ticket with us for the convention. One of them at first thought well of the idea, but after several days' delay he concluded that he would have to sacrifice too much in doing so to justify the step. During this delay a delegation of freedmen from Yazoo City came to me and asked me to consult to be a candidate on a ticket with one of their number. This I promised to do if they could induce some one of the native whites to take the other place. They replied that they had visited me at the suggestion of certain poor white men, who did not dare to be known as moving in the matter themselves, but would come out openly as soon as the ice had been broken by the new government. . . .

I consented to stand on a ticket with a freedman, a blacksmith named William Leonard, and Charles W. Clark, an ex-Union officer, who had been trying to plant in that neighborhood. The opposing ticket had been in the field two or three weeks, and the candidates had done some canvassing in the country districts as well as in Yazoo City.

It was on the last day before the election that our ticket was launched, so there would be no time for speech-making or other campaign work. But that was a mighty interesting campaign for all that, and some of the fruits of it remain to this day. That Yazoo graveyard cannot hide them all. . . .

AN ELECTION IN YAZOO

It is an historical fact, well known of course, that the reconstruction acts of Congress were passed to laws of the United States over the spiteful vetoes of that "tailor, Andy" Johnson.[36] It was not then, however, nor is it yet so generally well known that those acts were passed in spite of all the patronage of the President's great office, and that the agents appointed to execute them were more or less in sympathy with the fierce opposition to them which in the South existed among the former slave-holding class, with rare exceptions, and in the North assuredly extended beyond the ranks of the Democratic party, so called.

---

[36] "That tailor, Andy Johnson" was a derogatory term used by Yazoo's rich whites until they realized that the new President was taking their side against Congress. His menial employment was held up as proof that he was low class and contemptible.

In Yazoo, among "we all adventurers," it was enough to know that those acts had become laws. As for myself, I knew as little as one well could, and know anything of the fierce stress through which they had passed. That they voiced the mind and heart of the nation upon the questions they were intended and confidently (?) expected to solve,[37] I had no doubt. Therefore I was not bothered with any such questions as: "How will your action in consenting to be a candidate upon a ticket with a 'nigger' affect your standing with respectable people?"

Indeed, the only question that had given me any trouble was of an entirely different sort. It would have been stated thus: "Should you run away from this fight, and disaster befall the national cause, what will your old comrades in arms, and all the loyal people of the country say, who are acquainted with the true state of things here and with your known feelings and principles?"

Physically I had all my life been a coward. I presume this resulted from my training; for when a lad at school my father had warned me that he meant to punish me severely whenever it should come to his knowledge that I had been fighting with my school fellows—a "barbarous practice," he said. . . . During all my experience in the army I was never once able to get myself in range of the enemy's guns, except by sheer force of my will over my physical members, which were always stricken with palsy just before the battle, however firm they might become once the "ball" had opened. Therefore, though I had a faint conception of the *character* of the enemy, massed behind opposition to "nigro voting," no sooner had my resolution to become a "nigger candidate" been announced, than I at once felt all the physical symptoms remonitory of the "imminent deadly breach" between myself and "all the world"—in Yazoo.

Under and by the virtue of the authority vested in him by the *laws of the United States,* the commanding general had appointed three registrars for Yazoo County, whose duty it was, by those same laws, to make a list of the persons residing in that county who, under the law, were entitled to vote, and for several weeks prior to the conclusion I had reached as to my duty in the premises, these registrars had been preparing such a list. It had been completed, and the commanding general had issued his proclamation, according to law, setting the time when the election would be holden and prescribing the manner of conducting it.

Under that proclamation, the election would be held by those registrars, assisted by a corps of judges and clerks chosen from among the citizens of the county. According to the law it was requisite that one of those registrars should be present at each polling place one whole day,

[37] [Original author's footnote] The country has yet to learn that those much-maligned acts have succeeded in accomplishing God's purposes toward the negro far beyond the expectations of their framers.

and, as there were fifteen polling places it followed of necessity that the election for the entire county would require five days, and it had been so arranged.

For some time before it was to commence, printed posters had been distributed throughout the county and put up at all the crossroads and polling-places, in addition to the usual notice in the local newspapers. As our decision was not arrived at until the day before the election was to commence, and we could do nothing without tickets,[38] it was apparent that an election was likely to be held in three precincts of the county before we could get before the people. Besides, on examining our exchequer, we found there was not enough cash on hand with which to pay for printing the tickets. At one of the newspaper offices they flatly refused to print them without the cash in advance. But we succeeded at last, by promising not to tell, in getting a rather poverty-stricken devil to guarantee to have "a part" of the five thousand we wished struck off ready " 'gin night come on," to start with, and arrangements were soon made for forwarding the balance as our necessities might require. . . .

It was night before I got my supply, and was started off on horseback to travel twenty-seven miles to the place where the election for the following day, on my part of the line, was to be held.

One of a delegation of freedmen who had attended the meeting the night before accompanied me. He was employed on the plantation of Captain Bullfinch, a strong Union man during the war, and now a secret friend of our cause, whose residence was in the "hill country," about mid-way on our journey. It was late at night when we arrived at the plantation. Here my guide insisted that I should stop for the night and go on to the polling-place the following day. He knew his "old marsa's" feelings toward the Yankees. . . .

It had been sun up an hour before I got off [the next morning]. The ride was about fourteen miles. But I was at the polling-place before the voters began to arrive. Inquiring of the officers of election the supposed cause of their tardiness, I found that none could account for it. There had been only about one-fourth, or possibly one-third, of the registered voters of the precinct at the polling-place the day before who had voted, they said, and what struck me as more unaccountable still, was their assurance that "none of the whites were voting." Several of Captain Bullfinch's people had accompanied me, and after reflecting a few moments, I asked them for their opinion of the cause.

"Dey is afeer'd, Kunnel, de colud people is, an' da doan know yo' is y'here with dem. 'Sides, de white folks don' 'low'ed dar ain't g'wain ter be no 'lection, no how."

"Ah ha! that's it, eh?"

---

38 The candidates distributed printed tickets for the voters to use as ballots.

"Yes, sah, Mars Kunnel, dat's jes de way h'it ar', kase I done heerd um say down ter Benton, ter mars Leedam's sto' how dey g'wain fur ter keep all dey niggars frum votin' on da own 'count, kase dey wouldn't vote no how. 'Twan't no 'lection, dey 'low'd."

"Well," said I, calling him by name, "you go one way to some of your old fellow servants"; and then to another one, "you go another, and tell them all to come here, I wish to see them."[39]

In a moment they were off, on a fast trot, and I started out myself, following a blind path to see what I might be able to do in the way of finding the "lost" suffragans of Yazoo. I had proceeded about a mile, when, looking across a large open field, I saw what appeared to be a freedman, standing on the brow of a hill. "Now," I said to myself, "I'll call this man, and see if I can't enlist him in the search." Waving my hat toward him, in token of my wish to have him come to me, he started as if to do so, but in a very halting manner. As we approached, I could see that he was in great fear about something, and I spoke up in a kindly voice: "Uncle, why are you not at the election?"

The change in his manner reminded me of Uncle Isam, as he replied, "Doan know, marsa."

"Have you registered?"

"Yes, marsa; done got my paper."

"Where is it?"

"Low'd—Beez yo' de gen'leman whar gi'e it to me?"

"No, my name is Morgan."

At this, the change in his manner still further reminded me of Uncle Isam, especially as he came close up.

"Beez yo' de Colonel Morgan, whar lib yan in de 'Azoo City?"

"Yes."

"Wull, I d'car'! Dey done 'low'd yo' is dead wid de col'ra. Bress de good Marsta, yo' ain't. 'Low'd yo' might be de Kunnel when I done seed ye a coming yan, kase we done heerd from one ouah feller-servants yo' cloze by Benton. Mighty likely yo' mount a come dis y'here way."

But there were other surprises in store for me; for, seeing his free and changed manner, several freedmen who had remained hidden just over the hill from whence he had come, and entirely out of view until now, showed themselves. First, only their heads, as though peering at us, and now their bodies, standing. We walked up to them, when I found quite a large number, still lying upon the ground beyond the hill in a clump of trees.

These "outposts," becoming satisfied that I was, in fact, the person they had heard so much about, but "nebber seed t'wel yit," shouted to those over the hill to come and join us, which they very promptly did.

---

[39] [Original author's footnote] Now the "ball" had opened.

From their number I chose out several, whom I sent off after more, and the rest of us started for the polling-place. One of their number had a gun, a bird gun, which I requested him to take back home, assuring him that the government at Washington was holding this election. At all events, there would be no need of such weapons at the polls, and he cheerfully complied. . . .

I also gathered from them, as we walked along to the polling-place, among other things, that they had been told by their masters that there would be no election, and as if to prove the truth of the assertion, their masters had themselves remained at home. Some of these freedmen said they had heard threats made to the effect that if they went to the polling-places they would be killed. But, without previous concert, they had started to go, and falling in with each other on their several ways, they had become quite a numerous company by the time they reached the field where I found them.

Here they had halted to talk the subject over, and had resolved to send one of their number on to the polling-place to "sarch for de troof." Among their number was a preacher who had recently attended a conference, where he had been told of the proposed election and how it would be conducted.

Arriving at the place of voting we found several freedmen there who had been warned by the two whom I had sent out and quite a goodly number besides. My opponent had captured some of these, however, and secured their votes for himself. On my arrival there in the morning, he appeared as much at a loss to understand why the people generally had not turned out to vote as anyone else. Nor had he made any effort to find out—at least none such as I was making—and when the crowd which came with me arrived, of course he set out to capture them.

Mounting a wagon standing near the crossroads grocery, he began his efforts in that direction by a speech. . . . During the delivery of this speech there had been but slight manifestations of approval or sympathy from the freed people. They had remained almost as impassive as clay. When he ceased I got up on the wagon and replied briefly. . . . From the moment I began the interest of the freed people in my speech was apparent to all, and that interest continued to increase until they voiced their approval somewhat as follows:

"Dat's e talk, gen'lemens; yo' 'heah me. Dar! I tole ye hit wor' de Kunnel from de fust. Can't fool me.[40] Now yo's a tellin' de troof," etc.

Seeing my success, my opponent undertook to entice them to his support by offering to treat. But he signally failed in that also. The few white men present looked on with the supremest indifference, if not contempt.

[40] [Original author's footnote] Someone had told him I was not Colonel Morgan of Yazoo City, but another of the same name who had come from Jackson.

At the polling-place the next day there were a great many whites and two or three hundred freedmen. Having heard of the failure of their plan to "fool the darkies," they were now bent on coaxing, buying, or intimidating them at the polls, and the "pulling and hauling" process began early in the day. Failing to coax or buy them from voting, later in the day they began to threaten the freedmen. The lists of names of all who had registered were in the hands of the judges, who caused the name of each one to be checked off at the moment of casting the ballot, so that it was impossible to prevent their old masters from knowing the fact that such a one had voted. Therefore, all who would vote subjected themselves to such vengeance as their old masters might choose to inflict. . . .

A TRIUMPHANT VINDICATION

After the polls closed, and I was riding toward the polling-place of the next day, it being not yet dark, a shot fired from near the roadside passed whizzing by, so close to my head that I distinctly felt the force of the bullet. But it was not billeted with my name. It was long after dark when I reached Benton, but there were as many as three hundred freedmen awaiting my arrival just beyond the town, alongside the public highway. They had sent a runner to meet me, and to ask me to make them a speech. They said they had been unable to obtain any other place of meeting.

After talking a few moments to them, I rode out to the home of Captain Bullfinch, where I was hospitably received and entertained. It was the first time since I had left him, nearly two days before, that I had been thus received by a white man. The following day, the incidents at Benton were quite similar to those of the day preceeding. Our trials were not less on the next day, nor on the day following at Yazoo City, where this election was brought to a close.

When the ballots were all counted, it was found that the question, "Convention or no convention," was decided in the affirmative, by a vote of more than eighteen hundred "for" to only three "against." . . . It was also found that the "Morgan ticket" was elected by a vote of quite fifteen hundred, to less than four hundred for the "Yankee's ticket," as my opponents came to be called. The result staggered the natives [native whites, that is].

They had hoped to succeed in their plan of deceiving the negroes as to the importance of their votes upon that question by staying away from the polls themselves. When they discovered that they had failed, they deluded themselves into the belief that they could, by making fair promises to "our nigros," persuade them to have faith in their sincerity. And they showed their utter ignorance of the character of the *free* negro, by trying to bribe him not to vote, when the other two means had failed; and they added to their duplicity, treachery, and ignorance, still another quality, viz., brutality, when at last they resorted to intimidation to accomplish their purpose. This election demonstrated their possession of still another trait, viz., bossism. . . .

When the election was over the chairman of the "white man's" committee assured me that he had discovered his mistake [in boycotting the election] too late. I might, however, be certain that should I ever offer myself as a candidate for office in the county, he would not repeat it. This man further assured me that he was "amazed" at the intelligence exhibited by the negroes; confessed himself "mistaken" in his estimate of their character; confessed that he and his friends had intended to deceive them, believing it to be for the best good of all to do so; confessed that I had conducted my campaign "with perfect fairness," that he would have done just as I did had he been in my place, barring my refusal to fight; that had he been a "nigro" he would have done precisely as the negroes had, and voted for me. . . . [However, he remarked that] the radicals will lose their power in a few years, unless they can make up for defections, which are certain in the North as soon as the war feeling dies down a little, by additions from the South, and as the defection of "Andy" Johnson has shown that they cannot hope to gain that from the whites of the South they mean to lasso the whites with the negro vote and keep them in subjection until they have fully accomplished their purposes.

And then this Yazoo white statesman laughingly continued: "And as for you, and all like you, who join your faith to these radicals and to the nigro, they will have no more use for you then than they now have for the paper in their waste baskets. Then it will be our turn, and woe be to you."

I thanked this man for his advice. . . . "It's an honest difference of opinion," I said, "and you must allow me the hope, that while this is going on, we shall have large and voluntary accessions from your side to ours, right here, in Yazoo, and shall then be able to take care of ourselves."

Then he—"Don't fool yourself, young man. *We don't intend to allow you to gain any from our side that we can't get back when we shall need them.*"

———

THE CHAIRMAN'S WORDS were no idle threat—a time would come when he would deliver on his promise, in a manner so dramatic that Albert Morgan would have hardly believed it in 1867. After all, *he had won.* A Northern immigrant and an African-American blacksmith had been elected in the heart of Mississippi. Morgan could hardly be blamed for not thinking much of the Chairman's warning, for a revolution had truly begun. Only five years before, it had seemed as if a permanent slave republic would be established in the Southern states: Lee had thrashed McClellan, and Britain and France were considering recognition of the Confederacy. Now the former slaves were electors, sending their own and their allies off to draw up a new constitution for Jefferson Davis's home state.

Even as Morgan breathlessly rode from speech to speech in that memorable campaign, another young man was campaigning only a few dozen miles away in the town of Natchez. Though not many years apart in age, the two men had never heard of each other in 1867, despite their mutual enthusiasm for the Republican party. But within a year they would become steadfast friends and allies—coleaders of the revolution that was sweeping Mississippi.

His name was John R. Lynch. Though born a slave, he would become one of the most powerful men in the state before the end of the decade, and eventually one of the most important black men in the nation. Lynch's background bore the familiar, painful brand left by slavery. He was the son of a Louisiana plantation manager, Irish-born Patrick Lynch, and his slave concubine; the elder Lynch planned to have the boy and his mother freed upon his own death, but the pair were betrayed by the overseer who succeeded him. Only the arrival of the Union army in 1864 emancipated young John, who then went to work for the army and the navy. At the end of the war, he established himself as a photographer in Natchez, where he learned to read and write in a school established by an aid society.

In the first free election of 1867, Lynch was still too young to vote (having been born in 1847). But his fierce commitment to the promise of Reconstruction drove him into the campaign with the boundless energy that would characterize his long career in politics. In the passage that follows, he reflects upon that campaign in words that reflect his other salient traits: sharp analysis and shrewd judgment. He well understood, far better perhaps than the romantic Albert Morgan, that political necessity had led the North to throw open the gates of suffrage to blacks. He also saw the importance of white as well as black participation in the Republican party—participation that grew, as Morgan foresaw, as Reconstruction later piled up victory after victory.

For young John Lynch, however, the 1867 election was just a first, sweet taste of the career that would make him a congressman and a confidant of presidents.

A Free Election
by John R. Lynch

The rejection of the Johnson plan of reconstruction had clearly demonstrated that no halfway measures were possible. If the colored men were not enfranchised then the Johnson plan might as well be accepted. The Republican or Union white men at the South were not sufficient in numbers to make their power or influence felt. The necessities of the situation, therefore, left no alternative but the enfranchisement of the blacks. . . .

The first election held in Mississippi under the Reconstruction Acts took place in 1867, when delegates to a Constitutional Convention were elected to frame a new Constitution. The Democrats decided to adopt what they declared to be a policy of "Masterly Inactivity," that is, to refrain from taking any part in the election and to allow it to go by default. The result was that the Republicans had a large majority of the delegates, only a few counties having elected Democratic delegates. The only reason that there were any Democrats in the convention at all was that the party was not unanimous in the adoption of the policy of "Masterly Inactivity," and consequently did not adhere to it. . . .

But the Democratic party in the State was governed and controlled by the radical element of that organization—an element which took the position that no white Democrat could afford to participate in an election in which colored men were allowed to vote. To do so, they held, would not only be humiliating to the pride of the white men, but the contamination would be unwise if not dangerous. Besides, they were firm in the belief and honest in the conviction that the country would ultimately repudiate the Congressional Plan of Reconstruction, and that in the mean time it would be both safe and wise for them to give expression to their objections to it and abhorrence of it by pursuing a course of masterly inactivity. . . .

Of the Republican membership of the Constitutional Convention a large majority were white men—many of them natives of the State and a number of others, though born elsewhere, residents in the State for many years preceding the war of the Rebellion. My own county, Adams (Natchez), in which the colored voters were largely in the majority, and which was entitled to three delegates in the convention, elected two white men—E.J. Castello and Fred Parsons—and one colored man, H.P. Jacobs, a Baptist preacher. Throughout the State the proportion was about the same.

This was a great disappointment to the dominating element in the Democratic party, who had hoped and expected, through their policy of "Masterly Inactivity" and intimidation of white men, that the convention would be composed almost exclusively of illiterate and inexperienced colored men. Although a minor at the time, I took an active part in the local politics of my county, and, being a member of a Republican club that had been organized at Natchez, I was frequently called upon to address the members at its weekly meetings.

NOT MANY MONTHS in the future, young John Lynch would do more than speak to meetings—he would stand before them as a candidate with a fast-rising political career. A revolution was in bloom—and a recently educated former slave such as Lynch would soon have opportunities unimaginable only weeks before.

Meanwhile, a time of desperation settled over Mississippi. Hard-line white supremacists quickly realized the scope of their mistake, and they turned to their old tool, brute force, to stamp out the blossoming flower of liberty. Men such as the Morgans and their fellow Northerners—to say nothing of politically active blacks—now faced their old enemies in the new garb of the Ku Klux Klan. Never a centrally unified organization, the Klan grew up at the grass roots among white communities across the South in the late 1860s. Local groups of former Confederate soldiers and others (often led by wealthy planters) formed themselves into paramilitary squads, taking up the shared name, wardrobe, rituals, and terrorist tactics that spread the infamy of the K.K.K. across the nation.

Despite the atrocities and repression that blanketed the state, no help was forthcoming from the governor, the former Confederate general Benjamin G. Humphreys. Nor was the army much help: the garrison had been reduced by President Johnson to a mere 2,000 troops—and many of the officers and men sympathized with the Democrats. So as Albert Morgan set out for the constitutional convention and Charles remained in Yazoo City, the brothers were forced to wait out the crisis. If only they could survive—physically survive—they would be able to usher in a new age for the old heart of the Confederacy.

Siege
by Albert T. Morgan

It was through the trials and by such means as I have herein faithfully recounted that I became known to the whites of Mississippi as a "dictator," and among the blacks as a "savior." The convention was carried in the State and the delegates would assemble January 7th following, 1868, at Jackson, the capital. During this campaign I did not expend so much as one cent for "treats," or for any purpose calculated to induce anyone to vote our ticket. . . .

Meanwhile, reduced in circumstances as I was, I succeeded, by the sale of a quantity of refuse lumber that had been overlooked by Colonel Black, in raising money enough to purchase a suit of clothes to wear to the convention, and to pay my expenses in going there and for a week or so after my arrival in the capital.

On the morning of my departure I waited at the post office in the company of the postmaster and other friends, black and white—negroes and Yankees all—until the stage drove up. . . . But I was not allowed to go in peace; for, espying me as I got up into the stage, a handful of white urchins began halloaing, "O'oophie! O'oophie! Polecat!" . . . At that moment there appeared a dozen or more loungers near the corner, some of them full-grown men, others half-grown, who approached the stage door, and making horrid grimaces ejaculated, "Halloa, polecat![41] Whar ye goin', polecat! G'wain ter de nigger convention?" "Ha! ha! ha!" "He! he! he!" "Well, good-bye, Morgan. Take good car' yo'self. Haw! haw! haw!" Then the driver, having got his mail on board, cracked his whip, and away we sped on our journey of twenty-six miles to the railway station. . . .

At Benton there were similar cries after me as at Yazoo City, when we started; also at Deasonville, the next station, and at the railway depot. On entering the car, my identity was made known to other delegates on board, who were en route from counties in the northern part of the State, by these very cries; for nearly all of them had passed through a similar experience. In fact none of us were spared now that we were on board the train, but were marked for all manner of jest, scorn, or violent abuse, according to the temperament and gifts of our fellow-passengers, some of whom were en route to the capital to "see the fun." Very naturally these "outcasts" came together and formed a group by ourselves; for all the world over, misery loves company. . . .

During this time Charles and I passed through the most trying period of our experience in Yazoo. It was a season of trial, however, which bore more heavily upon him than me, and called out all the virtues of his grand character. After my departure for the convention, he succeeded in obtaining board in the home of a resident of the town—a widow lady of rare good breeding, benevolence, and courage. . . . No lady in the county was more highly thought of than she. But in an hour, as it were, this noble woman, battling for her children and her daily bread, was made an outcast. It came about in this way:

The postmaster, who was a Yankee, and the other Northern men had previously been received by her as boarders. But within sixty days from the admission to her house of General Greenleaf and Charles, the feeling in Yazoo had increased until it became such a reign of terror that even General Alvan C. Gillem, President Johnson's personal friend and trusted commanding general in the department, was induced to send a squad of

[41] [Original author's footnote] The epithet, "carpetbagger," had not yet been invented, or, if coined, had not yet reached the Yazoo channels of trade in such things. The "honor" of its invention is claimed for Virginia by some, and for Horace Greeley by others. However that may be, the epithet represents not so much a mollified state of feeling on the part of the enemy, as a change in their diplomatic methods, adopted for effect upon the "jury" at the North, then and ever since, in a measure, sitting at their (the enemy's) trial.

troops there for the protection of freedmen and loyalists. But the officer in command of these soldiers, upon his arrival, was seized by Colonel Black and his friends, "anti-Yankees," and welcomed at their houses, wined, dined, and petted by both sexes, until he became the drunken tool that he was for the furtherence of their purposes.

When they had thus wrought upon him, there was sent to that Southern widow lady the following note of warning: "Mrs. ——, you are keeping a den of infamy, which will be burnt down if you don't purge it out. An outraged Southern community won't stand it long. Beware!! K.K.K." This lady became hotly indignant at the outrage, and for a brief space resented it. . . . Upon receipt of the kuklux warning, [she] openly declared that she had never welcomed to her house more perfect gentlemen. . . .

Prompted by a desire to defend their landlady, Charles and General Greenleaf sought for quarters elsewhere in the town. . . . Yet it was not until after considerable maneuvering that these gentlemen were able to procure a lodging place. This was a suite of rooms near a livery stable, over the office of a lawyer, who plumed himself somewhat on his ancestry. They were obtained only through the intercession of a third party, a man who, at that time, was an officer of the United States. For the protection of the owner of those rooms, it had been allowed to leak out that they had been obtained by indirect means.

Now that a lodging place had been secured, still another difficulty presented itself, viz.: how to obtain food and service. . . . It began to look as though they would be starved into a surrender. . . . The anti-reconstructionists supposed that persistence in their policy of ostracism and intimidation would necessarily compel their full surrender or their retreat from the county. But they were again to be foiled; this time by the freed people. No sooner had they learned of this fresh outrage upon their friends, than a negro woman came forward and volunteered not only to provide the food, but also to cook and serve it for them *at actual cost*.

To their warning of the probable consequences to herself of such service to them, this woman replied: "Captain, I'z cooked fur my ole marstah all my days, an' he nebber gin me so much as a new dress when I quit um. Kase I wor free now. Sence dat I'z been cookin' fur de white genelmens an' a furnishin' of um thar food, an' I 'low I can do jez 'e same fur yo' all. . . . An' my son, yo' all knows *him,* he says, says he, 'Mammy, nary schools in dis y'here Azoo County 'fo' de Morgans come'd ter dis yar Azoo City, an' sho's yo' boh'n ef dey go from y'here, dat day de schools go wid um',' an' so dey would. I knows um. Kan't fool me, 'f I iz a nigger an' ain't got no larnin'. Jeems ha' got some, thank de blessed God a'mighty and yo' all Yankees. . . ."

But she had continued at this service not more than a few days, when, having to carry the food some distance, the enemy began first to coax, then to try to bribe, then to threaten, and all these failing, they actually inter-

cepted her upon the street and spilled her dishes. Certain freedmen, however, had foreseen such a result, and one of them, a shoemaker, and sort of
a pet with the whites, had been able to secure a room upon the ground
floor of the same building in which the outcasts lodged, and had moved
himself, family, and shop into it, so that when Aunt Sarah [the cook] could
no longer perform the service, the shoemaker's wife volunteered to supply
her place. . . . But the enemy's resources were equal to this emergency, for
those "anti-Yankees" not only withdrew their custom from this "nigger
cobbler,"—for such he had now become—their merchants refused to sell
him food supplies for his "Yankee boarders." . . .

In spite of the edict of the merchants the supplies were not cut off. . . .
For these provisions had been furnished secretly, some by the freed people, delivered through the blockade by hiding them under the clothes in
her basket; some by a certain merchant in the town, while the rest had
found their way to the hands of the shoemaker from boisterous, bull-
dozing "anti-Yankees," who, in their hearts, still retained their love of the
old Union cause.

About this time I visited them. Their quarters had been transformed
into an arsenal. There were two breech-loading Spencer rifles, a double-
barrelled shotgun, and two revolvers, seen nearby the head of the bed in
which they slept. Their windows were barred with iron, and the only
door of their apartment was doubly bolted with a huge brace for additional support. It was during this visit that I learned the facts above nar-
rated, and the additional fact that they were hourly expecting a violent
attack from the enemy, who, foiled in their effort to *starve* them out,
were now planning to *drive* them out or *kill* them. The latter alternative
it seemed had not been fully determined upon, and I was on the eve of
learning why for myself. . . .

NONE BUT BLACK AMERICANS ON GUARD TONIGHT

In those days it was deemed the safer policy by all Republican members
of that State convention to travel incognito and give no notice of their
intentions. . . . So they had not expected me at Yazoo on that day. I had
not been a half hour within the stronghold, when it was besieged by a
small army of friends, all colored men but one; for now even Northerners found it more to their interest not to recognize the outcasts socially,
by calling upon them at their stronghold. . . .

They had heard of my fight in the convention, they said; had heard
how the Democrats had defied the president of that body, the sergeant-
at-arms, and even "Stanton's hirelings." How they had drawn pistols,
and failed to shoot me because I was "a coward" and would not "draw
and defend myself." And they heard how a negro, Charles Caldwell, with

a little handful of his friends, armed only with pistols, had rallied to my side and made them scamper. . . .

That night I made a discovery. Just outside the sleeping room, on the porch, which was closed in on three sides and facing the only narrow stairway from the street to the porch, fully a dozen men, negroes, stood guard all night. There were but two pistols among them—old ones at that. They were armed with stout hickory clubs. That night I made another discovery. It was after ten o'clock, and when the last of our brave friends had quietly gone away. A wonderful solemnity rested over the stronghold, unbroken, save by an occasional shuffling of the men on guard, and a noise which sounded like the low ebb and flow of a rather animated conversation going on beyond brick walls. I asked Charles what the muffled sound was.

"Shall we uncover our secret to the radical delegate to the black-and-tan convention from the 'Azoo?" was his response, directed to the General.

"Certainly. Why not? I guess we can trust him, with our lives, our fortune, and our sacred honahs, by God, sir," was that outcast's reply, delivered with great mock solemnity of manner. By this time my curiosity was up. . . .

But by this time, certain other mysterious proceedings, instituted by [Charles] as this bit of play was going on, culminated, and lifting quite out of its place one of the planks in the floor of the room, exposing a bunch of cotton. . . . He raised the cotton from its place long enough to enable me to see into the room below. . . .

It was the lawyer with "an ancestry."

On looking from the other side of the aperture, I saw four men seated round a plain board table. One of them was Judge Isam, another Captain Telsub, another Aurelius Bings, Esq., and another was Major Sweet. An empty black bottle lay on one end of the table, while another nearly empty stood upon the other end, and several half-smoked cigars and pipes were strewn upon its surface, and on the floor nearby. They were all so near drunk that their speech was maudlin and aimless. . . .

There they were, Yazoo's best citizens, the leaders of the ku-klux-klan of that county, the night after receiving news of Stanton's victory over Johnson,[42] all upon the floor drunk. . . .

CHARLES HAS A NEW EXPERIENCE

As the work of the convention at Jackson progressed, and the time approached when that body should adjourn and the result of its labors be

---

[42] See chapter 9, "Prelude to an Impeachment," for a description of the struggle between Stanton and Johnson—a battle closely watched in Yazoo.

submitted to the people for their rejection or approval, Charles and General Greenleaf commenced organizing Loyal League Clubs and also the Republican party throughout the county.

The Loyal League Clubs established by them were organized in conformity to the constitution and by-laws of the National League in every particular. Their meetings were secret, and the outcasts were surprised by the number of applicants for membership from the old [white] Unionist element in the county.

About this time *The Clarion,* a newspaper published in the State capital and edited by Ethel Barksdale, who with Hons. W.P. Harris, A.G. Brown, and a majority of the anti-reconstruction element of the State, had banded together in what they themselves styled the Central Democratic Association of the State of Mississippi, published [an attack on] "the Loyal League Conspiracy." . . .

The revival of the reign of terror in Yazoo was one of the first fruits of those resolutions. The change was so sudden that the garrison [Charles, General Greenleaf, and their black protectors] was surprised.[43] The first sign of the approaching storm was observed by Charles one morning when he entered the post office for his mail. It came from a group of well-known boys and young men lounging about that corner, who revived their old cries of "O'oophie! Polecat!" "Old Morgan!" etc., etc., and as he came out and passed down the street they followed him.

Some of them had pistols, and one, just as they passed by some "ladies" standing in front of a door on Main Street, tried to trip my brother and throw him down, to the great delight of these fair ones. He must cross the bayou just above Mr. Goosie's ferry, and, this crowd of howling, teasing, cursing, cat-calling white youth pursued him into the ferry-boat, a long flat boat. Up to this time Charles had controlled himself perfectly. He had his revolver buckled to his person outside, and not concealed. They had several times called out to him, "Why don't you stan' yo' ground an' fight like a gentleman?" and had repeatedly called upon him to defend himself. . . .

As the ferryman was shoving the flat from the bank one of these white boys—son of one of the "leading citizens"—seized the ferryman's pole, and raising it made a rush for Charles, followed by the whole crowd, as though they meant to drive him from the further end of the flat into the rapidly running stream, where without help he would have been in great danger of drowning. Divining their purpose, Charles drew his weapon, and ordered them to "Halt! come nearer and I'll fire!" He had not even lost any part of his perfect self-control, and stood as calm and self-

[43] [Original author's footnote] During the brief era of good feeling, Yazoo had become so quiet that the outcasts abandoned their habit of going together whenever they went out.

possessed as if talking to the Sabbath-school. But alas! he had drawn a "deadly weapon"—had "exhibited it in a threatening manner." The boys at once ceased their pursuit, retired to their end of the flat, and Charles went on his way. . . .

Returning the next day to town, my brother was met by an officer who had a writ of some sort for his apprehension. Charles asked to be informed of the nature of the charge upon which he was to be arrested. This the officer at first declined to grant. But he shortly yielded, and announced that the order for his arrest was based upon the affidavit of ——, a son of the most prominent physician of the county, which affidavit charged my brother with "carrying a concealed deadly weapon," "exhibiting a deadly weapon," "violating city ordinance," "disturbing the peace, and assault."

Charles recognized the man as "a proper officer to make an arrest," and while denying the charges, he declared himself a law-abiding citizen, submitted to the demand without a murmur, was taken before the mayor, tried, and on the testimony of the prosecuting witness . . . was found guilty, fined on each count, and charged with all costs, the whole amounting to more than sixty dollars. Pending that *trial*, General Greenleaf, the postmaster, the freed people, together with some Northerners, who contributed secretly, took up a collection and thus raised the whole amount of the fine and costs, and paid the same promptly. They supposed that would be the end of the proceeding. . . .

The sequel showed that they meant to get [Greenleaf] too, by the same means as had been employed to entrap my brother. Only, those who now pursued the General were the kuklux fathers of the young kukluxes who had pursued Charles. So determined were they to aggravate him to make some sort of defense that they actually spat upon him, threw stones at him, and finally, getting close enough for the purpose, they struck him several times, and once squarely in the face.

THAT YAZOO JAIL IN 1868

Not long after *that* trial of my brother, another writ was issued, and he was taken again into custody on the very same charge upon which he had been tried by the mayor and fined, as I have shown. Bail was offered, but at that moment the same counsel who had prosecuted in the former case came forward and demanded that no person should be received as surety except such as could swear that they were worth "the amount of the bond *in real estate*, over and above their just debts and *all liabilities whatsoever*." . . .

Then the officer took Charles to jail. It had become the "common jail" now, and stress was placed upon the word "common" by the enemy, who shook hands with each other, and fairly gloated over their "victory." It was afternoon, and the march to the jail was amid the jeers, curses, and hurrahs of the anti-reconstructionists. . . . But his friends were not idle. The freedmen, under the leadership of the pastor of the little church we helped to build, with several of its officers and others, caused word to be sent to their friends in the country round to come to town forthwith, and in a short while the guard upon the stronghold, with augmented numbers, was on duty within easy reach of the jail, armed with their hardwood sticks.

The General and other Northerners were no less active, for they had information direct from Dave Woolridge's saloon and from other sources that the Captain [Charles] would be taken out and hanged during that night; and, from some words they had heard and certain actions of Captain Telsub, Judge Isam, and Colonel Black, they were satisfied it was not to be done by the ku-klux-klan of Yazoo.

From the moment this information reached the General, he began to work on the agent of the Freedman's Bureau—one who had recently been sent there—a very worthy officer but an extremely timid man, to convince him that it was his duty to interfere to save Charles. . . . "It is perfect folly for you gentlemen to continue your struggle here, with the President and commanding general against you. I'd abandon it altogether if I were in your places, and we'll have peace here at all events," said he. But the General was not dismayed. He got other Northerners to go and see the agent, and, learning of the General's efforts in that direction, the freedmen began to go to him.

While the town officer was taking my brother to jail, it was discovered that neither the sheriff, Colonel Finley, nor any of his deputies were in town, and some said they had not been at their office since the evening before. . . . This fact put a still more serious aspect upon the situation; for if what he had heard as coming from certain "family servants" was true, the sheriff and his deputies had purposely absented themselves. But there was a surprise in store for them all. The General had not thought of sending to the country for the freed people to come to town. . . . But shortly after the discovery of the sheriff's absence, the number of anxious freedmen in town suddenly increased, and before dark became a crowd. They were very orderly, no great excitement was apparent, but they were very determined. . . .

At last it was said the "niggers" were moving on the jail with the determination to take my brother out—rescue him—and soon a shout was heard "Take 'im out! Take Captain Morgan out that ar jail!" These shouts reached the ears of Mr. Fountain Barksdale. Now Mr. Barksdale was at the topmost round of the Yazoo business world. He knew all about the cause of these shouts. He knew that my brother was an honorable man, a law-abiding citizen, and innocent of any fault in this matter. So Mr. Barksdale began to think. He took off his spectacles and wiped them. At that moment one of his numerous clerks rushed in with the news that the "niggers" were going to burn the town unless Captain Morgan should be at once released. Mr. Barksdale was a nervous man. He did not wait to hear more, nor for his hat, but rushed almost frantically out upon the street and in the direction of the jail, shouting in his well-known thin tenor voice, "Turn him out! Turn Captain Morgan out a there! Where's the sheriff? Where's the sheriff? Where's the mayor? Turn him out! He's no business there! Turn him out, I say!" . . .

But there was no officer to be found. It was getting late, and the General and other Northerners had gone to make a final appeal to the bureau agent. This time with effect; for that officer began to see that it was indeed a serious matter. He at once sought out Colonel Black and Judge Isam and said to them: "I give you notice that if Captain Morgan is harmed tonight, in anyway, by anybody, I will make a written report to General Grant, through General Howard, and shall hold you two gentlemen responsible for whatever may happen."

Then Colonel Black: "What authority, by God, sir, have you for interfering in this matter? He is there by the decree of the courts of the land; by God, sir! He's a low-down, contemptible meddler, sir, consorting with our nigros, and inciting them to insurrection, by God, sir; and, by God, sir, an outraged Southern community won't stand it any longer, sir, by God, sir! He's no nigro."

But the General and other friends were close by, and for once the agent stood up like a man. . . . "I believe you do intend violence on Captain Morgan. Mark you, I'll be there, and you'll have at least two to hang," and the agent returned to his office.[44]

Within an half hour or so afterward Charles, accompanied by the General and the guard of the stronghold, walked into the agent's office to thank him for his services. . . . "The day after my confinement in the *common* jail, [Charles recounted,] Uncle Jonathan came into our stronghold, looking as if half scared to death. He had seen the kuklux. He knew it must be them. There were many men, 'a long string,' on horseback. They had ridden far and rapidly, for their horses were foaming. They carried guns. They came to the foot of the bluffs, where they met a man coming from town, with whom they conversed for some minutes, and then, with ranks somewhat demoralized, they turned about and rode away.[45] But I was no longer *in* the common jail of Yazoo, under a charge

44 [Original author's footnote] At the time the agent had not been made aware of what Mr. Barksdale was doing, therefore his conduct was rather heroic, for Colonel Black and his allies at Jackson, within that Central Democratic Association, were more powerful with General Gillem in such matters than anyone else outside of Washington.

45 [Original author's footnote] That same day we heard similar accounts from two other sources.

of assault with intent to kill; therefore they could do nothing that they could justify through the Associated Press dispatches and the headquarters of the commandant of this district, and thus my life was spared."

CHARLES'S FEVER

I don't think I ever before saw Charles in quite so savage a mood as he was at the close of his account of that "trial" and the subsequent proceedings. He paced up and down the floor of the stronghold for two mortal hours, during which he delivered himself of the most bitter invective against our Government that I ever listened to, or ever read; and what surprised me most was the perfect sympathy existing between him and the General. . . .

"I tell you, Albert, we must fight this thing out, if it takes our lives. The country doesn't understand it at all, and they won't understand it until we have furnished them proof upon proof, and they have come to see with their own eyes that the last state of the sick man of the South is worse than the first. Think of it! The negroes' only refuge is the Bureau, and you know how feeble, uncertain, and treacherous are the means of protection that affords them. . . . These same poor, despised negroes, after all, are our only protection, and they have proved their courage and fidelity to my entire satisfaction."

I thought this was a good place for me to put in a word, so I said, "Then you won't desert them and go home?"

"Desert them?" cried he. "From this time forth every black man in Yazoo is my brother, and every black woman . . . is my sister. God bless them! I would have as soon deserted Thomas at Nashville as desert them now."

"And I Meade at Gettysburg!" I involuntarily exclaimed. My brother's eloquence had made me forget his "fever."

"And I Grant on the Chickahominy, by God!" shouted the General, whose oath came out so round and full that it seemed to fit the place. Then we sang the "Star Spangled Banner," "John Brown's Body," and other patriotic airs, until Charles's "fever" passed quite off again.

JUST A LITTLE longer: that's all it would take. If the Morgans, the general, the freed people, and their white allies could only hold out just a little longer, a new age would begin for the old slave kingdom of Mississippi. The Morgans put it best, in the scene that closes the last selection, when they spoke in one breath of equality and patriotism, of civil rights for African Americans and loyalty to the Union. To so many Republicans in the spring of 1868, these things were linked inextricably.

Johnson's hostility toward Congress, and atrocities by the Ku Klux Klan and other groups, had driven Northern public opinion to a position that would have been considered extreme only a year before: blacks must have an equal seat at the national political table, or the terrible war would have meant nothing.

Albert had done his best at the constitutional convention to usher in the waiting age of freedom. Shortly after arriving in the state capital, the eloquent young veteran quickly became a leading force among the delegates. As historian Richard Nelson Current has shown, Morgan dominated the committee on suffrage, despite crippling bouts with chronic malaria. The most important question for the committee was not black suffrage—that was taken for granted—but rather who among the former Confederates should be stripped of their right to vote. Some Republicans favored a narrow exclusion, limiting the number to only those disfranchised by the Fourteenth Amendment (about 2,500 former high Confederate officials and military commanders in the state). Morgan pushed for a far stronger measure—one that, if passed, would have radically changed the future of Mississippi politics. He proposed to permanently disfranchise those who refused to swear, "I admit the political and civil equality of all men, so help me God."

Such a breathtaking step toward an egalitarian society went too far for some delegates at the raucous assembly. One, a conservative Northern white named Charles H. Townsend, reacted angrily, denouncing the president of the convention and challenging one of Morgan's allies to a fistfight. Then Albert stepped forward: lame though he was from that bullet through his thigh, sick though he was from lingering malaria, he faced off against Townsend on the capital grounds, surrounded by a crowd of shouting delegates. The two traded punches until a general brouhaha erupted, and constables arrived to clear away the brawling mob.

But Albert Morgan made his point. His proposal was adopted by the convention, and he was free to return to the nightmare that was consuming Yazoo City. Soon he would devote his attention to the campaign to convince Mississippi voters to adopt the new constitution.

Meanwhile, far from Yazoo County, America was changing in ways that the Morgans could hardly comprehend. The nation they had been raised in—with its economy of self-sufficient farmers and small, family-owned businesses (like their own father's grain warehouse)—was rapidly falling under the shadow of a new creature: the corporation.

II

MONEY

THE CUTTHROAT ECONOMY

7

DUEL OF THE ROBBER BARONS

In the spring of 1868 a peculiar duel began in New York's streets—in Wall Street, to be specific. It was a battle of titanic proportions, between utterly ruthless men with seemingly endless resources at their disposal. The city, then the state, then the nation watched breathlessly until the combatants staggered to a conclusion months later. It was a very strange contest: for all its vehemence, no one died, and while a few men may have been bruised a bit, none were seriously injured. And at the end much of the New York judiciary, state legislature, and most of the duelists themselves were left considerably richer. The prize was a business, the Erie Railroad; the weapons were money, stocks, and bonds; the battle-ground was a new type of organization, the corporation; and the contestants were a new kind of man—the robber baron.

Fascinating as it was in terms of human drama, the spectacular war for the Erie sounded a stark warning to the American public: the nation was changing, changing in ways that sharply contrasted with the rapid expansion of civil rights under Reconstruction. The national economy was undergoing a revolution launched by the Civil War as surely as the revolution in freedom in the South. Only a few years before, the economic system was based to a large degree on self-sufficient farms and small, family-owned businesses. Industry as we know it today was almost nonexistent. Of course, some large private firms and business partnerships were in operation, plantations dominated the South, and numerous mills and factories churned out manufactured goods. But even if the economy was not exactly egalitarian, workers could expect to earn enough to start their own shops or farms someday (except for the millions of slaves in the South). Corporations were rare; before the Civil War, a charter for a corporation required a special act of the state legislature, usually granted only for bodies providing a special service. Operating a canal, for example, or a major road.

Or a railroad. In the decades before the war, this newfangled means of transportation spread through such specially chartered corporations, often funded by state treasuries (and foreign capitalists). But the railroad corporations soon took on a life of their own, growing in directions virtually unimaginable at the outset. They accumulated massive amounts of capital to finance construction; enormous quantities of goods, materials, and men went into the operations and expansion of the various lines. Railroads emerged as America's first true national industry—and the men who rose to the top of these corporations soon mastered the mysterious arts of manipulating other people's money.

Then came the Civil War. It dramatically increased the demands on production in the North; it also required new means of concentrating and controlling the flow of money. As the largest businesses in operation, the railroads provided the expertise and the organizational model for the expanding, industrializing economy. The government speeded up this process of growth and modernization by introducing sweeping financial reforms: paper currency that was also legal tender, for example, which rapidly expanded the amount of currency in circulation and spurred the economy to grow more quickly. Congress enacted a national banking system in 1863, creating a unified financial structure. It also established a direct income tax, along with a high tariff to protect domestic manufacturing—and rich subsidies for the railroads.

By the time the war ended, the Southern vision of a plantation republic had collapsed and died; but the Jeffersonian vision of a nation of independent farmers was also breathing its last. Most Americans could still pretend that the dream had a future—but the high-profile battle for the Erie Railroad foreshadowed the end of the illusion. It proved how the corporation, when matched with a massive, wealthy industry, was concentrating enormous power in the hands of a few men.

Even as the freed people looked to a new age of civil equality, a very different era was dawning—an age of money power, when a vast gulf opened between the super rich and the rest, between those who could buy political might and those who merely voted. Alan Trachtenberg has called it the age of "incorporation," when the countryside was absorbed into a new social and economic system dominated by the conservative power of great wealth. From cotton mills to county banks, the nation fell into orbit around the financial center of New York, with its stock exchange and mighty banks. For many years to come, of course, most Americans could live outside the expanding grasp of the multiplying corporations; family farms would flourish for decades, and small businesses would always occupy niches in the economy. But the march toward concentration had begun. In the 1860s, few laws and regulations existed to hold back those who ran the great railroad behemoths, and so they waged their battles with a ruthlessness that earned them the title of robber baron.

Perhaps this vision of the great change that was beginning to grip the economy is too bleak. Certainly the rapid growth of transportation, of manufacturing, of the nation's wealth in general benefitted many people below the level of the corporate overlords. But a decade after the Civil War, Americans in the North lived in a noticeably less egalitarian society than they did in the decade before. A concentration of wealth and power had begun that gave the period the lasting name, the Gilded Age.[1]

[1] The name of the Gilded Age comes from the title of Mark Twain's first novel (cowritten with Charles Dudley Warner), a witty political satire published in 1873.

But to return to the war for the Erie. In July 1869, a young man named Charles Francis Adams, Jr. (son of the ambassador to England, grandson of John Quincy Adams, and brother of Henry Adams) wrote a remarkable article about the corporate struggle in the *North American Review,* a leading intellectual periodical. Vivid in prose, striking in its portraits of individuals, sharp in its insights, Adams's essay tells the dramatic tale of Erie better than anything written since. It is so remarkable, in fact, that it is the sole exception to the rule in this book that all selections are written by actual participants (though Adams apparently gained access to secret information about the Erie battle, including the company books). The exception is well worth making, for here is a gripping tale of money, power, and corruption.

A Chapter of Erie
by Charles Francis Adams, Jr.

The practice of piracy, it was thought, was battered and hung out of existence when the Barbary Powers and the pirates of the Spanish Main had been finally dealt with. But the freebooters have only transferred their operations to the land, and the commerce of the world is now more severely, though far more equally, taxed through the machinery of rings and tariffs, selfish money combinations at business centers, and the unprincipled corporate control of great lines of railway, than ever it was by depredations outside the law. . . . It is no longer the practice of Governments and Ministries to buy legislators; but individuals and corporations have of late not infrequently found them commodities for sale in the market. . . .

No better illustration of the fantastic guises which the worst of commonplace evils of history assume, as they meet us in the movements of the day, could be afforded than was seen in the events attending what are known as the Erie wars of the year 1868. Beginning in February and lasting until December, raging fiercely in the late winter and spring, and dying away into a hollow truce at midsummer, only to revive into new and more vigorous life in the autumn, this strange conflict convulsed the money market, occupied the courts, agitated legislatures, and perplexed the country throughout the entire year. Its history has not been fully written and probably never will be; yet it should not be wholly forgotten.

It was something new to see a band of conspirators possess themselves of a road more important than was ever the Appian Way, and make levies not only upon it for their own emolument, but through it on the whole business of a nation. Nor could it fail to be seen that this was by no means the end, but only the beginning. The American people cannot afford to glance at this thing in the columns of the daily press and then dismiss it from memory. It involves too many questions; it touches too nearly the national life.

The history of the Erie Railway has been a checkered one. Chartered in 1832, and organized in 1833, the cost of its construction was then estimated at three millions of dollars, of which but one million were subscribed. . . . At last, in 1851, eighteen years after its commencement, the road was opened from Lake Erie to tide-water. . . . Meanwhile the original estimate of three millions had developed into an actual outlay of fifty millions; the 470 miles of track opened in 1842 had expanded to 773 miles in 1868; and the revenue, which the projectors had "confidently" estimated at something less than two millions in 1833, amounted to over five millions when the road passed into the hands of a receiver in 1859, and in 1865 reached the enormous amount of sixteen millions and a half. The road was, in truth, a magnificent enterprise, worthy to connect the Great Lakes with the great seaport of America. Scaling lofty mountain ranges, running through fertile valleys and by the banks of broad rivers, connecting the Hudson, the Susquehanna, the St. Lawrence, and the Ohio, it stood forth a monument at once of engineering skill and of commercial enterprise.

Some seventeen or eighteen years ago, Mr. Daniel Drew first made his appearance in the Board of Directors of the Erie, where he remained down to the year 1868, generally holding also the office of treasurer of the corporation. Mr. Drew is what is known as a self-made man. Born in the year 1797, as a boy he drove cattle down from his native town of Carmel, in Putnam County, to the market of New York City, and, subsequently, was for years proprietor of the Bull's Head Tavern. Like his contemporary, and ally or opponent—as the case may be—Cornelius Vanderbilt, he built up his fortunes in the steamboat interest, and subsequently extended his operations over the rapidly expanding railroad system. Shrewd, unscrupulous, and very illiterate—a strange combination of superstition and faithlessness, of daring and timidity—often good-natured and sometimes generous—he has ever regarded his fiduciary position as director of a railroad as a means of manipulating its stock for his own advantage.

For years he has been the leading bear of Wall Street, and his favorite haunts have been the secret recesses of Erie. As treasurer of that corporation, he has, in its frequently recurring hours of need, advanced it sums which it could not have been obtained elsewhere, and the obtaining of which was a necessity. His management of his favorite stock has been cunning and recondite, and his ways inscrutable. Those who sought to follow him, and those who sought to oppose him, alike found food for sad reflection; until at last he won for himself the expressive sobriquet of the Speculative Director. Sometimes, though rarely, he suffered greatly in the complications of Wall Street; more frequently he inflicted severe damage upon others. On the whole, however, his fortunes had greatly prospered, and the outbreak of the Erie war found him the actual possessor of some millions, and the reputed possessor of many more.

In the spring of 1866 Mr. Drew's manipulations of Erie culminated in an operation which was at the time regarded as a masterpiece, but which subsequent experience has so improved upon that it is now looked on as an ordinary and inartistic piece of financiering. The stock of the road was at that time selling at about 95, and the corporation was, as usual, in debt, and in pressing need of money. As usual, also, it resorted to its treasurer. Mr. Drew stood ready to make the desired advances upon security. Some twenty-eight thousand shares of its own authorized stock, which had never been issued, were at the time in the hands of the company, which also claimed the right, under the statutes of New York, of raising money by the issue of bonds convertible, at the option of the holder, into stock. The twenty-eight thousand unissued shares and bonds for three millions of dollars, convertible into stock, were placed by the company in the hands of its treasurer, as security for a cash loan of $3,500,000. The negotiation had been quietly effected, and Mr. Drew's campaign now opened.

Once more he was short of Erie. While Erie was buoyant—while it steadily approximated to par—while speculation was rampant, and that outside public, the delight and the prey of Wall Street, was gradually drawn in by the fascination of amassing wealth without labor—quietly and stealthily, through his agents and brokers, the grave, desponding operator was daily concluding contracts for the future delivery of stock at current prices. At last the hour had come. Erie was rising, Erie was scarce, and the great bear had many contracts to fulfill, and where was he to find the stock? His victims were not kept long in suspense. Mr. Treasurer Drew laid his hands upon his collateral. In an instant the bonds for three millions were converted into an equivalent amount of capital stock, and fifty-eight thousand shares, dumped, as it were, by the cart-load in Broad Street, made Erie as plentiful as even Drew could desire. Before the astonished bulls could rally their faculties, the quotations had fallen from 95 to 50, and they realized that they were hopelessly entrapped. . . .

As a result of the transaction of 1866, Mr. Drew was looked upon as having effected a surprisingly clever operation, and he returned from the field hated, feared, wealthy, and admired. This episode of Wall Street history took its place as a brilliant success beside the famous Prairie du Chien and Harlem "corners," and but for subsequent events would soon have been forgotten. Its close connection, however, with more important though later incidents of Erie history seems likely to preserve its memory. Great events were impending; a new man was looming up in the railroad world, introducing novel ideas and principles, and it could hardly be that the new and old could not come into conflict. Cornelius Vanderbilt, commonly known as Commodore Vanderbilt, was now developing his theory of the management of railroads.

Born in the year 1794, Vanderbilt is a somewhat older man than Drew. There are several points of resemblance in the early lives of the two men, and many points of curious contrast in their characters. Vanderbilt, like Drew, was born in very humble circumstances in the State of New York, and received as little education. He began life by ferrying over passengers and produce from Staten Island to New York. Subsequently, he too laid the foundation of his great fortune in the growing steamboat navigation, and likewise, in due course of time, transferred himself to the railroad interest. When at last, in 1868, the two came into collision as representatives of the old system of railroad management and the new, they were each of them threescore and ten years of age, and had both been successful in the accumulation of millions—Vanderbilt even more so than Drew.

They were probably equally unscrupulous and equally selfish; but, while the cast of Drew's mind was somber and bearish, Vanderbilt was gay and buoyant of temperament, little given to thoughts other than of this world, a lover of horses and of the good things of this life. The first affects prayer-meetings, and the last is a devotee of whist. Drew, in Wall Street, is by temperament a bear, while Vanderbilt could hardly be other than a bull. Vanderbilt must be allowed to be by far the superior man of the two. Drew is astute and full of resources, and at all times a dangerous opponent; but Vanderbilt takes the larger, more comprehensive views, and his mind has a vigorous grasp which that of Drew seems to want. . . . It is impossible to regard Vanderbilt's methods or aims without recognizing the magnitude of the man's ideas and conceding his abilities. He involuntarily excites feelings of admiration for himself and alarm for the public.

His ambition is a great one. It seems to be nothing less than to make himself master in his own right of the great channels of communication which connect the city of New York with the interior of the continent, and to control them as his private property. While Drew has sought only to carry to perfection the old system of operating successfully from the confidential position of director, neither knowing anything nor caring anything for the railroad system except in its connection with the movements of the stock exchange, Vanderbilt has seen the full magnitude of the system, and through it has sought to make himself a dictator in modern civilization, moving forward to this end step by step with a sort of pitiless energy which has seemed to have in it an element of fatality. As trade now dominates the world, and the railways dominate trade, his object has been to make himself the virtual master of all by making himself absolute lord of the railways. . . .

Two great lines of railway traverse the State of New York and connect it with the West—the Erie and the New York Central. The latter communicates with the city by a great river and by two railroads. To get these two roads—the Harlem and the Hudson River—under his own absolute control, and then, so far as the connection with the Central was concerned, to abolish the river, was Vanderbilt's immediate object. First making himself master of the Harlem Road, he there learned his early lessons in railroad management, and picked up a fortune by the way. A few years ago Harlem had no value. As late as 1860 it sold for eight or nine dollars per share; and in January, 1863, when Vanderbilt had got the control, it had risen only to 30. By July of that year it stood at 92, and in August was suddenly raised by a "corner" to 179. The next year witnessed a similar operation. The stock, which sold in January at less than 90, was settled for in June in the neighborhood of 285. On one of these occasions Mr. Drew is reported to have contributed a sum approaching half a million to his rival's wealth. . . .

It was in the successful conduct of this first experiment that Vanderbilt showed his very manifest superiority over previous railroad managers. The Harlem was, after all, only a competing line, and competition was proverbially the rock ahead in all railroad enterprise. The success of Vanderbilt with the Harlem depended upon his getting rid of the competition of the Hudson River Railroad. An ordinary manager would have resorted to contracts, which are never carried out, or to opposition, which is apt to be ruinous. Vanderbilt, on the contrary, put an end to the competition by buying up the competing line. This he did in the neighborhood of par, and in due course of time, the stock was sent up to 180. Thus his plans had developed by another step, while, through a judicious course of financiering and watering and dividing, a new fortune had been secured by him.

By this time Vanderbilt's reputation as a railroad manager—as one who earned dividends, invented stock, and created wealth—had become very great, and the managers of the Central brought that road to him, and asked him to do with it as he had done with the Harlem and Hudson River. He accepted the proffered charge, and now, probably, the possibilities of his position and the magnitude of the prize within his grasp at last dawned on his mind. . . .

Physically, morally, intellectually, in population, wealth, and intelligence, all things tend to consolidation. One singular illustration of this law is almost entirely the growth of this century. Formerly, either governments, or individuals, or, at most, small combinations of individuals, were the originators of all great works of public utility. Within the present century only has democracy found its way to carry out the most extensive enterprises. And yet already our great corporations are fast emancipating themselves from the state, or rather subjecting the state to their own control, while individual capitalists, who long ago abandoned the attempt to compete with them, will next seek to control them. In this dangerous path of centralization Vanderbilt has taken the latest step in advance. He has combined the natural power of the individual with the factitious power of the corporation. The famous "L'état, c'est moi" of Louis XIV represents Vanderbilt's position in regard to his railroads. Unconsciously he has introduced Caesarism into corporate life. He has, however, but pointed out the way which others will tread. The individual will hereafter be engrafted on the corporation—democracy running its course, and resulting in imperialism; and Vanderbilt is but the precursor of a class of men who will wield within the state a power created by it, but too great for its control. He is the founder of a dynasty.

From the moment Vanderbilt stepped into the management of the Central, but a single effort seemed necessary to give the new railroad king absolute control over the railroad system, and subsequently over the commerce, of New York. By advancing only one step he could securely levy his tolls on the traffic of a continent. Nor would this step have seemed difficult to take. It was but to repeat with the Erie his successful operation with the Hudson River Road. Not only was it a step easy to take, but here again, as so many times before, a new fortune seemed ready to drop into his hand. . . . There was indeed but one obstacle in the way—the plan might not meet the views of the one man who at that time possessed the wealth, cunning, and combination of qualities which could defeat it, that man being the Speculative Director of the Erie—Mr. Daniel Drew.

The New York Central passed into Vanderbilt's hands in the winter of 1866–67, and he marked the Erie for his own in the succeeding autumn. As the annual meeting of the corporation approached, three parties were found in the field contending for control of the road. One party was represented by Drew, and might be called the party in possession—that which had long ruled the Erie, and made it what it was—the Scarlet Woman of Wall Street. Next came Vanderbilt, flushed with success, and bent upon his great idea of developing imperialism in public life. Lastly a faction made its appearance composed of some shrewd and ambitious Wall Street operators and certain persons from Boston, who sustained for the occasion the novel character of railroad reformers. This party, it is needless to say, was as unscrupulous and, as the result proved, as able as either of the others; it represented nothing but a raid made upon the Erie treasury in the interests of a thoroughly bankrupt New England corporation of which its members had the control. The history of this corporation, known as the Boston, Hartford, and Erie Railroad—a projected feeder and connection of the Erie—would be one curious to read, though very difficult to write. Its name was synonymous with bankruptcy, litigation, fraud, and failure. . . . Of late years, under able and persevering, if not unscrupulous management, the bankrupt, moribund company had been slowly struggling into new life, and in the spring of 1867 it had obtained, under certain conditions, from the Commonwealth of Massachusetts, a subsidy in aid of the construction of the road. One of the conditions imposed obliged the corporation to raise a sum from other sources still larger than that granted by the State. Accordingly, those having the line in charge looked abroad for a victim, and fixed their eyes upon the Erie.

As the election day drew near, Erie was of course for sale. A controlling interest of stockholders stood ready to sell their proxies, with entire impartiality, to any of the three contending parties, or to any man who would pay the market price for them. . . . Meanwhile the representatives of the Eastern interest played their part to admiration. Taking advantage of some Wall Street complications just then existing between Vanderbilt and Drew, they induced the former to ally himself with them, and the latter saw that his defeat was inevitable. Even at this time the Vanderbilt party contemplated having recourse, if necessary, to the courts, and a petition for an injunction had been prepared, setting forth the details of the "corner" of 1866.

On the Sunday preceding the election, Drew, in view of his impending defeat, called upon Vanderbilt. That gentleman thereupon very amicably read to him the legal documents prepared for his benefit, whereupon the ready treasurer at once turned about, and, having hitherto been hampering the Commodore by his bear operations, he now agreed to join hands with him in giving the market a strong upward tendency. Meanwhile the other parties to the contest were not idle. At the same house, at a later hour in the day, Vanderbilt explained to the Eastern adventurers his new plan of operations, which included the continuance of Drew in his directorship. These gentlemen were puzzled, not to say confounded, by the sudden change of front. An explanation was demanded, some plain language followed, and the parties separated, only to meet again at a later hour at the house of Drew. There Vanderbilt brought the new men to terms by proposing to Drew a bold *coup de main*, calculated to throw them entirely out of the direction. Before the parties separated that night, a written agreement had been entered into, providing that, to save appearances, the new board should be elected without Drew, but that immediately thereafter a vacancy should be created, and Drew chosen to fill it. He was therefore to go in as one of the two directors in the Vanderbilt interest, that gentleman's nephew, Mr. Work, being the other.

This program was faithfully carried out, and on the second of October Wall Street was at once astonished by the news of the defeat of the notorious leader of the bears, and bewildered by the immediate resignation of a member of the new board, and the election of Drew in his place. Apparently he had given in his submission, the one obstacle to success was removed, and the ever-victorious Commodore had now but to close his fingers on his new prize. Virtual consolidation in the Vanderbilt interest seemed a foregone conclusion.

The reinstallment of Drew was followed by a period of hollow truce. . . . The real conflict was now impending. Commodore Vanderbilt stretched out his hand to grasp Erie. Erie was to be isolated and shut up within the limits of New York; it was to be given over, bound hand and foot, to the lord of the Central. To perfect this program, the representatives of all the competing lines met, and a proposition was submitted to the Erie party looking to a practical consolidation and a division among the contracting parties of the earnings from the New York City travel. A new illustration was thus to be afforded, at the expense of the trade and travel to and from the heart of the continent, of George Stephenson's famous aphorism, that where combination is possible competition is impossible. The Erie party, however, represented that their road earned more than half of the fund of which they were to receive only one third. They remonstrated and proposed modifications, but their opponents were inexorable. The terms were too hard; the conference led to no result, and the war broke out afresh.

Then Vanderbilt, foiled in his attempt, went into Wall Street, prepared to make himself master of the Erie, as before he had made himself master of the Hudson River Road. The task in itself was one of magnitude. The volume of stock was immense; all of it was upon the street, and the necessary expenditure involved many millions of dollars. The peculiar difficulty of the task, however, lay in the fact that it had to be undertaken in the face of antagonists so bold, so subtle, so unscrupulous, so thoroughly acquainted with Erie, as well as so familiar with all the devices and tricks of fence of Wall Street.

The first open hostilities took place on the 17th of February. For some time Wall Street had been agitated with forebodings of the coming hostilities, but not until that day was recourse had to the courts. Vanderbilt had two ends in view when he sought to avail himself of the processes of law. In the first place, Drew's long connection with Erie, and especially the unsettled transactions arising out of the famous corner of 1866, afforded admirable ground for annoying offensive operations; and, in the second place, these very proceedings, by throwing his opponent on the defensive, afforded an excellent cover for Vanderbilt's own transactions on Wall Street. It was essential to his success to corner Drew, but to corner Drew at all was not easy, and to corner him in Erie was difficult indeed. . . .

It was, therefore, very necessary for Vanderbilt that he should, while buying Erie up with one hand in Wall Street, with the other close, so far as he could, that apparently inexhaustible spring from which such generous supplies of new stock were wont to flow. Accordingly, on the 17th of February, Mr. Frank Work, the only remaining representative of the Van-

derbilt faction in the Erie direction, accompanied by Mr. Vanderbilt's attorneys, Messrs. Rapallo and Spenser, made his appearance before Judge
Barnard of the Supreme Court of New York, then sitting in chambers,
and applied for an injunction against Treasurer Drew and his brother directors, restraining them from the payment of interest or principal of the
three and a half millions borrowed of the treasurer in 1866, as well as
from releasing Drew from any liability or cause of action the company
might have against him, pending an investigation of his accounts as treasurer; on the other hand, Drew was to be enjoined from taking any legal
steps towards compelling a settlement.

A temporary injunction was granted in accordance with the petition, and
a further hearing was assigned for the 21st. Two days later, however—on
the 19th of the month—without waiting for the result of the first attack,
the same attorneys appeared again before Judge Barnard, and now in the
name of the people, acting through the Attorney-General, petitioned for
the removal from office of Treasurer Drew. The papers in the case set forth
some of the difficulties which beset the Commodore, and exposed the existence of a new fountain of Erie stock. It appeared that there was a recently
enacted statute of New York which authorized any railroad company to
create and issue its own stock in exchange for the stock of any other road
under lease to it. Mr. Drew, the petition alleged, and certain of his brother
directors, had quietly possessed themselves of a worthless road connecting
with the Erie, and called the Buffalo, Bradford, and Pittsburg Railroad, and
had then . . . proceeded to supply themselves with whatever Erie stock they
wanted by leasing their own road to the road of which they were directors,
and then creating stock and issuing it to themselves in exchange, under the
authority vested in them by law.

The history of this transaction affords, indeed, a most happy illustration of brilliant railroad financiering. The road cost the purchasers, as financiers, some $250,000; as proprietors, they then issued in its name
bonds for two millions of dollars, payable to one of themselves, who now
figured as trustee. This person then, shifting his character, drew up as
counsel for both parties a contract leasing this road to the Erie Railway
for four hundred and ninety-nine years, the Erie agreeing to assume the
bonds. Reappearing in their original character of Erie directors, these
gentlemen then ratified the lease, and thereafter it only remained for
them to relapse into the role of financiers, and to divide the proceeds. All
this was happily accomplished, and the Erie Railway lost and someone
gained $140,000 a year by the bargain. The skillful actors in this much-
shifting drama probably proceeded on the familiar theory that exchange
is no robbery, and the expedient was certainly ingenious.

Commodore Vanderbilt, however, naturally desired to put some limit
to the amount of the stock in existence, a majority of which he sought to
control. Accordingly it was now further ordered by Mr. Justice Barnard

that Mr. Drew should show cause on the 21st why the prayer of the pe-
titioner should not be granted, and meanwhile he was temporarily suspended from his position as treasurer and director.

It was not until the 3rd of March, however, that any decisive action
was taken by Judge Barnard on either of the petitions before him. Even
then that in the name of the Attorney-General was postponed for final
hearing until the 10th of the month; but on the application of Work an
injunction was issued restraining the Erie board from any new issue of
capital stock, by conversion of bonds or otherwise, in addition to the
251,058 shares appearing in the previous reports of the road, and forbidding the guaranty by the Erie of the bonds of any connecting line of
road. While this last provision of the order was calculated to furnish food
for thought to the Boston party, matter for meditation was supplied to
Mr. Drew by other clauses, which specially forbade him, his agents, attorneys, or brokers, to have any transactions in Erie, or to fulfill any of
his contracts already entered into, until he had returned to the company
68,000 shares of capital stock, which were alleged to be the number involved in the unsettled transaction of 1866, and the more recent Buffalo,
Bradford, and Pittsburg exchange. . . .

Things certainly did not now promise well for Treasurer Drew and the
bear party. Vanderbilt and the bulls seemed to have it all their own way.
. . . So far from manufacturing fresh Erie and pouring it into the street,
[Drew] was to be cornered by a writ, and forced to work his own ruin in
obedience to an injunction. Appearances are, however, proverbially deceptive, and all depended on the assumption that some virtue did exist in
the processes of law, and that some authority was wielded by a New York
court. In spite of the threatening aspect of his affairs, it was very evident
that the nerves of Mr. Drew and his associates were not seriously affected.
Wall Street watched him with curiosity not unmingled with alarm; for
this was a conflict of Titans. . . . He seemed rushing on destruction. Day
after day he pursued the same "short" tactics; contract after contract was
put out for the future delivery of stock at current prices, and this, too, in
the face of a continually rising market. Evidently he did not yet consider
himself at the end of his resources.

It was equally evident, however, that he had not much time to lose. It
was now the 3rd of March, and the anticipated "corner" might be looked
for about the 10th. As usual, some light skirmishing took place as a prelude to the heavy shock of decisive battle. The Erie party very freely and
openly expressed a decided lack of respect, and something approaching
contempt, for the purity of that particular fragment of the judicial ermine
which—figuratively—adorned the person of Mr. Justice Barnard. They
did not pretend to conceal their conviction that this magistrate was a
piece of the Vanderbilt property, and they very plainly announced their
intention of seeking for justice elsewhere. With this end in view they be-

took themselves to their own town of Binghamton, in the county of Broome, where they duly presented themselves before Mr. Justice Balcom, of the Supreme Court. . . .

Taking advantage of the extreme complication [in New York's judicial structure], the Erie party broke new ground in a new suit. The injunction was no sooner asked of Judge Balcom than it was granted, and Mr. Frank Work, the Attorney-General, and all other parties litigant were directed to show cause at Courtlandville on the 7th of March; and meanwhile, Mr. Director Work, accused of being a spy of the enemy in the councils of Erie, was temporarily suspended from his position, and all proceedings in the suits commenced before Judge Barnard were stayed. The moment, however, that this order became known in New York, a new suit was commenced by the Vanderbilt interest in the name of Richard Schell; and Judge Ingraham cried check to the move of Judge Balcom, by forbidding any meeting of the Erie board, or the transaction of any business by it, unless Director Work was at full liberty to participate therein. The first move of the Drew faction did not seem likely to result in any signal advantage to their cause.

All this, however, was mere skirmishing, and now the decisive engagement was near at hand. The plans of the Erie ring were matured, and if Commodore Vanderbilt wanted the stock of their road, they were prepared to let him have all he desired. As usual the Erie treasury was at this time deficient in funds. As usual, also, Daniel Drew stood ready to advance all the funds required on proper security. One kind of security, and only one, the company was disposed at this time to offer—their convertible bonds under a pledge of conversion. The company could not issue stock outright, in any case, at less than par; its bonds bore interest, and were useless on the street; an issue of convertible bonds was another name for an issue of stock to be sold at market rates. The treasurer readily agreed to find a purchaser, and, in fact, he himself was just then in pressing need of some scores of thousands of shares.

Already at the meeting of the Board of Directors, on the 19th of February, a very deceptive account of the road, jockeyed out of the general superintendent, had been read and made public: the increased depot facilities, the projected double track, and the everlasting steel rails had been made to do vigorous duty; and the board had duly authorized the Executive Committee "to borrow such sums as might be necessary, and to issue therefor such security as is provided for in such cases by the laws of the State." Immediately after the Board of Directors adjourned, a meeting of the Executive Committee was held, and a vote to issue at once convertible bonds for ten millions gave a meaning to the very ambiguous language of the directors' resolve; and thus, when apparently on the very threshold of his final triumph, this mighty mass of 100,000 shares of new stock was hanging like an avalanche over the head of Vanderbilt.

The Executive Committee had voted to sell the entire amount of these bonds at not less than 72½. Five millions were placed upon the market at once, and Mr. Drew's broker became the purchaser—Mr. Drew giving him a written guaranty against loss and being entitled to any profit that might arise. It was all done in ten minutes after the Committee adjourned—the bonds issued, their conversion into stock demanded and complied with, and certificates for fifty thousand shares deposited in the broker's safe, subject to the orders of Daniel Drew. There they remained until the 29th, when they were issued, on his requisition, to certain others of that gentleman's army of brokers, much as ammunition might be issued before a general engagement. Three days later came the Barnard injunction, and Erie suddenly rose in the market. Then it was determined to bring up the reserves and let the eager bulls have the other five millions.

The history of this second issue was, in all respects, an episode worthy of Erie, and deserves minute relation. It was decided upon the 3rd, but before the bonds were converted Barnard's injunction had been served on everyone connected with the Erie Road or with Daniel Drew. The 10th was the return day of the writ, but the Erie operators needed even less time for their deliberations. Monday, the 9th, was settled upon as the day upon which to defeat the impending "corner." The night of Saturday, the 7th, was a busy one in the Erie camp. While one set of counsel and clerks were preparing affidavits and prayers for strange writs and injunctions, the enjoined vice-president of the road was busy at home signing certificates of stock, to be ready for instant use in case a modification of the injunction could be obtained, and another set of counsel was in immediate attendance on the leaders themselves. Mr. Groesbeck, the chief of the Drew brokers, being himself enjoined, secured elsewhere, after one or two failures, a purchaser of the bonds, and took him to the house of the Erie counsel, where Drew and the other directors and brokers then were. There the terms of the nominal sale were agreed upon, and a contract drawn up transferring the bonds to this man of straw— Mr. Groesbeck, meanwhile, with the fear of injunctions before his eyes, prudently withdrawing into the next room.

After the contract was closed, the purchaser was asked to sign an affidavit setting forth his ownership of the bonds and the refusal of the corporation to convert them into stock in compliance with their contract, upon which affidavit it was in contemplation to seek from some justice a writ of *mandamus* to compel the Erie Railway to convert them, the necessary papers for such a proceeding being then in course of preparation elsewhere. This the purchaser declined to do. One of the lawyers present then said, "Well, you can make the demand now; here is Mr. Drew, the treasurer of the company, and Mr. Gould, one of the Executive Committee." In accordance with this suggestion, a demand for the stock was then made, and, of course, refused; thereupon the scruples of the man of straw being all removed, the desired affidavit was signed. All business having now been disposed of, the parties separated; the legal papers were ready, the convertible bonds had been disposed of, and the certificates of stock for which they were to be exchanged were signed in blank and ready for delivery.

Early on Monday morning the Erie people were at work. Mr. Drew, the director and treasurer, had agreed to sell on that day 50,000 shares of the stock, at 80, to the firms of which Mr. Fisk and Mr. Gould were members, these gentlemen also being Erie directors and members of the Executive Committee. The new certificates, made out in the names of these firms on Saturday night, were in the hands of the secretary of the company, who was strictly enjoined from allowing their issue. On Monday morning this official directed an employee of the road to carry these books of certificates from the West Street office of the company to the transfer clerk in Pine Street, and there to deliver them carefully. The messenger left the room, but immediately returned empty-handed, and informed the astonished secretary that Mr. Fisk had met him outside the door, taken from him the books of unissued certificates, and "run away with them." It was true—one essential step towards conversion had been taken; the certificates of stock were beyond the control of an injunction. A day or two later the convertible bonds were found upon the secretary's desk, conveyed thither by an unknown hand; the certificates were next seen in Broad Street.

Before launching the bolt thus provided, the conspirators had considered it not unadvisable to cover their proceedings, if they could, with some form of law. This probably was looked upon as an idle ceremony, but it could do no harm; and perhaps their next step was dictated by what has been called "a decent respect for the opinions of mankind," combined with a profound contempt for judges and courts of law.

Early on the morning of the 9th, Judge Gilbert, a highly respected magistrate of the Second Judicial District, residing in Brooklyn, was waited upon by one of the Erie counsel, who desired to initiate before him a new suit in the Erie litigation—this time, in the name of the Saturday evening purchaser of the bonds and makers of affidavits. A writ of *mandamus* was asked for. This writ clearly did not lie in such a case; the magistrate very properly declined to grant it, and the only wonder is that counsel should have applied for it.

New counsel were then hurriedly summoned, and a new petition, in a fresh name, was presented. This petition was for an injunction, in the name of one Belden, the business partner of Mr. Fisk, and the documents then and there presented probably as eloquent an exposure of the lamentable condition into which the once honored judiciary of New York had fallen as could possibly have been penned. The petition alleged that some time in

February certain persons, among whom was especially named George G. Barnard—the justice of the Supreme Court of the First District—had entered into a combination to speculate in the stock of the Erie Railway, and to use the process of the courts for the purpose of aiding their speculation; "and that, in furtherance of the plans of this combination," the actions in Work's name had been commenced before Barnard.

It is impossible by any criticism to do justice to such audacity as this; the dumb silence of amazement is the only fitting commentary. Apparently, however, nothing could be stated of his colleague across the river that exceeded the belief of Judge Gilbert, for after some trifling delays . . . the Erie counsel returned to New York with a new injunction, restraining all the parties to all the other suits from further proceedings, and from doing any acts in "furtherance of said conspiracy"—in one paragraph ordering the Erie directors, except Work, to continue in the charge of their duties, in direct defiance of the injunction of Judge Ingraham, and in another, with an equal disregard of Judge Barnard, forbidding the directors to desist from converting bonds into stock. . . .

All was now ready. The Drew party was enjoined in every direction. One magistrate had forbidden them to move, and another magistrate had forbidden them to stand still. . . . Strategically considered, the position could not be improved, and Mr. Drew and his friends were not the men to let the golden moment escape them. At once, before even in New York a new injunction could be obtained, fifty thousand shares of new Erie stock were flung upon the market. That day Erie was buoyant—Vanderbilt was purchasing. His agents caught at the new stock as eagerly as at the old, and the whole of it was absorbed before its origin was suspected, and almost without a falter in the price. Then the fresh certificates appeared, and the truth became known.

Erie had that day opened at 80 and risen rapidly to 83, while its rise even to par was predicted; suddenly it faltered, fell off, and then dropped suddenly to 71. Wall Street had never been subjected to a greater shock, and the market reeled to and fro like a drunken man between the blows of these giants, as they hurled about shares by the tens of thousands, and money by the million. The attempted "corner" was a failure, and Drew was victorious—no doubt existed on that point. The question was, could Vanderbilt sustain himself? In spite of all his wealth, must he not go down before his cunning opponent? When night put an end to the conflict, Erie stood at 78, the shock of battle was over, and the astonished brokers drew breath as they waited for the events of the morrow.

The morning of the 11th found the Erie leaders still transacting business at the offices of the corporation in West Street. It would seem that these gentlemen, in spite of the glaring contempt for the process of the courts of which they had been guilty, had made no arrangements for an orderly retreat beyond the jurisdiction of the tribunals they had set at defiance. They were speedily roused from their real or affected tranquillity by trustworthy intelligence that processes for contempt were already issued against them, and that their only chance of escape from incarceration lay in precipitate flight. At ten o'clock the astonished police saw a throng of panic-stricken railway directors—looking more like a frightened gang of thieves, disturbed in the division of their plunder, than like the wealthy representatives of a great corporation—rush headlong from the doors of the Erie office, and dash off in the direction of the Jersey ferry. In their hands were packages and files of papers, and their pockets were crammed with assets and securities. One individual bore away with him in the hackney-coach bales containing six millions of dollars in greenbacks. Other members of the board followed under cover of the night; some of them, not daring to expose themselves to the publicity of a ferry, attempted to cross in open boats concealed by the darkness and a March fog. Two directors, who lingered, were arrested; but a majority of the Executive Committee collected at the Erie station in Jersey City, and there, free from any apprehension of Judge Barnard's pursuing wrath, proceeded to the transaction of business.

Meanwhile, on the other side of the river, Vanderbilt was struggling in the toils. As usual in these Wall Street operations, there was a grim humor in the situation. Had Vanderbilt failed to sustain the market, a financial collapse and panic must have ensued which would have sent him to the wall. He had sustained it, and had absorbed a hundred thousand shares of Erie. Thus when Drew retired to Jersey City, he carried with him seven millions of his opponent's money, and the Commodore had freely supplied the enemy with the sinews of war. He had grasped at Erie for his own sake, and now his opponents promised to rehabilitate and vivify the old line with the money he had furnished them, so as more effectually to compete with the lines which he had already possessed. . . .

Vanderbilt, however, had little leisure to devote to the enjoyment of the humor of his position. The situation was alarming. His opponents had carried with them in their flight seven millions in currency, which were withdrawn from circulation. An artificial stringency was thus created in Wall Street, and while money rose, stocks fell, and unusual margins were called in. Vanderbilt was carrying a fearful load, and the least want of confidence, the faintest sign of faltering, might well bring on a crash. He had a hundred thousand shares of Erie, not one of which he could sell. He was liable at any time to be called upon to carry as much more as his opponents, skilled by long practice, might see fit to produce. . . . His nerve, however, stood him in at least as good stead as his financial resources. Like a great general, in the hour of trial he inspired confidence. While fighting for life he could "talk horse" and play whist. . . .

As to the useless lumber of conflict, consisting chiefly of the numerous judges of the Supreme Court of New York and their conflicting processes of law, this can be quickly disposed of. Judge Gilbert was soon out of the field. His process had done its work, and the Erie councilors hardly deigned upon the 18th, which was the day fixed for showing cause, to go over to Brooklyn and listen to the indignant denunciations on the part of their Vanderbilt brethren, as with a very halting explanation of his hasty action, Judge Gilbert peremptorily denied the request for further delay, and refused to continue his injunction. . . . If Judge Gilbert was out of the fray, however, Judge Barnard was not. The wrath and indignation of this curious product of a system of elective judiciary cannot be described, nor was it capable of utterance. . . . The magistrate became more partisan than were the paid advocates before him, and all seemed to vie with one another in their efforts to bring their common profession into public contempt. Day and night detectives in the pay of suitors dogged the steps of the magistrate, and their sworn affidavits, filed in his own court, sought to implicate him in an attempt to kidnap Drew by means of armed ruffians, and to bring the fugitive by violence within reach of his process. Then, in retaliation, the judge openly avowed from the bench that his spies had penetrated into the consultations of the litigants, and he astonished a witness by angrily interrogating him as to an affidavit reflecting upon himself, to which that witness had declined to make oath. . . . When the Vanderbilt counsel moved to fix a day on which their opponents should show cause why a receiver of the proceeds of the last over-issue of stock should not be appointed, the Judge astonished the petitioners by outstripping their eagerness, and appointing Vanderbilt's own son-in-law receiver on the spot. . . .

All this time injunctions were flying about like hailstones; but the crowning injunction of all was one issued by Judge Clerke, a colleague of Judge Barnard, at the time sitting as a member of the Court of Appeals at Albany, in reference to the appointment of a receiver. . . . He enjoined [Judge Barnard] the individual and he enjoined [Judge Barnard] the judge; he forbade his making any order appointing a receiver, and he forbade the clerks of his court from entering it if it were made, and the receiver from accepting it if it were entered. This extraordinary order, the signing of which by any judge in his senses admits no explanation, the Erie counsel served upon Judge Barnard as he sat upon the bench, and, having done so, withdrew from the courtroom; whereupon the judge immediately proceeded to vacate the order, and to appoint a receiver. . . .

Finally the maze had become so intricate, and the whole litigation so evidently endless and aimless, that, by a sort of agreement of the parties, Judge Ingraham, another colleague of Judge Barnard, issued a final injunction of universal application, as it were, to be held inviolable by common consent, under which proceedings were stayed, pending an appeal. It was high time. . . .

The result of this extraordinary litigation may be summed up in a few words. It had two branches: one, the appointment of a receiver of the proceeds of the hundred thousand shares of stock issued in violation of an injunction; the other, the processes against the persons of the directors for a contempt of court. As for the receiver, every dollar of the money this officer was intended to receive was well known to be in New Jersey, beyond his reach. Why one party cared to insist on the appointment, or why the other objected to it, is not very apparent. . . . The contempt cases had even less result than that of the receivership. The settlement subsequently effected between the litigants seemed also to include the courts. . . . When the terms of peace had been arranged between the high contending parties, Barnard's rage by degrees subsided, until at last he ceased to rage at all. The penalty for violating an injunction in the manner described was finally fixed at the not unreasonable sum of ten dollars, except in the cases of Mr. Drew and certain of his more prominent associates; their contumacy his Honor held to be too great to be estimated in money, and so they escaped without any punishment at all. The legal profession alone had cause to regret the cessation of this litigation; and as the Erie counsel had $150,000 divided among them in fees, it may be presumed that even they were finally comforted.

It is now necessary to return to the real field of operations, which had ceased on the morning of the 11th of March to be in the courts of law. As the theater widened, the proceedings became more complicated and more difficult to trace, embracing as they did the legislatures of two States, neither of them famed for purity. In the first shock of the catastrophe it was actually believed that Commodore Vanderbilt contemplated a result to open violence and acts of private war. There were intimations that a scheme had been matured for kidnapping certain of the Erie directors, including Mr. Drew, and bringing them by force within reach of Judge Barnard's process. It appeared that on the 16th of March some fifty individuals, subsequently described in an affidavit filed for the special benefit of Mr. Justice Barnard, as "disorderly characters, commonly known as roughs," crossed by the Pavonia Ferry and took possession of the Erie depot. From their conversation and inquires it was divined that they came intending to "copp" Mr. Drew, or in plainer phraseology, to take him by force to New York, and expected to receive the sum of $50,000 as a reward for doing so. . . . From day to day new panics were started, until, on the 19th, Drew was secreted, a standing army was organized from the employees of the road, and a small navy equipped. The alarm spread through Jersey City; the militia was held in readiness; in the evening the stores closed and the citizens began to arm; while a garrison of about a hundred and twenty-five men intrenched themselves around the directors in their hotel. On the 21st there was another alarm, and the fears of an attack continued, with lengthening intervals of quiet, until the 31st, when the guard was at last withdrawn. . . .

The first serious effort of the Erie party was to intrench itself in New Jersey, and here it met no opposition. A bill making the Erie Railway Company a corporation of New Jersey, with the same powers they enjoyed in New York, was hurried through the legislature in the space of two hours, and after a little delay was signed by the governor; and the astonished citizens of the latter State saw their famous broad-gauge road metamorphosed before their eyes into a denizen of the kingdom of Camden and Amboy. . . . The new act of incorporation, however, was but a precaution to secure for the directors of the Erie a retreat in case of need; the real field of conflict lay in the legislature of New York, and here Vanderbilt was first on the ground.

The corruption ingrained in the political system of New York City is supposed to have been steadily creeping into the legislature at Albany during several years past. The press has rung with charges of venality against members of this body; individuals have been pointed out as the recipients of large sums; men have certainly become rich during short terms of office; and, of all the rings which influence New York legislation, the railroad ring is certainly supposed to be the most corrupt and corrupting. . . . Probably no representative bodies were ever more thoroughly venal, more shamelessly corrupt, or more hopelessly beyond the reach of public opinion than are certain of those bodies which legislate for republican America in this latter half of the nineteenth century. Certainly, none of the developments which marked the Erie conflict in the New York legislature of 1868 would tend to throw doubts on this conclusion. . . .

The investigation phase was the first which the Erie struggle assumed in Albany. During the early stages of the conflict, the legislature had scented the carnage from afar. There was "money in it," and the struggle was watched with breathless interest. As early as the 5th of March, the subject had been introduced into the State Senate, and an investigation into the circumstances of the company called for. This committee had its first sitting on the 10th, at the very crisis of the great explosion. But before the investigation was entered upon, [Senator and committee member] Mattoon thought it expedient to convince the contending parties of his own perfect impartiality and firm determination to hold in check the corrupt impulses of his associates. With this end in view, upon the 9th or 10th he hurried down to New York, where he had an interview with the leading Erie directors. . . .

Naturally enough, Mr. Drew and his associates took it into their heads that the man wanted to be bought, and even affirmed subsequently that, at that one interview, he had in pretty broad terms offered himself up for sale. . . . [Two reports, one hostile to the Erie party, one backing it, had been offered to Mattoon for his signature.] To a man of Mr. Mattoon's conscious probity such a position must have been one of terrible responsibility. He expressed a desire to think the matter over. It is natural to suppose, that in his eagerness privately to gain information, Mr. Mattoon had not confined his unofficial visits to the Drew camp. At any rate, his mind was in a state of painful suspense. Throwing the theory of double bribery aside as unsustained by direct evidence, the other theory, that of offended virtue, will alone account for the fact that, after arranging in consultation on Tuesday for a report favoring the Drew party, on Wednesday he signed a report strongly denouncing it, and, by so doing, settled the action of the committee. Mr. Jay Gould must have been acquainted with the circumstances of the case, and evidently supposed that Mr. Mattoon was "fixed," as he subsequently declared that he was "astounded" when he heard that Mr. Mattoon had signed this report. . . .

Indeed, Vanderbilt had thus far as much outgeneraled Drew in the manufacture of public opinion, as Drew had outgeneraled Vanderbilt in the manufacture of Erie stock. His whole scheme was one of monopoly, which was opposed to every interest of the city and State of New York, yet into the support of this scheme he had brought every leading paper of New York City, with a single exception. Now again he seemed to have it all his own way in the legislature, and the tide ran strongly against the exiles of Erie. The report of the investigation committee was signed on April 1st, and may be considered the high-water point of Vanderbilt's success. . . .

But when fairly roused by a sense of danger, the Drew party showed at least as great a familiarity with the tactics of Albany as with those of Wall Street. The moment they felt themselves settled at Jersey City they had gone to work to excite a popular sympathy in their own behalf. The cry of monopoly was a sure card in their hands. . . . An active competition with the Vanderbilt roads, by land and water, was inaugurated; fares and freights on the Erie were reduced on average by one third; sounding proclamations were issued; "interviewers" from the press returned rejoicing from Taylor's Hotel to New York City, and the Jersey shore quaked under the clatter of this Chinese battle. The influence of these tactics made itself felt at once. By the middle of March memorials against monopoly began to flow in Albany.

While popular sympathy was thus roused by the bribe of active competition, a bill was introduced into the Assembly, in the Erie interest, legalizing the recent issue of new stock, declaring and regulating the power of issuing convertible bonds, providing for a broad-gauge connection with Chicago, and the guarantee of the bonds of the Boston, Hartford, and Erie, and finally forbidding, in so far as any legislature could, the consolidation of the Central and Erie in the hands of Vanderbilt. . . . In a few days the bill was adversely reported upon, and the report adopted in the Assembly by the decisive vote of eighty-three to thirty-two. This was upon the 27th of March. The hint was a broad one; the exiles must give closer attention to their interests.

As soon as the news of this adverse action reached Jersey City, it was decided that Mr. Jay Gould should brave the terrors of the law, and personally superintend matters in Albany. Neither Mr. Drew nor his associates desired to become permanent residents of Jersey City; nor did they wish to return to New York as criminals on their way to jail. Mr. Gould was to pave the way to a different return by getting the recent issue of convertible bonds legalized. That once done, Commodore Vanderbilt was not the man to wage an unavailing war, and a compromise, in which Barnard and his processes of contempt would be thrown in as a makeweight, could easily be effected. A rumor was therefore started that Mr. Gould was to leave for Ohio, supplied with the necessary authority and funds to press vigorously to completion the eighty miles of broad-gauge track between Akron and Toledo, which would open to the Erie the much-coveted connection with Chicago. Having hung out this false light, Mr. Jay Gould went on his mission, the president of the company having sometime previously drawn half a million dollars out of the overflowing Erie treasury.

The mission was by no means unattended by difficulties. In the first place, Judge Barnard's processes for contempt seemed to threaten the liberty of Mr. Gould's person. He left Jersey City and arrived at Albany on the 30th day of March, three days after the defeat of the Erie bill, and two days before Mr. Mattoon had made up his mind as to which report he would sign. Naturally his opponents were well satisfied with the present aspect of affairs, and saw no benefit likely to arise from Mr. Gould's presence in Albany. The day after his arrival, therefore, he was arrested on the writ issued against him for contempt of court, and held to bail in half a million dollars of his appearance in New York on the following Saturday. He was immediately bailed, of course, and for the next few days devoted himself assiduously to the business he had in hand. . . .

The full and true history of this legislative campaign will never be known. If the official reports of investigating committees are to be believed, Mr. Gould at about this time underwent a curious psychological metamorphosis, and suddenly became the veriest simpleton in money matters that ever fell into the hands of happy sharpers. . . . He dealt in large sums. He gave to one man, in whom he said "he did not take much stock," the sum of $5,000, "just to smooth him over." This man had just before received $5,000 of Erie money from another agent of the company. It would be therefore interesting to know what sums Mr. Gould paid to those individuals in whom he did "take much stock." Another individual is reported to have received $100,000 from one side, "to influence legislation," and to have subsequently received $70,000 from the other side to disappear with the money; which he accordingly did, and thereafter became a gentleman of elegant leisure. One Senator was openly charged in the columns of the press with receiving a bribe of

$20,000 from one side, and a second bribe of $15,000 from the other; but Mr. Gould's foggy mental condition only enabled him to be "perfectly astounded" at the action of this Senator, though he knew nothing of any such transactions. Other Senators were blessed with a sudden accession of wealth, but in no case was there any jot or tittle of proof of bribery. Mr. Gould's rooms at the Develin House overflowed with joyous company, and his checks were numerous and heavy; but why he signed them, or what became of them, he seemed to know less than any man in Albany. This strange and expensive hallucination lasted until about the middle of April, when Mr. Gould was happily restored to the normal condition of a shrewd, acute, energetic man of business; nor is it known that he has ever since experienced any relapse into financial idiocy.

About the period of Mr. Gould's arrival in Albany the tide turned, and soon began to flow strongly in favor of Erie and against Vanderbilt. How much of this was due to the skillful manipulations of Gould, and how much to the rising popular feeling against the practical consolidation of competing lines, cannot be decided. The popular protests did indeed pour in by scores, but then again the Erie secret-service money poured out like water. Yet Mr. Gould's task was sufficiently difficult. After the adverse report of the Senate committee, and the decisive defeat of the bill introduced into the Assembly, any favorable legislation seemed almost hopeless. Both houses were committed. Vanderbilt had but to prevent action, to keep things where they were, and the return of his opponents to New York was impracticable, unless with his consent; he appeared, in fact, to be absolute master of the situation. . . .

The lobby was now full of animation; fabulous stories were told of the amounts which the contending parties were willing to expend; never before had the market quotations of votes and influence stood so high. The wealth of Vanderbilt seemed pitted against the Erie treasury, and the vultures flocked to Albany from every part of the State. Suddenly, at the very last moment, and even while special trains were bringing up fresh contestants to take part in the fray, a rumor ran through Albany as of some great public disaster, spreading panic and terror through hotel and corridor. The observer was reminded of some great defeat, as that on the Chickahominy or at Fredericksburg. In a moment the lobby was smitten with despair, and the cheeks of the legislators were blanched, for it was reported that Vanderbilt had withdrawn his opposition to the bill.

The report was true. Either the Commodore had counted the cost and judged it excessive, or he despaired of the result. At any rate, he had yielded in advance. In a few moments the long struggle was over, and that bill which, in an unamended form, had but a few days before been thrown out of the Assembly by a vote of eighty-three to thirty-two, now passed it by a vote of one hundred and one to six, and was sent to the Governor for his signature. Then the wrath of the disappointed members turned on Vanderbilt. Decency was forgotten in a frenzied sense of disappointed avarice. That same night the *pro rata* freight bill, and a bill compelling the sale of through tickets by competing lines, were hurriedly passed, simply because they were thought hurtful to Vanderbilt; and the docket was ransacked in search of other measures calculated to injure or annoy him. An adjournment, however, brought reflection, and subsequently, on this subject, the legislature stultified itself no more.

The bill had passed the legislature; would it receive the Executive signature? Here was the last stage of danger. For some time doubts were entertained on this point, and the last real conflict between the opposing interests took place in the Executive Chamber at Albany. There, on the afternoon of the 21st of April, Commodore Vanderbilt's counsel appeared before Governor Fenton, and urged upon him their reasons why the bill should be returned by him to the Senate without his signature. The arguments were patiently listened to, but when they had closed the Executive signature placed the seal of success upon Mr. Gould's labors at Albany. Even here the voice of calumny was not silent. . . . The very sum which had been paid, as it was pretended, was named; the broker of Executive action was pointed out, and the number of minutes was specified which should intervene between the payment of the bribe and the signing of the law.

Practically, the conflict was now over, and the period of negotiation had already begun. . . . Early in April Mr. Drew took advantage of that blessed immunity from arrest which the Sabbath confers on the hunted of the law, to revisit familiar scenes across the river. His visits soon resulted in conferences between himself and Vanderbilt, and these conferences naturally led to overtures of peace. Though the tide was turning against the great railroad king, though an uncontrollable popular feeling was fast bearing down his schemes of monopoly, yet he was by no means beaten or subdued. His plans, however, had evidently failed for the present. It was now clearly his interest to abandon his late line of attack, and to bide his time patiently, or to possess himself of his prey by some other method. The wishes of all parties, therefore, were fixed on a settlement, and no one was disposed to stand out except in order to obtain better terms. The interests, however, were multifarious. There were four parties to be taken care of, and the depleted treasury of the Erie Railway was doomed to suffer.

The details of this masterpiece of Wall Street diplomacy have never come to light, but Mr. Drew's visits to New York became more frequent and less guarded, and, by the middle of April, he had appeared in Broad Street on a weekday, undisturbed by fears of arrest, and soon rumors began to spread of misunderstandings between himself and his brother exiles. It was said that his continual absences alarmed them, that they distrusted him, that his terms of settlement were not theirs. It was even asserted that his orders on the treasury were no longer honored, and that he had, in fact, ceased to be a power in Erie.

Whatever truth there may have been in these rumors, it was very evident his associates had no inclination to trust themselves within the reach of the New York courts until a definitive treaty, satisfactory to themselves, was signed and sealed. This probably took place in the neighborhood of April 25th; for on that day the Erie camp at "Fort Taylor," as their uninviting hotel had been dubbed, was broken up, the President and one of the Executive Committee took steamer for Boston, and the other directors appeared before Judge Barnard, prepared to purge themselves of their contempt.

The details of the treaty which had been concluded between the high contracting parties were not divulged to the Board of Directors until the 2nd of July. Upon that day Mr. Eldridge announced the following terms of settlement: Commodore Vanderbilt was to be relieved of fifty thousand shares of Erie stock at 70, receiving therefore $3,500,000 in cash, and $1,250,000 in bonds of the Boston, Hartford, and Erie at 80. He was also to receive a further sum of $1,000,000 outright, as a consideration for the privilege the Erie Road thus purchased of calling upon him for his remaining fifty thousand shares at 70 at any time within four months. He was also to have two seats in the Board of Directors, and all suits were to be dismissed and offenses condoned. . . .

While Vanderbilt and his friends were thus provided for, Mr. Drew was to be left in undisturbed enjoyment of the fruits of his recent operations, but was to pay into the treasury $540,000 and interest, in full discharge of all claims and causes of action which the Erie Company might have against him. The Boston party, as represented by Mr. Eldridge, was to be relieved of $5,000,000 of their Boston, Hartford, and Erie bonds, for which they were to receive $4,000,000 of Erie acceptances. . . . A total of some $9,000,000 in cash was drawn from the treasury in fulfillment of this *settlement,* as the persons concerned were pleased to term this remarkable disposition of property intrusted to their care.

Messrs. Gould and Fisk still remained to be provided for, and to them their associates left—the Erie Railway. These gentlemen subsequently maintained that they had vehemently opposed this settlement, and had denounced it in the secret councils as a fraud and an outrage. This would seem in no way improbable. The rind of the orange is not generally considered the richest part of the fruit; a corporation on the verge of bankruptcy is less coveted, even by operators in Wall Street, than one rich in valuable assets. However, the voice of a clear majority was for peace. Mr. Eldridge counted out his bonds and received his acceptances, and thereupon he resigned his positions as director and president. The Boston raiders then retired, heavy with spoil, into their own North country, where, doubtless, in good time they will introduce the more highly developed civilization of the land of their temporary adoption. Mr. Vanderbilt apparently ceased to concern himself with Erie; and Daniel Drew, released from the anxieties of office, assumed for a space the novel character of a disinterested observer of the operations of Wall Street. Thus, in the early days of July, Messrs. Fisk and Gould found themselves beginning life, as it were, in absolute control of the Erie Railway, but with an empty treasury and a doubtful reputation. . . . Millions were necessary, and must at once be forthcoming.

The new officials were, however, men of resources and were not men of many scruples. The money must be raised, and recent experience indicated a method of raising it. Their policy, freed from the influence of Drew's vacillating, treacherous, and withal timid nature, could now be bold and direct. The pretence of resistance to monopoly would always serve them, as it had served them before, as a plausible and popular cry. Above all, their councils were now free from interlopers and spies, for the first act of Messrs. Gould and Fisk had been to do away with the old board of auditors, and to concentrate all power in their own hands as president, treasurer, and controller. Fortunately for them it was midsummer, and the receipts of the road were very heavy, supplying them with large sums of ready money; most fortunately for them, also, a strange infatuation at this time took possession of the English mind.

Shrewd as the British capitalist proverbially is, his judgment in regard to American investments has been singularly fallible. . . . They now, after all the exposures of the preceding months, apparently because it seemed cheap, rushed into Erie, and the prices in New York were sustained by the steady demand for stock on the foreign account. Not only did this curious infatuation, involving purchases to the extent of a hundred thousand shares, cover up the operations of the new ring, but, at a later period, the date of the possible return of this stock to Wall Street was the hinge on which the success of their culminating plot was made to turn.

The appearance of calm lasted but about thirty days. Early in August it was evident that something was going on. Erie fell suddenly ten percent; in a few days more it experienced a further fall of seven percent, touching 44 by the 19th of the month, upon which day, to the astonishment of Wall Street, the transfer books of the company were closed preparatory to the annual election [for the board of directors.] As this election was not to take place until the 13th of October, and as the books had thus been closed thirty days in advance of the usual time, it looked very much as though the managers were satisfied with the present disposition of the stock, and meant, by keeping it where it was, to preclude any such unpleasantness as an opposition ticket. . . .

The election took place at the usual time, and the ring in control voted themselves without opposition into a new lease on power. Two new names had meanwhile appeared in the list of Erie directors, those of Peter

B. Sweeney and William M. Tweed. The construction of the new board may be stated in a few words, and calls for no comment. It consisted of the Erie ring and the Tammany ring, brought together in close political and financial alliance. . . . This formidable combination shot out its feelers far and wide; it wielded the influence of a great corporation with a capital of a hundred millions; it controlled the politics of the first city of the New World; it sent its representatives to the Senate of the State, and numbered among its agents the judges of the courts. Compact, disciplined, and reckless, it knew its own power and would not scruple to use it. . . .

Comment would only weaken the force of this narrative. It sufficiently suggests its own moral. The facts which have been set forth cannot but have revealed to every observant eye the deep decay which has eaten into every part of our social edifice. No portion of our system was left untested, and no portion showed itself to be sound. The stock exchange revealed itself as a haunt of gamblers and a den of thieves; the offices of our great corporations appeared as the secret chambers in which trustees plotted the spoilation of their wards; the law became a ready engine for the furtherance of wrong, and the ermine of the judge did not conceal the eagerness of the participation; the halls of legislation were transformed into a mart in which the price of votes was higgled over, and laws, made to order, were bought and sold; while under all, and through all, the voice of public opinion was silent or disregarded. . . .

Modern society has created a class of artificial beings who bid fair soon to be the masters of their creator. It is but a very few years since the existence of a corporation controlling a few millions of dollars was regarded as a subject of grave apprehension, and now this country already contains single organizations which wield a power represented by hundreds of millions. These bodies are the creatures of single States; but in New York, in Pennsylvania, in Maryland, in New Jersey, and not in those States alone, they are already establishing despotisms which no spasmodic popular effort will be able to shake off. . . . Even now the system threatens the central government. The Erie Railway represents a weak combination compared to those which day by day are consolidating under the unsuspecting eyes of the community. A very few years more and we shall see corporations as much exceeding the Erie and the New York Central in both ability and will for corruption as they will exceed those roads in wealth and in length of iron track. . . . Already the disconnected members of these future leviathans have built up States in the wilderness, and chosen their attorneys Senators of the United States. Now their power is in its infancy; in a very few years they will re-enact, on a larger theater and on a grander scale, with every feature magnified, the scenes which were lately witnessed on the narrow stage of a single State. The public corruption is the foundation on which corporations always depend for their political power. . . . The lobby is their home, and the lobby thrives as political virtue decays.

COMMODORE VANDERBILT'S DEFEAT did not end the hostilities. Indeed, a fresh round of financial skirmishes and Wall Street battles erupted as the new masters of Erie demonstrated their prowess (at the expense of English investors, among others). But Vanderbilt's admission of failure, together with Drew's expulsion from the Erie board, marked a turning point in Wall Street's history. No one could ignore the power of these robber barons—power over judges and legislators, over investors and average citizens. And when the smoke cleared away, two men stood victorious—two enormously skilled, utterly unscrupulous men: the dour and calculating Jay Gould, and the flamboyant gambler Jim Fisk. Anyone who watched their performance could be sure that they would be heard from again.

As Adams writes, comment can only weaken the force of this narrative. Yet his own concluding observations were remarkably prescient. The rise of the corporation marked a sharp break with the past—as sharp a break, in its own way, as the end of slavery. As shown in the war for the Erie, the corporation, when coupled with the enormous size and wealth of the railway industry, placed unprecedented power in the hands of a few individuals. Even so, those men might never have earned the title "robber baron," had they not treated the public, and their own companies, with such contempt as they amassed staggering wealth. They strewed astonishing corruption in their wake as they marched like conquerors through the halls of government.

Corruption itself was nothing new to American politics. Historian Mark Wahlgren Summers even argues that the corruption of the Gilded Age was exaggerated when considered in light of past decades of graft, nepotism, and political patronage. But the corruption of antebellum years was retail; after the Civil War it reached wholesale proportions, rising with the expanding economy. The railroads pointed the way to the massive industries of the future; their pioneering legal form, the corporation, created a new model for business organization; and their reckless masters showed how ruthlessly great wealth could be used. And no one would prove more ruthless than Jay Gould and Jim Fisk—the most skilled, the most underhanded of the robber barons, lifted to the front rank through their triumph in the Erie war and in subsequent operations.

But the Erie was no exception: even as Vanderbilt battled Drew, Gould, and Fisk, the Crédit Mobilier conspiracy was unfolding within the Union Pacific, the giant railway that was about to complete the nation's first transcontinental line. Crédit Mobilier was a construction firm that did no work; the creation of Thomas C. Durant, a leading figure in the

Union Pacific, it received the exclusive contract to build the company's railway lines.[2] Crédit Mobilier subcontracted the work out, and massively overcharged the railroad (which was heavily subsidized by the federal government). The results were astonishing: Crédit Mobilier invested only $2,700,000, yet it reaped $23,366,319 in profit. When the scandal finally broke, investigators found that dozens of congressmen owned large amounts of the dummy company's stock.[3]

One more railway deserves our attention. Just as the Erie spawned Jay Gould and Jim Fisk, as the Union Pacific gave birth to the Crédit Mobilier and a whole litter of corrupt congressmen, so too did the mighty Pennsylvania Railroad deliver to the world an unusual individual—one who would surpass them all in his skill and power. He was a different kind of man, one destined to build companies rather than loot them. Though he little knew it in the hectic 1860s, one day he would lead the way in the creation of modern industrial America. His name was Andrew Carnegie.

---

[2] Durant named it after the famous French banking concern as a public relations ploy.

[3] Representative George S. Boutwell appears to be one of the few influential members of Congress to have turned down an offer of stock in Crédit Mobilier.

8

THE MAKING OF AN INDUSTRIALIST

Self-made men, it seems, are most often made by chance. Certainly that was the case with a young Scottish immigrant who sat shivering in the O'Reilly telegraph office in Pittsburgh on a January day in 1853. He clearly had capability: he was quick, confident, and cheerful, an intelligent man able to make a future for himself. But the extraordinary future he actually found began with a message from Thomas A. Scott, the superintendent for the western division of the greatest railroad in America, the Pennsylvania. Scott had just received permission from corporate headquarters to establish his own personal telegraph office, and he knew just the lad to run it for him: that bright young clerk named Andrew Carnegie.

For all of Carnegie's abilities, his departure from the O'Reilly office to the personal staff of Thomas Scott made possible his remarkable path to wealth and fame. As an employee of the Pennsylvania Railroad, Carnegie took a place in the most powerful corporation in America (it was said that the Pennsylvania legislature never adjourned until J. Edgar Thomson, the railway's president, had run out of business for it to attend to). As assistant to Scott, a man soon to be the second most powerful official in the Pennsylvania, Carnegie had a personal connection with the world of industry and finance. With his affectionate mentor at his side, the young man built up a network of contacts with bankers, railway men, and manufacturers.

And so Carnegie, the beneficiary of chance and hanger-on of the powerful, saw the opportunity before him and he grabbed it with both hands. He began to make his own investments, learning the role of entrepreneur. His gregarious charm, which had worked so well on Scott, smoothed his way in the business community—and he delivered on his promises, placing his money shrewdly, repaying his debts, and making money for his partners. Scott himself regularly contributed capital to Carnegie's ventures. But through his early career, Carnegie began feeling a path away from railroading (as much as that was possible in the economy of the 1860s) and toward manufacturing.

He discovered a love for making things, second only to his love for making money. In those early years, as a nation seethed first with war and then with the tense peace of Reconstruction, the former telegraph clerk took his first steps toward becoming something more than a wealthy man—something more than a Daniel Drew or a Jay Gould, who looted the corporations in their charge. Rising out of the railroad world of robber barons, Carnegie took his first steps toward becoming a new kind of man: an industrialist.

A Railroad Man Discovers Iron
by Andrew Carnegie

After my return to Pittsburgh it was not long before I made the acquaintance of an extraordinary man, Thomas A. Scott, one to whom the term "genius" in his department may safely be applied. He had come to Pittsburgh as superintendent of that division of the Pennsylvania Railroad. Frequent telegraphic communication was necessary between him and his superior, Mr. Lombaert, general superintendent at Altoona. This brought him to the telegraph operator at nights, and upon several occasions I happened to be the operator.

One day I was surprised by one of his assistants, with whom I was acquainted, telling me that Mr. Scott had asked him whether he thought that I could be obtained as his clerk and telegraph operator, to which this young man told me he had replied: "That is impossible. He is now an operator."

But when I heard this I said at once: "Not so fast. He can have me. I want to get out of a mere office life. Please go and tell him so." The result was I was engaged February 1, 1853, at a salary of thirty-five dollars a month as Mr. Scott's clerk and operator. . . .

RAILROAD SERVICE

Mr. Scott was one of the most delightful superiors that anybody could have and I soon became warmly attached to him. He was my great man and all the hero worship that is inherent in youth I showered upon him. I soon began placing him in imagination in the presidency of the great Pennsylvania Railroad—a position which he afterwards attained. Under him I gradually performed duties not strictly belonging to my department. . . .

Mr. Scott was promoted to be the general superintendent of the Pennsylvania Railroad in 1856, taking Mr. Lombaert's place; and he took me, then in my twenty-third year, with him to Altoona. . . . Mr. Scott remained at Altoona for about three years when deserved promotion came to him. In 1859 he was made vice-president of the company, with his office in Philadelphia. What was to become of me was a serious question.

Would he take me with him or must I remain at Altoona with the new official? The thought was to me unbearable. To part with Mr. Scott was hard enough; to serve a new official in his place I did not believe possible. The sun rose and set upon his head so far as I was concerned. The thought of my promotion, except through him, never entered my mind.

He returned from his interview with the president at Philadelphia and asked me to come into the private room in his house which communicated with the office. He told me it had been settled that he should remove to Philadelphia. Mr. Enoch Lewis, the division superintendent, was to be his successor. I listened with great interest as he approached the inevitable disclosure as to what he was going to do with me. He said finally: "Now about yourself. Do you think you could manage the Pittsburgh Division?"

I was at an age when I thought I could manage anything. I knew nothing that I would not attempt, but it had never occurred to me that anybody else, much less Mr. Scott, would entertain the idea that I was as yet fit to do anything of the kind proposed. I was only twenty-four years old, but my model was Lord John Russell, of whom it was said he would take the command of the Channel Fleet to-morrow. So would Wallace or Bruce. I told Mr. Scott I thought I could. . . . The order appointing me superintendent of the Pittsburgh Division was issued December 1, 1859. . . .

In 1861 the Civil War broke out and I was at once summoned to Washington by Mr. Scott, who had been appointed Assistant Secretary of War in charge of the Transportation Department. I was to act as his assistant in charge of the military railroads and telegraphs of the Government and to organize a force of railway men. . . . It was supposed that the war would soon be over; but it was seen shortly afterwards that it was to be a question of years. Permanent officials in charge would be required. The Pennsylvania Railroad Company was unable to spare Mr. Scott, and Mr. Scott, in turn, decided that I must return to Pittsburgh, where my services were urgently needed, owing to the demands made upon the Pennsylvania by the Government. We therefore placed the department at Washington in the hands of others and returned to our respective positions.

BRIDGE-BUILDING

During the Civil War the price of iron went up to something like $130 per ton. Even at that figure it was not so much a question of money as of delivery. The railway lines of America were fast becoming dangerous for want of new rails, and this state of affairs led me to organize in 1864 a rail-making concern at Pittsburgh. There was no difficulty in obtaining partners and capital, and the Superior Rail Mill and Blast Furnaces were built. In like manner the demand for locomotives was very great, and with Thomas N. Miller[4] I organized a prosperous and creditable concern—locomotives made there having obtained an enviable reputation throughout the United States. . . .

When at Altoona I had seen in the Pennsylvania Railroad Company's works the first small bridge built of iron. It proved a success. I saw that it would never do to depend further upon wooden bridges for permanent railway structures. An important bridge on the Pennsylvania Railroad had recently burned and the traffic had been obstructed for eight days. Iron was the thing. I proposed to H.J. Linville, who had designed the iron bridge, and to John L. Piper and his partner, Mr. Schiffler, who had charge of bridges on the Pennsylvania line, that they should come to Pittsburgh and I would organize a company to build iron bridges. It was the first company of its kind. I asked my friend, Mr. Scott, of the Pennsylvania Railroad, to go with us in the venture, which he did. Each of us paid for a one-fifth interest, or $1,250. My share I borrowed from the bank. Looking back at it now the sum seemed very small, but "tall oaks from little acorns grow."

In this way was organized in 1862 the firm of Piper and Schiffler which was merged into the Keystone Bridge Company in 1863—a name which I remember I was proud of having thought of as being most appropriate for a bridge-building concern in the State of Pennsylvania, the Keystone State. From this beginning iron bridges came generally into use in America, indeed, in the world at large so far as I know. My letters to iron manufacturers in Pittsburgh were sufficient to insure the new company credit. Small wooden shops were erected and several bridge structures were undertaken. Cast-iron was the principal material used, but so well were the bridges built that some made at that day and since strengthened for heavier traffic still remain in use upon various lines.

The question of bridging the Ohio at Steubenville came up, and we were asked whether we would undertake to build a railway bridge with a span of three hundred feet over the channel. It seems ridiculous at the present day to think of the serious doubts entertained about our ability to do this; but it must be remembered this was before the days of steel and almost before the use of wrought-iron in America. The top cords and supports were all of cast-iron. I urged my partners to try it anyhow, but I remember well when President [Thomas L.] Jewett of the railway company visited the works and cast his eyes upon the piles of heavy cast-iron lying about, which were parts of the forthcoming bridge, that he turned to me and said: "I don't believe these heavy castings can be made to stand up and carry themselves, much less carry a train across the Ohio River."

---

4 Thomas Miller was an old friend, and also a railroad man.

The Judge, however, lived to believe differently. The bridge remained until recently, though strengthened to carry heavier traffic. . . .

In Linville, Piper, and Schiffler, we had the best talent of the day— Linville an engineer, Piper a hustling, active mechanic, and Schiffler sure and steady. Colonel Piper was an exceptional man. I heard President Thomson of the Pennsylvania once say he would rather have him at a burnt bridge than all the engineering corps. There was one subject upon which the Colonel displayed great weakness (fortunately for us) and that was the horse. Whenever a business discussion became too warm, and the Colonel showed signs of temper, which was not seldom, it was a sure cure to introduce that subject. Everything else would pass from his mind; he became absorbed in the fascinating topic of horseflesh. If he had over- worked himself, and we wished to get him to take a holiday, we sent him to Kentucky to look after a horse or two that one or the other of us was desirous of obtaining, and for the selection of which we would trust no one but himself. . . .

Talking of the Colonel reminds me of another unusual character with whom we were brought in contact in these bridge-building days. This was Captain Eads, of St. Louis, an original genius *minus* scientific knowl- edge to guide his erratic ideas of things mechanical.[5] He was seemingly one of those who wished to have everything done upon his own original plans. That a thing had been done one way before was sufficient to cause its rejection. When his plans for the St. Louis Bridge [across the Missis- sippi] were presented to us, I handed them to the one man in the United States who knew the subject best—our Mr. Linville. He came to me in great concern, saying: "The bridge if built upon these plans will not stand up; it will not carry its own weight."

"Well," I said, "Captain Eads will come to see you and in talking over matters explain this to him gently, get it into proper shape, lead him into the straight path and say nothing about it to others."

This was successfully accomplished; but in the construction of the bridge poor Piper was totally unable to comply with the extraordinary require- ments of the Captain. At first he was so delighted with having received the largest contract that had yet been let that he was all graciousness to Cap- tain Eads. It was not even "Captain" at first, but " 'Colonel' Eads, how do you do? Delighted to see you." By and by matters became a little compli-

---

[5] Carnegie is writing of Captain James B. Eads, and he is quite inaccurate about Eads's scientific knowledge. Eads was one of the great mechanical geniuses who seemed to populate nineteenth-century America. He *was* eccentric, however, and his exacting demands upon the Keystone Works clouded Carnegie's view of his abilities. Eads's design was extremely advanced, and he succeeded in making the ironworkers produce each part according to his plans. However, Carnegie's account shows the tension between the bridge's architect and its builders.

cated. We noticed that the greeting became less cordial, but still it was "Good-morning, Captain Eads." This fell till we were surprised to hear "Pipe" talking of "Mr. Eads." Before the troubles were over, the "Colonel" had fallen to "Jim Eads," and to tell the truth, long before the work was out of the shops, "Jim" was now and then preceded by a big "D". . . .

When the work was finished, I had the Colonel with me in St. Louis for some days protecting the bridge against a threatened attempt on the part of others [the company chartered to operate the bridge] to take possession of it before we obtained full payment. When the Colonel had taken up the planks at both ends, and organized a plan of relieving the men who stood guard, he became homesick and exceedingly anxious to return to Pittsburgh. He had determined to take the night train and I was at a loss to know how to keep him with me until I thought of his one vulnerable point. I told him, during the day, how anxious I was to obtain a pair of horses for my sister. I wished to make her a present of the span, and I had heard that St. Louis was a noted place for them. Had he seen anything superb?

The bait took. He launched forth into a description of several spans of horses he had seen and stables he had visited. I asked him if he could possibly stay over and select the horses. I knew very well that he would wish to see them and drive them many times. . . . Nothing on earth would induce that man to leave the city until he saw those horses fairly started and it was an even wager whether he would not insist upon going upon the steamer with them himself. We held the bridge. "Pipe" made a splendid Horatius. He was one of the best men and one of the most valuable partners I ever was favored with, and richly deserved the rewards which he did so much to secure.[6]

The Keystone Bridge Works have always been a source of satisfaction to me. Almost every concern that had undertaken to erect iron bridges in America had failed. Many of the structures themselves had fallen and some of the worst railway disasters in America had been caused in that way. Some of the bridges had given way under wind pressure but nothing has ever happened to a Keystone bridge, and some of them have stood where the wind was not tempered. There has been no luck about it. We used only the best material and enough of it, making our own iron and later our own steel. We were our own severest inspectors, and would build a safe structure or none at all. When asked to build a bridge which we knew to be of insufficient strength or of unscientific design, we resolutely declined. Any piece of work bearing the stamp of the Keystone

[6] The great St. Louis bridge, completed on April 15, 1874, was indeed one of the great engineering feats of the age, a span of 515 feet across the Mississippi River.

Bridge Works (and there are few States in the Union where such are not to be found) we were prepared to underwrite. . . .

THE IRON WORKS

The Keystone Works have always been my pet as being the parent of all the other works. But they had not been long in existence before the advantage of wrought over cast-iron became manifest. Accordingly, to insure uniform quality and also to make certain shapes which were not then to be obtained, we determined to embark in the manufacture of iron. My brother and I became interested with Thomas N. Miller, Henry Phipps, and Andrew Kloman in a small iron mill.[7] Miller was the first to embark with Kloman and he brought Phipps [a talented but poor bookkeeper] in, lending him eight hundred dollars to buy a one-sixth interest, in November, 1861. I must not fail to record that Mr. Miller was the pioneer of our iron manufacturing projects. We were all indebted to Tom, who still lives[8] and sheds upon us the sweetness and light of a most lovable nature, a friend who grows more precious as the years roll by. . . .

Andrew Kloman had a small steel-hammer in Allegheny City. As a superintendent of the Pennsylvania Railroad I had found that he made the best axles. He was a great mechanic—one who had discovered what was then unknown in Pittsburgh, that whatever was worth doing with machinery was worth doing well. His German mind made him thorough. What he constructed cost enormously, but when once started it did the work it was intended to do from year's end to year's end. In those early days it was a question with axles generally whether they would run any specified time or break. There was no analysis of material, no scientific treatment of it.

How much this German created! He was the first man to introduce the cold saw that cut cold iron the exact lengths. He invented upsetting machines to make bridge links, and also built the first universal mill in America. All these were erected at our works. When Captain Eads could not obtain the couplings for the St. Louis Bridge arches (the contractors failing to make them) and matters were at a standstill, Kloman told us that he could make them and why the others had failed. He succeeded in making them. Up to that date they were the largest semicircles that had ever been rolled. Our confidence in Mr. Kloman may be judged from the fact that when he said he could make them we unhesitatingly contracted to furnish them.

[7] A more detailed history of the founding of these iron works, the seed of Carnegie's future steel empire, follows in the next selection. However, here he gives a detailed impression of the personalities involved.

[8] Miller died in 1911.

I have already spoken of the intimacy between our family and that of the Phippses. In the early days my chief companion was the elder brother, John. Henry was several years my junior, but had not failed to attract my attention as a bright, clever lad. One day he asked his brother John to lend him a quarter of a dollar. John saw that he had important uses for it and handed him the shining quarter without inquiry. Next morning an advertisement appeared in the *Pittsburgh Dispatch:* "A willing boy wishes to work."

This was the use the energetic and willing Harry had made of his quarter, probably the first quarter he had ever spent at one time in his life. A response came from the well-known firm of Dilworth and Bidwell. They asked the "willing boy" to call. Harry went and obtained a position as errand boy, and as was then the custom, his first duty every morning was to sweep the office. . . . It was the old story. He soon became indispensable to his employers, obtained a small interest in a collateral branch of their business; and then, ever on the alert, it was not many years before he attracted the attention of Mr. Miller, who made a small investment for him with Andrew Kloman. That finally resulted in the building of the iron mill in Twenty-Ninth Street. He had been a schoolmate and great crony of my brother Tom. As children they had played together, and throughout life, until my brother's death in 1886, these two formed, as it were, a partnership within a partnership. They invariably held equal interests in the various firms with which they were connected. What one did the other did.

The errand boy is now one of the richest men in the United States and has begun to prove that he knows how to expend his surplus. Years ago he gave beautiful conservatories to the public parks of Allegheny and Pittsburgh. . . .

Unfortunately Kloman and Phipps soon differed with Miller about the business and forced him out.[9] Being convinced that Miller was unfairly treated, I united with him in building new works. These were the Cyclops Mills of 1864. After they were set running it became possible, and therefore advisable, to unite the old and new works, and the Union Iron Mills were formed by their consolidation in 1867.[10] I did not believe that Mr. Miller's reluctance to associate again with his former partners, Phipps and Kloman, could not be overcome, because they would not control the Union Works. Mr. Miller, my brother, and I would hold the controlling interest. But Mr. Miller proved obdurate and begged me to buy his interest, which I reluctantly did after all efforts had failed to induce him to

[9] See the next selection for a more detailed account of this bitter dispute.

[10] This was a standard Carnegie maneuver: when faced with competition, he frequently started a rival company that would either take over the competitor, or else force the competitor to take over it (at a hefty price, of course).

let bygones be bygones. He was Irish, and the Irish blood when aroused is uncontrollable. Mr. Miller has since regretted (to me) his refusal of my earnest request, which would have enabled the pioneer of all of us to reap what was only his rightful reward—millionairedom for himself and his followers.

THE FULL HISTORY of Andrew Kloman and his mill is a fascinating tale of mechanical genius and savage jealousy.[11] The German was indeed brilliant with iron, as Carnegie writes. But he was also a creature possessed by greed and suspicion. He first established his mill with his brother Anthony; Thomas Miller came in as a silent partner to provide capital for expansion during the Civil War, to meet the demand for artillery pieces and gun carriages. Miller did business with the Kloman brothers as purchasing agent for the Fort Wayne Railroad, so he could not invest directly; instead, he hid his interest by placing it in the name of young Henry Phipps, Jr. (also known as Harry). Phipps was a gifted but poor accountant; he eagerly seized the opportunity to join in a growing manufacturing firm. Andrew Kloman, however, was not content.

His first target was his brother Anthony. Unlike Andrew, Anthony liked the good life too well; he didn't have the stomach for long hours of diligent work, despite the heavy wartime demand. Determined to force his brother out but short of money to do it, Andrew Kloman asked Miller to fund the buyout. Miller agreed, and now openly invested in the firm. He worked out a deal in which Anthony sold his one-third interest to both Phipps (who bought half with money loaned by Miller) and Tom Carnegie (Andrew's younger brother).

Kloman's suspicion, however, only burned higher. First he turned his angry eye on Phipps. The terrified young accountant deflected suspicion over to his former mentor, Thomas Miller; as historian Joseph Frazier Wall writes, Phipps played Iago to Kloman's Othello. Miller was secure in his share of the company, but the feud disrupted business; all of Pittsburgh watched the discord in the prospering iron mill.

Determined to settle the dispute, Miller brought in his old friend Andrew Carnegie. The Scottish immigrant was a busy man, supervising the western division of the Pennsylvania Railroad along with his other businesses and investments; but he agreed to serve as arbitrator. Carnegie worked out a deal that mollified Kloman and Phipps, but left Miller at a disadvantage: under the agreement, the two hostile partners could give Miller sixty days' notice, and then Phipps could buy out his share. Miller

11 The information in this section, and about Carnegie throughout the book, can be found in Joseph Frazier Wall's biography, *Andrew Carnegie* (Oxford University Press, New York: 1970).

resisted, but finally gave in to Carnegie's persistent persuasion once Phipps swore that he would never invoke this clause.

Within a few months, Phipps broke his word and delivered the sixty days' notice. In retaliation, Andrew Carnegie brought the enraged Miller into the new Cyclops iron works. The name was fitting, as Wall writes, for it had its single eye focused on Kloman's mill. For Miller, it was the final chapter of his bitter dispute; for Carnegie, it was just the beginning of his venture into iron and steel.

Betrayal
by Thomas N. Miller

Mr. Carnegie and I had returned from a four months' tour abroad, and Kloman solicited me to buy his brother out. Doing so I proposed to take Mr. [Tom] Carnegie in, with Kloman one-third, myself one-third, Phipps one-sixth, and Carnegie one-sixth. Kloman objected and further said he desired only one partner and that one myself. Carnegie was satisfied as to himself, but urged Phipps to be retained.

I so strongly took this position that I alarmed Kloman, and . . . he turned to Phipps. It was then that avarice, exceeded only by ingratitude, led to my betrayal. . . .[12] This action of Kloman and Phipps led to litigation and, finally, to the compromise made by Andy [Carnegie], and the 60-day clause and its violation within a few months to Mr. Carnegie's great chagrin, as he stated in his presentation of the case to my attorneys: "I put the clause in so that the interest of Miller would fall to Phipps, who had solemnly assured me that he would never touch it, as he owed all he had in the world to Miller."

The violation of this clause led to the building of the Cyclops mills by Andy, myself, and others [mostly the other partners in the Keystone Bridge Works], as he (Andy) was mortified beyond measure at the way I had been treated. The Cyclops was not a failure, but it was scarcely running when the other mill owners [Kloman and Phipps] proposed consolidation; the offer came from them. Andy was ill; we had spent more than we anticipated, though not in debt. I was still in the other mill through Andy's brother, so when Andy broached consolidation I replied promptly, "I'll do anything you desire save personal association with my old protege."

We did consolidate and I became the largest owner, but as a director never attended board meetings, satisfied to leave Andy, who was chair-

---

[12] Kloman placed a notice in the newspaper saying that Miller was not nor ever had been a part of the firm, and was not authorized to do business in its name.

man, to look after affairs. Later, for good reasons, the stockholders, to get my personal services to the board, left the objectionable party [Phipps] out against Andy's protest, but still later, when Andy succeeded in getting him back to fill a vacancy, then I asked Andy to buy me out as he was wedded to one I could not associate with; and Andy did buy me out, but at my own price, and I was glad to get out at that time.

Apart from sentimentalism, Andy was right in standing for the other director, for, as one old bank president says, "No one could keep a check longer in the air without funds to meet it," and I had not that faculty. Andy took no advantage of me. He never did; all was strictly straightforward negotiations. The only fault I found, and in the business world it is rarely deemed a fault, was that to Andy, Napoleon that he was in business, a blunder was worse than a crime. He could forgive the one; he could never excuse the other, and we started as business associates on this line. Since then he has parted with the other [Kloman] with a sigh, saying, as I fancy, "Et tu brute!"

The whirligig of time brings its revenge to see $500 loaned to a friend turned to the burden of $50,000,000. Surely that is sweet revenge. No one, though, can truly say that Mr. Carnegie's wealth burdens him like ordinary mortals. He has a wonderful faculty of enjoying life. . . . To my many friends who daily sympathize with me that I am not a multi-millionaire I simply say that, like the "Vicar of Wakefield," I am "passing rich on"—just what St. Paul prayed to be.

The Birth of an Industry
by Andrew Carnegie

We were young in manufacturing then and obtained for the Cyclops Mills what was considered at the time an enormous extent of land—seven acres. For some years we offered to lease a portion of the ground to others. It soon became a question whether we could continue to manufacture iron with so small an area.

Mr. Kloman succeeded in making iron beams and for many years our mill was far in advance of any other in that respect. We began at the new mill by making all shapes which were required, and especially such as no other concern would undertake, depending upon an increasing demand in our growing country for things that were only rarely needed at first. What others could not or would not do we would attempt, and this was a rule for our business which was strictly adhered to. Also we would make nothing except of excellent quality. We always accommodated our customers, even although at some expense to ourselves, and in cases of dispute we gave the other party the benefit of the doubt and settled. These were our rules. We had no lawsuits.

As I became acquainted with the manufacture of iron I was greatly surprised to find that the cost of each of the various processes was unknown. Inquiries made of the leading manufacturers at Pittsburgh proved this. It was a lump business, and until stock was taken and the books balanced at the end of the year, the manufacturers were in total ignorance of the results. . . . I felt as if we were moles burrowing in the dark, and this to me was intolerable. I insisted upon such a system of weighing and accounting being introduced throughout our works as would enable us to know what our cost was for each process and especially what each man was doing—who saved material, who wasted it, and who produced the best results.

To arrive at this was a much more difficult task than one would imagine. Every manager in the mills was naturally against the new system. Years were required before an accurate system was obtained, but eventually, by the aid of many clerks and the introduction of weighing scales at various points in the mill, we began to know not only what every department was doing, but what each one of the many men working at the furnaces was doing, and thus to compare one with another. One of the chief sources of success in manufacturing is the introduction and strict maintenance of a perfect system of accounting so that responsibility for money or materials can be brought home to every man. Owners who, in the office, would not trust a clerk with five dollars without having a check upon him, were supplying tons of material daily to men in the mills without exacting an account of their stewardship by weighing what each returned in the finished form.

The Siemens Gas Furnace had been used to some extent in Great Britain for heating steel and iron, but it was supposed to be too expensive. I well remember the criticisms made by older heads among the Pittsburgh manufacturers about the extravagant expenditure we were making upon these new-fangled furnaces. But in the heating of great masses of material, almost half the waste could sometimes be saved by using the new furnaces. The expenditure would have been justified, even if it had been doubled. Yet it was many years before we were followed in this new departure; and in some of those years the margin of profit was so small that the most of it was made up from the savings derived from the adoption of the improved furnaces. . . .

My investments now began to require so much of my personal attention that I resolved to leave the service of the railway company and devote myself exclusively to my own affairs. I had been honored a short time before this decision by being called by President Thomson to Philadelphia. He desired to promote me to the office of assistant general superintendent with headquarters at Altoona under Mr. Lewis. I de-

clined, telling him that I had decided to give up the railroad service altogether, that I was determined to make a fortune and I saw no means
of doing this honestly at any salary the railroad company could afford to
give, and I would not do it by indirection. When I lay down at night I
was going to get a verdict of approval from the highest of all tribunals,
the judge within.

I repeated this in my parting letter to President Thomson, who warmly
congratulated me upon it in his letter of reply. I resigned my position March
28, 1865, and received from the men on the railway a gold watch. . . .

Since then I never worked for a salary. A man must necessarily occupy
a narrow field who is at the beck and call of others. Even if he becomes
president of a great corporation he is hardly his own master, unless he
holds control of the stock. The ablest presidents are hampered by boards
of directors and shareholders, who can know but little of the business.

THE CONTRAST BETWEEN the stock exchange manipulations of men
such as Drew, Gould, and Fisk and the close attention to manufacturing
of Andrew Carnegie could hardly be sharper. Carnegie was a man obsessed with building his organizations, with collecting talented staff, with
the details that expanded profits and strengthened his businesses. He had
seized the opportunity created by the connections given him by Thomas
Scott; then he made his own way, leaving the salaried life of railroad work
behind, but taking the connections with him.

But even if he could jettison his old job, he could not escape the gravitational pull of the Pennsylvania Railroad. Manufacturing was overshadowed by the railroad world, which created much of the demand for iron
and steel (Carnegie's own iron works—now dubbed the Union Mills—
specialized in train axles). Even more important were his personal ties to
Thomas Scott and J. Edgar Thomson, two of the wealthiest and most
powerful businessmen in the country. Carnegie had taken a first step toward his destiny of steel; but in the meantime he dabbled in this business
and that, relying heavily on the backing of his two mentors for confidence, advice, and capital. There were still many roads open to Andrew
Carnegie—and he would soon be tempted down the robber baron's path
of intrigue on Wall Street.

III

CRISIS

THE YEAR
1868

9

PRELUDE TO AN IMPEACHMENT

In December 1866, as the battle between the Congress and President Andrew Johnson broke out in full fury, Representative George Boutwell received a summons from Secretary of War Edwin Stanton. At the age of fifty-two, the secretary was a singular figure: a native of Ohio, he had first come into the cabinet in 1860 as a Democrat. He was a staunch Unionist, however, and Lincoln eventually selected him to lead the War Department (in part to expand the political base of his Republican administration). Stanton proved himself to be one of the most capable and unpopular men in government. He ruled his department with an iron fist, stamping out corruption, insisting on efficiency, and occasionally pushing policies at odds with Lincoln's own. He also emerged as an ironclad Radical. So when Johnson set about reestablishing white rule in the defeated South, Stanton stood in his way.

As he sat down with Boutwell in the War Office, he had no thoughts for the financial misadventures of Wall Street, the struggles of unknown Yankees in Yazoo County, or even the fine points of policy as they were worked out in Congress. Something else brought the two men together in this atmosphere of crisis. They both knew that the reach of the federal government was short, that the closest thing to a national bureaucracy was the post office. The Radicals had only one tool to implement their plans for the South—one institution, built by Stanton himself through long years of war: the U.S. Army.

But there was the stumbling block. The greatest, indeed the only, weapon available to Congress was in the hands of its opponent, Commander in Chief Andrew Johnson. As Stanton leaned forward to speak to Boutwell, then, he had little to say about civil rights or suffrage; his words were aimed at a plan to strip the President of the sword he held, and return it to the Republican grip. It was the beginning of a shadow war of intrigue that paralleled the public battles of Reconstruction. Unfortunately for all concerned, it was to be this covert campaign, and not the struggle over the great issues, that would culminate in the impeachment and trial of the President of the United States of America.

Army Maneuvers
by George S. Boutwell

When I arrived in Washington to attend the meeting of Congress at the December session, 1866, I received a note from Mr. Stanton asking me to meet him at the War Office with as little delay as might be practicable. When I called at the War Office, he beckoned me to retire to his private room, where he soon met me. He then said that he had been more disturbed by the condition of affairs in the preceding weeks and months than he had been at any time during the war. He gave me to understand that orders had been issued to the army, of which neither he nor General Grant had any knowledge. He further gave me to understand that he apprehended an attempt by the President to reorganize the Government by the assembling of a Congress in which the members from the seceding States and the Democratic members from the North might obtain control through the aid of the Executive. He then said that he thought it necessary that some act should be passed by which the power of the President might be limited.

Under his dictation, and after such consultation as seemed to be required, I drafted amendments to the Appropriation Bill for the Support of the Army, which contained the following provisions: The headquarters of the General of the Army were fixed at Washington, where he was to remain unless transferred to duty elsewhere by his own consent or by the consent of the Senate. Next, it was made a misdemeanor for the President to transmit orders to any officer of the army except through the General of the Army. It was also made a misdemeanor for any officer to obey orders issued in any other way than through the General of the Army, knowing that the same had been so issued. These provisions were taken by me to Mr. Stevens, the chairman of the Committee on Appropriations. The bill was approved by the President the second day of March, 1867. His approval was accompanied by a protest on his part that the provision was unconstitutional, and by the statement that he approved the bill only because it was necessary for the support of the army.

———

BOUTWELL AND STANTON devised an ingenious plan—a subtle stroke that seemingly did little to diminish the President's authority as Commander in Chief, yet ensured that the implementation of his orders would remain in friendly hands. The two men avoided the blatant step of requiring that all orders go through Secretary Stanton, for he was a highly visible and controversial figure, openly hostile to Johnson's policies. Instead, they determined that the President's control of the military should be funneled through the army's senior officer—a man who had won universal respect and admiration that transcended politics, a man whom the Republicans looked to as their deliverer from Johnson's reign: Ulysses S. Grant.

Grant remains one of the great enigmas of American history. A man of humble birth, he had been an unimpressive student at West Point and an undistinguished peacetime soldier, standing out only during the combat of the Mexican War, in which he served as a highly capable junior officer. He had resigned from the army amid rumors of a drinking problem, and embarked on a miserable life as a civilian failure. Had the Civil War not erupted he might well have died an early and unnoticed death. But the war did indeed erupt, and West Point graduates with fighting experience came into high demand. For Grant, it was an incredible stroke of luck.

Grant proved himself a commander of shrewd intelligence and un-equaled resilience. The military restored him to a carefully structured world that seemed to sustain him, and the conflict gave him a sense of purpose he had clearly lacked as a civilian. His campaigns provided what he craved—*objectives*—and he drove toward each one with unshakable calm and unalterable stubbornness. After he successfully brought the Civil War to its conclusion, he looked for new objectives to conquer—and an adoring public offered him one, as Johnson's troubled adminis-tration hobbled toward its end: the presidency of the United States.

But who was Grant, and what did he stand for? It would not be the last time the nation would ask that of a respected general as he edged to-ward the political arena. But the problem with the victor of Appomattox was that he was notoriously taciturn, keeping his lips clenched around his cigar rather than mouthing proclamations in the manner of George B. McClellan, the last Civil War general to step into presidential politics. Some Radicals were suspicious of the man, especially after he had issued a postwar report on the South that seemed friendly to the defeated Con-federates. But he was the conquering hero; his name was synonymous with Unionism; and few Republicans could believe that he sympathized with Johnson.

And so Boutwell and Stanton inserted Grant into the workings of pol-itics through their plan to make him the valve for Johnson's control of the army. The general, however, saw his future in the White House, and he took counsel of his ambitions as he balanced on the narrow rail be-tween Johnson's angry, imperious demands and the fierce Radical oppo-sition. His unexpected adroitness at political infighting appeared about the time Boutwell passed his bill, when Johnson responded by trying to trick Grant into leaving the country so he could replace him with Gen-eral William T. Sherman (a notorious political conservative).

After that intrigue, Grant would run up against another. When Con-gress passed the army appropriation bill, it passed another law to place its hand over Johnson's grip on the cabinet and federal bureaucracy. It was called the Tenure of Office Act. It dictated that the president could not *remove* officials he had appointed, or install temporary replacements, without the consent of the Senate. Ever wily, Johnson sought to challenge the law by pitting the national hero and Republican favorite against the Radical kingpin in his administration—he promptly removed Stanton from the post of Secretary of War and offered the job to Grant. Here was sublety itself, a truly ingenious stroke. Would the quietly ambitious Grant accept the appointment, with all its power, and alienate the Radicals? Would the Republican Congress vote against their cherished commanding general?

The answers can be found in the memoirs of Julia Dent Grant, the general's wife. Left unpublished until the late twentieth century, her account offers unique insight into the mind and actions of the general—such as they can be found anywhere, for the silent commander rarely spoke his thoughts even with his own spouse. Her words (which begin here with the couple's move into a new house in Washington after the Civil War) shed light on the shrewdness of the stolid man of the hour. He was often underestimated by contemporaries and historians, who failed to see the intelligence and ambition behind his military or political campaigns. But Julia (herself the daughter of a Southern Democratic family) reveals the rich complexities of the silent, smoking figure: the anti-flamboyant man of the people who now mixed with Eastern high society, the seemingly apolitical general who adroitly positioned himself between the conservative President and the Radical Congress. Here this forceful woman shows how her husband calmly steered toward the White House, even as the Capitol drifted into the hurricane of impeachment.

The General's Tactics
by Julia Dent Grant

An upholsterer came down from Philadelphia and placed all the furniture, hung the curtains, etc., so that by the middle of January, 1866, we were snugly located in our lovely Washington home, from which time on we enjoyed—yes, we enjoyed—society, friendship, and love. . . .

Our receptions were brilliant. Our dinners (I do not know how my reputation as a good housewife came about, as I always felt that in that respect I was not as good as I should be) were fairly good and always pleasant. Our reception days were gala days indeed. The house would not hold our guests. The New York papers used to make wonderful cartoons of General Grant's house and surroundings on reception days and of General Grant's hand after the reception. We only *heard* pleasant words and *saw* smiling faces. We entertained many friends and many distinguished soldiers and statesmen. Our sons were going to school in Burlington most of the time, only being at home for the holidays, and were making good progress in their studies. Nellie and Jess went to school in the city.

While in Washington, I saw much of President Johnson's family. The ladies were always cordial and friendly with me. . . . I saw much of the family at the Executive Mansion. Mrs. Johnson was a retiring, kind, gentle, old lady, too much of an invalid to do the honors of the house, which care and pleasure she gladly transferred to her two daughters, Mrs. Patterson and Mrs. Stover, but she always came into the drawing room after the long state dinners to take coffee and receive the greetings of her husband's guests. She was always dressed elegantly and appropriately. . . .

On another occasion[1] . . . the President wished to send him [General Grant] to Mexico on a diplomatic mission, which the General declined, saying, "Mr. President, this is entirely a civil mission, and I really feel that someone else would fill the position more to your satisfaction than I possibly could. I therefore decline the honor which you wish to confer upon me." Mr. Johnson ignored this modest protest and directed Mr. Seward to prepare instructions for General Grant's mission to Mexico; at a meeting of the cabinet later, the President opened the subject by asking Mr. Seward if he had the instructions ready for General Grant.

The papers were produced, and then General Grant said: "Mr. President, I thought you understood that I declined this mission." Whereupon Mr. Johnson expressed great indignation and, with elevated voice, and striking the table with his clenched hand with considerable force, exclaimed turning to his attorney general, "I want to know if there is anything in the commission of the Lieutenant General that gives him the power to refuse to obey the order of the President of the United States?"

The General at once calmly but firmly replied: "I can answer that question, Mr. President, and without consulting your attorney general. I am an American citizen and I can accept or decline *any* appointment the President may offer me." General Sherman was sent on this mission to Mexico. I remember his saying to General Grant on his return, "There was no mission, nothing to do. But after they failed to get you out of the country, I was sent simply to save appearances." . . .

At this time the President's chair proved to be no sinecure, Mr. Stanton hectoring and thwarting him in every possible way. I remember when at Doubling Gap, Pa., where General Grant had left me with the children for a change of air, we expected him time and time again and great preparations were made for him, but we were always disappointed, and at last

[1] This passage, describing Johnson's attempt to send Grant away to Mexico, has been moved for chronological continuity.

he telegraphed me to come home. The General met me at Baltimore. When I asked him why he disappointed us and told him of the preparations made for his amusement, he said: "Well, Stanton was hectoring the President, and I could not leave, as he feared some trouble." He said further: "I think matters are at a standstill, as I think I have pacified the President by explaining Mr. Stanton's manner to him."

The next morning, as we were about to start to church, a messenger arrived from the White House asking for the General's immediate presence. The General did not return until two o'clock, when he informed me that Mr. Johnson had appointed him secretary of war. He said Johnson had been thinking it all over, had worked himself up to a white heat of indignation, had made up his mind to remove Stanton, and had asked him if he would accept the porfolio of secretary of war. He said: "And I consented to do so, as I think it most important that someone should be there who cannot be used." He said further: "Stanton would have gone and on a double-quick long ago if I had been President. He was very offensive, voting *'nay'* to every suggestion made by the President."

After luncheon, we drove out to the Soldiers' Home, where Mr. Stanton and family were spending the summer. Mr. Stanton was absent, and, after waiting an hour, we started home on the road leading from the south gate of the Soldiers' Home to Seventh Street; there we met Mr. Stanton in his carriage. The General got out and stood on the step of Mr. Stanton's carriage and told him of the President's determination. Mr. Stanton exclaimed: "Ah, I expected it. He could do nothing else and keep his self-respect." The General told him also that the President had offered him the War Department portfolio and that he thought it best to accept, as in his (the President's) present humor it was difficult to tell whom he might appoint. The General said further: "I thought, Mr. Stanton, it was but just to inform you so that you might not be unprepared and might arrange your actions, papers, etc."

I regret to say that the great war secretary entirely forgot this courteous act when a few months later he was reinstated by the Senate. He hastened to the office and took possession, thus entangling General Grant in a very disagreeable controversy with the President, who said that he (General Grant) had promised to keep the portfolio until he was relieved by the President. Whereas, when Mr. Johnson had himself suggested this plan, the General, apprehending some complication, had very respectfully replied: "Mr. President, the law is explicit on this subject," but Mr. Johnson seemed to think that the General should have kept the keys until he informed him of Mr. Stanton's reinstatement.[2]

[2] In this first confrontation with Congress over the Tenure of Office Act, Johnson backed down. He knew now for certain that Grant would not support him—and that the Senate was willing to deny the War Department even to the hero.

And now I must not fail to tell of how General Grant happened to be at the President's levee the evening of January 13, 1868, the night the Senate reinstated Stanton as secretary of war, every circumstance of which I so perfectly remember. I had some ladies visiting me who were very anxious to attend this levee, so I asked the General to be our escort. He, to my surprise, demurred, saying: "I would like to gratify you, but, really, under the circumstances, I do not think I ought to go." I, not knowing to what he referred, urged him, saying: "The ladies would be so disappointed, as we were all dressed to go." He then reluctantly consented.

Just as we were leaving the house, a messenger arrived from the Capitol with a note, which the General read by the gaslight in front of the house. The General hesitated again and said he really ought not to go, as he feared the President would look upon his presence as an expression of sympathy. Not knowing the importance of this implied sympathy, we still urged our desire to go. On our way home, the General said he really felt embarrassed when the President grasped his hand so cordially. The General went early the next morning to his office and to his astonishment found Mr. Stanton already in the war office. Mr. Stanton never once remembered the courtesy, the etiquette, observed and strictly adhered to, when he was displaced and Grant appointed. . . .

Mr. Johnson now became involved in grave political troubles. The South needed and demanded much; the North watched his every move with jealous eyes. Too much precious blood had been shed, too much treasure wasted, for the great sin of rebellion to be too lightly condoned by the government so lately threatened. And it was now that the impeachment trial took place. . . .

There can be no harm in my alluding here to the sentiment so prevalent about this time for a strong centralization of power, which was more than once talked of to me, citing more than one precedent for a man in General Grant's position seizing his opportunity. When I told the General all this, he was very indignant and said *he* would like to see anyone *try it*. It was constantly remarked that General Grant must be our next President, and I knew well that if any cabinet officer should try Grant as Stanton had tried Johnson there would be another impeachment trial, if that was what Mr. Johnson was tried for. It is certainly a very solemn act to bring the ruler of sixty millions of people, placed there by their voluntary votes, before a tribunal for trial as a criminal. . . .

The General was almost constantly surrounded by men of distinction and importance. Our home circle was almost broken up. The two older boys were in school at Burlington, Nellie and Jesse had tutors at home, and when we were not giving dinners ourselves, we were dining out. I remember a great ball at the French minister's and many others. Those four years are to me a pleasant memory of dinners, balls, and receptions, of pleasant people who said kind things, and some pleasant visits away from Washington.

GENERAL GRANT AVOIDED being a tool of the White House, and he had steered clear of alienating Congress (or his family, for that matter, for Julia's father was an outspoken Southern Democrat). He knew that his ambitions were best served by maintaining his posture as an apolitical soldier as the great confrontation moved forward, inexorably, to its dramatic conclusion. The rigid Johnson and the outraged Republicans could abide each other no longer, and so the nation arrived at an unprecedented, shocking moment: the trial of a President.

10

THE TRIAL OF
PRESIDENT ANDREW JOHNSON

Article II, Section 4 of the Constitution of the United States of America is at once highly specific and terribly vague: "The President, Vice President, and all civil Officers of the United States, shall be removed from Office on Impeachment for, and Conviction of, Treason, Bribery, or other high Crimes and Misdemeanors." It details two particular offenses, then strangely throws the door open to just about anything: high crimes *and* misdemeanors. Unfortunately, it says nothing about impeaching a President for announcing that whites must rule and blacks must serve, or for pursuing policies hostile to the unified will of Congress, or for sheer pigheaded incompetence. If the framers of the Constitution had chosen to specify such things as "high crimes and misdemeanors," American history might well have taken a different turn in 1868. For in that year, Andrew Johnson stood trial—and Andrew Johnson may well have been the worst President the nation has ever seen.

Today the history of Johnson's impeachment and trial, like the history of Reconstruction itself, is often seen through a distorted lens, one ground and refined through long years of Southern myth-making. We have been left with an image of crazed extremists in Congress trying to overthrow a brave President. Even John F. Kennedy described Thaddeus Stevens as "the crippled, fanatical personification of the extremes of the Radical Republican movement," and President Johnson as "the courageous if untactful Tennessean who . . . had committed himself to the policies of the Great Emancipator to whose high station he had succeeded." Never mind that the "fanatical" Stevens was a principled fighter for African-American rights, with beliefs that even the most conservative would freely accept today—never mind that a modern-day campaign on Johnson's platform would permanently end any politician's career: the myth was deeply ingrained in American consciousness, and Kennedy's book (*Profiles in Courage*) won the Pulitzer Prize.

As recounted in previous chapters, President Andrew Johnson had actually deepened the trauma of the Civil War. When the fighting ended, white Southerners stood ready to accept social changes they knew the North would demand—some ex-Confederate leaders even endorsed black suffrage. Northerners looked forward to a new era of peace and freedom, as did millions of newly liberated African Americans. But Johnson's policies stalled the arrival of the new era. A Southerner and a Democrat, he seemed to want a return to prewar conditions, minus only slavery. Southern whites leaped at their chance, passing sweeping laws to suppress and control blacks, organizing armed gangs to keep them down. And Johnson tolerated all of it.

On one hand, perhaps African Americans had Johnson to thank for unifying moderates and Radicals. His unyielding opposition to any expansion of rights for the former slaves removed the ground for compromise. His backstage efforts to use his powers of appointment to undo Republican Reconstruction policies—the law of the land, thanks to the overriding of his vetoes—infuriated even conservatives.

For a year before the impeachment, Radicals had been trying to make the intransigent President stand trial. George Boutwell led the first attempt, but failed. Finally, in 1868, they succeeded. Unfortunately, it was on the ground Johnson himself selected—the Tenure of Office Act. While Congress was out of session in late 1867, he once again ordered Secretary of War Stanton to vacate his post. Stanton refused, and in February 1868 the President literally forced him out of office, replacing him with Lorenzo Thomas, the Attorney General. By then the Senate had reassembled, and it voided the change—but this time Johnson refused to abide by its decision. Thomas was no Grant; he remained in office as long as the President ordered him to do so. For Republicans in Congress and across the nation, it was the last straw.

In February 1868, the House of Representatives moved to impeach (that is, to indict) Andrew Johnson of high crimes and misdemeanors. As Johnson hoped, however, nine of the eleven articles of impeachment related to his violation of the Tenure of Office Act, a law that many moderates were somewhat uncomfortable with, as it encroached on an area traditionally ceded to the executive branch. Only two articles—drawn up by Thaddeus Stevens and Benjamin Butler (a former Union general and a skilled Radical congressman from Massachusetts)—explicitly dealt with the real question at hand: Johnson's opposition to Republican Reconstruction laws and policies. These two charged him with denying the powers of Congress and trying to bring it into disgrace.

As Eric Foner writes, there were great weaknesses in this impeachment. It essentially accepted the idea that President Johnson could only be tried for criminal offenses, rather than for creating the present Constitutional crisis. There were also weaknesses in his defense, for his lawyers simultaneously argued that he had complied with the law, for it did not apply in this case (as Lincoln, not Johnson, had appointed Stanton); and that the law was unconstitutional, and so Johnson had violated it to test it before the Supreme Court. In the end, the question really came down to the will of the Senators who sat in judgment to perform the unprecedented act of removing a sitting President from office.

Two of the congressmen who took part in that great struggle were Shelby M. Cullom, representative from Illinois, and John Sherman, senator from Ohio. Both were moderate Republicans, rather than Radicals; Cullom in particular came to regret his bold acts of 1868, as he reflected on that year later in his life. Yet both accurately tell of their feelings at the time, of the excitement of the impeachment, and the breathless anticipation of the verdict—as senators switched sides, wavered, and all came down to a single vote.

Impeachment
by Shelby M. Cullom

The row continued in the Fortieth Congress. Bills were passed, promptly vetoed, and immediately passed over the President's veto. Many of the bills were not only unwise legislation but were unconstitutional as well. We passed the Tenure of Office bill; we attempted to restrict the President's pardoning power; and as I look back over the history of the period, it seems to me that we did not have the slightest regard for the Constitution. . . .

To make the feeling more intense, just about this time Johnson made his famous "swing round the circle," as it was termed.[3] His speeches published in the opposition press were intemperate and extreme. He denounced Congress. He threatened to "kick people out of office," in violation of the Tenure of Office Act. He was undignified in his actions and language, and many people thought he was intoxicated most of the time, although I do not believe this.

The radicals in both the House and Senate determined that he should be impeached and removed from office. They had the votes in the House easily, and they thought they could muster the necessary number in the Senate, as we had been passing all sorts of legislation over the President's veto. When the subject was up, I was doubtful, and I really believe, strong Republican that I was, that had it not been for Judge Trumbull I would have voted against the impeachment articles. I advised with the Judge, for whom I had profound respect. I visited him at his house. I explained to him my doubts, and I recall very clearly the expression he used in reply. He said: "Johnson is an obstruction in the Government and should be removed." . . .

It seems to me difficult to realize that it was as far back as March 2,

[3] This was the name given to a national tour Johnson made in 1866, during which he made several speeches violently denouncing Congress.

1868 that I addressed the House in favor of the impeachment articles. I think I made a pretty good speech on that occasion and supported my position pretty well. I took rather an extreme view in favor of the pre-dominance of the legislative department of the Government, contending that the executive and judiciary departments of the Government, while they are finally responsible to the people, are directly responsible to the legislative department.

The first and principal article in the impeachment proposed by the House was the President's issuance of an order removing Edwin M. Stanton as Secretary of War, he having been duly appointed and com-missioned by and with the advice and consent of the Senate, and the Senate having been in session at the time of his removal. I contended then, on the floor, that such a removal was a violation of the Consti-tution and could not be excused on any pretext whatever, in addition to being a violation of the Tenure of Office Act. I do not intend to go into the details of the various articles proposed by the House; suffice it to say that they were mainly based on the attempted removal of Mr. Stanton and the appointment of Mr. [Lorenzo] Thomas as Secretary of War.

I was very serious in concluding my speech. My words were . . . "His opposition to the laws of Congress on the subject of reconstruction has cost this nation thousands of loyal men who have been murdered in the South on account of their devotion to the flag, and millions of money which is to be added to the enormous public debt to be cast upon the necks of the people. Shall the nation endure it longer? Shall we struggle on and on until the welcome day comes when his term shall expire? The people say 'No'. . . ."

Needless for me to say, that as the subject continued feeling remained at a high pitch in the House. It was debated from day to day. Stevens was urging the impeachment with all the force at his command; some were doubtful and holding back . . . ; some changed—for instance, James G. Blaine, who was taunted by Stevens and sneered at for his change of front. Under the law then existing the President of the Senate succeeded a Vice-President who became, by death or removal of the President, President of the United States. The radicals in complete control—and I have no doubt that Stevens had a hand in it—elected the most radical of their member as President of the Senate—Ben Wade, of Ohio. Johnson removed, Wade would have been President, and the extreme radicals would have been in supreme control of the legislative and executive de-partments of the Government.

This condition is what made Mr. Blaine hesitate. He told me on one occasion: "Johnson in the White House is bad enough, but we know what we have; Lord knows what we would get with old Ben Wade there.

I do not know but I would rather trust Johnson than Wade."[4] But in the end Blaine supported the impeachment articles, just as I did, and as Senator Allison and other somewhat conservative members did, all feeling at the same time a little doubtful of our course.

Stevens, Logan, Boutwell, Williams, and Wilson were appointed managers on the part of the House, and solemnly and officially notified the Senate of the action of the House of Representatives in impeaching the President of the United States. The Senate proceeded without delay to resolve itself as a High Court of Impeachment, for the purpose of trying the President of the United States for high crimes and misdemeanors.

A Vote to Convict
by John Sherman

The trial of this impeachment by the Senate was an imposing spectacle, which excited profound interest during its continuance. It was soon developed that the gravamen of the charges was not the removal of Stanton, but was the attempt of the President to force General Lorenzo Thomas into a high office without the advice and consent of the Senate.

In the trial of this impeachment I wished to be, and I think I was, absolutely impartial. I liked the President personally and harbored against him none of the prejudice and animosity of some others. I knew he was bold and rash, better fitted for the storms of political life than the grave responsibilities of the chief magistrate of a great country. His education, such as it was, was acquired late in life, when his character was formed and his habits fixed. Still, his mind was vigorous and his body strong, and when thoroughly aroused he was an able speaker; his language was forcible and apt and his influence over a popular audience was effective. I disliked above all things to be a judge in his case. I knew some of my associates were already against the President, and others were as decided in his favor. I resolutely made up my mind, so far as human nature would admit, to fairly hear and impartially consider all the evidence produced and all the arguments made.

The counsel for the President were Henry Stanbery, B.R. Curtis, Jeremiah S. Black, William M. Evarts, William S. Groesbeck, and Thomas A.R. Nelson. The managers on the part of the House of Representatives were John A. Bingham, George S. Boutwell, James F. Wilson, John A. Logan,

---

[4] Fear of a Wade presidency swayed more than one vote in the Senate during Johnson's trial. The biggest objection to him was his strong support for a protective tariff and an expansion in the quantity of paper currency.

Thomas Williams, Benjamin F. Butler, and Thaddeus Stevens. The trial lasted nearly two months, was ably conducted on both sides. . . .

I voted for conviction for the reasons stated in the opinion given by me. I have carefully reviewed this opinion and am entirely content with it. I stated in the beginning my desire to consider the case without bias or feeling. . . . I stated the grounds of my conviction that the action of the President, in placing Lorenzo Thomas in charge of the office of Secretary of War without the advice and consent of the Senate, was a clearly illegal act, committed for the purpose of obtaining control of that office. I held that the President had the power to remove Secretary Stanton, but that he had not the power to put anyone in his place unless the person appointed was confirmed by the Senate.

Did the act of March 2, 1867, commonly known as the "tenure of office act," confer this authority? On the contrary, it plainly prohibits all temporary appointments except as specially provided for. . . . I felt bound, with much regret, to vote "guilty" in response to my name.

The Verdict
by Shelby M. Cullom

The trial dragged on from day to day. Part of the time the Senate considered the matter in executive session. The corridors were crowded; and I remember with what astonishment we heard that Judge Trumbull had taken the floor denouncing the proceeding as unworthy of a justice of the peace court. The Illinois delegation held a meeting, and Logan, Farnsworth, and Washburne urged that we unite in a letter to Judge Trumbull, with a view to influencing his vote for conviction, or of inducing him to withhold his vote if he could not vote for conviction. A number of our delegation opposed it, and the letter was not sent. . . .

All sorts of coercing methods were used to influence wavering Senators. Old Bob Schenck was the chairman of this movement, and he sent telegrams broadcast all over the United States to the effect that there was great danger to the peace of the country and the Republican cause if impeachment failed, and asking the recipients to send to their Senators public opinion by resolutions and delegations. And responses came from all over the North, urging and demanding the impeachment of the President.

It is difficult now to realize the intense excitement of that period. General Grant was there, tacitly acknowledged as the next nominee of the Republican party for the presidency. He took no active part, but it was pretty well understood from the position of his friends such as Logan and Washburne,[5] that the impeachment had his sympathy; and in the Senate Conkling was especially vindictive. Grimes, Fessenden, and Trumbull led the fight for acquittal. Many were noncommittal; but in the end the struggle turned on the one doubtful Senator, Edmond G. Ross of Kansas.

It was determined to vote on the tenth article first, as that article was the strongest one and more votes could be mustered for it than any other. It was well understood that the vote on that article would settle the matter.

More than forty-three years have passed into history since that memorable day when the Senate of the United States was sitting as a Court of Impeachment for the purpose of trying the President of the United States for high crimes and misdemeanors. The occasion is unforgettable. As I look back now, I see arising before me the forms and features of the great men who were sitting in that high court: I see presiding Chief Justice Chase; I see Sumner, cold and dignified; Wade, Trumbull, Hendricks, Conkling, Yates; I see Logan as one of the managers on the part of the House; I see old Thad Stevens, weak and wasted from illness, being carried in—all long since have passed to the beyond, the accused President, the members of the high court, the counsel. . . .

As the roll was called, there was such a solemn hush as only comes when man stands in the presence of Deity. Finally, when the name of Ross was reached and he voted "No"; when it was understood that his vote meant acquittal, the friends of the President in the galleries thundered forth in applause.

And thus ended for the first, and I hope the last, time the trial of a President of the United States before the Senate, sitting as a Court of Impeachment for high crimes and misdemeanors.

BY ONE VOTE, Johnson had escaped the disgrace of being the only President to be impeached, convicted, and removed from office. Immediately afterward, Stanton resigned his office, and the President asserted himself once again within his cabinet. Meanwhile, millions of voters screamed in outrage at the seven Republican senators who had voted to acquit. Questions were raised as to whether they had been bought. In fact, no money seems to have changed hands, but a number of Senator Ross's close friends were suddenly appointed to lucrative federal posts. Here, however, another myth of the impeachment grew up—that the seven men became the Seven Martyrs, cast out of their party for their be-

[5] Congressman John A. Logan was a Radical activist who had been a very effective general under Grant's command during the Civil War. Congressman Elihu Washburne was Grant's oldest political ally; he had secured for Grant an appointment as a general when the Civil War broke out.

trayal. Actually all remained active, and campaigned for Grant for President that fall.

The anticlimax of Johnson's acquittal brought to an end the mighty battle between Congress and the White House. The President's career was shattered as his party spurned him. An election loomed in the fall, and everyone's favorite was the conquering general of the Union, Ulysses S. Grant. Another symbol of the great fight passed away that year as well: Thaddeus Stevens, the brave, sharp-tongued champion of equal rights. Though later writers would condemn him after Reconstruction fell into disrepute, Americans in 1868 recognized him as a principled hero. When he died in August, he lay in state in the Capitol, drawing a vast crowd of mourners; only Lincoln's casket attracted more. A man of his beliefs even in death, he was buried (at his request) among African Americans, in an integrated cemetery in Pennsylvania.

But the daily battle for freedom continued in countless towns and counties across the South. For millions of Southern Republicans, white and black, it remained to be seen what the acquittal of Andrew Johnson would really mean.

11

VICTORY IN DEFEAT:
MISSISSIPPI IN 1868

In the summer of 1868, a striking new figure entered Yazoo County; within weeks he would emerge as a hero to local blacks, and a villain to most whites. Today his name is found in few serious works of history, let alone school textbooks, and most likely he will never appear in the African-American pantheon alongside Frederick Douglass and Martin Luther King, Jr. But in the small world of Yazoo City and its surrounding acres, this young man seemed larger than life, a fearless, imposing, eloquent figure who literally laughed at his enemies' revolvers and lynch ropes. His name was William H. Foote, and while he may be forgotten today, he was one of the finest of countless black leaders who helped create Reconstruction at the grass roots.

William Foote was only twenty-five when he appeared in Yazoo County, but already he was the subject of rumors about his dramatic past. Some said he had studied at Ohio's Oberlin College (where Albert Morgan had enrolled). Others said he had actually fought for the Confederacy; he had been born free in Vicksburg, and he was clearly proud of being a man of the South. Whatever the rumors, however, he was now an outspoken Republican, a bold advocate of the idea that African Americans needed to stand up and assert themselves in Mississippi politics. In William Foote, Albert Morgan discovered an important new ally and sometime rival—for Foote always refused to let blacks be taken for granted in the Republican party.

In the summer of 1868, however, Morgan deeply appreciated the power and passion of his new friend. A critical election approached: a vote to ratify the state constitution that Morgan had helped write. The atmosphere across the entire length of Mississippi was tense: conservative white leaders had learned from their mistake in abstaining from the previous election, and they were determined to control the results of this one. For over a century they had held blacks in the bonds of slavery; now they believed that they could hold them down for one day more.

The Ku Klux Klan appeared in full force. First organized in Tennessee in 1866, the collection of terrorist gangs spread across the South—and Mississippi became a Klan stronghold. Nightly raids left a trail of dead and mutilated blacks across the state. White immigrants from the North, including the Morgans, felt its hand as well—though generally with less force and frequency. Democratic leaders drew up plans to control the counting of ballots, just in case the violence and intimidation failed to work as well as planned.

African Americans might well have asked, Where was the army? The election was mandated by the Reconstruction Act, and the military was both its protector and executor. But in Mississippi only 2,000 troops remained to patrol the entire state. Furthermore, the military commander for the region, General Alvan C. Gillem, was a native Southerner and a close friend of President Andrew Johnson. He sympathized with the most reactionary wing of the Democratic party, and he ensured that the election was largely supervised by conservative officers who disliked the very idea of black suffrage. When reports of Gillem's conduct reached the ears of General Grant, he replaced him with General Irwin McDowell, a man who believed in carrying out a free election. But it was too late; he had no time to reverse Gillem's well-laid plans. Nor would he have time to reverse the election's results, for President Johnson stepped in and restored Gillem to office only a month later.

Johnson might have been a lame duck in Washington, but his authority was still felt in Mississippi. Congress or no Congress, General Grant or no General Grant, the most hard-line, reactionary, racist segment of the white Democratic party held sway as the new constitution went up for a vote. The Republicans were not idle; they organized clubs and associations across the state, bringing alive a rich political culture in almost every African-American community. In Yazoo County, Albert Morgan and the newly arrived William Foote faced a ferocious battle—one that would send them reaching for their pistols as well as ballots.

A Constitution, the Klan, and the Courageous Mr. Foote
by Albert T. Morgan

By the time the new constitution was ready for submission to the "qualified registered voters of the State" for ratification or rejection, Charles, the General, and a handful of Unionists, who after Stanton's victory over Johnson openly espoused the cause of reconstruction, had succeeded in organizing a Loyal League or a Republican club in nearly every center of population in the county. Thus, for the first time, there was a Republican party in Yazoo. The reader knows through what trial and what sacrifice. Charles was its recognized head; its soul. The General, by common consent, was its chief counselor, while the postmaster and other Northerners, together with the Unionists and the pastor of the little "nigro church" with its official membership, constituted the organizing force.

The delegates to the convention were its representatives. Nine hundred and ninety-nine of every thousand of its membership had never yet voted the Republican ticket.

W.H. FOOTE VS. THE "HUMAN HORNET"

That general election in Mississippi, when all the people participated for the first time, will long be remembered in Yazoo. The governor and all State and county officers, with rare exceptions, were opposed to any reconstruction of the State, and zealous supporters of their own "plan," which was founded upon the idea that, as the State had failed by rebellion to take itself out of the Union, the only act necessary to entitle the people to a share in the government of the whole country was the surrender of their arms. . . . They did *not* mean to surrender by their own act their *legal* claim to be reimbursed from the national treasury to the full extent of the market value of the slaves emancipated by the will of the nation; they did not mean to stop their successors from resolving that, after all, slavery *had not* been destroyed. They did mean to dodge the question, and they did it. . . .

This new constitution dodged nothing. Under its provisions the negro was a man, and all men were to be equal in their right to life, liberty, and the pursuit of happiness. Recognizing the institution of concubinage prevailing in the State as more demoralizing to the family and more destructive of manhood and womanhood than even that slavery which had been "destroyed," this new constitution declared that "All persons who have not been married, but who are now living together, cohabitating as man and wife, shall be taken and held for all purposes in law as married. . . ."

This new constitution would have been accepted without a dissenting voice by the people of California, Iowa, Wisconsin, Ohio, Pennsylvania, Massachusetts, or Maine, as the equal of their own in the propriety and wisdom of its provisions. Yet the people of Yazoo divided upon it so bitterly that one portion of the whites became savage in their efforts to defeat it, while another lent themselves to all manner of devices, by cajolery, by bribery, and by intimidation, to the same purpose.

Opposed to them were Charles, the General, five other Northerners, a handful of Unionists, the freed people—the Republican party of Yazoo. As the laws forbade freed people to own or acquire lands, there was but one plantation in the "hill portion" of the county where the Republican party could hold meetings, and there were but two in the "swamp portion." All other places of meeting were upon the broad highway, in the little negro church we helped to build, the Yankee stronghold, secretly in the cabins of the freed people. . . .

Of the Democrats, one party rode through the county as K.K.K.s, threatening and endeavoring to *scare* the freed people from their right to vote. They did not dare kill, because of the sterling qualities of the Freedman's Bureau agent.[6] But freedmen were whipped and bundled out of their houses without warning and driven upon the highway. On election day the "chairman" of the Democratic party and his numerous coadjutors fastened themselves upon Charles and the General, and assumed to be their "protectors" and "defenders" against calumny or person violence, thinking by this means to arouse a suspicion in the minds of the freed people that, at the last moment, they had been either converted, bribed, or driven to join the side of "the people." And such reports were circulated far and near.

Merchants deliberately rolled out of their warehouses barrels of flour, huge sides of bacon, or pork or tossed out pairs of shoes, boots, pants, coats, hats, dresses, nay, money, which was freely and openly tendered to the freed people. . . .

"The human hornet"[7] was omnipresent, irresistible, irrepressible. Now on horseback, hunting for voters coming from the country, now running towards Charles or the General, as though he would ride them down to give "the chairman" or some one of his aides an opportunity to interfere for their protection, Henry Dixon was a host in himself. So persistent were the chairman and his aides in their attentions to Charles and the General, so often did they have to "interfere" to "protect" them, so completely were they hemmed in and deprived of their power of locomotion by the crowd pressing about them, the day must have been lost but for the sagacity, courage, and fidelity of the freedmen themselves.

One of these, W.H. Foote, was as active, zealous, and effective for the Republicans as Dixon was for the Democrats. He went everywhere—into the most violent and bloodthirsty crowds of whites—with head erect, brave words of cheer for friends, and only defiance for enemies. He was a "newcomer," and little known.[8]

His audacity shocked the whites as the sudden appearance of some unexpected and invincible force upon the battlefield will shock the grand army about to clutch a great victory. Planters, merchants, doctors, lawyers, all who did not know him, said: "Why! look at that nigro; who is he? He has the audacity of a white man! Where is he from?" Before they had time to rally, Foote would have accomplished his business—retaken some hapless freedman captured by the Democrats, inspired him to

6 [Original author's footnote] There was but one Republican hung during that campaign.

7 Henry Dixon (the "human hornet") was the leader of the most violent faction of white Democrats in Yazoo County.

8 [Original author's footnote] He was a native of Vicksburg.

fidelity just as he was ready to surrender, and would be gone to some other quarter of the town on similar duty.

Hearing that a large body—about four hundred voters—on their way to vote had been halted by Dixon and others of his party, just over the brow of Peak Tenariffe, he procured a horse, rode out to the place, and when met by Dixon with a threat that if he interfered they would shoot him, he replied, "Shoot and be damned!" Then, turning to the freedmen, he cried out, "Men, this is our day. The new constitution is our freedom as well as that of our former masters. If ye reject it, ye reject liberty. Follow me!" They all obeyed.

Dixon and his party had told these freedmen that Captain Morgan, the General, and all the other Yankees "done sold out and left the country" that very morning, and if they went to town there would be bloodshed, because the white people would never submit to be governed by their slaves. Surprised and overwhelmed by the audacity of Foote, nearly the whole party had deposited their ballots before the enemy could recover. Then there would have been bloodshed but for the cool head and brave heart of Charles.

Learning of what had been done, the party that held him prisoner for above three hours broke, and joining their comrades from other points were about to break the "line," as the long file of Republican voters which Foote had rescued was called. Being released, and divining the cause, Charles pursued them, and arrived upon the ground just in time to place himself between the angry and now half-crazed whites and Foote and a handful of freedmen, who, armed mostly with sticks, were "stanin' thar groun'" and "talkin' back" to the whites in a manner most exasperating—to them. Seeing Charles's movement, several of the guard who had done but little else during the election but keep near him and the General, and certain other very solid freedmen, gathered close in about him, literally making a shield for him of their bodies.

But his cool, calm, unimpassioned words—he had purposely left his pistol at home that day—stilled the storm after a brief spell. The whites put up their pistols. Foote and one or two of his party put up theirs. The sticks went back into service as canes, and so, through similar trials, hairbreadth escapes, and exhibitions of sagacity, fidelity, and courage, the election passed and the day in Yazoo was won for the Republicans, without the loss of life. . . .

DEFEATED BUT NOT CAST DOWN

Although Yazoo and a number of other counties were carried for the constitution in the State, it failed of ratification. And as soon as the struggle was over, I found the "little garrison of the Yankee stronghold" in mourning. But the town was in holiday attire, and in place of angry words, threatening gestures, fierce looks, and opprobrious epithets, I was greeted all the way there and upon my arrival with only laughter and ridicule, accompanied with requests intended to be sarcastic.

"How are *yew*, Morgin?"

"Say, got any money left over from yo'r last investment?" . . .

"G'wain back on Tokeba?"

"How's the saw-mill business?" . . .

"Got yo' carpet-bag packed?"

"When ye g'wain to start?"

"Have you found out what O'oophie means yet?"

The only response made by the little garrison was as complete a surprise to the enemy as any of the anti-reconstructionists had yet suffered. When they came downtown next morning the first thing which attracted their notice was "the old flag," flying from a window of the stronghold. There was no mistaking it. There it moved in all its original glory. "Not a stripe erased, not a star obscured." And from its folds rang out, in tones so loud and clear that none mistook their meaning, "The little garrison of the Yankee stronghold in Yazoo may die—it will never surrender."

This was the first "Yankee flag" that the air had been permitted to kiss in Yazoo since the "Yankee soldiers" of General Sherman withdrew from that region. The only one planted in the faces of Yazoo rebels by a private citizen since that one which the Unionist had hauled down in 1860, in obedience to the "will of the people" of Yazoo. . . . Taken all aback by it the rebels lost their cunning. The white boys threw stones at the flag, white male rebels scoffed at it, white female rebels abandoned that street as if infected with small-pox. . . .

Grand old flag! for so it seemed to the freed people. Men, women, and children who beheld it with upturned faces, moistened eyes, and grateful hearts, while they gathered from its ringing tones the courage to hope or, as they often did, stop in the street, lift from their heads the ragged covering they called a hat, and give three cheers for the "Flag of Freedom." . . .

HOW, WHY, AND WHEN THE SOUTH SOLIDIFIED

The vote of Mississippi would not be counted at the ensuing election for President—thanks to the kuklux and anti-reconstructionists, who by fraud, violence, and murder had defeated our new constitution—unless, as many in Yazoo insisted ought to be done, the "sovereign white" people went forward and held the election in their own way, as in times before the war, and trusted to a Democratic President and Congress, which they affected to believe would be triumphantly elected by the North, to recognize its validity. . . .

[They had] finally come to believe what had been told them over and over again by the entire Southern press and by *all* the white leaders, that the Congressional plan had been engineered through Congress, and was being sustained by only a handful of fanatics like Sumner and Stevens, together with the "licentious" and "free love" elements of the country, represented by such women as Harriet Beecher Stowe, and such men as Henry Ward Beecher. . . .

Every utterance by a Northern Republican of note, or by a Northern Republican journal, that was in fact hostile to emancipation or negro suffrage, or that could be made to so appear, was quoted throughout the press of the South, and commented on with direct application to the local leaders in the reconstruction movement. Every Northern newspaper account of violence at the North upon negroes, or of hostility to them, was copied by the Southern newspapers and turned upon the reconstructionists. . . . All these facts, when taken together, made it clear to the [native white] Unionists, with rare exceptions, that the thing we sought for there in Yazoo, after the defeat of the new constitution, had little support anywhere, North as well as South, except among the negroes and a baker's dozen of fanatical leaders in Congress, whose strength with the Northern people would be found to lay with that dim and uncertain margin which existed between downright lunatics and shrewd far-seeing, self-seeking, money-making Yankees. Therefore the white race in Yazoo solidified.

To be sure there were then, as there are now, at least two parties among the whites. One believed that slavery was unconstitutionally destroyed, and that therefore the North would have to pay for the slaves— if only the South would hold out just a little longer. The other party was composed of those who had no faith in the sincerity of Northern professions of regard for sympathy for Unionists or negroes, and meant to look out for number one.

We believed, indeed felt certain, that we knew to the contrary. We believed, almost knew, that Grant would be elected. It was thus a question of endurance. . . .

THE WAR OF THE BADGES

The freed people had observed that the Democrats were wearing Seymour and Blair[9] badges, and heroically started a fund for the purchase of

9 Horatio Seymour and Frank Blair were the Democratic candidates for President and Vice-President, respectively, in 1868. Blair was openly racist, vowing to use the army to restore "white people" to power and denouncing blacks as "a semi-barbarous race" that wanted to "subject the white women to their unbridled lust."

some Grant and Colfax badges. The little garrison were able to contribute a few last dimes for such a purpose, and with the aid of a handful of Northerners, poor as ourselves, and a few Unionists, a sufficient amount was finally gotten together to pay for several hundred. . . .

"Jes' to let um know we doan' 'low ter s'render," as Uncle Peter put it, these badges were to be worn squarely upon the left breast, and as nearly over the heart as convenient. By changing about every patriotic freedman and Unionist in the county would be able to wear one of the badges at the least one whole day before the election. . . . These badges so excited the ire of the enemy that several of our brave friends got themselves into serious trouble on account of them. Woe to the hapless freedman caught wearing one beyond the shadow of the flag flaunting from the Yankee stronghold! If upon the highway he was sometimes seized by the very first "repentant" rebel who met him and whipped or, at the least, robbed of the priceless treasure.

Some not only talked back, they also struck back, and the Bureau agent had a number of cases before him growing out of such conflicts. Grave, dignified, "high-toned, honorable gentlemen" debated seriously whether those wearing them ought not to be arrested under the act of their legislature of 1865–66 prescribing a fine or imprisonment or both in the discretion of the court for "insulting gestures largely, or acts" of "freedmen, free negroes, or mulattoes" against a white man, woman, or child, and many denounced the "practice" as "incendiary," and liable to incite a "wah of races."

Mr. Foote, as he was called by the freedmen, *Foote* as he was termed by the whites for his defiance of them, had wrung from even the Democrats so much concession to his dignity, bravely, almost defiantly, wore one, sometimes two, pinned to the lapel of his coat and insisted upon walking upon the pavement while doing so, in utter disregard of Dixon's oft-repeated commands to "walk in the middle of the street, where other niggers go."

These badges were the cause of domestic troubles almost without number; for if a freedman, having obtained one, lacked the courage to wear it at home on the plantation in the presence of "ole marsa and missus," or of the overseer, his wife would often take it from him and bravely wear it upon her own breast. If in such cases the husband refused to surrender it, as was sometimes the case, and hid it from her or locked it up, she would walk all the way to town, as many as twenty or thirty miles sometimes, and buy, beg, or borrow one, and thus equipped return and wear it openly, in defiance of husband, master, mistress, or overseer. . . .

Those badges were also the cause of endless trouble in the families of the anti-reconstructionists; for the white man's concubine, the mistress's maid, and their cook were liable to appear in the family circle any day with "Grant's picture" upon their breasts. Their children, mingling and uniting together like any other "happy family," divided into hostile factions, and their quarrels and wranglings often led to bloodshed—from the nose of some over-sensitive white boy of the "recognized" side of the family, or from the backs or legs of some too presumptuous "brat" or "pickaninny" of the "unrecognized" side of the family. . . .

But the day of our deliverance was at hand.

BOTTOM RAIL ON TOP

The operations of the ku-klux-klan, as well as its organization up to this time, had been secretly carried on. But now, so strong was their faith that the "Democratic white man's national ticket" would be elected,[10] this organization began a series of public demonstrations—just before the day of election—by way of preparation for future service, as we feared. . . . The night riders of Yazoo had postponed the execution of their "decrees" against the little garrison of the Yazoo stronghold, fearing its effect upon the "god-and-morality party," and now confined their visits to the unprotected cabins of the freed people, some of whom they dragged from their beds, whipped, forced to surrender their badges, or to take an oath never again to meet with the Loyal Leagues, Republican clubs, or try to vote.

By that means, and by parading the streets until after midnight, blowing tin horns and beating tin pans, they expected to create such a terror in the minds of the freed people as would deter them from coming to the succor of the garrison in the Yankee stronghold, when the final assault should be made upon it.

But their racket had an opposite effect. It did not drive the freed people from the town nor prevent them visiting the stronghold in large numbers the two days preceding the election, and on that day, armed with their hard wood sticks. It did, however, disturb the "solid men" of the town in their slumbers, and the *Banner* warned them that they were misdirecting their efforts. That so incensed the "Grand Cyclops" that in its next issue that paper apologized. . . .

But now our deliverance had come.

The first glimmer of light from the sun of the advancing new era which we beheld cast such a shadow over the faces of the Democrats that . . . its reflection lighted up the faces of the freed people, old and young. . . . Long practice had made them expert in reading the faces of the white people, and their judgment upon the meaning of the various shadings in color, as they came and went, was unerring. The "Chairman of the

---

[10] In the presidential election of 1868, the Democrats declared themselves the "white man's ticket."

County Democratic Committee" and the "Grand Cyclops" were the first to receive the news [of Grant's election] and at once went off and got drunk. . . . The planters from the country got drunk before starting homeward, and yelled from the backs of their horses as they rode away, reeling to and fro in their saddles, "Hurrah for Grant! Hurrah for hell!" "O'oophie! Polecat! Carpet-bagger!" and, if perchance they met a group of freedmen, they would stop—as some did—and, as gravely as their maudlin tongues would permit, inform them:

"Bottom rail on top now, sho 'nuff."

Or perhaps inquire of them: "What you all g'wain to do now with yo' god, Mawgin—make him Gov'nur?" If the response was "Yes," as it often was, the rejoinder, as often as not, would be: "That's right, stan' by yo' friends. Hurrah for Mawgin! Hurrah for hell! Ya'er'hah'r'r'r! O'oophie! Polecat!" And ride on.

And its effect upon the freed people surprised everyone, even the Yan-kee garrison. . . . Instead of boisterous or even appropriate manifestations of joy at the election of Grant and Colfax, the only sign of their delight was manifested in their faces. . . . "It'll be a long time before the race'll shut off all feeling of dependence upon the white race. Great many of this present generation never will. Besides, as for me, though I consider my-self just as good as any white man that ever lived, I was raised with the Southern people, and I don't expect them to grow out of their ways much faster than the nigros do out of theirn," Mr. Foote explained. . . .

A WAR REMINISCENCE

Charles appeared to enjoy the change more than anyone else. He no longer had seasons when he seemed to look only at vacancy. On the con-trary, he had an object in view which claimed his attention without vari-ation, and when Congress met he accompanied other members of a committee to Washington for the purpose of presenting the "Mississippi case" to that body. . . .

As for our faithful [former] hands, who had sustained us no less gal-lantly in our political struggle than formerly they had done in our strug-gles on Tokeba, some had been able to eke out a scanty living at odd jobs; some had hired themselves under contracts made before the Bureau agent to native [white] planters in the neighborhood, or had succeeded in obtaining small patches of land to work on their own account. Of this last number, Uncle David was the most successful. . . .

As for Colonel Black, having failed to secure the requisite labor to work Tokeba himself, he had lost a year's rent and one good year's crop, and walked the streets leaning upon his cane, with all the evil spirit sub-dued, except when whisky spirits had possession of him. As for Mrs.

Black, she mourned in sackcloth and ashes the "degeneracy of the times" and her "hard fate." . . . As for the "Grand Cyclops," two continued in their practice of the law "in all the courts of Mississippi," and all of them agreed to "wait and see what would turn up next." . . .

As for the "radical delegates to the black-and-tan convention from Yazoo," Captain Clark accompanied Charles to Washington, the blacksmith rented a small building in Yazoo City, and with the remnant of his convention warrants opened a shop on his own account. And as for me—

On the first day of the battle of Gettysburg, after fighting from early morning to near nightfall, I received a wound which stretched me out upon a cot in a little room in Baltimore, so that for months I could not sit up nor turn over. When at last, the kind, skillful surgeon gave me leave to do so, I was placed in a chair by an open window, from which I could see the hurrying throngs of men, women, and children, the railway train arriving from a distance, the hills and forests beyond, a glorious November sunset, and heard the nurse say I would be allowed to "go home soon," I forgave the rebel who shot me, forgot the sores upon my back, everything in the thrill of the moment, and cried. So now, in this moment of restfulness and joy, I forgave the chairman of the Yazoo County Democratic Committee; the Barksdales, Harrisons, and Kellogs, their poor return for our firm's liberal patronage during our struggle with Colonel Black and his aiders and abettors; Dave Woolridge, who through the "friendship of the whites" had added a hotel to his saloon, and now allowed me to know that I could have my meals at his house . . . ; and even the enemy, male and female, whom I had met in better times and under more favorable auspices, who now began by ones and twos to see me gradually as we passed upon the street, and I returned their salutations, however faint as at first they were, cordially. "The war is over," I said, "let us have peace."

I forgot Tokeba, the "black-and-tan convention," the kuklux, the blows, curses, epithets; the jibes, jeers, and the scorn; all, except the "human hornet"; Ben Wicks, the planter of "many thousand acres and many hundred slaves" formerly; Major Bob Sweet, the bull-dozer; Harry Baltimore, the irreconcilable; Joe Telsub, the K.K.K. commander; Colonel Black; and a few others, who would neither allow me to forgive nor forget, but kept up to the end a spiteful and revengeful warfare. . . .

The change in the character of our quarters—from a "stronghold" to "apartments"—which took place on the departure of my brother for Washington, came near costing the remnant of the little garrison their lives. This was the winter of 1868–69. It occurred about midnight. The General and I had been more than usually absorbed in our legal studies, and had not yet retired. The first note of warning was a shuffling of feet upon the pavement below—the same where our guard to the Sabbath-school used to form—and a low, suppressed tone of command: "Halt, right dress, front, order arms, parade rest." While these commands were being hurriedly given, we sprang to the window, peeped out through the shutters, and saw not less than thirty, perhaps forty men, all disguised in black hoods and gowns, so that they could not have been identified by a passerby, and armed with guns and pistols, and what appeared to be wooden guns—such as are used in drill practice.

Although since the announcement of Grant's election our former precautions had been abandoned, we still kept our Spencers and revolvers within easy reach from the bed. Seizing these and hastily placing an additional prop against the door, we stood ready, "cocked and primed" for an attack almost by the time the klan were at a parade rest. Their only way of approach to our rooms was up the narrow flight of steps between the adjoining building and that in which we were, immediately in front of them, or by going around through the yard of the livery stable and up a narrow, rickety stairway at the rear, which led from the ground to our back gallery. In either case they would have to cross the back gallery a few steps before reaching the door. . . .

We waited in breathless suspense for the first warning of approach up the stairway. After waiting a moment and hearing none, and fearing their purpose might be to fire the building, the General crossed over to the front window to see what the kukluxes were doing. He at once made a sign for me to come to him, which I did. On looking out I saw one whom I took to be Captain Telsub, of the "Cyclops," at the head of the file, in close, whispered conversation with several of the "line" who had gathered about him. They appeared to be divided in opinion about something; for, as the Captain, who was apparently in command, gesticulated in an animated manner with head or hand toward the entrance of the stairway, as if he would go up himself if others would follow, some of those about him would point with equal emphasis toward the window, through the cracks and holes in the plain board shutters of which we were peering down upon them. . . . Finally, several of those in the "line" turned as though they would go away, and the commander yielded, gave the command "attention," "shoulder arms," "right face," and then, uttering altogether a deep groan, followed by curses, they marched away silently as they came.

They had scarcely passed out of sight when we heard a gentle tap at our door. Surprised by this, we did not answer it directly. Then came another, accompanied with a low tone, "Me, let me in."

It was the shoemaker [from downstairs]. The kukluxes had disturbed him, and he had arisen and peeped out, then seized his pistol and listened, while his wife slipped out the back way—to give the alarm to the guard. While thus listening, the shoemaker had been able to satisfy himself that it was the rays of light coming through our shutters which had warned the band that we were not asleep, and that fact had deterred them from their purpose. Shortly afterward there were at least a dozen of our stalwart friends on the back gallery and in our rooms, the greater part of whom remained all night. This was the last appearance of the enemy in disguise.

When next he rode on his raids, he needed no disguise and marched in solid column, nine hundred strong, armed with Winchester rifles, needle guns, double-barrelled shotguns, and with ropes over the pummels of their saddles, and pistols and knives in their belts.

SEQUEL

But I was yet to experience the sequel to that last visit of the kuklux. The General was out of town on some errand, and the only person present was Captain Bishop, a Northerner who, seeing the way we were just coining money with our sawmill on Tokeba in the year 1867, had brought down a portable steam sawmill, and set it buzzing in the brake next to ours. He, too, had passed through such a series of trials as had nearly bankrupted him, and, as others had sometimes done, had come over to lie on our bed, seek consolation from us, and minister to our craving for fellowship and intelligent sympathy.

He had fallen asleep, when there came a rather sharp knocking at the door. On opening it, I was startled by the presence there, on our rear gallery, of several of the irreconcilables, headed by Dave Woolridge and the ex-sheriff. . . . In a bold, brusque manner these two leaders entered our room, the ex-sheriff slightly behind the "nigro" [Woolridge]. Whereupon the following dialogue took place between us:

"Colonel Mawgin, you've been slandering the white people of this Azoo County long enough, and I'm y'here to ask you to take it back, and by—"

Then the ex-sheriff—"And ou' people—"

At that instant the manner of my callers had become so threatening that it amounted to a violent assault, especially when, half advancing, Dave made a movement as though to draw the long sword from his heavy cane while he stood as if about to spring upon me; the ex-sheriff keeping well up with him, while those upon the gallery huddled at the doorway.

Taking in the situation at a glance, and without waiting for the ex-sheriff to finish his sentence, I sprang through the narrow doorway to the adjoining room—the sleeping apartment of the outcasts—seized a loaded navy revolver, and yelling to the sleeping Captain, "Come on, Bishop!" levelled it cocked at the ex-sheriff and shouted: "Get out of here!"

Meanwhile, the Captain, who had been somewhat disturbed by their entrance, though still but half awake, stood at my back with a Spencer, and they "got." We followed only to meet our old stalwart guard hurrying through the rear yard and up the back steps as the last one of the ku-kluxes bustled down the narrow passageway onto the street in front.

Some explanation of the two last assaults upon our quarters may be desirable. We were still "consorting" with negroes "from choice." The desperate element among the anti-reconstructionists . . . were still on a hunt for a "last ditch" in which to spill the "last drop" of their chivalric blood, "by God, sah."

AFTER STANDING OFF the surprise assault, Albert Morgan soon realized that he had passed through the worst—the day of deliverance was indeed at hand. Johnson, General Gillem, and the Democratic party may have stymied the new constitution in Mississippi, but elsewhere in the South the revolution marched steadily forward.[11] Eight Southern states had their ballots counted in the presidential election of 1868, having passed their new constitutions, earning readmission to the Union. Indeed, the national balance was tipped by 450,000 black voters, who cast their ballots virtually unanimously for Grant (the General won with only a 300,000-vote majority).

But the Mississippi experience of fraud and intimidation was repeated elsewhere. The climate for the election had been set by the Democratic vice-presidential candidate, Frank Blair, who attacked Republicans for putting white Southerners under the thumb of "a semi-barbarous race of blacks who are worshippers of fetishes and polygamists." Though presidential candidate Horatio Seymour disapproved of his running mate's language, Southern whites cheered. They did more, in fact: in Louisiana and Georgia, they stole the election through violence and fraud much like that seen in Mississippi's constitutional vote: eleven counties in Georgia with large black majorities recorded not a single Republican ballot.

But the day of deliverance had come. A Republican was now bound for the White House—a man whose name was a rallying cry for those who had stood by the Union through four years of war, for those who had been freed at war's end. The Gilded Age, the age of Reconstruction, was now the age of Grant.

---

[11] The fraud in Mississippi's constitutional ratification vote was apparent to observers. Republicans had a majority of at least 17,000 in the state, as demonstrated by future elections; yet the Democrats defeated the constitution by 7,000 votes.

IV

HOPE

A REPUBLICAN IN THE
WHITE HOUSE
1869

12

THE INAUGURATION OF A GENERAL

When that single saving vote was cast in the great impeachment trial, President Andrew Johnson had won virtually nothing. In terms of policy, he was already beaten. Congress had long since enacted its plan for Reconstruction over his vetoes; his own men had whispered to hesitant senators during the trial that the President would do nothing more to stand in the way after an acquittal. That was not entirely true, of course, but it was clear to all that he was more a dead than a lame duck. His hopes for reelection evaporated; even the Democrats longed to be rid of him. Johnson served out his remaining months quietly, as all eyes turned to his obvious successor: General Ulysses S. Grant.

But who was Grant? Physically, he impressed no one: he was a stocky five foot eight, with stooped shoulders and a perpetually weary expression. He was an outstanding horseman, but this would be counted as more a vice than a virtue in the years ahead (whenever he devoted time to his love for good riding animals). Intellectually, he left no impression either, for he rarely opened his mouth except to puff on the cigar always at hand.

What the country definitely knew was that Grant had saved the Union in his role as commanding general during the final year of the Civil War. Of course, a grumbling campaign had already begun among defeated Confederates to denigrate his accomplishment: they said that Grant was a butcher with his men, that he had simply relied on superior numbers, that he had artlessly bludgeoned the genius General Lee into submission. But the public in 1868 knew better: they had followed four years of war with intense interest, and they knew the details of his individual victories as well as the long sweep of his campaigns. They had seen that only Grant, of all the Union generals, had been able to marshal the sprawling federal forces and carry out a grand strategy for victory.

It had been a demonstration of leadership on a national scale—and now the nation craved leadership more than anything else. The tedious reign of the quarrelsome, obstinate, infuriating Johnson led many voters to wish for the purity of the simple, silent conqueror: a man who had risen to glory without ostentation, who had worn a mud-spattered private's uniform as he commanded the world's mightiest army, who had humbled the arrogance of the slaveowning South.

But the qualities demanded of a wartime general are different from those of a peacetime president, and the nation knew little of what else Grant had to offer. His early life offered no encouragement: after a promising start as a junior officer in the Mexican War, he had resigned from the army during the peace that followed, then failed to make anything of himself as a civilian. Even more troubling (for Republicans) was his lack of a political pedigree. Lincoln had been a founder of the Republican party; and even though the Republicans in Congress hated Johnson, at least they knew where he stood. But Grant was pure enigma.

He did, however, possess the most important ingredient of all: ambition, ambition driven by his long years of obscurity. William S. McFeely, Grant's insightful biographer, has illustrated how deeply he felt the pain of his antebellum failure. But his success in the Civil War had revolutionized both his career and his sense of himself. As a triumphant general, he had basked in the love and praise of the nation. Now he consciously moved forward into the circles of the wealthy and influential, seeking a path to new attainments—pursuing power less for its own sake than for the recognition, the adulation, that it brought. The unspeaking, cigar-smoking general seemed the personification of simplicity; yet beneath his tired expression boiled a strange mix of need and ambition. Nor was political skill itself missing from his arsenal, as seen previously in his deft handling of President Johnson.

So when the Republican party elevated the man who saved the Union to lead the Union, Ulysses S. Grant was more than willing to be lifted up. The war had demonstrated that what he needed was an objective. Forts Henry and Donelson, Vicksburg, or Lee's army: the man who had failed in peace came fully alive, often displaying true genius, when calculating how to capture a designated target. Now the Republicans offered a different kind of objective, one that matched his need for public affection as well as his sense of duty.

The closest witness to his campaign and inauguration was his wife, Julia Dent Grant. She was the daughter of a Southern farmer (who would soon move into the White House with the Grant family), and not without ambition herself. She, too, had felt the humiliation of the long years of obscurity, and she happily soaked up the attention that descended upon her as the general became President. Her account of those hectic months sheds light on her husband's character and on the military circle he still traveled in (led by General Sherman, a sharp-tongued conservative with a notorious hatred for the press). She also reveals what Grant usually did *not* do: discuss his innermost thoughts with his wife. But hers is a rare look at life inside the White House, at the challenges facing a new first lady, at the inner world of a couple well matched in determination and drive.

An Election and a New Home
by Julia Dent Grant

In the winter of 1867–68, I often heard that General Grant was to be nominated for the presidency. I gloried in his position as general-in-chief and preferred it to all others. A soldier had always been my ideal, and I could not bear the idea of giving up his military office for a civil one. The Republican hosts were hurrying to Chicago [for their national convention]. I leaned over his chair and said to him: "Ulys, do you wish to be President?" He replied: "No, but I do not see that I have anything to say about it. The convention is about to assemble, and, from all I hear, they will nominate me; and I suppose if I am nominated, I will be elected."

"And then," I said, "if you are elected, do you think you can give satisfaction? The interests of the people are so widely different; to satisfy one section you must hurt another. Think well of all this, dear Ulys. Think of President Johnson. What a time he has had."

"Oh, Johnson!" he said. Then he earnestly repeated, "I do not want to be President, but I feel that if I am nominated I must accept as a duty and I feel, too, that if I am elected I can give to the widely separated interests and sections of the country more satisfaction than any other man. The South will accept my decision on any matters affecting its interests more amiably than that of any other man. They know I would be just and would administer the law without prejudice." And yet, I had the reputation of having urged the General to accept!

The convention met, and Grant was nominated. Then followed receptions of committees, regiments of soldiers, serenades, delegations from North, East, South, and West, and from every state in the Union. My poor flowers, in which I took such delight, were trampled and crushed under foot again and again, until at last I gave up replacing them. . . . I was intensely interested in the success of our ticket. I became an enthusiastic politician. No delegation was too large, no serenade too long.

The Democratic papers said: "General Grant was no soldier, had never won a victory."[1] Would you believe it! They said: "Grant was not a soldier. It is true there had been victories when he had command, but it was all *luck,* not skill." Mr. Felt of Galena said these statements reminded him of a story of a woodman who chopped and split two or three cords of wood to the other men's one. When their attention was called to this, they said: "Oh, yes, but he is a lucky man." The General's luck, I think, was in his hard knocks. Only think of it! my soldier was no soldier! only a lucky man!

---

[1] Most newspapers in the mid-nineteenth century openly affiliated with one party or the other, and their reporting reflected their political biases. The viciousness of political campaigns at this time was staggering, and would not be matched until the day when groundless insinuations could be quickly spread by fax machine.

They said he was an inebriate and not even an honest one: that he did not pay for his drinks. Of course, I was filled with righteous indignation. One morning while at Galena, I read the following in a paper: "General Grant is now lying confined in his residence at Galena in a state of frenzy and is tearing up his mattress, swearing it is made of snakes."[2] And there sat my dear husband, dressed in his white linen suit, calmly smoking and reading his paper and smiling at my wrathful indignation, saying: "I do not mind that, Mrs. Grant. If it were true, I would feel very badly, perhaps as badly as you do."

General Sherman said to me once, soon after the nomination, "Mrs. Grant, you must now be prepared to have your husband's character thoroughly sifted." "Why General," I exclaimed, "General Grant is my Admirable Crichton. He does all things well. He is brave; he is kind; he is just; he is true." The General, smiling at my enthusiasm, said: "Oh, my dear, it is not what he has done, but what *they will say* he has done, and they will prove too that Grant is a very bad man indeed. The fact is, you will be astonished to find what a bad man you have for a husband." And I was astonished, but, like the General, I grew not to mind it.

The General was triumphantly elected and on March 4, 1869, was inaugurated President of the United States. General Grant left his residence on I Street in his own carriage accompanied by some friends. I know he did *not* ride up to the Capitol with the ex-President. He absolutely refused to do so. I went with a large party to the Capitol, where I heard the oath of office and listened with pride and emotion to the first inaugural address of my husband, the President. He stood for a moment, then bowed his acknowledgment to the wild huzzas of the great throng gathered around the Capitol. He received the greetings of a few friends standing near, then he turned and, hastening towards me, he stooped and kissed me on the cheek and, with a pleasant smile, handed me his *first* inaugural address. He passed on and drove in his own carriage to the White House. I returned with my party to our residence on I Street.

After the President had announced his cabinet, I think his first official act was to appoint his old friend and comrade-in-arms Sherman his successor as general-in-chief of all the armies. This General Grant did in opposition to, in fact against, the earnest protests of many senators and members of Congress, among them Mr. Blaine. They all begged him to pigeonhole this commission, which they said had been created for him (Grant), and he ought to keep and occupy the position again when his term of office as President should expire. But the President said: "No, Sherman must succeed me. I shall send his name in at once, and I hope he will be confirmed without fail." And so General Sherman became general of the armies. It was Grant that made Sherman general-in-chief. . . .

---

[2] A reference to delirium tremens (Grant was known for his taste for liquor).

I found the White House in utter confusion. I felt greatly discouraged, but after a few weeks it began to assume an appearance of order. The servants I had in my home were thoroughly demoralized. Perhaps they thought they were incapable of doing the work in the White House. I was forced to let most of them go, and took with me only my maid, a little girl from Galena; our housekeeper, Mrs. Muller, a most faithful and excellent woman; and faithful Albert Hawkins, our coachman, who is now serving his sixth term as presidential coachman to General Harrison.

Order soon came out of chaos, and by autumn the house was in beautiful condition. I love the dear old house and, if I could have my way, would never have it changed. Eight happy years I spent there—so happy! It still seems as much like home to me as the old farm in Missouri, White Haven.

After much thought and fatigue, I at last had the furniture arranged in suites, so that each room would have its own set. I found it scattered widely in the upper chambers. Chairs and lounges were recovered; the hall carpets, which were much worn and so ugly I could not bear to look at them, were replaced. I also had the reception room to the right of the front entrance thoroughly renovated to be used as a waiting room. We found it had been used as a rendezvous for messengers, ushers, and sweepers, into which they brought their lunch baskets. They also heated their luncheons and smoked their pipes there. These men were both astonished and chagrined when they received orders that thereafter they must appear in dress suits and white gloves. They must take their meals at home and would not be allowed to smoke while on duty at the Mansion; any infringement of the above orders would meet with instant dismissal. Of course, this was largely commented upon by the papers, but it made no difference. The men were well paid and there was no reason why they should not look as neat and respectable as those serving in the houses of private gentlemen.

I was somewhat annoyed by the fact that the grounds back of the Mansion were open to the public. Nellie and Jess, the latter just learning to ride on a velocipede, had no place to play, and no place to walk save on the streets. Whenever we entered these grounds, we were followed by a crowd of idle, curious loungers, which was anything but pleasant. I inquired of the General if the grounds were public. "No," he said. "Then may I have the gates closed?" "Certainly," he said, and the gates were closed. Of course, a ripple of comment followed: "The Grants are getting a little too exclusive." But the children and I had that beautiful lawn for eight years, and I assure you we enjoyed it.

The first reception I held was in the Red Drawing Room. I felt a little shy. I had seen the ladies of the Johnson family receive there and I followed their example and stationed myself back of a white marble table, on which lay a large bouquet. Some of my acquaintances (among whom were dear Mrs. Emory and Mrs. Blair) came in early and at once remonstrated, saying, "Mrs. Grant, you are not going to receive here! If you could only see the throng of visitors already waiting the opening of your doors! Come at once, do, to the Blue Drawing Room."

To this I consented. A column of visitors began passing. They all looked happy and greeted me very kindly. I soon felt at home, as I knew nearly everyone present. Many inquiries were made for the President, "our President." After the first day, I prevailed on the President to assist me, which he willingly did. He came in at the last half of the reception and was usually accompanied by his cabinet officers, my reception day being one of his cabinet days.

One day as I sat in the library already dressed for my reception, one of the ushers appeared at the door and, bowing low, said: "Madam, if any colored people call, are they to be admitted?" I, after a moment's thought, said: "This is my reception day. Admit all who call."

A NEW ERA had begun—an era of hope. Though a large minority of Democrats remained obstinately opposed, the majority of Americans breathed a sigh of relief now that Republicans controlled both the White House and Congress. The bitter partisan battles of the Johnson era were past; the ability of ex-Confederates to resist the new order was damped down, though not snuffed out. And the new President was a proven leader, a man of decisive action.

And yet, wisps of trouble appeared early in the national bonfire of celebration. Julia Dent Grant's seemingly gracious decision at the end of the last selection, for example, foreshadowed problems in her husband's policies. She *allowed* African Americans to be admitted to her receptions, but she *invited* none; she went on to write that Washington's blacks were courteous enough to stay away, sparing her any embarrassment. Grant himself displayed little if any prejudice on a personal level, and he often demonstrated a strong sense of justice in his dealings with African Americans; but whether he would remain true to his instincts remained to be seen. In 1869, however, he was still a shining beacon of hope.

Unfortunately, Congress awarded him a less cordial reception. The post-Civil War years were an age of intense partisan feeling in America, and Grant's lack of a Republican political background troubled Congressional leaders. Accustomed to making his decisions in private after listening to his advisers, he failed to consult the politicians on Capitol Hill before selecting his cabinet. Instead, he turned to two small groups: his tight circle of army subordinates from Civil War days, and the wealthy businessmen who had befriended him in recent years. As a result, his appointments, which included some very capable men, looked to the nation like a pool of military cronies and merchant kingpins. His choices were Congressman Elihu Washburne (who had sponsored Grant's appointment as general at the start of the Civil War) for secretary of state; Alexander T. Stewart, a department store owner and perhaps the nation's wealthiest man, as secretary of the treasury; Jacob D. Cox, a former army subordinate, for secretary of the interior; John A. Rawlins, the President's closest friend and wartime assistant, as secretary of war; Adolph E. Borie, a wealthy Philadelphia businessman, as secretary of the navy; Ebenezer R. Hoar, a Republican party stalwart, as attorney general; and John A.J. Creswell, another party man, as postmaster general.

His silence was a mistake: Congress had never been more powerful than after its near-climactic showdown with Andrew Johnson, and it resented Grant's utter failure to consult the Senate about his choices, prior to sending their names in for ratification. Furthermore, party loyalty was considered the first qualification for a presidential appointment, but only two of the new men were Republican loyalists. Senator Charles Sumner decided to deliver a smart slap to the administration's snout by blasting the most important appointment—Alexander T. Stewart, the new secretary of the treasury. Stewart was staggeringly rich, and he and his wife had befriended the Grants; but he was not known to be much of a Republican. Senator Sumner uncovered a law, dating back to the late eighteenth century, that barred anyone who was engaged in trade from running the treasury department. Grant accepted the defeat, and instead appointed the capable Radical congressman George S. Boutwell. But resentment of Sumner's interference smouldered in the general's mind.

Another quick turnabout shook the administration as well. For some reason, Elihu Washburne quickly resigned as secretary of state, and became minister to France. Rumor had it, reports William McFeely, that Grant had hastily promised the state department's top post to his old mentor immediately after his election victory, then realized the rural Illinois representative would be ill suited to the job. Washburne accepted the demotion, and served capably in his new position. In his place came Hamilton Fish, a former governor of New York whose wife was well acquainted with Julia Grant. Fish turned in an admirable performance in his dealings with foreign countries, but his aristocratic, conservative mind-set made him deeply suspicious of Reconstruction.

With Grant's cabinet finally in place, two members of that body vividly recall the actions and character of the new President and his assistants. The first is one of his most respected men—George S. Boutwell, the new secretary of the treasury. Boutwell's portrait offers rich insight into the inner qualities of this almost impenetrable man, who even now was giving new hope to the nation.

The Character of the President
by George S. Boutwell

President Grant looked upon the members of his Cabinet as his family for the management of civil affairs, as he had looked upon his staff as his military family for the conduct of the army, and he regarded a recommendation for a Cabinet appointment as interference. His first Cabinet was organized upon that theory, somewhat modified by a reference to locality.

Mr. [Adolph] Borie, who became Secretary of the Navy, was a most excellent man, but he had had no preparation either by training or experience for the duties of a department. Of this he was quite conscious, and he never attempted to conceal the fact. He often said: "The department is managed by Admiral Porter, I am only a figure-head." In a few months he resigned. His associates were much attached to him. He was a benevolent, genial, well-informed man. His successor, Mr. [George] Robeson, was a man of singular ability, lacking only the habit of careful, continuous industry. . . .

The appointment of Governor Fish to the Department of State gave rise to considerable adverse comment. The chief grounds of complaint were that he was no longer young and that recently he had not been active in political contests. He had been a Whig when there was a Whig Party, and he became a Republican when the Republican Party was formed. As a Whig he had been a member of the House of Representatives and of the Senate of the United States, but he had not held office as a Republican, nor was he known generally as a speaker or writer in support of the policies or principles of the party. His age, then about sixty, was urged as a reason against his appointment. His selection as Secretary was extremely fortunate for General Grant and his administration. Governor Fish was painstaking in his office, exacting in his demands upon subordinates, without being harsh or unjust, diligent in his duties, and fully informed as to the traditions and usages of the department. Beyond these administrative qualities he had the capacity to place every question of a diplomatic character upon a foundation at once reasonable and legal. . . .

[As to President Grant himself,] there was never in his career any ostentatious display of power, never any exercise of wanton or unnecessary authority. He disliked controversy even in conversation, and his reticence when not in the company of habitual companions and trusted friends was due in part to his rule of life on that subject. . . .

The humanitarian side of his nature was strong, but it was not ostentatiously exhibited—indeed it was concealed rather than proclaimed. It was made known to me by his interest and by his lack of interest in appointments in the Treasury Department. Of salaried places he controlled the appointment of General Pleasanton as commissioner of internal revenue, and of that only. On several occasions he suggested the designation of a person named for employment in some menial or non salaried service. The person was in every instance the widow or daughter of some soldier of the war. At intervals, not widely separated, he would bring the subject to my notice. Thus, without a comment, I was forced to follow his suggestions.

The purity of his conversation might have been a worthy example for the most carefully trained person in etiquette and morals. My intercourse with General Grant was intimate through many years, and never on any occasion did he repeat a story or a phrase that contained a profane remark or carried a vulgar allusion. He had a relish for untainted wit and for genial humor, and for humor he had some capacity. He was not an admirer of Mr. Sumner and a trace of irony may be found in a remark attributed to him: When someone said: "Mr. Sumner does not believe in the Bible," General Grant said: "No, I suppose not, he didn't write it."

General Grant was attracted by a horse driven by a butcher. He purchased the animal at the cost of five hundred dollars. He invited Senator Conkling to a drive behind the new horse. The Senator criticized the animal, and said: "I think I should prefer the five hundred dollars to the horse." "That is what the butcher thought," said General Grant.

He was sincere and devoted in his friendships, but when he discovered that his confidence had been misplaced, a reconciliation became impossible. With him there could be no genuine forgiveness, and his nature could not tolerate any degree of hypocrisy. All voluntary intercourse on his part had come to an end. . . .

The imperturbability of spirit which was indicated in his conversation and movements was deep-seated in his nature. I was with him in a night trip to New York, when the train was derailed in part. As the wheels of the car struck the sleepers, he grasped the back of the seat in front of him and remained motionless, while many of the passengers added to their peril by abandoning their seats. One time General Grant received a pair of large roan horses from his farm in Missouri. He invited me to take one of the horses and join him in a ride on the saddle. I declined the invitation. I was then invited to take a seat with him in an open wagon. When we were descending a slight declivity one of the horses laid his weight on the pole and broke it, although the parts did not separate. General Grant placed his foot upon the wheel, thus making a brake and saving us from a disaster. General Grant's faculties were at command on the instant and under all circumstances.

ONE MORE VOICE joins the chorus that remembers the enigmatic President—one more view to ponder in assessing the man who led the nation at this critical point. Jacob D. Cox, an old officer of Grant's and now the secretary of the interior, understood something about the man often missed by both contemporaries and historians: the importance of his closest friends to his sense of direction, to his sense of right and wrong. And no friend was more important than General John A. Rawlins—the dying, tuberculosis-ridden secretary of war.

The American republic stood at a critical crossroads. The congressional plan of Reconstruction was finally taking effect in the South—but white resistance stood prepared to tear it apart by brute force. The economy in the North, and by extension the nation, was increasingly falling under the sway of powerful corporations, led by the mightiest railroads. Issues that now seem arcane—particularly the question of paper currency versus hard money (specie, or gold coinage)—directly affected the lives and prosperity of millions. Public corruption, dating back to before the Civil War, was rising to a crescendo, as seen in the war for the Erie Railroad. As Grant faced this turbulent landscape, his moral compass, John A. Rawlins, lay crippled by the most dreaded disease of the century.

Cox himself was a conservative Republican, and he often disagreed with the passionate, compassionate, dying general from rural Illinois. But he deeply appreciated the role played by Rawlins in Grant's life. His portrait is moving and revealing, offering insight into why the steadfast commander of the victorious Union army led an increasingly troubled administration as President.

Grant Loses His Conscience
by Jacob D. Cox

General Rawlins had died at the beginning of September, 1869, and his death was an irreparable loss to Grant and to the administration. Other men might fill the office of Secretary of War, but no other man could be found who could be the successful intermediary between General Grant and his associates in public duty. His friendship for his chief was of so sacredly intimate a character that he alone could break through the taciturnity into which Grant settled when he found himself in any way out of accord with the thoughts and opinions of those around him. Rawlins could argue, could expostulate, could condemn, could even upbraid, without interrupting for an hour the fraternal confidence and good will of Grant.

He had won the right to this relation by an absolute devotion which dated from Grant's appointment to be a brigadier-general in 1861, and which had made him the good genius of his friend in every crisis of Grant's wonderful career. This was not because of Rawlins's great intellect, for he was of only moderate mental powers. It was rather that he became a living and speaking conscience for his general; as courageous to speak in a time of need as Nathan the prophet, and as absolutely trusted as Jonathan by David.

In military problems Grant had a strong and almost intuitive sagacity in determining upon the path to victory; not always the easiest or the most economical in blood and treasure, but a sure one when his own indomitable courage and will had clear scope. He silently listened to the discussion of such men as Sherman and McPherson, he patiently turned the matter over in his own thoughts, and after a while enounced a decision which showed the aid he got from intelligent debate, while it was clearly marked with his own directness of purpose and boldness of action. Rawlins knew how to bring on such helpful discussion in Grant's presence. He knew how to reinforce the influence of those who deserved to be trusted, and to expose insidious and false friendship. He had blunt, wrathful words of objurgation for those who put in Grant's way temptations which he knew to be dangerous.

A moral monitor and guide not hesitant at big oaths and camp expletives seems a strange type of man, but no one could deny that Rawlins's heart was as true and his perception of the thing demanded by the honor and the welfare of his chief was as clear as his manners and words often were rough.

It will not need argument to show how useful such a friend and counselor might be as a Cabinet officer. He could give warnings that no one else could utter; he could insist upon debate and information before settled purposes should be adopted; he would know of influences at work that others would learn of only when some important step was already taken; his own openness of character would make him frank in action with his colleagues, and an honorable representative of their general judgment and policy. Rawlins might have differed from Mr. Fish as to the foreign policy of the government, especially in regard to Cuba,[3] but he would have seen to it that no kitchen cabinet committed the President to schemes of which his responsible advisers were ignorant. Indeed, there was no danger that a kitchen cabinet could exist till Rawlins was dead.

———

"NO ONE COULD replace John Rawlins," writes William McFeely. "The meaning of the death of John Rawlins to Ulysses Grant lay not in the removal of an honest voice of humanitarian conscience, great though that loss was. Grant had never seen Rawlins as a mere adviser; he was a friend." With the loss of that friend, he leaned on other advisers and acquaintances—but none shared Rawlins's single-minded devotion to Grant's own welfare. Ulysses and Julia now spent more and more time

[3] Cuba was seething in revolt against the colonial rule of Spain; Secretary of State Fish took a characteristically conservative view of the situation, and wished to avoid involvement, while the passionate Rawlins wanted to aid the Cuban rebels.

with the wealthy, conservative families of New York and Philadelphia; assistants such as Orville Babcock—a man who would emerge as the personification of Gilded Age morality—stepped into the breach left by Rawlins's death. The advice of Secretary of State Fish, who had little time for African Americans, played an ever greater role in Grant's decisions. But the former general in chief did not simply go to pieces at the death of his friend; he possessed his own moral force, which in his first term would make him the embodiment of freedom in the teeming South.

13
MISSISSIPPI RISES

Albert Morgan and John Lynch were exultant. Through four long years they had fought the forces of white supremacy—in election rallies, in court, in tense confrontations on streets red with the mud of Mississippi clay. Now General Ulysses S. Grant, slayer of the slave republic, was taking the oath of office as President, and triumph could not be far behind. But it was another general who tilted the battle in the state—a recently arrived New England Yankee, the new military governor Adelbert Ames.

General Ames was one of those rare individuals who arrive on the historical scene perfectly equipped to shift the course of events. As historian Richard Nelson Current writes, "He embodied the traditions of his Pilgrim and Puritan ancestors"—the son of a sea captain, a world traveler, an outstanding student, a firm abolitionist, a shining star as a cadet at West Point. At the first battle of Bull Run, he won the Congressional Medal of Honor for refusing to flee the field along with the rest of the panic-stricken Union army. Shot in the thigh, he stood his ground, issuing orders to his artillery battery until he collapsed from loss of blood. Like Albert Morgan, he fought in some of the bloodiest battles of the war: the Peninsula campaign, Antietam, Fredericksburg, Gettysburg, Petersburg, and the capture of Fort Fisher. He earned the rank of major general of volunteers, with a regular army rank of lieutenant colonel.[4] After the war, he served with occupation forces in South Carolina. "I am still at my duties," he wrote to his parents, "which consist in little more than aiding the agents of the Treasury Department and the Freedmen's Bureau in trying white men for killing negroes, of which work we have more than we can well do."[5]

Along with his courage and sense of moral purpose, Ames also possessed another important attribute: political connections. He was a close friend—and soon to be son-in-law—of one of the most powerful Radical Republicans in the House of Representatives, Benjamin Butler of Massachusetts. Butler himself had been perhaps the worst general in the Union army, but he proved to be one of the most effective politicians in the years that followed. The portly, bug-eyed, balding congressman was a

---

[4] The regular army remained a separate organization from the regiments of volunteers who swelled the military to hundreds of times its peacetime size.

[5] Quoted in Richard Nelson Current, *Those Terrible Carpetbaggers* (New York: Oxford University Press, 1988). This book is the source of much of the information presented here about Ames.

paradox particularly characteristic of the age: he relentlessly pursued impeccable policies, pushing for full and equal rights for African Americans—but he was also a master of the darkest political arts, and it was rumored that he was hip-deep in corruption. He also had helped mastermind the failed attempt to throw Andrew Johnson out of the White House.

On June 15, 1868, Ames had been ordered by General Irwin McDowell (his old commander at the first battle of Bull Run) to take over as military governor of Mississippi. Ames immediately ran into two problems: first, the civilian governor, Benjamin G. Humphreys (a former Confederate general), refused to leave office. Second, President Johnson replaced McDowell with General Alvan C. Gillem. Gillem had been commander of the region until only a month before, when Grant (as commanding general) ordered McDowell to take his place; but Johnson overrode him, because Gillem was a conservative who strongly sympathized with white-supremacist Democrats in the state. As a result, Ames found himself hamstrung until after Grant's inauguration in March 1869.

The very first day after the inaugural, the new President named Adelbert Ames to command of the military district that included Mississippi, replacing General Gillem. As both provisional governor *and* military commander, with Congress *and* the White House at his back, he now moved forcefully to sweep away the old order. The coming revolution, Ames knew, would be no one-man operation: thousands of local leaders, white and black, from William Foote to Albert Morgan to John Lynch, were waiting for this opportunity to remake Mississippi from the grass roots up. And these were exactly the men he sent for, after he had safely seen the obstinate General Humphreys out the door of the governor's mansion.

Mississippi was rising. A new generation of Southerners, led by Lynch and Morgan, were about to turn the old heart of the Confederacy into the best-run state in all of Reconstruction, and perhaps in the nation. In the passages that follow, these men describe the great advent of change. First to speak is Lynch, the former slave and Republican activist from Natchez who found himself launched into a career in politics. He reveals the local organizing that actually effected the revolution made possible by the arrival of General Ames—as well as the lingering traces of the days when rich planters ran the state (seen in the requirement that officeholders post a bond backed by real estate, which almost no blacks owned). The second voice belongs to Morgan, who vividly portrays the fight for Reconstruction as it was won on the local level, in the streets and fields of Yazoo County. Never vindictive, Morgan sought to expand the base of the Republican party by drawing in Southern whites. Though he had tried to ban former Confederate officers from voting in the state's new constitution, he now refused to accept the lucrative office of sheriff, deferring to a local white man. It was a statesmanlike decision, but one he would have cause to regret.

A General Takes Charge
by John R. Lynch

One of the first acts of Congress after the Presidential election of 1868 was one authorizing the President to submit Mississippi's rejected Constitution once again to a popular vote. The same act authorized the President to submit to a separate vote such clause or clauses of said Constitution as in his judgment might be particularly obnoxious to any considerable number of the people of the State.

It was not and could not be denied that the Constitution as a whole was a most admirable document. The Democrats had no serious objections to its ratification if the clause disfranchising most of their leaders was eliminated. When it became known that this clause would be submitted to a separate vote, and that the Republican organization would not insist upon its retention, no serious opposition to the ratification of the Constitution was anticipated. And, indeed, none was made.

The time fixed for holding the election was November, 1869. In the meantime the State was to be under military control. General Adelbert Ames was made Military Governor, with power to fill by appointment every civil office in the State. Shortly after General Ames took charge as Military Governor the Republican club at Natchez agreed upon a slate to be submitted to the Military Governor for his favorable consideration, the names upon said slate being the choice of the Republican organization of the county for county and city officials. Among the names thus agreed was that of the Rev. H. P. Jacobs[6] for Justice of the Peace.

It was then decided to send a member of the club to Jackson, the State capital, to present the slate to the Governor in person in order to answer questions that might be asked or to give any information that might be desired about any of the persons whose names appeared on the slate. It fell to my lot to be chosen for that purpose; the necessary funds being raised by the club to pay for my expenses. I accepted the mission, contingent upon my employer's granting me leave of absence.

Natchez at that time was not connected with Jackson by railroad, so that the only way for me to reach the capital was to go by steamer from

6 Rev. Henry P. Jacobs was a typical grassroots leader of the freed people. In 1856 he took his family on a daring escape north from slavery in Alabama. He was ordained a Baptist minister and moved to Natchez after the war, and eventually became Lynch's political rival in Adams County.

Natchez to Vicksburg or to New Orleans, and from there by rail to Jackson. The trip, therefore, would necessarily consume the greater part of a week. My employer—who was what was known as a Northern man, having come there after the occupation of the place by Federal troops—not only granted me leave of absence but agreed to remain in the city and carry on the business during my absence.[7]

When I arrived at the building occupied by the Governor and sent up my card, I had to wait only a few minutes before I was admitted to his office. The Governor greeted me cordially and treated me with marked courtesy, giving close attention while I presented as forcibly as I could the merits and qualifications of the different persons whose names were on the slate. When I had concluded my remarks the Governor's only reply was that he would give the matter his early and careful consideration.

A few weeks later the appointments were announced; but not many of the appointees were persons whose names I had presented. However, to my great embarrassment I found that my own name had been substituted for that of Jacobs for the office of Justice of the Peace. I not only had no ambition in that direction but was not aware that my name was under consideration for that or for any other office. Besides, I was apprehensive that Jacobs and some of his friends might suspect me of having been false to the trust that had been reposed in me, at least so far as the office of Justice of the Peace was concerned.

At first I was of the opinion that the only way in which I could disabuse their minds of that erroneous impression was to decline the appointment. But I found out upon inquiry that in no event would Jacobs receive the appointment. I was also reliably informed that I had not been recommended nor suggested by anyone, but that the Governor's action was the result of the favorable impression I had made upon him when I presented the slate. For this, of course, I was in no way responsible. In fact the impression of my fitness for office that my brief talk made upon the Governor was just what the club had hoped I would be able to accomplish in the interest of the whole slate. . . .

After consulting, therefore, with a few personal friends and local party leaders, I decided to accept the appointment although, in consequence of my youth and inexperience, I had serious doubts as to my ability to discharge the duties of the office which at that time was one of considerable importance.

Then the bond question loomed up, which was one of the greatest obstacles in my way, although the amount was only two thousand dollars. How to give that bond was the important problem I had to solve, for, of course, no one was eligible as a bondsman who did not own real estate.

---

7 Lynch's employer, N. H. Black, spent most of his time operating a plantation, and relied entirely on Lynch to run the photography business.

There were very few colored people who were thus eligible, and it was out of the question at that time to expect any white property owner to sign the bond of a colored man. But there were two colored men willing to sign the bond for one thousand dollars each who were considered eligible by the authorities. These men were William McCary and David Singleton.

The law having been duly satisfied in the matter of my bond, I was permitted to take the oath of office in April, 1869, and to enter upon the discharge of my duties as a Justice of the Peace, which office I held until the 31st of December of the same year, when I resigned to accept a seat in the lower branch of the State Legislature to which I had been elected the preceding November. When I entered upon the discharge of my duties as a Justice of the Peace, the only comment that was made by the local Democratic paper of the town was in these words: "We are now beginning to reap the ravishing fruits of Reconstruction."

Victory in Yazoo
by Albert T. Morgan

But the incidents adverted to in the last two chapters [of Morgan's memoirs], while certifying to the desperation and the cunning, also demonstrates the cowardice of the "last ditchers," who, forgetting their oft-repeated pledge to die in it, cleared that historical gully at one bound in their flight for the woods upon the inauguration of President Grant, one of the first acts of whose administration was the appointment of Adelbert Ames, who had been on duty in the State for some time, to succeed Alvin C. Gillem, Johnson's confidant, in the command of the district.

This appointment was received by the kukluxes very much as they had received the news of Grant's election, only "it doubled them all up." The only sign anywhere visible of resistance to his authority was made by the governor, Benjamin G. Humphreys, and he resisted only to the point of drawing out a show of force in the form of two United States soldiers, with fixed bayonets, who one morning showed themselves at the capital, under the command of the "military satrap's[8] underlings." He graciously surrendered "to overpowering force" . . . calmly biding the time when "disenthralled, redeemed" Mississippi should be able to "reassert herself. . . ." All the kukluxes of Yazoo at once imitated the example of their

---

8 [Original author's footnote] General Ames at once made himself known to the K.K.K.s as a satrap.

chief—the "human hornet" and three others alone excepted—and peace reigned throughout the borders of Yazoo.

The remnant of the little garrison now abandoned their old quarters. The General and his family began housekeeping, and I, by express invitation of Mrs. Blank, took board at the house of the lady whose home but little more than a year before had been converted into a "den of infamy" by the presence of my brother and the General.

General Ames's knife cut deep, but the band at the helm in Washington was as steady as Ames's surgery was courageous and skilled. Charles and Captain Clark were still at the national capital. The new military commander, who had heard of the "little Yankee garrison of Yazoo," tendered to me the office of sheriff and tax collector of the county.[9] This I declined, somewhat to his surprise, and when a reason was asked, I said: "I shall prefer to be in the legislature, if I am to be in office under the new regime."

"The sheriff's office in Yazoo County, I am told, is worth in fees and commissions six to ten thousand per year—is that not so?"

"I believe it is."

"Your compensation as a member of the legislature is likely not to exceed a thousand per year."

"True," I replied. "But I do not wish office for the money there may be in it. Until the government to be set up in the stead of the old one shall be established, I shall prefer to be in the legislature, where I think I may be able to do more good."

From that moment this "satrap" became my steadfast friend. He asked me to suggest a name for the place, and also names for all the other offices to be filled in Yazoo County. I then suggested the name of F.P. Hilliard for sheriff.

"Who is he?" said the commanding general.

"An old Unionist, and one who, though not very staunch, has nevertheless been friendly to our 'little garrison.' " . . .

"I think you're making a mistake, but if you request it I'll appoint Mr. Hilliard." I subsequently asked for it, and he was appointed.

General F. E. Franklin was appointed probate judge of the county, a Unionist was appointed to the office of chancery clerk, only second in fees to the sheriff's office, and when they had all been filled, the Unionists—all natives or ex-slaveholders—held all the "offices of profit" in the county.

Then the Northerners said—"Morgan, you're a fool!" and the enemy said—"fool!" and the chairman of the County Democratic Association

9 [Original author's footnote] Under the constitution and laws then in force, the sheriff was ex-officio tax collector of his county.

said—"fool!" I borrowed money enough to see me through, until after the forthcoming election, and began the cultivation of my new field.

At this point, the general commanding asked me to tender to Charles, on his behalf, the office of sheriff and tax-collector for Washington County. That suited me, and I at once telegraphed my brother the fact, advising him to accept it. He accepted.

Then I said, surely we may now have lasting peace in Yazoo, and I began to dig deeper in my new field. . . .

A BRIEF SUMMARY

Across the very threshold of this field lay the following fundamental axiom of the enemy, to wit: "Experience has demonstrated that the white races are the superior, the colored the inferior"; and also its corollary in their system of political ethics, viz.: "Therefore it is God's will that the colored continue in subjection to the white races."

I had felt the full force of the effect of the enemy's attempt to re-establish in Yazoo and in the State the policy which was the logical out-come of that barbarous assumption. The consequences to me had been all the more disastrous because of Charles's assumption at the beginning of our life in the South, that the rebels had been conquered the moment they were disarmed; whereas the fact was, as they all, from babes to Colonel Black, persisted in maintaining, at all times and under all circumstances, that they had only been overpowered.

My experiences had taught me . . . that Colonel Black and his allies were at all times able to demonstrate their right to voice the sentiments and the purposes of "we all" Southerners. At the same time, the physical endurance, industry, loyalty, and trustful appreciation of our hands; the political foresight of the mass of the freed people of the county . . . ; the courage and devotion of the guard of the stronghold; the frenzy for knowledge of the great mass; and the fidelity and patriotism of all during those four years had convinced me that the freed people of the county were the superiors of their former masters in physical strength, in manly courage, in political sagacity, and in love of country, and not inferior in any of the elements of good citizenship. . . .

A CHAPTER OF MISSISSIPPI STATE POLITICS

It mattered nothing to us whether they were negro or mulatto, Northern or Southern, Irishman, Dutchman, Jew, rebel, white, yellow, or red. Were they loyal now? Were they true? Could they weep over the crimes against their colored fellow-citizens committed in the name of liberty, by this mottled tyrant and hybrid of slavery—that Mississippi conspiracy—as bitter tears as over the spectacle of "a white lady cooking her own bread"?

Indeed and in truth this was a new field of labor. But there was a significance attached to the election of Grant to the Presidency which to us went further and meant much more than his personal triumph. It caused us to believe that the heart of the nation was in sympathy with the garrison of that Yazoo stronghold. . . .

But at this point, a little handful of Northern men of the State discovered that the Republican party had been "too proscriptive," and lacked "respectable leadership," and they very soon were known to be having lengthy consultations with members of that "Central Democratic Association." Whether upon their own motion or by invitation of the Democratic Association, I am not able to say. It was said at the time, and it was well known, that Mr. Ethel Barksdale, editor of the *Clarion,* was a chief counsellor and leader in this movement. It was also well known at the time that these very respectable Northern gentlemen professed to have "influence with Grant," and that they had succeeded in making Mr. Barksdale believe that they had such influence.

As the time approached, therefore, for the election when our new constitution would again be submitted to a vote of the people, by the aid of those Northern gentlemen that Central Democratic Association discovered that, after all, the new constitution was good enough for them, if only certain "proscriptive clauses" could be eliminated.

Whereupon, certain members of that association[10] met these very worthy and "highly respectable Republicans" in what was christened a "Conservative National Republican Convention." The result of their efforts to give to the "Republican party of the State a respectable leadership," was the following ticket: For Governor—Lewis Dent, *"carpet-bagger,"* and President Grant's brother-in-law. For Lieutenant-Governor—E. Jeffords, *"carpet-bagger."* . . . It was said that their nominee for governor resided in Coahoma County, Mississippi; but he was never a resident of the State, certainly not of that county. . . .

Our Republican convention met soon after, and it nominated the following ticket: For Governor, James L. Alcorn; for Lieutenant-Governor, R.C. Powers; for Secretary of State, James Lynch, colored[11]; for State Auditor, H. Musgrove; for State Treasurer, W.H. Vasser; for Attorney General, Joshua S. Morris; for Superintendent of Public Education, H.R. Pease. . . .

Our nominee for Governor was an old slaveholder—one who had come into our camp. Mr. Vasser and Mr. Morris were also old citizens and slaveholders who had joined our side. Mr. Lynch was the most bril-

---

10 [Original author's footnote] Otherwise called conspirators.

11 There was no relation between John Lynch and James Lynch.

liant orator of his time in Mississippi. The others were "carpet-baggers." Along with those "proscriptive clauses," which the President decided to submit to a separate vote, was section 5 of article 12, that clause prohibiting the State from loaning the State's credit. It was understood that the supporters of the Dent ticket had procured this action.

But this appears to have been about all they succeeded in doing in the way of influencing President Grant, although their candidate for Governor was his brother-in-law; for while our convention was in session the commanding general was invited in. General Ames replied as follows: "Gentlemen, you have my sympathy and my support." . . . From that moment the Dent ticket began to lose confidence in itself; for, seeing that it had failed to capture President Grant, the conspirators themselves lost respect for it. . . .

THE PRETTY PICKLE OF THE ENEMY

Our party in the county had met in convention, pronounced in favor of universal amnesty [for former Confederates] and also in favor of the retention of section 5, article 12 of the constitution. It had also pronounced in favor of the Alcorn ticket, as against the Dent ticket, and had nominated a full county ticket, nearly half of whom were native white men.[12]

The General and Captain Clark had been nominated for the State House of Representatives. I had been nominated for the State Senate. The convention also passed a resolution highly commendatory of the action of President Grant and of General Ames.

I was not altogether satisfied with our ticket. But it was the best we could do. Mr. Hilliard, our sheriff, and one other were the only persons of the class known as "best citizens" whom we could induce, even with "fat offices," to come out on our platform, which was the State platform. . . . Some insisted that Mr. Hilliard was never one of Yazoo's best citizens, that he was originally from the North, and while it was true that he had been a slaveholder, he had owned no more than half a dozen or so, and was a "common sort of fellow." Now that he was on our ticket he was in his true place—a scalawag.

The other was a preacher. He had been owner of quite a large "slave family." Parson Sivrup was a good man, they all agreed. But he could never be coaxed into saying right out in meeting that he was a Republican. He could say so very freely in private, though, and this was something to be thankful for.

---

[12] Even though Morgan freely admitted the failings of the local white Unionists, he felt strongly that the Republican party had to attract biracial support.

The other ticket was Republican too. But then it was styled the "National Republican ticket," except when it was called "the Conservative ticket." In the North, no Republican could have taken the least exception to that name.

With us it meant altogether more than its name implied. It signified that its following were Republicans, with a mental reservation; if they could at the same time be conservatives. In Mississippi, conservatism meant opposition to change, and that meant opposition to any tampering with Yazoo laws and customs, or interferences with Yazoo practices; therefore, the conspirators became *National* Republicans. It sounded well at the North, and in Mississippi it was, after all, but a name. And to cap the climax, even in Yazoo they nominated a "nigger" to go to the legislature. . . .

Their nominee for the State Senate was Major W.D. Gibbs. He came of a very ancient and very distinguished family. He was a very large planter, and supposed to be quite wealthy. The "nigger" candidate had been this gentleman's slave—also the slave of his father before him. He was still living there on the same old home-place working "fur ole mars jez' 'e same 'ez b'fo' de wah, no differn." His name was Reuben Pope. They called—everybody called him Reuben, except ole mars, who had always addressed him as Rube—but neither in "slave time," nor since "freedom came for all," had Rube ever been half the trouble to Major Gibbs as now; for the Major had pledged himself to make a thorough canvass of the county, and having been provided with the necessary outfit, together these two, the Major and Reuben (master and slave), traveled up and down through the swamp country chiefly—for there were more freedmen in the swamp than in the hills—holding meetings on all the large plantations. Here is just where the Major made a mistake. He should have "sont" Reuben. As it was Reuben had waited on the Major so long that it had become "second nature" to do so, and so could not help waiting on him now, nor could he help calling the Major "mastah."

Ever since our stronghold experience, our party had carried a flag along for use at our meetings. In this canvass, the boys would have a drum and fife. Therefore, with our band and our flag, we were able to make a most attractive display. Seeing this and being determined to keep up with "them damn Yankees" for at least once in their lives, the enemy undertook to get up a band too. . . . But just here the Major made a fatal blunder. Instead of carrying the flag himself, or hiring a "po' white" to do so, he entrusted it to Reuben. This was the way they traveled. The Major, with one of his chief supporters—very often it was Captain Telsub, or Major Sweet, or Ben Wicks—rode on ahead in their carriages. The band followed with Reuben and the flag in the band wagon.

This was too much. The patient, long-suffering freed people could not stand it any longer. . . . Reuben as standard-bearer for the *Democrats* was too much. It broke the back of the major's camel. Poor Reuben! It soon got so that no one had any chickens for him, or any place for him to lay his head. The white folks couldn't—just couldn't have him in their beds, nor at their tables. Now they were in a pretty pickle. The Major and his friends could not understand what it was possessed "our nigros." . . .

Although Grant was president, and peace prevailed throughout the borders of Yazoo, during this memorable campaign the irreconcilables were still an element of discord, and on two occasions resorted to violence. They are worthy of a place here only because they illustrate the truth of what has gone before as respects the aggressive elements in the ranks of the enemy. . . .

The first occurred at the place of registration.

As usual, Charles, though no longer a resident of the county, the General, and myself were the target of the enemy, who taunted the freedmen with running after and supporting for office men who owned no real estate in the county. A blacksmith who owned no *taxable* property, being a freedman, ventured to respond to the taunt from a certain Dr. Pompous, by inquiring:

"Doctor, 'whar yo' tax 'ceipt?"

Of course, a "freedman, free negro, or mulatto" had no right to ask such a question. It was a misdemeanor by law, for, if not insulting in terms, it was doubtless so in "gestures largely, or acts," or "about" to become so. However, as the freedman had ventured he was in for it, and stood up to it like a man, while his comrades began to gather close around him. They could anticipate the result, you see.

Dr. Pompous was not prepared for this. Why should he be? He had never had just such an experience before, probably. But the doctor was equal to the emergency, and quickly and hotly exclaimed, "Why, you damned nigger! How dare you insult me in that manner! I'll teach you something, by God."

There was, however, another surprise in store for him. The blacksmith stood his ground and squared himself with great double fists for defense, as the doctor made a rush toward him. This so enraged the white man that he quite forgot the place and the occasion, and in great fury fairly leaped at the blacksmith. His passage, however, was barred by fully a dozen strong freedmen, who caught him some around the legs, some around his arms and body, while others pushed him back with their hands. Not a blow did they strike. Seeing the freedmen thus rally to the support of the blacksmith, the doctor's white neighbors and friends rallied in his behalf, and some of them out with their pistols.

At this critical juncture the registrar (who, under the law, was a *Federal* peace officer) sprang between them, and seizing the doctor ordered the freedmen to disperse.

"Ordered the freedmen to disperse! Well, what did they do to the whites?" Nothing. . . . You see, it was a concession by the officer, that the white man had been insulted, and a compliment to him for his forbearance in not shooting "the nigger" instead of trying to whip him. . . .

This [insult] was only understood by those of the crowd who knew that the doctor had paid no taxes since the war, and that the blacksmith had paid each year a poll tax of five dollars, a street tax of five dollars, and other taxes, amounting to five dollars more. . . .

The second one occurred at the hustings. . . .

WHEN THE "NIGGERS" DID NOT RUN

As my reader has already inferred, the enemy hoped to conquer "our nigros" by dividing them, and they had been induced to put Reuben Pope on their "Conservative National Republican" ticket for the legislature with that object solely in view. In their political school, the end always justifies the means, and although Reuben was a very bitter pill, considering the end to be gained they could swallow him. They could go further. Under the spell of their anticipations, they could wrap Reuben up in the grand old flag and swallow the whole bundle. . . .

The "black folks" for so long had been witnesses of "old mars' " contempt for the flag, that it had not occurred to them as within the range of possible events that the "white folks" could so far deceive themselves as to suppose for a moment that its use for such a purpose would be accepted by anyone as evidence of real change of heart on the part of their former masters. "Ole mars' 'low nigger got no sense 'kase he ha' got no larnin'," Uncle Peter explained while "argufying" that feature of the campaign with some equally shrewd companions. And Uncle Peter was right; for the old flag had an opposite effect from what was intended. But the enemy were not dismayed. . . . Uncle Peter shook his head and vowed, "Darz sholy sump'en g'wain ter drap, sartin. Yo' jes' lis'en ter whar I'z a tellin' yo' all. Dem 'ar white genl'mens has no mo' money ter trow 'way den we all po' niggers, min' dat. I'z a talken now. Uncle Peter is. I tell yi' jes' you take car' yo'self. Dey is getten ready fur some mischuf, day is; I knows um; can't fool me if I is a nigger and got no larnin'. I wor bornd wi' um, I was."

These sage observations of Uncle Peter were called forth by the announcement that the enemy had challenged me to a joint discussion of the issues of the day with Major Gibbs. Anticipating this challenge and also the line of the Major's argument, I prepared myself with certain incontestable documentary evidence: ammunition that there had as yet been no favorable opportunity for me to use, and I cheerfully accepted the enemy's proposal for a series of mass meetings.

The first of these was at Dover Crossroads, in the southern part of the county, and in the neighborhood of the Major's home. The arrangement was for my opponent to lead off with an hour; I was to follow with an hour and a half, and he to close with a half hour. The audience was composed of about five hundred colored men, women, and children, and perhaps as many as forty or fifty whites assembled in the open yard about the front of the crossroad white folks' church, from the front of which was our speaker's stand.

There were not more than a half-dozen white Republicans present, most of whom were seated on the platform. All the white Democrats— "National Republicans"—were upon the outskirts of the crowd, save only the Major, who of course had a seat with me upon the platform. Of course there were no white ladies at all present. . . .

The Major had the advantage of me from the start, for he was able to say that they all knew him, knew his family. He was no stranger. I could only say in reply to that part of his speech, that I had been for four years a resident of the county, and was already tolerably well known. I hoped they would know me better after a while.

The Major had said that he could appreciate their situation, their poverty, their distress. If only they, the colored people, would "t'ar themselves away from their false leaders," and trust him, he not only could do, but truly would do a "heap mo'" for them than any stranger could. . . . The Major had declared that nobody but Yankees had prejudice against the freed people on account of their color. This, he insisted, was true, because even Fred. Douglass, "the greatest black man that ever lived, and the man who made the radical party," had only a few days before been refused a seat at the table in a hotel up North; "the same place where Colonel Morgan, their god, came from." . . . For one, he had no prejudice. "No Southerner had any prejudice against the color which God gave nigros, and which they could no mo' help than they could fly." They all knew his black mammy, Aunt Sally. Why! she had suckled him, and loved her to that day as much as his own dear mother, almost. . . . [13]

About the moment I began my reply to this part of the Major's speech, a young country white man, a stranger to me, who had climbed upon the stand in rear of me, touched my elbow and whispered in my ear, inquired—"Colonel, yo' got a pistol?"

[13] [Original author's footnote] I have heard a great many native Southern men speaking to mixed assemblies of colored and white men, and have never yet listened to one who did not make the same claim to kindly consideration by the blacks. [Much of the debate between the two candidates has been cut here.]

"Yes," said I, for I had that morning provided myself with one.

"Thar's g'wain to be trouble y'here today, Colonel, an' if yo'll gie it ter me I'll stan' by ye."

I thanked the young man for his kindly offer, but thought I could defend myself, and so informing him, I resumed my talk. . . . [During the speech,] some one of the whites exclaimed: "Yo' don't own no land."[14]

I had heard similar exclamations before during my talk, and was now prepared to answer it. "Do all your candidates own land?"

It was agreed that Reuben did not, and I suggested that there were four on their State ticket who were believed not to own any land in the State, and besides, there were at least two on their county ticket who did not. I had understood, I said, that my opponent for the Senate owned none in the State or elsewhere.

This was laughed at. I begged them not to laugh, for, without wishing to be personal, I thought I could prove that the Major owned not an acre of land. Then I brought out my documents and read from the sworn statement of my opponent himself, made before a registrar in bankruptcy that the only property he *owned or controlled* was a horse, saddle and bridle, saddlebags, double-barrelled shotgun, and a navy Colt's revolver!

This announcement, authenticated by the seal of the court, produced a decided sensation, for my opponent resided upon a large and valuable plantation, which, however, shortly before going into bankruptcy, by some "hocus pocus" had become the property of his wife in name.

I might have added that Mr. Mix, the tailor at Yazoo City, had informed me that the Major obtained credit of him for an elegant suit of clothes only a short time before taking the benefit of the bankruptcy act, and included the amount in his schedule of indebtedness filed in that court, and had paid the bill by notice of his discharge by that court of all liability therefor.

Shortly after the interruption by the young countryman which I have mentioned, two men, strangers then to me, came out from the little group of the enemy which had collected at the front of the corner store just over the way, bringing with them a half-drunken fellow—judging by his manner—of whom they let go as they approached the mass of freed men and women in front of me.

This half-drunken fellow elbowed his way violently through the mass, pushing along with himself what appeared to be a half-witted or half-drunken black man that had come into view from a quarter unknown to me, until he reached a point directly in front and below me. His approach had been so violent that it had greatly disturbed the people along his way, and having reached the point indicated, he commanded the negro to curse me.

14 As mentioned earlier, the existing state laws (and white political prejudices) were stilted in favor of landowners.

"Tell 'im he's—hic-a-hic—liar; God damn him."

His tone was one of suppressed anger, and though I resolved not to allow it to interrupt me, he repeated it so often that the portion of the audience about him were greatly disturbed by it, and became somewhat indignant when in reply to a polite request of one of the leading colored men present that he should keep still, he exclaimed, "You're a damned lyin' son of a bitch."

I had kept right on with my remarks, not regarding the offender further than to keep watch of him, and of the group of the enemy at the store front, amongst whom were some guns. But the colored man who had addressed him, now joined by two or three others, made a motion as if to take hold of his arm. At that instant the bulldozer whipped out a pistol and fired at the colored man, who would have fallen to the ground had he not been caught by a comrade.

Upon the instant I sprang from the platform amongst them, followed by two of the white Unionists, and some from the group about the store rushed toward us.

There were as many as ten, perhaps thirty, shots fired, on both sides, and when the battle was over the women and children, most of whom ran at the first discharge, came back on the grounds from out of the bushes nearby and from the road beyond, about the moment that the Major and I had reached a conclusion that it would be just as well that I should agree not to finish my speech there on that day, if he would not claim his right to close, and I promised to let it be known from our side that he had done all he could to stop the row.

The only man killed was the bulldozer, who had not retreated more than ten steps when he fell, and was dead before the battle was over. The man he shot, however, became a cripple for life from the very bad wound just below the groin.

Mr. Foote had received but a slight scratch, a woman thought she had been hit, and I escaped without anything more than the smell of fire upon my clothes. I had merely stood my ground, and had not fired. It had ended almost as soon as it began, and the "niggers" did not run, either.

The news of the battle reached town before we could notwithstanding we drove pretty rapidly. . . . Mr. Barksdale and certain other "law-abiding citizens" had already held a hasty consultation, and recommended to the sheriff the employment of a large number of extra deputies to enable him to put down the "insurrection already begun," pledging him the aid of "every good Democrat" in the county to keep the enemy quiet, if only he would "protect them against the nigros," who, it was feared, having once tasted the sweets of self-preservation, would fly into all sorts of license unrestrained.

The sheriff to "humor them," solemnly promised to protect them and the "white women and children from the cradle up," and swore in some few extra deputies to that end. But the "insurrection" ended where it began, with the bulldozer, and our joint discussion ended also, and that was thereafter the most peaceful, good-natured campaign ever held in the county, and the election the most quiet, orderly, and fair ever held before or since in Yazoo County.

General Grant was President and General Ames was *military* governor then, and though the vote was large, the new free constitution was ratified *unanimously,* and the Republican ticket was elected by an overwhelming majority, and there was perfect peace in Yazoo. . . .

OUR FIRST "NIGGER CONSTABLE"

Mr. Foote, early in the administration of General Ames, had been made a constable. One day one of Harry Baltimore's hands came to town and lodged complaint with our Republican magistrate against that "high-toned, honorable gentleman" for beating him, and for setting his dogs on him. The magistrate issued his warrant for the arrest of General Baltimore, and placed it in the hands of Mr. Foote for execution.

Now, the magistrate and General Baltimore were white men. Foote was a negro—so-called—but he executed that warrant with such courage and discretion that, during his trial, General Harry Baltimore felt called upon to say, in open court, that while the magistrate was a "damned thief," Mr. Foote was a high-toned, honorable gentleman; for he could do no other way than "try to execute the damned warrant."

Mr. Foote had another experience that year. A young white man set out to "teach him a lesson," but he learned one of Foote instead; for Mr. Foote whipped him. This was 1869.

We made great strides forward that year. Our varied contests with the enemy up to this time were likely to prove the best instructors. Some of the officers of election were young men who had been educated in the school taught in the little church we helped to build. . . .

Already during the five years since the war, Mr. W.H. Foote, James Dixon, Houston Burrus, Frank Stewart, and scores more of Yazoo freedmen were demanding the same courteous treatment on the streets, in the stores, and at their homes for their wives as common decency exacted for other ladies from the public, the merchant and his clerks, or callers at their residences.

At first this was met with contempt and often drew out acts of greater license from those white men who had always acted upon the privilege which their color gave them under the old rule, to enter a negro's house without knocking and stand or sit with hat on, and, when evil nature prompted, to suggest an intrigue with wife, mother, sister, or daughter. The old rule permitted a white man to pinch or put an arm around a colored woman while shopping, or openly invite an intrigue, or when she was on the street to stare at, make remarks to or about her of an insulting character, or, as was sometimes the case, openly invite an intrigue, and when resented by the lady, press it by some coarse speech or action.

Mr. Foote was never known to allow his wife to be thus insulted without resenting it in such a manner as would forever deter the intruder from repeating it. He prided himself on the fact that he was a "Southern gentleman," and he acted upon the "Southern rule" of an eye for an eye, and a tooth for a tooth, to the bitter end. . . .

All hostility to the agents at work in the planting of the provisions of [a new] rule was repressed merely not by the power of the rule nor of its agencies, nor yet of the great mass of the freed people behind it, but by the respect which the rank and file of the enemy had for the Federal power in the hands of a President who was in sympathy with a loyal Congress and the heart-beats of the American nation. It was repressed only as the appetite of the wolf is while the lambs are within the fold and the shepherd on guard is awake.

Mr. Foote, Frank Stewart, James Dixon—no relative of the "human hornet"—and many others of the Yazoo freedmen were not lambs, but the mass were. . . . It was evident to me that Mr. Foote's policy would not cure the evil. It would for a time protect himself and his family from open insult so long as the dread of the Federal power remained a factor in repressing the instincts of the wolf, but not any longer. So I said then, so I say now, and so my patient reader will say when we separate.

Surveying the entire field, my only hope was in the *steady, unswerving power from without*. I trusted implicity in that power; for, had not the watchword been of our fathers, from the day when they threw overboard the tea in Boston Harbor, "Eternal vigilence is the price of liberty"? Why should I doubt their [the North's] fidelity to it? Why should I question their love for or faith in our cause? Why should I suspect them of faint-heartedness now, of all times the most fructuous of happy results for the champions of universal liberty, a harvest season for mankind never yet equalled on the face of modern earth? I could not doubt, I did not question, I would not faint, and bent my head lower still under the heavy yoke, while I set my plow to deeper and still deeper furrows in my new field. . . .

SIGNS OF A NEW CROP OF MEN AND WOMEN IN YAZOO

The season had been a good one. The crop was even larger than the year preceding, and better than all, the freed people were nearly all getting a fair share for making it. The year before they had purchased new clothing, new beds and blankets, new cooking utensils, etc.; horses and mules, and some shotguns for hunting purposes. This year they were beginning to buy—land!

It made all things lively in Yazoo City. The number of small traders was rapidly increasing. Theretofore, a half hundred men had owned the bulk of cultivated land in the county, and furnished their laborers, as well as their plantations, by orders on their factors in New Orleans, or at one or the other of three houses in Yazoo City, of which Mr. Barksdale's was the chief. Now, however, the laborers were making their own purchases, and they sought for the cheapest dealers.

Thus it came about that the business and commercial fabric was undergoing a reconstruction no less in its farreaching consequences than that worked out in politics. All was transition, change, and the intelligent, cultivated young [white] men, as well as their elders, looked out upon a future they were not competent to penetrate any distance at all, for their eyes had been trained in other and wholly different glasses than those required for the purpose. . . .

One thing was certain, if that state of things should continue many years, the "African" *would* own the country. The only thing to prevent it, would be *a fair competition with him for the right to own it*. This meant honest effort, manly labor on the part of the *white man*.

Would the white man prove himself to be the equal of the negro? It was an interesting question to me. It was an entertaining one, also; for, to "own this whole country" meant to own a country surpassing the valley of the Nile in extent and in richness. It was a question I delighted to study, and I felt grateful for the prospect that I was to be a participant in the race, and a sharer in the harvest. . . .

Now that peace had come again, and we were in places of power; now that the curses, contempt, and blows of the enemy had changed to smiles and caresses . . . Our new "radical sheriff" was the first under the new regime to receive any sort of recognition from Yazoo City "society." His family began to elevate themselves accordingly, for so it is, I am told, the wide world over. . . . Our new sheriff, having kept himself and family out of active participation in the former contests, was less "objectionable," a less embarrassing subject, though he often complained to me of the outrageous slights, even insults, put upon himself and family because he had taken office of the radicals. His wife was a proud, haughty woman, and felt these things most keenly. . . .

Whenever, out of hunger for some sort of social companionship, I ventured upon the "ragged edge" of the Yazoo social order, all my former teachings, my sacred theories, my inborn principles got up such a rebellion within my soul that I turned at the very threshold, and ran as far away from the edge of this social precipice as my conscience would carry me under the thump, thump, thump of my aching heart.

Now that Grant was President and in "sympathy with fanaticism," now that the free constitution . . . had been unanimously ratified, now that the trick of the enemy had failed to prevent the "nigro rising," quite to the top, now that . . . Foote, the General, the ex-bureau agent, and myself, all "polecats," were the lawmakers for Yazoo, now that the "freedman, free negro, or mulatto" sat on the jury, that his poll-tax had been reduced to two dollars, that he was no longer more liable to arrest for failure to pay it than "ole mars," that the auction block for "runaways" had been destroyed, that "our nigros" could testify in court against a white man, that Uncles Peter, David, Jonathan, and the late "little garrison" not only had the right, but were enjoying it, to buy and carry arms, that they were already buying land, that rape of a negro girl by a white man was a rape, that the white man's "black sweetheart" began to "kick against the pricks," now that all these things were no longer *in futuro* but *in esse,* and now that all present danger that "our nigros" were "about to rise" with intent to "kill all the white men, women, and children from the cradle up" had passed into the limbo of the forgotten kukluxes and the dead Dover bulldozer, I deemed it high time that I should take a wife.

———

THE TALE OF Morgan and his bride is a remarkable one—a true Reconstruction love story, to be covered in chapters to come. But we can appreciate his desire to settle down: the penniless outcast Yankee was now a state senator and major political leader (though still penniless). As Morgan recounts in the almost religious recitation at the end of the selection above, Mississippi society was being torn up by the roots. The change must have seemed biblical indeed to the long-suffering African Americans, for the last had indeed become first. William H. Foote, the free black man of Vicksburg, was made a constable in Yazoo; John R. Lynch, the former slave from Natchez, was made justice of the peace, and nurtured greater ambitions.

And yet, the importance of federal intervention cannot be overstated. "My only hope," writes Morgan, "was in the *steady, unswerving power from without.*" Ex-Confederate whites had a monopoly on armed force in the South, absent the occupying troops of the U.S. Army. Until Congress put the region under military control, former slave drivers controlled all of the government machinery; in the case of Mississippi, there was still no relief until Grant became President and entrusted the troops to a dedicated, principled commander. Federal intervention was absolutely essential for blacks to overcome these obstacles, as another generation discovered a century later during the civil rights movement. Thousands of ruthless white Democrats were biding their time, cultivating men such as Sheriff Hilliard, waiting for Washington to tire of its protective chores.

Despite the clouds ahead, there was no question that the black majority of Mississippi basked in a new day. Reconstruction had truly arrived, ringing in one of the greatest moments of hope in American history.

V

SPECULATION

HIGH TIDE OF THE ROBBER BARONS

14

BLACK FRIDAY

The remaking of the South was the farthest thing from Jay Gould's mind in the spring of 1869. The Mephistopheles of Wall Street, as he was later dubbed, was now approaching the height of his power: in the last year alone he had ousted Drew, bested Vanderbilt, and cemented an alliance with the corrupt Tammany Hall ring—the circle of Democrats that sat atop the city of New York as if it were a pile of loot. But as with Morgan and Lynch, the inauguration of Grant gave the young robber baron a surge of hope—or at least a whiff of enormous opportunity. The beloved general had hardly finished his inaugural address when Gould launched a breathtaking scheme, one that turned on that most ancient obsession: gold.

Before the Civil War, the price of gold was a rather simple matter. The government minted gold coins—each composed of its face value in the metal.[1] A gold dollar might fluctuate in buying power—it might buy fewer sacks of flour this year than last—but the price of gold was determined by the act of coining. Of course, the amount of gold available did not grow with the expanding economy; it was a natural resource, and its availability was determined by mining. This often led to a shortage of money; poor and remote farmers complained year after year about the lack of currency.

To meet the demand, states and local banks issued banknotes—slips of paper that promised the bearer an equivalent amount of specie (gold or silver, but usually gold) if the notes were turned in to the issuing bank. Of course, banks issued notes far in excess of their actual holdings of gold, since it was unlikely that all the banknotes would be returned at once. The market value, in gold dollars, of these notes fluctuated with the reputation of the issuing institution, its specie reserves, etc.

The Civil War caused a crisis in this decentralized, gold-based currency system. Panic gripped the economy, and people began to hoard precious metals. Customers began returning their notes to banks, demanding payment in specie; reserves of gold dropped to dangerously low levels. The national treasury was almost emptied. In 1862, Congress took action. It passed the Internal Revenue Act, including sweep-

---

[1] Silver was also used in antebellum coinage, but it had been largely driven out of circulation by the time of the Civil War.

ing excise taxes, an inheritance tax, and the first income tax in American history. It established a Bureau of Internal Revenue to administer the influx, and set up a system of national banks. But equally important was another bill passed in 1862, the Legal Tender Act.

The Legal Tender Act established a national currency—a paper bill, immediately dubbed the greenback—that was *not* backed dollar for dollar by specie. No one could demand payment in gold for their paper notes. And as the name of the act indicates, the greenback was legal tender; unlike the notes of private banks, it could not be refused as payment. As James McPherson writes, the law "asserted national sovereignty to help win a war fought to preserve that sovereignty." Gold dollars continued to exist, and customs duties were still payable only in specie (precious metals remained the international medium of exchange), but the greenback was an instant success. The currency supply was managed adroitly; investor confidence in federal bonds rose; and the economy grew rapidly with the more adequate supply of banknotes.

But the innovation created economic distortions unlooked for by the creators of the Legal Tender Act—distortions that would draw the attention of Mr. Gould in 1869. Gold now had a price: a dollar's worth of gold was no longer simply a gold dollar. A market for gold opened in New York (the Gold Room, as it was dubbed) where speculators bought and sold greenbacks and gold. During the war, the price of gold served as a barometer of investor confidence in the Union cause; when the Union army suffered a defeat, the value of the greenback dropped. But the Gold Room also took on a central role in the exchange of greenbacks from the domestic economy for specie used in foreign trade.

After the war, pressure grew for doing away with the greenback and restoring the nation to "hard money"—gold coins and specie-backed banknotes. In favor of the rollback were wealthy Eastern businessmen (who liked the fiscal stability and low inflation that accompanied hard money) along with social conservatives (one banker declared that "gold and silver are the only true measure of value," since "these metals were prepared by the Almighty for this very purpose"). On the other side were rural, especially Western farmers who thrived on the expanded money supply created by the greenback. Inflation was a good thing for them; if a dollar is worth less, it is easier to get, and bills are easier to pay. And some businessmen worried that eliminating greenbacks would tie up gold in the domestic economy, making it less available for foreign trade, which was conducted strictly in specie.

Under President Johnson, the fiscal conservatives held sway, and the treasury department began selling gold and buying greenbacks, taking them out of circulation. Grant's new treasury secretary, George S. Boutwell, held much the same view, and he continued the slow process of returning the currency to specie.[2] But the new President was much harder to figure out: an old Westerner himself, he understood the problems of insufficient cash, but he was also a newfound friend of conservative Eastern businessmen such as Alexander Stewart.

As Jay Gould mused upon these facts, he struck upon his dramatic scheme—a financial conspiracy that shocked the nation in its audacity. In April of 1869, he called upon his friend and partner James Fisk, Jr., to explain the plan. The two were an odd pair: about the same age (Gould thirty-three, Fisk thirty-four), they presented a marked contrast in personalities. Gould was the genius of the two—a thoughtful, small, slender man, given to gardening and history, as well as utterly unscrupulous fiscal maneuvering. Fisk was the colorful one, the bold public face of the conspiratorial duo. As William McFeely so aptly describes him, he was "probably not equally bright but surely as bold . . . a celebrator of the joys of being rich. A brassy dresser, a forthright storyteller, a flamboyant gambler, and a vulgar (that is, successful) womanizer. . . . Fisk was apt to tell the truth if he could not think of any good reason not to." Victors in the war for the Erie, they made perfect partners for a plot that combined shrewd inside maneuvering and brash public relations.

Their plan: to drive up the price of gold to unprecedented levels. Their means: by influencing President Grant, the Western man of destiny, to stop selling gold and buying greenbacks. Their obstacle: Treasury Secretary George Boutwell, the high-minded and fiscally conservative manager of the administration's financial policies. To accomplish their purposes, the pair stopped at nothing—drawing in everyone from Abel R. Corbin, the husband of Grant's sister, to the First Lady. From April through September, they pursued their plot—winning the nickname "the gold bugs" in the newspapers—until the market finally came crashing down on a day known as Black Friday.

The Gold Bugs
by George S. Boutwell

So much time has passed since September 24, 1869, that there may be a large public who may become interested in a review of the events of the

---

[2] Boutwell was a leading Radical Republican; his conservative fiscal views show that the Radicals were united only in their belief in justice for African Americans. Some extended their ideas to sympathy for the plight of cash-poor farmers in the West; others, such as Boutwell, saw no connection between federal intervention in civil rights, which he favored, and federal intervention in the economy, which he frowned upon.

spring and summer of that year which culminated in Wall Street, New York, in the transactions and experiences of the day known as "Black Friday."

When the Forty-First Congress assembled in December of that year, the House of Representatives directed the Committee on Banking and Currency "to investigate the causes that led to the unusual and extraordinary fluctuations of gold in the city of New York, from the 21st to the 27th of September, 1869." . . . From [its] report it appears that certain persons in the city of New York entered into an arrangement, or understanding, or combination, as early as the month of April, 1869, for the purpose of forcing the price of gold artificially to a rate far beyond what might be called the natural price.

The committee . . . characterized the combination as a conspiracy. Technically and in a legal point of view the parties concerned could not be treated properly as conspirators. It does not appear that they contemplated the violation of any law, but only a policy by which gold might be advanced from time to time, and out of which advance large sums of money might be realized by those who were holders of gold. Upon that theory Jay Gould and James Fisk, Jr., who were the leaders and organizers of the combination, with their associates, made large purchases of gold. . . .

It appears in the review[3] that Mr. Gould originated the scheme of advancing the price of gold and that Mr. Fisk was his principal coadjutor. It also appears that Mr. Fisk entered into the arrangement upon the basis of friendship for Mr. Gould, and not in consequence of an opinion on his part that the scheme was a wise one. Mr. Gould had two main purposes in view: first, the profit that he might realize from an advance in gold; and, second, the advantage that might accrue to the railroad with which he was connected through an increase of its business in the transportation of products from the West. As set forth in Mr. Gould's letter [to Boutwell], he entertained the opinion, which rested upon satisfactory business grounds, that an advance in the price of gold would stimulate the sale of Western products, increase the business of transportation over the railways, and aid us in the payment of liabilities abroad. . . .

When I entered the Treasury Department in March, there had not been sales of gold nor purchases of bonds by the Treasury Department as a policy, and but few transactions on either side had been made by my predecessors in office. As early as the 12th day of May I commenced the purchase of bonds for the sinking fund and for the reduction of the interest-bearing public debt. . . .

The President accepted the idea that the management of the Treasury Department was in my hands, and from the first to last, he was influenced by a military view that an officer who was charged with the conduct of a business, or of an undertaking, should be left free to act, that he should

[3] This paragraph has been moved for narrative continuity.

be made responsible, and that, in case of failure, the consequences should rest upon him. It happened, and as a plan on my part, that neither the President nor the Cabinet was made responsible for what was done in the Treasury Department. . . .

In the line of these views, it happened that I announced my purpose to purchase bonds in May, 1869, without conference either with the Cabinet or the President. When the announcement was made, there was a slight advance in bonds. In order that the business interests of the country might not be influenced by an apprehension that changes might take place in the policy of the Department, I announced . . . at the beginning of each month the sales of gold and the purchases of bonds that were to be made during the coming month. Those announcements were sent out on the evening of Sunday, either the last Sunday of the closing month or the first Sunday of the opening month. . . .

Unfortunately, this policy was made the basis of the proceedings in New York which culminated in "Black Friday." The parties interested—I do not call them conspirators—assumed that for thirty days the policy of the department as to the sale of gold would remain unchanged, and on that basis they proceeded to make arrangements for the advance in gold. Not satisified with that policy, which was designed to save the business community from unnecessary apprehensions, an attempt was made to induce me to make an announcement for two or three months. Such suggestions were made in letters that I received from interested parties in the city of New York.

Speculation in gold was not all on one side. There were speculators who were anxious to break down the price of gold, and between the lines I could read the condition of the respective parties from whom I received letters. Under date of September 23, I received a letter from a prominent house in New York in which the writer said: "I am actuated to again portray to you the state of financial affairs as they now exist in this city. The speculative advance in gold has brought legitimate business almost to a standstill, owing to the apprehension of a corner, which from appearances may appear at any moment."

It did not follow that the writer was "short on gold," as the phrase is. I had, however, in my possession at that time a list of persons in New York who were supposed to be contestants, some for an advance in gold and others for a fall. In this connection I may say that it was no part of my policy to regulate affairs in Wall Street or State Street or Lombard Street. Until it became apparent that the operations in New York affected largely and seriously the business interests of the country, and until it became apparent that the Treasury receipts were diminished by the panic that had taken possession of the public, I refrained from any interference with those who were engaged either in forcing up or forcing down the price of gold. . . .

[Here] unfolds the policy which had guided Gould and Fisk and their associates from April to the culmination of their undertaking, the 24th day of September. As far as I know, the effort had been directed chiefly to the support of the false theory that the President was opposed to the sale of gold, especially during the autumn months, when a large amount of currency is required, or in those days was supposed to be required, for "the moving," as it was called, of the produce of the West to the sea coast for shipment to Europe. They even went so far as to allege that the President had ordered the Secretary of the Treasury to suspend the sale of gold during the month of September, for which there was no foundation whatever. Indeed, up to the 22nd of September, when I introduced the subject of the price of gold to the President, he had neither said nor done anything. . . .

At a meeting, which was accidental as far as the President was concerned, on board one of Fisk and Gould's Fall River steamers when he was on his way to Boston in June of that year to attend the Peace Jubilee, an attempt was made to commit General Grant to the policy of holding gold. I was present on the trip with the President. What happened on the boat may best be given in the language of Mr. Fisk and Mr. Gould.

Mr. Fisk, in his testimony before the [Congressional] committee, said: "On our passage over to Boston with General Grant, we endeavored to ascertain what his position in regard to the finances was. We went down to supper about nine o'clock, intending while we were there to have this thing pretty thoroughly talked up, and, if possible, to relieve him from any idea of putting the price of gold down."

Mr. Gould's account before the committee was as follows: "At this supper the question came up about the state of the country, the crops, prospects ahead, etc. The President was a listener; the other gentlemen were discussing. Some were in favor of Boutwell's selling gold, and some were opposed to it. After they had all interchanged their views, someone asked the President what his view was. He remarked that he thought there was a certain amount of fictitiousness about the prosperity of the country, and that the bubble might as well be tapped in one way or another. . . . We supposed from that conversation that the President was a contractionist. His remark struck across us like a wet blanket."

The error of Fisk and Gould and their associates, from the beginning to the end of the contest, was in the supposition that the President was taking any part in the operations of the Treasury concerning the price of gold. If he expressed any opinions outside in conversation, there were no acts on his part in harmony with or in antagonism to the views he entertained. . . . Their policy was directed to two points: first, to influence the President, if possible, to interfere in a way to advance the price of gold; and, second, to satisfy their adherents and opponents that the President had either so interfered or would so interfere.

Even Fisk and Gould may at a period of time have rested in the belief that the President either had interfered or that he would interfere. Their confidence was in Mr. A.R. Corbin, a brother-in-law of the President, who under the influence of various considerations, which appear to have been personal and pecuniary to a very large extent, lent himself to the task of influencing the President. As a matter of fact, his attempts were very feeble and misdirected and of no consequence whatever. Indeed, such is my opinion of the President, and such my belief as to his opinion concerning Mr. Corbin, that nothing which Mr. Corbin did say, or could have said, did have or could have had the least influence upon the President's opinion or conduct. It is, however, also true that Fisk and Gould employed Corbin and gave him consideration in their undertakings out of which he realized some money. I received information also, which may not have been true, that they suggested to him that he might become president of the Tenth National Bank, which had a very conspicuous part in the events which culminated in Black Friday.

An attempt to strengthen the impression that it was the purpose of the President to prevent the sale of gold was made through an article prepared by Mr. Corbin, probably under the direction of Mr. Gould and others, which appeared finally, with some alterations and omissions, in the New York *Times* of the 25th of August. It appears to have been the purpose of the parties interested to mislead the *Times* as to the authorship of the article, and they secured the agency of Mr. James McHenry, a prominent English capitalist, who called at the *Times* office and presented the article to Mr. Bigelow, the editor, as the opinion of a person in the intimate confidence of the President. The article was put in type and double leaded. When so prepared, suspicions were aroused, and the financial editor, Mr. Norvell, made very important corrections, taking care to omit sentences and paragraphs that contained explicit statements as to the purposes of the President. . . . Among the statements made which were preserved in the article were these . . . "So far as current movements of the Treasury are concerned, until the crops are moved it is not likely Treasury gold will be sold for currency to be locked up." . . .

The most unpleasant incident of the gold speculation of 1869 was the fact that General Butterfield, the assistant treasurer in the city of New York, was so far involved as to lead the President to ask for his resignation.

GOULD AND FISK had cast their net wide. They failed to snare the President himself, but they snatched up several of those around him. Foremost was Abel Corbin, his bumbling brother-in-law, who was given a large stake in the gold purchases being made by the pair; his constant efforts to convince Grant to stop gold sales failed miserably, as Boutwell suggests. But he not only lobbied the President personally—he also arranged several opportunities for Gould and Fisk to run into Grant, supposedly by accident, so they could press their own case. Another key figure was Daniel Butterfield, who had been appointed to his treasury post—the second most important in the department—at Corbin's urging. Finally, there was the person closest to the President: First Lady Julia Grant.

It was not the first or the last time that wealthy men would lobby the President and his immediate family, but it was certainly the brashest effort in history. When Gould and Fisk failed to sway Grant, they pursued a tie to his wife. With Corbin as the conduit, they apparently set up a large account for Julia. Fisk later testified that Gould had sold $500,000 worth of gold for the First Lady, gaining her a profit of about $25,000. Some have doubted this claim; yet the records of the Adams Express Company indicate a sizeable cash delivery to the White House—for Julia Dent Grant—about this time.

Was the First Lady involved in the plot to run up the gold market? Certainly Gould and Fisk put out the word that she was, to lend credence to their claims that Grant had agreed to limit sales of government gold. It would have taken little effort on her part: a nod in response to Corbin's whispered offer, and the conspirators would put up the cash for the investment. A few weeks later, as the market rose, they could have sold the gold that was held in her name, and she had an easy $25,000. And there is another factor to consider: she had suffered years of relative deprivation before the Civil War, and now she wished to circulate with her wealthy new friends in style. As William McFeely writes, "She knew little of the ways of the New York financial world, but she knew everything about being deprived of money. She believed fervently that her Ulysses—and she—deserved well of the Republic, and she lived in a world that, in large part, saw rewards in terms of money."

Perhaps the presence of her finger in the honey jar explains an unusual incident in September, as the final collapse of the gold speculation approached. Gould and Fisk knew that their public deception about Grant's involvement could only last so long. They began to grow desperate to secure a solid commitment from the President, so they could drive the market still higher before pulling out. Accordingly, they ferociously pressured the weak Abel Corbin to get a flat declaration of support from Grant in the early days of fall. Corbin sent an urgent letter to Grant by special messenger. It arrived as the chief executive was playing croquet with friends and his wife's relatives in Washington, Pennsylvania. This final, desperate appeal was too much for the taciturn general. The frenzy in New York, the constant lobbying, the participation of Corbin, Butterfield, and now his wife—it finally went past his endurance. Usually

Grant deferred to his strong-willed spouse; but this time there would be no saying no to the furious President.

An Urgent Letter
by Julia Dent Grant

Our eight years in the Executive Mansion were delightful, but there were some dark clouds in the bright sky. There was that dreadful Black Friday. The papers seemed to say I knew something of it, but I did not—only this. One day, while visiting a cousin at Washington, Pa., a banker there, I sat in the library writing letters. General Grant entered and asked: "Whom are you writing to?" I answered, "Your sister." He said; "Write this." Then he dictated as follows: "The General says, if you have any influence with your husband, tell him to have nothing whatever to do with [Gould and Fisk]. If he does, he will be ruined, for come what may, he (your brother) will do his duty to the country and the trusts in his keeping." I signed, "Sis."

He said: "Seal and send the letter by the first mail." And I did. That is all I knew about it then. After the letter was sent, the General told me he had received a letter from his brother-in-law just before he came into the library, and supposing it had been brought up by one of my cousin's clerks, who always brought the General's mail, he then opened it and seeing it was from Corbin, glanced up at the man and said, "all right," meaning to dismiss the messenger and that there was no answer, who repeated, "All right?" The General nodded.

Directly, General Horace Porter, then on duty with my husband, entered and asked the General if the letter he had just received was important. "No, it is from Corbin," General Grant said. "Did you read it carefully?" Porter asked. "Do you know it was sent by special messenger from New York?"

"No," the General said, "was not that one of [William W.] Smith's clerks?" "No," said General Porter, "what did you say to him?" "Nothing. I said, 'all right,' meaning there was no answer and that he could retire." Porter said: "Yes! the messenger said he would at once telegraph your answer 'all right.' "

The General said to me: "I have read the letter carefully now and I find it is an earnest plea for a certain financial policy, which you know he continually urges, saying if I will adopt it, it will make money plentiful and consequently make my administration popular. I always felt great respect for Corbin and thought he took much pleasure in the supposition that he was rendering great assistance to the administration by his valuable service. I blame myself now for not checking this (as I thought) innocent vanity. It is very sad. I fear he may be ruined—and my poor sister!" And sure enough, when we arrived in Washington, the papers announced a fearful financial panic in New York, and, as I remember, the President did his duty, his whole duty, on that occasion.

———————

THE GOLD BUGS were ecstatic when they received the telegraphed response, "all right." But then came the letter from Julia Grant, dictated by the President himself. The implication was clear—the administration would soon act to end the speculation. "Mr. Corbin," Gould coldly declared, "I am undone if that letter gets out." He handed over a check for $100,000 to the panic-stricken Corbin to convince him to remain in the market; if the President's brother-in-law sold his holdings, the market would quickly collapse. Then the steel-willed young man went to Wall Street, where he forced the price of gold still higher.

The end was near, and Gould was already making plans for his successful departure from the frenzied trading of the Gold Room. But in the closing days, he worked assiduously to convince others that the price would keep climbing. He spread word that Corbin was still in; he sent off letters to Boutwell, trying to convince him to hang on to the treasury's gold; he pushed the Tenth National Bank, an institution he held tightly in his grasp, to dangerously extend itself in giving credit to gold speculators.

Meanwhile, the treasury secretary and the President had arrived at the same conclusion: it was time for a fall. Soon after Grant returned from Pennsylvania, the two men met in Washington, and decided upon the actions that would bring on the mad panic known as Black Friday.

———————

The Panic
by George S. Boutwell

Under date of September 20, I received a letter from Gould to which I made no reply. Aside from the topics to which he directed my attention in the letter, is the unavoidable inference from the context as a whole that Gould had then no faith in the statements [he had] given to the public that the President was in any manner pledged to interfere and prevent the sale of gold. . . .

As early as the 20th of September, I had evidence satisfactory to me that the Tenth National Bank in the city of New York was a party to the speculation in gold, and that its assistance was rendered largely through the certification of checks drawn by the brokers and largely in excess of the balances due them upon the books of the bank when the certifications were made. It appeared from the evidence submitted that these certifications of checks in excess of the balances due to brokers amounted to about $18,000,000 on the 22nd and 23rd of September, when the speculation was at its height.

For the purpose of arresting the process and checking the speculation in gold, I detained the comptroller of the currency and three competent clerks after the close of business on the 22nd of September. The clerks received commissions as bank examiners, and were instructed to go to New York that night and take possession of the Tenth National Bank at the opening of business in the morning, and to give directions that the habit of certifying checks in excess of the balances due must be suspended. It was my expectation that the enforcement of that rule would, or might, end the speculation, inasmuch as the purchasers of gold would be unable to meet their obligations, and therefore it would be out of their power to create them. This expectation was not realized. Whether the certification went on at the Tenth National Bank in defiance of the order, or whether other banks were so connected with the speculation that checks were certified elsewhere, was not known to me.

I called upon the President after business on the 23rd of September, and made a statement of the condition of the gold market in the city of New York, as far as it had been communicated to me during the day. I then said that a sale of gold should be made for the purposes of breaking the market and ending the excitement. He asked me what sum I proposed to sell. I said: "Three million dollars will be sufficient to break the combination."

He said in reply: "I think you had better make it $5,000,000."

Without assenting to his proposition or dissenting from it, I returned to the department, and sent an order for the sale of $4,000,000 of gold the next day. The order was to the assistant treasurer in these words: "Sell $4,000,000 gold to-morrow, and buy $4,000,000 bonds." The message was not in cipher, and there was no attempt to keep it secret. It was duplicated, and sent by each of the rival telegraph lines to New York.[4] Within the space of fifteen minutes after the receipt of the despatch, the price of gold fell from 160 to 133 [dollars per ounce], and in the language of one of the witnesses, "half of Wall Street was involved in ruin." . . .

Under date of the 24th day of September,[5] I received a letter from my special and trusted correspondent in the city of New York in which I find this statement: "This has been the most dreadful day I have ever seen in this city. While gold was jumping from forty-three to sixty-one [that is, from $143 per ounce to $161] the excitement was painful. Old, conserv-

[4] Boutwell was worried that Butterfield in particular would hold the telegram until he could notify Gould and Fisk.

[5] This paragraph and the next two have been moved for narrative continuity.

ative merchants looked aghast, nobody was in their offices, and the agony depicted on the faces of men who crowded the streets made one feel as if Gettysburg had been lost and the rebels were marching down Broadway. Friends of the Administration openly stated that the President or yourself must have given these men to feel you would not interfere with them or they would never dare to rush gold up so rapidly. In truth, many parties of real responsibility and friends of the Government openly declared that somebody in Washington must be in this combination." . . .

Another extract from Fisk's testimony gives a graphic view of his condition when the crash came: "I went down to the neighborhood of Wall Street Friday morning. When I got back to our office you can imagine I was in no enviable state of mind, and the moment I got up street that afternoon I started right round to old Corbin's to rake him out. I went into the room, and sent word that Mr. Fisk wanted to see him in the dining-room. I was too mad to say anything civil, and when he came into the room, said I, 'Do you know what you have done here, you and your people?' He began to wring his hands, and 'Oh,' he says, 'this is a horrible position. Are you ruined?' I said I didn't know whether I was or not; and I asked him again if he knew what had happened. He had been crying, and said he had just heard; that he had been sure everything was all right; but that something had occurred entirely different from what he had anticipated. Said I, 'That don't amount to anything. We know that gold ought not to be at thirty-one [$131 per ounce], and that it would not be but for such performances as you have had this last week; you know damn well it would not if you had not failed.' I knew that somebody had run a saw right into us, and said I, 'This whole damn thing has turned out just as I told you it would.' I considered the whole party a pack of cowards; and I expected that, when we came to clear our hands, they would sock it right into us. I said to him, 'I don't know whether you have lied or not, and I don't know what ought to be done with you.'

"He was on the other side of the table, weeping and wailing, and I was gnashing my teeth. 'Now,' he says, 'you must quiet yourself.' I told him I didn't want to be quiet; I had no desire to ever be quiet again. He says, 'But, my dear sir, you will lose your reason.' Says I, 'Speyers has already lost his reason; reason has gone out of everybody but me.' " . . .

For the moment, the condition in Wall Street and the Gold Exchange seemed to justify the statement of the person whose language has just been quoted. As a matter of fact, however, many of the people involved recovered from the panic, and were able to meet their obligations. Some were gainers, probably, by the proceedings of the month of September, and some were losers. As I have already said, I had no purpose to help anybody or to hurt anybody, and I interfered in Wall Street only when the operations that were going on there involved innocent parties who were engaged in legitimate business, and also imposed upon the Government a sacrifice in the loss of revenue.

Following the downfall of the combination, there appeared in the newspapers statements and imputations which reflected upon the President and his family as to their relations to the gold operations. Mr. Corbin's connection was established beyond controversy, but the evidence which established his relations to the parties engaged in the gold speculation was also conclusive as to the fact that the President had no connection with it, and that he was not in any way interested in any policy calculated to advance the interests of the combination.

———

ONE MAN FLOURISHED in the crash—and it should be no surprise that his name was Jay Gould. After convincing everyone else to drive up the market to its peak, he quietly and anonymously sold off his holdings. Unlike his confederates Fisk and Corbin (who survived, but took a terrible loss) or such political insiders as Butterfield, Gould walked away from the panic with millions.

Black Friday was a strange scandal. No laws were broken. Neither Grant nor Boutwell succumbed to the incessant lobbying. But these events demonstrated critical weaknesses in America's financial structure. The economy was booming, but almost every aspect of the republic's finances were concentrated in one city, New York. There, the nation's biggest banks clustered together, holding deposits from every state; there, most foreign trade flowed in or out of the country; and there the assistant U.S. treasurer regulated the complex interchange between greenbacks and gold—the first used only in domestic transactions, the latter being the only medium of foreign exchange.

Even the use of greenbacks, however, failed to meet the needs of the American economy. There was so little currency in circulation that a sudden turn in the markets—Gould's assault on gold, for example, of Vanderbilt's massive purchase of Erie stock—could constrict the whole country. And the Treasury Department was staffed by political appointees, such as Butterfield; Boutwell did a fine job, but one bad official could topple the rickety tower rising in Wall Street and send it crashing across America.

The nation had a narrow escape, then, but a foreboding one. One man had led the economy to the brink of disaster with ruthless skill. Once again, Jay Gould had shown himself to be a master of conspiracy in an age of conspiracy, as a tiny clique of wealthy men had played with the financial policies of a great nation. It was another sign that the grand old republic was falling under the shadow of an elite answerable to no one.

———

15

ANDREW CARNEGIE, DEALMAKER

The name Carnegie means steel. It conjures up images of massive factories, vast iron and coal mines, far-flung railways carrying raw materials in one direction and finished rails and beams in another—all within a single corporate empire. The name Carnegie means to us something far different from that of Gould, who viewed company treasuries the way Jesse James (a contemporary) viewed banks; it symbolizes the urge to build, to perfect, to expand a business. Or so it does today. As the 1860s passed away into the 1870s, however, the future empire builder threw himself down another path entirely.

Even as the young entrepreneur established his first manufacturing firm, he discovered the joys of manipulating money. No sooner were his iron mills up and running in Pittsburgh than he moved to New York, the nation's financial capital. There he thrilled to the role of dealmaker: selling bonds, securing mergers, raiding rival corporations. Indeed, Carnegie proved to be strikingly, ruthlessly adept at the arts of the robber baron, winning the admiration of Jay Gould himself. With his confident charm, he won more success in the European financial market (the source of much of America's investment capital) than perhaps anyone in his day.

In the account that follows, Carnegie describes his vibrant career as a Wall Street financier. He clearly relishes his many deals with European investors: the quiet negotiations with educated, cultured men, the agreements settled over a glass of sherry, the staggering commissions he earned. He also reveals his own ruthless approach to business. Carnegie was an early investor in the first sleeping car manufacturer—a company that soon discovered that its patents were being stolen by George Pullman, who was rapidly rising to dominate the industry. In a situation such as this, Carnegie knew when to fight, and when to force his opponent (and his partners) into a merger.

Later still, he launched a takeover of the Union Pacific Railroad, which started a decisive split with his old mentor Thomas Scott—though in these reminiscences, he reverses the roles played by the two men. Carnegie never let sentimentality stand in his way, as he proved when his old friend Scott appealed for help on the threshold of the panic of 1873. All together, he offers a vivid picture of a man steadily marching toward a life not as an industrialist, but as a master of the deal.

Stocks and Bonds
by Andrew Carnegie

Our business continued to expand and required frequent visits on my part to the East, especially to New York, which is as London is to Britain—the headquarters of all really important enterprises in America. No large concern could very well get on without being represented there. My brother and Mr. Phipps had full grasp of the business at Pittsburgh. My field appeared to be to direct the general policy of the companies and negotiate the important contracts.

My brother had been so fortunate as to marry Miss Lucy Coleman, daughter of one of our most valued partners and friends. Our family residence at Homewood was given over to him, and I was once more compelled to break old associations and leave Pittsburgh in 1867 to take up my residence in New York. The change was hard enough for me, but much harder for my mother; but she was still in the prime of life and we could be happy anywhere so long as we were together. Still she did feel the leaving of our home very much. We were perfect strangers in New York, and at first we took up our quarters in the St. Nicholas Hotel, then in its glory. I opened an office in Broad Street. . . .

After a time new friendships were formed and new interests awakened and New York began to be called home. When the proprietors of the St. Nicholas opened the Windsor Hotel uptown, we took up our residence there and up to the year 1887 that was our New York home. . . . Among the educative influences from which I derived great advantage in New York, none ranks higher than the Nineteenth Century Club organized by Mr. and Mrs. Courtlandt Palmer. The club met at their house once a month for the discussion of various topics and soon attracted many able men and women. . . .

I had lived long enough in Pittsburgh to acquire the manufacturing, as distinguished from the speculative, spirit. I was surprised to find how very different was the state of affairs in New York. There were few even of the businessmen who had not their ventures in Wall Street [that is, in the stock market] to a greater or less extent. I was besieged with inquiries from all quarters in regard to the various railway enterprises with which I was connected. Offers were made to me by persons who were willing to furnish capital for investment and allow me to manage it—the supposition being that from the inside view which I was enabled to obtain I could invest for them successfully. Invitations were extended to me to join parties who intended quietly to buy up the control of certain properties. In fact the whole speculative field was laid out before me in its most seductive guise.

All these allurements I declined.[6] The most notable offer of this kind I ever received was one morning in the Windsor Hotel soon after my removal to New York. Jay Gould, then in the height of his career, approached me and said he had heard of me and he would purchase control of the Pennsylvania Railroad Company and give me one half of all profits if I would agree to devote myself to its management. I thanked him and said that, although Mr. Scott and I had parted company in business matters, I would never raise my hand against him. Subsequently Mr. Scott told me he had heard I had been selected by New York interests to succeed him. I do not know how he had learned this, as I had never mentioned it. I was able to reassure him by saying that the only railroad company I would be president of would be one I owned. . . .

My first important enterprise after settling in New York was undertaking to build a bridge across the Mississippi at Keokuk. Mr. Thomson, president of the Pennsylvania Railroad, and I contracted for the whole structure, foundation, masonry, superstructure, taking bonds and stocks in payment. The undertaking was a splendid success in every respect, except financially. A panic threw the connecting railways into bankruptcy. They were unable to pay the stipulated sums. Rival systems built a bridge across the Mississippi at Burlington and a railway down the west side of the Mississippi to Keokuk. The handsome profits which we saw in prospect were never realized. Mr. Thomson and myself, however, escaped loss, although there was little margin left. . . .

The reputation obtained in the Keokuk bridge[7] led to my being applied to by those who were in charge of the scheme for bridging the Mississippi at St. Louis, to which I have already referred. This was connected to my first large financial transaction. One day in 1869 the gentleman in charge of the enterprise, Mr. Macpherson (he was very Scotch), called at my New York office and said they were trying to raise capital to build the bridge. He wished to know if I could not enlist some of the Eastern railroad companies in the scheme. After careful examination of the project I made the contract for the construction of the bridge on behalf of the Keystone Bridge Works. I also obtained an option upon four million dollars of first mortgage bonds of the bridge company and set out for London in March, 1869, to negotiate their sale.

During the voyage I prepared a prospectus which I had printed upon my arrival in London, and having upon my previous visit made the ac-

6 This statement is typical of Carnegie's autobiography: he is imparting his later outlook, after he had concentrated all of his efforts in manufacturing, to his earlier life, which was rife with financial speculation. The incident described here followed Carnegie's raid on the Union Pacific, which appears shortly.

7 A reputation built on the technical achievement of building the bridge, which had a 380-foot span.

quaintance of Junius S. Morgan, the great banker, I called upon him one morning and opened negotiations. I left with him a copy of the prospectus, and upon calling next day was delighted to find that Mr. Morgan viewed the matter favorably. I sold him part of the bonds with the option to take the remainder; but when his lawyers were called in for advice a score of changes were required in the wording of the bonds. Mr. Morgan said to me that as I was going to Scotland I had better go now; I could write the parties in St. Louis and ascertain whether they would agree to the changes proposed. It would be time enough, he said, to close the matter upon my return three weeks hence.

But I had no idea of allowing the fish to play so long, and I informed him that I would have a telegram in the morning agreeing to all the changes. The Atlantic cable had been open for some time, but it is doubtful if it had yet carried so long a private cable as I sent that day. It was not an easy matter to number the lines of the bond and then going carefully over them to state what changes, omissions, or additions were required in each line. I showed Mr. Morgan the message before sending it and he said, "Well, young man, if you succeed in that you deserve a red mark."

When I entered the office the next morning, I found on the desk that had been appropriated to my use in Mr. Morgan's private office the colored envelope which contained the answer. There it was: "Board meeting last night; changes all approved." "Now, Mr. Morgan," I said, "we can proceed, assuming that the bond is as your lawyers desire." The papers were soon closed.

While I was in the office Mr. Sampson, the financial editor of *The Times*, came in. I had an interview with him, well knowing that a few words from him would go far in lifting the price of the bonds on the Exchange. American securities had recently been fiercely attacked, owing to the proceedings of Fisk and Gould in connection with the Erie Railway Company, and their control of the judges in New York, who seemed to do their bidding. I knew this would be handed out as an objection, and therefore I met it at once.

I called Mr. Sampson's attention to the fact that the charter of the St. Louis Bridge Company was from the National Government. In case of necessity appeal lay directly to the Supreme Court of the United States, a body vying with their own high tribunals. He said he would be delighted to give prominence to this commendable feature. I described the bridge as a toll-gate on the continental highway and this appeared to please him. It was all plain and easy sailing, and when he left the office, Mr. Morgan clapped me on the shoulder and said, "Thank you, young man; you have raised the price of those bonds five percent this morning."

"All right, Mr. Morgan," I replied, "now show me how I can raise them five percent more for you."

The issue was a great success, and the money for the St. Louis Bridge Company was obtained. I had a considerable margin of profit upon the negotiation. This was my first financial negotiation with the bankers of Europe. Mr. Pullman told me a few days later that Mr. Morgan at a dinner party had told the telegraphic incident and predicted, "That young man will be heard from." . . .

While visiting the Continent of Europe in 1867 and deeply interested in what I saw, it must not be thought that my mind was not upon affairs at home. Frequent letters kept me advised of business matters. The question of railway communications with the Pacific had been brought to the front by the Civil War, and Congress had passed an act to encourage the construction of a line. The first sod had just been cut at Omaha and it was intended that the line should ultimately be pushed through to San Francisco. One day in Rome it struck me that this might be done much sooner than was then anticipated. The nation, having made up its mind that its territory must be bound together, might be trusted to see that no time was lost in accomplishing it. I wrote to my friend Mr. Scott, suggesting that we should obtain the contract to place sleeping-cars upon the great California line. His reply contained these words: "Well, young man, you do take time by the forelock."[8]

Nevertheless, upon my return to America, I pursued the idea. The sleeping-car business, in which I was interested, had gone on increasing so rapidly that it was impossible to obtain cars enough to supply the demand. This very fact led to the forming of the present Pullman Company.[9] The Central Transportation Company was simply unable to cover the territory with sufficient rapidity, and Mr. Pullman beginning at the greatest of all railway centers in the world—Chicago—soon rivaled the parent concern. He had also seen that the Pacific Railroad would be the great sleeping-car line of the world, and I found him working for what I had started after. He was, indeed, a lion in the path. Again, one may learn from an incident which I had from Mr. Pullman himself, by what trifles the important matters are sometimes determined.

The president of the Union Pacific Railway was passing through Chicago. Mr. Pullman called upon him and was shown into his room. Lying upon the table was a telegram addressed to Mr. Scott, saying,

[8] In 1859, Carnegie had obtained a one-eighth interest in the Woodruff Sleeping Car Company, which supplied the Pennsylvania Railroad. The founder, Thomas T. Woodruff, created the first sleeping cars and held most of the patents. In 1862, Carnegie reorganized the firm as the Central Transportation Company; together with Scott, Thomson, and others, he took control from Woodruff himself.

[9] George Mortimer Pullman arrived in Chicago from upstate New York in 1855. A better entrepreneur than an inventor, he largely stole Woodruff's design. After initial failure, he later added lavish decorations and creature comforts to his cars, and achieved tremendous success.

"Your proposition for sleeping-cars is accepted." Mr. Pullman read this involuntarily and before he had time to refrain. He could not help seeing it where it lay. When President Durrant entered the room he explained this to him and said: "I trust you will not decide this matter until I have made a proposition to you."

Mr. Durrant promised to wait. A meeting of the board of directors of the Union Pacific Company was held soon after this in New York. Mr. Pullman and myself were in attendance, both striving to obtain the prize which neither he nor I undervalued. One evening we began to mount the broad staircase in the St. Nicholas Hotel at the same time. We had met before, but were not well acquainted. I said, however, as we walked up the stairs: "Good evening, Mr. Pullman! Here we are together, and are we not making a nice couple of fools out of ourselves?"

He was not disposed to admit anything and said, "What do you mean?"

I explained the situation to him. We were destroying by our rival propositions the very advantages we desired to obtain.

"Well," he said, "what do you propose to do about it?"

"Unite," I said. "Make a joint proposition to the Union Pacific, your party and mine, and organize a company."

"What would you call it?" he asked.

"The Pullman Palace Car Company," I replied. This suited him exactly; and it suited me equally well.

"Come into my room and talk it over," said the great sleeping-car man.

I did so, and the result was that we obtained the contract jointly. Our company was subsequently merged in the general Pullman Company and we took stock in that company for our Pacific interests. Until compelled to sell my shares during the subsequent financial panic of 1873 to protect our iron and steel interests, I was, I believe, the largest shareholder in the Pullman Company.

This man Pullman and his career are so thoroughly American that a few words about him will not be out of place. Mr. Pullman was at first a working carpenter, but when Chicago had to be elevated he took a contract on his own account to move or elevate houses for a stipulated sum. Of course he was successful, and from this small beginning he became one of the principal and best-known contractors in that line. If a great hotel was to be raised ten feet without disturbing its hundreds of guests or interfering in any way with its business, Mr. Pullman was the man. He was one of those rare characters who can see the drift of things, and was always to be found, so to speak, swimming in the main current where movement was the fastest. He soon saw, as I did, that the sleeping-car was a positive necessity upon the American continent. He began to construct a few cars at Chicago and to obtain contracts upon the lines centering there.

The Eastern concern [the Central Transportation Company] was in no condition to cope with that of an extraordinary man like Mr. Pullman. I soon recognized this, and although the original patents were with the Eastern company and Mr. Woodruff himself, the original patentee, was a large shareholder, and although we might have obtained damages for infringement of patent after some years of litigation, yet the time lost before this could be done would have been sufficient to make Pullman's the great company of the country. I therefore earnestly advocated that we should unite with Mr. Pullman, as I had united with him before in the Union Pacific contract.

As the personal relations between Mr. Pullman and some members of the Eastern company were unsatisfactory, it was deemed best that I should undertake the negotiations, being upon friendly footing with both parties. We soon agreed that the Pullman Company should absorb our company, the Central Transportation Company, and by this means Mr. Pullman, instead of being confined to the West, obtained control of the rights on the great Pennsylvania trunk line to the Atlantic seaboard. This placed his company beyond all possible rivals. Mr. Pullman was one of the ablest men of affairs I have ever known, and I am indebted to him. . . .

Success in these various negotiations had brought me into some notice in New York, and my next large operation was in connection with the Union Pacific Railway in 1871. One of its directors came to me saying that they must raise in some way a sum of six hundred thousand dollars (equal to many millions to-day) to carry them through a crisis; and some friends who knew me and were on the executive committee of that road had suggested that I might be able to obtain the money and at the same time get for the Pennsylvania Railroad Company virtual control of that important Western line. I believe that Mr. Pullman came with the director, or perhaps it was Mr. Pullman himself who first came to see me on the subject.

I took up the matter, and it occurred to me that if the directors of the Union Pacific Railway would be willing to elect to its board of directors a few such men as the Pennsylvania Railroad would nominate, the traffic to be thus obtained for the Pennsylvania would justify that company in helping the Union Pacific. I went to Philadelphia and laid the subject before President Thomson. I suggested that if the Pennsylvania Railroad Company would trust me with securities upon which the Union Pacific could borrow money in New York, we could control the Union Pacific in the interests of the Pennsylvania. Among many marks of Mr. Thomson's confidence this was up to that time the greatest. He was much more conservative when handling the money of the railroad company than his own, but the prize offered was too great to be missed. Even if the six hundred thousand dollars had been lost, it would not have been a losing investment for his company, and there was little danger of this because we were ready to hand over to him the securities which we obtained in return for the loan to the Union Pacific.

My interview with Mr. Thomson took place at his house in Philadelphia, and as I rose to go he laid his hand upon my shoulder, saying: "Remember, Andy, I look to you in this matter. It is you I trust, and I depend on your holding all the securities you obtain and seeing that the Pennsylvania Railroad is never in a position where it can lose a dollar."

I accepted the responsibility, and the result was a triumphant success. The Union Pacific Company was exceedingly anxious that Mr. Thomson himself should take the presidency, but this he said was out of the question. He nominated Mr. Thomas A. Scott, vice-president of the Pennsylvania Railroad, for the position. Mr. Scott, Mr. Pullman, and myself were accordingly elected directors of the Union Pacific Railway Company in 1871.

The securities obtained for the loan consisted of three millions of the shares of the Union Pacific, which were locked in my safe, with the option of taking them at a price. As was to be expected, the accession of the Pennsylvania Railroad party rendered the stock of the Union Pacific infinitely more valuable. The shares advanced enormously. At this time I undertook to negotiate bonds in London for a bridge to cross the Missouri at Omaha, and while I was absent upon this business Mr. Scott decided to sell our Union Pacific shares. I had left instructions with my secretary that Mr. Scott, as one of the partners in the venture, should have access to the vault, as it might be necessary in my absence that the securities should be within reach of someone; but the idea that these should be sold, or that our party should lose the splendid position we had acquired in connection with the Union Pacific, never entered my brain.[10]

I returned to find that, instead of being a trusted colleague of the Union Pacific directors, I was regarded as having used them for speculative purposes. No quartet of men ever had a finer opportunity for identifying themselves with a great work than we had; and never was an opportunity more recklessly thrown away. Mr. Pullman was ignorant of the matter and as indignant as myself, and I believe that he at once reinvested his profits in the shares of the Union Pacific. I felt that much as I wished to do this and to repudiate what had been done, it would be unbecoming and perhaps ungrateful of me to separate myself so distinctly from my first of friends, Mr. Scott.

At the first opportunity we were ignominiously but deservedly expelled from the Union Pacific board. It was a bitter dose for a young man to swallow. And the transaction marked my first serious difference with a

10 Carnegie is telling a completely reversed version of this incident, probably to make it fit with his later conviction that stock speculation is a great evil. In fact, it was Carnegie himself who sold the stock as it skyrocketed in price; Scott, who had been elected president of the mighty railroad, was furious.

man who up to that time had the greatest influence with me, the kind
and affectionate employer of my boyhood, Mr. Thomas A. Scott. Mr.
Thomson regretted the matter, but, as he said, having paid no attention
to it and having left the whole control of it in the hands of Mr. Scott and
myself, he presumed that I had thought it best to sell out. . . .

BUSINESS NEGOTIATIONS

Complete success attended a negotiation which I conducted about this
time for Colonel William Phillips, president of the Allegheny Valley Railway at Pittsburgh. One day the Colonel entered my New York office and
told me that he needed money badly, but that he could get no house in
America to entertain the idea of purchasing five millions of bonds of his
company although they were to be guaranteed by the Pennsylvania Railroad Company. The old gentleman felt sure that he was being driven
from pillar to post by the bankers because they had agreed among themselves to purchase the bonds only upon their own terms. He asked ninety
cents on the dollar for them, but this the bankers considered preposter-
ously high. Those were the days when Western railway bonds were often
sold to the bankers at eighty cents upon the dollar.

Colonel Phillips said he had come to see whether I could not suggest
some way out of his difficulty. He had pressing need for two hundred and
fifty thousand dollars, and this Mr. Thomson, of the Pennsylvania Railroad, could not give him. The Allegheny bonds were seven percents, but
they were payable, not in gold, but in currency, in America. They were
therefore wholly unsuited for the foreign market. But I knew that the
Pennsylvania Railroad Company had a large amount of Philadelphia and
Erie Railroad six percent gold bonds in its treasury. It would be a most
desirable exchange on its part, I thought, to give these bonds for the
seven percent Allegheny bonds which bore its guarantee.

I telegraphed Mr. Thomson, asking if the Pennsylvania Railroad Company would take two hundred and fifty thousand dollars at interest and
lend it to the Allegheny Railway Company. Mr. Thomson replied, "Certainly." Colonel Phillips was happy. He agreed, in consideration of my
services, to give me a sixty-days option to take his five millions of bonds
at the desired ninety cents on the dollar. I laid the matter before Mr.
Thomson and suggested an exchange, which that company was only too
glad to make, as it saved one percent interest on the bonds.

I sailed at once for London with the control of five millions of first
mortgage Philadelphia and Erie Bonds, guaranteed by the Pennsylvania
Railroad Company—a magnificent security for which I wanted a high
price. And here comes in one of the greatest of the hits and misses of my
financial life.

I wrote the Barings from Queenstown that I had for sale a security which even their house might unhesitatingly consider. On my arrival in London I found at the hotel a note from them requesting me to call. I did so the next morning, and before I had left their banking house I had closed an agreement by which they were to bring out this loan, and that until they sold the bonds at par, less their two and a half percent commission, they would advance the Pennsylvania Railroad Company four millions of dollars at five percent interest. The sale left me a clear profit of more than half a million dollars.

The papers were ordered drawn up, but as I was leaving Mr. Russell Sturgis said they had just heard that Mr. Baring himself was coming up to town in the morning. They had arranged to hold a "court," and as it would be fitting to lay the transaction before him as a matter of courtesy they would postpone the signing of the papers until the morrow. If I would call at two o'clock the transaction would be closed.

Never shall I forget the oppressed feeling which overcame me as I stepped out and proceeded to the telegraph office to wire President Thomson. Something told me that I ought not to do so. I would wait till to-morrow when I had the contract in my pocket. I walked from the banking house to the Langham Hotel—four long miles. When I reached there I found a messenger waiting breathless to hand me a sealed note from the Barings. Bismarck had locked up a hundred millions in Magdeburg. The financial world was panic-stricken, and the Barings begged to say that under the circumstances they could not propose to Mr. Baring to go on with the matter.

There was as much chance that I should be struck by lightning on my way home as that an arrangement agreed to by the Barings should be broken. And yet it was. It was too great a blow to produce anything like irritation or indignation. I was meek enough to be quite resigned, and merely congratulated myself that I had not telegraphed Mr. Thomson.

I decided not to return to the Barings, and although J.S. Morgan & Co. had been bringing out a great many American securities I subsequently sold the bonds to them at a reduced price as compared with that agreed to by the Barings. . . . Of course in this case I made a mistake in not returning to the Barings, giving them time and letting the panic subside, which it soon did. When one party to a bargain becomes excited, the other should keep cool and patient. . . .

Soon after being deposed as president of the Union Pacific [in 1872], Mr. Scott resolved upon the construction of the Texas Pacific Railway. He telegraphed me in New York to meet him at Philadelphia without fail. I met him there with several other friends, among them Mr. J. N. McCullough, vice-president of the Pennsylvania Railroad Company at Pittsburgh. A large loan for the Texas Pacific had fallen due in London and its renewal was agreed to by Morgan & Co., provided I would join the other parties to the loan.

I declined. I was then asked whether I would bring them all to ruin by refusing to stand by my friends. It was one of the most trying moments of my whole life. Yet I was not tempted for a moment to entertain the idea of involving myself. The question of what was my duty came first and prevented that. All my capital was in manufacturing and every dollar of it was required. I was the capitalist (then a modest one, indeed) of our concern. All depended upon me. My brother and his wife and family, Mr. Phipps and his family, Mr. Kloman and his family, all rose up before me and claimed protection.

I told Mr. Scott that I had done my best to prevent him from beginning to construct a great railway before he had secured the necessary capital. I had insisted that thousands of miles of railway lines could not be constructed by means of temporary loans. Besides, I had paid two hundred and fifty thousand dollars cash for an interest in it, which he told me upon my return from Europe he had reserved for me, although I had never approved the scheme. But nothing in the world would ever induce me to be guilty of endorsing the paper of that construction company or of any other concern than our own firm.

I knew that it would be impossible for me to pay the Morgan loan in sixty days, or even to pay my proportion of it. Besides, it was not that loan by itself, but the half-dozen other loans that would be required thereafter that had to be considered. This marked another step in the total business separation which had to come between Mr. Scott and myself. It gave me more pain than all the financial trials to which I had been subjected up to that time.

It was not long after this meeting that the disaster came and the country was startled by the failure of those whom it had regarded as its strongest men. I fear Mr. Scott's premature death [May 21, 1881] can measurably be attributed to the humiliation which he had to bear. He was a sensitive rather than a proud man, and his seemingly impending failure cut him to the quick. Mr. McManus and Mr. Baird, partners in the enterprise, also soon passed away. These two men were manufacturers like myself and in no position to engage in railway construction. . . .

Notwithstanding my refusal to endorse the Morgan renewal, I was invited to accompany the parties to New York next morning in their special car for the purpose of consultation. This I was only too glad to do. Anthony Drexel was also called in to accompany us. During the journey Mr. McCullough remarked that he had been looking around the car and had made up his mind that there was only one sensible man in it; the rest had all been "fools." Here was "Andy" who had paid for his shares and did not own a dollar or have any responsibility in the matter, and that was the position they all ought to have been in.

Mr. Drexel said he would like me to explain how I had been able to steer clear of these unfortunate troubles. I answered: by strict adherence to what I believed to be my duty never to put my name to anything which I knew I could not pay at maturity; or, to recall the familiar saying of a Western friend, never to go in where you couldn't wade. This water was altogether too deep for me.

———

WHAT A MAN was Carnegie. By 1873, he had bought out the sleeping car inventor Woodward, forced a merger with the patent thief Pullman, undercut his partners in the Union Pacific takeover, and turned against his old mentor Scott. He had inserted himself as financier and bond salesman for his own bridge-building ventures and his friends' railroads, pocketing hundreds of thousands of dollars in commissions. Clearly no one knew how to play the game better, or more ruthlessly, than Andrew Carnegie—as Jay Gould, the master himself, acknowledged when he sought the Scotsman's help in running the Pennsylvania.

That request came immediately after the Union Pacific incident—an incident telling in more ways than one. "I have never bought or sold a share of stock speculatively in my life," Carnegie writes in his memoirs— a statement proven patently false by his unloading of the transcontinental railroad's securities after the takeover by Scott, Thomson, Pullman, and himself. He reconciles this misstatement with the facts by misstating the facts themselves—he completely reverses the roles played in the stock sale, claiming it was Scott, not himself, who cashed in on the sudden rise in the Union Pacific shares. "It never entered my brain," he writes, to sell them. But is he deceiving his readers, or himself? This period of his career so sharply contrasts with his later devotion to steelmaking that he had to reinvent it in his own mind. Writing from the perspective of long years as an empire builder, he could not acknowledge to himself his youthful devotion to the role of the robber baron—or that he, not Scott, had severed the ties between mentor and pupil.

The contrast between these two phases in Carnegie's career, however, are less stark in reality than in the distinctions he himself drew between speculation and manufacturing. The fortune he piled up from these diversified financial transactions gave him the resources of money and reputation that allowed him to launch his great move into steel. For as Scott nearly drowned in the crisis of 1873 (covered later in this book), Carnegie had already begun this strategic shift—establishing an enterprise that would change the face of American industry for the next century.

———

VI

POLITICS

GRANT'S FIRST TERM
1869–1873

16

AN ISLAND, A SENATOR,
AND A CABINET SEAT

Grant's friend was dying. In September 1869, John A. Rawlins lay stretched out on his bed in Washington, coughing the last of his life away in a final battle with tuberculosis, the dreaded plague of the nineteenth century. At the side of the ailing secretary of war sat General William T. Sherman, the commander of the army, along with Jacob D. Cox, the secretary of the interior: the three men were old companions from Civil War days, when all had served under Ulysses S. Grant. But the President himself was far to the north, in Saratoga, New York; there he received word that Rawlins had little time left. A hurried departure, a succession of delayed trains, and the stolid chief executive arrived in the capital only to learn that his closest friend had died exactly an hour before.

The death of Rawlins undoubtedly shook Grant more than the surprise attacks his armies had endured at Shiloh or the Wilderness, and far more than the taciturn general could ever express. His friend had not possessed the intellectual spark of Sherman; nor did he have the stature and wealth of the New York and Philadelphia businessmen who now surrounded the President. But he was something that none of these men could be—he was the better angel of Grant's nature, a man who understood the best of his companion's instincts. William McFeely has described Rawlins as "an honest voice of humanitarian conscience," and that he was: as Cox revealed previously, he could frame a debate before his commander, screening out the self-serving and manipulative voices, and drawing forth the deep sense of justice and decisiveness that Grant possessed. He could harangue the general, whisper to him, shout at him, in a way that no other was ever allowed to. He became the living embodiment of Grant's conscience. It was no small irony that he died at almost the same moment that the President turned a deaf ear to his family's self-interested pleadings and ordered an end to Gould and Fisk's gold speculation—one of his finest acts as President.

Ulysses would not be without a close companion for long. Before the first shovel of dirt hit the top of Rawlins's casket, another adviser, another old subordinate from wartime days, stepped forward to take his place. He was the president's private secretary, bearing a name that could have been plucked from the ripest Victorian novel: Orville E. Babcock. On the surface, Babcock might have resembled Rawlins in some ways. Both were outgoing, talkative, and closely attuned to the inner mind of their commander. But in motive and action, the private secretary could not have offered a starker contrast with the late secretary of war. Where Rawlins knew how to draw out Grant's strengths, Babcock knew how to play on his vulnerabilities. Where Rawlins would stoke Grant's fires of righteousness, Babcock would turn the heat of presidential power to his own profit. Where Rawlins helped Grant bend his mind to decisive action, Babcock played on his desperate need for an objective, pointing him to where his efforts would benefit Babcock most. In short, he was precisely that type of man that Rawlins had sought to shield Grant from.

Babcock's career of intrigue and venality began even before the death of Rawlins, when he hit upon an objective for the President to pursue. And Grant's need for one was indeed great. After all, the old fighting commander could look about himself in the White House and ask, What was there to do? Reconstruction was proceeding apace; while he did much, in his first term, to speed the process along (appointing Adelbert Ames as a military district commander in the South, for example), there was little new ground to be broken there. In economics, advisers such as Secretary of the Treasury George Boutwell advocated retrenchment rather than an aggressive policy, an idea supported by his newfound wealthy friends. So when Babcock began to whisper a plan into the President's ear, Grant listened. As the shrewd private secretary sketched it out, it seemed just the thing—a positively exciting prospect. Yes, the general who had captured Vicksburg and Richmond could now be the President who annexed Santo Domingo.[1]

Santo Domingo? The idea today seems preposterous. But the absurdity of annexing the island republic stems in part from the fact that it never happened. After all, the United States had only recently purchased Alaska, a distant, seemingly frozen peninsula with almost no American settlers. Later the nation would absorb Hawaii, the Philippines, and Puerto Rico, three sets of islands filled with people who did not speak English; two would remain more or less permanently American. Furthermore, the attempt to acquire Santo Domingo was belittled by both contemporaries and many historians because that republic was populated by dark-skinned inhabitants, a fact that did not suit the Anglo-Saxon establishment.

Nevertheless, the annexation campaign proved to be a classic episode of the Gilded Age—an adventure in unauthorized cowboy diplomacy by Orville Babcock, who had purchased large tracts of land on the island, counting on a rapid rise in value. The effort was also opposed by men of the highest principles, particularly Senator Charles Sumner, the powerful voice of racial equality and the politician Grant disliked the most. As

[1] Today known as the Dominican Republic. The nomenclature for this nation was unsettled in nineteenth-century Washington; some referred to it as San Domingo, others as Santo Domingo.

George Boutwell revealed previously, the President (a man of humble origins who hated ostentation) could not stand the loftiness of the windy, Boston-bred senator, no matter how consistently noble his beliefs.

Grant honestly thought the purchase of Santo Domingo would provide an outlet for African Americans who found conditions unbearable in the South. Migration, after all, was the traditional American solution to social problems; not coincidentally, this was also the era of the last great Western movement. Sumner thought the idea was ridiculous; black Americans had built the civilization below Mason-Dixon, and now they deserved to fully enjoy it. The senator lent more than his eloquent voice to the debate: he was chairman of the Senate Foreign Relations Committee, and no treaty could be ratified over his opposition.

Adding to the complexity of the situation was the fact that Grant's own secretary of state, Hamilton Fish, also opposed the annexation. He was a skilled diplomat, but he was also a particularly elitist Easterner, and he loathed the idea of absorbing an impoverished island of black people. He also bridled at Babcock's effort to run a private foreign policy in the Caribbean. Moreover, Fish and Sumner were old friends. But the secretary of state was embroiled in an entirely different set of international problems. He was trying to settle a bitter dispute with England over the wartime depredations of Confederate cruisers, built and armed in British ports; scores of American merchant ships had been destroyed by these English creations. The United States demanded reparations; talk of war was in the air. The secretary was willing to settle for a lump sum of money, but Sumner created difficulties by insisting on Canada (a British possession) as the price of peace. Grant could hardly care less about these negotiations, but they offered a useful means of driving a wedge between the two old friends—a wedge that could serve the cause of annexing Santo Domingo.

In the passage that follows, cabinet member Jacob D. Cox reveals the tortuous political infighting that resulted from the effort to purchase Santo Domingo. Now forgotten by all but specialists, the episode was a critical turning point in Grant's transition from exalted, decisive general to partisan, scandal-ridden President. The chief executive was never short on political skills, but this issue—and his wily friend Babcock—gradually pulled him down a path of political intrigue that would eventually swallow his once-promising administration.

Grant's Political Duel
by Jacob D. Cox

In the early months of Grant's administration there was at Washington a representative of the Baez government in San Domingo [*sic*], named

Fabens.[2] That country was in a revolutionary condition, and it was not certain that Baez would be able to maintain himself against his rival, Cabral, who was at the head of an armed force in the interior of the island. Fabens professed to be negotiating for the purchase of some of the old arms which filled our arsenals after the close of the civil war. He was, however, constantly suggesting the annexation of San Domingo to the United States, and Mr. Fish from time to time reported these overtures, and the annoyance which the persistence of Fabens gave him. The annexation scheme met with little favor in the Cabinet, and Congress showed itself consistently opposed to it. The objections were various, and were based on grounds of general policy as well as on the particular circumstances of the case and of the time.

First, there were those who held firmly that the only sound policy of the United States is a strictly continental one, coupling a leading influence on the mainland of America with deliberate abstinence from distant extensions of territory. Second, there were those who, in view of the fact that the dominant population of the island was of the negro race, felt that the problems involved in our own great emancipation were quite as large as this generation could satisfactorily handle.[3] Third, still others thought that as the whole island of Hispaniola was divided between the two republics of Hayti [sic] and San Domingo, jealous of each other, the one speaking only French, the other only Spanish, the acquisition of the Spanish half would necessarily be followed by the annexation of the whole, each contingency seeming to excel the other in troublesome complications. Fourth, men of statesmanlike character felt deeply the inconsistency of opening a new scheme of West India colonies while the treaty with Denmark for the purchase of St. Thomas,[4] negotiated by Mr. Seward, was still pending. . . . Lastly, there were some scrupulous enough to be deterred from favoring annexation because Baez was forbidden by the constitution of his country from negotiating it; and who believed with Charles Sumner that it would be wrong to the people of the colored race to take from them the territory which gave them the opportunity to work out the problem of their capacity for independent self-government.

[2] Buenaventura Baez was the president and dictator of Santo Domingo. J.W. Fabens and William Cazneau were Texans who were lobbying in Washington for annexation. As Cox indicates, Baez was battling a revolt at the time. Under President Johnson, Secretary of State William H. Seward had attempted to annex Santo Domingo; in addition, he had obtained a treaty to purchase the Danish West Indies.

[3] Cox speaks delicately here of the fact that many white politicians (including Cox himself) did not want to add an island full of black people to the American republic.

[4] Denmark had agreed to sell what are now the U.S. Virgin Islands to the United States; Congress failed to ratify the treaty, however, and the islands would not pass into American hands until World War I.

The discussion of the subject at Cabinet meetings had been free, and although Grant was a listener rather than a participant in the debate, there was a general acquiescence in the opinion of Mr. Fish that a cordially friendly attitude to the actual government in San Domingo, with decided discouragement to all intervention and filibustering, should be our policy. This was so well understood that there was no hesitation in talking about the matter in this sense, and in letting it be known that the administration had taken this line of conduct.

One day, however, the President casually remarked that the navy people seemed so anxious to have the bay of Samana as a coaling station that he thought he would send Colonel Babcock down to examine it and report upon it as an engineer. Babcock, as will be remembered, was one of the group of young army officers who, having been members of Grant's military staff, were retained in duties near his person during his presidency. His position was nominally that of assistant private secretary. His army service had been creditable, and he was a very intelligent and competent military engineer. The suggestion of sending him on the errand was not welcome to those who were anxious to avoid complications, but there was no objection raised, and the acquiescence was a silent one. It was stated that no publicity would be given to the mission, and that a confidential report upon the country, its people, its harbors, would be useful.

Before Babcock was ready to go, the President, in the same casual way, remarked that the New York merchants who had control of the trade with the island had courteously tendered to Babcock free passage on one of their ships. This showed that somebody was giving publicity to the mission, but it had greater significance in showing that the State Department had no part in its management. Mr. Fish, evidently surprised, remarked that it seemed to him very undesirable that Colonel Babcock should be the guest of the merchants having trading interests in San Domingo, whilst he was upon a confidential investigation for the President. General Grant acquiesced, and said he would direct the navy to give Colonel Babcock transportation, as vessels were going down to join the West India squadron. Still again, a day or two later, it was said that, as Babcock did not speak Spanish, a well-known officer of the Inspector General's department would accompany him. Lastly, it appeared that Mr. Columbus Cole, then a Senator from California, was to be of the party on this new voyage of discovery to Hispaniola.

As the members of the Cabinet were carefully discreet in their reticence, the increase of the party and of the apparent importance of the mission caused a certain uneasiness, especially as rumors began to fly about that business speculations were involved, and that the official character of the affair was much less than its real significance. The members of the government felt loyally bound to suppress their own doubts, and to attribute to the excitability of the quidnuncs the rumors of important purposes connected with Babcock's voyage.

After some weeks' absence, Babcock's return was announced by the New York newspapers, with suggestions of interesting results. On seeing this, I called upon Mr. Fish at the State Department the same afternoon. He sent his private secretary from the room, and closed the door; then coming toward me with manifest feeling, he said, "What do you think! Babcock is back, and has actually brought a treaty for the cession of San Domingo; yet I pledge you my word he had no more diplomatic authority than any other casual visitor to that island!" An earnest discussion of the situation followed, in which we agreed that the proper course was to treat Babcock's action as null, and to insist upon burying the whole in oblivion as a state secret; this being the only way, apparently, to save him from the grave consequences of a usurpation of power. It did not occur to either of us, in view of the past history of the matter, that the President would assume the responsibility for the illegal act of his messenger.

In the informal discussion of the subject which incidentally occurred before the next Cabinet meeting, the view Mr. Fish had taken seemed to be the general one, and it was expected that he would present it when we should be assembled. When the heads of departments came for the purpose to the President's room at the White House, they found Babcock already there, showing to each, as he arrived, specimens of the ores and products of the island, and descanting upon its extraordinary value. He met a rather chilling reception, and soon left the room.

It had been the President's habit, at such meetings, to call upon the members of the Cabinet to bring forward the business contained in their portfolios, beginning with the Secretary of State. This would at once have brought the action of Babcock up by Mr. Fish's disclaimer of all part in the matter, and his statement of its utter illegality. On this occasion, however, General Grant departed from his uniform custom, and took the initiative. "Babcock has returned, as you see," said he, "and has brought a treaty of annexation. I suppose it is not formal, as he had no diplomatic powers; but we can easily cure that. We can send back the treaty, and have Perry, the consular agent, sign it; and as he is an officer of the State Department it would make it all right."

This took everybody so completely by surprise that they seemed dumfounded. After an awkward interval, as nobody else broke the silence, I said, "But, Mr. President, has it been settled, then, that we *want* to annex San Domingo?" The direct question evidently embarrassed General Grant. He colored, and smoked hard at his cigar. He glanced at Mr. Fish on his right, but the face of the Secretary was impassive, and his eyes were fixed on the portfolio before him. He turned to Mr. Boutwell on his left, but no response met him there. As the silence became painful, the President called for another item of business, and left the question unanswered. The subject was never again brought up before the assembled Cabinet.

It would naturally be supposed that a breaking-up of the Cabinet would follow; but on the mere suspicion of such differences as I have described, strong party influences were set at work to prevent a rupture. General Grant became, afterward, so thorough a party man that it is necessary to recall by positive effort of memory that his position was looked upon as very uncertain when his administration began. His report to President Johnson on the condition of the Southern States had indicated that he was not in sympathy with the congressional plan of reconstruction, which was the burning question of the time. Party leaders were nervous lest he should prove unwilling to conduct his administration in harmony with them, and in case of a break they feared a total loss of party control in the country. Members of the administration were therefore urged strenuously to make no issue on what might be regarded as a personal wish of the President, and they shared the opinions of their party friends enough to make them feel the importance of avoiding collision. The probability that the treaty could not be ratified made the dropping of the subject more easy.

The position of Mr. Fish was the most difficult one. He was on terms of intimate friendship with Charles Sumner, the chairman of the Committee on Foreign Relations in the Senate, and both official propriety and personal feeling had made him frankly open in discussing diplomatic affairs with the Senator. He had honestly treated the talk of Dominican annexation as mere gossip, without solid foundation, and now he suddenly found his sincerity in question, under circumstances which forbade him to say how gravely the State Department had been compromised. The situation seemed so intolerable that he took the very natural course of tendering his resignation. The President was far from wishing this result, though it did not make him abandon the annexation scheme. His strong request that Mr. Fish should not insist, joined to the pressure from outside to which I have alluded, made a postponement, at least, of the question of the resignation. The other members of the government could more easily ignore the subject, and immerse themselves in the special duties of their own departments.

The treaty which was finally submitted to the Senate was signed on November 29, 1869, and was transmitted for ratification in December. The President had been committed to the strange promise to use his personal influence to secure its acceptance, and the efforts to do this through direct application to Senators was one of the things which was felt to be most objectionable at the time.[5] It opened the way to bargaining for votes, and directly compromised the dignity of the Executive. The nomination of [Attorney General] Judge Hoar to the Supreme Court

---

5 Another reminder of how different political propriety was at that time: the President was expected to appoint loyal party men to civil service positions, but he was criticized for negotiating openly with senators over legislation.

was so nearly coincident with the transmittal of the treaty that it is fair to regard it, in part, as an attempt to conciliate adverse influences. It lay before the Senate for some time, and confirmation was finally refused in the early part of February, 1870.

The efforts to secure ratification of the treaty languished during the winter and spring; but after the time had elapsed within which the purchase of St. Thomas must be completed, and that embarrassment was supposed to be out of the way, a very active effort was made to bring the San Domingo scheme to a successful termination. The headquarters of this activity were in the private secretary's office at the Executive Mansion. Papers and files from the State Department were sent for and retained without even the formality of using the President's name and authority, so that Mr. Fish was obliged to protest against the irregularity, and demand that it be stopped. He was ready, he said, to attend the President with any papers in his department at any time, but he could not permit their custody to be transferred to any other place.

Notwithstanding the effort to conduct the business as an exceptional one, in which only acquiescence on the part of the Secretary was expected, Mr. Fish found his position so irksome that he again tendered his resignation in writing. I happened to be present, and saw the earnestness with which General Grant repelled the idea of there being any necessity for it. Manifestly he had not appreciated Mr. Fish's embarrassments, and seemed to think it was an easy matter to pass over the irregularities whose importance he did not rightly estimate. He insisted upon a delay, and it was later understood that a definite arrangement was made that the Secretary of State should be untrammeled in the conduct of all other business of the department, and relieved of the annoyances in this matter, of which he had complained.

The President was by no means lacking in personal regard for Mr. Fish, and estimated highly the value of his character, his knowledge of the world, his facility of intercourse with foreign representatives, and his tact in dealing with officials of all classes. He insisted that Mr. Fish must not leave him, and that the difficulties of the situation would soon be ended by the disposal of the treaty in one way or another. Unless ratified by the 1st of July, it would expire by its own limitations.

When Judge Hoar's nomination to the bench had been defeated, in the winter, he [Hoar] again sent word by closest friends that his resignation [as attorney general] would be at the President's disposal; but General Grant saw nothing to make a change in their relations desirable, and the subject was dropped, definitively, as I supposed. Delicacy had prompted the judge thus to speak through others, so that no feeling of personal regard might make the President hesitate to express his wish. More than four months had elapsed, and the Attorney-General, like the other members of the administration, had devoted himself to the work of his own office, forgetting as far as possible everything, including San Domingo, which did not directly affect his own responsibilities.

One afternoon in June I had gone home from my office to dinner, and about seven o'clock received the New York papers which the messenger usually brought to my house after the arrival of the Eastern mail. Opening a copy of the *Times*, I was amazed to see the announcement that the Attorney-General had resigned, and that his resignation had been accepted by the President. I knew that nothing had been further from Judge Hoar's thoughts two or three days before, and there had not, since the winter, been any suggestion or intimation of such a thing from other quarters. I could hardly believe my eyes. That such changes in the administration could be made without an announcement to its members, leaving them to learn it from the public press, was incredible.

Hastily taking my hat, I went from my house on Capitol Hill down through the park to catch the horse-car on Pennsylvania Avenue and go to Judge Hoar's lodgings, which were on F Street, not far from the Treasury building. At the lower park gate I almost ran into Senator Henry Wilson of Massachusetts, who actually buttonholed me. "See here, Mr. Secretary," he said, "tell me what this means!"

"What do you refer to?"

"The Attorney-General's resignation, of course," was the reply. Nonplussed how to answer, and shrinking from revealing the fact that I was more ignorant than he, I took refuge in commonplaces about the natural result of there being two Cabinet officers from one State, and the known wish of the judge to retire whenever this should cause embarrassment. "I know all that," said he, "but we thought that talk had gone by, and I am greatly disturbed lest it means a breaking-up which may lead we can't tell where."

I tried to reassure him by saying I thought there was no such danger, that we all had confidence in Grant's honesty and patriotism, and it would turn out that there was nothing more in it than I had intimated. He shook his head seriously and doubtingly; then turned on me with, "But what do you know of the new man whose name was sent in this afternoon?"

Worse cornered than ever, as I could not even guess who had been nominated, and had never heard a name officially mentioned in connection with a possible vacancy in the office, I could only mumble, "Oh, I think you'll find he's all right," and the approaching street-car giving me an escape I added, "But you must excuse me; I must catch this car," and broke away from him, repeating to myself Chancellor Oxenstiern's famous saying.

Reaching the Attorney-General's lodgings, I opened the conversation almost in the words Senator Wilson had used to me: "Well, judge, what *does* this mean?"

"Sit down," he said, "and I will tell you." The recollection of what he said is so vivid that I may safely say that I give it in his own words: "I was sitting in my office yesterday morning, attending to routine business, with no more thought of what was to come than you had at that moment, when a messenger entered with a letter from the President. Opening it, I was amazed to read a naked statement that he found himself under the necessity of asking for my resignation. No explanation of any kind was given, no reason assigned. The request was as curt and as direct as possible. My first thought was that the President had been imposed upon by some grave charge against me. A thunder-clap could not have been more startling to me. I sat for awhile wondering what it could mean—why there had been no warning, no reference to the subject in our almost daily conversations. The impulse was to go at once and ask the reasons for the demand; but self-respect would not permit this, and I said to myself that I must let the matter take its own course, and not even seem disturbed about it. I took up my pen to write the resignation, and found myself naturally framing some of the conventional reasons for it; but I stopped, and destroyed the sheet, saying to myself, 'Since no reasons are given or suggested for the demand, it is hardly honest to invent them in the reply'; so I made the resignation as simple and unvarnished as the request for it had been."

Before sending it to the White House, Judge Hoar, to avoid any possibility of its becoming public by his act, made a copy with his own hand, and locked up the letter and the answer in a private drawer of his desk. In the afternoon he had occasion to submit papers in some pardon cases to the President, and went to the Executive Office for the purpose. Meanwhile the acceptance of the resignation had been sent to him, and this was so framed as to convey the sentiments of personal good will and high respect which no one in near relations to them doubted that General Grant actually felt. This letter was published, with the brief resignation. The equally brief request for the resignation has never been given to the public. The omission, as every one must see, wholly changes the effect of the correspondence.

On meeting Judge Hoar, the President enlarged to some extent upon his personal confidence in him, and the real regret with which he severed their relations, and now frankly connected his own action with the exigency in which he found himself, and the necessity, to carry out his purposes, of securing support in the Senate from Southern Republicans, who demanded that the Cabinet place should be filled from the South. He reminded the Attorney-General of what had passed in the winter, relative to his resigning, and said he had assumed that this connection of things should be understood without further words. Judge Hoar assured him that the explanation removed any painful impression that might have been made at first, that his only wish was that the administration might be a success in every respect, and that no personal interest of his should for a moment stand in the way of it. He then, however, took the liberty of saying that he thought he knew the class of men who had desired his removal,[6] and he hoped, for the President's own sake, that he had chosen his successor, since otherwise he would be subjected to a pressure in favor of unfit men which might prove most embarrassing to him. General Grant naively admitted that he had not yet given any thought to that part of the matter, but appeared to be struck with the wisdom of the judge's suggestion, and himself asked that the whole matter remain strictly confidential till he could reflect upon it, when he would call it up again.

On the next morning (which was that of the day on which I was having the evening interview I am narrating) that Attorney-General was again in his office attending to business, when he was once more surprised by an interruption. This time it was by a well-known correspondent of the New York *Tribune*, who sent in his card with an urgent request to be admitted. Feeling a vague suspicion that it might prove embarrassing, Judge Hoar peremptorily excused himself. His clerk returned after a moment, evidently disturbed, and said, "I beg your pardon, Mr. Attorney-General, for coming back, but the gentleman says that if you will look at his paper he thinks you will see him." The judge took the offending paper, and found it was a dispatch from the editor of the *Tribune* to the correspondent, saying, "The *Times*, this morning, says the Attorney-General has resigned, and his resignation accepted; why have we not heard from you?" Puzzled for a moment how to act, ready wit came to his aid in a characteristic way, and he said to the clerk, with a significant smile, "Mr. Pleasants, you may give the gentleman any information you are possessed of."

The Attorney-General's office, at that time, was in the south front of the Treasury building, and his anteroom, with the usual approach to it, was on the side toward Fourteenth Street. A private door, however, led to the south portico, and no sooner was his clerk gone than Judge Hoar put on his hat, and, going out by this way, took the short path across the park to the Executive Mansion. Being admitted, he said, "Mr. President, I have come to tell you that somebody about you betrays you." He then told the story of the dispatch from New York. General Grant was deeply stirred by it, and saying he would severely punish the breach of confidence, went into the private secretary's room to investigate. He soon returned, mollified, and explained that the secretaries could account for the leak only by supposing that some unauthorized person must have got access in the outer office to the letterpress copybook in which was the acceptance of the resignation.

6 Hoar and Cox both had become quite conservative, and harbored prejudices against Southern Radical Republicans.

The idea of a secret guarded in that way made the matter too amusing for comment, if not for credence, and the judge contented himself with recalling what he had said the day before of the desirability of decisive action. The President said he had been thinking of Mr. Akerman, of Georgia, who had been appointed district attorney for Georgia, and whom Judge Hoar had spoken well of when he had been a candidate for the judgeship of the Southern circuit. He asked whether the judge did not think he would be a fit man. Judge Hoar replied that he believed Mr. Akerman to be an honest man and a good lawyer; but he added, "It would hardly be proper for me, Mr. President, to say what should be the standard of fitness for the attorney-generalship of the United States."

He took his leave, and Mr. Akerman's nomination was immediately made. It was necessary that it should be authenticated by the great seal, so it went to the State Department before it was sent to the Senate, and Mr. Fish thus learned of the change among his colleagues. I have stated how I learned it.

My conversation with Judge Hoar was on the evening of Thursday, the 16th of June, and at the next regular Cabinet meeting it was so confidently assumed that the President would enter into explanations of the serious step taken that, by common consent, no other business was brought forward. Judge Hoar was not present, and each Secretary, as called upon, answered that he had nothing to offer. The President waited a moment, as if somewhat surprised, and then simply remarked that if there was no business to be done, the meeting might as well adjourn. It did so, and no reference to the subject, of any sort, was ever made by General Grant in the presence of his assembled advisers. Judge Hoar remained in office some weeks (a short absence intervening) till Mr. Akerman could be ready to assume his duties. He brought the new Attorney-General to the Cabinet room and introduced him to his colleagues; then turning to the President, he said, "Having presented my successor, I will take my leave, wishing the most abundant success to your administration." General Grant replied that although he should not see the judge again in that place, he hoped to meet him elsewhere frequently.

It was part of current information on which I fully relied, though I cannot give its source as explicitly as I can that of my other statements, that General Grant's interviews with Senators from the Southern States had been marked by great directness of dealing. The "carpet-bag" Senators were men of different characters and qualities. There were some, like General Willard Warner of Alabama, whose motives no one would impugn, whether he took sides with the President or with Mr. Sumner. Senator Warner's colleague was, justly or unjustly, looked upon as a type of a different class of politicians; and it was in negotiation with such a one, representing his class, that Grant learned the demands of these Senators. He was told that they desired to please him and to support his plans, but, considering Mr. Sumner's controlling influence with their colored constituents, it would be at no small political peril to themselves if they opposed that Senator on the San Domingo question. Instead of receiving help of the administration in matters of patronage, which might smooth over home opposition, they found themselves less influential than they had a right to expect. Reciprocity was necessary if the President desired their aid. When asked in what departments they found a lack of consideration, the Attorney-General's was named, and it was strongly urged that Judge Hoar should be displaced by a Southern man acceptable to them.

I had promised Judge Hoar to make a visit to Concord, when he went home near the end of June, to attend Harvard College commencement; he being one of the governing Fellows of the university, and his son, Mr. Sherman Hoar, taking his first degree that year. . . . General Sherman was also in Boston at the time, and I was invited with him to dinner by the Saturday Club, of which Judge Hoar was a member. Emerson, Longfellow, Lowell, and Holmes were all there, and I need not say it was an occasion to remember. It only concerns my present story, however, to tell what occurred just before we parted. Mr. Longfellow was presiding, and unexpectedly I found that he was speaking to me in the name of the Club. He said that they had been much disturbed by rumors then current that Mr. Motley [ambassador to Great Britain] was to be recalled from England on account of Senator Sumner's opposition to the San Domingo treaty. They would be very far indeed from seeking to influence any action of the President which was based on Mr. Motley's conduct in his diplomatic duties, of which they knew little, and could not judge; but they thought the President ought to know that if the rumor referred to was well founded, he would, in their opinion, offend all the educated men of New England. It could not be right to make a disagreement with Mr. Sumner prejudice Mr. Motley by reason of the friendship between the two. I could only answer that no body of men had better right to speak for American men of letters, and that I would faithfully convey their message.

On my return to Washington, I first made known to Mr. Fish the duty that had been committed to me. Not only did he interpose no objection to it; he expressed an earnest wish that it might change the President's purpose. I took an early opportunity of reporting to General Grant what the eminent men of the Saturday Club said to him. His only reply was, "I made up my mind to remove Mr. Motley before there was any quarrel with Mr. Sumner." This he said in an impatient tone, as if repelling interference.

Senator Wilson also had visited Boston, and had been told of the request made by the Saturday Club. He called on me, and asked whether I intended to fulfill it. I answered that I undoubtedly should. He then told me that he had been asked to support my statement, and that he should do so most earnestly. In pursuance of this purpose, he wrote a friendly but strong letter of remonstrance to the President, dated on the 5th of July.

Mr. Fish's relations to Mr. Sumner were still friendly, and Judge Hoar was and continued to be the friend of both; but the progress of the San Domingo business had put Mr. Fish in a false position, apparently, and having yielded to the President's urgency that he should remain in the Cabinet, he could not, at the moment, explain fully to Mr. Sumner the seeming changes of his attitude. It is in the nature of such differences that they grow larger, and in the following winter they led to an open rupture between the old friends. I myself have never doubted that Mr. Fish's stay in the State Department was a sacrifice of personal feelings to a sense of duty to the country; and that, despite the complications and annoyances which I have had to recount, every lover of the country has reason to rejoice that he remained at his post. His confidence in and regard for Judge Hoar were such as to be decisive, a little later, in placing the latter upon the commission to negotiate the remaining differences with Great Britain. The President also retained and increased his respect for the judge, but by that time the Secretary of State was recognized as having the rightful initiation in the formation of such a commission.

It ought to be added that whatever may seem singular in the conduct of this business by General Grant was not at the time attributed to any wrong purpose by those who were closest to him. He lacked the faculty of conversational discussion, which is the very essence of the successful conduct of business where cooperation is necessary. In military matters the objective is usually a very definite one, and the end being clearly aimed at, the intervening steps arrange themselves when there is true courage and tenacity of purpose. In civil affairs there would be danger that such a rule would run into the pernicious maxim that the end justifies the means. A very different kind of knowledge, both of men and of affairs, is needed to conduct properly the civil business of the state.

COX WAS EXACTLY right: Grant was perfect for the position of wartime commander, but particularly ill suited to the fuzzy give-and-take of peacetime politics. He pursued Santo Domingo as if it were Richmond in 1864, and Senator Sumner as if he were General Lee. If there was any weapon he could use to strike at his opponent, he used it; if there was any ally he could lay low, he attacked him.

The happy irony of this disturbing clash was that Attorney General Ebenezer Hoar was replaced by a far more effective man. Hoar—despite a proud abolitionist background—had proved himself particularly weak in combatting the Ku Klux Klan in the South. When his position was undermined by his association with Sumner, a new senator from Mississippi, by the name of Adelbert Ames,[7] suggested a fresh face might do more good. He selected Amos T. Akerman, one of the unsung heroes of Reconstruction. Akerman was a white native of New Hampshire who had lived his entire adult life in Georgia, and he had risen to prominence in the years that followed the war. He seemed just the man for the job.

As attorney general, he moved swiftly and effectively to smash the Klan. He had new means at his disposal, too, for Congress created the Justice Department in June 1870. In April 1871 it launched a searching investigation of Klan atrocities in the South, and quickly passed the Ku Klux Klan Act (supported by Grant once Boutwell forcefully argued with his chief). Akerman personally directed prosecutions in South Carolina, helping squash the brutal outrages there. He also sought to build up the Republican party throughout the South, as the best guarantee of protecting African Americans over time. Akerman well deserved to be called "the finest champion of human rights in the Grant administration," as William McFeely has described him.

The elitist Secretary of State Fish was annoyed by the crusading new attorney general, and he whispered against him constantly. Akerman could not survive the intrigue, and he was forced to resign on December 13, 1871. It was another early sign of the crumbling moral foundations of Grant's presidency. Akerman himself noted of his cabinet counterparts, "Even such atrocities as Ku-Kluxery do not hold their attention . . . the Northern mind being active and full of what is called progress runs away from the past."

The removal of Akerman confirmed the emerging balance in the administration. Two men now grasped Grant's ear: the dignified, deeply conservative Secretary of State Fish, and the open-minded, sticky-fingered Babcock. It was one more irony in a presidency built on irony that each man had grave flaws built into his strengths. Fish proved himself an adroit diplomat, yet the characteristics that enabled him to negotiate with English lords as an equal were intertwined with an elitism that made him deeply suspicious of Reconstruction. Babcock possessed little if any racism—unlike Fish, he could speak with the Latin American dictator Baez with no distaste—yet he seems to have gone through life repeating the refrain, "What's in it for me?" He quickly discovered that, as the president's private secretary, there was quite a lot.

But to return to Grant's duel with Sumner, for it was far from over: The scene of the action shifted to the Senate chamber, where administration stalwarts such as Senator John Sherman moved against the man who was fighting the treaties with England and Santo Domingo. Sherman knew that Grant was more than angry about the resistance to his pet project: he

---

[7] See chapter 18 for an account of Ames's rise to the United States Senate.

was deeply wounded, for he had called on Sumner personally, visiting his house to lobby for the Santo Domingo annexation. The senator had made approving noises; the next day, he continued his opposition.

It was this failure that led Grant to negotiate with such Southern senators as Adelbert Ames over the attorney generalship and other matters. Furthermore, Sumner's vehemence in demanding blood and Canada from Britain raised the specter of war with England. The senator certainly had a point, for the British (who often threw their moral compass overboard on the seas of international relations) had behaved abominably during the Civil War; but his old friend Fish longed for a peaceful settlement to the dispute. Under these conditions, the White House passed word to the Republican caucus in the Senate that Sumner must be dealt with.

A Coup in the Senate
by John Sherman

Prior to the meeting of Congress in December 1870, a controversy had arisen between Senator Sumner and Secretary Fish which created serious embarrassment, and I think had a very injurious influence during that and succeeding sessions of Congress. Mr. Sumner had long been chairman of the committee on foreign relations, and no doubt exercised a domineering power in this branch of the public service. Mr. Fish and Mr. Sumner had differed widely in respect to the annexation of San Domingo and certain diplomatic appointments and former treaties, among them the highly important English negotiation for the settlement of claims growing out of the war.

On these topics the President and Mr. Sumner could not agree. Mr. Sumner insisted that the hasty proclamation by Great Britain of neutrality between the United States and the Southern Confederacy was the gravamen of the *Alabama* claims. The President and Mr. Fish contended that this proclamation was an act of which we could not complain, except as an indication of an unfriendly spirit by Great Britain, and that the true basis of the *Alabama* claims was that Great Britain, after proclaiming neutrality, did not enforce it, but allowed her subjects to build cruisers, and man, arm, and use them under the cover of the rebel flag, to the destruction of our commercial navy.[8]

This difference of opinion between the President and Mr. Sumner led

[8] The *Alabama* and other Confederate warships built in England were manned almost entirely by British sailors, led by a few Southern officers. Sumner thought the cession of Canada to the United States would be the just compensation for the cruisers' attacks; Mr. Fish was willing to settle for a payment.

to the removal of John L. Motley, our minister to England, who sided with Sumner, and unquestionably intensified the feeling that had arisen from the San Domingo treaty.

As to that treaty it was a conceded fact that before the President had become publicly committed to it he had, waiving his official rank, sought the advice and counsel of Mr. Sumner, and was evidently misled as to Mr. Sumner's views on this subject. The subsequent debating, in both open and executive session, led to Mr. Sumner's taking the most extreme and active opposition to the treaty, in which he arrayed with great severity the conduct of the naval officers, the Secretary of the Navy, Mr. Fish, and the President. This was aggravated by alleged public conversations with Mr. Sumner by "interviewers," in which the motives of the President and others were impugned. In the meantime, the social relations between the Secretary of State and Mr. Sumner had become impossible; and—considering human passion, prejudice, and feeling—anything like frank and confidential communication between the President and Mr. Sumner was out of the question.

A majority of the Republican Senators sided with the President. We generally agreed that it was a false-pretended neutrality, and not a too hasty proclamation of neutrality, that gave us an unquestionable right to demand indemnity from Great Britain for the depredations of the *Alabama* and other English cruisers. And as for the San Domingo treaty, a large majority of Republican Senators had voted for it—though I did not; and nearly all of us had voted for the commission of inquiry of which Mr. Wade was the chief member.

When we met in March, it was known that both these important subjects would necessarily be referred to the committee on foreign relations. . . . In the Republican conference the first question that arose was as to Mr. Sumner. He was the oldest Senator in consecutive service. He was eminent not only as a faithful representative of Republican principles, but as especially qualified to be chairman of our foreign relations. He had long held that position, and it was not usual in the Senate to change the committees, but to follow the rule of seniority. . . .

In deciding Mr. Sumner's case, in view of the facts I have stated, two plans were urged: First—to place him at the head of the new and important committee of privileges and elections, leaving the rest of the committee of foreign relations to stand in the precise order it had been, with one vacancy to be filled in harmony with the majority. Second—to leave Mr. Sumner to stand in his old place as chairman, and to make a change in the body of the committee by transferring one of its members to another committee, and fill the vacancy by a Senator in harmony with the majority. My own opinion was that the latter course was the most polite and just; but the majority decided, after full consideration and debate, upon the first alternative. . . .

This affair created feeling in the Senate which it is difficult now to realize, but it was decided in a Republican caucus, in which there was an honest difference of opinion. We foresaw, whichever way it should be decided, that it would create—and it did create—bad feeling among Senators, which existed as long as Mr. Sumner lived.

FISH GOT HIS treaty; Grant did not. The British settled the dispute with a large payment in gold, and not with a large transfer of land. Canada remained a possession of Queen Victoria, destined to become an independent country (though it would persist in the strange custom of hailing the English monarch as its own). But if Sumner failed to get the ice-rimmed domain to the north, as he so dearly desired, Grant also failed to get the palm-fringed island to the south. The senator had seen to that. So the President took what revenge he could, securing the removal of his crusty opponent from his committee chairmanship.

Grant had transformed himself from general to President, and the result was not appealing. As military commander, he had been calm, decisive, unpretentious, and almost unfailingly victorious. As President, he began to descend into personal disputes, political intrigue, and the occasional heavy-handed display of power, as he and Julia hobnobbed with the wealthy. As general, his closest adviser had been the compassionate, deeply moral Rawlins; as President, he spent his private hours with the shifty, acquisitive Babcock. Much of the old Grant still persisted, of course; he was still an unostentatious man, an individual who displayed little if any personal prejudice with regard to race or class. But under the whispering tutorship of Babcock and the pressures of Washington itself, he increasingly became a political beast.

Cox noted the change: the general who was initially considered politically doubtful by the Republican elders emerged as a highly partisan party figure. Indeed, William McFeely has called him the first true Republican President (for even Lincoln, the pioneer, was an old Whig). Though never fully consistent in his actions, Grant began to make appointments to build party strength and loyalty, and he sought to enforce party discipline. His efforts were spurred on by the defeat of the Santo Domingo treaty, and by an attempt to build a rival party—the Liberal Republicans—by Missouri Senator Carl Schurz.

Increasingly, party politics, and especially the critical state of Missouri, absorbed Grant's attention. For now he had a new objective, one that he would spend every effort and even break a few rules attaining. More than anything else, he wanted to be reelected President of the United States.

17

THE BIRTH OF A RING

Not many days after John Rawlins's death, a harbinger of doom visited Washington. It was a man, actually, a confident, speculative schemer who could have sprung straight from Twain's novel *The Gilded Age*. His name was General John McDonald, and he soon took up a central role in a massive conspiracy that would shatter the Grant administration and help unravel Reconstruction.

At the time, he was engaged in a classic speculator's trade, buying and selling claims made against the government for actions in the Civil War. During the conflict, military officials took civilian goods for the use of the troops, issuing vouchers that promised payment. Since many doubted the possibility of actually collecting on these IOU's, McDonald bought them at far less than their face value, counting on his own ability to obtain full payment from the government. He also traded in claims made by citizens who had suffered losses or injuries as a result of the war; he would pay these poor individuals for the right to press their cases and keep whatever he collected. After a sudden turn of fortune in his ghoulish business, however, he found himself at the White House, hat in hand.

The increasingly political President and his acquisitive secretary Orville Babcock each saw an opportunity in McDonald's misfortune—an opportunity to tighten Grant's control of the Republican party in Missouri. This in itself was not unusual. It was considered quite normal for the President to use his powers of patronage and appointment to build up the party. But the key to his control of Missouri would involve something else: bribes paid by whiskey distillers to the superintendent of internal revenue in return for the right to underreport their production, so they could evade the heavy taxes on spirits. And McDonald was to be that superintendent.

Historian Charles Wahlgren Summers has shown that these distillery kickbacks dated back to the Lincoln administration; under Johnson, the payments had been particularly heavy. But according to McDonald—the man who would direct what became known as the Great Whiskey Ring— the difference under Grant was in the political purposes to which the money was put. As he mentions in this account, Missouri was torn by political feuds, and Senator Carl Schurz was organizing the Liberal Republicans to oppose the President's grip on the party. Missouri was a critical state, and the White House could not afford to lose it. And never before was the ring so well organized, so vast in extent.

Some historians have been skeptical about McDonald's claims, thanks in part to the extra dose of doubt thrown onto charges made against presidents. But much of his account is unquestionably true; furthermore, he paints an image of Grant consistent with the man who fought a duel of intrigue with Sumner and outmaneuvered Johnson. And at no point does McDonald say that the President personally profited from the ring or directed its activities. As in all other areas of the government, Grant placed a trusted man in charge, knowing the essentials of what he had to do, and left to him the task of carrying it out. Babcock, on the other hand, saw an opportunity for personal gain, and he did not hesitate to seize it.

McDonald's account, then, is highly credible, and it deserves attention. More than that, it offers a gripping tale of bribery, backroom deals, and political intrigue, culminating in the reelection of the President.

The Origins of the Great Whiskey Ring
by John McDonald

The great whiskey frauds culminating in 1875 are a part of the history of American politics. No ring was ever before formed embracing such a gigantic scope and including among its chief instigators and members such distinguished government officials. The original intention of the organizers, adopting suggestions from the highest authority in the land, was to make the ring co-extensive with the nation, with headquarters in all the large cities, for the purpose of raising a campaign fund with which to advance the interests of President Grant in his aspirations for a second term. . . . During congressional and municipal campaigns, however, a part of this fund was always used in the interests of Republican candidates.

HOW I BECAME SUPERVISOR

In the years 1868–69, I was engaged in Washington City collecting war claims against the government and buying up quartermasters' informal vouchers. I conducted this business with much success, but in September of the latter year, being a passenger on the ill-fated train on the Erie Railroad which burned at Mast Hope, Pa., with such destruction to life and property, I lost my trunk containing over $9,000,000 of these claims. My individual loss approximated $300,000, to recover which I went to President Grant for the purpose of obtaining from him a note of introduction to Jim Fisk, then manager, and Jay Gould, then President of the Erie Railroad Co. Grant declined to give me the note. . . .

During my conversation with the President, I mentioned the fact that several of my friends in St. Louis had requested me to make application for one of the Supervisorships [of internal revenue], an office created by Congress, July 20, 1868. . . . President Grant responded at once, saying: "Well, McDonald, I would like to give you one of those places, and if you will accept, all you will have to do is to return to St. Louis and procure some recommendations, make your application, and forward your papers."

Having received such a decided and unexpected promise, I began to think seriously of accepting the position, and returned to St. Louis at once. . . . In a few days, I had prepared a very large list of recommendations, which together with my application I carried in person to President Grant. He examined my papers with great care and then had them filed with Commissioner Delano, and on October 5th, 1869, my commission as Supervisor of Internal Revenue was issued. . . . On the 12th of November, 1869, I took possession of the Supervisor's office, having charge of the district embracing Arkansas and the Indian Territory, with headquarters at Little Rock. . . .

The Republican party in Missouri, at the time I became a revenue officer, was harassed by dissensions, and the especial virulency of the *Missouri Democrat* sowed the seeds of a growing discord among the adherents of the administration. The President was greatly annoyed at these apparently irreconcilable differences among his friends, and to restore harmony within the party he sent for me, and after a lengthy discussion of these difficulties, he decided to attach the state of Missouri to my district and make my headquarters at St. Louis. . . .

The President had confidence in my ability to pacify the disturbing elements, and frankly confessed that it was necessary for me to direct my best efforts in this direction, as his success for a second term lay chiefly in the demand for his renomination coming from the West. The change pleased me because St. Louis was my home, and headquarters in that city would be much more agreeable for many reasons.

Immediately after assuming charge of the revenues of Missouri, I had a conversation with Wm. McKee, senior proprietor of the *Missouri Democrat*, in which he admitted that his opposition to the President was caused by Grant's persistence in appointing persons to office in St. Louis contrary to his (McKee's) expressed wishes, and against the best policy of the party in the state. He was especially bitter against Ford, the [tax] Collector, and asserted that he was entitled to the benefits bestowed upon the party by his paper. Several other conversations occurred between us in which contingencies were provided for.

In the early part of April 1870, I took a trip South and remained absent for some time; upon my return, among the communications awaiting my attention was the following, enclosed in a letter of instructions from Acting Commissioner Douglass:

ST. LOUIS, MO., APRIL 4TH, 1870

DEAR SIR:

You had better examine Mr. Ford's affairs at once, as well as L. Card's distillery; if you do so, as it ought to be done, you will find something which will *astonish* you.

{Private}   R.D. SIMPSON

In this connection it is proper that the reader understand the fact that nearly every distillery was, at that time, libeled and shut up, and the revenue was coming in at an exceedingly slow rate; but I at once acted upon the suggestion of this letter and thoroughly investigated Mr. Ford's books, and also the distillery. During the progress of this investigation, which was made without the suspicion of Mr. McKee, [a bitter] editorial appeared in the *Missouri Democrat* of August 20, 1870. . . .

The full intent of this editorial was not doubtful. McKee was anxious for the removal of several revenue officials distasteful to him, and particularly C.W. Ford, the Collector, who was such a warm bosom friend of the President's that only extraordinary influences could accomplish his removal. Hence the editorial was in the nature of a threat, a part of which was carried out by Mr. McKee in the organization of the Liberal party in Missouri the following fall.

A very sudden change now transpired, which transformed the elements of discord into happiest reconciliation. In the investigation I prosecuted at Ulrici's distillery (formerly run by Card & Lawrence, as referred to in Simpson's letter of information), a most glaring fraud was unearthed, viz. the discovery of 48,000 bushels of grain which had been used for distillation and unaccounted for to the government. The magnitude of this fraud was equal to stealing directly from the government the sum of $117,600, and I at once accused Mr. Ford of guilty knowledge in the disposition of that money.

After a season of skillful evasion, Mr. Ford admitted the frauds, and exhibited the deepest humility and remorse of conscience. I reported to Mr. McKee the result of my investigation, and from that moment on he was anxious for the retention of Mr. Ford in the Collector's office, and expressed his sorrow at having published in his paper the editorial just referred to. . . .

For some time before this McKee had made suggestions to me about organizing a ring among the revenue officials in St. Louis to derive profits from illicit distilling, but Ford prevented a consummation of this intention; and after Ford was detected in connection with Concannon, his deputy, in defrauding the government, he still refused to treat with McKee, because of the antagonisms which had existed between them. The matter was then laid before President Grant, together with an explanation of McKee's opposition to the administration. Soon afterwards Ford signified his willingness to meet and arrange details with McKee, which (I can state with only circumstantial proof) was caused by instructions by the President to Mr. Ford.

Having come to an understanding, arrangements were completed by which McKee, Ford, and myself were to control all federal appointments in Missouri, the Senators at that time (Hon. Frank Blair and Hon. Carl Schurz) not being in sympathy with the administration, and were subsequently ignored by the President. . . .

[In the spring of 1871,] we [McKee, Ford, and McDonald] proceeded to Washington together.[9] Before our arrival Babcock, being notified of our coming, made arrangements for McKee and Ford to dine at the White House. This they did, but I was not one of the party, having declined so as to allow the President, McKee, and Ford to talk the matter over free from the restraint which I was afraid my presence would impose. They returned to me at the Ebbett House about seven o'clock p.m. and informed me that they had passed a most agreeable time with the President, though they had not spoken to him upon politics but had made an engagement to meet him again, in company with myself, at eight o'clock p.m.

At the appointed hour we visited the White House, when, after saluting Mrs. Grant, in company with the President we retired to the Blue Room and spent a long while thoroughly canvassing the political issues in the West, and particularly our scheme for creating a campaign fund. The President distinctly informed both Mr. Ford and Mr. McKee that he had intrusted certain matters to me, that he understood everything, and that whatever we wanted would be forthcoming upon request. Mr. McKee then told the President that the quartermaster in charge of the Government stores at St. Louis might be dispensed with and the interests of the party promoted by the appointment of a more influential working Republican. The President replied: "Well, name your man and I will see Belknap and have him appointed." Mr. McKee then named Maj. E.B. Grimes, who was then stationed in the extreme West, as the successor.

The following day McKee, Ford, and myself called on Secretary [of War] Belknap, who upon our entrance remarked: "What do you fellows want; another quartermaster at St. Louis, eh? I understand that you are in control of matters out West, and what I can do, which I presume is not much, will be done with promptness." McKee and Ford returned to St. Louis highly delighted with their visit, and fully satisfied that they had harbored a most unjust suspicion against me, which they tried to atone for by giving me their implicit confidence thereafter. . . .

9 This passage on the visit to Washington, consisting of this paragraph and the next three, have been moved for narrative and chronological continuity.

The revenue was honestly collected and returned until the fall of 1871, when, at the suggestion of Mr. McKee, one Conduce G. Magrue was imported from Cincinnati to manage the illicit distilling, and to arrange for the collection of the asssessments to be made on the distillers and rectifiers. Magrue's qualifications for this position were of the highest order, as he had successfully conducted two or three enterprises of like character before. His introduction to St. Louis was, ostensibly, as an agent for some paving company in the East.

The Ring would have begun operations much earlier than it did, had it not been for the fact that every distillery in St. Louis was libeled, with the single exception of Ulrici's, at which Ford's crookedness was first discovered. A removal of these libels, necessary to a release that would permit the distilleries to run again, required the labor of several months. . . .

There was, I repeat, an understanding between the President, McKee, Ford, Joyce [John A. Joyce, McDonald's private secretary], and myself that a Ring should be formed, the proceeds from which should constitute a campaign fund to advance the interests of the administration. . . .

President Grant, being ambitious for a second term, saw the necessity of reclaiming the [St. Joseph, Missouri] *Herald* and [the St. Louis] *Democrat*[10]. . . . I was the instrument used by the President in each case to pacify and win over the recalcitrant sheets. Being well fortified with instructions, I saw Col. Bittinger [editor and owner of the St. Joseph *Herald*], and finding him plastic to essential overtures, promised to place him in a position by which he might be a beneficiary of a fund created through illicit distilling in St. Joseph. In addition to this promise to permit the St. Joseph distilleries to run crooked, I also agreed to secure for him an appointment as consul to one of the important cities of England.

C.B. Wilkinson, also one of the proprietors of the *Herald*, had a claim against the government amounting to nearly $10,000, in his settlement upon going out of the office of Collector in about 1865. This claim (I was told by Wilkinson) had been ignored. . . . I promised to collect the claim, and to give the paper certain federal patronage,[11] if the *Herald* would renounce its liberal course, and come out strong for the administration.

My offers were accepted, and when I went to Washington I told President Grant of my arrangements, and drew his attention to the condition of Wilkinson's claim. I further told him that Mr. Wilkinson was especially

[10] In 1872 the *Democrat* was bought out, and McKee left the paper and started a new one, the St. Louis *Globe*. The new management at the *Democrat* was far less friendly to the Grant administration than it had been under McKee (once he had joined the Whiskey Ring, that is). Not many months later the *Democrat* sold out to the *Globe*, and the two papers were consolidated.

[11] The single most important form of government patronage for newspapers was the issuing of printing contracts.

anxious to secure this money, as he would then be enabled to increase the power of his paper.

The President replied: "There will be no trouble about that, for I will see Mr. Boutwell and have the matter attended to."

Upon my return to St. Louis, I reported to Mr. Wilkinson the readiness of the government to settle the claim, and in two weeks thereafter I appeared in Washington with Wilkinson, and took him to the Treasury Department. Upon meeting Mr. Boutwell, the Secretary, Wilkinson announced the object of his visit, whereupon the Secretary replied: "Yes, I have already been spoken to about that matter; if you will come back about two o'clock we will fix your claim," and calling a messenger he sent out for the Comptroller and the papers in the case. Wilkinson kept the engagement, and at the appointed hour he received a draft on the Assistant Treasurer at New York for the full amount of the claim.

Thus the engagement with the *Herald* was consummated, and to more thoroughly seal the compact and utilize Bittinger and Wilkinson the latter was, in February 1873, appointed Collector of the revenue at St. Joseph, and the machine there went into full operation under the new regime. The district had been running crooked, however, for some time before, but now the earnestness of the illicit distillation was pronounced and bold. Con. Magrue having arrived in St. Louis in September 1871, everything was then fixed for the manufacture of illicit whiskey throughout the district.

The first money derived from illicit distilling was in September 1871, the month Magrue appeared in St. Louis to put the machinery of the Ring into operation. I cannot give the minute details of the collection and disbursement of the illicit fund for the reason that there was no rule established for the government of the Ring members in their operations. One month an assessment of $20,000 may have been levied on the distillers and rectifiers and during the next five months five times that sum may have been called for. Much depended upon the demand made by General Babcock for division among the administration conspirators, and the demand for local purposes.

In addition to this, the Washington segment of the Ring was in the habit of sending agents into my district for the sole purpose of blackmail. I have no doubt that Hogue, Brasher, and others who appeared here as revenue agents were sent by Babcock and Rogers, the deputy commissioner (whom I conversed with and received almost admissions of the fact), for the purpose of scaring the St. Louis distillers into the payment of large sums of money for their silence. More than $100,000 was paid out of the fund in this way and that some of this money went into the White House has always been my positive belief.

AN ILLICIT FORTUNE flowed through Babcock's hands during the days of the whiskey ring. The shrewd and unscrupulous presidential secretary was never slow to find an angle of personal profit in any government activity—and the possibilities of a secret ring of distillers and tax inspectors did not escape him. Grant turned away, preferring not to see his friend indulge in the corruption that characterized the age.

Meanwhile, the political power of the ring grew. Newspaper editors fell over themselves in the quest for bribes, happily turning over their editorial policies for so generous a president. As the election of 1872 drew near, many of Grant's friends feared for the result, remembering the very close race he had barely won four years before, when he had been saved by the votes of African Americans in the South. But the President knew better; as vague as he might have been on the details, he understood that a vast and intricate organization was laboring in his favor.

Here two accounts immediately follow one another. The first is by George W. Childs, a well-to-do publisher who fancied himself one of the President's closer companions. He was one of many who feared for his friend's reelection, and marveled at his calm. The second is again by General John McDonald, the mastermind of the Great Whiskey Ring. With fascinating detail, he describes the workings of the operation, as it continued to churn out illicit funds even after the election ended. The conspirators swelled with greed as they continued their work month after month, with little fear of discovery. They even began to fear that Grant might take a dim view of their doings, and sought to curry his favor with expensive gifts. Everything went smoothly, but McDonald was not entirely satisfied. He might well have asked, When would it all end?

The President's Predictive Powers
by George W. Childs

With regard to election matters General Grant was a close observer, and had a wonderful judgment respecting results. One particular case may be cited. During the canvass of his second term (towards the end part of it) there began to be doubts throughout the country of his election. Senator [Henry] Wilson, who was then running on the ticket for Vice President, and who was a man of the people and had had a good deal of experience in election matters for forty years, made an extensive tour through the country, and came to my house just afterwards, very despondent. He went over the ground and said that the result was in a great deal of doubt.

I hastened to see General Grant, and told him of this feeling, particularly as it impressed Senator Wilson. The general said nothing, but sent for a map of the United States. He laid the map on the table, went over it with a pencil, and said, "We will carry this State, that State, and that State," until he nearly covered the whole United States. It occurred to me he might as well put them all in, and I ventured the remonstrance, "I think it would not be policy to talk that way; the election is now pretty near at hand."

When the election came, the result was that Grant carried every State that he said he would—a prediction made in the face of the feeling throughout the country that the Republican cause was growing weaker, and in spite of the fact that the candidate for Vice President on the ticket with Grant, who was deeply interested in the election, had visited various parts of the country, South and West, and had come back apprehensive and dispirited.

General Grant was very magnanimous to those who differed with him, and when I asked him what distressed him most in his political life, he said, "To be deceived by those I trusted." *He had a great many distresses.*

The Ring in Operation
by John McDonald

In the fall of 1873 an explosion occurred which well nigh disrupted the Ring and seriously disturbed the loyalty of the *Globe*.[12] . . . I will explain the cause: As previously stated, Grant's collusion with the Ring consisted in his utilization of corrupt money to secure his re-election. After this purpose was accomplished I was anxious to see the Ring organization dissolved because its ramifications were so extensive, and included such a vast number of men of every character that I was in constant dread of public exposure.

Time and again I talked with McKee and the other managers urging upon them the danger of our position and the bad policy of continuing the corruption after our purposes were accomplished. I laid the matter before Grant who referred me to Babcock whose judgment he relied upon. McKee, in the meantime, became very much offended at my determination to break up the Ring, and finding the administration rather according to my wishes he brought the pressure of his paper against me and was loud in his demands for my removal, being unable to accomplish which he attacked the third-term idea. At length, by seductive argument, the administration concurred in McKee's opinion that the Ring could be run successfully by creating a fund to advance Grant's third-term aspirations. When this view became pronounced I at once accepted the pur-

12 As noted previously, the St. Louis *Globe* was established by McKee in 1872; not many months later the *Globe* and *Democrat* consolidated.

pose as a self-sufficient one and harmony again prevailed among all members of the Ring. . . .

The Whiskey Ring did not confine its operations to St. Louis, but was in full activity in all important cities. In New Orleans there was a gigantic Ring under the immediate supervision of James N. Casey, Collector of the Port of that city who was President Grant's brother-in-law. . . .

Nothing transpired . . . important to record here, until the death of Col. C.W. Ford, the Collector, which occurred at the residence of T.B. Blackstone, in Chicago, October 24th, 1873. Among the telegrams I sent to the friends of Col. Ford, notifying them of his death. . . .

CHICAGO, OCT. 25TH, 1873

HIS EXCELLENCY, U.S. GRANT, Washington:
Hon. C.W. Ford died at the residence of Mr. Blackstone at six o'clock last evening; his remains go to Monroe, Mich., this evening at five o'clock. *I have made provision for the safety of his private papers* and effects. I will be in St. Louis Monday.

MCDONALD

Being fully aware of the fact that there had been correspondence between the President and Col. Ford concerning the management of the Whiskey Ring and the distribution of the campaign fund, I telegraphed to the President in this manner in order to dissipate any anxiety which might be felt at these letters falling into the hands of other parties. . . .

The arrangements were now so complete and no special political necessity appearing for the use of the funds collected from the distillers and rectifiers, the Washington end of the line begun to let their wants be known. I made a regular report, generally each month, to the President, of the manner in which the whiskey money was used. Owing to the very useful position W.O. Avery, Chief Clerk of the Internal Revenue Bureau, occupied, and for advancing us information, he was made the first beneficiary of the fund in Washington. About November 15th [1873] Joyce sent Avery a letter containing $500, it being, I repeat, the first Washington remittance. . . .

A report obtained currency some time in the latter part of August [1874], that St. Louis would soon be visited by another revenue agent, and hearing nothing from Washington, I had Joyce send the following telegram:

ST. LOUIS, AUG. 26th, 1874

COL. W.O. AVERY, Chief Clerk Treasury Department, Washington.
Are friends coming west? See H. (Holt), and give me soundings.

(SIGNED) "A."

To this dispatch there was no answer, and fearing that Avery's induction into an office in which his superior [the new Secretary of the Treasury Benjamin H. Bristow] was then making efforts, or at least contemplating measures that would expose the Whiskey Ring, had resulted in a contrariwise influence, and that he was afraid to give us the information we desired, Joyce sent him a letter, in which the following sentence occurred: (The exact date of the letter I am unable to give from memory, and we rarely retained copies of either letters or telegrams) "If you have any doubt of the propriety of sending this information, see Gen. Babcock, or, if he is not in the city, see G." This meant for Avery to repeat his wishes to Babcock or President Grant, and they would furnish the necessary information to us.

Upon receipt of this letter, Gen. Babcock being absent from Washington, Col. Avery took it to the President, who, after reading the contents, wrote the following endorsement on the back of the letter.

"Joyce and McDonald are reliable and trustworthy.
Let them have the information they want."

(SIGNED) U.S. GRANT

One of the prime motives which actuated Col. Avery in going to the President for his endorsement was to obtain a color of authority for revealing secrets of the Department. He was thoroughly known to the fact that the President was cognizant of all the tricks of the Whiskey Ring, and was, in fact, a member of it; he also realized that his position was a new one, with which he did not yet have that familiarity that would hide all his acts, and his first duty, he felt, was to obtain the confidence of the Secretary. The reports of intended raids from revenue officers continued to circulate. . . .

MY RIDE WITH THE PRESIDENT

Col. Joyce, even after his appointment as revenue agent, remained in my district and continued to act as my confidential secretary. He was a shrewd and thoroughly reliable man and withal one of much cunning and spontaneous resource. I intrusted him not only with all my secrets but left the arrangement of all details furthering the interest of the Ring in his hands. He was especially intimate with Gen. Babcock, and during the visit of the Presidential party [to St. Louis] in October, Col. Joyce and Gen. Babcock were almost inseparable. They canvassed future contingencies and the need of money by the White House officials. . . .

[On December 5, 1874] I started for Washington, but on the preceding day Col. Joyce collected the sum of $5,000 from the distillers and rectifiers which he requested me to deliver to Gen. Babcock, in accordance with the understanding between them, when the latter was in at-

tendance at the St. Louis Fair. This money, as I saw it counted, was in
bills of the denominations of $1,000 and $500.

I reached Washington on the morning of December 7th, and directly
after office hours went to the White House. The first person I met there
was Gen. Babcock, whom I found seated at his desk in the Secretary's
room, and after passing the usual greetings I took the money from my
pocket and handed it to him, with the remark: "Here is $5,000 which
Joyce collected from the boys for your benefit just before I left St.
Louis." He took the package and placed it in his pocket without counting the money, with many expressions of gratitude, remarking that he
understood the source from whence the money came.

During this time a committee from the two branches of Congress were
waiting upon the President to inform him of the opening of Congress,
and their readiness to receive his official communications. When the
committee left the Executive Chamber, the President followed one of the
Senators to the head of the stairs and there took leave of the committee.
I was standing in the ante-room awaiting an opportunity to speak to him
when he turned about and, seeing me, extended a cordial greeting. He
asked me how long I would remain in the city, and to call upon him each
day while in Washington. I replied that my stay would be but a few days.

He then spoke freely concerning the team [of horses] and rig I had
sent him, saying that his gratitude was unbounded, and pronounced the
horses the finest, by far, in Washington. Said I, "General, I have some papers in connection with the team which, with my explanation, I wish to
give you." . . .

Having disposed of the receipts and made the President apparently secure
from the prying curiosity of newspaper correspondents, who always see in
these gifts stepping-stones to political preference, we changed our conversation to a discussion of political matters in the West. I told him that I had
just given Gen. Babcock $5,000 which, I remarked, is a part of the proceeds
of our campaign fund in St. Louis. He assured me it was all right, as he had
intrusted Babcock with the details of Western matters, and whatever we did
with him (Babcock) would be quite satisfactory to all, and added: "I will see
to it personally, however, that you get all the changes you want."

I then explained to him what an uncompromising "old hog" (as I used
the term) McKee was proving himself to be; that we were compelled to
give him $500 to $1,200 every week in order to pacify him and keep his
paper for us in the coming campaign. His reply was: "Well, you must do
the best you can and depend upon me to do all for you at this end of the
line you may require."

While we were thus engaged a messenger came and informed the President that his team was at the door waiting for him. He asked me to walk
downstairs with him and take a look at the horses. I did so, and showed the
ostler how to draw the curb rein to make them drive properly. While we

were looking at the horses, [Internal Revenue Bureau] Commissioner Douglass came by and spoke to us, but after passing a few remarks he walked on. President Grant then requested me to get in and take a drive with him, which I did, going to nearly Bladensburg, and, returning, making a circuit of the city and driving through all the principal streets. During our ride the conversation turned to political matters, and chiefly upon his prospects for a third term. He mentioned the names of several parties who, he thought, might possibly be candidates. Among these were Gov. Morgan of New York, Morton, Conkling, Logan, and Blaine, the latter being then Speaker of the House. He criticized each of these and appeared satisfied that his chances were much better than were those of the parties discussed.

Upon our return from the ride I went back to the White House with the President, and while the colored attendants were brushing our clothes, a messenger-boy informed me that Gen. Babcock was in his office and wished to see me. I left the President in the reception room and went up stairs, where I met Gen. Babcock alone. He first asked me if I had talked freely with the President in relation to appointments out West and the arrangements generally in my district. I replied that I had, and that the President promised to make any appointments or changes of officers I desired. I asked him what [Treasury Department investigators] Brooks and Hoge were doing or were going to do. His answer was that he did not know, but would find out on the following day and advise me. He assured me that he was not going to allow them to go to St. Louis on a "blackmailing trip," as, said he, "we want all the money you can raise now ourselves.". . .

Shortly after my return to St. Louis, in December 1874, I told Col. Joyce that it would be very well to make another small contribution to the President and Gen. Babcock. To do this we procured a box of the finest cigars we could find and enclosed in the box with the cigars a $1,000 bill, which we sent by express addressed to Gen. Babcock. In due time, Col. Joyce received a letter from Babcock acknowledging receipt of the cigars with the enclosure, to which was added a few lines to the effect that "we," referring to Grant and himself, "enjoyed the excellent flavor of those cigars."

AS GRANT'S FIRST term ended and the second began, the conspirators could well be satisfied. They had helped reelect their man, and had strengthened his grip on the party. The wily Babcock had found a new path of intrigue and self-enrichment, while the President himself indulged in thoughts of a third term. But in the flourishing Whiskey Ring the seeds of Grant's destruction had been planted—though a few more seasons would pass before the poisoned fruit would fall from the vine.

18

THE MISSISSIPPI TRIUMPH

Albert Morgan was in love. It was not a feeling he had grown accustomed to over the last few years: anger, righteous indignation, despair, and exultation had been the colors of his emotional palette. But times were changing in Mississippi. Even though the Klan still haunted the red clay roads of the state's backwater counties, even though the Democrats had lost none of their fire, no one could question that the land of Jefferson Davis was undergoing a revolution. The voters had ratified the new constitution; Republicans occupied public offices from the county courthouse to the governor's mansion. Huge tasks lay at hand: laws dating back to slavery needed to be overturned; taxation that favored rich plantation owners demanded reform. It was the perfect moment, Morgan thought, to take a bride.

The marriage of the brave young immigrant from Wisconsin—now a state senator in Mississippi—was a true Reconstruction love story, a matter not only of personal satisfaction but of political importance. Almost everything Morgan did in those early years of Grant's administration resounded throughout the community. Local African Americans—men and women with pride, but without arms, education, or wealth—had stood by him as together they fought and suffered for the sake of justice. Unionist Southern whites and immigrant Yankees had measured his bravery and political skill on countless occasions. With little opposition, he rose to lead the Republican party in the county.

So when Morgan took a wife, it meant something, and it means something still. Then as now, his life captured the reality of Reconstruction at the grass roots, as he and his allies dealt with the practical issues that truly made a difference in average persons' lives. As Congress passed sweeping laws and the nation ratified amendments to the Constitution, the Republicans of Yazoo County reassessed taxes, repaired roads, built schools, and plowed under the color line that had been a fact of life in the South for two centuries.

In the account that follows, Morgan makes issues such as tax rates and county budgets fascinating as they can only be in an era such as this. He also reveals the complexity of political life in Yazoo, as an intense debate developed within the black community over the need to follow its own leadership. The young Yankee shows sympathy for the feelings of those who questioned white leaders for a black majority—indeed, he had broken with other Northerners when he chose to run for the constitutional convention on a ticket with an African-American man. But together with most black leaders, he spoke out against racial separatism—and on his wedding day he proved how deeply he believed the gospel he preached.

Yazoo, Reconstructed
by Albert T. Morgan

I resolved to visit my brother [in Washington County]. It lay on the opposite side of that Delta, and on the great "Father of Waters." . . . [The two brothers met and heatedly discussed the political situation in Washington County. Albert Morgan felt that his brother Charles had been duped by local white Democrats, who claimed that local African Americans were unsuited to political leadership. Gradually, Albert convinced his now-angry brother that he had been seduced by the same forces that almost had lynched him in Yazoo.]

Then Charles stopped short in the dirt road over which we were walking through plowed fields, and turning upon me a most doleful countenance, exclaimed: "Look here! are you going to marry that rebel woman?"

It was my brother's turn to scold now, so he appeared to think, at least, and he seized his opportunity with a zest that showed me how deep was his interest in any step I might take so vital to my future happiness as my marriage.

"Why!" I exclaimed, "Charles, what's the matter with you?"

"Matter enough, I should think, from all I can hear."

"Well, what have you heard?"

"Why! all this talk about your engagement to Miss ——, what's her name?"

"So—you've—heard—that—too, have you? Pray, who told you?"

"Several have mentioned it to me. It was only last week that Colonel Withers, the biggest old reb in this county, on his return from a trip down the river told me he had heard that you were engaged to her."

"Well, what did he have to say about it?"

"Oh, he thought it an excellent idea; good way to close up the bloody chasm, you know, and all that sort of nonsense. He actually congratulated me upon it. Pretty fellow, you to talk to me about allowing these assassins to blindfold me! For my part I'd much rather submit to that operation by a man than any woman I ever saw."

"Ha, ha, ha! had you?"

"Better look sharp, boy."

"Charles, my dear, big brother, will you promise not to go back on me?"

"Well, you're my brother, of course, but then why haven't you said something about it before?"

"Ah! I see. You mean your consent. Well, I ask you now. Have I your consent to marry the only girl in this wide world that I care a 'tinker's baubee' for, as Colonel Black used to say?"

"What an old hyena he is!"

"But you're off the subject, Charles."

"My consent? Why, you're of age, man. As you make your bed, you must lie, you know."

"Yes, I've heard that remark before, and shall doubtless hear it again. But you must promise not to disown me, do you?"

"Y-e-a-s. Yes, I'll promise, but—"

"Look me in the eye, old polecat. I am anxious to see how you take it—steady now! You are *mistaken*, my brother! God willing I am going to marry a 'nigger' schoolmarm."[13]

MORE REVELATIONS

My brother's eyes did not drop at my announcement. They did search my very soul. He must have been content with what he saw at the bottom, for, taking my arm in his, in that affectionate, brotherly way, which was all the more precious to me because it was not often he did it— Charles was not very demonstrative in his affections—he pulled me around, and we resumed our walk.

"Your cigar has gone out, I see" [said Charles]. . . .

"I'll throw it away shortly. Fact is, I've promised Carrie to quit it altogether before our wedding day."

"Well, that's a good beginning, anyhow."

"Good; now tell me about yourself, Charles; why don't you get married?"

"You haven't told me who it is yet that is to take the place of your cigar."

"Oh, do you recollect a certain Sabbath-school you visited with me in Jackson last fall?"

"The one that had so many unrecognized children of 'first citizens of Mississippi' in it?"

"The same; by the way, I had not learned all about her day-school then; the truth is, my brother, there are children of Governors, United States Senators, members of Congress, of the 'High Court of Errors and Appeals,'[14] of the Legislature, and of sheriffs, justices of the peace, doctors, lawyers, ministers, merchants, planters, school teachers, blacksmiths, carpenters, and general laborers in that school. Would you believe it?"

[13] At this point the reader should hardly need reassurance that Morgan uses the racist insult ironically.

[14] [Original author's footnote] Now styled the Supreme Court.

"Yes, I don't doubt it; it's just so here. . . ."

"The first time I visited it there were seventy-odd pupils, by actual count."

"Is it possible! And but one teacher?"

"Only my girl."

"I wonder how she manages them all?"

"Do you recollect a remark you made of her as we left the Sabbath-school that day?"

"I don't know that I do; I remember that I thought her a most heroic girl—"

"And said she'd make a better member of the legislature than any of those you saw in that august body."

"Ha, ha! Yes, I recollect."

"Well, I'm going to make her my wife. . . ."

"You haven't told me where she's from yet."

"She's from Syracuse, New York."

"Good place to come from, by George!"

"I see you are determined to have the whole story. Her mother has been a widow several years; had a large family on her hands; lost her eldest boy and main support in one of the last skirmishes about Petersburg. Ever since 1864 they've all been teaching—the mother and four children—in the South. They live together—the mother and two daughters—at Jackson. Carrie is the most—perhaps I ought not to say most successful, where all have done so nobly—but certainly the most popular teacher there, unless I except one or two most estimable Quaker ladies. Certain it is that she has not only won the love of all the freed people, she has also won the profound respect of the enemy, who treat her with great deference, notwithstanding her calling. Mr. Barksdale, Judge Potter, and many of the solid men of the capital city have manifested their appreciation of her tact, skill, ability, and devotion in many ways. She is as tireless in her work as she is skillful. Think of it, she not only manages that large day school—sometimes numbering a hundred—but she attends to her religious duties, superintends—at least leads—the Sabbath-school, runs a temperance society, and has put in execution various other plans for the social elevation of the freed people."

"I don't see how she stands such a strain."

"My dear boy, the cause in which she is engaged—the cause. Just think of it; there are not half teachers enough for those hungry, starving children. Then too she is a wonderful creature, that girl of mine; never has been sick a day in her life! Never has taken a dose of any kind of medicine! Her breath is as pure and sweet as if it came from off a bed of spring violets."

"Ha, ha, ha! Haw, haw, haw! You forget yourself, my boy. That should be secret."

"Don't care, we're engaged; guess a fellow can kiss a girl after they've been engaged as long as we have."

"How long is that?"

" 'Bout a year."

"Well, I guess you do love her. . . . Albert, have you considered all the obstacles in the way of such a step?" My brother all at once became very grave and awfully solemn, which was heightened, if possible, by my reply, for I retorted thus:

"Obstacles! What obstacles, pray? Ought there to be any obstacles in the way of my marriage to such a girl?"

"There should not be, but in Ohio it is a penitentiary offense for a white man to marry a woman of African ancestry. And now that I think of it, I apprehend that you'll find it quite difficult to escape the same penalty here in Mississippi, unless by some hocus-pocus you can prove yourself to be of the same blood. Considering your complexion and features, particularly your nose, that would be as difficult an undertaking as the former, in my opinion, and—"

All Charles's serious aspect had now vanished, and I could see that he was preparing to retaliate on me for having on a certain occasion called him a jail-bird. Anticipating which I interrupted him.

"My dear brother, you're a long way behind the times."

"Behind the times! Well, I judge that you at least mean to keep ahead." . . .

"But it is true, Charles, old boy; the battle was fought in this country when the rebellion collapsed at Appomattox. Garrison, Phillips, Lucretia Mott, Gerrit Smith, Sumner, and a small army of heroic souls have won all the honors. There is now no law in Mississippi standing between my betrothed and me. There are none now to forbid the banns. African slavery on this continent is dead."

"Are you sure there is no law?"

"More than a month ago I introduced into the Senate a bill repealing all laws upon that subject, and five days afterward that bill, having passed both houses, was approved by the Governor."

"Is it possible! I haven't heard a word about it."

"It is a fact." . . .

A WEDDING

Shortly afterward the records of the Circuit Court of Hinds, the capital county of Mississippi, bore the fact of my marriage to Miss Carrie V. Highgate, on August 3, 1870. The bond required was about the same as that exacted of my brother, a failure to give which had resulted in his incarceration in a murderer's cell in that Yazoo common jail. But now that

Grant, instead of Johnson, was President, and the new constitution had been ratified unanimously, and the black code had been repealed, and the "nigros" had "done riz," I had no trouble at all to give it. Within one week from the day we began keeping house in Yazoo, wife and I—how strangely that contrasts with "Yankee stronghold". . . .

During this season "we all Yankees," "nigros," and "scalawags" in Yazoo gathered the first fruits of all our planting in that county during the Reconstruction period, and with high hopes for the future prepared the ground for other seed, and prayed for the blessed showers of love from on high to quicken them. . . .

PROGRESS OF THE FREED PEOPLE

But that which seems to me the most gratifying feature of the period of which I am now writing, is the marvelous progress made by the freed people in the art of self-government. I presume that many of my readers[15]—if indeed I have many—will smile incredulously at this point; they have often done so before in the course of this story. That cannot be helped. All have my free consent to smile, to laugh, or to cry whenever the mood shall prompt them. This is said to be a free country, and I believe in its fundamental institutions. But I am digressing, and am reminded that I have left only space for facts.

About the close of our political campaign in 1869, and from then on, there were frequent arrivals at Yazoo of persons from the North and from adjoining States, all of whom brought with them a universal panacea for the woes of the people, "both black and white." Some came "highly recommended" to some one or more of the State official dignitaries, others came bearing no other testimonials than the merits of the politic nostrums they had to introduce. This class was of both races, and of all shades of politics, complexion, calling, and employment or profession. Some openly espoused the cause of "the people," and became "good citizens"; in other words, Democrats. Others as openly espoused the cause of "the people," and became "scum"—carpetbaggers; in other words, Republicans. There were a few who espoused the cause of "ou' color," and at once began to find fault with both Democrats and Republicans.

One of these was a quite intelligent colored man, whose parents had passed through the color crucible at the North and still felt the pain of the burn. By way of illustrating the fact that he had inherited their remembrance of Yankee prejudices and their secret contempt of the Yankee character, he began almost immediately upon his arrival at Yazoo an effort to gather the

15 The author wrote his account in 1884, when Reconstruction was already widely discredited among the white public, North and South alike.

freed people into a separate political organization. To accomplish this purpose, he gravely assured them that their liberties did not depend upon the
leadership of any man or set of men, but upon themselves; that they were
under no obligations whatever to any person, or to any party for their freedom, because freedom was the natural state of man, and their emancipation
was evidence merely that the country had come to the point of recognizing
the fact. The obligation, therefore, was all on the other side, and could not
be discharged until the white man, who had always lived upon the negro's
toil, went a step farther and made some sort of restitution.

According to his philosophy, the fact that the freedom and citizenship
of the negro had been put into the Constitution and laws of the country
was ample guarantee of its permanence, and, as the colored people of
Yazoo were largely in the majority, two to one, they ought, therefore, to
rule. Had he stopped here he might have made some headway amongst
"ou' color" in Yazoo. But he did not, and continued to advance in the
unfolding of his scheme, until he had openly denounced me as a fraud,
and not a true friend of the colored people. Then he found it to his interest quite suddenly to leave the county, which he did, and returning
North spread the news amongst "ou' color" that the carpetbaggers at the
South were not only deluding the poor freed people to their ruin, but
were an intolerable nuisance to the State. In proof of this he cited his
own case, and declared that I had incited the "poor, ignorant freed people"—my dupes—to drive him away, because I feared the presence in the
county of "intelligent gentlemen of color." Now, the truth is I knew
nothing of the affair until long afterwards. . . .

There were other aspiring colored young men from the North, more
wise than those of the class to which the one I have mentioned belonged.
These came seeking honest employment, or waited until they became acquainted with the people until they attempted to lead. Several of this
class became useful citizens, engaged in merchandising, planting, or
school teaching, and thus grew to be real helps in the work of clearing
the old ground and in cultivating and harvesting the crops that grew
upon it. These were recognized and preferred by the people according to
their merits. At this time, Mississippi and other Southern States enjoying
free governments, offered a tempting field for ambitious and worthy
young colored men at the North, where nearly all the doors to the trades
and higher employments, in private as well as in public life, were closed
against them. I was not at all surprised that they came flocking to Mississippi and Yazoo. For one I was glad to have them come. . . .

But in Yazoo, colored men from the North found a match for themselves
in many of the freed people, whose sterling good sense and practical knowledge of affairs in some measure made up for their lack of school training.
Our local elections afforded ample means for testing these qualities, and for
bringing out the comparative merits of the two. Northern colored men,

even in Yazoo, had to contend with the prejudices of the freed people, which often were as bitter as the prejudices of the native whites against "we all Yankees." So that unless the Northern colored men could make his race argument or reasoning in favor of segregation do service for him, the freedman who aspired for leadership was likely to carry off the prize. . . .

AN ACCOUNT OF MY STEWARDSHIP, 1869 TO 1874

The smallest political subdivision in Mississippi is the county government. "Town meetings" are unknown there. There are township territorial subdivisions, but no township governments. For this reason the county officers and the county "rings" are the most powerful factors in State politics. . . . By the old constitution, during the slave regime, the county board was styled the Board of County Police; by our new constitution the county board was styled the Board of County Supervisors. The change was in name merely. . . .

Thus the board of supervisors would be the most important position in our new government. I resolved to guard that position myself, and having asked for it, I was appointed supervisor for Beat No. 3—the Yazoo City beat—by General Ames, and was made president of the board by the voice of my colleagues. This was 1869. . . .

I think the reader will agree with me that I have not had very much to say of myself as leader and "dictator" in Yazoo. But we have now reached a point where I must give some account of my stewardship, and tell the reader what I, backed by the loyal true of our brave crew, did in Yazoo during the period of my trust. I shall be brief, and I shall begin with our party's management of the county finances.

At the beginning of our term of office, the board discovered that not only was there no money in the treasury, but that the total indebtedness of the county could not be ascertained for lack of proper records. We were able to know, beyond a doubt, that it amounted to quite ten thousand dollars. It might be thirty thousand. It was in the shape of county warrants, which up to that moment had sold down as low as forty-five, and rarely went higher than sixty-five cents on the dollar. But a small patch of the county poor farm was being cultivated. The county poor house was a hovel. . . . The courts were being held in a little, old hall.[16] The only protection for the valuable county records were the brick walls of this hall, and a watchman. The highways had been neglected; some of them were impassable. The bridges were nearly all old, and sadly in need of repair. Populous settlements were deprived of access to the county seat for several months in the year for want of bridges, unless men could spare

---

[16] [Original author's footnote] Over a store-room.

from their business the time requisite for a tedious, circuitous, and expensive journey, partly by private teams, and partly by irregular river packets. The county jail was a rickety old brick contrivance, with a board fence, half rotted down, and toppling over in places. . . .

There was not a free public school-house in the county. Mississippi was an old State when Nebraska was peopled only by Indians and hunters, but in 1869 there was hardly an organized county in what is now the State of Nebraska that had not a better free school building than any house used for school purposes in Yazoo County in 1869, and it was among the first organized counties in the State—a center of population, of wealth, and of commerce. The only school-houses in use were such as had been erected for private schools, and some that had been erected with so much of the proceeds of the sixteenth-section school lands as had not been stolen by Yazoo slave-lords. . . .

Had the county finances been in good shape, there would have been obstacles enough in the way of a successful establishment of the new government to make it a doubtful experiment. With the county heavily in debt, its paper so greatly depreciated that only those inside the county ring would deal in it, and extensive immediate outlays absolutely necessary for the proper security of the county records, the dispatch of the business of the county, especially of the courts, the construction of bridges, etc., etc., to work at the same time for the establishment of free schools appeared to many of the Unionists a "suicidal undertaking," to some of the Northerners, a hopeless task, and to the enemy, an outrage, for which the people of the county "without regard to color" would hold the perpetrators responsible to the full extent of the law and outraged public sentiment. Many well-meaning friends said, "We must not attempt to do all at once." . . .

The truth is, that while the assessed value of the property of the county, from 1865 to 1869, was in round numbers four and a half millions, it could not have been purchased of its owners for less than twenty millions. By way of illustration, Tokeba, for which we paid seven dollars per acre rent in 1866 and 1867, and would have continued to pay the same sum through 1868, but for the determination of Colonel Black and the enemy to "get rid a' them damned Yankee sons of bitches now," was assessed at one dollar per acre for some, and none at a higher rate than eight dollars per acre. . . . My recollection is that there was not an acre assessed at so high a figure as twelve dollars. Yet the Northerners who rented them [the county's plantations] in 1866 and 1867 paid ten dollars per acre annual rent for the cultivated lands. . . . Therefore, I proposed that we revise and correct the inequalities in the present assessment rolls and make a slight increase in the total valuation while doing so.

This was done. Plantations like Tokeba were increased in value upon the roll to two, eight, and twelve dollars per acre; those like the Paynes' to two, ten, and fifteen dollars per acre, according to the land and improvements; while those that had been assessed at too high a rate, correspondingly, were reduced in value upon the assessment roll. The result was an increase of the total valuation of the real and personal property of the county in round numbers to five millions. . . .

The enemy employed legal counsel and fought these innovations, as they were termed, step by step, but in vain. I had anticipated this opposition and, in the selection of members for this vital point in our loyal government, had procured the appointment of two colored men, who, with myself, constituted a majority of the board. It may be remarked as a little singular that I should have been willing to entrust so sacred an interest to the chance of an alliance between two "ignorant nigros," as they were called by the enemy, and the old ex-slaveholder on the board. A little reflection, however, will satisfy the reader that I acted from correct principles.

It is true that, as a rule, Southern men, whether Unionists, Conservatives, or irreconcilables, have always maintained that the negro is unreliable when placed in charge of an important trust. Most of such people maintain, even to this day, that he is not only unreliable, but incapable. But here were two freedmen—men who had been slaves until the war freed them—one of them could barely read, who could not sign his name, the other of whom could write only about as well as he could read, and that was very poorly, and yet I trusted them implicitly. In the first place, I knew that the freed people were in truth craving an opportunity to educate their children. I believed that these men, in such a position, would represent faithfully the known wishes of their "own color."

I also believed that the great mass of freed people did in truth appreciate their freedom, and would be as prompt to condemn wastefulness or extravagance on the part of their representatives as the whites, *if not more so*. And, although the color of one was "light," and his eyes gray, the color of the other black, with black eyes, I felt that I could trust them. They both had worked hard since the war, and saved their money, and upon the very first opportunity had purchased land.

The result proved the wisdom of my choice, for while the Northerner on the board wavered several times during the contest, and while the ex-slaveholder often got very hot, indignant, and "outraged," the voices of the two colored men were always on the side of right.

First the enemy tried to coax, then to bribe, and then to drive them from me, but, without a particle of coaxing, or of convincing, or of bull-dozing from me, or any of my friends, these men stood firm as a rock upon the naked line of duty, swerving neither to the right nor to the left, and I here testify that they discharged their duties faithfully, ably, and most creditably to themselves and the county. The fact is, they were *men*, with the instincts common to good, well-meaning men. They were also *citizens*, and they appreciated the fact. They were *public officers* in charge of a sacred trust. They were *representatives*, and they understood that fact, and they bowed loyally to the known will of their constituents. . . .

RESULTS

The reader has already seen what was accomplished by the enemy during the years of its control prior to the war, and in the four years which followed that event, in the way of county improvements. In this chapter I shall endeavor to faithfully set down what was accomplished by "we all radicals," in the six years of my "dictatorship."

By the beginning of 1875, the requisite repairs upon the county highways and bridges had been completed, and new bridges built, so that in that respect the county had never before enjoyed equal facilities. Improvements upon the poor-farm buildings had been made, the farm put in cultivation, system and order enforced in its management and among its inmates, and the institution became nearly self-sustaining. The capacity and security of the jail had been enlarged with the addition of safe iron cells. The new courthouse, costing quite seventy thousand dollars, had been erected and paid for as the work progressed, and had been accepted by a committee of the oldest and best members of our Yazoo bar association. Everybody said it was a credit to the county.

The county indebtedness had at no time exceeded the annual levy for current expenses. The finances had been managed in such a way that within the first year of our control, county warrants went up to par, and remained there during the entire period, with only short exceptions. At the close of 1873, there were outstanding obligations amounting to quite thirty thousand dollars, but nearly if not quite the entire sum would be absorbed by the tax levy for that year. . . .

Yazoo City was an incorporated town, its government under the control of the Republicans, who were in the majority. As in the county so it was here; extensive improvements had been wrought; new sidewalks, pavements, and gutters, had been made; and, above all perhaps, a new steam fire-engine had been provided. Our Yankee postmaster, aided by a few public-spirited fellow-citizens, was foremost in all these good works. . . .

On all these improvements our party leaders had been practically a unit, and the great body of the freed people had stood squarely by us. I am sorry to say that there was not the same harmony among "we all Republicans" upon the school question. By the annual message of Governor James L. Alcorn for 1871, it appears that there were schools open in Yazoo County from 1865 to 1870 as follows:

1865—For white pupils, 6; for colored, 3.
1866— .... 8; ....5.
1867— .... 8; ....2.
1868— ....12; ....3.
1869— ....14; ....6.
1870— ....14; ....6.

None of these were free public schools, and those for the colored people were organized and supported entirely by the bureau, or by Northerners, or by the freed people themselves. . . .

There was no violent opposition to the establishment of the [free public school] system in Yazoo County. The difficulty was of another kind. The school board of the county was composed of very worthy and capable men, Unionists and Northerners, and one colored man. At its head was the county superintendent, a Yankee who had been a bank president . . . but he possessed the same failing as most Northerners who settle there sooner or later seem bound to discover. He was conscientious in the discharge of his duties, but was extremely desirous of having the good opinion of "Southerners."[17] He was also anxious to have the good opinion of the colored people, and I have no doubt meant to do for their best good in his management of that branch of our county government, but the white Southerners associated with him were extremely timid. They went forward with their work as though their first duty was to consult the enemies of the system, and although our board of supervisors repeatedly assured the school board of their willingness to levy for whatever amount they could wisely use, their three first annual estimates were far below what they should have been.

In addition to this—while the number of educable children in the county, according to the assessor's returns in 1872, was, whites, 2,180; colored, 4,183—up to and including 1872 this board had established twenty-five schools for the colored, and had given forty-one to the white children. And as if to cap the climax, in 1873 they actually proposed a reduction of the tax levy for school purposes.

The colored people were beginning to clamor against this partiality, and the politicians among the enemy were taking advantage of what apparently was our neglect of the colored people, and, as I was at the head in the management of affairs, were holding me responsible for it.

To have attempted to set up a system which mixed the races in the schools, nearly everybody said, would lead to a "war of the races," so separate schools had been provided by State law. The colored people did not complain of this, but they did demand equal school facilities. In justice to them they should have had the forty-one, and the whites have been content with twenty-five schools; if no more than sixty-six could be provided. There was no reason at all, nor had there been, for this slow progress in that vital work.

But at best, the system at first was only tolerated by the whites, because they could not help themselves. The question now was, whether they should be allowed to strangle it while we had charge. I resolved to take the responsibility of saying no. Therefore when the superintendent's term ex-

[17] [Original author's footnote] He afterward married a most estimable lady of that State.

pired I recommended and procured the appointment of my brother in his place. Now, this was not my brother the "jail-bird," but another one.

Soon after Charles's transfer to Washington County, the ex-bureau agent was also transferred to a field where his services were more likely to be helpful to our cause than in Yazoo, where, it was said, we had more than our share of good material. Shortly afterward, however, General Greenleaf and our Republican magistrate died, and went straight to heaven, I believe. All these transfers so reduced the little garrison that Mr. Foote, the old guard, and myself were left the sole survivors in the county.

During this period my brother William came down to visit me. Things had grown to be so much brighter-hued in Yazoo, that I had little difficulty to induce him to remain and to unite his fortunes with me in my new home. It was this brother whom I got appointed superintendent.

The result was a marked change in the conduct and growth of the free-school system. . . . My brother's heart was in the good work as thoroughly as my own. He sent North for teachers. Under the new management there were no steps backward. On the contrary, in 1875, the close of my brother's term, according to the official reports, there were in the county free schools as follows: white, 45; colored, 63; total, 108. Of teachers employed, there were: white, 79; colored, 23. Of school-houses and rooms, there were 109. Sixty of these houses had been erected and paid for during the period. There had not been a day from 1869 to 1875 when the holder of a warrant on the school fund could not demand and receive in lawful money of the United States the full amount expressed upon its face. . . . In spite of all the obstacles in the way of its growth, in 1875 the system in Yazoo was a complete success, a fact acknowledged by all except possibly a handful of the most violent of the irreconcilables. . . .

The enemy, while we planted, looked on in amazement and gradually descended through all the stages from bitter, implacable foes, blunt frenzy, helpless indifference and enmity, to placid acquiescence, to secret, and finally, before the election of 1875, to open support. Members of the Yazoo bar, even Mrs. Black's attorney, confessed that the business of the courts had never been more ably or more satisfactorily conducted; that the laws had never been more faithfully or more justly executed; that the county had never before enjoyed greater peace; and the planters and the rank and file of the enemy all agreed that the county had never been more prosperous.

There were, however, a few exceptions to this universal voice, viz.: Colonel Black, the human hornet, Ben Wicks, Major Sweet, et al. But we had shouldered the load and carried it in triumph.

AFTER LONG YEARS of persecution and failure, Morgan at last found success. He found it all the sweeter because he achieved more than a political victory—by any measure, the movement he led had made Yazoo

County a better place to live. He set a personal example in his marriage to Carrie Highgate. For centuries, white men had mated with black women, taking them as unacknowledged concubines; Morgan was disgusted by the practice, and when he fell in love, he changed state law to make his union an open and honorable one.

Of course, the path of Reconstruction in Yazoo wound around the obstructions of history. Though a minority both locally and statewide, the white population could still block or slow down reforms, forcing compromises. School segregation offers an example. The question of mixed schools was fiercely debated, but in the end Republicans of both races decided that half a loaf was better than none, and submitted to white demands for segregated schools.

Indeed, hindsight can often prove as much a curse as a benefit in considering the advances of Reconstruction. Sharecropping, for example, later became a symbol of economic oppression. But it came into existence at this time at the insistence of black farmers. African Americans longed for autonomy, for the freedom to work unsupervised, with their own families, in their own way; sharecropping was a relief from the wage-labor gang system that replaced plantation slavery. White landowners complained about being forced to accept the change; but gradually they learned to bind their tenants with debt.

Similarly, the fact that the proportion of blacks in public office was consistently lower than their share of the population seems unfair; but to African Americans in the 1860s and '70s, the fact that former slaves held office at all represented a mind-boggling revolution. And their share of offices grew over time. At first, they were held back by a number of factors: immigrant Northern and local Unionist whites aggressively took charge of the Republican party in every Southern state, for instance. Also, most states continued to require that officeholders post a bond backed by real estate; since landowning had been illegal or practically impossible for blacks in most states, few could comply. But rising prosperity and self-assertiveness led to an ever larger share for African Americans as Reconstruction progressed.

One African American held office in Mississippi from the arrival of General Ames through the end of the era—John R. Lynch, freedman of Natchez. Ever since Ames had appointed him justice of the peace, Lynch had been gaining prominence in his town and in surrounding Adams County. The fact that a former slave held the post swelled its importance in the black community: African Americans brought him every sort of problem, from family disputes to conflicts with employers. And his position in the local Republican party grew as well. Though still in his early twenties, Lynch soon won election to the state House of Representatives.

In the passage that follows, Lynch recalls the early years of the Reconstruction government in Mississippi, as he and other legislators sought to remake the state. As Albert Morgan did in Yazoo County, Lynch faced a daunting task. For decades, the state had been run by the planter elite, and every aspect of law had been oriented to meet their wishes. Now schools had to be constructed, roads rebuilt, and the racist Black Code swept away. The new government hoped to modernize the economy and aid railroad construction.

But the planter class had hardly disappeared. In fact, one of its foremost representatives, James L. Alcorn, ran for office as the Republican candidate for governor. The selection of Alcorn reflects a strategy adopted by most local Republican parties throughout the South; white elites had dominated the region for so long, and controlled so much of its wealth, that party leaders felt they could only succeed if they won the support of at least a segment of this group. Most states would soon see deep divisions in their parties as a result of this outreach. But Alcorn had been outspoken in his call for black rights; in office, he worked with African-American officials such as Lynch. He was still a rich planter, however, and he believed more than anyone else that white support was the key to success in Mississippi. More and more, Alcorn would emerge as the conservative rival of General Adelbert Ames, the conscientious godparent of the Reconstruction government.

In the meantime, it seemed to Lynch that a new age had indeed come to pass in the heart of the old South. He exulted in the electoral triumph over the party of the Ku Klux Klan, and in the sweeping new laws he helped enact. And nothing gave him greater pride than seeing an African American become United States Senator, taking the seat once held by Jefferson Davis himself.

Building a New Mississippi
by John R. Lynch

The election resulted in an overwhelming Republican victory. That party not only elected the State ticket by a majority of about 30,000 but it also had a majority in both branches of the State Legislature. The new administration had an important and difficult task before it. A State Government had to be organized from top to bottom; a new judiciary had to be inaugurated—consisting of three Justices of the State Supreme Court, fifteen Judges of the Circuit Court, and twenty Chancery Court Judges—who had all to be appointed by the Governor with the consent of the Senate and, in addition, a new public school system had to be established.

There was not a public school building anywhere in the State except in a few of the larger towns, and they, with possibly a few exceptions, were greatly in need of repairs. To erect the necessary school houses and to reconstruct and repair those already in existence so as to afford educational facilities for both races was by no means an easy task. It necessitated a very large outlay of cash in the beginning, which resulted in a material increase in the rate of taxation for the time being, but the Constitution called for the establishment of the system, and of course the work had to be done. It was not only done, but it was done creditably and as economically as possible, considering the conditions at that time. That system, though slightly changed, still stands—a creditable monument to the first Republican State administration that was organized in the State of Mississippi under the Reconstruction Acts of Congress.

It was also necessary to reorganize, reconstruct, and, in many cases, rebuild some of the penal and charitable institutions of the State. A new code of laws also had to be adopted to take the place of the old code and thus wipe out the black laws that had been passed by what was known as the Johnson legislature, and in addition bring about other changes so as to make the laws and statutes of the State conform with the new order of things. This was no easy task. . . .

[At the election in Natchez in Adams County,] Jacobs was . . . nominated for member of the [State] House of Representatives without opposition, his associates being John R. Lynch [the author] and Capt. O.C. French, a white Republican. The ticket as completed was elected by a majority of from fifteen hundred to two thousand, a Republican nomination in Adams County at that time being equivalent to an election.[18]

When the Legislature convened at Jackson the first Monday in January, 1870, it was suggested to Lieutenant-Governor Powers, presiding officer of the Senate, that he invite the Rev. Dr. Revels to open the Senate with prayer. The suggestion was favorably acted upon. That prayer— one of the most impressive and eloquent prayers that had ever been delivered in the Senate Chamber—made Revels a United States Senator.[19] He made a profound impression upon all who heard him. It impressed those who heard it that Revels was not only a man of great natural ability, but that he was also a man of superior attainments.

The duty devolved upon that Legislature to fill three vacancies in the United States Senate: one, a fractional term of about one year—the remainder of the six-year term to which Jefferson Davis had been elected before the breaking out of the Rebellion—another fractional term of about five years, and the third, the full term of six years, beginning with the expiration of the fractional term of one year. The colored members

[18] At the county Republican convention, Lynch and his followers defeated the nomination of his chief rival, Rev. Henry P. Jacobs, to the state Senate. Lynch persuaded Rev. Hiram R. Revels to run for the office; after losing the nomination to Revels, Jacobs agreed to run for a state House seat instead.

[19] At this time U.S. senators were still elected by state legislatures.

of the Legislature constituted a very small minority not only of the total membership of that body but also of the Republican members. Of the thirty-three members of which the Senate was composed four of them were colored men: H.R. Revels of Adams [County]; Charles Caldwell, of Hinds; Robert Gleed, of Lowndes; and T. W. Stringer, of Warren. Of the hundred and seven members of which the House was composed about thirty of them were colored men. . . . But the colored members insisted that one of the three United States Senators to be elected should be a colored man. The white Republicans were willing that the colored men be given the fractional term of one year, since it was understood that Governor Alcorn was to be elected to the full term of six years and that Governor Ames was to be elected to the fractional term of five years.

In this connection it may not be out of place to say that, ever since the organization of the Republican party in Mississippi, the white Republicans of that State, unlike some in a few of the other Southern States, have never attempted to draw the color line against their colored allies. In this they have proved themselves to be genuine and not sham Republicans—that is to say, Republicans from principle and conviction and not for plunder and spoils. They have never failed to recognize the fact that the fundamental principle of the Republican party—the one that gave the party its strongest claims upon the confidence and support of the public—is its advocacy of equal political rights. If that party should ever come to the conclusion that this principle should be abandoned, that moment will merit, and I am sure it will receive, the condemnation and repudiation of the public.[20]

It was not, therefore, a surprise to anyone when the white Republican members of the Mississippi Legislature gave expression to their entire willingness to vote for a suitable colored man to represent the state of Mississippi in the highest and most dignified legislative tribunal in the world. The name of the Rev. James Lynch was first suggested. That he was a suitable and fit man for the position could not be denied. But he had just been elected Secretary of State for a term of four years, and his election to the Senate would have created a vacancy in the former office which would have necessitated the holding of another State election and another election was what all wanted to avoid. For that reason his name was not seriously considered for the Senatorship.

The next name suggested was that of the Rev. H.R. Revels and those who had been so fortunate as to hear the impressive prayer that he had delivered on the opening of the Senate were outspoken in their advocacy of his selection. The white Republicans assured the colored members that

[20] Lynch is only partially correct in this statement about the Republican party in Mississippi. Governor Alcorn soon began to court the support of native whites, appointing some Democrats to public offices. The party split into factions—a conservative one led by Alcorn, a progressive one by Ames.

if they would unite upon Revels, they were satisfied he would receive the vote of every white Republican member of the Legislature. Governor Alcorn also gave the movement his cordial and active support, thus insuring for Revels the support of the State administration. The colored members then held an informal conference, at which it was unanimously decided to present the name of Rev. H.R. Revels to the Republican Legislative Caucus to fill the fractional term of one year. The choice was ratified by the caucus without serious opposition.[21]

In the joint Legislative session, every Republican member, white and colored, voted for the three Republican caucus nominees for United States Senators—Alcorn, Ames, and Revels—with one exception, Senator William M. Hancock of Lauderdale [County], who stated in explanation of his vote against Revels that as a lawyer he did not believe that a colored man was eligible to a seat in the United States Senate. But Judge Hancock seems to have been the only lawyer in the Legislature—or outside of it, as far as could be learned—who entertained that opinion.

IMPORTANT EDUCATIONAL AND POLITICAL MEASURES

In addition to the election of the three United States Senators, this Legislature had some very important work before it, as has already been stated. . . . The entire State Government in all its branches had to be reconstructed and so organized as to place the same in perfect harmony with the new order of things.

To accomplish these things money was required. There was none in the treasury. There was no cash available even to pay the ordinary expenses of the State government. . . . To raise the necessary money to put the new machinery in successful operation one of two things had to be done: either the rate of taxation must be materially increased or interest-bearing bonds must be issued and placed upon the market, thus increasing the bonded debt of the State. Although the fact was subsequently developed that a small increase in the bonded debt of the State could not very well be avoided, yet, after careful deliberation, the plan agreed upon was to materially increase the rate of taxation.

This proved to be so unpopular that it came near losing the Legislature to the Republicans [that is, the Democrats nearly won] at the elections of 1871. Although it was explained to the people that this increase was only temporary and that the rate of taxation would be reduced as soon as some of the schoolhouses had been built and some of the public institutions had

[21] Since Revels had run for the state legislature and won with Lynch's backing, his election to the U.S. Senate can be seen as a victory for Lynch in the factional politics of the state's Republican party.

been repaired, still this was not satisfactory to those by whom these taxes had to be paid. They insisted that some other plan ought to have been adopted, especially at that time. . . . This was especially true of those who had been the owners of large landed estates and of many slaves. . . . These were men who had made and molded public opinion, who had controlled the pulpit and the press, who had shaped the destiny of the States; who had made and enforced the laws—or at least such laws as they desired to have enforced—and who had represented the State not only in the State Legislature but in both branches of the National Legislature at Washington. . . . It was not only a difficult matter for them to adjust themselves to the new order of things and to the radically changed conditions, but no longer having slaves upon whom they could depend for everything, to raise the necessary money to prevent the decay, dissipation, and the ultimate loss or destruction of their large landed estates was the serious and difficult problem they had before them. . . .

But since Governor Alcorn, under whose administration and in accordance with whose recommendation this increase had been made, was a typical representative of this particular class, it was believed and hoped that he would have sufficient influence with the people of his own class to stem the tide of resentment, and to calm their fears and apprehensions. That the Republicans retained control of the Legislature as a result of the elections of 1871—though only by a small majority in the lower house—is conclusive evidence that the Governor's efforts in that direction were not wholly in vain. . . .

Governor Alcorn also recommended—a recommendation that was favorably considered by the Legislature—that there be created and supported by the State a college for the higher education of the colored boys and young men of the State. This bill was promptly passed by the Legislature, and, in honor of the one by whom its creation was recommended, the institution was named "Alcorn College."

The presidency of this much-needed college was an honorable and dignified position to which a fair and reasonable salary was attached, so the Governor, who had the appointing power, decided to tender the offer to Senator H.R. Revels upon the expiration of his term in the Senate. I had the honor of being named one of the first trustees of this important institution. . . .

As evidence of the necessity for such an institution, it will not be out of place to call attention to the fact that when the writer was first elected to Congress in 1872, there was not one young colored man in the State that could pass the necessary examination for a clerkship in any of the Departments at Washington. Four years later the supply was greater than the demand, nearly all of the applicants being graduates of Alcorn College. . . .

The knowledge I had acquired of parliamentary law not only enabled me to take a leading part in the deliberations of the Legislature, but it resulted in my being made Speaker of the House of Representatives that was elected in 1871.

SPEAKER JOHN LYNCH: It was a remarkable title for a man who had been born in slavery, who had lived for a time as a fugitive from his birth-place, who had settled penniless in Mississippi. But Lynch was clearly a remarkable man. His eloquence and intellect had lifted him to statewide leadership. But his rise to the powerful position of speaker would not be easy.

Alcorn's governorship split the Republican party in Mississippi. A rich planter himself, schooled in the whites-only politics of the antebellum South, he believed that the party could only survive if it attracted conserva-tive white support. He held this conviction despite the well-known fact that blacks were a majority of the state population. Alcorn removed as many as half of Adelbert Ames's appointees, replacing them with Democrats as often as Republicans. He moved to block proposals from such legislators as state Senator Albert Morgan—killing off, for example, a plan to ban school seg-regation. In so doing, he alienated many black and Radical white Republi-cans; more than one complained that even under Reconstruction, those who had rebelled in the Civil War were gaining more than those who had stayed loyal. Even worse, Alcorn's efforts failed: he only attracted the weak support of no more than a few thousand former Whigs.

The division in Mississippi reflected a rift that shattered Republican or-ganizations throughout the South. In Georgia in 1868, white Republi-cans joined with Democrats to evict black delegates from the state constitutional convention. That state, along with Florida, then appor-tioned electoral districts to minimize the influence of black voters. Gov-ernor Robert K. Scott of South Carolina initially appointed a fair number of black officials—notably trial judges—but he later reversed himself, de-spite the large African-American majority in his state. Alabama's party split between conservative followers of Governor William H. Smith and Radical adherents of Senator George Spencer. In Virginia, whites man-aged to overturn Reconstruction almost immediately. North Carolina and Tennessee froze blacks out entirely from many areas of government.

Louisiana suffered, as Eric Foner has written, "the most byzantine fac-tional struggles" of the entire South. Republicans were split in any number of ways: immigrant Northerners against native whites, whites against blacks, and freeborn African Americans (many French-speaking residents of New Orleans) against former slaves. Blacks formed a majority of the state popu-lation, but the New Orleans freeborn elite felt it was their right to lead the freed people, an assumption many former slaves resented. Furthermore, Governor Henry Warmoth (a Northern man) fought one bitter feud against a ring of officials led by federal marshal Stephen B. Packard and Collector of the Port James F. Casey (another presidential brother-in-law), and a second against his own (black) lieutenant governor, P.B.S. Pinchback.

This infighting terribly damaged the Republican party locally and across the South. Warmoth sought white support, appointing Democrats to local positions. Packard and Casey struggled with him for control of the legislature—Marshal Casey actually had Warmoth arrested in 1872, and the governor used the state militia to physically occupy the statehouse. Warmoth found himself impeached, and Pinchback became the nation's first black governor. And throughout the intrigue-ridden conflict, corruption seeped through the state government.

To the weary citizens of Louisiana, the Republican split across the river in Mississippi must have seemed faint trouble indeed. In fact, to the weary citizens of New York (who had just seen their legislature purchased intact by Jay Gould), the government of this Reconstruction state must have seemed like paradise. Despite the divisions, Republicans made tremendous progress in reforming and rebuilding. And even conservative Alcorn was willing to accommodate black voters on more than one occasion—acceding to the election of Senator Revels, for example.

But Radical Republicans revolted against Alcorn's appeal to white Democrats, collecting instead around the newly elected Senator Adelbert Ames. The two men faced off in Washington after Alcorn arrived as Revels's successor, and they became bitter enemies. In the halls of Congress, they took opposite sides on the debate over laws to suppress the Ku Klux Klan—Alcorn belittling Klan violence, and Ames denouncing it. Before long, Ames decided that he must return to Mississippi to run for governor to root out his rival's influence and appointees.

But first, the state witnessed a groundbreaking political contest—for a man born in bondage was a candidate for speaker of the House of Representatives. In the account that follows, Lynch makes clear how the factional split between Ames and Alcorn hindered his election. But one thing he does not discuss so openly: his own political skills. Lynch must have been a far more gifted legislator and negotiator than he lets on in his dispassionate description, for he managed to win over the crucial support of the very man who was doing his best to color the Republican party white.

The Contest for Speaker
by John R. Lynch

The elections being over, and a Republican majority in both branches of the Legislature being assured, Governor Alcorn was then prepared to vacate the office of Governor, to turn over the administration of State affairs to Lieutenant-Governor Powers and to proceed to Washington so as to be present at the opening session of Congress on the first Monday in December, when he would assume his duties as a United States Senator.

The Legislature was to meet the first Monday in the following January—1872. As soon as the fact was made known that the Republicans would control the organization of the House, the Speakership of that body became agitated. If Speaker [H.W.] Warren had been reelected he would have received the Republican caucus nomination without opposition, but his defeat made it necessary for a new man to be brought forward for that position. A movement was immediately put on foot to make me the Speaker of the House.

Upon careful examination of the returns it was found that of the one hundred fifteen members of which the House was composed there were seventy-seven whites and thirty-eight colored. Of the seventy-seven whites, forty-nine had been elected as Democrats and twenty-eight as Republicans. The thirty-eight colored men were all Republicans. It will thus be seen that, while in the composition of the Republican caucus there were ten more colored than white members, yet of the total membership of the House there were thirty-nine more white than colored members. But in the organization of the House, the contest was not between white and colored, but between Democrats and Republicans. No one had been elected—at least on the Republican side—because he was a white man or because he was a colored man, but because he was a Republican.

After a preliminary canvass the fact was developed that the writer was not only the choice of the colored members for Speaker of the House, but of a large majority of the white Republican members as well. They believed—and voted in accordance with that belief both in the party caucus and in the House—that the writer was the best-equipped man for that responsible position. This fact had been demonstrated to their satisfaction during the two sessions of the preceding Legislature.

The nomination of the writer by the House Republican caucus for Speaker was a foregone conclusion several weeks before the convening of the Legislature. With a full membership in attendance fifty-eight votes would be necessary to perfect the organization. When the Republican caucus convened sixty members were present and took part in the deliberations thereof. Four of the Republicans-elect had not at that time arrived at the seat of government. The two Independents from Carroll [County] refused to attend the caucus, but this did not necessarily mean that they would not vote for the candidates thereof in the organization of the House. But since we had sixty votes—two more than were necessary to elect our candidate—we believed that the organization would easily be perfected the next day, regardless of the action of the members from Carroll County.

In this, however, we were sadly disappointed. The result of the first vote for Speaker of the House was as follows:

Judge Chandler of Noxubee [County], who had been elected as a regular Republican with four other white Republicans—all of whom attended and took part in the caucus the night before—refused to vote for the nominee of the caucus for Speaker, but voted instead for Chandler. . . .

While the deadlock was in progress, Senators Alcorn and Ames suddenly made their appearance on the scene of action. They had made the trip from Washington to use their influence to break the deadlock, and to bring about an organization of the House by the Republican party. But Senator Alcorn was the one that could render the most effective service in that direction, since the bolters were men who professed to be followers of his and loyal to his political interests and leadership.

As soon as the Senator arrived he held a conference with the bolters, including Messrs. Armstead and Streeter—the two independents from Carroll. In addressing those who had been elected as Republicans and who had attended and participated in the caucus of that party, the Senator did not mince his words. He told them in plain language that they were in honor bound to support the caucus nominees of their party, or that they must resign their seats and allow their constituents to elect others that would do so.

With reference to the Independents from Carroll, he said the situation was slightly different. They had been elected as Independents under conditions which did not obligate them to enter the Republican caucus or support the candidates thereof. They had pledged themselves not to support the Democratic caucus nominees, or to aid that party in the organization of the House. Up to that time they had not made a move, nor given a vote that could be construed into a violation of the pledge under which they had been elected, but they had publicly declared on several occasions that they had been elected as Independents or Alcorn Republicans. . . . If this was true [Alcorn told them] then they should not hesitate to take the advice of the man to support whose administration they had been elected. He informed them that if they meant what they said the best way for them to prove it was to vote for the Republican caucus nominees for officers of the House, because he was the recognized leader of the party in the State and that the issue involved in the elections was either an endorsement or repudiation as Governor. . . .

The two Carroll County Independents informed the Senator that he had correctly outlined their position and their attitude . . . but that they were apprehensive that they could not successfully defend their action and explain their votes to the satisfaction of their constituents if they were to vote for a colored man for Speaker of the House.

"But," said the Senator, "could you have been elected without the votes of colored men? If you now vote against a colored man—who is in every way a fit and capable man for the position—simply because he is a colored man, would you expect those men to support you in the future?" The Senator also reminded them that they had received very many more colored than white votes; and that, in his opinion, very few of the white men who had supported them would find fault with them for voting for a capable and intelligent colored man to preside over the deliberations of the House. "Can you then," the Senator asked, "afford to offend the great mass of the colored men that support you in order to please an insignificantly small number of narrow-minded whites?"

The Senator assured them that he was satisfied that they had nothing to fear as a result of their action in voting for Mr. Lynch as Speaker of the House. He knew the candidate favorably and well and therefore did not hesitate to assure them that if they contributed to his election they would have no occasion to regret having done so. The conference then came to a close with the understanding that all present would vote the next day for the Republican caucus nominees for officers of the House. This was done. The result of the ballot the following day was:

Lynch, Republican caucus nominee 63
Chandler, Independent Republican....................................49
Necessary to elect..57

It will be seen that Judge Chandler received the solid Democratic vote while Lynch received the vote of every voting Republican present, including Chandler and the two Independents from Carroll. . . .

At the conclusion of the session, the House not only adopted a resolution complimenting the Speaker and thanking him for the able and impartial manner in which he had presided over its deliberations, but presented him with a fine gold watch and chain—purchased with money that had been contributed by members of both parties and by a few outside friends—as a token of their esteem. On the outside case of the watch these words were engraved: "Presented to Hon. J. R. Lynch, Speaker of the House of Representatives, by the Members of the Legislature, April 19, 1873." That watch the writer still has and will keep as a sacred family heirloom.

———————

DURING HIS SPEAKERSHIP, Lynch helped give Mississippi one of the best-run state governments in the nation. Indeed, his service in the legislature secured him election to the United States Congress and a place as one of the leaders of the state party. And yet today his name is forgotten by all but specialists.

A Republican in Mississippi in 1873 might have laughed at the idea that Lynch would one day be forgotten or even discredited. The party was triumphant after years in the wilderness. But forces were already gathering to overthrow the revolution, and to wipe its memory from the books. The Democrats were learning that openly racist slogans did not play well in the North. Instead, a new refrain found its way into the press and into politicians' speeches: corruption, corruption, corruption.

Yes, corruption existed in Southern governments. It ranged from bribes of legislators to railroad stock speculation by officials who were responsible for state aid for railroads. It was particularly prominent in states where factional fighting was at its worst, particularly Louisiana and South Carolina. But corruption was a characteristic of post-Civil War government in general, not Reconstruction specifically. Nothing that occurred in the South came close to the wholesale bribery of the Erie Railroad episode in New York, or the staggering graft of the Tweed ring in New York City. The most serious national conspiracies, such as the Whiskey Ring and the Crédit Mobilier plot, had nothing at all to do with Reconstruction. Furthermore, Democrats shouldered their way to the trough of corruption as eagerly as Republicans—without the balancing effect of such leaders as Charles Sumner, Adelbert Ames, or Albert Morgan. The Democrats raised the issue as a reason to sweep away Reconstruction—but it might as well have been a reason to do away with government in general.

As further evidence for their charge, Southern whites pointed to large salary increases that Republicans voted for themselves when they gained office. But public pay was artificially low to begin with; it had always been assumed that officials would be wealthy planters who could support themselves. Under Reconstruction, officeholders were often men who were poor, such as former slaves, or who were made to suffer for their political activism. The Morgans, as a typical example, had been tossed out of their thriving planting and lumber enterprise; African-American artisans and shopkeepers found that well-to-do whites stopped patronizing their businesses. Once in office, they depended on their salaries for a living income.

When viewed from the perspective of 1873, then, Reconstruction was notable not for misrule, not for corruption, but for the astonishing revolution brought about in a deeply conservative, racially divided society. In Mississippi, an African American had broken a path into the United States Senate; another served as speaker of the state House of Representatives. A university open to black students had been constructed, and schools and economic opportunities appeared throughout the state. The world had turned upside down in a mere five years. Perhaps some had already begun to suspect that it was too good to last.

VII

TWILIGHT

GRANT'S ADMINISTRATION
TREMBLES
1873–1875

19

PANIC

Another year of glory in an age of glory: so the dawn of 1873 must have seemed to four very different men scattered far about the country. Each had flourished during Ulysses S. Grant's first four years in the White House; each could look forward to even greater triumphs as the slump-shouldered general took the oath of office for the second time. In Mississippi, Albert T. Morgan took pride in the reconstruction of Yazoo County; now his own leader, Adelbert Ames, was a candidate for governor, and Morgan himself contemplated a run for sheriff, the most powerful local office. In Washington, John R. Lynch listened to Grant's inaugural speech with a particularly personal sense of satisfaction—for this former slave was now the youngest member of the U.S. House of Representatives. In St. Louis, John McDonald counted out his personal take from the flow of illicit distillery kickbacks, and mused about the bribes he had sown to help reelect the President. And in Pittsburgh, financier and manufacturer Andrew Carnegie had already embarked on a venture that would change not only his own life, but American history.

Within a year, the ambitions of all four men would tremble on the edge of disaster. The particular disasters facing each of the four came from separate sources—yet the crises in industry, politics, and corruption would eventually combine to shake Grant's once-promising administration to its foundations and bring Reconstruction to a shuddering halt. As each man recognized the coming storm, he fought it to the best of his ability; by the time 1874 passed away, their lives would be balanced on a slender rail between triumph and catastrophe.

None of the four better knew how to walk that rail than Andrew Carnegie. Since the Civil War, he had been reaching his hand into one business after another—perhaps not turning everything he touched into gold, but certainly making more than enough money to enrich his partners and himself. He prospered in iron works, bridge building, bond sales, and company takeovers. He could play the part of the manufacturer, the master of the mill, or the refined yet ruthless financier with equal ease and gregarious charm. Indeed, Carnegie had attracted the attention of none other than Jay Gould.

But Carnegie had to part ways with the robber baron, both literally and figuratively. He was a very different man from Mr. Gould, deriving an entirely different sort of satisfaction out of his business dealings.

Where Gould was a predator, Carnegie was a builder. Even in finance, Gould honed bonds and stock certificates into weapons for attack, while Carnegie fashioned them into intricately designed structures—interwoven webs of companies, creditors, and commissions, channeling the flow of profit to Carnegie himself from every point. How much sweeter, then, if he could not only build an intangible company framework, but create something solid and real. And nothing is more solid than steel.

Steel seemed a natural product for Carnegie, with his background in iron making. As of 1870, however, steel had few customers in American industry—and in 1870, American industry primarily meant the railroads. Iron was weaker and more brittle; iron rails required replacement far more often than steel ones. But iron was affordable, and steel was not. Before the Civil War, not one American mill turned out steel rails.

The steel-making process itself was well established. As early as 1856, Henry Bessemer of England found a way to produce steel by blowing cold air through molten pig iron. His method burned out the elements that make iron inferior to steel—silicon in particular. The Bessemer process, however, left phosphorus—another contaminant—untouched. He had unknowingly used iron ore that was unusually low in phosphorus when he made his discovery. The rarity of this type of ore made steel far too expensive for mass production.

Carnegie, however, was intrigued. He experimented with small Bessemer works, and snatched up patents for methods to bond steel with iron—methods that ultimately proved faulty. His iron works turned out small quantities of steel for specialized orders, but the market never seemed to grow. Phosphorus-free iron was simply too expensive. Furthermore, Bessemer found himself locked in a court battle with William Kelly of Kentucky; Kelly had discovered the same process years before the Englishman had, and he owned the American patent to it. "Blocked by both nature and law from using the Bessemer process," as Joseph Frazier Wall writes, American manufacturers and customers stuck with iron.

If this situation had not changed, perhaps Carnegie never would have concluded to concentrate all his efforts in manufacturing. Perhaps he would have continued his successful life as a dabbler in iron, bridges, and bonds, ending in an early retirement and historical anonymity. But both nature and the law soon opened the gate to Carnegie's destiny. Kelly and Bessemer reached a settlement, and agreed to pool their patent rights. Then vast new iron fields—yielding wonderfully phosphorus-free ore—were opened in the upper peninsula of Michigan. The iron deposits had been discovered in the 1840s, but not until 1868 did chemists discover the superb quality of the ore.

As of 1872, however, few Bessemer plants were yet to be found in the United States. With limited production, costs remained high; with high costs, the demand remained low. In that year, however, Carnegie himself visited the greatest steel works of England. In the light of the vast molten flow of iron and steel, he knew that his instincts had been right—steel was the future. The only question was how to make it in sufficient quantities, at low enough cost. When he returned, he threw himself into the project that would consume the rest of his life.

One factor was to prove both his greatest strength and his almost fatal weakness as he began: the importance of the railroads. The railways would be by far his biggest customer, consuming rails by the tens of thousands; no other companies matched their wealth and scale. Carnegie himself had been a railroad man, a product of the greatest of the great corporations, and he personally knew the heads of all the major lines. But this fact was also a measure of the economy's weakness. One industry dominated the stock market; one industry shaped the prosperity of millions. If there was to be a failure in one of the major railroads, the entire house of cards could fall—possibly sweeping Carnegie's rising house of steel along with it.

In the passage that follows, the rising tycoon describes how he gradually withdrew from the life of the bond salesman and returned with full force to his iron and bridge works. With increasing clarity, he saw a vision of an empire of steel—a vision he pursued with his brother Tom, the cantankerous German engineer Andrew Kloman, and the bookkeeping genius Mr. Phipps. But their empire-to-be almost crashed to the ground as panic gripped the nation.

Steel
by Andrew Carnegie

I had made repeated journeys to Europe to negotiate various securities, and in all I sold some thirty millions of dollars worth. This was at a time when the Atlantic cable had not yet made New York a part of London financially considered, and when London bankers would lend their balances to Paris, Vienna, or Berlin for a shadow of a difference in the rate of interest rather than to the United States at a higher rate. The Republic was considered less safe than the Continent by these good people. My brother and Mr. Phipps conducted the iron business so successfully that I could leave for weeks at a time without anxiety.

There was danger lest I should drift away from the manufacturing to the financial and banking business. My successes abroad brought me tempting opportunities, but my preference was always for manufacturing. I wished to make something tangible and sell it and I continued to invest my profits in extending the works at Pittsburgh.

The small shops put up originally for the Keystone Bridge Company had been leased for other purposes and ten acres of ground had been secured in Lawrenceville on which new and extensive shops were erected. Repeated additions to the Union Iron Mills had made them the leading mills in the United States for all sorts of structural shapes. Business was promising and all the surplus earnings I was making in other fields were required to expand the iron business. I had become interested, with my friends in the Pennsylvania Railroad Company, in building some railways in the Western States, but gradually withdrew from all such enterprises and made up my mind to go entirely contrary to the adage not to put all one's eggs in one basket. I determined that the proper policy was "to put all good eggs in one basket and then watch that basket."

I believe the true road to preeminent success in any line is to make yourself master in that line. I have no faith in the policy of scattering one's resources, and in my experience I have rarely if ever met a man who achieved preeminence in money-making—certainly never one in manufacturing—who was interested in many concerns. The men who have succeeded are men who have chosen one line and stuck to it. It is surprising how few men appreciate the enormous dividends derivable from investment in their own business. . . .

I have tried always to hold fast to this important fact. It has been with me a cardinal doctrine that I could manage my own capital better than any other person, much better than any board of directors. The losses men encounter during a business life which seriously embarrass them are rarely in their own business, but in enterprises of which the investor is not master. . . . As for myself my decision was taken early. I would concentrate upon the manufacture of iron and steel and be master of that. . . .

As we had been compelled to engage in the manufacture of wrought-iron in order to make bridges and other structures, so now we thought it desirable to manufacture our own pig iron. And this led to the erection of the Lucy Furnace in the year 1870—a venture which would have been postponed had we fully appreciated its magnitude. We heard from time to time the ominous predictions made by our older brethren in the manufacturing business with regard to the rapid growth and extension of our young concern, but we were not deterred. We thought we had sufficient capital and credit to justify the building of one blast furnace.

The estimates of its cost, however, did not cover more than half the expenditure. It was an experiment with us. Mr. Kloman knew nothing about blast-furnace operations. But even without exact knowledge no serious blunder was made. The yield of the Lucy Furnace (named after my bright sister-in-law) exceeded our most sanguine expectations and the then unprecedented output of a hundred tons per day was made from one blast furnace, for one week—an output that the world had never heard of before. We held the record and many visitors came to marvel at the marvel.

It was not, however, all smooth sailing with our iron business. Years of panic came at intervals. We had passed safely through the fall in values following the war, when iron from nine cents per pound dropped to three. Many failures occurred and our financial manager had his time fully occupied in providing funds to meet emergencies. Among many wrecks our firm stood with credit unimpaired. But the manufacture of pig iron gave us more anxiety than any other department of our business so far. The greatest service rendered us in this branch of manufacturing was by Mr. Whitwell, of the celebrated Whitwell Brothers of England, whose blast-furnace stoves were so generally used. Mr. Whitwell was one of the best-known visitors who came to marvel at the Lucy Furnace, and I laid the difficulty we were experiencing before him. He said immediately: "That comes from the angle of the bell being wrong."

He explained how it should be changed. Our Mr. Kloman was slow to believe this, but I urged that a small glass-model furnace and two bells be made, one as the Lucy was and the other as Mr. Whitwell advised it should be. This was done, and upon my next visit experiments were made with each, the result being just as Mr. Whitwell had foretold. Our bell distributed the large pieces to the sides of the furnace, leaving the center a dense mass through which the blast could only partially penetrate. The Whitwell bell threw the pieces to the center leaving the circumference dense. This made all the difference in the world. The Lucy's troubles were over. . . .

THE AGE OF STEEL

Looking back today, it seems incredible that only forty years ago (1870) chemistry in the United States was an almost unknown agent in connection with the manufacture of pig iron. It was the agency, above all others, most needful in the manufacture of iron and steel. The blast-furnace manager of that day was usually a rude bully, generally a foreigner, who in addition to his other acquirements was able to knock down a man now and then as a lesson to the other unruly spirits under him. He was supposed to diagnose the condition of the furnace by instinct, to possess some almost supernatural power of divination, like his congener in the country districts who was reputed to be able to locate an oil well or water supply by means of a hazel rod. He was a veritable quack doctor who applied whatever remedies occurred to him for the troubles of his patient.

The Lucy Furnace was out of one trouble and into another, owing to the great variety of ores, limestones, and coke which were then supplied with little or no regard to their component parts. This state of affairs became intolerable to us. We finally decided to dispense with the rule-of-thumb-and-intuition manager, and to place a young man in charge of the furnace. We had a young shipping clerk, Henry M. Curry, who had distinguished himself, and it was resolved to make him manager.

Mr. Phipps had the Lucy Furnace under his special charge. His daily visits to it saved us from failure there. Not that the furnace was not doing as well as other furnaces in the West as to money-making, but being so much larger than other furnaces its variations entailed much more serious results. I am afraid my partner had something to answer for in his Sunday morning visits to the Lucy Furnace when his good father and sister left the house for more devotional duties. But even if he had gone with them his real earnest prayer could not but have had reference at times to the precarious condition of the Lucy Furnace then absorbing his thoughts.

The next step taken was to find a chemist as Mr. Curry's assistant and guide. We found the man in a learned German, Dr. Fricke, and great secrets did the doctor open up to us. Ironstone from mines that had a high reputation was now found to contain ten, fifteen, and even twenty percent less iron than it had been credited with. Mines that hitherto had a poor reputation we found to be now yielding superior ore. The good was bad and the bad was good, and everything was topsy-turvy. Nine-tenths of all the uncertainties of pig-iron making were dispelled under the burning sun of chemical knowledge.

At a most critical period when it was necessary for the credit of the firm that the blast furnace should make its best product, it had been stopped because an exceedingly rich and pure ore had been substituted for an inferior ore—an ore which did not yield more than two-thirds of the quantity of iron of the other. The furnace had met with disaster because too much lime had been used to flux this exceptionally pure ironstone. The very superiority of the materials had involved us in serious losses.

What fools we had been! But then there was this consolation: we were not as great fools as our competitors. It was years after we had taken chemistry to guide us that it was said by the proprietors of some of the furnaces that they could not afford to employ a chemist. Had they known the truth then, they would have known that they could not afford to be without one. Looking back it seems pardonable to record that we were the first to employ a chemist at blast furnaces—something our competitors pronounced extravagant.

The Lucy Furnace became the most profitable branch of our business, because we had almost the entire monopoly of scientific management. Having discovered the secret, it was not long (1872) before we decided to erect an additional furnace. This was done with great economy as compared with our first experiment. The mines which had no reputation and the products of which many firms would not permit to be used in their blast furnaces found a purchaser in us. Those mines which were able to obtain an enormous price for their products, owing to a reputation for quality, we quietly ignored. A curious illustration of this was the celebrated Pilot Knob mine in Missouri. Its product was, so to speak, under a cloud. A small portion of it only could be used, it was said, without obstructing the furnace. Chemistry told us that it was low in phosphorus, but very high in silicon. There was no better ore and scarcely any as rich, if it were properly fluxed. We therefore bought heavily of this and received the thanks of the proprietors for rendering their property valuable.

It is hardly believable that for several years we were able to dispose of the highly phosphoric cinder from the puddling furnaces at a higher price than we had to pay for the pure cinder from the heating furnaces of our competitors—a cinder which was richer in iron than the puddled cinder and much freer from phosphorus. Upon some occasion a blast furnace had attempted to smelt the flue cinder, and from its greater purity the furnace did not work well with a mixture intended for an impurer article; hence for years it was thrown over the banks of the river at Pittsburgh by our competitors as worthless. In some cases we were even able to exchange a poor article for a good one and obtain a bonus.

But it was still more unbelievable that a prejudice, equally unfounded, existed against putting into the blast furnaces the roll-scale from the mills which was pure oxide of iron. This reminds me of my dear friend and fellow-Dunfermline townsman, Mr. Chisholm, of Cleveland. We had many pranks together. One day, when I was visiting his works at Cleveland, I saw men wheeling this valuable roll-scale into the yard. I asked Mr. Chisholm where they were going with it, and he said: "To throw it over the bank. Our managers have always complained that they had bad luck when they attempted to remelt it in the blast furnace."

I said nothing, but upon my return to Pittsburgh I set about having a joke at his expense. We had then a young man in our service named Du Puy, whose father was known as the inventor of a direct process in iron-making with which he was then experimenting in Pittsburgh. I recommended our people to send Du Puy to Cleveland to contract for all the roll-scale of my friend's establishment. He did so, buying it for fifty cents per ton and having it shipped to him direct. This continued for some time. I expected always to hear of the joke being discovered. The premature death of Mr. Chisholm occurred before I could apprise him of it. His successors soon, however, followed our example.[1]

I had not failed to notice the growth of the Bessemer process. If this proved successful I knew that iron was destined to give place to steel; that the Iron Age would pass away and the Steel Age take its place. . . .

The question of a substitute for iron rails upon the Pennsylvania Railroad and other leading lines had become a very serious one. Upon cer-

[1] It was Phipps, ever the careful bookkeeper, who kept track of waste products and investigated what could be done with them. He initiated the program of buying up other companies' roll scale and remelting it.

tain curves at Pittsburgh, one the road connecting the Pennsylvania with the Fort Wayne, I had seen new iron rails placed every six weeks or two months. Before the Bessemer process was known I had called President Thomson's attention to the efforts of Mr. Dodds in England, who had carbonized the heads of iron rails with good results. I went to England and obtained control of the Dodds patents and recommended President Thomson to appropriate twenty thousand dollars for experiments at Pittsburgh, which he did. . . .[2] But there was nothing to be compared with the solid steel article which the Bessemer process produced.

Our friends of the Cambria Iron Company at Johnstown, near Pittsburgh—the principal manufacturers of rails in America—decided to erect a Bessemer plant. In England I had seen it demonstrated, at least to my satisfaction, that the process could be made a grand success without undue expenditure of capital or great risk. Mr. William Coleman, who was ever alive to new methods, arrived at the same conclusion. It was agreed we should enter upon the manufacture of steel rails at Pittsburgh. He became a partner, and also my dear friend Mr. David McCandless, who had so kindly offered aid to my mother at my father's death. The latter was not forgotten. Mr. John Scott and Mr. David A. Stewart, and others joined me; Mr. Edgar Thomson and Mr. Thomas A. Scott, president and vice-president of the Pennsylvania Railroad, also became stockholders, anxious to encourage the development of steel. The steel-rail company was organized January 1, 1873.

The question of location was the first to engage our serious attention. I could not reconcile myself to any location that was proposed, and finally went to Pittsburgh to consult with my partners about it. The subject was constantly in my mind and in bed Sunday morning the site suddenly appeared to me. I rose and called to my brother: "Tom, you and Mr. Coleman are right about the location; right at Braddock's, between the Pennsylvania, the Baltimore and Ohio, and the river, is the best situation in America; and let's call the works after our dear friend Edgar Thomson. Let us go over to Mr. Coleman's and drive out to Braddock's."

We did so that day, and the next morning Mr. Coleman was at work trying to secure the property. Mr. McKinney, the owner, had a high idea of the value of his farm. What we had expected to purchase for five or six hundred dollars an acre cost us two thousand. But since then we have been compelled to add to our original purchase at a cost of five thousand dollars per acre. There, on the very field of Braddock's defeat, we began the erection of our steel-rail mills. In excavating for the foundation many relics of the battle were found—bayonets, swords, and the like. . . .

---

[2] Carnegie's experience with the Dodds process, as with his other attempts at improving regular iron rails, was not successful.

In naming the steel mills as we did the desire was to honor my friend Edgar Thomson, but when I asked permission to use his name his reply was significant. He said that as far as American steel rails were concerned, he did not feel that he wished to connect his name with them, for they had proved to be far from creditable. Uncertainty was, of course, inseparable from the experimental stage; but, when I assured him that it was now possible to make steel rails in America as good in every particular as the foreign article, and that we intended to obtain for our rails the reputation enjoyed by the Keystone bridges and the Kloman axles, he consented. . . .[3]

The works were well advanced when the financial panic of September, 1873, came upon us. I then entered upon the most anxious period of my business life.

———

PANIC. THE WORD had filled the headlines once before in Grant's presidency, when Secretary of the Treasury George Boutwell had broken the gold conspiracy of Gould and Fisk. In 1869, however, Black Friday could only briefly fluster the nabobs of Wall Street. In 1873, the panic ushered in a nationwide depression.

The origins of the crisis could be found in the Northern Pacific Railroad, a transcontinental line then marching west across the northern Great Plains. The Northern Pacific served as a sort of Gilded Age lodestone, attracting to it the most colorful and important figures of the era. Its surveying parties plotted a path down the Yellowstone River, through the heart of unceded Sioux territory; they were ferociously attacked by bands of warriors led by Hunkpapa chief Sitting Bull, among others. The railroad men were defended by troops under the command of the flamboyant General George Armstrong Custer, who received his introduction to the country where the Sioux would kill him only a few years later. In the east, the leading businessmen of the day invested in Northern Pacific securities, which were handled by the firm of Jay Cooke & Company. Cooke might be considered a more respectable counterpart to the Gould of the same first name—a wizard with money who had helped the federal government finance the Civil War.

Unfortunately, the Northern Pacific also attracted another product of the Gilded Age: exaggerated expectations. The vast expense of constructing a line through thousands of miles of wilderness was a pessimist's delight; eventually the company's securities could no longer be sold. On September 18, 1873, Jay Cooke went bankrupt. The country was stunned—for the

[3] Carnegie had more than sentimental reasons for naming the new works after his old mentor and longtime financial backer. As head of the Pennsylvania Railroad, Thomson would be his single largest customer for steel rails.

banker who had kept the Union government afloat had failed himself. Creditors called in loans; suppliers demanded payment for invoices; depositors tried to close their bank accounts. Money—especially gold—was pulled out of circulation as people hoarded against the crisis. The Treasury Department might have calmed the storm; but Boutwell had ascended to the Senate, and his successor, William Richardson, was a passive incompetent.

Depression rolled across the nation; by most accounts, it lasted until 1879, though its effects lingered far longer. William McFeely writes that, between 1873 and 1876, the wages of city workers fell twenty-five percent, but the cost of food fell only five percent (deflation is a product of economic depression, as money becomes scarce). At least one million people found themselves unemployed, out of a total of forty million. The nation seethed with unrest; in New York's Tompkins Square, a riot of the impoverished erupted, to be quelled by rampaging policemen.

In the twentieth century, economists would conclude that a depression should be met with inflationary policies—an increase in currency to balance the hoarding that results from panic. A fluctuating level of money would become one of the most important tools for regulating the economic cycle. In the panic of 1873, many Americans—strapped by the raw shortage of currency—came to a similar conclusion. They noisily campaigned for an increase in legal tender; they even formed a political organization known as the Greenback party, which won a number of seats in Congress. But the conventional wisdom of the twentieth century and the popular slogan of the nineteenth was nothing more than common foolishness to most businessmen in the 1870s.

And businessmen were taking over politics. In the years after the Civil War—especially with the establishment of Reconstruction—the Republican party increasingly identified itself with conservative, monied interests. Rural and morally motivated activists found themselves on the outside, for the party of the Radicals was transforming into the party of the wealthy. Alan Trachtenberg has identified this trend as a part of a process of "incorporation." There would be no more rail-splitting, self-taught country lawyers rising to the White House; as Trachtenberg writes, "a new breed of men—of unprecedented personal wealth and untrammeled power," dominated the life of the nation, and their instrument was the Republican party.

The fight for the heart of the party was not fully won by the time of the great panic, but the end was definitely in sight. In December 1873, for example, Iowa Republican Congressman George W. McCrary introduced a bill to establish a commission to regulate railroad rates. Farmers of both parties liked the idea, but the Republican leadership was appalled. Even the moderates felt that McCrary's idea went against Republican principles—or what were rapidly becoming Republican principles. The interests of business came first.

Nowhere was that fact more clearly seen than in the debate over the money supply during those dark days of 1873–74. And no one demonstrated the spread of the conservative orthodoxy better than Senator John Sherman, a man of notoriously moderate temperament. Sherman recognized the suffering the country was enduring, but he was no man to go against the teachings of the hard–money men who ruled the Eastern establishment. To those who had money, specie was gold, metaphorically as well as literally. The floating value of the paper dollar unsettled wealthy businessmen—they believed in nothing but precious metals, and they pushed for a return to gold-backed currency even in the midst of the crisis. It was a catastrophically bad idea: a return to specie would only further limit the amount of money in circulation. Nevertheless, this was the view that captured the minds of such financial experts as Sherman and such financial failures as President Grant. The policy would not be without political repercussions.

The Panic of 1873
by John Sherman

During the first four years of General Grant's administration the financial condition of the United States was eminently prosperous. . . . [The] improvement of the public credit was accompanied with a large reduction of internal taxes and duties on imported goods. The business of the country was prosperous, the increase and extension of railroads and the development of new industries was marked, indicating great prosperity.

All this was subsequently changed by the happening of a panic in September 1873. The cause of this was attributed to over-trading, to the expansion of credits, and to the rash investments made in advance of public needs. This panic commenced by the failure of Jay Cooke & Co. of Philadelphia, an enterprising firm of high standing, then engaged in selling the bonds of the Northern Pacific Railroad Company.

I was engaged at that time, with a committee of the Senate . . . in examining many plans of public improvements. . . . Roscoe Conkling, of New York, was a member of that committee. We were at Buffalo when the failure of Cooke & Co. was announced. We all felt that for the present, at least, our duties as a committee were at an end. The panic spread so that in a month all industries were in a measure suspended. The wildest schemes for relief were proposed, in and out of Congress. The panic spread to the banks, which were compelled in self-defense to call in their loans, to withhold their circulating notes, and contract their business. As usual on the happening of such a panic, an appeal was made to the treasury for relief, a demand was made for an increase of the volume of the United States notes, and that the Secretary of the Treasury should use the money of the government to buy exchange. . . .

When Congress convened in December 1873, the wildest schemes for relief to the people were demanded. More than sixty bills, resolutions, and propositions were introduced in the Senate in respect to the currency, the public debt, and national banks, all bearing upon the financial condition of the country, expressing every variety of opinion, from immediate coin payments to the wildest inflation of irredeemable paper money. All these were referred to the committee on finance . . .

Finally, after more than three months' study and debate, a majority of the committee agreed upon a measure and directed me to report it to the Senate. It fixed the maximum limit of the United States notes at $382,000,000.[4] It provided for a gradual payment of these notes in coin or in five per cent bonds, at the option of the Secretary of the Treasury, from the 1st of January, 1876. It was entitled "An act to provide for the redemption and reissue of United States notes and for free banking." . . .

The bill led to a long continuous debate which extended to the 6th of April, 1874. Several amendments were offered which enlarged the maximum of notes to $400,000,000, and greatly weakened the bill as a measure of resumption of specie payments. By reason of these amendments many of those who would have supported the bill as introduced voted against it on its passage, I among its number. . . . The bill was taken up in the House of Representatives on the 14th of April, 1874, and without any debate on its merits, was passed by the vote of 140 yeas and 102 nays.

On the 22nd of April, President Grant returned the bill to the Senate with his veto. . . . Thus, for that session, the struggle for resumption [of specie payments] ended; but the debate in both Houses attracted popular discussion, which tended in the right direction. The evil effects of the stringency in monetary affairs, the want of confidence, the reduction in the national revenue, the decline of domestic productions, all these contributed to impress Congress with the imperative necessity of providing some measure of relief. Instead of inflation, of large issues of paper money by the United States and the national banks, there grew up a conviction that the better policy was to limit and reduce the volume of such money to an amount that could be maintained at par with coin. . . .

During this period[5] a party sprang up composed of men of all parties called the Greenback party, who favored an increase of United States

[4] Even taking inflation into account, the fact that the total amount of paper currency in circulation was less than 400 million dollars shows how small the national economy was in the 1870s—indicating why the collapse of *one* banking firm could trigger a nationwide panic and depression.

[5] This paragraph has been moved for chronological continuity.

notes, and the payment of all United States notes and securities in such notes. This difference of opinion continued until the resumption of specie payments in January 1879. . . .

The election of Members of Congress in 1874 resulted in the choice of a large majority of Democrats in the House of Representatives of the 44th Congress, the term of which commenced on the 4th of March, 1875. . . . This political revolution was no doubt caused largely by the financial panic of 1873, and by the severe stringency in monetary affairs that followed and continued for several years. I do not deem it necessary to refer to the political questions that greatly excited the public mind during that session. Congress was largely occupied in political debate on questions in respect to the reconstruction of the states lately in rebellion, upon which the two Houses [the Democratic-controlled House and the Republican-controlled Senate] disagreed.

———

A DEMOCRATIC HOUSE? The idea would have seemed preposterous in the heady days that followed Grant's resounding reelection in 1872. Yet the depression that followed the panic of 1873 was profound indeed, and the Eastern businessmen who had captured the Republican party scarcely knew how to make things better. Driven to desperation, the public responded: it kicked out the party of Thaddeus Stevens, and ushered in the men who had followed Andrew Johnson.

As millions stared poverty in the face and thousands saw their fortunes disappear, one man survived. Andrew Carnegie was just the sort to thrive in the crisis: bold with strategy, cautious with money, a master of negotiations who could charm nervous creditors or snap them to attention with a well-timed threat. He was also ruthless, and it was during this massive crisis that he let his one-time father figure, Thomas A. Scott, sink under the burden of his own imprudence.

Not everyone in Carnegie's growing steel empire possessed his steely nerves. Andrew Kloman in particular bridled at having to take direction from the Scotsman. But through the crises of economics and personal feuds, Carnegie steered safely onward to create the very archetype of modern industry—and one of the greatest manufacturing fortunes the nation had ever seen.

———

The Founding of an Empire
by Andrew Carnegie

The works were well advanced when the financial panic of September, 1873, came upon us. I then entered upon the most anxious period of my business life. All was going well when one morning in our summer cottage, in the Allegheny Mountains at Cresson, a telegram came announcing the failure of Jay Cooke & Co. Almost every hour brought news of some fresh disaster. House after house failed. The question every morning was which would go next. Every failure depleted the resources of other concerns. Loss after loss ensued, until a total paralysis of business set in. Every weak spot was discovered and houses that otherwise would have been strong were borne down largely because our country lacked a proper banking system.

We had not much reason to be anxious about our debts. Not what we had to pay of our own debts could give us much trouble, but rather what we might have to pay for our debtors. It was not our bills payable but our bills receivable which required attention, for we soon had to be meeting both. Even our own banks had to beg us not to draw upon our balances.

One incident will shed some light upon the currency situation. One of our pay-days was approaching. One hundred thousand dollars in small notes were absolutely necessary, and to obtain these we paid a premium of twenty-four hundred dollars in New York and had them expressed to Pittsburgh. It was impossible to borrow money, even upon the best collaterals; but by selling securities, which I had in reserve, considerable sums were realized—the company undertaking to replace them later.

It happened that some of the railway companies whose lines centered in Pittsburgh owed us large sums for material furnished—the Fort Wayne road being the largest debtor. I remember calling upon Mr. Thaw, the vice-president of the Fort Wayne, and telling him we must have our money. He replied: "You ought to have your money, but we are not paying anything these days that is not protestable."

"Very good," I said, "your freight bills are in that category and we shall follow your excellent example. Now I am going to order that we do not pay you one dollar for freight."

"Well, if you do that," he said, "we will stop your freight."

I said we would risk that. The railway company could not proceed to that extremity. And as a matter of fact we ran for some time without paying the freight bills. It was simply impossible for the manufacturers of Pittsburgh to apply their accruing liabilities when their customers stopped payment. The banks were forced to renew maturing paper. They behaved splendidly to us, as they always have done, and we steered safely through. But in a critical period like this there was one thought uppermost with me, to gather more capital and keep it in our business so that come what would we should never again be called upon to endure such nights and days of racking anxiety.

Speaking for myself in this great crisis, I was at first the most excited and anxious of the partners. I could scarcely control myself. But when I finally saw the strength of our financial position I became philosophically cool and found myself quite prepared, if necessary, to enter the directors' rooms of the various banks with which we dealt, and lay our entire position before their boards. I felt that this could result in nothing discreditable to us. No one interested in our business had lived extravagantly. Our manner of life had been the very reverse of this. No money had been withdrawn from the business to build costly homes, and, above all, not one of us had made speculative ventures upon the stock exchange, or invested in any other enterprises than those connected with the main business. Neither had we exchanged endorsements with others. Besides this we could show a prosperous business that was making money every year.

I was thus enabled to laugh away the fears of my partners, but none of them rejoiced more than I did that the necessity for opening our lips to anybody about our finances did not arise. Mr. Coleman, our good friend and true, with plentiful means and splendid credit, did not fail to volunteer to give us his endorsements. In this we stood alone; William Coleman's name, a tower of strength, was for us only. . . .

When the cyclone of 1873 struck us we at once began to reef sail in every quarter. Very reluctantly did we decide that the construction of the new steel works must cease for a time. Several prominent persons who had invested in them became unable to meet their payments and I was compelled to take over their interests, repaying the full cost to all. In that way control of the company came into my hands.

The first outburst of the storm had affected the financial world connected with the Stock Exchange. It was some time before it reached the commercial and manufacturing world. But the situation grew worse and worse and finally led to the crash which involved my friends in the Texas Pacific enterprise, of which I have already spoken. This was to me the severest blow of all. People could, with difficulty, believe that occupying such intimate relations as I did with the Texas group, I could by any possibility have kept myself clear of their financial obligations.

Mr. Schoenberger, president of the Exchange Bank at Pittsburgh, with which we conducted a large business, was in New York when the news reached him of the embarrassment of Mr. Scott and Mr. Thomson. He hastened to Pittsburgh, and at a meeting of his board next morning said it was simply impossible that I was not involved with them. He suggested that the bank should refuse to discount more of our bills receivable. He was alarmed to find that the amount of these bearing our endorsement and under discount was so large. Prompt action on my part was necessary to prevent serious trouble. I took the first train for Pittsburgh, and was able to announce there to all concerned that, although I was a shareholder in the Texas enterprise, my interest was paid for. My name was not upon one dollar of their paper or any other outstanding paper. . . . My only obligations were those connected with our business; and I was prepared to pledge for it every dollar I owned, and to endorse every obligation the firm had outstanding.

Up to this time I had the reputation in business of being a bold, fearless, and perhaps a somewhat reckless young man. Our operations had been extensive, our growth rapid, and although still young, I had been handling millions. My own career was thought by the elderly ones of Pittsburgh to have been rather more brilliant than substantial. I know of an experienced one who declared that if "Andrew Carnegie's brains did not carry him through his luck would." But I think nothing could be farther from the truth than the estimate thus suggested. I am sure that any competent judge would be surprised to find how little I ever risked for myself or my partners. When I did big things, some large corporation like the Pennsylvania Railroad Company was behind me and the responsible party. My supply of Scotch caution never has been small; but I was apparently something of a daredevil now and then to the manufacturing fathers of Pittsburgh. They were old and I was young, which made all the difference.

The fright which Pittsburgh financial institutions had with regard to myself and our enterprises rapidly gave place to perhaps somewhat unreasoning confidence. Our credit became unassailable, and thereafter in times of financial pressure the offerings of money to us increased rather than diminished, just as the deposits of the old Bank of Pittsburgh were never so great as when the deposits in other banks ran low. It was the only bank in America which redeemed its circulation in gold, disdaining to take refuge under the law and pay its obligations in greenbacks. It had few notes, and I doubt not the decision paid as an advertisement.

In addition to the embarrassment of my friends Mr. Scott, Mr. Thomson, and others, there came upon us later an even severer trial in the discovery that our partner, Mr. Andrew Kloman, had been led by a party of speculative people into the Escanaba Iron Company. He was assured that the concern was to be made a stock company, but before this was done his colleagues had succeeded in creating an enormous amount of liabilities—about seven hundred thousand dollars. There was nothing but bankruptcy as a means of reinstating Mr. Kloman.

This gave us more of a shock than all that had preceded, because Mr. Kloman, being a partner, had no right to invest in another iron company, or in any other company involving personal debt, without informing his partners. There is one imperative rule for men in business—no secrets from partners. Disregard of this rule involved not only Mr. Kloman himself, but our company, in peril, coming as it did atop the difficulties of my Texas Pacific friends with whom I had been intimately associated. The question for a time was whether there was anything really sound. Where could we find a bedrock upon which we could stand?

Had Mr. Kloman been a businessman it would have been impossible ever to allow him to be a partner with us again after this discovery. He was not such, however, but the ablest of practical mechanics with some business ability. Mr. Kloman's ambition had been to be in the office, where he was worse than useless, rather than in the mill devising and running new machinery, where he was without peer. We had some difficulty in placing him in his proper position and keeping him there, which may have led him to seek an outlet elsewhere. He was perhaps flattered by men who were well known in the community; and in this case he was led by persons who knew how to reach him by extolling his wonderful business abilities in addition to his mechanical genius—abilities which his own partners, as already suggested, but faintly recognized.

After Mr. Kloman had passed through the bankruptcy court and was again free, we offered him a ten percent interest in our business, charging for it only the actual capital invested, with nothing whatever for good-will. This we were to carry for him until the profits paid for it. We were to charge interest only on the cost, and he was to assume no responsibility. The offer was accompanied by the condition that he should not enter into any other business or endorse for others, but give his whole time and attention to the mechanical and not the business management of the mills.

Could he have been persuaded to accept this, he would have been a multimillionaire; but his pride, and more particularly that of his family, perhaps, would not permit this. He would go into business on his own account, and not withstanding the most urgent appeals on my part and that of my colleagues, he persisted in the determination to start a new rival concern with his sons as business managers. The result was failure and premature death. . . .

PARTNERS

When Mr. Kloman severed his connection with us there was no hesitation in placing William Borntraeger in charge of the mills. It has always been with especial pleasure that I have pointed to the career of William. He came direct from Germany—a young man who could not speak English, but being distantly connected with Mr. Kloman was employed in the mills, at first in a minor capacity. He promptly learned English, and became a shipping clerk at six dollars per week. He had not a particle of mechanical knowledge, and yet such was his unflagging zeal and industry for the interests of his employer that he soon became marked for being everywhere about the mill, knowing everything, and attending to everything.

William was a character. He never got over his German idioms and his inverted English made his remarks very effective. Under his superintendence the Union Iron Mills became a most profitable branch of our business. . . . Early hours in the morning and late in the dark hours at night William was in the mills. His life was there. He was among the first of the young men we admitted to partnership. . . .

William once sold to our neighbor, the pioneer steelmaker of Pittsburgh, James Park, a large lot of old rails which we could not use. Mr. Park found them of a very bad quality. He made claims for damages and William was told that he must go with Mr. Phipps to meet Mr. Park and settle. Mr. Phipps went into Mr. Park's office, while William took a look around the works in search of the condemned material, which was nowhere to be seen. Well did William know where to look. He finally entered the office, and before Mr. Park had time to say a word William began: "Mr. Park, I vas glad to hear dat de old rails what I sell you don't suit for steel. I will buy dem all from you back, five dollars ton profit for you."

Well did William know that they had all been used. Mr. Park was nonplussed, and the affair ended. William had triumphed. . . .

Mr. Phipps had been head of the commercial department of the mills, but when our business was enlarged, he was required for the steel business. Another young man, William L. Abbott, took his place. . . .

Mr. Curry had distinguished himself by this time in his management of the Lucy Furnace, and he took his place among the partners, sharing equally with the others. There is no way of making a business successful that can vie with the policy of promoting those who render exceptional service. We finally converted the firm of Carnegie, McCandless, & Co. into the Edgar Thomson Steel Company, and included my brother and Mr. Phipps, both of whom had declined at first to go into the steel business with their too enterprising senior. But when I showed them the earnings for the first year and told them if they did not get into steel they would find themselves in the wrong boat, they reconsidered and came with us. It was fortunate for them as for us. . . .

The mills were at last [in 1874] ready to begin and an organization the auditor proposed was laid before me for approval. I found he had divided the works into two departments and had given control of one to Mr. Stevenson, a Scotsman who afterwards made a fine record as a manufacturer, and control of the other to a Mr. Jones. Nothing, I am certain, ever affected the success of the steel company more than the decision which I gave upon that proposal. Upon no account could two men be in the same works with equal authority. An army with two commanders-in-chief, a ship with two captains, could not fare more disastrously than a manufacturing concern with two men in command upon the same ground, even though in two different departments.

I said: "This will not do. I do not know Mr. Stevenson, nor do I know Mr. Jones, but one or the other must be made captain and he alone must report to you." The decision fell upon Mr. Jones and in this way we obtained "The Captain," who afterward made his name famous wherever the manufacture of Bessemer steel is known.

The Captain was then quite young, spare, and active, bearing traces of his Welsh descent even in his stature, for he was quite short. He came to us as a two-dollars-a-day mechanic from the neighboring works at Johnstown. We soon saw that he was a character. Every movement told it. He had volunteered as a private during the Civil War and carried himself so finely that he became captain of a company which was never known to flinch. Much of the success of the Edgar Thomson Works belongs to this man.

In later years he declined an interest in the firm which would have made him a millionaire. I told him one day that some of the young men who had been given an interest were now making much more than he was and we had voted to make him a partner. This entailed no financial responsibility, as we always provided that the cost of the interest given was payable only out of profits.

"No," he said, "I don't want to have my thoughts running on business. I have enough trouble looking after these works. Just give me a hell of a salary if you think I'm worth it."

"All right, Captain, the salary of the President of the United States is yours."

"That's the talk," said the little Welshman.

Our competitors in steel were at first disposed to ignore us. Knowing the difficulties they had in starting their own steel works, they could not believe we would be ready to deliver rails for another year and declined to recognize us as competitors. The price of steel rails when we began was about seventy dollars per ton. We sent our agent through the country with instructions to take orders at the best prices he could obtain; and before our competitors knew it, we had obtained a large number—quite sufficient to justify us in making a start.

So perfect was the machinery, so admirable the plans, so skillful were the men selected by Captain Jones, and so great a manager was he himself, that our success was phenomenal. I think I place a unique statement on the record when I say the result of the first month's operations left a margin of profit of $11,000. It is also remarkable that so perfect was our system of accounts that we knew the exact amount of the profit. We had learned from experience in our iron works what exact accounting meant. There is nothing more profitable than clerks to check up on each transfer of material from one department to another in process of manufacture. . . .

MILLS AND THE MEN

The one vital lesson in iron and steel that I learned in Britain was the necessity for owning raw materials and finishing the completed article ready for its purpose. Having solved the steel-rail problem at the Edgar Thomson Works, we soon proceeded to the next step. The difficulties and uncertainties of obtaining regular supplies of pig iron compelled us to begin the erection of blast furnaces. Three of these were built, one, however, being a reconstructed blast furnace purchased from the Escanaba Iron Company, with which Mr. Kloman had been connected. As is usual in such cases, the furnace cost us as much as a new one, and it never was as good. There is nothing so unsatisfactory as purchases of inferior plants. . . .

While testing the ores of Virginia we found that these were being quietly purchased by Europeans for ferro-manganese, the owners of the mine being led to believe that they were used for other purposes. Our Mr. Phipps at once set about purchasing that mine. He obtained an option from the owners, who had neither capital nor skill to work it efficiently. A high price was paid to them for their interests, and (with one of them, Mr. Davis, a very able young man) we became the owners, but not until a thorough investigation of the mine had proved that there was enough manganese ore in sight to repay us. All this was done with speed; not a day was lost when the discovery was made. And here lies the great advantage of a partnership over a corporation. The president of the latter would have had to consult a board of directors and wait several weeks and perhaps months for their decision. By that time the mine would probably have become the property of others.

We continued to develop our blast-furnace plant, every new one being a great improvement upon the preceding, until at last we thought we had arrived at a standard furnace. Minor improvements would no doubt be made, but so far as we could see we had a perfect plant and our capacity was then fifty thousand tons per month of pig iron.

The blast furnace department was no sooner added than another step was seen to be essential to our independence and success. The supply of superior coke was a fixed quantity—the Connellsville field being defined. We found that we could not get on without a supply of the fuel essential to the smelting of pig iron; and a very thorough investigation of the question led us to the conclusion that the Frick Coke Company had not only the best coal and coke property, but that it had in Mr. Frick himself a man with a positive genius for its management. He had proven his ability in starting as a poor railway clerk and succeeding. In 1882 we purchased one half of the stock in this company, and by subsequent purchases from other holders we became owners of the great bulk of the shares.

There now remained to be acquired only the supply of iron stone. If we could obtain this we should be in the position occupied by only two or three of the European concerns. We thought at one time we had succeeded in discovering in Pennsylvania this last remaining link in the chain. We were misled, however, in our investment in the Tyrone region, and lost considerable sums as the result of our attempts to mine and use the ores of that section. . . .

Our chemist, Mr. Prousser, was then sent to a Pennsylvania furnace among the hills which we had leased, with instructions to analyze all the materials brought to him from the district, and to encourage people to bring him specimens of minerals. . . . One day he sent us a report of analyses of ore remarkable for the absence of phosphorus. It was really an ore suitable for making Bessemer steel. Such a discovery attracted our attention at once. The owner of the property was Moses Thompson, a rich farmer, proprietor of seven thousand acres of the most beautiful agricultural land in Center County, Pennsylvania. An appointment was made to meet him upon the ground from which the ore had been obtained. We found the mine had been worked for a charcoal blast furnace fifty or sixty years before, but it had not borne a good reputation then, the reason no doubt being that its product was so much purer than other ores that the same amount of flux used caused trouble in smelting. It was so good it was good for nothing in those days of old.

We finally obtained the right to take the mine over at any time within six months, and we therefore began the work of examination, which every purchaser of mineral property should make most carefully. We ran lines across the hillsides fifty feet apart, with cross-lines at distances of a hundred feet apart, and at each point of intersection we put a shaft down through the ore. I believe there were eighty such shafts in all and the ore was analyzed at every few feet of depth, so that before we paid over the hundred thousand dollars asked we knew exactly what there was of ore. The result hoped for was more than realized. Through the ability of my cousin and partner, Mr. Lauder, the cost of mining and washing was reduced to a low figure, and the Scotia ore made good all the losses we had incurred in the other mines, paid for itself, and left a profit besides. In this case, at least, we snatched victory from the jaws of defeat. . . .

The rapid substitution of steel for iron in the immediate future had become obvious to us. Even in our Keystone Bridge Works, steel was being used more and more in place of iron. King Iron was about to be deposed by the new King Steel.

———

BY THE END of the 1870s, Andrew Carnegie was well on his way to being the premier steelmaker in the nation. He had steered his way from crisis to crisis, emerging stronger at the end of each. More than that, he had brought his concern into the new day of vertically integrated industry; his firm controlled sources of coal and iron, enormous plants, and distribution networks. It was a change that was increasingly overtaking all of American business: at the same moment, John D. Rockefeller was monopolizing the petroleum industry in his Standard Oil Company, making use of his own special relationship with the railroads. Carnegie could look around him and see that he had, indeed, built something tangible.

As much as he can be admired for his keen business sense, for the enormous scope of his achievements, he helped usher a host of mixed blessings into American history. The average citizen's vision of becoming a self-employed craftsman disappeared within his own lifetime, to be replaced by wage labor in factory towns. The self-made steel king ruthlessly crushed unions, most infamously at his vast Homestead mills in 1892, when his armed guards battled disgruntled workers.

The panic of 1873 unleashed a depression that swept everything along with it. The Republicans lost the House of Representatives, the public lost their savings, the South would soon see Reconstruction tremble on the brink. But Carnegie survived, and with him survived a dawning age of massively powerful industrialists, when everyone faced a new set of expectations. His own account of his battle with Kloman is revealing in this respect. To Carnegie, Kloman had committed the ultimate sin by striking out on his own. Strange criticism from someone whose single principle in life was that he would never work for another man again.

20

THE SHADOWS DEEPEN, PART I:
MISSISSIPPI

As Grant took his second oath of office, Adelbert Ames and Albert Morgan conferred about the troubling state of Mississippi. The two made a natural pair: both had served valiantly in the Union army for the duration of the Civil War; both had moved to the South from the far North after the hostilities ended; both were senators—the first a sitting U.S. senator, the latter recently retired from the state legislature; and both were idealists who defied the thieving "carpetbagger" stereotype perpetrated by the Democratic press and politicians. Together they had gone far toward building a new Mississippi, in which the color line was a thing of the past. Yet all around them were signs of danger.

Albert Morgan's achievements have appeared in this volume in his own words; Adelbert Ames's were no less significant. As United States senator, Ames had helped secure passage of the Ku Klux Klan Act, a powerful extension of federal protection to the freed people that cut against decades of constitutional practice. He had negotiated with Grant to secure a place as attorney general for Amos Akerman, who proved extremely effective in enforcing the law, breaking the back of the Klan in South Carolina and elsewhere. In January 1873, Ames introduced a bill to desegregate the military: "Now that he [the African American] is a citizen," he thundered to the Senate, "he ought to be permitted to serve in one regiment or another, as he sees fit, as the white man or an Indian or a man of any other race is permitted to do." He was far ahead of his peers: the bill failed, and segregation in the army would continue until President Harry Truman, a Democrat, issued an executive order to end it in 1948.

Despite these advances, despite the reelection of the President who first sent Ames to Mississippi, Reconstruction was clearly in trouble. On the national scene, the constant snarl of Democratic attacks had risen to a roar, swaying the opinion even of Republicans. New York *Tribune* journalist James S. Pike, a man with a strong antislavery record, journeyed to South Carolina in 1873; he sent back a stream of articles that condemned the state government as "the most ignorant democracy that mankind ever saw," under the control of "a mass of black barbarism." Pike turned his reports into a best-selling book called *The Prostrate South*. The fact that Pike now voiced openly racist views, or that he had based his attacks

325

on interviews with hostile white politicians, did nothing to lessen the impact of his writing among a Northern public increasingly uncomfortable with the egalitarian revolution in the South.

That same year, an even more important publication appeared: the Supreme Court decision in the *Slaughterhouse Cases.* Justice Samuel F. Miller's decision gutted the Fourteenth Amendment, declaring that most rights of citizenship were still reserved to state control, despite the Amendment's guarantee of *national* citizenship. The result threw into doubt the whole series of groundbreaking laws recently passed to protect individual liberty. African-American rights were suddenly, unexpectedly, rocked off their foundations.

Meanwhile, Republican governments in the upper South were swept away as early as 1869 and 1870. Maryland and West Virginia went first, to be followed by Virginia, Tennessee, and Missouri. The resurgent Democrats in these states wrote new laws and constitutions that led the way in undermining the power of blacks at the ballot box. Poll taxes and property ownership were demanded of voters, thus excluding most African Americans, and electoral districts were reapportioned to limit or eradicate black influence. These laws also reduced the rights of poor whites, but the Democratic leadership had never cared for the impoverished of any race.

In the border states, however, blacks formed a distinct minority of the voting population; the Republicans had been bolstered by state laws that disfranchised former Confederates. In an effort to win more white support, they repealed those limitations, unleashing an avalanche of Democratic votes. Deeper in the South, African Americans constituted a far larger portion of the public, and it was here that white supremacists campaigned with the torch, pistol, and noose. Massive violence and intimidation led to Democratic victories in 1870 in North Carolina, Alabama, and Georgia. Enforcement of the Ku Klux Klan Act helped restore Republicans to a share of state government in the first two, but Georgia was permanently lost—or "redeemed," in the perverse vocabulary of Southern Democrats. There they quickly enacted ballot requirements that almost erased black votes in a state with a very narrow white majority. The Georgia government also eliminated county governments where African Americans were a large majority, replacing them with state-appointed boards. And the Democrats had campaigned as the party of "home rule."

Even in states where Republicans survived in power, where blacks were a majority, vicious party feuds weakened state governments and tarnished the image of Reconstruction. South Carolina suffered terrible political infighting—but nothing could match Louisiana. As mentioned earlier, rival factions there fought ferociously for power. The election of 1872 was so bitterly disputed that two rival governors and legislatures swore themselves in, each claiming to be the rightful government. Grant had to send in federal troops to settle the dispute by force. It was indeed a shameful episode—magnified by the Democratic press in the North to cast a shadow over Reconstruction and black suffrage in general.

No one was more disgusted by events in Louisiana than Senator Ames. As historian Richard Nelson Current recounts, the Mississippi Republican traveled across the river to observe its 1872 campaign, and came back with new worries and determination. "Warmoth has sold the state to the Democracy," he wrote. Indeed, where Governor Henry Warmoth, a Republican, had not already appointed Democrats to office, white supremacists took power by force. In Grant Parish, local African Americans feared that Democrats would seize the government; accordingly, they dug trenches around the town of Colfax, the county seat, and formed themselves into militia units. On Easter Sunday, heavily armed whites overran the town, slaughtering hundreds—"including," Eric Foner notes, "the massacre of some fifty blacks who lay down their arms under a white flag of surrender."

"It causes two different and conflicting emotions to rise up within me," Ames wrote, "the one, to abandon a life of politics where such things alone find place, and another, to buckle on my armor anew that I may better fight the battle of the poor and oppressed colored man." And whispering in his ear, urging him on to further battle, was Albert Morgan, the veteran of so many bitter fights with "the enemy." As discussed previously, Mississippi's own Republican party had split into factions, and it was in danger of falling completely under the sway of the conservative wing led by former governor and current senator James L. Alcorn.

Ames's followers needed him at home. Ridgley C. Powers, Alcorn's handpicked successor, was governor now, and he continued his leader's policies of appeasing white Democrats. Ames himself wanted to prove that he had broad support (since U.S. senators were voted in by state legislatures, he had yet to win a statewide election). So when Morgan and others urged him to run for governor in the election of 1873, he agreed, settling in the town of Natchez (where John Lynch would be his congressman) with his wife Blanche Butler Ames—the daughter of Republican leader Benjamin F. Butler—and his two young children.

In the Republican state convention, Ames trounced Powers and received the party nomination. Alcorn rose to the occasion, declaring *himself* a candidate for governor as an independent, with Democratic support. But the former military hero overshadowed the polished Southern planter. Richard Nelson Current writes that he impressed even Democratic newspapers: one commented, "We have heard no Republican speaker who has so favorably impressed us as a *speaker*. His speech was certainly, in a literary point, superior to Gen. Alcorn's speech made here some time back." On election day, he polled 70,000 votes to Alcorn's 50,000.

Even as Morgan urged Ames to run for governor, Yazoo Republicans urged *him* to run for sheriff, the most powerful local office. In fact, the county situation directly paralleled what had happened at the state level. Like the statewide Republican leadership, Morgan wanted to broaden the party's base to include white voters; at both levels, a former slaveholder was selected for the most powerful office (Alcorn for governor and F.P. Hilliard for sheriff); and at both levels the handpicked candidate proved a disappointment, deciding to appeal to unrepentant Democrats. For much the same reasons as Ames decided to step down from the U.S. Senate to run for governor, Morgan descended from the state senate to run for sheriff.

The election should have been the finest moment in local history—for political life was reaching unprecedented richness and maturity. The campaign no longer simply pitted black against white: One group of African Americans—led by none other than William H. Foote and the African Methodist Episcopal Church—opposed Morgan in an effort to show that blacks need not depend on white leadership. A valid point, but young Albert was not the condescending Yankee often found in Southern Republican parties. And events soon proved that solidarity, not division, was required if African Americans were to retain power at all.

In the passage that follows, Morgan insightfully ties local Democratic thinking to national developments. His opponents keenly observed events in the North, and they were patient enough to await the opportunity to destroy everything he had built. After they failed to prevent him from taking office as sheriff, they began to test a new strategy, one that surpassed anything they had tried before. The final result was Reconstruction writ small: initial triumph, dogged opposition, a shocking tragedy, and a conclusion filled with foreboding.

An Election and a Killing
by Albert T. Morgan

The election of 1873 was in a certain sense the climax in our State of "radical rule," so called by the enemy. It was the year when the varied progressive influences converging from different and often widely separate centers of thought, interest, and action, converging upon Mississippi, with none other than weapons of truth, met and for a third time overcame the enemy upon the ground of his own choosing.

Up to this time Mr. Hilliard had held the most lucrative office in the county—that of sheriff and the ex-officio tax collector—uninterruptedly, or for a period beginning in 1869, and continuing more than four years. Notwithstanding our disagreement upon the school and other questions, I had given him a hearty and unfaltering support. I had done this not because of any especial personal regard for him, or that he entertained for me, nor because I was under any obligations whatever to him, but solely because I desired to lay the foundations of our party upon a broader basis than mere race lines (which would have restricted its membership to the colored people, led by a handful of "Yankees"), and believed that an exhibition of unfaltering political friendship for Mr. Hilliard would at least be accepted by the native whites as evidence of the sincerity of my professions in that regard. I had given five years to the cause of Reconstruction in Yazoo and in the State without other reward than the consciousness of having done well; and the empty honors of an office that, while entailing the gravest responsibilities upon me and the hardest kind of work, did not afford me a personal support. My creditors were clamorous for their money, and everyone called me a fool for giving to others the fruits of my toil and trials instead of preserving at least some share for myself.

The same friends who could not at all understand why we had failed on Tokeba, now could not understand why I was not yet able to pay my debts. They read in the papers that the carpetbaggers were all getting rich, and was I not one of that class? Besides, the old guard had become dissatisfied with Mr. Hilliard. So had nearly all the freed people, who blamed him for not taking a more active part in behalf of free schools. Mrs. Hilliard and her daughters had become leading members in the leading white folks' church, and in Yazoo society. It was said that the sheriff was rich; that he had saved "nigh on to fifty thousand dollars."

But be that as it may, the time had come when I had expected, from the very outset, to ask for my reward. The State was reconstructed in all the departments of government, and peace and quiet prevailed. But my friends among the white Unionists, the Northerners, and especially the old guard, together with the great body of the freed people, anticipating what would be my wishes in the premises, were already using my name as Mr. Hilliard's successor, and when the convention met I was placed in nomination for that office by acclamation. It was the most intelligent body of Republicans ever assembled in the county. The contrast between it and the first Republican convention held in the county was indeed striking. Every one of the delegates had been chosen at numerously attended primaries, and nearly all of them could read, and a large majority could both read and write. There were at least three colored men of the number who were worth, in real estate and livestock, not less than ten thousand dollars each, all of which they had made at planting. There was also a sprinkling of native whites, among them planters, merchants, and one lawyer, all of whom had been slaveholders. . . .

My term had expired in the Senate. I enjoyed no means or facilities whatever for influencing either those delegates, or the masses who had sent them there, to vote for me, other than my name and the memory among them of my services. Without money or patronage at my disposal, and with convictions of duty respecting party leadership which forbade my making promises of reward contingent upon my election, at the close of my four years' term in the Senate, I was as powerless to reward friends or to punish foes within our party as my baby boy, then two years old.

But though Mr. Foote was a warm advocate of Mr. Hilliard's re-election, he, together with the official membership of the A.M.E. Church which had got a foothold in Yazoo too,[6] had been for weeks canvassing the county in Mr. Hilliard's interest, supplied, as was at the time openly proclaimed and well known, with "ample funds" for all manner of expenses, it all failed, and, as the denizens of Yazoo County will remember to this day, the shout went up from the convention upon the vote nominating me, "nearly lifted the roof from the courthouse," as everybody said. . . .

It also gives me great pleasure to add that although my share of the expenses of the campaign from first to last for tickets, for travelling, and all other expenses did not exceed one hundred dollars; although I made no canvas at all among the people, and but one speech during the campaign which followed the nomination; although the day of the election and for several days before I had been ill in bed and under the care of a physician; and although the enemy made Mr. Hilliard their candidate and placed upon their ticket with him for *all* county offices and many of the district offices *none but* colored men, my majority over him was nearly two thousand in a vote of thirty-one hundred.

The truth is that the irreconcilables had all along intended to use Mr. Hilliard for my overthrow. To this purpose was due the social eminence to which his family so suddenly attained, and the hearty support of their organ, the *Democrat*.

The result made them very mad indeed; for they now had to carry a double dose of "nigro rule." The first was at Dover, when they saw with their own eyes that the freedman, free negro, and mulatto dared shoot to kill. The next was now, when they realized that I had not misjudged the negro, that he was capable of not only feeling but also of expressing gratitude.

But all of a sudden, certain of them professed to have had a revelation. It was in the election news from Ohio. "Old Bill Allen" had "done rize up," and Ohio had gone Democratic! Seeking for the cause of this change, they discovered that in June 1873, a new departure in politics was taken when the *Democratic* convention in Allen County, of that State, passed a resolution declaring that corruption in political parties had become chronic, and that "both political parties have demonstrated that they are powerless to check or control existing tendency toward the utter demoralization of the

6 [Original author's footnote] Upon the close of the campaign of 1869, the irreconcilables suddenly became especial admirers of Mr. Foote, often contrasting him with "them low down Yankees," and always to the disparagement of the Yankees. This, with the prejudices he already possessed, together with the tendency of his church to segregation, had great influence upon him, and by 1873 he was an avowed advocate of a party that should be made up of "Southerners and nigros" to the exclusion of "Northerners."

politics of the country," also that a convention had been held at Columbus and participated in by both Democrats and Liberals. It had—

> "*Resolved,* That we insist upon a strict adherence by the General Government to the constitutional limitations of its power, and we demand home government in all local affairs."

Also, that a Democratic State convention followed, which nominated William Allen for governor, and—

> "*Resolved,* That the Democratic party seeks to revive no dead issues, but stands by its principles, which are suited to all times and circumstances. . . . It defends the reserved rights of the States and of the people, and opposes the centralization that would impair or destroy them."

Mr. Allen's majority was but about 800. Under ordinary circumstances, the fact could have had no particular significance in the South. But the circumstances were extraordinary. The convention in Allen County where the "Ohio movement" originated was a *Democratic departure.*[7] The excuse for it and for the Liberal convention which followed sprang from a widespread disgust of the corrupt practices, apparent in *both* the great political parties *at the North.* The "bloody shirts" of Georgia, Alabama, Tennessee, Louisiana, and other Southern States had frequently been unfurled and made to do service in Northern elections for the Republicans, until thousands of the most conscientious and enlightened members of the party thought they saw in everyone of them—those "bloody shirts"—a trick by thieves for the perpetuation of their opportunity to rob the country through the channels of politics.

The investigations which had followed in New York and other cities, in States and in Congress, had uncovered to the country the fact that corruption did prevail to an alarming extent in both parties. Some traced the cause to the war, others traced it back to "Federal interference" in States at the South, while there were those who declared that the root of the matter was in the extension of the suffrage so as to include the negro. Taking advantage of this feeling, a man of undoubted personal and political sincerity and integrity was brought to the front in Ohio and placed upon a platform which, while it embraced a plank covering the grievances of Republicans, also embraced planks which met the demands of extreme and irreconcilable Democrats everywhere, South as well as North.

7 The "Ohio Idea," or the "New Departure" as it was also called, abandoned overt appeals to white supremacy, and recast the attacks on Reconstruction as an appeal for "home rule." As Morgan writes, the approach was bolstered by the publicity given to public corruption, common in both North and South.

The fact was, that many voted for the man without regard to the platform upon which he stood, as a protest against the corrupt tendencies of the times. That elected him. This result was accepted by the irreconcilables in Yazoo as proof that the day of their deliverance from what *they* still called a "carpetbag negro usurpation" was at hand. For was not Ohio a "hotbed of abolitionism," the "home of Giddings," the very "backbone of radical power" at the North?

So they talked to each other while they shook hands and congratulated themselves; so they talked to the freed people, while felicitating themselves on the prospect that after all the time was not a great way off when they should be again able to "whip a nigger"; so some of them jocularly said to me while good humoredly inviting me to "read the handwriting on the wall." I insisted that they were mistaken; that the result was a protest against corruption, not against our Mississippi nor our Yazoo government; at which they would remind me of that resolution of the Liberals favoring "home government" and protesting against Federal usurpations of power. But, pointing to our majorities, I would always reply, "what is ours but home government—the rule of the majority?" Notwithstanding all the progress we had made, all the examples we had afforded of the capacity of the negro for self-government, their response to this was always a kind of grin accompanied with a look which said, "Morgan, you may be honest, but you're green," and a final word, which was rarely more than "yo'll see."

Notwithstanding the fact that my candidacy for the sheriff's office meant an increase of taxes for school purposes, largely increased facilities for the education of the children of the freed people, and was a rebuke to Mr. Hilliard and his supporters for their neglect of this cause, out of a total registered "white vote" of more than 1,500 and of a total vote cast of 3,137, he received but 431, while I received 2,365. The fact is I received nearly, if not quite, as large a number of white votes as he. The Grange organization in the county was at that time in the zenith of its power and I know that the head of that organization and many of its members voted for me. . . .

When the bond was complete[8] and the time provided by law for me to qualify and enter upon the duties of my office had arrived, I appeared before the proper officer, took the oath of office required by law and made the usual personal notice to Mr. Hilliard. He then for the first time informed me that he had resolved not to surrender the office to me.

The only court then in session in the county was our board of supervisors. . . . Mr. Hilliard was then in attendance upon the board. Prepared with the certificate of the proper officers, showing my election to the office by the people, showing also the record of my bonds and of my oath of

[8] To step into the office of sheriff, Morgan had to post a bond of $20,000, backed by real estate. The amount was largely covered by freedmen who had become landowners in the past few years.

office, and that the day had arrived when by law the term of the incumbent, Mr. Hilliard, should expire, and when I should become the lawful sheriff, and, showing that I was the lawful sheriff, I went before that body and demanded to be recognized by them as sheriff in fact. It was at this juncture that Mr. Hilliard appeared with counsel, and asked that I be not recognized. Upon the hearing before the board, it was legally established that Mr. Hilliard had given me no notice whatever of his intention to contest my right to the office; that he had not filed in any court any notice whatever of contest; that he did not deny my election, and that the only ground upon which he attempted to defend his refusal to turn over to me the keys of the office room was the fact that a legal question was pending in the Supreme Court of the State, regarding the legality of the election.[9]

Mr. Hilliard, his counsel, and the board at the time well knew that the question pending in the Supreme Court involved only the legality of the election for State officers, and had no relation whatever to county officers. Mr. Hilliard and all the rest knew that by the Constitution and laws his term was for but two years, and that that term expired that very day. So the board decided, and therefore declared, that I was the sheriff, in law and in fact, and they commanded me to attend them at their sessions, thus dismissing Mr. Hilliard.

One of the arguments presented by his counsel at that hearing fairly illustrates the animus of their entire proceeding. That counsel stated that certain rumors had come to his ears to the effect that I had threatened, if Mr. Hilliard should refuse to turn over the keys of his office to me, to send to the country for the colored people—even he called them colored people now—to come to town, when I would use them for an assault upon the building. And then he begged the board to consider what might be the consequences of such an act. "For," as he declared, "our people are not yet prepared to tolerate that method of asserting one's right to an office," and the result might be a bloody conflict—"a war of races."

Now, four years had passed since that alarm was last heard in Yazoo. Its revival, considering all the circumstances, awakened some laughter. . . . Well, I must be brief. Mr. Hilliard promptly yielded to the order of the board so far as to "withdraw," and I was at once installed in his place. That evening when he left his office room and went home, he placed three men on guard inside it. Under the law he was the trespasser, and I had undoubted authority to arrest him and hold him as such. Had he made any formal contest, no matter how absurd the grounds of it might

[9] Governor Ridgley Powers had sued to prevent Adelbert Ames from taking office. In a last-ditch attempt to continue his term, he argued that the election should have been delayed until 1874; the courts overturned his protest, which only applied to the statewide election in the first place.

have been, it would have been different. He had made no contest at all, formal or otherwise, except to appear before the board as I have related.

I appointed some deputies and continued all the next day to act as sheriff for the board (whose sessions would continue for some days, it being a regular stated meeting) and for the county. That night a friend of Mr. Hilliard brought me direct from him an offer of $5,000 to allow him to remain in the office thirty days longer. This was in amount the same as the offer of Captain Telsub on a former occasion. . . .

I became exasperated. It was impossible for me to sleep that night, only by fits and starts. All night long I kept revolving in my mind what had I done to cause this man to have so low an opinion of my judgment, as for a moment to suppose that I would fail to see that my acceptance of his offer would not only deprive me of the office forever, but also would forever blast my name; or that he should for a moment suppose that seeing this I could be such a dastard as to accept such a fate for such a consideration. I had accepted the jeers, the scorn, the blows of the enemy during the reign of the kuklux. But that was in behalf of a cause that had made Mr. Hilliard sheriff and, as everybody said, a rich man; that was when Mr. Hilliard, "the poor Unionist," came by the backyard to our stronghold to sympathize with its little garrison. This was now, when Mr. Hilliard, after having enjoyed the fleshpots from our planting until he was fat, and after having been fawned upon by the enemy until his family had grown vain and proud, and he had lost his head, had become a tool for their uses, to the overthrow of Morgan, the destruction of our party, and the ruin of our cause. . . .

My wakefulness greatly worried my poor wife, who "couldn't understand it at all." I had taken the liberty, which so many husbands take, to keep the worst of the bad news from her. What could it mean? What had happened? Was I not the sheriff? Had I not been installed in office by the only court then in session in the county? Was there to be any further trouble? I explained as best I could, and yet, though she is a rather quick-witted woman, she still failed to see. The only thing about it was that Mr. Hilliard still kept the keys to the sheriff's office, and had men on guard over the room. . . .

That morning I went to the courthouse earlier than usual, and went to the sheriff's room. The door was open and no one in except a young man, Mr. Hilliard's nephew. Walking in I informed him that I was the sheriff of the county and should remain in the office. He might, if he pleased, bear my message to Mr. Hilliard, to come and get any personal effects he might have there. Without making any resistance at all the young man withdrew, and left the building.

Less than two hours afterward Mr. Hilliard was a corpse, and one of my deputies so badly wounded that fears were entertained for a long time that he would not recover. But he did.

THE MANNER OF IT

The death of Mr. Hilliard occurred in this manner: He was at home when informed that I had entered, and with my deputies was in full possession of the sheriff's office room. It was said that he became very much excited and ran down to the office of his attorney, with whom he held a hasty consultation. Meantime quite a number of his personal and political followers gathered upon the street nearby. From these and from others who were summoned by him a crowd, estimated by some to number twenty and by others twenty-five, was hastily formed for the avowed purpose of "recapturing" the room. During this time Mr. Foote, still a strong partisan of Mr. Hilliard, came to the office. Finding me and my deputies in quiet possession, he became very greatly excited and cursed some of my men, so that to avoid him the office door was closed against him. Then he rang the courthouse bell and went away.

The point where Mr. Hilliard formed his men was two squares distant and around a corner, so that the first knowledge I had of their purpose was his appearance at the head of the street upon which was the courthouse, in front of his followers, hurrying toward us and presenting a most violent array. Seeing this some of the citizens scampered away. Others remained. There was no time for consultation, even for thinking, for in a moment they would be at the courthouse. My first impulse sprang from a desire to preserve the peace and to save my brother William and my friends and deputies who remained, numbering six persons all told, from violence. Instantly acting upon it, I ordered them all within the room, to close and bolt the door from the inside, and to remain there, no matter what happened.

Then I started alone to meet the crowd, and meeting them halfway, calling Mr. Hilliard by name, in a loud voice, I warned him that I was the sheriff; that I had possession of the office; that I had left my deputies in charge of it; and that he should halt. Mr. Hilliard not only saw me, but he must have heard me, for I was almost in front of him. But he refused to halt, and hastening his speed kept on. Then I made the same announcement to his followers, some of whom also heard me, for they hesitated. But Mr. Hilliard turned and shouted to them to follow him, which they did. While thus endeavoring to halt the crowd, they all passed by me.

It was now impossible for me to regain the courthouse ahead of them, so I followed, hoping that when they should reach the office, finding it closed against them, they would wait for me. But they did not, and Mr. Hilliard and some of his friends violently forced open the door, breaking the panel, and one of them fired into the room. The shot was returned from inside. At the moment I reached the steps leading into the main hall of the building (the same steps over which Hilliard and his party had passed an instant before), saw him reeling away from the now open office door, and was met with a blinding flash and crushing noise. But the ball had opened, and when it ended, which could not have been more than five minutes afterward (it did not seem more than one), I had cleared the courthouse and yard of the last one of them, except my former friend, who lay bleeding and senseless upon the floor of the hall, near the front door, where he fell.[10]

Right here, and before stopping to grieve over the fate of Mr. Hilliard, even before we stop to mark the grave of civil peace . . . I gladly tarry to do an act of simple justice to the negro. Three of the men in that room when I left it were negroes. I had not gone ten steps on my way to meet the angrily advancing crowd, when I was followed by one of these who, as I was afterward told by the others in the room, could not be restrained from following me, and declared that I should not go alone to meet them. That "nigro" followed me all the way and was close at my side throughout the conflict. My deputy on the inside, who was wounded and who in spite of it stood up like a man to the last, was also a "nigro." The only one of Mr. Hilliard's friends who stood by him with fidelity and who was the last man to leave the courthouse, was "that nigro Foote." The last one of Mr. Hilliard's bourbon allies ran almost at the first fire; some of them in their haste cleared the high iron picket fence of the yard at one bound.

When it was over, my first thought was for Mr. Hilliard and my wounded deputy, and I promptly dispatched a messenger for surgical aid. But before this duty had been accomplished I was notified that a complaint of some sort had been made against me before the mayor. I promptly inquired of that officer what the nature of the complaint was, and was informed that it was murder. . . .

Then there followed such a revival of the scenes witnessed by the little Yankee garrison of Yazoo in 1868 and 1869, as speedily transformed the little town of Yazoo City into a seething caldron of warring political forces. The appetite of the irreconcilables for office and power, sharpened by more than four years of enforced abstinence, overcame their discretion, made them blind to all the proprieties of the occasion, arrayed them in open defiance of all law, and obliterated in their bosoms all sense of justice.

It would be a day or two before the chancellor [a civil court circuit judge] arrived. During this waiting all manner of rumors were set afloat, all calculated to inflame public sentiment against me. The charge that I had wantonly shot down Mr. Hilliard without giving him any "show for his life,"[11] was added to until it took this form: "While *Sheriff* Hilliard was off his guard Morgan stole into his office and shot him down like a dog." Also this other form: "Hilliard was first shot by one of Morgan's nigros. Then, while endeavoring in his almost helpless condition to escape from the courthouse, he was met at the door by Morgan, who deliberately placed his pistol at the *sheriff's* head and fired three shots into him." . . .

10 In the confusion of the fight, Morgan did fire his revolver several times.

11 [Original author's footnote] A common phrase in Yazoo.

It then became apparent to me that the leaders among the irreconcilables had resolved on taking possession of the county government, and were sanguine of their ability to use the chancellor in the accomplishment of their purpose. Just how they would proceed was not yet quite clear. Neither our Senator nor either of my counsel appeared to anticipate any such purpose, and the Senator was strong in his belief that it could be easily thwarted if it should be found to exist.

But the result proved the correctness of my judgment. The irreconcilables kept their own counsels. The first step to their goal lay over Hilliard's body. His bitterest enemies were chief among the mourners at his funeral, and they overlooked on that occasion none of the devices known to Southern political conspirators for stirring the hearts of "our people."

No one doubted that I would remain and stand my trial, and so the committing magistrate—the mayor—had instructed that I be not confined, but allowed to remain at my home until the hearing before the chancellor could occur. But no sooner had the ceremonies at the grave been concluded than there arose a demand for my close confinement. Major Sweet, Captain Telsub, and the human hornet were foremost in giving voice to that demand. . . . So, for the sake of peace, and that I might not appear to anyone to show want of respect for the laws, I voluntarily informed the mayor that he need not hesitate to lock me up in the jail. . . .

I had not been shut up in a cell but was allowed the freedom of the jailor's apartments. Upon discovering this the irreconcilables found in the fact new cause of complaint against our Republican officials and insisted that I be locked up in a cell. This was done, and very soon afterward the discovery was made by the irreconcilables that I was not in the murderer's cell but in one of the common cells. . . .

[Acting against the law, the] chancellor assumed that he not only had the authority to do so, but that it was his duty to appoint a sheriff and tax collector for the county. A strange coincidence was the fact that at the moment the chancellor made that discovery there appeared before him a man whom the leaders of the irreconcilables recommended as in every respect worthy of the place. . . . Now, this applicant, thus recommended and here ready in court to assume the robes of office so soon after my incarceration, was none other than the former chairman of the County Democratic Committee, one of the irreconcilables; a man in whom the enemy put such trust that, when called on to name a member of the board of registrars for the registration of voters and for the holding of elections in the county, they had chosen him.[12] He was the same who

12 [Original author's footnote] Under the law passed by our free State government, both parties were entitled to representation on that board, which was composed of three members. In Yazoo "we all" Republicans had always freely accorded to our opponents the privilege of choosing for themselves who should represent them on the board.

had signed and delivered to me the certificate of election to the office, Geo. M. Powell. Having at the beginning yielded to the mob spirit, the chancellor was now a slave to the mob; so, notwithstanding the Republicans of the county outnumbered the Democrats two to one, this chancellor appointed a trusted leader of the Democrats.

A NEGRO "RISING"

Up to the moment of Mr. Powell's appointment by the chancellor, there had been no "rising" of the negroes. But now they came pouring into town in large numbers, and presented a most defiant attitude. The demand of the [white] mob for the appointment of a new jailor was immediately complied with by the chancellor's new sheriff. But the negroes planted themselves across the street just above the jail, and openly and fearlessly proclaimed that the new jailor should not act. Taught by their experiences in 1867, 1868, and 1869, the negroes believed that all these proceedings pointed directly to the death of myself and deputies at the hands of the mob. . . .

By the action of the colored people at this juncture, the situation became extremely critical. They were armed only with their hardwood sticks, excepting only a few who had pistols, but the enemy could see that they were not only very numerous, but also very determined. The chancellor's new sheriff could have summoned his following and speedily cleared the streets, because they had or could quickly procure arms for the purpose. But he hesitated to do this. The new State government, with Ames at its head, was already installed in power.

The new legislature, having a large Republican majority, was in session in Jackson, and the friends I had made during my service in the constitutional convention and in the State senate were devising means to check the insurrection in Yazoo. The human hornet and his friends were anxious to "clear the streets of the nigros," but the chancellor's sheriff, having assumed the duties of that office under color of his appointment, was responsible for the peace. He hesitated to attack these negroes, and two whole days were spent in efforts to "pacify them." But they could neither be purchased nor cajoled. . . .

The enemy finding that the colored people could not be moved from their purpose, began negotiations looking to my transfer from our Yazoo jail to that of some other county. This was finally effected and I was secretly taken from the jail and conveyed to that of Hinds County, at the capital, which was my own selection. Now the State authorities began to act.[13] The chancellor had been appointed to fill a vacancy caused by the

---

[13] The newly inaugurated Governor Ames visited Morgan in his cell, and acted quickly to reverse the county coup launched by the Yazoo Democrats.

death of his predecessor. The appointment was withdrawn or revoked and another appointed in his place. The chancellor's sheriff was promptly removed, and the governor appointed my brother William to his place, "to continue during the disability of the lawful sheriff," myself.

The chancellor's sheriff for a time resisted, and the human hornet and his aides fumed and raved terribly at this new "outrage" put upon them, but all to no purpose; for at the expiration of two months I was again in full possession of my office. My deputies had been released from jail and perfect peace reigned throughout Yazoo. . . .

Ames being governor, and the important offices of the county having been by his firm policy removed from the reach of the starving sleuth-hounds of slavery, there was no longer anything to tempt the irreconcilables of Yazoo to violence. . . . But no sooner had I resumed the duties of my office than some of the most violent of the irreconcilables became fawning suitors after favors. The rough characters again disappeared, and the open, manly irreconcilables again went into hiding and "bided their time." Peace had come again to Yazoo, and I resumed my planting in the old stubble-ground. . . .

Eighteen hundred and seventy-four was a memorable year in Yazoo politics. The "Ohio idea," respecting "local self-government" and local sovereignty vs. the sovereignty of the individual, so aptly illustrated in that State in the person of Governor Allen, was bearing rich fruitage in Mississippi, where it was most happily illustrated in the person of the human hornet, Colonel Black, Judge Isam, Captain Telsub, and George M. Powell.

The Republican idea, represented in Mississippi in the person of Governor Ames, had done battle with the Ohio idea on its chosen field in Mississippi, our Yazoo stubble-ground, and overcame it. Peace had come again in Yazoo. But just outside our borders, on the south, in the county of Warren, the Ohio idea and certain other ideas appeared to stay. They were to have a charter election in the city of Vicksburg, Warren County, and for months in advance of it the irreconcilables had been preparing for the "war of races," which they assumed was about to occur.

Now those irreconcilables in Vicksburg, like their brethren in Yazoo, professed to believe in local self-government, and all the time protested against outside interference. But while openly doing that they were secretly making provision for as much aid for their cause from outside as they should need for their purposes. All sorts of false reports of "nigro risings," "nigros threatening to burn the city," and so forth were manufactured by them and published throughout the State in their newspapers and by special couriers. As a result of these measures, about the first of August reports came to me that there were three "independent military companies" being organized in the southern part of the county, and that they were "patrolling" their respective neighborhoods, disarming colored men whenever they were found with any kind of weapon, arresting some, and terrorizing all.

To ascertain the truth of those reports, I sent out two deputies, both white men and ex-Confederate officers, and a colored man, into the neighborhood of these "companies" with instructions to quietly travel about among the people and ascertain the truth. One of the deputies reported to me that he had found a "company" of white men under arms and drilling. He knew the "captain" quite well, and was informed by him that the organization was not for service in Yazoo County, but in response to calls for help from the white citizens of Vicksburg, who were hourly expecting an attack by a "mob of infuriated nigros," who were "threatening to burn the town." . . . Among the number were some of the worst as well as the best young white men of the county. [One of them] was a brother of the human hornet. The man sent to Dover made a similar report as to the Dover company, except that its members appeared not to be at all ashamed of what they were doing, and gloried in it. . . . The third organization, nearer to Vicksburg than the other two, was "out on a scout" with their Warren County brethren, and could not be got at.

Now every member of those companies, and their aiders and abbetors, knew that I was the sheriff and chief peace officer of the county, yet not a word had reached my ears of the cause of their complaint, from any one of their number, until I sought for it as I have related. My first information of their organizations came from a colored man living near Dover, who had got his squirrel gun taken away from him by members of the company.

Reports of "nigro insurrection" again became common throughout the State. One was reported in Tunica County, about the center of the swamp region, and General Chalmers, in command of an army recruited largely from Memphis and other parts of Tennessee and which was variously estimated in the public prints at from two to ten thousand white men, crowded on steamers chartered at Memphis for the purpose, hurried to the scene, creating terror and consternation among the negroes wherever they appeared. Democratic newspapers throughout the State, and the South, contained vivid accounts of the "ravages of the negroes." . . . We employed different means for suppressing the "rising" about to occur in Yazoo at this juncture.

The *Democrat* appeared with a blood in the eye editorial on the affidavit of one Simon Battaile, which it published, and which exposed what Simon said he knew of a "deep-laid, dark, and damnable plot" on the part of the negroes to "rise" and so forth, and the *Democrat,* and also the *Banner,* called on "our people" to arm and prepare for it.

Now it so happened that Simon was one I had for several days been searching for with a warrant for his arrest on a charge of grand larceny. But here he was now, "exposing" this so-called "nigro rising." In less than twenty-four hours I had Simon in jail, where he confessed to me that he knew nothing of any "rising" more than he had heard that the colored people were preparing for a celebration[14] of some sort to be held at Yazoo City. He had done this thing in order to secure the aid and sympathy of the "best citizens" to help him out of his own trouble.[15]

The prompt exposure of Simon's part in the conspiracy of the irreconcilables to compel "our nigros to rise," which was made in the columns of our Yazoo *Republican,* postponed the rising, however. During this time the excitement prevailing at other points in the State, which had been created by the efforts of the irreconcilables to "send their aid and assistance" to their brethren at Vicksburg, who were engaged in a "last ditch struggle" for the "supremacy of the white race, and the preservation of Southern civilization and honah, by God, sir," was not general in Yazoo. It was made so, however, by the arrival of a steamboat from Vicksburg, which brought an appeal from "our people" there for arms. It continued on up the river, stopping at all the principal landings, spreading the appeal and gathering up all the double-barrelled shotguns and rifles that were offered for the purpose.

Upon its return I went on board and saw the captain, who informed me that he was gathering the weapons for the defense of himself and his crew, for defense against a "mob of nigros gathered upon the river's bank" below Sartartia [*sic*], for the purpose of capturing his boat when it should return to Vicksburg. I placed a deputy, an ex-Confederate officer, on the boat with instructions to accompany it to the county line, and to arrest all persons who might appear with arms to do violence against it, or anyone on board. He did so, got off at the line, and returned by land. He reported that he had not been able to find any negroes with arms. On the contrary, they all appeared to be in distress at the violent proceedings of some of the whites, who were leaving that part of the county with their arms for the purpose of giving aid to their brethren at Vicksburg.

All of the proceedings I have mentioned occurred about the same time. I was able to preserve the peace of the county and protect the colored people only by ceaseless watchfulness and tireless effort, day and night. I employed at my own expense a number of special deputies, through whom I was able to keep myself informed of the plans and purposes of the enemy. One of the armed companies had already separated to their homes. To the "captain" of the Dover company I wrote [a clear and stern warning]. . . .

The night-riding and interference with peaceable colored people suddenly ceased, but the result was due, doubtless, not so much to the respect of this "captain" or of his followers for my authority, as to the fact

14 [Original author's footnote] A frequent annual gathering upon the close of the summer's work, and before cotton picking commences.

15 [Original author's footnote] The sequel proved their fidelity to him, for he escaped the legal penalty for his crime of grand larceny.

that the election at Vicksburg had passed, the irreconcilables there had triumphed, and assistance was no longer needed. But their victory had cost them dear, for it was at the time said that fully one hundred colored people were killed before they surrendered to the "superiah strategy and statesmanship" of their former masters.[16]

In Yazoo my efforts were seconded by all the colored people and by nearly all the whites who were not of the irreconcilables, or of the sleuth-hound class. A largely attended "peace-meeting" was held in the town, at which our Senator, our postmaster, the pastors of the colored churches, Mr. Foote,[17] . . . and myself were speakers.

———

A NARROW TRIUMPH in 1873, in the face of the most blatant perversion of law, brought Albert Morgan into the sheriff's office—but it was a victory overshadowed by a forbidding future. After five solid years of Reconstruction, the hard-line Democrats were still willing to resort to brute force to drive the Republicans out. In fact, their failure in Yazoo proved to be another lesson in their evolving strategy for destroying the free government of the state. The Vicksburg election of 1874 provided a test of their new tactics—widespread, brutal intimidation by tightly organized paramilitary companies, followed by perfect peace on the actual day of balloting.

The approach was the brainchild of Congressman Lucius Quintus Cincinnatus Lamar, foremost leader of the Democratic party of Mississippi and a man who matched his Latin names with a Roman appetite for blood in politics. Lamar understood what his predecessors did not: the need to maintain positive public relations with the North. He saw that economic depression and corruption scandals distracted the Yankee public from events in the South; Northern politicians were looking for an excuse *not* to send in troops. He made conciliatory speeches in Washington even as he plotted mass insurrection in Mississippi. In Vicksburg, he and his comrades perfected the method of draping an appearance of calm across the end of a campaign of terror.

Violence was not simply a matter of preference for Mississippi Democrats—it was a necessity if they were to drive out the Republican government. They faced two problems in winning elections: first, blacks were a majority, and second, Adelbert Ames turned out to be a superb governor. As Richard Nelson Current writes, he developed a balance between in-

---

[16] [Original author's footnote] The following was wired by one of the victors at that election to the chairman of the Yazoo Democratic Committee, which may explain the kind of assistance required there. The word "coon" signifies negro.

"Coons in the kanebrakes. We have taken a hundred scalps and are masters of the situation.—R.O. LEARY, *Mayor.*"

[17] Since the divisive election of 1873, Foote and Morgan had allied again.

spired progressivism and old-fashioned frugality. In his inaugural address, he called for the elimination of illiteracy, the distribution of land to African Americans, the expansion of manufacturing, and "rigid economy" in government. He made little headway with his land program, but he did end many state handouts to private companies. For example, he issued an executive order to assess and tax the previously tax-exempt railroads. He also secured a public role for women by getting the legislature to pass a local-option law for alcohol sales. It required anyone seeking a liquor license to present a petition signed by a majority of both men and women in the local district. "One of the finest features of the law is its recognition of the voices of the women of the State," the governor said. "It recognizes their equal ability with male counterparts."

Ames was the Democrats' worst nightmare: a capable, conscientious, utterly uncorrupt leader—and a Medal of Honor winner as well. So they quietly honed their strategy, running the first successful test in Vicksburg. Nor did they operate in isolation: the 1874 election across the border in Alabama was marked by much the same violence. Planning and money flowed across state lines, as the party planned its final assault on Reconstruction.

John Lynch recognized the trouble, and he determined that something had to be done. He was certainly in the right place to make a stand—the former slave, former photographer, former justice of the peace was now a member of the United States Congress. But despite his eloquent speeches and cloakroom lobbying, he faced the same factors that now favored the Democrats: a North wearied by economic woe and a Republican party torn by infighting. On the national scene, things seemed to go from bad to staggeringly bad. The collapse of the Freedmen's Savings and Trust Company (known as the Freedmen's Bank) in June 1874 was a particularly cruel blow; it not only took with it the meager financial resources of countless freed slaves and black institutions, it also further discredited the efforts made to assist African Americans since emancipation.

An even greater loss came with the death of Charles Sumner, that tireless, eloquent voice of freedom. The senator died in March; Lynch and his fellow black congressmen redoubled the fight for Sumner's greatest unfinished legacy—a new civil rights bill to ban segregation in everything from public transportation to private cemeteries, from public schools to jury selection. Governor Ames's father-in-law, Benjamin Butler, had introduced the bill; Lynch delivered a powerful speech in support. Two months after Sumner's death, Congress passed it—an unprecedented law that was enforced almost nowhere, a sad if noble marker of the quickly retreating tide of equality.

Lynch could see that things were growing gloomy indeed: when he returned to Mississippi for the election of 1875, he recognized the signs of impending disaster all about him.

Trouble on the Horizon
by John R. Lynch

In the 43rd Congress, which was elected in 1872 and which would expire by limitation March 4, 1875, the Republicans had a large majority in both Houses. In the House of Representatives of the 44th Congress, which was elected in 1874, the Democratic majority was about as large as was the Republican majority in the House of the 43rd Congress. The Republicans still retained control of the Senate, but by a greatly reduced majority.

During the short session of the 43rd Congress, important legislation was contemplated by the Republican leaders. Alabama was one of the States which the Democrats were charged with having carried in 1874 by resorting to methods which were believed to be questionable and illegal. An investigation was ordered by the House. A committee was appointed to make the investigation, of which General Allbright of Pennsylvania was chairman. This committee was authorized to report by bill or otherwise. After a thorough investigation, the chairman was directed and instructed by the vote of every Republican member of the committee, which constituted a majority thereof, to report and recommend the passage of what was called the Federal Elections Bill. This bill was carefully drawn; following substantially the same lines as a previous temporary measure, under the provisions of which what was known as the Ku Klux Klan had been crushed out, and order had been restored in North Carolina.

It is safe to say that this bill would have passed both Houses and become a law, but for the unexpected opposition of Speaker Blaine. Mr. Blaine was not only opposed to the bill, but his opposition was so intense that he felt it his duty to leave the Speaker's chair and come on the floor for the purposes of leading the opposition to its passage. This, of course, was fatal to the passage of the measure. After a desperate struggle of a few days, in which the Speaker was found to be in opposition to a large majority of his party associates, and which revealed the fact that the party was hopelessly divided, the leaders in the House abandoned the effort to bring the measure to a vote.

Mr. Blaine's motives in taking this unexpected position, in open opposition to the great majority of his party associates, has always been open to speculation and conjecture. His personal and political enemies charged that it was due to jealousy of President Grant. Mr. Blaine was a candidate for the Republican presidential nomination the following year. It was a well-known fact that President Grant was not favorable to Mr. Blaine's nomination, but was in sympathy with the movement to have Senator Roscoe Conkling, of New York, Mr. Blaine's bitterest political enemy, nominated. Mr. Blaine was afraid, his enemies asserted, that if the Federal Elections Bill—under the provisions of which great additional power would have been conferred upon the President—had become a law, that power would be used to defeat his nomination for the Presidency in 1876; hence his opposition to the bill.

But whatever his motives were, his successful opposition to that measure no doubt resulted in his failure to realize the ambition of his life—the Presidency of the United States. . . . His opposition to that bill practically solidified the Southern delegates in that convention against him, and as a result he was defeated for the nomination, although he was the choice of a majority of the Northern delegates. . . .

Although I was not favorable to his nomination for the Presidency at any time, my relations with Mr. Blaine had been so cordial that I felt at liberty to seek him and ask him, for my own satisfaction and information, an explanation for his action in opposing and defeating the Federal Elections Bill. . . . He requested me to come to the Speaker's room immediately after the adjournment of the House that afternoon.

When I entered the room Mr. Blaine was alone. I took a seat only a few feet from him. I informed him of the great disappointment and intense dissatisfaction which his action had caused in defeating what was not only regarded as a party measure, but which was believed by the Republicans to be of vital importance from a party point of view, to say nothing of its equity and justice. I remarked that for him to array himself in opposition to the great majority of his own party associates—and to throw the weight of his great influence against such an important party measure as the Federal Elections Bill was believed to be—he must have had some motive, some justifiable grounds of which the public was ignorant, but about which I believed it was fair to himself and just to his friends and party associates, that he give some explanation. "As a Southern Republican member of the House, and as one that is not hostile or particularly unfriendly to you," I said, "I feel that I have a right to make this request of you."

At first he gave me a look of surprise, and for several seconds he remained silent. Then, straightening himself up in his chair, he answered: "I am glad, Mr. Lynch, that you have made this request of me, since I am satisfied you are not actuated by any unfriendly motive in doing so. I shall, therefore, give a frank answer to your question. In my judgment, if that bill had become the law the defeat of the Republican party throughout the country would have been a foregone conclusion. We could not have saved the South even if the bill had passed, but its passage would have lost us the North; indeed, I could not have carried even my own State of Maine, if that bill had passed. In my opinion, it was better to lose the South and save the North, than to try through such legislation to save the South, and thus lose both North and South. I believed that if we saved the North we could then look after the South. If the Southern Democrats are foolish enough to bring about a Solid South the result will be a Solid North against a Solid South; and in that case the Republicans have nothing to fear. You now have my reasons, frankly and candidly given, for the action taken by me on the occasion referred to. I hope you are satisfied with them."

I thanked Mr. Blaine cordially for giving me the desired explanation. "I now feel better satisfied with reference to your action upon that occasion," I assured him. "While I do not agree with you in your conclusions, and while I believe your reasoning to be unsound and fallacious, still I cannot help giving you credit for having been actuated by no other motive than to do what you honestly believed was for the best interest of the country and the Republican party."

STATE CAMPAIGN OF 1875

When I returned to my home after the adjournment of Congress in March, 1875, the political clouds were dark. The political outlook was discouraging. The prospects of Republican success were not at all bright. There had been a marked change in the situation from every point of view. Democrats were bold, outspoken, defiant, and determined. In addition to these unfavorable indications I noticed that I was not received by them with the same warmth and cordiality as on previous occasions. With a few notable exceptions they were cold, indifferent, even forbidding in their attitude and manner. This treatment was so radically different from that to which I had been accustomed that I could not help feeling it keenly. I knew it was indicative of a change in the political situation which meant that I had before me the fight of my life.

My advocacy and support of the Federal Elections Bill, commonly called the "Force Bill," was occasionally given as the reason for the change; but I knew this was not the true reason. In fact, that bill would hardly have been thought of but for the fact that Mr. Blaine, the Republican speaker of the House, had attracted national attention to it through his action in vacating the chair and coming on the floor of the House to lead the opposition to its passage. This act on the part of the statesman from Maine made him, in the opinion of many Southern Democrats, the greatest man that our country had ever produced—George Washington, the Father of the Republic, not excepted. . . .

I was well aware of the fact at the time that it was the result of the State and Congressional elections at the North in 1874 that had convinced Southern Democrats that Republican ascendency in the National Government would soon be a thing of the past—that the Democrats would be successful in the Presidential and Congressional elections of 1876 and that that party would, no doubt, remain in power for at least a quarter of a century. It was this, and not the unsuccessful effort to pass a Federal Elections Bill, that had produced the marked change that was noticeable on every hand. Every indication seemed to point to a confirmation of the impression that Democratic success at the Presidential election was practically an assured fact.

There had been a disastrous financial panic in 1873 which was no doubt largely responsible for the political upheaval of 1874; but that was lost sight of in accounting for the result. In fact they made no effort to explain it except in their own way. The Democrats had carried the country; the reasons for this they construed to suit themselves. The construction they placed upon it was a national condemnation and repudiation of the Congressional Plan of Reconstruction, and they intended to govern themselves accordingly.

The election in Mississippi in 1875 was for members of Congress, members of the Legislature, and county officers, and also a State Treasurer to serve out the unexpired term of Treasurer Holland, deceased. My own renomination for Congress from the Sixth (Natchez) District was a foregone conclusion, since I had no opposition in my own party; but I realized the painful fact that a nomination this time was not equivalent to an election. Still, I felt that it was my duty to make a fight, let the result be what it might. . . .

The administration of Governor Ames was one of the best the State had ever had. The judiciary was quite equal to that which had been appointed by Governor Alcorn. The public revenues had been promptly collected, and honestly accounted for. There had not only been no increase in the rate of taxation, but, to the contrary, there had been a material reduction. Notwithstanding these things the Democrats, together with the radical element in charge of the party machinery, determined to seize the State Government *vi et armis*; not because it was at all necessary for any special reason, but simply because conditions at that time seemed to indicate that it could be safely done.

A DARK CLOUD obscured the shining star of Reconstruction. By early 1875, Mississippi stood out clearly as the best-run state in the South, if not the nation as a whole. Thanks to the heroism and skill of men such as Albert Morgan, John Lynch, and Adelbert Ames, it had survived the disasters that had already overwhelmed most of the Reconstruction governments. Indeed, it had gone on to rebuild itself as no other state had, with a lack of corruption that New Yorkers, for example, could only dream of. But the Democrats had learned their lesson; when the time came for the election of 1875, they would strike with a ruthlessness scarcely seen anywhere in American history. For Republicans, the question was whether the distracted President and the now-divided Congress would stand by them one more time.

21

THE SHADOWS DEEPEN, PART II:
THE RING TAKES FRIGHT

Nothing has a single cause in history. So it was with the death rattle of the age of Grant—a towering yet rickety structure of hope and greed, constructed from golden nails and rotten planks. It shook with the winds of economic depression, of the reforming spirit, of personal ambition, of raw hatred and violence. In 1875, however, one John McDonald of St. Louis had little time to ponder abstract forces: his troubles had a single name, and the name was Benjamin Bristow.

The gales of economics had blown Mr. Bristow into Grant's cabinet, almost against the President's will. Some time earlier, the highly capable George Boutwell had resigned from his post as treasury secretary to take his place as the new United States senator for Massachusetts. He had been replaced by William Richardson. But Richardson was soon undermined by yet another scandal: as assistant secretary of the treasury, he had signed up a man named John D. Sanborn to work on commission to find delinquent taxpayers. Sanborn earned plenty, but he only identified culprits already known to the treasury department. Richardson's opponents seized upon the Sanborn scandal as an excuse to force him out of office: his real crime, in their eyes, was that he was a soft-money man, in favor of expanding the supply of greenbacks. The Republican party was increasingly becoming the party of a business establishment that wanted low-inflation, specie-backed currency. And so the party elders thrust into Grant's arms Benjamin Bristow, a man untarnished by scandal and glowing with a luster of gold.

As Bristow took charge of the treasury department on June 2, 1874, the Whiskey Ring saw no reason to worry. John McDonald had the operations well in hand in St. Louis, Orville Babcock had the ear of President Grant, and their man J. W. Douglass controlled the Internal Revenue Bureau. Bristow's contractionist policies might hurt the average farmer and worker, but that mattered little to the men in the bribery-and-kickback business. But they soon discovered, as William McFeely writes, that "Bristow possessed that sticky double commodity, principle and ambition, and he was in the uncommon position of being able to rise to the first while advancing to the second." The treasury secretary found that he could best win the public's acclaim not by destroying the green-back supply, but by wiping out the Whiskey Ring.

In the passage that follows, ringmaster John McDonald describes the panic that followed word of Bristow's investigation. He offers an inside look at the frenzied response of the frightened conspirators: the cryptic telegrams, the secret meetings. He and his assistant Colonel Joyce worked feverishly to stop it—but Grant had other ideas. The old soldier knew what it was like to be surrounded and surprised by enemy forces, and he had always won by calmly proceeding with his own plans. As General William T. Sherman said, Grant never gave a thought to what the foe was up to, over the hill and out of sight. Furthermore, he was fiercely loyal to his friends and subordinates. So when McDonald and Joyce panicked at the onset of Secretary Bristow, the President refused to retreat, choosing instead to fight it out on that line if it took all summer—or the rest of his term.

A Worrisome Investigation
by John McDonald

On the 26th of January, 1875, Mr. Bristow, who had circulated suspicions that the Government was being defrauded out of the revenue on whiskey manufactured in several large cities in the country, decided to inaugurate an investigation by ordering a change of supervisors, so that frauds would undoubtedly appear, because of the lack of understanding between the distillers and the new officials; or, if there were any honest supervisors, they would readily detect the manner in which the frauds were being perpetrated.

Let me remark, however, that everyone engaged in the illicit whiskey frauds knew that Bristow's investigation meant something; that he was exceedingly anxious to ferret out the guilty parties and bring them to punishment; hence, every act of his was watched with painful interest, and we were compelled to use the full influence of the President to keep Bristow from enforcing orders which would be certain to expose the Ring and every member of it.

When this order for a change of supervisors was issued (to take effect Feb. 15th), by which I should have been transferred to Philadelphia, I realized the necessity of having it countermanded at once, to accomplish which I sent the following dispatch:

St. Louis, Feb. 3d, 1875

Hon. J.W. Douglass, Internal Revenue Office, Washington:
Don't like the order; it will damage the Government and injure the
administration. Will explain when I see you.

John McDonald

On the day after I transmitted this telegram, I sent Col. Joyce to Washington to influence the countermanding of this order, but before his departure I was gratified by the receipt of the following telegram:

Washington, Feb. 4th, 1875

Gen. Jno. McDonald, St. Louis:
The order transferring you to Philadelphia is suspended until further
orders.

(Signed) J.W. Douglass, Commissioner

Immediately after receiving this, the following dispatch was repeated
to me over the wires, which showed me at once the cause for the unexpected telegram from the Commissioner:

Executive Mansion,
Washington, Feb. 4th, 1875

J.W. Douglass, Internal Revenue Office.
Sir:—The President directs me to say that he desires the circular
order, transferring Supervisors of Internal Revenue, be suspended,
by telegraph, until further orders.

(Signed) Levi P. Luckey

(NOTE—Luckey was Assistant Secretary to the President.)
Upon receipt of this Col. Joyce, before departing, sent the following
dispatch:

St. Louis, Feb. 4th, 1875

To Gen. O.E. Babcock, Washington:
We have information that the enemy weakens. Push things.
(Signed)   Sylph [18]

Col. Joyce then left for Washington for the purpose of seeing the President, and our friends there, with relation to the order. The President

18 "Sylph" was a code name the members of the Ring used to communicate with
each other by telegraph.

suspended the order that we might have the necessary time to straighten out our crooked affairs, but concluded at that time to permit the transfer order to go into effect when we should inform him that affairs would permit it without exposure. But we had all things in such excellent working condition in St. Louis that I was anxious to avoid a change. It was with this understanding Col. Joyce started for Washington. . . .

After his arrival in Washington, Col. Joyce went direct to the President and to Gen. Babcock, and to them explained the situation and the views I entertained, as here indicated. After receiving their assurances that all our wishes should be respected, even at the expense of Bristow's serious displeasure, Col. Joyce sent me [a reassuring] dispatch. . . . Notwithstanding the favorable turn affairs had taken at Washington, yet there was a feeling of great dread, because I was sure that Bristow was determined to push his investigation by some adroit means.

In the early part of March I ascertained that Geo. W. Fishback, formerly proprietor of the *Missouri Democrat,* was in Washington, and my suspicions were aroused that his visit was in the capacity of an informer. My reasons for entertaining such an idea were based upon a circumstance which transpired some time previously, to which I must direct the reader's attention. It was pretty generally known in St. Louis that just prior to the absorption of the *Democrat* by the *Globe,* the proprietors of the former were often in sore straits for the necessary money to continue the publication of the paper. In one of these impecunious moments Mr. Fishback came to my room at the Planters House, and after a little preliminary conversation, introduced the object of his visit. He explained to me the financial embarrassment from which his paper suffered and urged me to loan him the sum of $5,000 for ninety days, in consideration of which he proffered me the support of the *Democrat.* In his pleadings he remarked that he could not see why I should refuse him the use of a few thousand dollars of the Government's money.

My reply to him was that I was not a bonded officer; that I did not handle a dollar of the Government's money as my duties were entirely supervisory. Finding all other resources failing him, he finally submitted to me an editorial article highly commendatory of my official acts as Supervisor, and exalting my influence as a Republican, and told me that if I would let him have the money he would print the article in the editorial columns of the *Democrat* the following day. But to all his entreaties I turned a deaf ear, not regarding the influence of his paper as at all consequential. From that time Mr. Fishback became an active and insidious enemy of mine, and through intimate social relations he held with one of the distillers, he obtained some information concerning the conduct of the Ring.

With this explanation my anxiety to learn the object of his visit to Washington at this particular time is obvious. I therefore wrote to Gen. Babcock, telling him of my fears and asking him to casually meet Fishback and learn what he was doing. In reply to this enquiry I received [assurances that he was there on innocuous business] . . .

For a short while I was satisfied, but when I began considering the information Fishback was in possession of I felt certain that the distiller from whom he had learned so much had not neglected to tell him also that Babcock was a member of the Ring. Then the fact dawned upon me that Fishback's appearance of friendship and his assertion that he was looking after river improvements was only used to deceive Babcock as to his real purpose. My suspicions were then resting upon important facts as was afterwards proven. Mr. Fishback became a strong supporter of Bristow and gave him all the information in his possession, besides which he suggested to the Secretary a means for verifying his statements, by appointing a man who had been a commercial reporter of the *Democrat* as special agent to examine the receipts and shipments of grain and whiskey at St. Louis for the past several years.

We had been running the distilleries crooked from the time Col. Joyce returned from Washington until some time in March, when the pacific condition of our affairs was suddenly interrupted by the appearance of revenue agent Yaryan, whose ostensible purpose was the investigation of railroad back taxes. But he was suspected and the distilleries shut down at once, while Yaryan, to carry his deception further, left St. Louis for Richmond, Ind., but returned after an absence of only a few days. During Yaryan's absence, Holmes, a clerk in the Fraud Division of the Internal Revenue Bureau, came to St. Louis, explaining his visit as connected with the Knights Templar business. But his story was not believed and a sharp watch was kept upon his movements, and I soon learned that he was there as an aid to Yaryan to make an investigation. . . .

THE RING TAKES FRIGHT

The visit of Yaryan in March and April, 1875, was the first effective step taken to lay bare the frauds of the Whiskey Ring. Yaryan had already . . . discovered enough fraud to have exposed the illicit combination, but it is perhaps doubtful whether he could have secured a conviction of any of the members save, possibly, two or three distillers, upon the evidence he had then collected. But the circle in which the organization was now uneasily operating grew constantly smaller. . . .

My serious alarms were excited that some treachery was being practiced, and to discover the source I determined to go to Washington and confer with the President. Accordingly, on the evening of the 19th [of April], I left St. Louis for the Capital. Upon my arrival there, on the morning of the 21st, I found that the President, Gen. Babcock, and Secretary Belknap, were in Boston attending the Jubilee. I stopped at the Arlington House, where I met Senator Dorsey of Arkansas, and to him I told my story of the manner in which Secretary Bristow was interfering with my affairs.

The Senator advised me to join him in a determined effort to influence the President to dismiss Bristow, a suggestion which, if I had acted upon, would have undoubtedly prevented any exposure of the Ring; but, without disclosing to him the methods I had intended to pursue, I left him and called at the Treasury Department, where I formally met Secretary Bristow, addressing him with only a single inquiry, viz.: "Did you send Mr. Holmes into my district?" His reply was: "If my memory serves me right, I did."

I left him without conversing any further, and went over to the Internal Revenue Bureau where I met Commissioner Douglass, and with him I held an interview in which I sought to learn who was responsible for the appearance of revenue agents in my district. Taking a seat beside his desk I asked him what Holmes and Yaryan were doing in my district without my being informed first of their coming. He replied: "Why, they are not in your district; Mr. Holmes is now in the department."

I informed him of his mistake, but to be convinced, he sent a messenger to Holmes's room, and there learned that he had been granted a leave of absence for a few days by Secretary Bristow. This confused the Commissioner, especially after I told him that the Secretary had informed me, only a few moments before, that he had sent Holmes into my district.

The Commissioner arose in a somewhat excited manner, and remarked that he would see the Secretary and learn why he had not been consulted in this matter. He went over to see Secretary Bristow, while I awaited his return. He was absent about half an hour, and when he came back I saw a marked change in his appearance. He seemed loth to announce the result of his visit to the Secretary, and when I inquired of him what had passed between them, he said: "Well, General, the fact is, I cannot tell you just now; but will explain everything before you leave Washington. But I can assure you that no damage to you will result from the investigation." I then left the Commissioner, and spent the remainder of the day at the Washington Club House, playing billiards and talking to officials.

On the following morning, as I entered the dining hall of the Arlington House, I was somewhat surprised to see there some St. Louis friends and Senator Dorsey, whom I greeted, and then I noticed Secretary Bristow seated at a table across the room, and when he caught my gaze he motioned to me to come over to his table. When I approached him, he insisted upon me taking a seat at his table, which I did, when the following conversation occurred.

Said he: "How are you getting on with revenue matters in your district?"

I replied that I was collecting all the revenue—and this was true at the time, for all the distilleries were running straight then.

He pressed the query further, by adding: "How long have you been collecting all the revenue in your district?"

I answered: "Ever since the arrival of the officers you last sent into my district. But," said I, "I presume you get daily reports from those agents" (referring to Yaryan and Holmes), "now at St. Louis, and know fully as much as I do."

"Yes," he replied, "I get reports from out there, and have collected considerable evidence."

I inquired of him the nature of his evidence, but he responded by saying: "Well, I can't exactly tell you that, but I have got a barrel of it" (at the same time spreading his arms, and bringing his fingers together in a gesture, showing it was so large round), "but as yet it implicates only the distillers and dealers."

Then I inquired if he was after the officers, too.

"Oh, no," he replied, "I am only trying to collect the revenue. I have been aware of the fact that for a great while the revenue has not been collected." And he added: "What portion of the revenue has been collected in your section of the country?"

I answered that in my opinion, about two thirds. He then asked me if I didn't think it could all be collected. I told him it might be under certain circumstances; he then desired to know what circumstances were essential. I answered him by saying that the first thing necessary would be an entire change of officers, and an increase of the number of officers as the labor was too great for the number then employed.

He further consulted my opinion respecting my belief in the ability of the same number of officers to collect the revenue, provided the officers were honest. To this I made answer that if the officers would renounce politics and could secure honest subordinates it might be possible, but, I added, as the service is now organized I think it extremely doubtful if you can increase the collections. . . .

His next enquiry was: "Have you come to Washington with the intention of resigning?"

I replied that I had not. "But," said I, "I have canvassed the situation in my own mind since my arrival here and concluded to have a talk with the President and Gen. Babcock, and, if they do not change my mind, I shall resign, as I do not wish to fight a buzz-saw in this matter."

He asked me what I meant by the use of such an expression. My answer was that he was my superior officer and had authority to send men into my district and make investigations whenever he should choose, and that I could not retain my self-respect and permit that to be done without their coming with instructions to report to me; that I was a friend of the President and of Gen. Babcock and that whatever I had done in my district was in good faith.

He assured me that he was not fighting the President's friends but was only seeking to collect the revenue. . . . He was anxious to learn if the

Government officers at St. Louis could be relied upon to prosecute parties guilty of violations of revenue laws.

I replied that they could, but I doubted the expediency of the Government bringing suits against the distillers and rectifiers for two reasons, which I explained as follows: These men, said I, have been led to believe that the money they have paid upon the whiskey they have illicitly manufactured was used for political purposes, and that their operations have been sanctioned not only by the district officers, but also by that power which recognizes no superior; that prosecutions would result in closing the distilleries and thereby entirely close that source of revenue. The second reason I assigned was its inexpediency because of the injury it would entail upon the Republican party by arraying against it the most efficient workers within its ranks.

He told me that, while he was anxious to preserve and secure the further success of the Republican party, that he made his duties as an officer of the nation paramount to his allegiance to party, and that, regardless of political results, he would collect the revenue.

I admired the sentiments of the Secretary, as I told him, but I also expressed to him my grave doubts of his ability to withstand a fight which his contemplated actions invited, and assured him that his first efforts would arouse a political spirit like an avenging Nemesis, and that his opposition would come from a higher power than perhaps he had considered. . . .

This last answer of mine somewhat confused him for, after a pause which indicated a gathering of ideas, he asked me if I had seen the President since my arrival in Washington. I replied that I had not, but that I was waiting his return from Boston, and was anxious to see him.

Then, with some anxiety pictured in his face, he inquired if I intended talking with the President upon this matter in the same direct and pointed manner I had spoken with him (the Secretary).

Said I: "General, I shall talk to the President not only as plainly as I have talked with you but I shall be much less reserved in my conversation with him."

He then asked if, after my intended interview with the President, I would return to him and report the substance and result of my conversation. My reply was that I would repeat to him so much of the interview as would be agreeable to the President, but that, as the matter would be canvassed between us in a confidential manner, I could not betray any trusts.

The Secretary remarked that he was aware that I occupied a more intimate and influential relation with the President than any other person in the West.

This closed our conversation, which had lasted about two hours. When I went out into the hotel office, I learned that the President and Gen. Babcock had returned from Boston; so I went directly to the White House, where I was fortunate, upon entering the Executive room, to find the President alone. I drew a chair up near him, and after passing a very few words of general remark, I proceeded directly to disclose the object of my visit.

I first explained to him that my district was being visited by revenue agents without my knowledge; that there was a veil of secrecy over the actions of the Secretary in matters wherein I was deeply interested and in which I should have been consulted, and that this secrecy also prevented the Commissioner of Internal Revenue from giving me instructions, so that there was a rapidly widening breach in the revenue service; that if the policy outlined by Secretary Bristow should be pursued, it would result in the destruction of the Republican party.

To this the President replied that he had talked with the Secretary concerning the collection of information by revenue agents, but that his idea was that the evidence thus gathered should not be used against the revenue officers, but only against the distillers and businessmen; that he had thought such action even a wise party act.

To this I replied by assuring him that the officers were too intimately associated with the distillers and rectifiers to escape an exposed connection should prosecutions be begun; that these men had been the largest contributors to the campaign fund when the collections were applied to that purpose, but that for a long time past the money thus raised had gone into the pockets of individuals, as he well knew. In addition to this, I reminded him that if the prosecutions were based upon conclusive evidence, that the distillers and rectifiers would not alone suffer, but that the officers and *everyone having guilty knowledge* would be liable to the same punishment. I told him further that these agents, in getting this evidence, would be certain, almost, to leak some of their information, which would run directly into the newspapers.

To this the President responded that the papers were so full of scandals that unless the proof were furnished, their reports would hardly be credited by the public. He told me that when the agents made their investigations, their reports could easily be controlled in the Department, and that they should be.

I argued with him that the safest plan would be to recall the agents, because, said I, if they get this evidence, it is certain, sooner or later, to obtain publicity. I also gave him my impressions concerning the intentions of Secretary Bristow, which were that, if unrestrained, the investigations would be most searching, and with a mountain of searing evidence, it could not be hidden from the public. I further told him that the Secretary had already assured me he had "a barrel" of information, sufficient to convict a large number of the distillers and rectifiers.

The President then said: "What disposition, in your judgment, should be made of the evidence?"

My reply was that it ought to be shoved into a red-hot stove.

Said he: "Well, I hardly think it would be policy to burn it up," but, said he, "don't you think it would be a good plan to have it all sealed up securely and placed in a vault where no one could get at it?"

I answered, that would subserve present necessities, but that it would be resurrected sometime, when there was a change of officers. He then told me he would prevent a further accumulation of the evidence by having the agents recalled, and that he would confer with the Secretary as to the most desirable means for preventing any of the evidence from becoming public.

I responded by saying: "Well, General, if you have an understanding with the Secretary, you can control things." He acknowledged that he had no understanding with the Secretary, but that, at all events, the evidence would be controlled.

I remarked: "You and the Secretary ought to work together."

His response was: "Yes, we ought to; but if we don't, one of us will have to quit, and it will not be me."

I said: "No, I don't presume it will be you, as your time is fixed by the public, and the Secretary's tenure depends upon individual pleasure." He then asked me what effects Bristow's action would have in other districts, and upon the party. I told him that, as he understood everything that had been going on in my district, it was only necessary for me to assure him that the same condition of affairs existed throughout the entire country and in every district; that if the matter were allowed to reach the public it could no more be stopped than the waves of the ocean before the wind; that it would expose the internal operations of the Republican party, the sources from whence its life was derived, and that the party would collapse like a balloon rent by lightning.

He manifested much anxiety, and was, indeed, sorely agitated. His response to my opinion was: "Well, it *must* be stopped." . . .

The President expressed his anxiety to have me . . . tell the Secretary to carefully guard the evidence he had against the possibility of publicity until he (Grant) could confer with him (Bristow) as to its disposition. I replied to him that I would go over and see the Secretary and report in the evening or following morning. I then arose to go, and as I did so, made the remark that I had a package of money for Gen. Babcock, which I intended to deliver.

"Yes," he replied, "Bab" (as he almost always called Gen. Babcock), "is in his office."

I walked into the private secretary's room but found it full of visitors, so that I did not speak to Gen. Babcock for a few moments. When I caught his attention I greeted him, and in a *sotto*-voice, informed him that I had a package for him.

He told me that, as he had just returned from Boston and was very busy, he could not talk with me then, but asked me to dine with him at 5 p.m.; that his family was out of the city and that he would be alone.

I then left the White House and started to the Treasury Department, but, on the plateau between the White House and Treasury, I met Secretary Bristow on his way to see the President. We stopped and entered into a conversation, in which I informed him that I had just left the President, having been engaged with him ever since leaving the breakfast table.

He asked me if I had talked freely with the President. I told him that I had, and thereupon repeated to him nearly everything the President had told me, including his desire to have the evidence referred to carefully guarded until the President should confer with him. I did not forget to tell Mr. Bristow that I had told the President the best disposition to make of the evidence was to shove it into a red-hot stove, but that the President thought a better plan would be to seal it up securely and place it where there was no possibility of anyone seeing it.

Mr. Bristow smiled, and remarked that he had not secured the evidence for such a purpose, and then asked me to go over to his office and wait for his return, as he desired to talk further with me. . . .

I went over to the Secretary's office and waited there nearly an hour before Mr. Bristow returned. When he came in we held a general conversation in which we went over the same subject as in the morning and my conference with the President. I then asked him if he had consulted with the President with regard to the disposition of the evidence. He replied that the subject had been mentioned. I then asked him if the President had suggested to him the destruction of the evidence, or sealing it up to prevent its publicity or use. His reply was that the matter was talked about but no conclusion had been reached. I inquired of him if he and the President had disagreed. He said that the President's views were not exactly like his own, but thought they would be in accord in the course of a few days.

I became convinced that the Secretary was not talking to me without reserve, and that he was keeping his own decisions from me, so I began making inquiries to ascertain what he proposed to do in my district; whether he intended making seizures, etc. He told me that he thought he would seize the property of the distillers and rectifiers, against whom he had evidence. I suggested to him a more advisable course in submitting a proposition that would compromise the trouble. I told him that I thought these men would pay up all the back taxes and settle with the government, which would prevent them from being broken up. He told me that he had not thought of this, but that he should consult the best interest of the Government before taking any final action.

Here we dropped the subject, and he requested me to call upon him frequently while in the city that we might talk further upon the matter. After assuring him that I would, we parted.

From the Secretary's office I called on Commissioner Douglass with whom I had some conversation, in the course of which I told him that after considering the indignities of Mr. Bristow, I had concluded to resign. He said he did not blame me for having such an intention, and assured me that he had a strong inclination to do the same thing.

I did not remain long with the Commissioner, and went over to the Washington Club House, where I played billiards and talked with friends until 5 o'clock, p.m., when I went to Gen. Babcock's residence. I found Gen. Babcock and Gen. Horace Porter at the house together, but in order to meet me privately Gen. B. invited me to go upstairs with him to see a newly fitted-up room, and a bullfinch which he had recently purchased. . . .

When we were alone he offered me a chair and we sat down and had a lengthy conversation. But before we had talked long I drew a package containing $5,000 from my side pocket and gave it to him. This money had been collected by Col. Joyce before his departure for Kansas City and given to me for delivery to Gen. Babcock, as I was then expecting to visit Washington. He thanked me for the money, saying at the same time, "Well, it isn't much, but it is very acceptable at this time."

At this juncture the doorbell rang to tell the General that there was a gentleman at the door who wished to see him. He went downstairs, but after an absence of a few minutes he returned with a piece of paper in his hand, which he handed to me with the remark, "There, now, General, you see how our money goes." I looked at the paper and saw that it was a receipt for $500, signed by Krounce, the Washington correspondent of the *New York Times*. He then explained to me that the money was paid for the appearance of an article in the *Times* in relation to some change of officers in Boston, which this article was intended to prepare an excuse for.

I told him that he ought not to grumble if he got value received. He replied that it was not grumbling, but that the demands for money were so numerous that at times he was sorely puzzled to raise necessary funds. We then conversed upon the subject matter I had discussed with Secretary Bristow and the President. I repeated to him my intention to resign and get out of the service.

He advised me to do so, saying at the same time that if I would leave St. Louis and go to New York, that we could arrange schemes there to make a great deal more money than we had derived from the Whiskey Ring; that I would be worth a great deal more to them in New York (meaning himself and the President) than I was in the West. We talked perhaps half an hour when he took me into the front room and showed me the bullfinch, which sang until I was perfectly enraptured with it. He then told me that he had purchased the bird for my wife.

We went downstairs, and shortly afterwards dinner was announced. While dining, Secretary [of War] Belknap came in and, on invitation, sat down with us. After dinner, Belknap and Porter left, and Gen. Babcock and I went into the billiard room and played billiards, and continued our conversation on the contemplated action of Secretary Bristow, until nearly midnight. . . . He also informed me that an effort was being made to dismiss Belknap, but he said that scheme would not work. He talked considerably about me going to New York, but did not say what special position he wanted me to occupy. . . .

I left Gen. Babcock and went into the Executive room, where I met the President, with whom I had some further conversation on the Bristow investigation. I asked him if he had conferred with the Secretary on the matter of the evidence collected.

He replied that he had talked some to the Secretary about it, but not enough to settle the matter. He said that he was not fully convinced of Mr. Bristow's intentions, though, said he, "The Secretary seems to be a little arbitrary, but there shall be no trouble."

Said I: "General, you don't mean for me to infer that the Secretary is manifesting open hostility to you?"

"Oh no, no," replied the President, "not that, but he merely shows a decided wish to have his own way, which will not be permitted, unless he changes present apparent inclinations."

"Well," I remarked, "I should like to get an idea of what I may expect, so as to be prepared for any policy."

The President spoke up quickly, saying: "If any new phase develops important for you to know, I will write you at once."

I interposed an immediate objection, telling him that he must not think of writing, as my correspondence was liable at any time to fall into the hands of detectives, reminding him that already two or three important letters addressed to me had been intercepted or stolen. After a few moments further conversation, I told the President that I had made up my mind, after considering the matter fully, to tender my resignation. His reply was: "Oh, don't do that, I assure you that no trouble growing out of this matter will affect you, and besides, I don't know who could fill your position out there, taking care of the newspapers, etc." I replied to him that I would again consult with the Secretary and Commissioner, after which I would let him know definitely what I proposed to do. . . .

I went to the Club House where I drafted my resignation . . . I took the letter over to the Secretary [Bristow] and showed it to him. He pronounced it a fine letter, and said that while he had hardly expected me to take such a step, yet he thought it a proper one. I sat and conversed with him quite a time, repeating much that had previously passed between us. I told him that my impression was he was getting into deep water, but that I proposed to step aside and let him sail his own boat. Another remark I made was in declaring that while I was in politics I always made everything subservient to party, and that all my efforts had been centralized in making the Republican party a success.

His reply was that that was an element in the party which was doing it a great injury; that an honest collection of the revenue and a thorough discharge of official duties would do much more towards perpetuating the party than a distribution of money obtained by corrupt practices. "Yes," said I, "my ideas are so different from those of others in the party, that it is better for me to get out"; that I would tender my resignation and return to St. Louis that night. . . .

I left the Secretary and again went to the Club House, where I remained until about four o'clock, when I returned to the White House. As I entered the front door I met the President and Mrs. Grant coming out to take a ride, the team which I had given the President being in waiting for them. I addressed the President, telling him that I had my resignation with me which I wished to give him. He replied, "Well, I am just going out riding; can't you come in to-morrow?" I told him that I intended leaving Washington that night and that I would like for him to receive my resignation then. "Well," said he, "if that is so, why, you can hand it to me."

I gave him the letter and he stepped aside to read it. Mrs. Grant and I then entered into a short conversation in which she assured me that the team I had given the President had afforded them more pleasure than anything they had ever possessed. . . . When the President had examined the letter a few moments he turned to me and with a significant smile on his face he remarked, as he placed it in the inside pocket of his coat: "I'll take care of this," leaving the inference that he would not accept my resignation unless it became necessary, a circumstance he did not anticipate. . . . Soon afterwards I took the train for St. Louis, since which time I have never seen Mr. Bristow. . . .

Immediately upon my return from Washington I held a conference with all the U.S. Revenue officers in St. Louis with relation to their resignations. Col. Joyce tendered his resignation about the 27th, and Collector Maguire adopted the same course in a day or two after. I went directly to Wm. McKee, who was still publishing the *Globe*, on Third near Pine street, and explained the situation to him thoroughly. He manifested the greatest alarm, and begged me to see him daily and report the actions of the government. I was then in almost daily correspondence with Gen. Babcock, and upon receipt of his letters I would take them down to the *Globe* office, where I usually found Mr. McKee and Collector Maguire, and together we would read them.

The draw-strings of the Government kept squeezing the Ring tighter, and we began seriously to reflect upon the probability of our own punishment. In my correspondence with Gen. Babcock I did not neglect to acquaint him with our fears, and ask his interposition to prevent a collapse that would entail disaster.

"THE DRAW-STRINGS of the government," as McDonald calls them, did indeed draw tighter and tighter around the Ring. And yet Grant hesitated. He was in a far tighter place than he had ever been during the

Civil War; his friends knew that he would rather be surrounded by enemy troops, as he had been at Belmont or Vicksburg, than hemmed between his own treasury secretary and his congressional opponents. Perhaps, he mused, the investigation might be allowed to run a limited course, to make a great show of honesty by snaring a few guilty men.

But not all—for no matter what we think of McDonald's veracity, there can be little doubt that Grant knew Babcock was in illicit whiskey money up to his chin, and Babcock was one of the few friends he had left. Increasingly he felt besieged: his foes were calling for the heads of his loyal subordinates; the people had repudiated his leadership and elected a Democratic House of Representatives; his feud with the late Senator Sumner had even damaged his relationship with congressional Republicans. Distracted and embittered, he would have trouble simply paying attention when, that same dark year, an armed insurrection exploded in the heart of the fallen Confederacy.

VIII

DARKNESS

THE REPUBLICAN FAILURE

1875–1877

22

THE GREAT MISSISSIPPI REBELLION

The time had come for an end to Reconstruction in Mississippi. As 1875 began, this chilling fear ran through two men who knew the state well—as well as anyone, in fact, for they had helped make it what it was. One black, one white, one a United States congressman and the other a county sheriff, both Republicans and both believers in the equality of all races: John Lynch and Albert Morgan had fought for almost a decade to revolutionize a place where a minority of the population had long held the majority in slavery. The slavery was gone for good, but the white minority had never given up its determination to resume control.

Congressman L. Q. C. Lamar knew that 1875 was a good year to strike. His thousands of fellow Democrats had been organizing, arming, and drilling in military tactics for many months; his strategy had been perfected in the local election in Vicksburg; his comrades in neighboring Tennessee and Alabama had just destroyed their own Reconstruction governments, using similar means. Most important of all, the possibility of federal intervention was at a minimum. It was only with the help of Washington that blacks had ever come into their political inheritance—otherwise they could never have overcome the wealth and firepower commanded by the white elite. But an economic depression had swept Democrats into the House of Representatives, and President Grant was besieged by a corruption investigation that even now was reaching into the White House itself.

What could the Republicans do? Governor Ames, Sheriff Morgan, and Congressman Lynch asked themselves that daily, as 1874 passed away into an increasingly violent 1875. Could the state militia handle the Democratic gangs? The white militiamen could not be trusted, and purely black units might alienate the last remaining white Republicans. The only hope was in regular army troops—but who would believe that a true rebellion had broken out once more in the South?

The Armed Companies
by Albert T. Morgan

According to estimates made by myself in the fall of 1874, there were at that time three hundred colored men owning real estate in Yazoo

County. These holdings varied from a small house and lot in town, to more than two-thousand-acre tracts of cotton and corn land. Several of the colored planters were in quite independent circumstances. Their wives and their daughters no longer worked in the cotton and corn fields. Each one owned a carriage, not always of the best pattern, to be sure, but ample for the family and sufficiently elegant in appointments for country uses. . . . Many more colored men owned livestock; horses, mules, cows, sheep, hogs, and chickens were innumerable. The total real value of the property of the colored people of Yazoo at that date, was not less than a million and a half dollars. They were in truth rising. Indeed, there was danger that "our nigros" would, before long, own the whole county.

Besides, the overthrow of free government in the surrounding States, particularly in Alabama and Tennessee, was forcing the more enterprising colored families into Mississippi, where, under our Republican government, there was better security for persons, and more certain returns for their toil. This negro immigration was styled by the irreconcilables, a "black cloud threatening the supremacy of the white race." The marvelous fecundity of that race, their physical strength and powers of endurance, their wonderful progress in the science of politics, and their boundless ambition, as fully recognized by the leading minds among the enemy as by myself, and much more than by the people of the Northland, had completely changed the character of the *free* negro question from one of doubt and sincere apprehension of his ability to survive, to one of the white man's ability to do so while in the presence of the negro and while the conditions of existence were equal. The greatest minds in the State, on the "superior side of the line," were gravely debating the question, which would be the wiser policy for the white man, emigration and the abandonment of the State to the negro, or a general arming of the white race with the purpose of checking by force the "threatened supremacy" of the negro race. To such persons these were the only alternatives.

Trained in the school of slavery—African slavery at that—they could not bring themselves to contemplate the possibility of an equal race with equal burdens, between the dwellers upon the two sides of the arbitrary caste line, which the existence of that system of slavery had made essential to its perpetuity. . . . While the questions were being thus discussed, the enemy had another revelation. This time I was able to read the handwriting on the wall, but I shut my eyes and stubbornly refused to do so.

Massachusetts gone Democratic? Surely that was a lying dispatch, I would never believe it. But the next morning it was not a lie. It was the solemn truth. Ah! how it hurt. All day the news came worse and worse, and the hurt grew worse. The irreconcilables could not believe their eyes. The enemy said it was too good to be true. The next day there was more of the same sort.

Then reading through their tears of exultation, the irreconcilables began to crow, and all the enemy to cackle. My! reading through my tears, how they did burn. But that would never do. I was captain of the ship—"dictator." It would not do to whine. Already Uncles Peter and Jonathan and Pomp and the pastor of the little church we had helped to build, and the "guard," and all the rest were asking me what it all meant. What should I say? What ought I to say? Putting on a bold front I said it meant that the enemy had captured our magazine, but we still held the fort. Therefore it meant nothing.

The tidal wave not only engulfed Massachusetts, it swallowed up the House of Representatives in Congress. Friends, colored men, came from "way below Sartartia, 'jinin' on to Warren County," from Dover, from Silver Creek, from Bentonia, and from "way yan in Homes county," to learn from me what the matter was. "Ole boss"—it was boss and no longer "mars," with many colored men in 1874—"Ole boss actin' very queer 'bout something or other," some said. "The Captain boun' to say they has got we all now," others said, "kase de Yankees gone back on us." Mr. Foote, Mr. Burrus, Mr. Dickson, Elder Jackson, Rev. Mr. Gibbs, sister Rachel, and most of the solid colored people looked grave and anxious. They not only read the news for themselves, they interpreted it.

The enemy not only read, they were "jubilating." They came from everywhere, on horseback, by "companies," in carriages, and on foot. Their leaders interpreted the news to them while speaking from the balconies, dry goods boxes, and from wagons, in the light of huge bonfires, far into the night. MASSACHUSETTS had "wheeled into line!" had "repudiated the carpetbagger!" had "put its protest on record against nigro rule!" The "carpetbaggers and scalawags would have to go now!" Less than two weeks before, the most brilliant orator of that occasion, in a private conversation with me, had professed the superiority of Northern civilization over that of the South, expressed regret for the past conduct of himself and Southern leaders, and led me to hope that he would at an early day declare himself a Republican—but it was all over now. . . .

GRANT'S PROMISE

In Vicksburg, particularly in Warren County, there had been Republican maladministration. Therefore the irreconcilables succeeded in carrying the whites almost en masse into a contest which they openly and boastfully proclaimed was one for the "supremacy of the white race," and so styled their organization the "white man's party." The result there was accepted by the irreconcilables, and by many others, throughout the State as evidence of the greater efficacy of such an organization for the overthrow of the Republican power in Mississippi. "Independent military companies" in Yazoo, as we have seen, made their first appearance August 1874, and in that portion of the county which was nearest to Vicksburg. We have also seen that their professed object was to send "aid" to their brethren at Vicksburg.

In the town of Yazoo City, where the vote had always been close, the Democrats that year succeeded in electing their ticket. The irreconcilables claimed the result as a triumph of the "Vicksburg color line policy." But the mass of the whites denied that it was, and manifested considerable hostility to that policy. We have also seen what was the immediate effect upon Yazoo of the tidal wave that engulfed Massachusetts.

But no sooner had the crowd of Johnnie Rebs dispersed to their homes than our Yazoo world resumed its normal state. On the surface all was peace and good-will. But it was my duty to know what was going on underneath the surface. I knew that the men who as often as once a week quietly rode out of town to the fair grounds, or to the flats below Peak Tenariffe, or to those above town, were a secret military organization, and were engaged at target practice. I also knew that every effort possible was being put forth to persuade quiet, law-abiding young white men in the town to join this company; that in the country, similar organizations were being formed, and that the very best young white men were being induced, upon one pretext or another, to join them; that white women were foremost in the work of recruiting for those companies, and that the changes taking place in the official membership of the county grange were proof of a design to make use of the machinery of that organization for the promotion of a movement for a reorganization of parties upon the race, or "color line." . . .

It was impossible for me not to see in all these preparations a settled purpose on the part of the irreconcilables to take possession of the government by force if necessary. And although it was my duty as captain of the ship to maintain a confident exterior, I knew that Major Gibbs was speaking the truth when he warned me, on the occasion I have mentioned, that such was not only their intention, but that they also believed in their ability to accomplish their purpose; for, as the major, and others like him during that period often declared, "we all hold the strings to Uncle Sam's moneybag, at Washington, now."

I visited the capital and stated to the Governor the facts I have here related, and was not at all surprised to learn from him that he was constantly in receipt of similar information from other Republican strongholds. The signs all pointed one way. There could be no mistaking them. I attended a caucus of the Republican members of the legislature, called to consider the situation, and made use of my knowledge of the plans and purposes of the enemy in behalf of a measure which the Governor had suggested for organizing and arming the militia of the State, so that in case of riot or insurrection, he would have the means with which to defend his own authority, and execute the laws. Two-thirds of the members of that caucus were personally known to me, and had been witnesses to my faithful services in behalf of the establishment of our free

State government. Many of them were my warm, personal friends. They believed everything I said respecting the situation in Yazoo, and what was made known as to other localities. Yet nearly every colored member who spoke upon the subject opposed arming the militia.

The two principal reasons assigned by them for opposition were: First, it would tend to arouse race antagonisms. Second, they had faith in General Grant, and believed that he would come to their aid should they be attacked. . . .

Perfect peace reigned throughout Mississippi, and the warning voice of the governor, and others, found an echo only in the laughter, derision, and curses of the Barksdales, the Georges, the Singletons, Lamars, *et als.,* who meekly, everywhere and at all times, declared that they would never consent to obtain power through such means as they were most foully and wickedly charged with preparing to use. But no sooner had the legislature adjourned than affairs took on a different aspect. The gentle, cooing Democratic doves ruffled their feathers and cawed like hungry carrion crows. . . .

The changed manner of the enemy throughout the State so alarmed Republicans that a hasty consultation was held at the capital and a committee dispatched to visit the President, lay all the facts before him, and learn what would be his course in the event of a general insurrection against the constituted authorities. Returning, this committee reported, and their words were passed from one to another of the local leaders, that the President had assured them of his full sympathy and had promised to protect our government and the right of Republicans to vote to the utmost of his authority. But he had also said that the people of the North had grown tired of these appeals for help from the South. It would therefore be necessary that it should be clearly such a case as, under the Constitution, would justify his exercise of Federal power in our behalf. To make such a case it must be made clearly to appear that the enemy were actually using force, not merely threatening to do so, and that its application was so widespread and violent that the State authorities were powerless to control it.

That was satisfactory to "we all" Republicans. There were few cowards in our ranks. Resting secure in "Grant's promise," for so the President's assurances were regarded, they prepared to meet the enemy, feeling that, should they be killed, their deaths would not have been in vain.

In Yazoo, our party had never before been so united. The conduct of the irreconcilables after the death of Mr. Hilliard and especially that of those who had won victory at Vicksburg upon the color line had greatly alarmed the members of the A.M.E. Church, and they were now among my staunchest supporters. So far as I knew I was the unanimous choice of our party for re-election [in 1875]. . . .

All knew of the organization of white independent military companies, and of the very extensive arming that had been going on. Some had seen whole boxes of Winchester rifles and shotguns brought into the county for distribution to these companies. Mr. James M. Dixon[1] and Mr. Houston Burrus mentioned an effort made by the human hornet, by tumbling before them as they walked down Main Street a pile of dry-goods boxes, to compel them to quit the sidewalk, walk in the street, or fight.

It was 1868 come again, but our party was stronger now than then. One of the members of that committee was an ex-Confederate captain; another, our Senator, and the colored men upon it could read and write. All the important offices of the county were in the hands of our party. Ames was governor, Grant was still President, and we had his promise. . . .

[Despite the lies of the Democrats,] there were not only not sixteen hundred army guns in the entire county, there were not sixteen in the possession of the colored people. There were no armed military or other companies or organizations amongst them. The colored people of Yazoo were wholly without arms except now and then an old pistol or squirrel gun. Many good people at the North have blamed them for that, as though it was evidence of their incapacity for self-government. These friends forget. They forget that when the war closed General Howard and other Federal officers having authority in the South advised the freed people not to purchase guns, because it might offend their old masters, and get them into all sorts of trouble; that every missionary sent among them advised the same course; and that General Grant and all of us did. These friends also further forget that everyone giving such advice accompanied it with an assurance that the government at Washington would protect them against violence from the rebels.

The Quandary
by John R. Lynch

After the nominations had all been made, the campaign opened in dead earnest. Nearly all the Democratic clubs in the State were converted into armed military companies. Funds with which to purchase arms were believed to have been contributed by the National Democratic organization. Nearly every Republican meeting was attended by one or more of these clubs or companies—the members of which were distinguished by red shirts, indicative of blood—the attendance being for the purpose, of course, of "keeping the peace and preserving order." To enable the Dem-

[1] James M. Dixon was a local Republican leader. Born in slavery in North Carolina around 1835, he became a Methodist preacher and was appointed to the Yazoo County Board of Supervisors by Ames in 1869. One of Morgan's key allies, he also served in the state House of Representatives and on the county school board. He was a typical Reconstruction success story, owning a 250-acre farm by 1875.

ocrats to carry the State a Republican majority of between twenty and thirty thousand had to be overcome. This could be done only by the adoption and enforcement of the most questionable methods. It was a case in which the end justified the means, and the means had to be supplied.

The Republican vote consisted of about ninety-five percent of the colored men, and of about twenty-five percent of the white men. The other seventy-five percent of the whites formerly constituted the flower of the Confederate Army. They were not only tried and experienced soldiers, but they were fully armed and equipped for the work before them. Some of the colored Republicans had been Union soldiers, but they were neither organized nor armed. In such a contest, therefore, they and their white allies were entirely at the mercy of their political adversaries.

Governor Ames soon took in the situation. He saw that he could not depend upon the white members of the State militia to obey his orders, to support him in his efforts to uphold the majesty of the law, and to protect the law-abiding citizens in the enjoyment of life, liberty, and property. To use the colored members of the militia for such a purpose would be adding fuel to the flames. Nothing, therefore, remained for him to do but to call on the National administration for military aid in his efforts to crush out domestic violence and enforce the laws of the State. He did call for such aid, but for reasons that will be given later it was not granted.

The Revolt
by Albert T. Morgan

I had lately several times seen the human hornet [Henry M. Dixon] . . . and once, just before the day of our meeting, we met and passed each other on the street. His face was so white and pale, his lips so clenched and livid, his gait so nervous and meteoric that I shall never forget the shock he gave me, nor the sulphuric odor in his trail. From that moment I believed that he had been chosen to kill me when the opportunity should arrive. . . . On the day of the meeting, the pastor of the A.M.E. Church, of the church on the hill we helped to build, and other leading colored men came to me with further evidence of the purpose of the enemy to attack our meeting that night, and many craved my consent for the Republicans to go armed. This I not only refused to give, but forbade them to do so, and I expressly advised them to carry their Bibles instead.

They saw as clearly as I that the storm was at hand, but they could not know as I did its extent and power. It was my duty to shield them and preserve the peace. At the same time, as a citizen and a candidate for reelection, it was my duty to attend the meeting and make the speech. . . . There was some consolation for me in the fact that my wife and children were absent at our summer home at Holly Springs,[2] and knew nothing of my peril.

On my way to the meeting the human hornet crossed my path, and there was the same sulphuric odor in his trail that I had the last time before observed. The hall was lighted by small tallow dips. Except upon the speaker's platform, where there was a lamp and several candles, the light was dim. There were present our Senator, the ex-confederate captain, and several more native white Republicans, perhaps a hundred colored men, the mass of whom were in the raised seats in front of the platform, and one of my deputies, an ex-confederate officer.

I had just commenced my speech when there filed into the hall, in regular order, as if by preconcert and arrangement, some seven or eight of the most substantial white men of the town, and took their seats all together immediately in front of me. . . . Following this "committee" came the human hornet, Fritz Halder, and others of the violent class, who lounged about inside the doorway. Almost from the first the former began interrupting me, and sometimes to dispute my statements. This was politely objected to by someone in the audience. But I suggested that they be allowed to ask questions, and I promised to try and answer. At this point the human hornet withdrew, and almost immediately returned, bringing with him a reckless, worthless colored man, whose property had been levied upon by the delinquent tax collector for unpaid taxes.

This colored man found his way to near the middle of the audience, and then began a bitter denunciation of me. He was requested to sit down, whereupon the human hornet rushed to his side, and while in the attitude of drawing his pistol, proclaimed the right of the fellow to go on, and his purpose to protect him in it. Even this did not disturb the Republicans in the audience, all of whom preserved a calm and orderly exterior, however great their indignation, and I felt so confident of their ability to maintain this attitude that I was encouraged by it to persevere in the policy of submission to the insults and wrongs of the enemy, as Charles and the General had so successfully done in 1867 and 1868, particularly in their Sabbath-school. I felt sure that it was all done to provoke some of us to resistance, when, as during the reign of the kuklux, they would seize upon it as sufficient pretext for any violence they might choose to inflict. Therefore I proceeded in what I had to say in great caution. . . .

The result showed that I had miscalculated the extent of the enemy's trust in their majority in the House of Representatives at Washington. I had not believed that they would dare to kill unless some sort of violent resistance to their methods was offered by someone. There was the weak point in my armor, and it was at that point they surprised me. For after

[2] [Original author's footnote] This was a popular resort for persons unable to go any farther North, and who wished to escape the summer epidemic of the swamps.

the battle of nerve had proceeded for perhaps half an hour, certain of the "committee" appeared to get restless, the hornet became exasperated, and upon my mentioning the name of the chairman of our board of supervisors,[3] he exclaimed in accents of fire, "He's a thief! He's a thief!"

Some persons sitting at the right of the platform, and a full twenty-five feet from the hornet, replied, "Oh! no! no!" rapidly.

Instantly the hornet, with the rapidity of a meteor, and with pistol in hand rushed toward the person. Then there was a shot, and then a volley, all within an instant of time. The lights on that side of the hall went out, those upon the platform burned brightly.

There are those who refuse to believe in special providences. What was this? . . . I did not run. On the contrary, observing the violent movement of the hornet, I turned toward him and commanded peace. At that instant the first shot was fired, and before I could take two steps toward them, the volley. I stood, fronting them, in the full glare of the lights upon the platform, when that volley was fired, and the hornet and his aides were not more than twenty feet distant.

That volley was fired directly at me, and each bullet was aimed to kill. What was it?

The end piece of the little plain, pine board table, at which I was standing when the first shot was fired, afterward contained three bullet holes. The window facing and the wall at the back of the platform was literally peppered with bullet marks. The day following, when asked by his admiring associates, "why in hell he allowed Morgan to escape," the hornet, puzzled and confused by his failure to kill me, declared, "I stood just so"—describing his position at the front and right of the platform, which put him directly in my front as I turned and commanded the peace, and was not twenty feet distant from me—"and emptied every barrel of my two navies[4] at the ——— ." . . .

AFTER THE BATTLE

Did I shoot? Yes, twice; but while standing thus in the bright light upon the platform the light in which the hornet and his party were went out. It was said that the enemy put out the lights. I am inclined to think, however, that the dim light of the few tallow dips upon that side of the hall was obscured by the dense smoke from the rapid discharge of the enemy's pistols. At all events, it became so dark there that I could see no one. Then it was that I got out of range of their pistols by way of the window at the back of

[3] [Original author's footnote] This man was the most popular Republican with the enemy there was in the county.

[4] "Navies" refers to his pair of .36 caliber Colt Navy revolvers.

the platform, to a ladder which reached from it over a narrow court to the roof of the hotel adjoining. The ladder gave way under me and I fell to the pavement, full twelve feet below. Shocked and dazed for a moment, I quickly recovered and climbed back into the hall. . . .

The hall was not yet entirely empty. Men were still hurrying away from it by the rear stairway, and Mr. Mitchell lay at full length upon the floor. I spoke to Dick (everyone called him Dick), and it would seem that he recognized my voice, for he raised his eyes to mine.

It was a murderous bullet. Entering the neck from the rear, it ranged downward, touching the spine in its course. The pistol from which it was fired had been placed so close to the neck, that the flame from the powder ignited his coat collar, and powder was burned into the skin. . . .

Mr. Foote was badly wounded in the side, but had made his escape. There were others wounded, but Dick was the only one killed. Our Senator and all the other white Republicans had left the hall. My deputy, Mr. Redding, remained in care of Dick. He at once informed me that the hornet and his party left the hall by the front way as soon as I escaped through the window. I had not been two minutes here when some colored men, who were searching for me, came and informed me that the main street was full of armed white men, and that they were searching for me. On the street at the rear of the hall were quite a large number of my colored friends who remained to "die by you, Colonel." They were not armed; some few may have had pistols. But what could we do against that mob of whites, some of whom I could see with guns in their hands, hurrying toward the market-house?

These friends of mine did not fail to comprehend the meaning of it all. They meant what they said. They would have followed me in an effort to arrest the hornet and his aides, but that I would not attempt to do.

Finding my way home, I had not been there five minutes when the house was thronged with colored friends, some of whom had stood by our little garrison in its darkest hours, and among them the pastor of that other church. All were anxious that I should make a stand and fight the mob. But to their prayers and entreaties I held firmly to my resolve, and advised them all to go home, go to bed, and advise every colored man they could see or get word to, to do the same, and upon no pretext whatever come to town.

"What yo' goin' to do, sheriff?"

"Stay right here in my own house."

"Day'll be 'yhere and kill yo' sure."

"Never mind me, you all go home, as I tell you."

"Never 'low to leave the colonel that way—never! Die first!"

Then I reasoned with them, pointing out to them the folly of fighting those well-armed companies, and reminding them that every one of our white friends had vanished. After reason and persuasion failed, I commanded them. Then they departed; some cursing, some crying. The last one had but just disappeared through the backyard, when tramp, tramp, tramp, sounded the tread of the hornet's company upon the pavement, approaching my house.

This was my castle. Fortunately, only a few days before, I had purchased a fresh supply of cartridges for my Spencer rifle, and with this, and other weapons ready at hand (the very same we had armed our ancient stronghold with), I would be able to make at least a show of resistance. Now they were upon the gallery and banging against the door. My hostler, Frederick Harris, opened it and they entered.

"Whar's Colonel Mawgin?"

"Doa'n know, Mars Dixon, 'deed I don't, Kunnel hav'n bin y'here sez de meetin' I 'low."

Evidently they believed him, for, after spying about upon the first floor a moment, they went away regularly as they came, tramp, tramp, tramp, keeping step for all the world just like a company of trained soldiers. . . . But all night long I heard every little while the tramp of squads of men marching.

The next day, looking out from the window of my stronghold, I could see them. They were as well armed, and under as perfect discipline, apparently, as any troops of our late armies were. Including the cavalry company from the country, there were not less than three hundred armed white men in the town. Their weapons were Winchester rifles, needle-guns,[5] double-barrelled shotguns, and pistols.

There were not armed colored men anywhere that I could see, or hear of, and scarcely any at all to be seen upon the streets. This was a great relief to me, for it showed their faith in me, and took away the only pretext there was for the presence of armed whites, whose numbers, nevertheless, were constantly increasing. The enemy promptly caused a warrant to be issued, charging me with attempting to murder Dixon, placed it in the hands of the hornet and his aides, offered a large reward for me, dead or alive, visited the capital of the State, Holly Springs, and other points where I might possibly be found in search of me, marched to the courthouse and took possession of it and of my office—upon the ground that the sheriff was a fugitive from justice—assembled the board of aldermen of the town and caused an appropriation of a thousand dollars to be made for pay of the soldiers, established a cordon of pickets around the town, with instructions to allow no colored man without a pass to enter or depart from it, and by such and various and sundry other means, usurped full and complete authority. Still "our nigros" refused to "rise."

The details of this insurrection would, doubtless, make mighty interesting reading for the general public. They would fill a volume. I have not space for them.

5 "Needle-gun" was a popular term for a single-shot, breechloading hunting rifle, especially the Sharps and Springfield models.

Trusting in the President's "promise," I had remained in the town because, when the United States troops came, it would be essential to the
success of their mission that some semblance of lawful government remained. I believed that the presence of no more than two United States
soldiers, with authority from the President to act for the preservation of
the peace, and for the protection of the lawful government, would be sufficient to cause the enemy to disperse to their hiding places, when I could
once more resume the functions and duties of my office, Republicans
might once more return to their homes, and we could proceed with our
canvass. Once it was rumored about that the troops were coming. The
effect of this rumor was enough to induce the hornet and his company
to quit the courthouse, and abandon my office; but it was a false report.
Immediately afterward the town resumed its warlike appearance, and the
enemy's methods were resumed with renewed vigor.

From my hiding place I could see the rows of bright, shining army
guns near the market house, stacked, and with sentries on guard over
them, precisely as I have so often seen them in our old army camps, and
on our marches against the rebels in those other war days. I could also
see armed bodies of mounted men riding out on their scouting expeditions to the country for the purpose of suppressing "nigro risings" that
were "about to occur." These parties usually went armed to the teeth,
and carrying ropes at their saddles.

During all those long days and nights of waiting and watching, my
friends in the town remained true to me. Some were in the ranks of the
enemy, and rode with the hornet on his raids. They knew of my hiding
place [now at his brother's house], and whenever the enemy came too
near, drew them upon some other trail. But this could not always last.

On the eleventh day, the leaders of the enemy became convinced that I
was still in the town, and arrangements were made for a final search. This
time they would invade my stronghold. They had kept a vigilant watch upon
it for several days, and the four corners of that square were guarded with
extra pickets; but my friends were keen and watchful. That night just before
the hour for posting the pickets, I was to endeavor to escape from town.
The plan was for Fred to have my sorrel mare saddled and ready with the
stable door open, and nothing left for me to do but mount and ride away.
Friends were stationed on each corner between my stronghold and the stable, with pre-arranged signals in case of detection or immediate danger.

So, disguised in some old clothes, at that hour when the shadows of
our long Yazoo twilight cover the old town with a mask, I walked from
my brother's house full two squares to the stable, found the faithful sorrel, just as faithful Fred had promised she would be, mounted her, and
rode away. People whom I knew were passing to and fro. But none knew
me, until just as I began the ascent by the plank road of the long hill back
of the town, just opposite the little church we helped to build, where a

sentry with musket at a right shoulder shift, one of the enemy, startled perhaps my mare out of her listless, drowsy gait, recognized me. . . .

As though he had received a direct revelation, this white, armed with a Winchester rifle, turned on his heel and ran away as rapidly as his legs could carry him toward headquarters, the market house. Now I was free, for the sorrel was a fleet-footed beast. Nine miles out, I passed some friends, colored people, who were having a prayer meeting at the church nearby. They warned me that Bentonia was guarded in the same way as Yazoo City, by a white company, and one of their number volunteered to guide me by a circuitous route, through the fields, to a point beyond the town, thus enabling me to escape that danger.[6]

Before 10 A.M. the next day I was at the capital. Here I found our Senator, and also found refugees from all parts of the State. The State was one vast camp of armed white leaguers. In Hinds County [the capital county] as many as one hundred Republicans, it was said, had been killed. The Governor's office was thronged with men who had come to him for help. . . .

Not only was Mississippi one vast armed camp of white leaguers, all the surrounding States were ready to "send their aid" to their brethren in Mississippi. . . . The Governor's intention to send two companies of militia into Yazoo was abandoned because of the greatly superior force of the enemy. . . . Their brethren in Alabama . . . were not only standing by their arms, ready to move at the click of a wire, but had chartered trains to convey them to the "scene of conflict." Others like them and like those in Yazoo were ready in Warren, Madison, Hinds, Holmes, and other counties to do the same thing. In the face of this array the Governor's two companies of militia, one white, the other black, could not contend. It was certainly not the fault of the colored company that it did not try. My old friend, Charles Caldwell, was its captain. They were at all times ready to go. . . .[7]

What follows relating to the doings of the enemy in Yazoo, I shall have to state upon hearsay. I shall, however, set down nothing but that which came to me from perfectly reliable friends, from official sources, and through the press.

Shortly after I left, as I have described, it would seem that the colored men became somewhat restless. It was reported that some were lying in wait below the town to shoot the hornet. The following day "Captain"

[6] [Original author's footnote] I afterward learned that I had not been gone from that "nigro church" twenty minutes when a body of mounted cavalry from Bentonia rode up and inquired for me.

[7] Caldwell actually did march his men through the countryside, though he had little success in stemming the Democrats' revolt. On Christmas Day in 1875, a white friend lured him into a store in Clinton, where Caldwell was murdered.

Taylor's company of cavalry rode through that neighborhood. Next day the body of a [black] Republican was found hanging to a tree. . . .

Such scenes soon became of frequent occurrence, until leading Republicans had been killed in every supervisor's district of the county. Colored men were forced to assist at some of them, as in the case of Horace Hammond [the victim mentioned in the previous paragraph], where some of the [coroner's] jury were colored men. In one instance the coroner's jury was made up from the number who did the hanging. Their verdict, however, was the same as in the case of Hammond: "Came to his death by hanging by parties unknown."

The hanging of [James G.] Patterson has attracted some notice beyond the borders of Yazoo. He was my friend, an intelligent, cultivated, orderly, peace-loving man. He was one of the three members from our county in the State House of Representatives. I knew him personally and well. I never heard him use profane or vulgar language. His habits were exceptionally good. I never knew or heard that he used intoxicating liquors. It is said that as chairman of the Republican club in his neighborhood in former campaigns he had made arrangements, regardless of the threats of the enemy, for a Republican meeting. . . . [To prevent it, he was hung, and the Democratic press blamed it on other African Americans.]

Every leading white Republican remaining in the county surrendered and published the fact over his own signature, and then sent word to me that they had done so in the hope of preventing further bloodshed, and of saving their own property and lives. One organized a company, and took his place in line with the white leaguers, "to kill niggers when necessary," and to aid in suppressing the "risings" which were "about to occur."

The chairman of the county Democratic committee entered the United States post office and caused all communications addressed to leading Republicans relating to the canvass and to the approaching election to be destroyed—burned.

At last, when election day arrived and the result was announced, the ticket of the enemy had received (so it was declared) 4,044 votes. There were two votes for me, but as was announced at the time, these were cast by the hornet, who explained that it would "not do to be too damned unanimous." Perhaps this was the real reason for the three votes cast by the enemy in 1867.

The enemy's rejoicings over this result were as extravagant as their jubilations over the result of the election of Massachusetts the year previous, or as their violent efforts to win it. The hornet was elevated into a sort of demigod, and all sounded his praises. A movement was set on foot to raise a fund with which to purchase a suitable testimonial of their appreciation of his services. . . . This fund was quickly raised, and upon the testimonial—a massive silver pitcher—was engraved the following:

To
The Bravest of the Brave,
Captain HENRY M. DIXON

Presented to him by his Democratic fellow-citizens of Yazoo County, as an humble testimonial of their high appreciation of his brilliant services in the redemption of the county from radical rule in 1875.

The *Banner* said: "Let no man dare say that a nobler man ever lived." Then a great county gathering was held, at which were present Ethel Barksdale and Otho R. Singleton, both now in the House of Representatives at Washington, and L. Q. C. Lamar and J. Z. George, present United States Senators from that State. Before these distinguished persons, the hornet and his company were paraded, dressed, and armed as when on their hanging expeditions, and there in the presence of the vast throng, over whom waved our grand old flag, received fresh from the lips of these, their true and tried captains and leaders, Barksdale, Singleton, George, Lamar, the thanks of "the people" of the county, "the people" of the State, and of "our people" everywhere, for their "glorious services" in behalf of "our sacred cause."[8] . . .

Throughout that period the Republicans were as helpless as babes. There was never any resistance at all by them to the violence of the enemy.

That campaign in Yazoo has been called "the coronation of the Mississippi plan." So it was; for in twenty-six other counties of the State that year the enemy were less humane. In some of that number Republicans resisted by violence the aggressions of the enemy, and were massacred in crowds of ten, twenty, fifty, and in one county, it was said quite one hundred were killed. But in Yazoo, instead of summoning the unarmed colored men against the disciplined and fully equipped ranks of the white league, the Republican leaders made their fight upon the picket-line, trusting to the reserves at the North to fill their places when they should be all killed, captured, or in retreat. Therefore, only leaders were killed in Yazoo, and only so many of them as was necessary to convince Republicans that their opponents would kill if necessary, that they had the power to kill, and that there were none to forbid it, or to punish them for it afterward. Therefore the mass of the Republicans remained silent and passive. Ohio and Massachusetts had gone Democratic. Had I summoned a posse of colored men and resisted, of course there would have been a general massacre in Yazoo, too. That I would not do. Therefore the hornet and all his aides were entitled to the thanks of mankind! The hornet received the thanks of "our people" on the occasion mentioned. His reward came later.

8 [Original author's footnote] It was here and by those distinguished statesmen (?) that Yazoo was christened the Banner county of the State.

By such means as I have here but faintly detailed, Yazoo and Mississippi were "redeemed." By such means Major W.D. Gibbs, my opponent in 1869, recovered his own without the aid of Reuben, and took his place in the State Senate; the attorney for Mars' Si, who was also for the State against Charles, and for Mr. Hilliard against me, was elected to the House; and Captain Taylor of the cavalry company was elected to be sheriff and tax collector.

Within twenty-four hours after their new government was installed in the places of "we all" Republicans, the county treasury was entered and every dollar of the school fund carried off.[9] To this day, it is said that the robbery was by "persons unknown." Then their grand jury, selected by the same means as were Gibbs, Taylor, and Mars' Si's attorney, on their solemn oaths, presented to the court "a true bill" for murder against me.

MORGAN FLED MISSISSIPPI to save his life—chased not by the Yazoo warrant for murder (he had stood and fought the Democrats in court before) but by the armed companies that had occupied the state. It was an astonishing sight: a finely planned and executed armed insurrection—a legally and fairly elected government of an American state overthrown by military force. It was so well run, in fact, that Lamar and other leaders knew just when to send their men back into hiding, creating the air of calm that convinced a weary Grant that he need not intervene.

Governor Adelbert Ames tried to get federal help—he tried so hard that the new attorney general, Edwards Pierrepont, grew annoyed. "The whole public are tired out with these annual autumnal outbreaks in the South," he told Ames, "and the great majority are ready to condemn any interference on the part of the government." It is a measure of the success of the Democrats' claims that they were fighting for "home rule," that the attorney general should see the defense of a free state against a military coup as "interference." And so the public was spared another tiresome intervention, as hundreds of African-American citizens swung by their necks from Mississippi trees and fell in pools of their own blood on Mississippi soil. The victorious Democrats could congratulate themselves that another state was "redeemed," redeemed from the villainy of racial equality.

And the man who basked in the glow of the successful campaign, the chief redeemer of them all, was Lucius Quintus Cincinnatus Lamar. His keen mind had given white Democrats the unified strategy to conquer their state back from the majority who were ruling it a little too well. But his true genius was to perfect a second face for presentation to the North. The man who had actually written the state law that took Mississippi out of the Union at the beginning of the Civil War, the man who breathed fire to

9 [Original author's footnote] About twenty-eight thousand dollars.

local Democrats, had delivered a stirring eulogy in Congress for Senator Charles Sumner when that stalwart Radical died in 1874. Even as Lamar plotted an insurrection, he won acclaim as a voice of conciliation.

Indeed, he succeeded in duping John F. Kennedy—our durable representative of conventional wisdom—who in *Profiles in Courage* praised the Southern Democrat even as he danced on Ames's grave. "No partisan, personal, or sectional considerations could outweigh his devotion to the national interests," the future President gushed; Lamar wanted "conciliation" and "the restitution of normal federal-state relations and the withdrawal of military rule." On the other hand, Kennedy declared, "no state suffered more from carpetbag rule than Mississippi." No better proof than this can be provided that history is indeed written by the victors. And Lamar *was* victorious—victorious not only in massacring hundreds of innocent African Americans, victorious not only in delivering his state once more into the hands of white supremacy, but victorious in recasting his own image.

Yet the conciliator image holds within it a certain bitter truth. Before the Civil War, Southern congressmen held the republic within their grasp; if not always in control of public policy, they certainly had a veto over it at all times. They spent the decade after their defeat in the Civil War trying to reassert elite white domination over their own states. At the end of the struggle, they once again had supreme local control—but their national position was gone forever. Lamar had forged the way to complete victory by striking an unspoken bargain: white rule in the South, in exchange for Northern dominance in national affairs.

But one last word awaits on the state of affairs in Mississippi—for Congressman John R. Lynch was not to share the fate of his friend Albert Morgan. In his district the election took quite an unexpected turn, one that offered a glimmer of hope in the darkness that fell over the South in 1875.

The Survivor
by John R. Lynch

When the polls closed on the day of the election, the Democrats, of course, had carried the State by a large majority—thus securing a heavy majority in both branches of the Legislature. Of the six members of Congress the writer was the only one of the regular Republicans that pulled through, and that by a greatly reduced majority. . . .

The election of the writer, it was afterwards developed, was due in all probability to a miscalculation on the part of some of the Democratic managers. Their purpose was to have a solid delegation. . . . But in my district the plan miscarried. In one of the counties [in Lynch's district] there were two conflicting reports as to what the Democratic majority was; according to one, it was two hundred and fifty; according to the other, it was five hundred. The report giving two hundred and fifty was, no doubt, the correct one, but the other would probably have been accepted had it been believed at the time that it was necessary to insure the election of the Democratic candidate. To overcome the majority in that district was more difficult than to overcome it in any of the other districts.

While their candidate, Colonel Roderick Seal, was quite a popular man, it was well known that I would poll a solid Republican vote and some Democratic votes in addition. Fortunately for me there was a split in the party in my own county (Adams) for county officers, which resulted in bringing out a very heavy vote. This split also made the counting of the ballots very slow—covering a period of several days. My name was on both tickets. The election took place on Tuesday, but the count was not finished until the following Friday evening. Hence the result for member of Congress in that county could not be definitely ascertained until Friday night.

The Democratic managers at the State capital were eager to know as soon as possible what the Republican majority in Adams County would be for Congressman, hence, on Wednesday evening, the editor of the local Democratic paper received a telegram from the Secretary of the Democratic State Committee, requesting to be informed immediately what the Republican majority for Congressman would be in Adams County. The editor read the telegram to me and asked what, in my opinion, would be my majority in the county. My reply was that I did not think it would exceed twelve hundred; thereupon he sent in the following report: "Lynch's majority in Adams will not exceed twelve hundred."

Upon receipt of this telegram the majority of two hundred and fifty instead of five hundred was deemed sufficient from the county heretofore referred to. If the Republican majority in Adams County would not exceed twelve hundred, the success of the Democratic Congressional candidate by a small but safe majority was assured on the face of the returns. Since Adams was the last county to be reported, no change could thereafter be made. When the count was finally finished in Adams it was found I had a majority of over eighteen hundred. This gave me a majority in the district of a little over two hundred on the face of the returns.

The disappointment and chagrin on the part of the Democratic managers can better be imagined than described. . . .

EFFECTS OF THE REFORM ADMINISTRATION IN MISSISSIPPI

Because the Democrats carried the election in Mississippi in 1875, they did not thereby secure control of the State Government. That election was for members of the Legislature, members of Congress, and county officers. Only one State officer was elected—a State Treasurer—to fill the vacancy created by the death of Treasurer Holland. All the other State officers were Republicans. But the Democrats could not afford to wait until Governor Ames's term expired. They were determined to get immediate control of the State Government. There was only one way in which this could be done, and that was by impeachment.

This course they decided to take. It could not be truthfully denied that Governor Ames was a clean, pure, and honest man. He had given the State an excellent administration. The State judiciary had been kept up to the high standards established by Governor Alcorn. Every dollar of the public money had been collected, and honestly accounted for. The State was in a prosperous condition. The rate of taxation had been greatly reduced, and there was every prospect of a still further reduction before the end of his administration. But these facts made no difference to those who were flushed with the victory they had so easily won. They wanted the offices, and were determined to have them, and that, too, without very much delay. Hence, impeachment proceedings were immediately instituted against the Governor and Lieutenant-Governor—not in the interest of reform, of good government, or of low taxes, but simply in order to get possession of the State Government. . . .

When the articles of impeachment were presented to the House, it was seen that they were so weak and so groundless that the Governor believed it would be an easy matter for him to discredit them even before an antagonistic legislature. With that end in view, he employed several of the ablest lawyers in the country to represent him. They came to Jackson and commenced the preparation of the case, but it did not take them long to find out that their case was a hopeless one. They soon found out to their entire satisfaction that it was not to be a judicial trial, but a political one, and that the jury was already prepared for conviction without regard to the law, the Constitution, the evidence, or the facts. Governor Ames was to be convicted, not because he was guilty of any offense, but because he was in the way of complete Democratic control of the State Government. . . .

Upon their advice, therefore, the Governor promptly tendered his resignation, which was promptly accepted. He then left the State never to return again. If the impeachment proceedings had been instituted in good faith—upon an honest belief that the chief executive had committed offenses which merited punishment—the resignation would not have been accepted. . . .

The sanguinary revolution in the State of Mississippi in 1875 was claimed to be in the interest of good administration and honest government; it was an attempt to wrest the State from the control of dishonest men—negroes, carpetbaggers, and scalawags—and place it in control of intelligent, pure, and honest white men. With that end in view, Geo. M. Buchanan, a brave and gallant ex-Confederate soldier, was through questionable and indefensible methods defeated for the office of State Treasurer, and Wm. L. Hemmingway was declared elected. Yet when the change took place it was found that every dollar of the public money was accounted for. During the whole period of Republican administration not a dollar had been misappropriated, nor had there been a single defalcation, although millions of dollars had passed through the hands of the fiscal agents of the State and the different counties.

How was it with the new reform administration? Treasurer Hemmingway had been in office only a comparatively short while when the startling information was given out that he was a defaulter to the amount of $315,612.19. William L. Hemmingway a defaulter! Could such a thing be possible? Yes, it was an admitted and undisputed fact. . . . Even after the defalcation was made known there was nothing to indicate that any of the money had been appropriated to his own use. Yet the money had mysteriously disappeared. Where was it? Who had it?

Hemmingway was tried, convicted, sentenced, and served a term in the State Prison; all of which he calmly endured rather than give the name of any person having connection with that unfortunate affair. All the satisfaction that the public can get with reference to it—other than the punishment to which Hemmingway was subjected—is to indulge in conjectures about it. One conjecture, and the most reasonable and plausible one, is that if Hemmingway had made a full confession it might have involved not only some men who were prominent and influential, but perhaps the Democratic State organization as well. For it was a well-known fact that in 1875 nearly every Democratic club in the State was converted into an armed military company. To fully organize, equip, and arm such a large body of men required an outlay of a large sum of money. . . .

The case of Treasurer Hemmingway is conclusive evidence that in point of efficiency, honesty, and official integrity the Democratic party had no advantage over the party that was placed in power chiefly through the votes of colored men. What was true of Mississippi in this respect is also true—in a measure, at least—of the other reconstructed States.

23

THE RING COLLAPSES

President Grant was angry. His two terms in the White House had brought nothing but frustration—a succession of insurmountable obstacles placed in his way by his enemies. And such enemies! The pompous, windy, and now late Senator Sumner, who started things off by blocking the appointment of Alexander T. Stewart, and then destroyed the annexation of Santo Domingo; the rigid, moralistic Senator Schurz, who had had the nerve to organize a rival party to oppose the President; and now one of his own cabinet members, Secretary of the Treasury Benjamin Bristow: so the bitter president must have mused. Bristow had targeted Grant's friends and subordinates John McDonald and Orville Babcock in the Whiskey Ring investigation; Grant was certain that the ambitious reformer was aiming even higher.

How much did the President know about the whiskey frauds? McDonald tells us he knew practically everything—and in this age, when almost no layers of bureaucracy insulated the chief executive from the daily workings of government, it is easy to believe McDonald's claims. There was also a tight partnership—even friendship—between Babcock and Grant. Much of the historical attention to the conspiracy has been devoted to the personal profit gained by the participants; but it was the *political* purpose of the ring that had the more serious implications. Hence Grant's anger and fear. He derived no money himself from the illicit operation, but he did gain the support of newspapers and politicians, thanks to its bribes and favors.

Grant also took the investigation as a personal affront. He had been a military man much of his life, spending several years as commander of what was, for a time, the world's most powerful army; he could not abide insubordination from his officers. As President, he saw Bristow as one of his lieutenants, and he took deep offense at his scourging investigation. At first, the politically savvy Grant had thought Bristow's efforts, if arrested in time, might rebound to his own advantage. But the treasury secretary would not stop—he seemed to feel none of the personal loyalty that the President demanded above all else. He appeared determined to send to jail Grant's last real friend, Orville Babcock, and perhaps take a stab at the chief of state himself.

McDonald could clearly see the anxiety, even paranoia, that now shrouded the White House like so many curtains pulled tight to keep out prying eyes. He appealed time and time again to his crony Babcock, who replied with reassurances, none of them reassuring. He could see that Grant would never let Babcock hang, for the President felt that an admission of his secretary's guilt would be an admission of his own guilt—and McDonald and Bristow both knew that Babcock was very, very guilty. In the end, Grant would even be willing to perjure himself for his closest friend—but someone had to pay the price.

Indictments and Convictions
by John McDonald

If a seeming but not real digression is pardonable I will here explain the very peculiar and anomalous attitudes of Commissioner Douglass [head of the bureau of internal revenue]: As has been here shown in an earlier part of this book, Douglass received his appointment almost directly through the influence of Whiskey Ring members. In the fall of 1874 Mr. Douglass discovered that Secretary Bristow had formed a determination to inaugurate a searching investigation of revenue matters in order to satisfy himself why the collections had so materially fallen off. When this course was decided upon Mr. Douglass was not slow to find that Mr. Bristow was not consulting him but was taking matters into his own hands.

This scared the Commissioner, and to prepare for an exposure which he felt was coming he changed his attitude and professed, suddenly, an almost consuming desire to ferret out every semblance of fraud. The investigation proceeded, however, without any special assistance of his, until Mr. Bristow was startled by proofs which showed conclusively that the Whiskey Ring had been in full operation for five years; not only this, but in searching through the pigeon-holes in the Commissioner's office, the Secretary found a large number of reports from revenue agents who had been sent into my district, and had explained the frauds that were being perpetrated. . . . This discovery decided the Secretary in his former opinion that the Commissioner had at least some guilty knowledge of the revenue frauds, and a change was at once determined upon. This was about the last day of April [1875], and without any consultations the Secretary dismissed Mr. Douglass, the office to be declared vacant on the 15th of May, on which day Hon. D.D. Pratt succeeded to the position.

On the 10th day of May [1875], Lucien Hawley and E.H. Chapman, armed with the proper authority from Washington, quietly dropped upon St. Louis, landing as it were in the midst of the distilleries and rectifying establishments, ten of which they seized without giving me any notice. . . . In the afternoon of the day on which the seizures were made Mr. Hawley called on me at my office, and handed me his letter of authority and instructions. . . .

Reports of every character were flying fast, some of which reached the President, and a constant irritation was the result. . . . Notwithstanding the fact that I tendered my resignation on the 23rd of April, it was not until a month later that it was accepted. Bristow urged my dismissal, because he was then well informed of my connection with the Ring and was equally well convinced of the President's connivance if not indeed his direct complicity with all the whiskey frauds. But with the hope that I might be able to cover a major part of the most damaging evidence, I was continued in office until the 25th of May. . . .

The doubtful reader may desire to know why, if the President was my co-conspirator, he accepted my resignation at all, and also why he did not interpose his authority and suppress Mr. Bristow when the Secretary's actions had assumed such a threatening attitude. Let me here explain: In my interview with the President in April, as reported, I gave him my opinion that if he permitted Secretary Bristow to continue his investigations, that no power could suppress the reports made by revenue agents; that this information would certainly leak out in some manner and that it would soon assume proportions for evil as irresistible as the waves of the ocean. The President did not so regard it, and his idea was that to make a specious showing of administration honesty would produce a favorable effect, and advance his political interests by procuring his renomination for the Presidency.

This idea obscured the results from him which I could see were sure to follow, and relying upon his power to run his vessel within an inch of the most dangerous breakers without coming in contact with the reef, he considered the glory that would reward him and, like the indolent oarsman who rides at first in the easy swirl of the seductive maelstrom, he realized only when it was too late the roaring charybdis he had been drawn into. . . .

When this came the President, fully realizing the danger his rash measures had seduced him into, drew my resignation from his side pocket, where it had lain for one month, and permitted the Secretary to accept it. His reliance henceforth was in my silence, and his natural good luck. Daily he advised with Gen. Babcock, and through him he communicated his wishes to me. And here I desire to call the attention of the reader to a fact which is very important, and which may possibly be overlooked by some, viz.: That the President does all his official correspondence through his secretary. It is perhaps difficult to define the lines of distinction between the communications of the secretary and the President in matters of doubtful character. . . .

In the early part of June the Grand Jury, then in session in St. Louis, returned an indictment against me, and also charged Joyce, Fitzroy, and Bevis, a distiller, charging us with "willfully and maliciously destroying public records." On the day after this was found, I was arrested by U.S. Marshal Newcomb, and gave bail in the sum of $5,000. But this step only increased the anxiety of the President and Gen. Babcock, and on the

17th I wrote Gen. B., informing him of my indictment, but conveying my assurance that he and the President could only be reached criminally through me, and whatever the ordeal might be, I should go through it without betraying them in the slightest. . . .

In the next letter, from Babcock, however, even as a bull-finch (B.F.)[10] he pipes like a craven, with notes of no doubtful import . . . :

JULY 14

DEAR FRIEND:

I am told some valuable information that was taken from a safe was sent to Cincinnati to the care of one Maj. Blackburn, a lawyer of that city, and that it is believed it can be purchased from him if enough money is paid. The price for it is high, but it is believed that it can be purchased if price enough is paid, and that they are trying to buy it.

YOUR FRIEND, B.F.

Does the reader want me to explain this panorama of Grant and Babcock's infamy; shift the scenes until all the black lines are plainly discernable? Well, while my pen is to it and the people grown more morbid by looking upon the great festering body of corruption which I have here exposed to their view, I'll show them more. "This valuable information" Gen. Babcock refers to, was stolen out of the safe of the U.S. District State Attorney's office at St. Louis, or at least I have been so informed. It consisted of evidence fully establishing my guilt and pointing to President Grant and Gen. Babcock as accessories. "They are trying to buy it," means that the President, together with himself and others in the Ring, were then negotiating with Blackburn for the evidence, and they desire me to contribute a part of the necessary money.

I did not regard the information spoken of as especially damaging, because I knew that if the government officers here really meant to convict me that there was so much evidence against us all that, like a river, it could not be exhausted by dipping up the water while the source remained. I replied to him in that manner, and the matter was not referred to again in our correspondence.

In the latter part of July, I left St. Louis and went up to my farm in Wisconsin, near Ripon, but was not allowed to remain there long as all the members of the Ring were now in deep distress, and they looked to me for assistance, sending me a dozen letters every day imploring me to return. Before leaving St. Louis for Wisconsin, I employed Judge Chester

[10] After Babcock made his gift of a bullfinch to McDonald's wife, he began to sign his secret letters "Bull-Finch" or just "B.F."

H. Krum to defend me from the charges preferred in the indictment already alluded to. . . .

I knew that Grant and Babcock were, in a measure, in my power, because they were my superiors and equally guilty with myself. So my conclusion was to let the White House end of the line take care of itself and to offer no further obstacle to Bristow's foray. My determination brought forth abundant fruit, by alarming the President and his chevalier scribe, who, being unable to account for my nonchalance, and quite at sea as to my intentions, learning of my return to St. Louis they took the train and arrived in the city on the 24th of September. The visit of the President and Gen. Babcock was made under circumstances that would disguise their real purposes from the public. . . .

My first notification of their arrival was through Maj. Grimes [an army officer who was the conduit for the secret correspondence], who came to me at the Planters House, where I was stopping, and taking me by the arms said, "There is a gentleman over the way who wishes to see you; will you go over with me now?"

I crossed the street with Maj. Grimes and followed him upstairs to a room over John Bonnett's restaurant. Upon entering the room I found Gen. Babcock, who cordially greeted me and then informed me that he had ordered a dinner and wine expressly for me. I saw that a very sumptuous repast had been provided for two and on his invitation I took a seat at the table. Maj. Grimes did not dine with us for, as I learned from the General, matters had been arranged for a strictly private conversation between us.

He began the interview by saying: "The old man (meaning Grant) and I have come out here to see what you have done. This thing has gone far enough and must stop right here. We have taken rooms at the Lindell, and at four o'clock this afternoon I want you to see the President privately and tell him exactly what you want." I did not make any reply at once so as to permit him to make a full statement. He said there had already been scandal enough, and he declared that the trouble would not be allowed to continue if "we" (the expression he used) "have to dismiss every man in the Government service." . . . He further remarked that the old man (Grant) was too easy, and that he wanted me to say to him that it was time to take the bull by the horns and stop the investigations and prevent a prosecution of any of the members. He gave it as his opinion that, inasmuch as Bristow, Wilson, Dyer, Henderson, etc., were appointees of the President, that they could be restrained by the President's wishes, especially if the matter assumed the position of "quit or go"; that a prosecution of the President's friends was a serious reflection upon the President, which could in no event be tolerated.

He talked in this manner for nearly an hour, and when he paused to hear my suggestions, I replied in substance that I had to disagree with him in all his propositions. Said I, "Judging, as you do, from Washington, it is impossible for you to comprehend what irresistible force the charges and demand for a complete investigation of fraud in connection with the illicit whiskey combination is being made. The time was when this trouble might have been averted, and I told the President when in Washington that if he did not muzzle or dismiss Bristow and call in all the revenue agents, that a wave of exposure would certainly engulf us all.

"No," said I, "it is worse than folly to speak of suppressing facts possessing such importance and pregnant with such terrible possibilities, those which, in part, have already reached the public and placed everybody in a fever heat of anxiety to hear it all." . . . I assured him, however, that the prosecutions could not extend to the President himself except through Col. Joyce and myself, and that he might depend upon me to carry the secrets I had like facts hidden under the mold of centuries. I advised him to return with the President to Washington, and to take no part in averting prosecutions which might be construed against them, and to leave the St. Louis boys to take care of themselves.

Somewhat surprised, he asked: "Why, General, what do you mean by that? Don't you want us to do anything out here for you?"

I replied: "The fact is, the papers have so worked up this matter that any action which you might take to prevent a complete exposure of the Ring would be only to invite your own ruin"; that they had already asserted that the President knew of the existence of the Whiskey Ring, and any interference from him now would confirm the truth of the charge with the public. . . .

I also told him that, under the circumstances, and especially considering my indictment, that it would be very indiscreet for the President to receive me at his rooms; but that I would call at the Lindell and see the President publicly, and as chance afforded, would ascertain from him whether he approved of my determination. I informed him of the fact that there were detectives watching the President himself, and that my footsteps were continually dogged by them. Said I, "You need not be surprised to see an account of our meeting and interview here published in the morning papers."

He replied that he had no fears of seeing any notice of this meeting, because, said he, "Maj. Grimes arranged this place of interview, and we came here together in a closed carriage." (It was subsequently shown that the President was under the surveillance of detectives, who reported all his acts and movements to Secretary Bristow. It was owing to my refusal to hold a private interview with him that he escaped being disgraced by such a circumstance.) Our conversation then drifted from the prospective trials to other private matters connected with our mutual interests. . . .

Our conversation lasted for more than two hours, during which we ate a very hearty dinner and consumed two bottles of wine. When we parted I repeated to him my determination not to see the President privately, but, I remarked, you may speak to him and ascertain how he receives my policy of action, and report to me at my room in the Planters House this evening.

True to our appointment, Gen. Babcock called on me, and related with much ecstacy how the President was delighted with my considerate ideas, and credited me with a wisdom that was so gratifying that it inspired him with the hope that my finesse would yet bring them out of their distressing dilemma. . . .

I saw no more of the General until the next day about eleven o'clock, when he called at my room and again renewed the conversation we had on the previous day. . . . He then enquired if I had fully considered the ordeal I should have to submit to in bearing the opprobrium of a conviction.

Said I: "That is part of the funeral I have considered; I have already been abused to the limit of newspaper possibility, and there is nothing to it now but standing up in court and passing through a few changes, and at most hear the turn of the bolt on my liberty."

At the mention of the "bolt," the General interrupted me by saying: "Oh! it will not come to that; they will never turn a key on you, because the old man (Grant) tells me that if they convict you, he will pardon you the moment the verdict is announced. Don't have any fears about that, but I can't believe this arbitrary action will ever be necessary." I told him that I expected the President to pardon me at once, in case of my conviction, and that it was because of this and the friendly obligations I owed him that I proposed to stand and take the full brunt of the law, in order that my fidelity might be proven. . . .

On the 27th, the day preceding the departures of the president and his party for Des Moines, Ia., Justice Miller, sitting for this district, rendered his opinion upon the demurrer to the indictments of Col. Joyce, Al. Bevis, Jos. Fitzroy, and myself, which concluded as follows: "Without delaying further, I will say that both Judge Treat and myself are of the opinion that the indictment is essentially bad, and the demurrer must be sustained."

Notwithstanding this decision we were placed under bonds to appear before the next Grand Jury. . . . In the latter part of the June term other indictments had been found against us charging conspiracy, which fact I neglected to state in the earlier and proper part of this narrative, so that when the demurrer to the indictment charging us with a willful destruction of public records was sustained, we were at once re-arrested upon a bench warrant and placed under bonds in the sum of $11,000, to answer to two indictments charging us with conspiracy and one charging us with destruction of public records. Col. Joyce was also indicted during the September term by the Grand Jury sitting in the western district, and his case was transferred to Jefferson City, where he was afterwards tried. . . . On the 23rd [of October] the trial was concluded and a verdict of guilty was returned against him "for failure to report official investigations." . . .

On the 2nd day of November, while in attendance at court, awaiting and expecting my arraignment, Col. Dyer and Gen. Henderson [the prosecutors] consulted with me as to the propriety of my pleading guilty and becoming a witness for the Government. They promised me immunity from punishment if I would adopt such a course, but I positively refused, knowing that their object was to secure the conviction of the President and Gen. Babcock through my testimony.

On Monday, the 15th, my case was called, and the court denying my application for a continuance, I was placed on trial, which continued until the following Monday, when a verdict of guilty was returned. . . .

My friends, without exception, pleaded with me to demand my pardon. Maj. Grimes received a letter from Gen. Babcock on the day of my conviction, in which he told Grimes to assure me that the President would pardon me immediately upon my request. But I refused the proffer of a pardon and if this fact were allowed to remain unexplained there is scarcely one of the thousands who will read this book that would give the slightest credence to this statement. My reasons were, nevertheless, of the most plausible character: At the particular time of which I am writing the most damaging charges were being made against the President and Gen. Babcock, and I knew that the Grand Jury was then investigating allegations against the latter, and the public was daily expecting his indictment. My position, serious as it was, did not make me forget what I conceived to be my duty. I had avowed my determination to protect the President and Gen. Babcock even at the sacrifice of my own feelings and humiliation. I realized that if the President granted me a pardon in the face of public opinion, which was very excited, that it would clearly establish the fact of my intimate affiliation with both Grant and Babcock, and the impeachment of one and conviction of the other would be a foregone conclusion. . . .

My personal discomforts, while in confinement, were not so great as those unacquainted with the circumstances might suppose. I was visited daily by nearly all my friends. . . . Among the daily callers at my citadel was E.W. Fox, at one time collector of the port of St. Louis, and, I believe, the inventor of wooden insoles in army shoes which, during the war, furnished such a blessed margin of profit to army contractors. . . . His visits were always very pleasant because he was a member of the Grand Jury which was then in session, and he never failed to tell me every day just how the investigation against Babcock was proceeding.

He was our mutual friend and was rewarded for it, as Grant had promised, in this manner: The people of St. Louis knew Fox too well to accept him as a government officer, so the only thing that remained was to appoint his son as consul to Brunswick, Germany, at a salary of $2,500 in gold per year. This son was only nineteen years of age at the time of his appointment, while the regulations require all consuls to be at least twenty-one years of age, but then he was large enough and the President couldn't afford to regard requirements when his own and Babcock's interests were risked against such stakes. Fox, however, did more than I have already mentioned. . . . Before the adjournment of the Grand Jury he succeeded in securing the adoption of a letter completely exonerating the President from any complicity or knowledge of the whiskey ring; but it was impossible for him to prevent Babcock's indictment so he could only do the next best thing: notify the President by telegraph the moment the indictment was found. . . .

On the day this letter [exonerating Grant] was adopted, Fox came to my department of the municipality [the jail] and, with joy beaming from his little grey eyes, he said: "Now General, what do you think of that? Hain't that policy and diplomacy; wasn't that one of the brightest ideas of the century?" etc. I agreed with him that it was a master stroke; in fact, he filled me to such an extent with the importance of his accomplishment, that I yielded to his solicitation and assurances of pecuniary distress, and loaned him the sum of $200, the memory alone of which remains as a momento of his insinuating address and magnanimous disposition. With this money Fox posted to Washington and secured his boy a consulship. . . .

On the 4th of November, the Grand Jury returned indictments against Wm. McKee, proprietor of the *Globe-Democrat,* and Constantine Maguire, revenue collector, charging them with conspiracy to defraud the Government. On the 13th of the same month, Col. Joyce was sentenced by Judge Krekel to a term of three and one-half years' imprisonment in the penitentiary and to pay a fine of $2,000. . . .

BABCOCK PLACED ON TRIAL

On the 24th of November, the case of Wm. O. Avery (who is now well known to the reader) was called, and both sides being ready the trial proceeded, Judge Chester H. Krum entering an appearance as counsel for the defendant. Avery's conviction was not secured until the 3rd of December, after a bitter fight in which the most exciting scenes occurred. . . . During the trial of Avery, Gen. Henderson took a more than prominent part—he assumed a most aggressive attitude [and insinuated that Grant was involved]. . . .

W.D.W. Barnard, a cousin of President Grant's, was in the court-room during the delivery of [his] speech, and regarding the language as a serious reflection upon the President, he sent a dispatch to Washington that night giving the offensive remarks in full. It should be remembered that this speech was made at a time when the Grand Jury was investigating charges against Gen. Babcock, and hence they had a double significance. The President and his coterie of barnacles felt outrages, nay—frightened at this boldness, and as they had long been seeking an occasion to get rid of Gen. Henderson, they accepted this as their opportunity. . . . [11]

It was the first indefensible step taken to prevent an honest and thorough prosecution of all the Whiskey Ring members, and the suspicions which before attached to the President now assumed the nature of well founded charges. The removal of Gen. Henderson from a position as assistant to the district attorney, in which he had distinguished himself by an energy and efficiency that struck terror to the heart of the illicit whiskey conspiracy, was not alone the last and desperate resort of an alarmed and implicated administration—it was a virtual confession of its own guilt. The President was betrayed by his personal fears into an act that stamped him with ineffaceable suspicion. . . .

On the 9th of December the Grand Jury concluded its lengthy session by returning an indictment against Gen. Orville E. Babcock. The excitement over this announcement was almost equal to that exhibited by the Northern people when they received the news of the capture of Richmond in 1865. It was a stroke of lightning, as it were, and everyone thought they saw the hand of justice hovering over the heads of those who were fortified by the influence which attaches to the Executive. . . .

On the 20th of January [1876], Wm. McKee was arraigned for trial. . . . Every step in the case was bitterly contested, and in St. Louis, where the defendant had occupied a high position for more than thirty years, the excitement was very great. The evidence was so overwhelming, however, that on the morning of February 1st a verdict of guilty was returned. On the same day Col. Constantine Maguire, having not the slightest hope for an acquittal, entered a plea of guilty. . . .

On February 8th, Gen. Babcock was placed on trial, charged with conspiracy to defraud the Government, there being five counts in the indictment. . . . This trial was one of the most remarkable and in many respects the most noteworthy of any ever held in America. Not that there were any intricate problems of jurisprudence involved, but because it arrayed the people directly against the Executive. It was essentially a fight between justice and the cormorants of power and mighty influence, and alas, that it must be said, justice was defeated.

The court-room was densely packed with interested people during every day of the trial, while the streets in the vicinity of the United States Courts were literally crowded with anxious persons eager to catch every floating rumor appertaining to the distinguished defendant. . . . On the ninth day of the Babcock trial the President's deposition was introduced in court and read. . . . In taking the deposition of the President I desire

[11] Henderson was removed from his post as assistant to the district attorney for taking "advantage of his position as special counsel of the government to assail the President, who was not on trial," as Attorney General Edwards Pierrepont wrote.

to call the attention of the reader to the fact that the President of the United States could not be compelled to testify, as all processes of U.S. Courts are in his name. . . . On Feb. 9th it was agreed between the counsel for Babcock and the Government that the deposition of the President would be taken orally, and in accordance with this stipulation Maj. Eaton was selected to represent the prosecution, and left for Washington on the evening of the 10th, for that purpose. . . . It must be understood that the distinguished witness could not be coerced and that Maj. Eaton could not, even if he had a disposition to do so, examine the President the same as a witness in a police court.

It is apparent all through the deposition that whenever Maj. Eaton pressed the President, he either did not remember or gave the Major to understand that he (the President) did not think it necessary. Secretary Bristow, although earnest and determined in his prosecution of Babcock, felt a delicacy in placing the President of the United States in a position where he would appear in the eyes of the nation as a co-defendant in this case. All parties concerned understood and appreciated the delicate position they were placed in, and that forty millions of people were looking at them through the medium of an independent press. All understood that the object of the President's deposition was to inform the court and the jury and through them each individual member of every home throughout the entire country the President's unbounded confidence in Gen. Babcock's integrity. . . .

At noon on the 24th the case was given to the jury and the court took a recess until three o'clock, when, upon reassembling, the jury returned into court and rendered their verdict of "not guilty." At this juncture Gen. Babcock arose and shook the hand of each juror with much warmth.

THE PRESIDENT SUCCEEDED: his best friend went free, despite overwhelming evidence, despite the conviction of his coconspirator John McDonald and many others. But it was a Pyrrhic victory indeed: no one doubted that the massive corruption of the era had reached into the White House itself.

Ulysses S. Grant's presidency shuddered toward its end, choked by many more scandals than the Whiskey Ring. One official after another had been forced out in disgrace, from Treasury Secretary William Richardson to Secretary of War William W. Belknap, who had sold off a lucrative Indian trading post for a handsome annuity. And so the conquering hero, the savior of the Republic, had been reduced to an ineffectual lame duck, saddled with a Democratic House, drained of credibility, and haunted by impeachment; the President had even descended so low as to testify (indirectly) to save the most unsavory figure in the unsavory city of Washington.

Nor did he wish to abandon that figure after his controversial acquittal. The evidence implicating Babcock was overwhelming, despite the verdict—yet the isolated Grant still clung to him. He only relinquished his friend when Secretary of State Fish confronted him with evidence that Babcock's career of graft dated back to the days of Black Friday; Babcock, along with Assistant Treasury Secretary Daniel Butterfield, had been on the take as Jay Gould manipulated the gold market. Grant reluctantly sent his former personal secretary away, providing him with a post as a lighthouse inspector along the Atlantic coast.

Despite all this, historian Mark Wahlgren Summers has argued that the corruption of the age of Grant is notable less for its existence than for the new determination to root it out. Public graft was a long-lived legacy of political patronage; when McDonald set up the whiskey conspiracy, he was rebuilding a long-standing illicit relationship between tax collectors and distillers, dating back to Johnson's and even Lincoln's administration. An earthquake of reform rattled this cozy tradition during Grant's presidency, from New York to St. Louis. Democrat Samuel J. Tilden won fame in the 1870s by sending to jail Jay Gould's old political partner, New York City boss William M. Tweed; Tilden went on to break up other conspiracies, such as the canal ring that skimmed money from the upkeep of New York's waterways. In 1871, reforming Senator Carl Schurz helped push through a bill to establish the Civil Service Commission, designed to reduce the political role played by public officials. Congress launched a number of investigations of corruption, as figures such as cartoonist Thomas Nast and writer Samuel Clemens (better known as Mark Twain) lampooned officials on the take.

But there is another side of this great reform campaign to consider, before we raise a tombstone over the Grant presidency, engraved with a pious condemnation of corruption. The reformist wing of the Republican party also happened to be the conservative wing; on the other hand, the politicians most likely to promote partisan activists for public office were often those most dedicated to Reconstruction. Politically motivated appointments had always been a tool of party control—why sacrifice that tool now, many Radicals reasoned, when the cause to be advanced was equal rights for African Americans? The bitter irony is that corruption and civil rights rose and fell together.

And so President Grant sat in the White House, silently smoking his cigars through his last year in office, isolated, friendless, alienated. Rawlins was long since dead; Babcock was sent away; McDonald was locked up in a rancid, vermin-infested prison, eventually to be freed with a last-minute pardon. In the West, General Sheridan, Howard, and other old army subordinates fought the last of the Indian wars—damping down Apache resistance, chasing down the Nez Percés of Chief Joseph, and fighting the Sioux and Northern Cheyenne in the very last region left unceded by Native Americans. Even here, success was marred by tragedy, as Indian warriors triumphed in the epic battles of the Rosebud and Little

Bighorn, wiping out the flamboyant Custer and almost three hundred men of the Seventh Cavalry. A dreary succession of marches and minor skirmishes finally convinced the Indians to surrender for the last time. And in the South, all but three Reconstruction governments had fallen, seemingly forgotten by the man in the White House, the man who had made them possible. Three free states left, three islands in the Southern sea of white supremacy: the only question was how much time remained before they, too, would be drowned in the flood.

24

1877: THE FINAL DISASTER

As the President sulked in the executive mansion, shielded from the ungrateful public by the iron gate that Julia had ordered closed, the Republican party elders plotted how to survive his political collapse. One of them—well, he was far from a party elder, stalwart though he was—observed with disgust: no one had come to the aid of Congressman John Lynch when he miraculously survived the insurrection in Mississippi. The Republican leaders could use his luck and his skill as they faced the election of 1876, for it would revolve around one last violent outbreak in the desperately divided South. But a black representative was the last man they wanted to hear from in that fateful campaign.

Congressman Lynch, however, might well have had the sympathies of Senator John Sherman; the ever-moderate Ohio Republican tended to view the Radicals with a wary eye, but he could rise to white-hot outrage at the atrocities perpetrated on African Americans. Like Lynch, he was not altogether pleased with former Speaker of the House James G. Blaine, the leading candidate for the Republican nomination; he was quite happy with the ultimate selection of Rutherford B. Hayes, who "from his early manhood," Sherman wrote, "has been an anti-slavery man." Henry Adams had another opinion of Hayes: a "third-rate nonentity," he sniffed. Eric Foner describes him as a "colorless" man "whose main claim to fame was managing to remain on good terms with all factions of the party." These were the ingredients of a safe nominee, not a bold leader willing to fight for the last remains of Reconstruction.

If Senator Sherman harbored any such doubts, he hid them well. As the campaign of 1876 developed, the Ohio Republican toured the nation, urging the party faithful to recall why they had fought the Civil War; he reminded them that the same men who had rebelled against the national government now were terrorizing the freed people, defying the results of the great conflict.

Unfortunately, those same men were active in the last three states where Reconstruction held sway: Louisiana, Florida, and South Carolina. The Democrats had learned the successful lesson of the Mississippi coup the year before; in 1876, they intended to burn, shoot, and hang their way to electoral victories in the holdout states, despite the black majorities in Louisiana and South Carolina and the large black minority in Florida. Grant in 1876 felt even less desire than the year before to use the army or federal marshals to enforce the law in the South—especially now that spare troops were being drained onto the northern plains to track down Sitting Bull and the other Indians who had annihilated Custer.

So went the most hotly disputed election in American history. Like most aspects of Reconstruction, it has gone down in most history books quite the opposite from the way it actually happened: the Republicans, it has long been said, sought to steal the electoral college votes of these three Southern states, despite Democratic majorities at the ballot box. Sherman's account makes clear, however, that the Democrats relied on the most brutal methods to secure their supposed victory. But the Republicans had been weakened, and Hayes and Grant hesitated at using force. So a deal was struck, a deal that Sherman is anxious to deny: a Republican would take the White House, and the Democrats could have the last three states left where African-American votes meant anything.

The Contested Election
by John Sherman

The Republican national convention of 1876 met at Cincinnati on the 14th of June of that year. After the usual organization the following eight nominations for President were made: Blaine, Morton, Conkling, Bristow, Hayes, Hartranft, Wheeler, and Jewell. . . . The vote for Hayes increased at each ballot until the seventh ballot he received 384 votes, a majority over all.

Undoubtedly Blaine was the favorite of the convention, but the antagonisms that existed between him and Conkling probably defeated his nomination. I still believe that the nomination of Hayes was not only the safest, but the strongest that could be made. The long possession of power by the Republicans naturally produced rivalries that greatly affected the election of anyone who had been constantly prominent in public life, like Blaine, Conkling, and Morton. Hayes had growing qualities, and in every respect was worthy of the high position of President. He had been a soldier, a Member of Congress, thrice elected as Governor of Ohio, an admirable executive officer, and his public and private record was beyond question. He was not an aggressive man, although firm in his opinions and faithful in his friendships. Among all the public men with whom I have been brought in contact, I have known none who was freer from personal objection, whose character was more stainless, who was better adapted for a high executive office than Rutherford B. Hayes. . . .

His [Democratic] opponent, Samuel J. Tilden, was a man of singular political sagacity, of great shrewdness, a money-making man who professed to represent, and perhaps did represent as fairly as anyone, the ideas of the New York politicians of the school of Van Buren and Marcy. I knew Mr. Tilden personally and very favorably, as we were members of a board of railroad directors which frequently met. He seemed to take pleasure in talking with me about political events, and especially of famous New York politicians, of whom Silas Wright and Mr. Van Buren were his favorites. He had acquired great wealth as the attorney of corporations, and was undoubtedly a man of marked ability and sagacity. He had taken an active part in defeating the corruption of Tweed in New York politics. He had been elected governor of the State of New York, and as the candidate of reform and honesty in politics.

The long and important session of Congress adjourned on the 15th of August. It had been the arena for long debates, mostly on political topics growing out of Reconstruction and financial measures heretofore referred to. The pending presidential contest also excited much debate in both Houses. The administration of General Grant had not been entirely satisfactory, and the long continuance of the Republican party in power was an element of weakness. The complaints, unavoidable in the most honest administration, and the disappointments of office-seekers, placed that party on the defensive.

The South had, by Reconstruction, been practically restored to political power, and the body of the negroes had been substantially disfranchised, though legally entitled to the suffrage. Riots and crimes of every degree were committed in the South, notably in Louisiana, South Carolina, and Florida. Organized mobs and violence had deterred many from voting, and in some cases had prevented even the semblance of a free election.

I entered actively into this canvass, more than in any previous one. Three days before the adjournment, I made my opening speech in Marietta, Ohio, in which I discussed fully the dangers of the restoration of the Democratic party to power, and the probability of their failure to enforce the constitutional amendments and the protection of the rights of the freedmen. I claimed that the election of Mr. Tilden would result in the virtual nullification of the constitutional amendments, and amount to a practical restoration to power of the old Democratic party. The revival of the rebel claims,[12] the refunding of the cotton tax, and the damages done to rebels were fully commented upon, as were the outrages committed upon freedmen during the second administration of General Grant, the organization of the Ku Klux Klans and the White League, and the boldness with which the laws were disregarded in the South.

It is now difficult to realize the condition of public affairs in all the

[12] Sherman refers to the claims by former slaveholders to financial compensation for the emancipation of their slave "property."

states then lately in rebellion. The people of the South are certainly entitled to the highest credit for the great change that has recently been
made in the government of their states, but it cannot be denied that during the ten years after the war their condition bordered on the despotism
of mob rule and violence. Financial questions, no doubt, entered into the
canvass, but in this respect Governor Tilden and Governor Hayes did not
materially differ, while public opinion in the Southern states was almost
a unit in favor of the larger use of paper money. Their bankrupt condition made this policy almost universal there.

I continued until the day of election to make speeches, not only in
Ohio but in several of the states. . . . I think it would be safe to say that
from the close of Congress until the day of election I spoke on nearly
every weekday in some one of the five or six states which I visited.

The result of the presidential election in November 1876 was extremely doubtful. It was soon asserted that the majority either way would
be very small, and that the probabilities were that Mr. Tilden was elected.
Zachariah Chandler, chairman of the national Republican committee,
however, confidently telegraphed on the morning after the election that
Hayes was elected by a majority of one in the electoral college. Further
reports developed that on account of intimidation, frauds, and violence
committed in the election in Louisiana, South Carolina, and Florida, the
vote of each of those states was doubtful, and could only be ascertained
by the reports of the returning boards.

All of their electoral votes were needed to give Hayes the majority of
one. Both parties claimed in each of the states a majority of the popular
vote. In the heated state of political feeling in those states, it was a matter of grave doubt whether the count of the vote might not result in violence, tumult, or war. On the evening of November 11, I received from
President Grant the following telegram:

PHILADELPHIA, PA., NOVEMBER 11, 1876.

RECEIVED at MANFIELD, O., 8:35 P.M.

SENATOR JOHN SHERMAN:
I would be much pleased if you would join other parties, who have
already accepted same invitation, to go to New Orleans to witness
the canvassing of the vote of Louisiana.

U.S. GRANT

I replied that I would go as soon as practicable, and received the following answer:

WASHINGTON, D.C., NOVEMBER 12, 1876

RECEIVED at MANFIELD, O., 4 P.M.

HON. JOHN SHERMAN:
Unless you can reach there by Friday morning [November 17] it will
be too late.

U.S. GRANT

I at once started for New Orleans, stopping on the way in Columbus to confer with Governor Hayes, who said he wished I would go to New Orleans and witness the count, but expressed in the strongest possible language his opposition to any movement on the part of anyone to influence the action of the returning board in his favor. He said if Mr. Tilden was elected, he desired him by all means to have the office. I proceeded to Cincinnati, where I met some of the gentlemen whom General Grant had requested to witness the count. When we arrived in New Orleans I found far less excitement in respect to the count than in Ohio. I there met the other gentlemen who had been, like myself, invited by General Grant. . . .

At New Orleans I was for the first time introduced to the members of the returning board, who, under the laws of Louisiana, were required to verify the count and whose return was final. We met also a large number of gentlemen who were there at the request of the national Democratic committee to perform the same duty that had been imposed upon us by General Grant. . . .

The returning board then proceeded to perform its duty under the law. . . . Whatever opinions may be expressed as to the correctness of the findings of the returning board, there can be no doubt that its proceedings were open, fair, and impartial. The board arrived at the conclusion that the Republican electors received a majority of the votes cast in Louisiana at that election, and were entitled to cast the vote of the state for the President of the United States.

During the great excitement over this controversy, and also over that in South Carolina and Florida, exaggerated statements without the slightest foundation of frauds and improper conduct on the part of the returning officers were made and published. As to the action of the returning board in Louisiana, I feel bound now, after a long lapse of time, to repeat what was reported to General Grant by the Republican visitors, that it made a fair, honest, and impartial return of the result of the election. In concluding our report we said:

"The proof of violence and intimidation and armed disturbance in many other parishes is of the same general character, although more general and decisive, as to the five parishes particularly referred to. In the others, these causes prevailed at particular polling places, at many of which the Republican vote was, to a considerable extent, pre vented. . . ."

Pending the action of the board, I wrote to Governor Hayes the following letter, giving a general view of the testimony:

STATE OF LOUISIANA, EXECUTIVE DEPARTMENT

NEW ORLEANS, NOVEMBER 23, 1876

MY DEAR SIR:

I have not written you sooner, for the progress of our visitation will be known to you through the papers sooner than from my letters, and the telegraph office here is more public than a sheriff's sale. We sometimes hear of private telegrams before they are delivered. . . .

We are now collecting the testimony as to the bulldozed parishes. It seems more like the history of hell than of civilized and Christian communities. The means adopted are almost incredible, but were fearfully effective upon an ignorant and superstitious people.[13] That you would have received at a fair election a large majority in Louisiana, no honest man can question. . . .

VERY TRULY YOURS,   JOHN SHERMAN.

I met Governor Hayes on my return and his conversation was to the . . . effect that he wished no doubtful votes and would greatly prefer to have Mr. Tilden serve as President if there was any doubt of his (Hayes's) election. The Republican visitors did not return until after the meeting of Congress at its regular session on the 4th of December, 1876. . . .

On the 18th of January, 1877, Mr. Edmunds, of the select committee of the Senate on the counting of electoral votes, submitted a report in writing with an accompanying bill. It was, with one exception, signed by the members of the committees of the two Houses without distinction of party. The bill provided in full detail a prescribed manner for counting the electoral vote. It was adopted by both Houses and voted for by a great majority, but believing it was extra constitutional, I, with other Republicans, did not vote for it. The history of the electoral commission provided for in this bill is part of the history of the country, and it is not necessary to here enter into it in detail. It is sufficient to say that it resulted in the counting of the votes of Louisiana, South Carolina, and Florida for Mr. Hayes, electing him President by a majority of one vote. . . .

[13] This comment, coming from a firm Republican supporter of Reconstruction, shows how deeply racism ran in the country in 1876—suggesting why the North was willing, in the end, to allow black suffrage to lapse.

When[14] Mr. Hayes was inaugurated as President, he found thirty-six states in the full and uncontested exercise of all the powers of states in the Union. In two states only were there contests as to who was governor. Both contests had existed from January to March 1877, while General Grant was president.

In South Carolina, Governor Chamberlain claimed to have been elected on the Republican ticket, and General Hampton on the Democratic ticket. The President is not made the judge of who is elected governor of a state, and an attempt to exercise such a power would be a plain act of usurpation. The constitution of South Carolina is much like that of Ohio. The count of the vote was to be made by the general assembly of the state. Unfortunately for Chamberlain a controlling question in the contest had been decided against him by a Republican court, and he was only kept in possession of the state house by the actual presence of United States troops in the building. He had appealed again and again to President Grant to recognize him as governor and to give him the aid of Federal troops in the enforcement of his claim, which General Grant had refused, seeking only to preserve the public peace.

When President Hayes was inaugurated both contestants were called to Washington and both were patiently heard and the questions presented were patiently and carefully examined. The President held that a case was not presented in which, under the constitution and the laws, he was justified in using the army of the United States in deciding a purely local election contest. The soldiers and bayonets of the United States were then withdrawn from the state house—not from the state, nor the capital of the state—but from the building in which the legislature that alone could lawfully decide this question must meet. This was all that was done by the President, and Governor Chamberlain, without further contesting his claim, abandoned it and left the state. . . .

The case of Louisiana was far more difficult. The local returning officers of that state had, after a full examination, certified to the election of the legislature, showing a Republican majority in both houses. This had been done by excluding from their return the votes of certain parishes and counties wherein intimidation, violence, and fraud had prevailed to an extent sufficient to change the result of the election. I was present, at the request of General Grant, to witness the count, and I assure you, as I have said officially, that the proof of this intimidation, violence, and fraud extended to murder, cruelty, and outrage in every form, was absolutely conclusive, showing a degree of violence in some of those parishes that was more revolting and barbarous than anything I could conceive of. . . . But it was equally clear that [the election board's] return was not conclusive upon the members

14 The passage that follows is the text of a speech Sherman delivered in 1877; he included it in his memoirs, rather than restate the events described.

elected, and that each house had the constitutional right to pass upon the returns and elections of its members, and to set aside the action of the returning board. The two houses, when organized, had also the power to pass upon the returns of the election of governor, and they alone and no one else. Neither the President of the United States nor the returning board has any power or right to pass upon the election of governor. And here the difficulty in the Louisiana case commences.

Governor Packard [the Republican] contends that a majority of the two houses, as duly returned, did pass upon the election of the governor, and did return that he was duly elected, but this was stoutly denied by Governor Nichols [the Democratic candidate]. This vital point was strongly asserted and denied by the adverse parties, and the legislature of Louisiana divided into two hostile bodies, holding separate sessions, each asserting its legal power and denouncing the other as rebels and traitors. Governor Packard and his legislature called upon President Grant for the aid of the army to put down insurrection and domestic violence; and here I confess that if I had been President, instead of General Grant, I would have recognized Packard and sustained him with the full power of the general government. My intense feeling, caused by the atrocities of Louisiana, may have unduly influenced me. But General Grant did not think this was his duty. . . . He would only maintain the peace. He would not recognize Packard as governor, but I know what is now an open secret, the strong bent of his mind and at one time his decision was to withdraw the troops, to recognize Nichols and thus end this dangerous contest. He did not do this, but kept the peace.

But during these two months the whole condition of affairs had slowly changed in Louisiana. The government of Packard had dwindled away until it had scarcely a shadow of strength or authority, except at the state house, where it was upheld by federal bayonets. The government of Nichols had extended its authority over the state and was in full existence as the *de facto* government of Louisiana, supported by the great body of white men and nearly all the wealth and intelligence of the state, and by the tired acquiescence of a large portion of the colored people, some of whom deserted Packard's legislature and entered that of Governor Nichols. The delay and hesitation of General Grant had been fatal to Packard, and when Hayes became President the practical question was greatly changed. One thing was clear, that a legislature had been duly elected in November previous, and was then in existence, though separated into two parts. If the members lawfully elected could be convened, they alone could decide the question of who was governor, without the intervention of troops, and their decision could be supported, if necessary, by the general government.

The most anxious consideration was given to this question. Days and weeks of anxious deliberation were given to it by the President and his cabinet. . . . [15] To aid in this [decision], a commission of the most eminent men, high in position, from different states, and distinguished for judicial impartiality, was selected and the result is known to all. They went to Louisiana, and with great difficulty brought together these hostile legislatures which met, organized, promptly settled the questions in dispute in favor of the government of Nichols, and thus ended this most dangerous controversy.

No other change was made, no other act done except, when the solution was almost accomplished, the few troops which had occupied the state house were withdrawn a few squares away to their barracks. Thus, in this peaceful appeal to the legislature of Louisiana, this controversy, which not only endangered the peace and safety of this state, but the peace and safety of the whole people of the United States, was settled. This is the sum and substance of all that was done in the Southern policy, as it is called, of the President.

Perhaps I ought to state that his policy has a broader motive than a mere settlement of a local election contest. It seeks to bring the North and South together again into conditions of harmony and fraternity, and by a rank appeal to the generous impulses and patriotic feeling of all classes of people in the South, to secure not only peace among themselves, but the equal protection of the laws to all, and security in the enjoyment of political and civil rights.

No doubt the result in Louisiana caused some disappointment to many Republicans throughout the United States who deeply sympathized with their Republican brethren in that state. In that feeling I did, and do, share, and yet I feel and know that every step taken by President Hayes was right. . . . Some are foolish enough to talk of his abandoning the colored people and their constitutional rights. President Hayes, from his early manhood, has been an anti-slavery man . . . and I believe this day that the policy he has adopted will do more to secure the practical enforcement of those rights than the employment of an army tenfold greater than the army of the United States.

————

SOME POLITICAL ALCHEMY still unknown to modern science must have entered into Sherman's calculations when he declared, "the policy he [Hayes] has adopted will do more" to secure civil rights for blacks "than the employment of an army tenfold greater than the army of the United States." In light of the century that followed the Compromise of 1877 (as Hayes's arrangement with Southern Democrats has been called), it is difficult to see how abandoning African-American voters to white supremacist rule could have done less to secure their rights. Indeed, one thing this age and its af-

[15] Hayes had appointed Senator Sherman as Secretary of the Treasury, so he took part in these debates.

termath make clear: the only way to guarantee equal rights for blacks was vigorous federal intervention. It worked during Reconstruction, and it would work again during the civil rights era of the 1960s.

The path blazed by Congressman L. Q. C. Lamar (now *Senator* Lamar) in Mississippi opened the way for the Democratic triumph of 1877. They failed to carry the presidency—but all the better for Southern whites, for why would they want a Yankee Democrat (a moralistic one at that) in the White House, when they could extract a heavy price from a Republican? Hayes took the oath of office in peace, and in return he allowed whites to do what they wished in the South, to sweep away the legally elected governments, to change their laws and constitutions to limit the political power of African Americans for good (at least for several generations).

But there were survivors—men who hung on throughout the South in small, unvanquished pockets of Republican, sometimes black, political power. It would take another twenty years for the full array of Jim Crow laws to come into effect in many states,[16] and traces of Reconstruction would linger in a county here or a township there. Some Southern black Republicans benefitted from their party's continued control of federal patronage and appointments. And in Mississippi there was no more important survivor than John Lynch.

Congressman Lynch not only won reelection during the catastrophic election of 1875, he went on to win a later term in 1882 (though he had to challenge the fraudulent ballot count). In the words of Eric Foner, he and two other African-American men "formed a triumvirate that dominated party affairs" in Mississippi after Reconstruction. He served as an auditor in the U.S. treasury department and as a delegate to almost every Republican national convention through 1900—and as the temporary chairman in 1884. Lynch became the first African American to deliver the keynote address to a major party convention (the next time would not be until 1968). The former slave prospered economically as well, acquiring a 1,500-acre plantation near Natchez, and eventually buying three more as well as several town lots.

But personal triumph was not enough for the eloquent Lynch—he wanted political survival for his people. The abandonment of Mississippi in 1875 staggered him: Had not the state been well-run? Had it not been a Republican bastion? Why had the Republican President, then, allowed an armed overthrow of its Constitutional government? To answer the question, we must flash back to the late days of Grant's administration, before the final catastrophe of 1877, when the young Mississippi survivor

16 Jim Crow laws (as segregation and disfranchisement laws were known) did *not* immediately follow the Republican defeat in the 1870s. Many arose a decade or more later, in response to the increasing assertiveness of the growing population of prosperous blacks.

came to the White House to press his case. Lynch got his answer—and a prophecy of the looming disaster that would soon throw the South into almost eighty years of darkness.

Mississippi Abandoned
by John R. Lynch

Shortly after I reached Washington in the latter part of November, 1875, I called on the President to pay my respects, and to see him on business relating to a Civil Service order that he had recently issued. . . . After paying my respects to the President, I brought this case to his attention. . . .

I then informed the President that there was another matter about which I desired to have a short talk with him, that was the recent election in Mississippi. After calling his attention to the sanguinary struggle through which we had just passed, and the great disadvantages under which we labored, I reminded him of the fact that the Governor, when he saw that he could not put down without the assistance of the National Administration what was practically an insurrection against the State Government, made application for assistance in the manner and form prescribed by the Constitution, with the confident belief that it would be forthcoming. But in this we were, for some reason, seriously disappointed and sadly surprised. The reason for this action, or rather non-action, was still an unexplained mystery to us. For my own satisfaction and information I should be pleased to have the President enlighten me on the subject.

The President said that he was glad I had asked him the question, and that he would take pleasure in giving me a frank reply. He said he had sent Governor Ames's requisition to the War Department with his approval and with instructions to have the necessary assistance furnished without delay. He had also given instructions to the Attorney-General to use the marshals and the machinery of the Federal judiciary as far as possible in cooperation with the War Department in an effort to maintain order and to bring about a condition which would insure a peaceable and fair election.

But before the orders were put into execution a committee of prominent Republicans from Ohio had called on him (Ohio was then an October State—that is, her elections took place in October instead of November). An important election was then pending in that State. This committee, the President stated, protested against having the requisition of Governor Ames honored. The committee, the President said, informed him in a most emphatic way that if the requisition of Governor Ames were honored, the Democrats would not only carry Mississippi—a State which would be lost to the Republicans in any event—but the Democratic success in Ohio would be an assured fact. If the requisition were not honored it would make no change in the result in Mississippi, but that Ohio would be saved to the Republicans. The President assured me that it was with great reluctance that he yielded—against his own judgment and sense of official duty—to the arguments of this committee, and directed the withdrawal of the orders which had been given the Secretary of War and the Attorney-General in that matter.

This statement, I confess, surprised me very much. "Can it be possible," I asked, "that there is such a prevailing sentiment in the North, East, or West as renders it necessary for a Republican President to virtually give his sanction to what is equivalent to a suspension of the Constitution and the laws of the land to insure Republican success in such a State? I cannot believe this to be true, the opinion of the Republican committee from Ohio to the contrary notwithstanding. What surprises me more, Mr. President, is that you yielded and granted this remarkable request. That is not like you. It is the first time I have ever known you to show the white feather. Instead of granting the request of that committee, you should have rebuked the men—told them that it is your duty as chief magistrate of the country to enforce the Constitution and laws of the land, and to protect American citizens in the exercise and enjoyment of their rights, let the consequences be what they may; and that if by doing this Ohio should be lost by the Republicans it ought to be lost. In other words, no victory is worth having if it is to be brought about upon such conditions as those—that it is to be purchased at such a fearful cost as was paid in this case."

"Yes," said the President, "I admit that you are right. I should have not yielded. I believed at the time that I was making a grave mistake. But as presented, it was duty on one side, and party obligation on the other. Between the two I hesitated, but finally yielded to what was believed to be party obligation. . . . But I was satisfied then, as I am now, that Mississippi could not have been saved to the party in any event and I wanted to avoid the responsibility of the loss of Ohio, in addition. This was the turning-point in the case.

"And while on this subject," the President went on, "let us look more closely into the significance of this situation. I am very much concerned about the future of our country. When the War came to an end it was thought that four things had been brought about and effectually accomplished as a result thereof. They were: first, that slavery had been forever abolished; second, that the indissolubility of the Federal Union had been permanently established and universally recognized; third, that the absolute and independent sovereignty of the several States was a thing of the past; fourth, that a national sovereignty had been at last created and established, resulting in sufficient power being vested in the general government not only to guarantee to every State in the Union a republican form of government, but to protect, when necessary, the individual citizen of the United States in the exercise and enjoyment of the rights and privileges to which he is entitled under the Constitution and laws of his country. In other words, that there had been created a National citizenship as distinguished from State citizenship, resulting in a paramount allegiance to the United States— the General Government—having ample power to protect its own citizens against domestic and personal violence whenever the State in which he may live should fail, refuse, or neglect to do so. . . . This has been my conception of the duties of the President, and until recently I have pursued that course. But there seems to be a number of leading and influential men in the Republican party who take a different view of these matters. These men have used and are still using their power and influence, not to strengthen but to cripple the President and thus prevent him from enforcing the Constitution and laws along these lines. They have not only used their power and influence to prevent and defeat wise and necessary legislation for these purposes, but they have contributed, through the medium of public meetings and newspaper and magazine articles, to the creation of a public sentiment hostile to the policy of the administration. . . .

"It requires no prophet to foresee that the national government will soon be at a great disadvantage and that the results of the war of the rebellion will have been in a large measure lost. In other words, that the first two of the four propositions above stated will represent all that will have been accomplished as a result of the war, and even they, for the lack of power of enforcement in the general government, will be largely of a negative character. What you have just passed through in Mississippi is only the beginning of what is sure to follow. I do not wish to create unnecessary alarm, nor to be looked upon as a prophet of evil, but it is impossible for me to close my eyes in the face of things that are as plain to me as the noonday sun."

It is needless to say that I was deeply interested in the President's eloquent and prophetic talk which subsequent events have more than verified. . . .

It was claimed by some,[17] believed by others, and predicted by many that by the time the election for President in 1876 would roll around it would be found that the Republicans had regained substantially all they had lost in 1874; but these hopes, predictions, and expectations were not realized. The Presidential election of 1876 turned out to be so close and doubtful that neither party could claim a substantial victory. While it is true that Hayes, the Republican candidate for President, was finally declared elected according to the forms of law, yet the terms and conditions upon which he was allowed to be peaceably inaugurated were such as to complete the extinction and annihilation of the Republican party at the South. The price that the Hayes managers stipulated to pay—and did pay—for the peaceable inauguration of Hayes was that the South was to

[17] This paragraph has been moved for chronological continuity.

be turned over to the Democrats and that the administration was not to enforce the Constitution and the laws of the land in that section against the expressed will of the Democrats thereof. In other words, so far as the South was concerned, the Constitution was not to follow the flag.

ON JULY 16, 1877, employees of the Baltimore & Ohio Railroad at Martinsburg, West Virginia, went on strike. They were protesting their second wage reduction in under a year in the midst of the depression— and they were not alone in their indignation. The strike soon spread to almost every part of the country; miners and steelworkers soon left their posts to show their support. The North was in an absolute uproar, in a way it had never been during the fall of Reconstruction. Crowds of workers and sympathizers filled the streets, while men from well-off families formed militia units to suppress the "insurrection," as it was called.

At the height of the national strike, President Hayes cordially received a notable visitor to the White House: Thomas A. Scott, Andrew Carnegie's estranged mentor and now president of the mighty Pennsylvania Railroad. The two men knew each other well; Hayes's close ties to the railway industry could be seen in the many corporate attorneys and directors who staffed his administration. After they conferred, the President issued his orders: U.S. troops (sent straight from the South, where they were no longer wanted) were marched into the streets of Buffalo and St. Louis, where they protected strikebreaking workers and broke up union meetings. "On July 29," Eric Foner writes, "the Great Strike had come to an end." Hayes jotted down in his diary: "The strikers have been put down by *force*." It was not surprising that Scott could secure that force from the White House: a few weeks before, he had played a key role in negotiating the final abandonment of Reconstruction in the Compromise of 1877.[18]

With the twin struggles of that year, the Great Strike and the Compromise, the long battle for the future—we might even say the soul—of America reached a climax. It had begun in 1865, as an openly racist President and Southern state governments faced off against a Republican party composed of African Americans and patriotic loyalists, led by men who believed that victory in the war should mean something more than the mere technical abolition of slavery. It had been fought by Democrats who openly called themselves "the white man's party" and Republicans who had come to see freedom and equality for blacks in the South as a continuation of the Civil War, as an essential expression of the national sovereignty they had given so many lives for at places with such names as Shiloh and Gettysburg.

Yet at the very height of the Republican triumph, the party descended

[18]The terms included a promise of federal aid for the troubled Texas Pacific railroad, which Scott also led.

into vicious infighting and corruption, led by the very man who had made the military victory in the Civil War possible; all the while, Democrats patiently waited, repeating an incessant chant that the freed blacks and their white allies in the South were not worthy of the exertions of the federal government. And the Northern economy changed as well—it was gradually absorbed into a new system dominated by rising industrial giants, massive firms headed by men of unprecedented wealth and power, men such as Thomas Scott. Men who took over the Republican party, supplanting the Radicals, replacing their calls for freedom with demands for hard money and protective tariffs.

In 1877, the Republican party had ceased to be the flagship of civil rights, and had instead emerged as the embodiment of wealthy respectability. Nostalgic reminders of the battles of the Civil War and Reconstruction could still win votes, but the exclusive rooms where policies took shape were reserved for the powerful. In this new party, the struggle in the South was a tiresome relic of the past; industrial titans such as Rockefeller's Standard Oil or Carnegie's steel empire were the important future. L. Q. C. Lamar and other Southern leaders knew better than to rile old Union sentiments; they spoke gently, soothingly, and agreed to a deal with the Northern elite.

Not that the legacy of Reconstruction entirely disappeared: here a black Republican still stayed in office, there an institution such as Alcorn State University managed to survive. Furthermore, the triumph of federal power remained, battered but intact: the Fourteenth Amendment, that dramatic extension of central authority, stayed in the Constitution, even if it was now interpreted almost out of existence by the Supreme Court. The Fifteenth Amendment remained as well, a seed of hope that would lie dormant for ninety long years. The reach of federal law had been permanently extended to individuals, backed by a fresh crop of new federal courts, the establishment of the Department of Justice, and the federal marshal system. The national bureaucracy doubled in size between 1871 and 1881. "With its new federal powers established during the Civil War and confirmed by the Union victory," Alan Trachtenberg writes, "the central government strengthened its hold over civil society in the very years that it remained relatively inactive in shaping the emerging society." That is, federal power grew even as Washington abandoned Southern blacks and Northern workers.

The battle was won, won by an alliance of Northern Republican businessmen and Southern Democrats. Yankee industrialists gave up the South and gained a strong national government that backed their own interests. Other forces would arise to oppose this arrangement, including the Populist party. But the pattern of American history for most of the ensuing century had been set. The only fight that remained was the struggle for memory.

IX

EPILOGUES

25

THE DEBATE

In December 1995, historian James M. McPherson noted an odd fact about American memory. "The American Civil War," he wrote in *The New York Review of Books*, "is a highly visible exception to the adage that victors write the history of wars. No defeated nation has had more numerous and ardent champions than the Confederacy." This is indeed strange, given the context of historical writing. You will find, for example, no textbooks in American classrooms that hail the loyalists who fought with the British against the Revolution, or that exalt the glory of the German Kaiser, let alone the Nazis. But the losing side in the Civil War has been treated very differently—and any reader who has reached this point will know why: the same Confederate commanders who led a rebellion against the United States were back in public office by 1877. They were back because they had won a fight even greater than the war itself.

The reviled rebels of 1865 were the statesmen of 1877: Southern Democrats had won not only the control of their state governments, they had secured the confidence of the Northern population. In the larger scope of Southern history, they were indeed the victors, and they set about writing the history—not only of the Civil War, but of the dramatic dozen years that followed. Their task had commenced even before the fall of the last Southern Republican governor: the depression-weary North swallowed unceasing tales of a "prostrate South," gasping under the heels of thieving carpetbaggers, conniving scalawags, and ignorant blacks. It was a short step from political harangues and distorted newspaper reporting to school textbooks, once white-line Democrats were back in power.

But the battle for memory was not won overnight. After the Compromise of 1877 a ferocious debate raged between ousted Southern Republicans and triumphant Democrats. This chapter can only offer a glimpse of it through four voices—two opponents and two defenders of Reconstruction, one white and one black on each side. First the critics: Mississippi Senator L. Q. C. Lamar—the same politician who plotted the violent overthrow of his state's government—and Booker T. Washington, the respected black educator.

Lamar's essay (which appeared in 1879 as a part of a forum on black suffrage in *The North American Review*, a leading intellectual periodical) displays all the hallmarks of his campaign to deceive the Northern public: he never argues that African Americans should be denied the vote—rather, he writes, they need to be *educated* until they are ready to lead themselves. Until then, they should happily follow their "natural leaders," the white elite. In his mind, slavery was a happy first step in that education. He also repeats what were already becoming established stereotypes: Reconstruction governments were bloated and corrupt; Northern immigrants were self-serving, greedy carpetbaggers; Southern white Republicans were shameless scalawags. It was a drumbeat of propaganda that would soon become conventional wisdom among even serious historians.

The second critique is, in a way, more interesting and more troubling. It comes from one of the most influential African Americans of the late nineteenth century, Booker T. Washington. Though still quite young during the era in question, he later turned against the legacy of Reconstruction as he attempted to establish the Tuskegee Institute in the white-ruled state of Alabama. Washington's conservative, inward-looking philosophy reflects a vibrant strain of thought in the black community that continues to this day—an ethic of self-help and self-development, shunning reliance on government intervention. But Washington carried that principle farther, rejecting the all-too-brief black experience of electoral politics. By the time he wrote, the white Democratic cliches about Reconstruction had become so pervasive, he accepted them himself. He saw political activism as a wasteful diversion from the practical tasks of education and economic development.

An Ignorant Negro Majority
by L. Q. C. Lamar

When you put the ballot in the hands of an ignorant negro majority as a means of education and progress, you must be patient while they learn their lesson. We of the South have borne all this, because we knew that the reaction must come. It has come. The results which you see to be so bad [the supposed misgovernment of Reconstruction] the negro has seen also. He has come back to us with the same blind impulse with which a few years ago he fled from us. He may be as ignorant a Democrat as he was an ignorant Republican, but years must yet pass before the ballot will have educated him fully into self-reliant, temperate citizenship; and what we of the South have borne, our friends of the North must bear with us, until the negro has become what we both want to make him. This is part of his education.

By a system, not one whit less a system of force or of fraud than that alleged to exist now, he was taken away from his natural leaders at the South, and held to a compact Republican vote. Granting—which I do not grant— that the present methods [of controlling black voters] are as bad as those then applied, the fault lies in the character of the vote. It is not educated to free action, and we must educate it to what it ought to be. Take the history of the race . . . and is there not progress, astonishing progress, when the material with which we are dealing is considered? Force and fraud [on the part of the Democrats] have been freely charged. Could anyone expect, did anyone expect, that such a tremendous political and social change—the sudden clothing of four million slaves with suffrage and overruling political power—could be made without violent disturbance and disorder? Had any such change ever been made in any free State without convulsion? Was it expected that, when the capital and character of a State were placed at the mercy of a numerical majority of ignorant and poverty-stricken voters it would present a model of peace and order? . . .

At this stage of progress, the negro vote cannot intelligently direct itself. It must and will follow some leader. Now, up to 1876, the Republican party, armed with all the authority of the Federal government, supplied those leaders. They were strangers in the States they governed. The moment that the compact vote upon which their power rested was divided, they abandoned their places, and in almost every case left the States in which they had ruled. The great mass of colored voters was left without guides. . . . The weapon of defense which had been given to the negro was thrown away by his leaders in their flight, and [Northern critics] can scarcely complain if it was picked up by the Democrats. . . .

The whole country has passed through a very painful experience in the solution of this question [of black suffrage], and no one can adequately describe the bitterness of the trial of the South; but she has borne it, and it seems to me that a statesman who loves this great country of which we are all citizens should feel that the time has come when a kindly judgment of each other's difficulties would bring us nearer that unanimity of action which alone aids the solution of a grave social and political problem.

I was born and bred a slaveholder, born and bred among slaveholders; I have known slavery in its kindest and most beneficent aspect. My associations with the past of men and things are full of love and reverence. In all history, never has a heavy duty been discharged more faithfully, more conscientiously, more successfully, than by the slaveholders of the South. But, if I know myself and those whom I represent, we have accepted the change in the same spirit. No citizen of this republic more than the Southerner can or does desire to see the negro improved, elevated, civilized, made a useful and worthy element in our political life. None more than they deplore and condemn all violence or other means tending to hinder the enjoyment of his elective franchise. The South took him, as he was sent to her, a wild and godless barbarian, and made him such that the North has been able to give him citizenship without the destruction of our institutions. The progress which he made with us as a slave will not be arrested now that he is a freeman—unless party passion and personal ambition insist upon using him as an instrument for selfish ends. . . .

So far I have to some extent, for the sake of argument, conceded the assumption that the negro vote has been subjected to the forcible control of the white race, but that I deny. . . . Let any intelligent Northern man review the history of the State governments of the South for the last ten years under Republican rule—the gross and shameless dishonesty, their exorbitant taxation, their reckless expenditure, their oppression of all native interests, the social agonies through which they have forced all that was good and pure to pass as through a fiery furnace; the character of the men—many of them—they have placed in power; and then say if such a state of things in a Northern or Western State would not have been a sure and natural precursor of a Republican defeat, so absolute and complete that the very name of the party would have become in that State a name of scorn and reproach. Then why should not that result have occurred in the South?

The Reconstruction Period
by Booker T. Washington

During the whole of the Reconstruction period our people throughout the South looked to the Federal government for everything, very much as a child looks to its mother. This was not unnatural. The central government gave them freedom, and the whole Nation had been enriched for more than two centuries by the labor of the Negro. Even as a youth, and later in manhood, I had the feeling that it was cruelly wrong, at the beginning of our freedom, to fail to make some provision for the general education of our people in addition to what the states might do, so that the people would be better prepared for the duties of citizenship.

It is easy to find fault, to remark what might have been done, and perhaps, after all, and under all the circumstances, those in charge of the conduct of affairs did the only thing that could be done at the time. Still, as I look back now over the entire period of our freedom, I cannot help feeling that it would have been wiser if some plan could have been put into operation which would have made the possession of a certain amount of education or property, or both, a test for the exercise of the franchise, and a way provided by which this test should be made to apply honestly and squarely to both the white and black races.

Though I was but little more than a youth during Reconstruction, I had the feeling that mistakes were being made, and that things could not remain in the condition they were then in very long. I felt that the Reconstruction policy, so far as it related to my race, was in a large measure on a false foundation, was artificial and forced. In many cases it seemed to me that the ignorance of my race was being used as a tool with which to help white men into office, and that there was an element in the North which wanted to punish Southern white men by forcing the Negro into positions over the heads of the Southern whites. I felt that the Negro would be the one to suffer for this in the end. Besides, the general political agitation drew the attention of our people away from the more fundamental matters of perfecting themselves in the industries at their doors and in securing property.

The temptations to enter political life were so alluring that I came very near yielding to them at one time, but I was kept from doing so by the feeling that I would be helping in a more substantial way by assisting in laying the foundation for the race through a generous education of the hand, head, and heart. I saw colored men who were members of the state legislatures, and county officers, who in some cases could not read or write, and whose morals were as weak as their education.

Not long ago, when I was passing through the streets of a certain city in the South, I heard some brick-masons calling out, from the top of a two-story building on which they were working, for the "Governor" to "hurry up and bring some more bricks." Several times I heard the command, "Hurry up, Governor!" "Hurry up, Governor!" My curiosity was aroused to such an extent that I made inquiry as to who the "Governor" was, and soon found that he was a colored man who at one time had held the position of Lieutenant-Governor of his state. But not all the colored people who were in office during Reconstruction were unworthy of their positions, by any means. . . .

Of course, the colored people, so largely without education, and wholly without experience in government, made tremendous mistakes, just as any people similarly situated would have done. Many of the Southern whites have a feeling that, if the Negro is permitted to exercise his political rights now to any degree, the mistakes of the Reconstruction period will repeat themselves. I do not think this would be true, because the Negro is a much stronger and wiser man than he was thirty-five years ago, and he is fast learning the lesson that he cannot afford to act in a manner that will alienate his Southern white neighbors from him.

WASHINGTON REJECTED UNIVERSAL suffrage, even arguing for literacy and property requirements that would have excluded most blacks from the polls under the friendliest government. He had swallowed whole the image of Reconstruction built up by men like L. Q. C. Lamar: when he saw a former lieutenant governor forced to work as a common laborer, he did not react with despair, but with disdain that such a common fellow had ever been in politics. He even accepted the mistaken view that most African Americans had been seeking political office, or public assistance, rather than working or seeking education. As far as both his and Lamar's views are concerned, the next two writers offer the best rebuttal—a virtual summary of the history recounted in this volume through the words of those who lived it.

First comes a familiar voice: John R. Lynch, the remarkable Mississippi man who rose from slavery to Congress. In 1913 he published his own account of the era, *The Facts of Reconstruction,* as a rebuke to the hostile view that had come to dominate even academic history. Here he offers a specific response to the charge that African Americans voted against the interests of whites, or that they blindly sought public office in the manner described by Washington. The struggle against Reconstruction was not a battle for good government, he argues, it was a battle for whites-only government.

Following Lynch comes Daniel H. Chamberlain, the former Republican governor of South Carolina (scene of some of the worst violence in the overthrow of Reconstruction). His essay, like that of L. Q. C. Lamar, appeared in the *North American Review* in 1879; though he himself had failed to secure black rights as governor of his adopted state, he proved to be an eloquent defender once he was out of office. Here he and Lynch offer the actual facts of Reconstruction.

The Facts of Reconstruction
by John R. Lynch

It is claimed that in States, districts, and counties in which the colored people are in the majority, the suppression of the colored vote is necessary to prevent "Negro Domination"—to prevent the ascendency of the blacks over the whites in the administration of State and local governments. This claim is based upon the assumption that if the black vote were not suppressed in all such States, districts, and counties, black men would be supported and elected to office because they were black, and white men would be opposed and defeated because they were white.

Taking Mississippi for the purposes of illustration, it will be seen that there has never been the slightest ground for such an apprehension. No colored man in that State ever occupied a judicial position above that of Justice of the Peace and very few aspired to that position. Of seven State officers only one, that of Secretary of State, was filled by a colored man, until 1873, when colored men were elected to three of the seven offices—Lieutenant-Governor, Secretary of State, and State Superintendent of Education. Of the two United States Senators and the seven members of the lower house of Congress not more than one colored man occupied a seat in each house at the same time. Of the thirty-five members of the State Senate, and the one hundred and fifteen members of the House—which composed the total membership of the State Legislature prior to 1874—there were never more than seven colored men in the Senate and forty in the lower house. Of the ninety-seven members of the Constitutional Convention of 1868 but seventeen were colored men. . . .

Colored men never at any time had control of the State Government nor of any branch or department thereof, nor even of any county or municipality. . . . The State, district, and municipal governments were not only in control of white men, but white men who were to the manor born, or who were known as old citizens of the State—those who had lived in the State many years before the War of the Rebellion. There was, therefore, never a time when that class of white men known as Carpetbaggers had absolute control of the State Government, or that of any district, county, or municipality, or any branch or department thereof. There was never, therefore, any ground for the alleged apprehension of negro domination as a result of a free, fair, and honest election in any one of the Southern or Reconstructed States. . . .

It could not be truthfully denied that Governor Ames was a clean, pure, and honest man. He had given the State an excellent administration. . . . Every dollar of the public money had been collected, and honestly accounted for. The State was in a prosperous condition. The rate of taxation had been greatly reduced, and there was every prospect of a still further reduction before the end of his administration. But these facts made no difference to those who were flushed with the victory they had so easily won [in 1875]. They wanted the offices, and were determined to have them, and that, too, without very much delay. Hence, impeachment proceedings were immediately instituted against the Governor and Lieutenant-Governor—not in the interest of reform, of good government, or of low taxes, but simply in order to get possession of the State Government.

Reconstruction and the Negro
by Daniel H. Chamberlain

If we turn now to an examination of the conduct and capacity of the colored race as shown during the period of its free exercise of the suffrage, it will appear that that race exhibited qualities entitling it to all the political privileges conferred by the reconstruction methods. It is necessary here to shut out the partisan clamor and misrepresentation of the day, and attend only to the authentic facts as grounds of judgment. First, then, it may be said that the colored race gave to the Southern States wise, liberal, and just constitutions. . . . The organic law of the ten States embraced in the Reconstruction Act of 1867 shows no instance of a purpose or effort to exclude any classes or individuals from an equal share of

all political privileges. The demands of public education were fully recognized and provided for. The methods and principles of taxation were
just and enlightened. The modes of selecting judicial officers were such
as prevail in the most prosperous States of the North. In a word, the constitutions of the reconstructed States would today command the most
unqualified approval of all competent and impartial judges and critics.

And the same conclusion would follow from an examination of the
general legislation in these States during the same period. It was, with
few exceptions, dictated by the public wants and suited to the public
needs. In the ordinary conduct of the practical affairs of government,
much must be said in approval of the spirit and methods which then prevailed. Elections were free, fair, and honest. Political canvasses were conducted by the colored race without violence, or disorder, or excessive
rancor. The power which they held they put fairly at hazard with each recurring election. They neither cheated nor intimidated nor sought to intimidate their opponents. Their popular assemblages listened with
respect and attention to the arguments of their bitterest political foes on
those rare occasions when their foes condescended to address them with
argument. Public order was maintained. Crime was detected and punished. Life and property was as safe as in most of the States.

There was a period of official corruption and profligacy in the States in
which the colored vote predominated, extending generally from 1869 to
1874. . . . In its worst stages it did not equal this description, given by
the Committee of Seventy of corruption in New York: "It has bought
Legislatures, controlled Governors, corrupted newspapers, defiled courts
of justice, violated the ballot-box, threatened all forms of civil and religious liberty, awed the timid rich, bribed the toiling masses, and cajoled
respectable citizens. . . ." Southern corruption . . . was never so powerful, daring, or pervasive as in other sections of the country. It never pol-
luted the sources of political power; it never violated the ballot-box; it
never bribed the "toiling masses." It may be said with perfect truth that
the colored voters of the South never sustained public men whom they
believed to be corrupt. . . .

From 1873 till 1876, when political power was violently wrested from
them, it is the truth of history that there was at the South a steady
progress toward good government, purity of administration, reform of
abuses, and the choice of capable and honest public officers in those
States in which the colored race had the most complete control. . . .

The fact of the present suppression and overthrow of colored suffrage at
the South is now made the ground of the argument that the race was not
equal to the duties of self-government. It is said that every people worthy
of freedom and self-government will have freedom and self-government. It
is said that the inability of a people to cope, in physical and material resources, with its enemies is proof that such a people is not entitled to re-

tain its political power. Such conclusions are as illogical as they are im-moral. Under the principles of our Government and of all just government, rights are not dependent on numbers or physical strength or material resources. . . .

The present political supremacy of the white race in at least five of the Southern States is the result of the violent exclusion or fraudulent suppression of the colored vote. No honest and well-informed man will question this. In South Carolina, Mississippi, and Louisiana, the result has been reached by a system of deliberate, organized violence in all its forms, supplemented and crowned by the most daring and stupendous election frauds. It is an intolerable affront to every sentiment of humanity or dictate of justice, to argue that any results secured by such means are less detestable than the atrocities and crimes by which they were wrought.

LYNCH AND CHAMBERLAIN may have been right, but they lost the debate. For the next century, writers ranging from novelists to serious historians would perpetuate the myth of Reconstruction as a terrible period. Moviegoers would digest a diet of films such as *Birth of a Nation* and *Gone With the Wind*, which distorted the era into something that could have come straight from the pen of L. Q. C. Lamar, though it would have been unrecognizable to Albert Morgan or John Lynch. Book after book would repeat what became conventional wisdom about Reconstruction, castigating the boldest defenders of freedom while hailing such men as Lamar himself. As late as 1995, *The New York Times* printed an article that declared, "Northern Republicans brought vengeance down on the South with a ferocity . . . putting it under military rule."[1] So complete was the white-line victory in the battle for memory that even Daniel Chamberlain himself came to reject Reconstruction in his old age, saying it produced "shocking and unbearable misgovernment" at the hands of "a backward or inferior race."

Needless to say, not everyone was swept up in the decades of rejection of the great battle for freedom. The views of Booker T. Washington were attacked by a growing number of African-American intellectuals around the turn of the century; W. E. B. Du Bois lent his brilliant mind to the study of the era—"a brief moment in the sun," as he called it—building a stream of dissident scholarship that never disappeared. Albert Morgan was

[1] This description reflects the longest-lingering (though still mistaken) criticism of Reconstruction: that the federal government imposed its will on the South and tried to artificially impose civil rights. Indeed, the *Times* writer seems to have been unaware of the fact that military administration ended as soon as each state ratified a constitution based on universal (male) suffrage. And such modern-day critics seem to forget that blacks were Southerners too, and very much wanted what Reconstruction offered.

forced to publish his recollections at his own expense—yet he bore the cost to bear witness to the truth. And John Lynch was tireless in his defense of the period, publishing books and articles up through the 1930s. Eventually, a new and far more accurate view of Reconstruction would flower in universities in the 1960s, '70s, and '80s; the interpretation presented in this volume reflects the accepted views of today's academic historians.

And yet, there is something terribly sad about the image of John Lynch in the 1910s: an old man living in exile in Chicago, huddled over his desk, angrily writing his eloquent articles—a tired figure working in virtual isolation, struggling to maintain a memory of truth in a world that chose to remember the lies. He knew the significance of his lonely work: as Eric Foner writes, "Few interpretations of history have had such far-reaching consequences as this [the racist, hostile] image of Reconstruction. . . . [It] did much to freeze the mind of the white South in unalterable opposition to outside pressures for social change and to any thought of . . . eliminating segregation or restoring suffrage to disfranchised blacks." And so they wrote, men like Morgan and Lynch, sending their works out into a world that neglected to read them, scattering seeds for a future generation to harvest in a second era of civil rights for all.

26

THE AFTERMATH

Northern Republicans

George S. Boutwell left Grant's cabinet in 1873 to become United States senator for Massachusetts. He served in the Senate until 1877. As a leading Radical, he never turned his back on the legacy of Reconstruction, and he remained an active party figure; as William McFeely has written, he was one of the most underestimated men of his age. He published his reminiscences in 1902, and died in 1905.

John Sherman moved in the reverse direction from Boutwell: he went from the Senate into the cabinet in 1877, having earned a place as treasury secretary through his loyalty to President Rutherford B. Hayes. After that bland, one-term chief executive left the White House in 1881, Sherman once again took a seat in the Senate. There, in one of those strange turns of history, the moderate expert on financial affairs proved to be something of a progressive, in his own compromise-seeking way. He secured passage of two important bills in 1890: the Sherman Silver Purchase Act and the Sherman Antitrust Act. The first expanded the supply of currency in circulation (though it was curtailed after the panic of 1893); the second made a groundbreaking effort to limit the power of massive corporations, and remains in effect to this day. In 1897, he served briefly as secretary of state for President McKinley, retiring in 1898. He died in 1900.

Jacob D. Cox left Grant's cabinet in October 1870. Cox had never been friendly to the Radical wing of the party (he had lost the governorship of Ohio in 1868 because of his support for Johnson on Reconstruction), and he proved to be a harsh critic of Grant as well. He linked himself to Carl Schurz's Liberal Republicans, and served in Congress from 1877–79. Cox moved into education, serving as dean of the Cincinnati Law School for sixteen years, beginning in 1881, and as president of the University of Cincinnati. He died in 1900.

Administration Figures

Oliver O. Howard helped found Howard University, a school for black students, in Washington in 1867; from 1869 to 1873, after the demise of the Freedmen's Bureau, he served as Howard's president. He also helped start Lincoln Memorial University in Tennessee. The one-armed "Christian general" saw himself as something of an emissary to the non-white races: during his presidency of Howard, for example, he traveled to Arizona, where he won the respect of Cochise and secured a just (if temporary) peace with the Apaches. But the general was hardly a model of twentieth-century multicultural tolerance. From 1874 to 1881, he served as commander of the Department of the Columbia, where he bungled negotiations with Chief Joseph's band of the Nez Percé tribe— sparking a war in which he and his men were humiliated by the Indian warriors. In 1886, he was promoted to major general and given command of the Division of the East. He retired in 1894 and died in 1909.

John McDonald suffered rather more than his friend and coconspirator **Orville Babcock.** McDonald submitted to a miserable year in a vermin-infested prison before being pardoned by Grant at almost the last moment of his presidency. He was so infuriated at his treatment (after all, he had faithfully kept quiet about the White House's involvement in the Whiskey Ring) that he promptly began writing his account of the illicit operation. Babcock, on the other hand, found himself banished from the White House after his acquittal—but a consolation prize eased the pain. Grant appointed him an inspector of lighthouses; and the wily Babcock, surprisingly, seemed to carry out his duties fairly faithfully. So faithfully, in fact, that he died in the line of duty, drowning in Mosquito Inlet, Florida, in 1884.

Julia Dent Grant and her husband **Ulysses S. Grant** saw their White House years rather differently. For the First Lady, they were a wonderful time spent at the center of high society; her son attended West Point, her daughter married an English aristocrat, and the rabble were kept out by the gate she had ordered closed. Ulysses was wearied by his difficult second term, but he did nothing to discourage an attempt by Republican stalwarts to nominate him yet again for the 1880 election. To his great misfortune, there were no more wars during his lifetime to call him back to what he did best: lead an army.

After a two-year tour around the world, Julia and Ulysses moved to New York, where the former general and President invested in a financial firm. It was a typical peacetime endeavor for Grant: it collapsed from fraud in 1884, leaving the couple penniless. Even worse, the old man was diagnosed with throat cancer, the legacy of a lifetime spent with a cigar in his mouth. But Mark Twain came to his aid by arranging for a lucrative contract for his memoirs, offering a last chance to leave money behind for Julia. Grant rose to the task, writing a brilliant two-volume work on his Civil War career. He completed the manuscript days before he died in 1885. Julia lived for almost twenty more years, dying in 1902. In 1897, an opulent tomb for the couple was constructed in Manhattan, overlooking both the Hudson River and the neighborhood of Harlem—so Grant would eventually tower in death over the race he had ultimately failed in life.

Businessmen

Andrew Carnegie expanded his steel empire through the end of the century, consolidating his grip on the industry during the depression of 1893–97. One by one, he snapped up his competitors or drove them out of business, even as he purchased iron mines, coke ovens, and transportation; he was greatly aided by his partnership with Henry C. Frick. He also ruthlessly battled unions. By 1900, the Carnegie Steel Company produced a quarter of the nation's steel. Carnegie looked forward to retirement; in his final coup, he sold his firm in 1901 to the newly formed U.S. Steel Corporation for the price of his choosing: $250 million. He then lived the life of a philanthropist, funding Carnegie Hall in New York, the Carnegie Institute of Washington, the Carnegie Foundation for the Advancement of Teaching, the Carnegie Endowment for International Peace, and almost 3,000 libraries. He died in 1919.

Jay Gould, Jim Fisk, Daniel Drew, and **Cornelius Vanderbilt** lived out very different lives. Fisk went first, in 1872: the flamboyant robber baron proved to be a little too successful with his favorite sideline, women. As William McFeely writes, "Jealous of Fisk's success with the beautiful Josie Mansfield, Edward Stokes entered the fashionable Grand Central Hotel and shot Fisk dead." The much cooler and cerebral Gould lived the longest, stretching out his career until 1892. Though expelled from the Erie Railroad in 1872, to the very end of his life he successfully manipulated the stock of various railways, particularly the Union Pacific, to his own profit. In between fell Cornelius Vanderbilt and Daniel Drew. The Commodore survived his Erie defeat, going on to connect Chicago and New York by rail in 1873; he founded Vanderbilt University as well, with a one-million-dollar gift. He died in 1877, leaving behind a very rich son, William Henry Vanderbilt. Drew, the furtive bear of Wall Street, did not fare so well. Ruined by the Panic of 1873, he passed on to his death in 1879 after having suffered the indignity of bankruptcy.

Other Northern Writers

Elizabeth Cady Stanton served as president of the National Woman Suffrage Association from 1869 to 1890, and of the National American

Woman Suffrage Association (which unified the nation's two main feminist organizations) from 1890 to 1892. The insertion of the word "male" into the Fourteenth Amendment seemed only to spur her on to further efforts. From 1868 to 1870 she coedited the magazine *Revolution,* and she tirelessly traveled the country, lobbying for the woman's right to vote. It was not always an attractive campaign: she sometimes indulged in openly racist comparisons of supposedly ignorant black men, who had the vote, and cultured white women, who did not. But she made progress as she pushed for equal treatment in every area of life. With Susan B. Anthony and Matilda Jocelyn Gage she amassed the first three volumes of the *History of Woman Suffrage* in the 1880s; her memoirs followed in 1898. She died in 1902.

Charles Francis Adams, Jr., in typical Gilded Age fashion, soon profited from his own expose of railroad corruption. He was named to the Massachusetts Board of Railroad Commissioners in 1869, where he served as chairman from 1872 to 1879. Given this privileged position, even he could hardly help speculating in railroad securities, which he did quite profitably during his years on the board. He was made chairman of the government directors of the Union Pacific in 1878 and became president of that railroad in 1884, but was kicked out of office by the still-active Jay Gould in 1890. Before he died in 1915, he managed to reform the public schools in Quincy, Massachusetts, and served on the Harvard Board of Overseers and as president of the Massachusetts Historical Society.

Southerners

Booker T. Washington made his way from the coal mines of West Virginia to the Hampton Institute in Virginia in 1872. After three years, he went on to teach school and study at the Wayland Seminary in Washington, D.C. In 1879, he became an instructor at Hampton; in 1881, he was selected to organize a school for African Americans at Tuskegee, Alabama. As leader of the Tuskegee Institute, he developed his philosophy of industrial education and self-help, eschewing politics as a path of advancement; economic equality, he argued, must precede a fight for political equality. In 1895, he delivered a controversial speech at Atlanta that starkly expressed these views, earning him the anger of W. E. B. Du Bois and the admiration of white leaders. In 1900, he founded the National Negro Business League to advance his idea of black economic self-reliance. He published a number of works on his life and philosophy. Washington died in 1915.

Lucius Quintus Cincinnatus Lamar moved from the United States House of Representatives in 1877 to the Senate, where he served until 1885. Long a dominating figure in the Democratic party both in Mississippi and nationwide (he wrote the law by which Mississippi seceded from the Union at the start of the Civil War), he was appointed secretary of the interior by President Grover Cleveland; he held that office until 1888. Lamar, the man who had masterminded the violent overthrow of the legally elected government of Mississippi, the man who saw to the destruction of African-American civil rights, ascended to the United States Supreme Court in 1888, serving as associate justice through 1893, when he passed from this world. Where he went is a matter for debate.

John R. Lynch served out his term in Congress, losing his bid for reelection in 1876. In 1882, he remarkably battled his way back into the U.S. House of Representatives, after contesting his supposed defeat. He remained a major force in Mississippi Republicanism, defying the white Democratic establishment. He amassed a total of four plantations, along with other parcels of real estate, and was admitted to the state bar in the 1890s. A regular delegate to the national Republican conventions, Lynch became the first black man to deliver the keynote address to a major party convention in 1884. He benefitted from Federal patronage as well, serving as an auditor in the treasury department under President Benjamin Harrison, and as paymaster in the regular army, beginning in the Spanish-American War in 1898. In 1912, he retired and moved to Chicago, and he died in 1939.

Adelbert Ames, though largely forgotten now, was certainly a leading figure in Reconstruction—a period that haunted his life and his record in history. After being driven from office by the Democrats in 1876, he moved to Northfield, Minnesota, where he joined his father's flour-milling business (and where Jesse James and his gang, all former Confederate guerrillas, were shot to pieces in a foiled bank robbery in 1876). Ames settled in Massachusetts, where he invested in textile mills and real estate; he also invented a number of gadgets and machines, ranging from a pencil sharpener to flour mill machinery. He rejoined the army during the Spanish-American War, serving as a brigadier general in the siege of Santiago de Cuba and the battle of San Juan Hill, fighting alongside Theodore Roosevelt and his cavalry regiment, the Rough Riders.

Ames, however, remained dogged by critics of Reconstruction, and he frequently wrote to correct the many unfriendly (and incorrect) accounts of his service in Mississippi. He even convinced one hostile historian, James W. Garner, to give him "grudging praise," as Richard Nelson Current writes. But Ames lived out his life comfortably, playing golf in Florida with John D. Rockefeller and other wealthy men. He died at age ninety-seven, on April 13, 1933.

Albert T. Morgan escaped Mississippi with his wife, his children, and his life. He felt lucky to do so. Penniless, he secured help from Blanche K. Bruce, the black United States senator from Mississippi. Senator Bruce was able to get Morgan a job as second-class clerk in the Pension Office. But the life-and-death struggle he had just endured aggravated his old war wounds and his malaria, and in 1879 he applied for an invalid pension. He devoted what energy he had to his great effort to tell the truth about Reconstruction; in 1884, the financially strapped Morgan published *Yazoo* at his own expense. But his haven soon collapsed: when Democrat Grover Cleveland won the presidency in 1884, Morgan discovered his new boss would be none other than L. Q. C. Lamar, the newly designated secretary of the interior.

Kicked out of his job, he took his family to Lawrence, Kansas. After five years of poverty, he left his wife behind and traveled to Colorado in 1890 to prospect for gold and silver, hoping to come back to her rich. He never succeeded. Ashamed, broken-hearted, he never had the courage to return to his family, which eventually moved to New York. He died penniless in a boarding house in Denver on April 15, 1922.

As for the couragous William Foote, the vicious Henry Dixon (the "human hornet"), and the rest of Yazoo County, Albert Morgan wrote the best epilogue himself in his memoirs. He recorded the sad fate of what was once the most promising county in the South, a place where, for a short while, the former slave really experienced freedom. He told the conclusion of the story with the same energy and humanity that he had shown while living it, during the ten years he had given to the soil and people of Mississippi. And he ends with a note of faith, of hope, of foresight to a time when the truth would finally win out.

Shattered Lives and Living Dreams
by Albert T. Morgan

The events mentioned in the last chapter occurred eight years ago. All the chief conspirators are still living [in 1884]: Barksdale, George, and Lamar. They are all in the Congress of the United States. Their dupes, Captain Telsub, the hornet, and Halder are dead; all died by violence. The death of each was most pitiful, tragic. The former was killed in Texas; a private quarrel, it was said. It was also said that upon his body were found some of the missing school funds of Yazoo County.

The hornet died a martyr to free speech, and while defending the negro's right to life, liberty, and the pursuit of happiness. For four years there had been but one political party in the county. The irreconcilables dominated that party absolutely, and they called it the Democratic party.

By their admirers throughout the State they were called the "Banner Democracy of the Banner County." That year, 1879, the hornet became the leader of the "disaffected," and champion of a movement designed to build up an opposition party. He had the encouragement and support of many of Yazoo's "best citizens." "Our nigros" were quick to seize upon that movement as opening a way out of the political slavery in which they were groaning, and rallied to that standard almost *en masse*.

The banner Democracy found in that fact proof, strong as holy writ, that the colored people were again "about to rise," and promptly set on foot precisely the same means as had been employed for the overthrow of our free State government. Rumors of "nigro risings" became once more frequent. The result was a large gathering of the "independent companies" at Yazoo City, July 25, 1879, when a formal demand was made upon the hornet that he should withdraw from his candidacy for the sheriff's office. To this demand he [caved in]. . . .

A challenge was to come, however. For immediately after "the great assembly of earnest, determined men" [as the newspaper called it] had been dispersed, Mr. Dixon announced that his withdrawal had been procured by force, and while he was *in duress,* therefore it was null and void.

But the banner Democracy was equal to this emergency. Another meeting was called. I have a souvenir of this event. It is a printed document, from which I extract the following. . . .

> "To sum up in brief our opinion and estimate of the character of the man Dixon, we declare as our deliberate opinion that he is a murderer, a gambler, a bully, a thief, a man of violence, of blood, of lies, a man who will pack juries, a low, unprincipled demagogue in politics, and an infidel in religion. . . . We further declare as our belief that the man Dixon appropriated to his own use some ($1,500 or $1,600) fifteen hundred or sixteen hundred dollars in money, warrants, and notes, which was taken from the body of the negro Patterson, who was hung on Silver Creek in 1875.[2] . . ."

It would seem that this declaration was adopted unanimously.

This souvenir was promptly inclosed in an envelope, post-marked Yazoo City, August 18, and was addressed to me in the well-known hand of Fritz Halder, who also wrote "compliments" in the upper left hand corner. . . . Before the souvenir reached me, indeed, the very next time the hornet appeared upon the main street, a man with a double-barrelled shotgun in his hands killed him. The man's name was Barksdale. He is, I

---

[2] [Original author's footnote] Our Republican legislator [mentioned in the last selection from Morgan's memoirs].

believe, a nephew of Congressman Barksdale, who was in Congress when Mississippi, with Jefferson Davis at their head, seceded from that body.

Some of the "best citizens" of Yazoo saw nothing but shame in it. Of the number was Mars Si's attorney for the State against Charles and for Hilliard against me; the very same who was elected in 1875, when Yazoo was "redeemed" by the means I have but so faintly set forth, to Patterson's vacant seat in the State legislature. From a letter written and published by him just after Mr. Dixon's death, I extract the following:

> "When is the bulldozing and intimidation to end? When are we to have a free, unawed aspiration for office, canvass, and election? When is our mother district to be unstained with the blood of the citizens, and when shall the graves cease to be filled with the dead on election years and occasions? When are the wails and cries of widoes [sic] and orphans to be unheard in party organizations and elections? Why the continued threats and intimidation against those who may see fit to organize the colored voters to vote any particular ticket, when there are no tickets but what are almost exclusively composed of old and tried white citizens of Yazoo County? They know and we know that there has been bulldozing, and even worse."

As may be inferred from the *Herald's* comments, the movement for an opposition party in Yazoo died with Mr. Henry M. Dixon. . . . One of the last acts of this man's life was the publication of the following card, which appeared in the *Herald* as an advertisement:

> "I again say that the supposed Patterson money was used to defray the current expenses for the eventful campaign of 1875. I further state $3,000 was used as a bribe to have the ballot-boxes stuffed, if necessary, and to issue certificates to Democratic candidates. . . . I consider that my conduct throughout the canvass of 1875 was indorsed by all Democratic citizens, and I do not fear that my character will suffer by any cowardly attack made for a political purpose.
> Respectfully, H.M. DIXON."

IN THE HANDS OF THE LORD

Four years later, it was Christmas eve, 1882, a "high-toned, honorable gentleman" named Posey, John T. Posey, "son of General Carnot Posey, of Confederate fame," attended a "negro ball" in Yazoo City. There he met and had a "personal altercation" with one John James, "a nigger." It is said that the quarrel was the result of a rivalry between Posey and James for the smiles of one of the belles of the ball. Posey insulted James and James struck

Posey. James was arrested, but Posey refused to prosecute. That is, Posey refused to publish the cause of the quarrel. He was a "gentleman," and James was only "a nigger." Besides, the belle was only a "nigro wench."

During these long years of woe, during these years of white supremacy in Yazoo, a spark of Federal authority remained. Mr. Bedwell, who had married a "Southern lady," was still postmaster, and Mr. Foote had been a deputy collector of internal revenue. Now "our best citizens" could tolerate Mr. Bedwell, but that "nigro Foote" was all the while a thorn in their side. His office as well as his person was concentrated incendiarism, a perpetual menace. How could "our nigros" be made to "keep thar place" with Foote in a place which, by divine right, belonged to a white? The situation was made more tragic by the fact that Foote dared, upon occasion, to shoot at a white.

Foote was allowed no peace in that office. He was frequently warned of plots of the "best citizens" to "get rid of that damned nigger revenue collector." The little Yankee garrison had already been got rid of. The old guard had all been killed or had died, or gone off to Kansas,[3] or had surrendered. . . . [Foote] alone remained. He had stood squarely by Mr. Dixon during his last raid [in creating an opposition party in 1879]. His friends were Southerners, and he had come to have an abiding hatred of the Yankees, whose failure in 1875 to come to the succor of our government, in its final struggle with the old slave oligarchs, had eliminated from his breast not only all hope of succor from the North, but also all respect for Northerners. Thus matters stood a year later, Christmas eve, 1883.

That evening John T. Posey set out, at the head of some congenial spirits from the "superiah" side of the line, to "whip a nigger." Naturally enough John James at that moment stood most in need of a thrashing. But James was employed at the meat market by one Lynch, the butcher, a "po' white." Learning of the intentions of Posey and his party, James with the full consent of his employer, and by his command, took refuge in the butcher shop.

Nothing daunted by this interference of a "po', no-count white man," Posey, at the head of his followers, went away and procured weapons. Meanwhile several of James's friends, colored men, came to his succor. Posey and his friends returned. At that moment the "po' white," the employer of James, was standing in front of his shop. As the Posey party approached he walked out into the street, held up his hands, and said, "You can't one of you go in my house. I ain't a-going to have any row in there."[4]

3 One of the notable responses by African Americans to their defeat in Mississippi was the so-called Exodusters movement: thousands migrated to Kansas, establishing their own settlements on the frontier.

4 [Original author's footnote] From the testimony of Posey's business partner, Thomas Williams, white Democrat, upon the "trial" which followed.

At this juncture Mr. Foote approached the Posey group. It would seem that he was alone. The handful of Posey's friends had grown into a crowd. At this moment an employee of Posey's appeared on the scene. . . . Then it was said Foote and a Yankee,[5] who was one of the Posey crowd, had an "altercation." Then Foote was knocked down; then the firing began.

Upon the "trial" it was said that some colored men had said before the firing, that if it should begin, it would not end as it did in 1875. It was said that Mr. Foote had said this. If so, Mr. Foote spoke more truly than he knew. It did not end as it did in 1875. It began with the death of John T. Posey, Carnot Posey, John's brother, a young man named Nichols, and Fritz Halder. The Yankee was wounded. All were white.

Who did the killing?

John Link, the above-mentioned witness, further testified upon that trial: "Posey rushed right up to the front door of Lynch's butcher shop. Mr. Halder arrested him on the sidewalk, almost immediately at Lynch's door. Posey told him to turn him loose, that he had no right to stop him." At this point the recollection of all the "high-toned" witnesses, so far as I have been able to learn, becomes confused except in the case of one, who said that after Foote was struck, and while falling, he fired his pistol. . . . Foote was present, at all events. He did not run away. He trusted in his cause and in his white Southern friends. James ran away, was pursued, and shot to death; "riddled with bullets." His employer, that "po' white," Foote, and some ten more colored men were charged with murder, arrested, and locked up in that Yazoo jail.

And this is the way it ended. I quote from a special dispatch to the St. Louis *Globe-Democrat,* dated Yazoo City, December 29, 1883, from which all the foregoing extracts from the testimony at the "trial" have been taken:

"Five o'clock, the hour set by some of the most active for moving on the jail, came and passed. It was very quiet, and some of the leading citizens claimed that there would be no trouble tonight. It was only a calm before a storm.

"Half a dozen mounted men galloped into town over the highway leading up the Yazoo Valley. Then came a delegation from Bentonia. Then others. At 6:10, just after dark, a squad of men, armed with shotguns, made their appearance on the lower part of Main Street. They moved up toward Jefferson, and as they marched others joined them. The column grew at every step. They turned up Jefferson and went a block; then they stopped. An old gentleman spoke to them and said, 'Boys, are you organized? Aren't you too early?'

"Somebody replied: 'We tried to hold them back, but they would start.'

5 [Original author's footnote] This Yankee was doubtless trying to prove that he was as "good a friend to the South" as anyone else.

"Half a block north there was another halt. Some of the more prudent counseled delay. A great chorus of 'noes' greeted this. 'Go ahead, go ahead; they'll get them all out if we don't hurry.' This last shout caught the popular sentiment. There was a great shout of 'Go on, go on,' then a cheer, which rang through the city. The crowd, grown to fully 200, pressed ahead at a rapid walk toward the jail. There was no masking, and not the slightest attempt at concealment. Men recognized each other by name and shook hands while they waited for the committee inside to bring out the prisoners. . . .

"After ten minutes' work the cell in which was Robert Swaze was opened, and he was led into the hall. He made no fight whatever, but stood erect while the noose at the end of a long rope was put around his neck. Then his hands were tied behind him. Two or three conflicting commands were given—one was for a squad to go downtown and get more rope. Somebody shouted, 'Shoot 'em.' This was yelled down. . . . 'Throw the end of the rope over the fence. We'll string him right up here.'

"The end was thrown over the fence, and a dozen inside caught hold and began pulling. Swaze was raised up to his tip-toes, and then the rope caught in a crack and stuck fast. 'This is cruel; why didn't you go to a tree?' somebody exclaimed. An active fellow mounted another man's shoulders, caught the top of the fence, and tugged at the rope, while the one on the outside held Swaze up. It seemed an hour. It was perhaps only a minute, until the rope was loosened again. Then it was pulled until Swaze was swung six inches off the ground. It caught again, but those outside said it was high enough, and the men inside stopped pulling. . . .

" 'Bring out that Internal Revenue Collector, we want him next,' came from the yard.

"It was not necessary, for the committee had already commenced on the doors where W.H. Foote was confined. Foote walked over and took a drink from a bucket of water, then placed himself with his left side against the wall and stood facing the spot where, as the door swung back, he would meet the first man who entered. Suddenly the door swung open. As it let in the crowd Foote raised his right hand with a missile in it and struck out. The first man went to the floor under the blow. Half a dozen were in before another blow could be given. Foote fought like a tiger.

"There was a shot, then another, and three more in quick succession. The light had gone out in the midst of the struggle, and as the shots were fired they illuminated the room in a single second, and showed confused struggling. Then all was quiet. The man who entered first and received Foote's blow was a young farmer named A. Fatheree,[6] from Free Run in this county. In the melee one of the bullets had struck him in the instep

6 [Original author's footnote] My recollection is that this is the same young man who in 1869 assayed to whip Foote, and got a whipping himself instead.

of the foot, making a very ugly wound. As soon as a light was brought in and Fatheree had been carried out Foote was examined. There were some signs of life. Six shots were fired with steady aim, and those who cared to enter the room satisfied themselves that the negro was dead. His forehead was shot away, and blood and brain covered a space of the floor a yard square. Nearly all the bullets had been sent into his head. He was so mutilated as to be scarcely recognizable. Foote undoubtedly made a fight to provoke the shooting, that he might die that way rather than be hung. . . ."

The next day. From the same:

"Close by Parker's body [another of the black men lynched that night] was the door opening into the cell where Foote made his desperate fight and forced those in front to shoot him. In daylight the remains seemed even more ghastly than they did last night. . . . When the crowd was heard coming toward the jail [the night of the attack,] an officer went to the door and said, 'Foote, I expect your time is coming. You hear them? Take it as easy as you can.'

"There was just the slightest tremor in his voice as he replied: 'Yes, I hear them; I'll try to take it quietly.' Then he quietly put out the light and waited. . . ."

When news of these deeds reached me I began the task of writing this book. Then I promised myself to not "wave the bloody shirt."[7] Nor have I. Let others do that. But if not for the living something remains for the dead. . . .

THE FORTY YEARS IN THE WILDERNESS ARE PASSING AWAY

Credit Mobilier, Pacific Mail, Sanborn Contracts, and Henry Ward Beecher had wrought their fatal spell upon the country. . . . [8] Massachusetts had gone Democratic. "Our people" had but six months more to wait. January following a government of their own choosing was installed in power throughout the State, and L.Q.C. Lamar was chosen United States Senator. We know by what means and at what cost. My friend Patterson's life and money were but a very small fraction of the whole. . . .

What with corruption that had become chronic in both the great political parties at the North, the tales of "outrage and wrong" perpetuated upon "our stricken brethren at the South" by "carpetbaggers and nigros," together with frequently recurring "nigro insurrections," our brave and

7 This was a common term for election appeals by Republican candidates in the 1860s, '70s, and '80s, who called forth the memory of the Civil War dead.

8 These were all episodes that discredited Republican rule; famous abolitionist Henry Ward Beecher was caught up during this period in a trial for adultery.

generous friends at the North grew "tired." The President dared not keep his "promise." The United States bayonets did not reach Mississippi. I did not reach the other shore. A robber, liar, and murderer—the Mississippi bulldozer—stood in the way, and from that day to this he has pursued his trade with most "superiah strategy and statesmanship."

Some of the survivors of the campaign of 1875 the bulldozer has silenced by cajolery, some he has bribed to silence, some he has silenced by threats, and some he has killed. But such as he could neither cajole, bribe, intimidate, nor kill, he has pursued with a malice, a cunning, and a persistency that has driven them from their homes and scattered them to the four corners of the earth.

Chisholm refused to surrender or run, and the bulldozer killed his daughter that he might make surer work with him. Gilmer refused, and he "filled him full of lead." Charles Caldwell refused, and he "shot him all to pieces," and wantonly slew his half-witted brother. Page refused, and he fired his home and slew him and all his children, from the elder son to the baby in the cradle. But why continue the list? I could add a hundred names more to it.

Ever since that day when Lamar, Barksdale, George, and Singleton *et als.*, met with "our people" in Yazoo, and publicly thanked Mr. Dixon and his company for their services in the "redemption" of that State, and Yazoo was declared the banner county, colored men there have been whipped, hunted by hounds, and killed, and their mothers, wives, daughters, and sweethearts have been reviled, seduced, raped, while Yazoo law gave them no redress. . . .

As I have said, after the white leagues broke up our meeting, September 1, 1875, a warrant charging me with an attempt to murder him was placed in the hands of Mr. Dixon, and a large reward was offered for me, dead or alive. I went about openly at the capital, and at Holly Springs, where my family were, and back and forth frequently, yet no attempt was made to arrest me. It is my belief that the warrant was not intended for any such purpose, but that it was intended as a means of excusing my assassination. . . .

General Greenleaf, our Republican magistrate, Mr. Foote, and Charles are dead. The reader knows already how all, except Charles, died. The only one who died by violence was Mr. Foote. Charles could not get away from that "wonderful country." Having withdrawn from leadership in politics, he was permitted to pursue, in Washington County, his "designs upon the country" in peace. When the great fever epidemic that devastated Greenville first appeared in the State, he was absorbed in the management of his lucrative business. He had passed safely through previous fever epidemics; he believed he could withstand this one. At all events he would not run away. So, while his wife and children had the fever and recovered, he died there. . . .

I submit that the American people are always prepared to do right when it clearly appears. I speak plainly, as it is my right and duty to do. . . .

I have never denied nor been ashamed of the fact that my wife and children have in their veins negro blood; "nigro taint" is the enemy's phrase. The only thing about it which grieves me is the fact that so many of our good girls and boys can see no difference between miscegenation as practiced at the South [through concubinage and rape by white men] and amalgamation through honorable marriage, or, seeing the true distinction, nevertheless prefer and honor the miscegenationist above the amalgamationist.

Wife and I have been married fourteen years; we have six children. During all the dreary years that have passed since the enemy, by force and murder, took possession of my new field, stole our grand old flag from us, and occupied our temples, this woman and these children have been my refuge.

The world moves, though Yazoo may remain a dead sea. History has changed the meaning of fame. Formerly it was a report, now it is a judgment. It will not always be true that "the heart which responds to the call of duty finds no rest except in the grave." Have patience—wait. The forty years in the wilderness are passing away.

Some day the telegraph, the telephone, and the printing press will assemble the world in one congregation, and teachers will appear to instruct all in the language and justice of truth.